ZONES OF STARS

OBSERVED AT

THE NATIONAL OBSERVATORY, WASHINGTON.

APPROVED BY

CAPT. G. A. MAGRUDER,

CHIEF OF THE BUREAU OF ORDNANCE AND HYDROGRAPHY;

AND PUBLISHED UNDER AUTHORITY OF

Presented by the
National Observatory,
Washington.

SUPERINTENDENT.

VOL. I.—PART I.

CONTAINING THE ZONES OBSERVED WITH THE MERIDIAN CIRCLE IN 1846.

WASHINGTON:
GEORGE W. BOWMAN, PRINTER.
1860.

INDEX.

INTRODUCTION.

Commander M. F. Maury, U. S. N.,
Superintendent of the Observatory.

Sir: In compliance with your instructions, I herewith present observations of zones, made with the Meridian Circle in the year 1846, arranged for convenient reference, and accompanied with the reductions and results. The zones of stars contained in the present volume—even when completed by the addition of those observed during the same year by the Transit and Mural—will make but a small portion of the series of observations commenced at the National Observatory, in pursuance of an order from the Secretary of the Navy, dated March 6, 1846, and which, in consequence of many other pressing duties, and the limited computing force allowed, it has been found impossible to reduce and prepare for publication at an earlier day. The series was originally designed to include all stars within the compass of our instruments, and crossing the meridian at an elevation of above eight degrees. The observations were continued without interruption until the year 1853, or until it had become apparent that the labors of the observers were only accumulating an amount of material which they had no means, within a reasonable time, of putting into a shape convenient for use. Previous to this time, however, the observations made in the years 1846 and 1847, had been copied from the observing books, the forms of reduction arranged, and some progress made in the reduction itself. This commencement was soon after interrupted, not again to be resumed till the autumn of 1859. The present volume contains all of the work which there has, as yet, been time to prepare for publication, and must be taken merely as the first fruit of a very comprehensive plan, the execution of which has only been impeded by lack of adequate force.

The observations with the Meridian Circle (the results of which make the first part of this volume) were made by Professor J. S. Hubbard and Lieutenant L. Maynard. It will be a necessary preliminary to describe the instrument with which they were made, the methods of observation, adjustment, and reduction, and to explain the tabular forms in which the data, the reductions, and results are now presented.

THE INSTRUMENT.

The Meridian Circle of the Observatory is now much changed from its original construction. The following description of it as it was in 1846, when these observations were made, is taken, with little variation, from the second volume of the Washington Astronomical Observations published in that year: "The foundation upon which it rests is of masonry, and similar to those of the Transit Instrument and Mural Circle. The piers are of granite. At each end of the axis and outside of each pier is a circle thirty inches in diameter, of which, one, the western, during the year 1846, is graduated only to fifteen minutes, and subdivided by a vernier to single minutes. This is the finding circle. To it is attached the clamp, the binding screw of which passes through the pier; the tangent screw for slow motion in declination, acting on the clamp, carries with it the circle and the telescope. This circle may be moved about its axis, and is adjusted so that the zero of graduation corresponds to the zenith. The reading for the equator is, when the finding circle is West, 321° 6′; when East, 38° 54′. The second circle is graduated to three minutes and subdived by four microscopes, lettered A, B, C, D, which read to single seconds, and, by estimation, to tenths of a second. This circle is left entirely free from clamps, and is never touched by the observer. The microscopes are held by four bearers, resting on the circumference of a smaller circle, which is supported by a prolongation of the axis of the instrument, but prevented from turning with it by means of a small bar proceeding downwards from the center:

this bar being confined between the two screws which, when the telescope is reversed, give the slow motion to the instrument. A spirit level attached to the bar and small circle, and called the Alidade level, is intended to detect any movement of the microscope system about the common center. This level, however, cannot be reversed, and experience has shown that its indications could not be trusted, as the presence of the observer's person, while reading the microscopes, affected it sensibly. And whenever a current of air passed through the room, it caused such changes of position in the bubble as to render unsafe any inference of change in the instrument, and the readings have been therefore entirely disregarded. One division of this level is equal to 2″.78. A similar level is attached to the other extremity of the axis near the finding circle, but no use has been made of it. From the top of each pier rises a small brass pillar to the height of 21.5 inches, through which passes a steel lever 15.5 inches long, parallel with the horizontal axis, and intended to remove by a counterpoise the additional weight of the alidade circle and microscopes from the axis of the instrument. From the side of one of these pillars also projects a small hook which serves to support the striding level when in position. The pillars fit in sockets at their base, instead of being permanent, as it is necessary to remove them before reversing the instrument. The main counterpoises bearing up the axis are applied through friction rollers and by means of short horizontal levers at points immediately adjoining and within the termination of the steel pivots. The telescope tube is 56 inches in length, being composed of the central cube and two brass cones, each 24 inches long, 7.2 inches diameter at the cube, and 3.8 inches diameter at the end. The broad rings containing the object-glass and eye-piece, fit accurately the extremities of the main tube, surface to surface, and are convertible; the change from object-end to eye-end being very easily effected, and the simplest means thus afforded for eliminating the effect of flexure. The object-glass has 4.5 inches of clear aperture, and 58.2 inches focal length. The optical performance of the telescope is most excellent, enabling the observer to use the highest magnifying power with advantage in the ordinary state of the atmosphere. The lower powers have generally been used only for observations of the sun and of faint stars, which would bear but feeble illumination. The eye-piece is arranged to have a vertical, as well as horizontal motion, and commands the whole field of view. The illumination of the field is effected by means of a small lamp attached to a bent arm, which enters the pier immediately below the finding circle, and the light is conveniently modified by a small piece of red glass fitted to the open end of the axis. The reversing apparatus, was attached to the piers by two cross pieces, which supported and steadied the screw. A slight experience, in 1845, was sufficient to show that this mode of reversing was too prejudicial to the permanence of adjustment to be continued with safety, and there being no other means at hand of effecting the reversal, the instrument was suffered to remain in one position during the year 1846. The value of one division of the striding level, as determined by means of the mural circle, was found to be 1″.681, or 0*s*.1121 in time." This value has been used in determining the inclination of the axis to the horizon, and also in the discussion of a series of observations, made in this and the preceding years, to determine the figure of the pivots, for the details of which the reader is referred to Washington Astronomical Observations for 1846, pp. xxxviii to xl. The circle is read by four microscopes, held by the bearers already mentioned. "In the focus of the eye-piece of each microscope are two parallel wires, about 10′ apart, which, when the circle is read, are placed so as to include between them the broad division marks of the limb—a mode of reading inferior in accuracy to that with cross wires, as in the Troughton microscopes." In the second volume of Washington Observations, already quoted, (pp. xli to liii,) will be found an investigation of the inequality of the micrometer screw, and errors of graduation, which it is not deemed necessary to insert in this place. As in these zone observations the circle was uniformly set near a division of the circle, the correction for runs of the microscope is inappreciable, and has been neglected. The diaphragm contained, in 1846, eleven transit wires and seven micrometer or declination wires; the transit wires being designated as follows: 1, 2, I, II, III, IV, V, VI, VII, 10 11; and the micrometer wires by the numbers, 1, 2, 3, 4, 5, 6, 7. The first of the transit wires is that over which, when the circle is east, the star first passes at its upper culmination. And the first of the micrometer wires is that which is uppermost in the field, with the circle east, and the observer looking southward.

The equatorial intervals of the transit wires (their distances from the mean wire,) for the whole of these observations is as follows:

M — 1 = +60.49s.		M — 11 —60.49s.
M — 2 = +49.31		M — 10 —49.31
M — I = +32.903		M — VII = —32.826
M — II = +21.791		M — VI = —21.934
M — III = +10.964	M — IV = — 0.026s.	M — V = —10.877

These values, with the exception of the two first and two last, (those at the extremities of the field,) have been deduced from transits of Polaris and δ Ursæ Minoris, and obtain for the middle or fixed wire. No transits were observed on the wires 1, 2, and there is no recorded determination of the value of the intervals between them and the mean wire. These intervals M — 1, M — 2, being only used as arguments for the reduction to the meridian, they have been set down at the same distances from the mean wire as 10 and 11.

"For the zone observations where the stars have been observed at various distances from the middle of the field, it becomes important to determine the errors of the transit wires throughout their whole length. For this purpose the following table has been deduced from the zones themselves."

	M—I.	M—II.	M—III.	M—IV.	M—V.	M—VI.	M—VII.	M—10.	M—11.
Rev.	s.	s.	s.	s.	s.	s.	s.	s.	s.
0	+32.99	+21.96	+11.03	—0.03	—10.94	—22.00	—32.94	—49.05	—60.42
10	.99	.93	.02	.03	.93	.01	.94	.13	.44
20	.99	.90	.02	.03	.92	.03	.95	.20	.46
30	.98	.87	.01	.03	.92	.05	.96	.26	.48
40	.98	.84	.00	.03	.91	.06	.97	.30	.48
50	.98	.81	.00	.03	.90	.04	.96	.30	.45
60	.97	.78	.01	.03	.90	.01	.94	.29	.40
70	.97	.75	.01	.03	.89	21.98	.91	.27	.33
80	+32.97	+21.72	+11.01	—0.03	—10.89	—21.95	—32.88	—49.25	—60.25

"The distances between the micrometer wires and the middle one have been determined by means of the collimating eye-piece and circle-readings, each wire being made to coincide with its own image, or that of wire 4. The mean of all the determinations gives:

	′ ″	*Rev.*
4 — 1 =	— 20 30.25 =	35.677
4 — 2 =	— 14 38.54 =	25.477
4 — 3 =	— 5 55.42 =	10.307
4 — 5 =	+ 5 46.13 =	10.038
4 — 6 =	+ 14 28.94 =	25.199
4 — 7 =	+ 20 19.03 =	35.351

"The value of a revolution of the micrometer screw has been obtained from the intervals of 4 — 3 and 4 — 5, by comparing the coincidences of wires 3, 4, and 5 with the fixed wire." The mean of all the determinations gives 34.483 for this value. There seems to have been no determination of the inclination, or of any irregularity in the intervals of the declination wires, during the year. The intervals have, therefore, been assumed as constant, and the wires as parallel and perpendicular to the meridian.

The revolutions of the micrometer screw are counted on a notched scale, placed in the focus of the telescope and in the edge of the field. The intervals between the notches of this scale are equal to one revolution of the screw, and every fifth notch is further marked by a hole opposite to it in the scale. A pointer moved by the micrometer screw and so adjusted that when it is in the interval between two notches, the index of the screw-head shall mark zero, serves to count the number of revolutions. The notch nearest the middle of the field, being one of the holed notches, is numbered 40. The scale counting in the same direction as the declination wires, that is, beginning at the upper edge of the field when the circle is east, and the observer looking southward, and counting from 0 to 80. The head of the micrometer screw is graduated to hundredths.

A fixed horizontal wire marks the middle of the field at or near the fortieth division of the scale. To this are referred all the angular measures of the telescope, and its relation to the micrometer scale is determined by noting the readings of the scale and screw-head, when the fourth declination wire is brought to coincide with it. This reading is recorded as the micrometric coincidence. In these observations it has always been a fraction greater than 40.

The collimating eye-piece heretofore mentioned, was constructed out of one of the eye-pieces of the instrument by inserting between its lenses a plane mirror perforated at the center and movable about an axis perpendicular to the optical axis of the telescope—the cell of the eye-piece being left open opposite the mirror to receive the light of a lamp held before it.

METHODS OF OBSERVATION AND ADJUSTMENT.

The Nadir Point upon which the observed altitudes depend has been determined by the collimating eye-piece—the fixed wire being brought to coincide with its image as seen through the telescope reflected in a basin of quicksilver, and the reading of the circle in this portion taken as the Nadir Point at the instant of observation. These coincidences were repeated five times at each determination, and the mean, corrected for runs, taken as final. The details of these observations will be found in the second volume of the Washington Astronomical Observations, already quoted. The result (N+180°) under the head of Zenith Point, with the corresponding value of the micrometer coincidence, comprehend all that it has been thought necessary to insert here.

The corrections for errors of level, azimuth, and collimation have been made according to the formula of Bessel, by which, supposing the telescope to be directed to any point where declination is δ, and that the axis of the meridian circle prolonged westward mark a point in the heavens whose declination is n, and its hour angle from the meridian counted westward ($90°—m$); the angle which the optical axis of the telescope makes with the axis of the instrument, counted also westward, being ($90°+c$,) we will have for the sum of these errors—

$$I = m + n. \text{ tang. } \delta + c \text{ sec. } \delta.$$

And if now we make b the inclination of the axis of the circle with the horizon and ($90°—k$,) its azimuth counted from the south westward; φ being the latitude of the observer, we have—

$$m = b \cos. \varphi + k \sin. \varphi.$$
$$n = b \sin. \varphi - k \cos. \varphi.$$

The quantity b is determined directly by the striding level, having regard to the error arising from inequality of the pivots, and the quantity ($b \pm c$) by the collimating eye-piece. By this process, without reversal of the instrument, (which during the year 1846 could not be safely effected,) we obtain the value of c, which is further corrected for the reduction to the mean wire and for diurnal aberration.

The value of ($n+c$) is obtained by either of the following formulas:

$$n + c = \frac{(\alpha - \tau) - (\alpha + 12^{h} - \tau)}{2 \text{ tang. } \delta}$$

$$n + c = \frac{(\alpha - \tau) - (\alpha' - \tau') + c\,(\text{sec. } \delta' - \text{tan. } \delta')}{\text{tan. } \delta - \text{tan. } \delta'}$$

In which α, δ, τ represent the right ascension, declination, and time of transit of a circumpolar star, and $\alpha' \ \delta' \ \tau'$ the right ascension, declination, and time of transit of an equatorial star. In determining the value of $(n+c)$ the transit of a circumpolar star was compared with all the others observed on the same night, these transits having been first corrected by the quantity c. (sec. δ—tang. δ.)

The value of m was then computed from the formula—

$$m = b \text{ sec. } \varphi - n \text{ tang. } \varphi.$$

The stand and rate of the clock, at the hour most convenient for the observations, were determined by comparing the corrected transits of fundamental stars with their tabulated places.

METHODS OF REDUCTION.

These include the determination for each zone, of the following quantities:

(1.) The correction for the error and rate of the clock.

(2.) The declination of the middle of the zone, or of the 40th division of the micrometer scale, corrected for the refraction dependent upon the state of the atmosphere at the commencement of the observations.

(3.) The difference of refraction between the middle of the zone and each 10th division of the micrometer scale at the commencement of the observations.

(4.) The corrections for changes in atmospheric conditions occurring during the observations.

(5.) The corrections for changes in the reading of the Circle during the observations.

(6.) The intervals of the transit wires, or their distances from the mean wire, answering to the declination of the middle of the zone, and to each 10th division of the micrometer scale. These intervals being computed from the equatorial intervals given at page VII.

(7.) The reductions to the mean places for 1850.0, for the declination of the middle of the zone, and for each 20th minute of right ascension contained in it; also the change in these reductions for each 10th division of the micrometer scale.

(8.) The sum of the corrections, for error of level, azimuth, and collimation, for the declination of the middle of the zone, computed by the formula—

$$I = m + n \text{ tang. } \delta + c \text{ sec. } \delta.$$

And the changes in this correction for each 10th division of the micrometer scale.

(9.) The reduction of the observed declination to the meridian $= -\frac{\sin.^2 \frac{1}{2} h. \sin. 2\delta}{\sin. 1''}$ where h is the hour angle and δ the declination of the star observed.

These different quantities having been computed, those dependent only upon the time were combined and the values of their sums interpolated for every 10th minute. Those dependent upon the declination of the observed body or its place in the zone being applied separately to each observation.

In reducing the observed right ascensions, the observed transits were first referred to the mean wire by means of the intervals described in (6.) Then using the following notation:

$\alpha =$ the right ascension of the observed star,
$T =$ its time of transit over the mean wire,
$\Delta\delta =$ the difference of declination from the middle of the zone,
$K =$ correction to the clock,
$I =$ correction for level, azimuth, and collimation at the middle of the zone,
$\Delta I =$ change in the value of I answering to $\Delta\delta$,
$M\alpha =$ reduction to mean place of 1850.0 for the middle of the zone,

ΔMa = change in the value of Ma answering to $\Delta\delta$.

We shall have, for the mean right ascension for 1850.0,

$$\alpha = T + K + I + \Delta I + Ma + \Delta Ma.$$

The quantity I being constant for the whole zone; K and M depending upon the time, and ΔI, ΔMa, upon the position of the observed star, or its difference of declination from the declination of the middle of the zone.

In reducing the observed declinations, the following method was adopted: The micrometer intervals were counted, not from the middle of the zone, but from 30′ north of it, so that their values have all the same sign as the declination. The corrections for differential refraction in the zone, and also the reductions to the mean place for 1850.0, being applied by differences, two arbitrary constants were introduced, n′, n″, the first greater than the whole of $M\delta$, and the other greater than the whole change of ρ, each with a negative sign. These constants avoid the liability to error arising from a change of sign in the quantities $M\delta$, ρ, in the same zone; using the following notation:

δ = mean declination of an observed star for 1850.0.

D = mean declination of the middle of the zone for 1850.0, supposing the refraction at the commencement of the zone to remain constant.

D D + 30′ — n' — n''.

i = the micrometer interval, or δ — (D + 30′.)

δ = difference between the declinations of the star and of the middle of the zone.

ρ differential refraction for $\Delta\delta$.

$M\delta$ = reduction to the mean place for 1850.0.

$\Delta M\delta$ = change in the value of $M\delta$; answering to $\Delta\delta$.

$\Delta\rho$ = correction for change of refraction during the observations.

ΔR. Correction for change of reading in the circle.

r. Reduction to the meridian.

We shall have—

$$\delta = -(D + i + (\rho + n') + (M\delta + n'') + \Delta M\delta + \Delta\rho + \Delta R + r.)$$

Of these quantities, D, i, r, are determined from the observations; $M\delta$, $\Delta\rho$, and ΔR, depend upon the time; and ρ and ΔMd upon $\Delta\delta$.

The process of reduction will be better understood from the following example of Zone III:

(A.)

		FROM REFRACTION TABLES.						
Circ. R'g............	276° 21′ 5″.60	Bar.	29.996 in.	log B. 0.01467	Diff. for		B. +.056	— 0″.98
Zen. Pt..............	359 59 58.79	At. ther.	51°.3	" t. 0.00189	"	"	t. — 4°.8	— 0.22
Coin., C	40″.070 = —2.41	Ex. ther.	41°.8	" T. 0.04748	"	"	T. — 5.0	— 4.93
Ap. zen. dist., Z..	83 38 55.60			" R. 2.62369	"	"	{ +23 'Z	—26.81
Co. lat...............	51 6 20.75						{ —23 'Z	+24.34
Red. to 1850.........	— 32.15			ι′ 0.00410				
Ref'n.................	— 8 11.99			ΔT 0.00013				
D.	—44 54 0.49						n.′ = — 4.49	
30′ — n′ — n″	+ 30 30.49			log. R′ 2.69196			n.″ = — 26.00	
D.	—44 23 30.0			R = 491″.99				

(B.)

VALUE OF INTERVALS OF THE TRANSIT WIRES IN ZONE III.

	I.	II.	III.	IV.	V.	VI.	VII.	10.	11.
Rev.	*s.*	*s.*	*s.*	*s.*	*s.*	*s.*	*s.*	*s.*	*s.*
0	46.91	31.24	15.73	—0.04	44.67	29.10	13.70	51.02	35.03
10	.83	.15	.69	.04	.71	.14	.77	.03	.12
20	.75	.06	.66	.04	.74	.16	.84	.04	.25
30	.67	30.97	.62	.04	.77	.18	.90	.06	.36
40	.60	.88	.59	.04	.80	.22	.96	.12	.49
50	.52	.78	.56	.04	.84	.29	.05	.23	.67
60	.44	.69	.54	.04	.87	.38	.15	.35	.88
70	.36	.60	.52	.04	.91	.48	.27	.49	36.12
80	46.29	30.57	15.50	—0.04	44.94	29.57	13.39	51.64	36.36

These values are derived from those given at page VII, by multiplying these last into the secant of 44° 53′ 28″.3, the declination of the middle of the zone.

Reductions to the mean place for 1850.0, for the declination — 44° 53′ 28″.3, and the right ascensions following:

(C.)

a.	Ma.	Mδ.	Δ
h. m.		″	″
9 20	+6.706	—32.15	
			— 4.76
40	6.869	36.91	
			9.18
10 0	7.059	41.33	
			13.28
20	7.279	45.43	
			16.96
40	7.526	49.11	
			20.22
11 00	7.797	52.37	
			23.09
20	8.092	55.24	
			25.47
40	8.407	57.62	
			—27.38
12 0	+8.741	—59.53	

(D.)

CORRECTIONS DEPENDENT ON TIME.

	IN RIGHT ASCENSION.				IN DECLINATION.			
a.	K.	I.	Ma.	ΣΔa.	ΔR.	Δρ.	Mδ.	ΣΔδ+n′.
								n—4.49
h. m. 9 20	+67.838	+1.209	+6.714	+75.761	.00	. . .	— 0.28	— 4.77
40	.840	.209	6.878	75.927	—0.78	—0.77	5.03	11.07
10 0	.851	.209	7.069	76.129	1.56	1.53	9.43	17.01
20	.862	.209	7.291	76.362	2.34	2.30	13.52	22.65
40	.872	.209	7.540	76.621	2.74	3.06	17.17	27.46
11 0	.883	.209	7.812	76.904	2.75	3.83	20.41	31.48
20	.894	.209	8.108	77.211	2.77	4.60	23.26	35.12
40	.904	.209	8.424	77.537	2.79	5.37	25.62	38.27
12 0	+67.915	+1.209	+8.759	+77.883	—2.81	—6.13	—27.50	—40.93

Ma and *Mδ*, in the above table, are corrected for the error of the clock K.

(E.)

CORRECTIONS DEPENDENT ON $\Delta\delta$.

	$\Delta M\alpha$.				$\Delta M\delta$.				Δ I.	ρ.	$(\rho + n'')$.
	9*h*.	10*h*.	11*h*.	12*h*.	9*h*.	10*h*.	11*h*.	12.0.			
Rev.	*s.*	*s.*	*s.*	*s.*	″	″	″		*s.*	″	″
0	—0.044	—0.038	—0.030	—0.019	+0.040	+0.027	+0.008	.000	+0.007	—26.81	—52.81
10	.033	.028	.022	.015	.030	.020	. . .	. .	.005	19.84	45.84
20	.022	.019	.015	.010	.020	.012	. . .	. .	.004	13.08	39.08
30	— .011	— .009	— .008	. . .	+ .010	+ .007	. . .	. .	+ .002	— 6.44	32.44
40	.000	.000	.000	.000	.000	.000	.000	.000	. . .	. . .	26.00
50	+ .011	+ .009	+ .008	. . .	— .010	— .007	. . .	. .	— .002	+ 6.32	19.69
60	.022	.019	.015	+0.010	.020	.012	. . .	. .	.004	12.44	13.56
70	.033	.028	.022	.015	.030	.020	. . .	. .	.005	18.43	7.57
80	+0.044	+0.038	+0.030	+0.019	—0.040	—0.027	—0.008	.000	—0.007	+24.34	— 1.66

The tables containing the corrections $\Sigma\Delta\alpha$, $\Sigma\Delta\delta$, were interpolated as follows:

(F.)

α.	$\Sigma\Delta\alpha$.	Diff. for 10*m*.	$\Sigma\Delta\delta + n''$.	Diff. for 10*m*.
h. m.				
9 20	+75.761		— 4.77	
		—0.080		—3.20
30	.841		7.97	
		.086		3.11
40	.927		11.07	
		.096		3.07
50	76.023		14.08	
		.106		2.93
10 0	.129		17.01	
		.113		2.85
10	.242		19.86	
		.120		2.79
20	.362		22.65	
		.125		2.50
30	.487		25.15	
		.134		2.31
40	.621		27.46	
		.139		2.11
50	.760		29.57	
		.144		1.91
11 0	.904		31.48	
		.151		1.87
10	77.055		33.25	
		.156		1.77
20	.211		35.12	
		.160		1.65
30	.371		36.77	
		.166		1.50
40	.537		38.27	
		.171		1.41
50	.708		39.68	
		+0.175		—1.25
12 0	+77.883		—40.93	

The manner of determining the quantities i and r, the micrometric interval, and the reduction to the meridian depending merely upon the readings of the micrometer, require no explanation. These being obtained, the mean right ascension of any observed star for 1850.0 will be $= T + \Sigma\Delta\alpha + \Delta M\alpha + \Delta I$; the quantity $\Sigma\Delta\alpha$ being taken from Table F, and $\Delta M\alpha$ and ΔI from Table E.

In like manner, the mean declination for 1850.0 of an observed star, will be

$$= -\ (D + i + r\ (+\rho + n' + \Delta M\delta) + (\Sigma\Delta\delta + n'')$$

$(\rho + n')$ and $\Delta M\delta$ being taken from table E, and $(\Sigma\Delta\delta + n'')$ from table F.

In the tabulated results, the sum of all the corrections to the observed right ascension is designated by a; and in the corrections to the observed declination,

$$i + r + (\rho + n' + \varDelta M\delta) = D: \text{ and } (\Sigma\varDelta\delta + n') = d.$$

EXPLANATION OF THE PRINTED OBSERVATIONS.

At the head of each zone is placed, the number of the zone; the date of the observations; the initial of the observer's name; (H for Professor Hubbard, M for Lieutenant Maynard;) the value of D, and of the constants n′ n″, above described.

In the body of the page, the first column from the left hand contains the number of the star in the zone, and the second column its magnitude.

The next nine columns, headed "seconds of transits," exhibit the seconds by the clock, at which the star passed the wires as numbered.

The twelfth column, headed T, shows the clock time of the transits reduced to the mean wire.

The thirteenth column, headed a, contains the sum of the corrections for reducing T to the mean right ascension for 1850.0.

In the fourteenth column, headed Micrometer, the roman numeral indicates the transit wire at which the declination of the star was observed. It is the argument for obtaining the reduction to the meridian. The second number is that of the micrometer wire used in observing the declination, and the following numbers show in revolutions and parts the position of that wire on the scale.

The fifteenth and sixteenth columns contain the reductions, which being added to D, give the mean declination of the observed star for 1850.0. In these reductions using the previous notation—

$$D = i + r + (\rho + n' + \varDelta M\delta.)$$
$$d = (\Sigma \varDelta \delta) + n''.$$

The two last columns show the resulting mean right ascensions and declinations for 1850.0.

The letters B, M, Z, on the right hand of the page, indicate that the stars against which they are placed may be found either in the catalogue of the British Association, the Madrass catalogue of Taylor, or in the catalogue of Argelander's Southern Zones. The asterisks on the left hand margin refer to notes at the end of the volume. And in regard to them, it is proper to state that the hand-books of the observers contain many notes relative to the state of the weather; to errors of reading which have been corrected by reference to the context; to groups and colors of stars; and other incidents which have been omitted, as not affecting the results.

At the bottom of every page, in which a zone is commenced, are given the readings of all the instruments, the circle, barometer, and thermometers, with the times at which they were taken; also, under the head of "corrections," the corrections for error of the clock, and their rates; the quantities m, n, c, used in determining the corrections for errors of azimuth, level, and collimation; also the zenith point and micrometer coincidence.

The reduction of these observations was commenced in the year in which they were made, and, under the direction of Professors Hubbard and Major, the observations had been copied from the observing-books, and the intervals of the transit wires, as also the reductions to the mean places for 1850 had been computed for each zone. The time of transit over the mean wire, designated by T, had also, for the greater part of the work, been determined.

On resuming the work in 1859, the reductions for all the zones, as before described, were computed and tabulated by myself. I also applied these reductions to the first twenty-six zones—completing the work thus far. While thus engaged, Professor Pendleton had revised and corrected the values of T found previously. He also computed this quantity for the zones where it had been omitted; and, from the twenty-sixth zone to the end, he applied the corrections, thus finishing the whole work. To insure as great accuracy as our means permitted, we both revised these parts of the first computation.

It will be perceived that a very considerable portion of the zones now published are in high south declination. The reason for observing them first has been that they require a more favorable atmosphere, will probably present the greatest difference of results, and demand more frequent observation to arrive at the necessary accuracy of determination. And here it is proper to state that, in these more southern zones, the estimates of magnitude, which are those of the observer at the time, will always depend upon the kind of weather in which they were made, and be on this account uncertain. In other respects, the present publication gives all the data from which the results have been derived, so that each observation may be computed separately—thus affording a check upon the more general methods described in the first part of this letter. The discrepancies between the results of observations of the same star made here, as well as those which have been discovered in comparisons with other catalogues, will be the subject of future examination. Such of them as have probably been occasioned by misreadings of the micrometer are mentioned in the notes at the end of the volume.

Very respectfully,

JAS. FERGUSON,
Assistant Astronomer.

NATIONAL OBSERVATORY, *October* 1, 1860.

D is the declination of the middle of the Zones.

D. = −24° 56′.

Right Ascension.	Zone.	Page.	No. Stars.
h. m. h. m.			
19 29 to 23 48	LXIX.	85	163
20 23 0 25	LXX.	89	94

D. = −25° 26′.

Right Ascension.	Zone.	Page.	No. Stars.
19 26 to 0 25	LXVIII.	82	166

D. = −25° 56′.

Right Ascension.	Zone.	Page.	No. Stars.
19 26 to 1 56	LXVI.	77	173

D. = −26° 27′.

Right Ascension.	Zone.	Page.	No. Stars.
15 3 to 15 46	XXXI.	38	17
15 29 16 49	XXXIII.	40	50
17 32 17 57	XLI.	47	18
20 0 21 1	XXXV.	42	17
21 1 23 0	L.	55	50

D. = −26° 56′.

Right Ascension.	Zone.	Page.	No. Stars.
15 52 to 21 5	XXVIII.	35	115
20 55 23 36	LXXI.	91	69

D. = −27° 26′.

Right Ascension.	Zone.	Page.	No. Stars.
20 42 to 1 42	LXII.	71	135
13 23 17 16	XXXV.	28	99
16 30 19 42	XXIV.	26	64
19 42 21 0	XXXIX.	45	40

D. = −27° 56′.

Right Ascension.	Zone.	Page.	No. Stars.
20 35 to 0 29	LX.	67	161
1 31 2 29	LXV.	77	37
15 22 16 8	XVIII.	20	21
15 26 18 11	XXVII.	33	100
18 6 18 59	XXXVII.	43	36
18 57 20 36	LXIII.	74	68
22 2 22 32	LIV.	59	18

D. = −28° 27′.

Right Ascension.	Zone.	Page.	No. Stars.
13 12 to 15 20	XXIII.	25	65
15 13 17 22	XXII.	24	47
18 29 21 4	LV.	60	62
21 12 0 6	LXXII.	72	92

D. = −28° 56′.

Right Ascension.	Zone.	Page.	No. Stars.
h. m. h. m.			
10 30 to 11 27	X.	9	29
12 3 16 58	XV.	16	161
14 2 15 0	XVII.	19	27
17 2 17 30	XXX.	38	20
17 30 19 26	XXXII.	39	50
18 34 20 31	XLVIII.	53	48
18 51 19 45	LII.	58	42
20 29 21 0	XLIII.	49	21
21 0 23 1	XLVI.	51	66

D. = −29° 28′.

Right Ascension.	Zone.	Page.	No. Stars.
11 11 to 12 30	VIII.	8	14
15 30 17 29	LX.	8	26
18 8 20 34	LI.	56	52
19 15 20 17	LXI.	70	32
20 15 0 29	LVIII.	64	91

D. = −39° 49′.

Right Ascension.	Zone.	Page.	No. Stars.
9 20 to 10 71	VII.	7	6

D. = −40° 26′.

Right Ascension.	Zone.	Page.	No. Stars.
9 49 to 16 38	XI.	9	128
15 7 15 59	II.	3	11
16 53 18 29	XXXVIII.	44	37
18 37 20 9	XXIX.	37	13
20 25 21 4	LXXIII.	75	10
21 25 22 19	LXXVIII.	98	19
22 28 0 28	LXXIV.	95	30

D. = −40° 50′.

Right Ascension.	Zone.	Page.	No. Stars.
11 4 to 15 19	VI.	6	41
14 59 17 48	XXI.	22	52
17 48 19 13	XLIX.	54	26
19 2 20 23	LIX.	66	24

D. = −41° 20′.

Right Ascension.	Zone.	Page.	No. Stars.
21 50 to 0 31	LXIV.	75	59
10 41 17 24	XIII.	13	90
13 2 13 40	XVI.	19	11
13 34 14 31	XX.	22	17
14 40 20 0	XXVI.	30	124
18 0 18 30	XLVII.	52	11
18 58 22 55	LVII.	62	52
19 58 21 26	LIII.	59	16

D is the declination of the middle of the Zones.

D. = $-41^\circ\ 51'$,

Right Ascension.					Zone.	Page.	No. Stars.
h.	*m.*		*h.*	*m.*			
13	4	to	17	0	XIX.	21	36
18	31		20	56	LVI.	61	50
21	11		23	52	LXXV.	96	24

D. = $-42^\circ\ 21'$.

15	41	to	16	8	XXXIV.	42	9
16	4		18	59	XLII.	47	61

D. = $-42^\circ\ 51'$.

16	4	to	18	1	XXXVI.	42	32
20	29		21	57	XLV.	50	24

D. = $-43^\circ\ 22'$.

0	37	to	4	54	LXXIX.	99	55
16	2		18	38	XIV.	15	43
21	4		23	26	LXXVI.	96	19
23	33		0	27	LXXX.	100	14

D. = $-43^\circ\ 52'$.

Right Ascension.					Zone.	Page.	No. Stars.
h.	*m.*		*h.*	*m.*			
9	40	to	10	34	XII.	12	13
16	3		17	13	XL.	46	15
19	36		21	43	LYVII.	81	24

D. = $-44^\circ\ 7'$.

14	9	to	15	1	IV.	5	17

D. = $-44^\circ\ 23'$.

9	15	to	15	29	V.	5	40
18	3		20	0	XLIII.	50	18

D. = $-44^\circ\ 53'$.

9	38	to	12	2	III.	4	34
10	29		11	34	I.	3	14
13	31		14	31	I.	3	16
20	24		0	44	LXXVII.	97	56

ZONES OF STARS

OBSERVED WITH

THE MERIDIAN CIRCLE

OF

THE NATIONAL OBSERVATORY.

1846.

Number.	Magnitude.	SECONDS OF TRANSITS. I.	II.	III.	IV.	V.	VI.	VII.	10.	11.	T.	a.	MICROMETER.	D.	d.	Mean Right Ascension, 1850.0.	Mean South Declination, 1850.0.
Zone I. April 3. H. $D. = -44° 23' 40''.0$. $n'. = -4''.99$. $n''. = -25''.00$.																	
											h. m. s.	s.	r.	' "	"	h. m. s.	° ' "
1	9	..	..	..	34.5	..	5.7	..	..	..	10 29 34.77	+70.96	IV. 5 50.470	—18 24.84	— 7.14	10 30 45.73	44 42 11.98
2	8.9	14.5	..	46.0	1.0	16.7	32.3	..	..	..	34 1.34	71.01	" 3 42.881	34 46.15	8.06	35 12.35	44 58 34.21
3	7.8	..	..	28.5	44.2	0.0	15.5	31.0	..	..	49 44.52	71.02	" 2 48.103	40 37.79	11.03	50 55.54	45 4 28.82
4	9	..	26.0	41.0	56.5	11.0	..	..	..	..	54 56.38	71.33	" 6 42.135	14 26.40	11.93	56 7.71	44 38 18.33
5	7.8	58.0	13.0	28.0	..	..	14.2	30.0	..	..	11 2 43.88	71.44	" 5 43.818	22 17.92	13.28	11 3 55.32	44 46 11.20
6	7	..	48.0	3.6	19.0	34.5	50.0	..	..	..	8 19.13	71.51	" 2 49.220	39 57.93	14.19	9 30.64	45 3 52.12 B.
7	8	..	..	..	39.0	55.0	10.0	..	..	..	9 39.42	71.56	" 5 52.505	17 12.85	14.40	10 50.98	44 41 7.25
*8	7.8	..	44.0	0.0	15.2	..	..	..	..	..	13 15.24	71.60	" 4 39.852	30 30.11	14.94	14 26.84	44 54 25.05
9	9	..	..	..	52.0	7.0	..	..	..	..	13 51.86	71.61	" 2 48.215	40 33.25	15.02	15 3.47	45 4 28.27
10	7.8	..	52.5	8.0	23.0	39.0	54.5	..	..	..	17 23.51	71.67	" 2 50.152	39 25.11	15.57	18 35.18	45 3 20.68 B.
*11	9	..	34.0	49.0	4.5	20.0	35.8	..	..	..	20 4.75	71.72	" 3 45.042	33 30.33	15.97	21 16.47	44 57 26.30
12	8.9	..	11.0	..	41.5	57.0	..	..	..	..	29 41.70	71.88	" 3 48.151	31 41.16	17.27	30 53.58	44 55 38.43
13	9	..	51.0	6.0	22.0	..	..	..	..	..	31 21.83	71.91	" 3 43.908	34 10.08	17.46	32 33.74	44 58 7.54
14	9	..	..	..	..	..	2.3	..	..	..	11 31 31.45	71.91	VI. 2 41.503	44 29.20	17.48	11 32 43.36	45 8 26.68
$D. = -44° 24' 0''.0$. $n'. = -12''.55$. $n''. = -26''.00$.																	
15	8.9	..	47.8	2.8	18.2	33.7	49.0	..	..	..	13 31 18.38	74.26	IV. 5 48.240	19 43.73	12.30	13 32 32.64	44 43 56.03 M.
16	9	..	1.0	16.0	32.0	47.2	..	..	..	..	33 31.83	74.31	" 6 38.570	16 32.85	12.22	34 46.14	44 40 45.07 M.
17	8.9	..	8.0	23.0	38.0	54.0	9.3	..	..	..	48 38.54	74.62	" 5 48.129	19 47.86	11.62	49 53.16	44 43 59.48
18	6.7	..	38.0	53.5	8.8	24.2	40.0	..	..	..	51 8.99	74.68	" 4 43.766	28 13.53	11.47	32 23.67	44 52 25.00 B.
19	9	..	58.0	13.2	29.0	44.4	59.0	..	..	..	59 28.85	74.84	" 1 46.076	47 47.37	10.98	14 0 43.69	45 11 58.35
20	9	..	22.0	37.2	53.0	8.2	24.0	..	..	..	14 2 53.02	74.91	" 1 37.738	52 40.56	10.74	4 7.93	45 16 51.30 M.
21	5.6	..	..	..	34.0	48.0	..	..	..	..	8 33.30	75.05	" 1 29.310	57 37.57	10.33	9 48.35	45 21 47.90 B.
22	7	..	..	..	..	9.5	25.0	40.5	..	..	9 54.66	75.05	V. 7 47.602	5 18.49	10.25	11 9.71	44 29 28.74 B.
23	9.10	..	..	41.8	57.0	..	..	..	..	..	12 57.18	75.13	IV. 3 43.409	34 29.09	10.00	14 12.31	44 58 39.09
24	7	..	47.5	..	..	33.8	49.4	..	..	..	16 18.55	75.20	" 5 51.700	17 40.94	9.72	17 34.75	44 41 50.66
25	7.8	..	..	0.8	..	32.0	47.5	..	..	..	15 16.76	75.16	" 6 52.780	8 13.41	9.79	16 31.92	44 32 23.20
26	8	..	28.0	44.0	..	14.4	29.2	..	..	..	18 59.02	75.24	" 6 42.718	14 6.37	9.48	20 14.26	44 38 15.85
27	9	..	14.4	29.5	45.5	0.8	16.5	..	..	..	24 45.43	75.38	" 3 45.555	33 13.05	8.93	26 0.81	44 57 21.98 M.
28	8.9	..	38.5	54.0	9.6	25.0	40.5	..	..	..	27 9.65	75.44	" 1 44.075	48 57.77	8.72	28 25.09	45 13 6.49 M.
29	8	..	45.0	0.0	15.2	31.0	46.4	..	..	..	29 15.64	75.46	" 2 41.553	44 28.25	8.45	30 31.10	45 8 36.70
30	9.10	..	11.5	27.0	43.0	58.0	..	..	..	..	14 31 42.69	75.52	" 3 45.920	33 0.43	8.25	14 32 58.21	44 57 8.68
Zone II. April 6. H. $D. = -39° 56' 50''.0$. $n'. = -12''.90$. $n''. = -12''.00$.																	
1	8.9	..	33.1	47.8	2.5	16.2	31.0	..	..	..	15 7 2.06	76.53	IV. 3 45.061	33 14.74	11.81	15 8 18.59	40 30 16.55 M.
2	8	..	..	..	..	..	..	34.0	..	..	7 50.93	76.51	VII. 6 37.530	17 2.56	11.73	9 7.44	14 2.29
3	6	..	48.0	2.0	16.2	31.0	45.0	..	..	..	10 16.38	76.57	IV. 7 41.280	9 0.08	11.38	11 32.95	6 1.46 B.
4	9	..	..	..	28.0	43.0	..	..	..	..	15 10 28.19	76.52	" 6 40.861	15 7.45	11.35	15 11 44.71	40 12 8.80 M.

CORRECTIONS.

	COR. TO CLOCK.	HOURLY COR.	m.	n.	c.	ZENITH POINT.	COINC.
	s.	s.	s.	s.	s.	° ' "	r.
April 3, at 12h....	+62.491	+0.008	+0.521	—0.342	+0.246	359 59 59.37	40.000
6, "	+63.261	+0.014	+0.521	—0.342	+0.246	359 59 57.66	40.081

INSTRUMENT READINGS.

	CIRCLE. A.	B.	C.	D.	Mean.	BAR.	THERMOM. At.	Ex.
h.	° ' "	"	"	"	"	I.	°	°
Zone I.—April 3, 10.6..	276 21 11.8	14.7	15.6	11.0	13.27	30.420	49.6	44.7
11.6..	13.3	15.0	16.0	14.6	14.72	30.424	46.6	42.6
13.5..	6.7	8.7	9.3	7.4	8.02	30.464	44.4	39.5
14.6..	6.4	8.5	10.0	8.3	8.30	30.480	43.8	38.8
Zone II.—April 6, 15.0..	280 45 1.4	3.0	6.0	3.5	3.47	30.386	52.6	48.0
16.0..	0.5	1.6	5.4	3.5	2.75	30.370	52.0	46.5

Number.	Magnitude.	Seconds of Transits. I.	II.	III.	IV.	V.	VI.	VII.	10.	11.	T.	a.	Micrometer.	D.	d.	Mean Right Ascension, 1850.0.	Mean South Declination, 1850.0.
Zone II. April 6. H. D. = −39° 56′ 50″.0. n′. = −12″.90. n″. = −12″.00. (Continued.)																	
											h. m. s.	s.	r.	′ ″	″	h. m. s.	° ′ ″
5	8.9	. .	15.2	29.0	43.5	57.5	12.2	. .	. .	. .	15 16 43.38	+76.55	IV. 6 48.231	−10 51.59	−10.43	15 18 0.93	40 7 52.02
6	6	. .	24.0	38.4	53.0	7.2	21.8	. .	. .	. .	20 52.83	76.77	" 2 44.320	42 28.97	9.85	22 9.60	39 28.82
*7	9	. .	. .	13.5	. .	33.0	. .	. .	. .	. .	25 28.18	76.84	" 3 40.618	35 48.99	9.15	26 45.02	32 48.14
8	9	. .	. .	41.0	. .	10.0	. .	. .	. .	. .	25 55.42	76.84	" 3 43.872	33 56.01	9.08	27 12.26	30 55.09 M.
9	9	. .	. .	. .	47.0	0.9	15.3	29.5	. .	. .	35 46.44	77.01	" 3 39.870	36 15.04	7.51	37 3.45	33 12.55
10	9	. .	5.0	19.6	34.0	48.5	2.2	. .	. .	. .	48 33.79	77.17	" 6 39.015	16 11.60	5.24	49 50.96	13 6.84
11	9	. .	. .	33.3	47.5	2.1	16.5	. .	. .	. .	15 59 47.56	77.40	" 2 38.060	46 7.84	3.24	16 1 4.96	40 43 1.08 M.
Zone III. April 13. H. D. = −44° 23′ 30″.0. n′. = −4″.49. n″. = −26″.00.																	
1	9	. .	5.0	21.5	. .	53.0	. .	. .	. .	. .	9 38 37.01	75.88	IV. 1 42.810	49 41.64	10.63	9 39 52.89	45 13 22.27 M.
2	8	. .	36.0	51.0	7.0	22.8	38.5	. .	. .	. .	39 7.19	75.90	" 1 42.210	50 3.03	10.69	40 23.09	45 13 43.72 M.
3	7	. .	21.0	36.2	52.0	7.2	23.0	. .	. .	. .	42 51.99	75.94	" 3 36.615	38 27.07	11.92	44 7.93	45 2 8.99 B.
4	7.8	. .	36.5	51.2	7.0	22.3	37.5	. .	. .	. .	47 6.99	76.03	" 7 37.941	10 58.22	13.20	48 23.02	44 34 41.42 B.
5	9	. .	. .	. .	. .	. .	. .	42.5	. .	. .	47 56.29	75.98	VII. 2 37.858	46 37.26	13.45	49 12.27	45 10 20.71
6	9	. .	18.0	33.2	48.5	4.2	20.0	. .	. .	. .	57 48.91	75.98	IV. 2 38.210	46 25.68	16.46	59 4.89	45 10 12.14
7	8.9	. .	. .	. .	. .	. .	47.2	2.5	. .	. .	59 16.69	76.15	VI. 6 41.829	14 37.90	16.80	10 0 32.84	44 38 24.70
8	8	. .	17.5	33.3	49.0	4.2	19.8	. .	. .	. .	10 2 48.87	76.15	IV. 2 50.130	39 26.80	17.79	4 5.02	45 3 14.59
9	9	. .	. .	. .	. .	. .	40.0	55.0	. .	. .	3 9.42	76.19	VI. 6 48.833	10 32.26	17.91	4 25.61	44 34 20.17
10	9	. .	29.3	45.0	1.0	16.0	. .	. .	. .	. .	12 0.63	76.26	IV. 4 40.818	29 57.15	20.51	13 16.89	44 53 47.66 M.
11	9	. .	. .	5.5	21.5	36.5	. .	. .	. .	. .	14 21.29	76.28	" 2 43.602	43 15.88	20.97	15 37.57	45 7 6.85
12	9	. .	. .	21.0	. .	52.0	7.5	. .	. .	. .	18 36.73	76.35	" 5 40.140	24 28.27	22.20	19 53.08	44 48 20.47
13	9	. .	. .	21.5	37.5	53.0	8.4	. .	. .	. .	18 37.52	76.36	" 5 43.780	22 20.30	22.21	19 53.88	44 16 12.51
14	9.10	. .	26.0	41.0	. .	12.5	. .	. .	. .	. .	23 57.02	76.39	" 1 42.574	49 49.79	23.64	25 13.41	45 13 43.43
15	9	. .	. .	8.0	24.0	39.3	55.3	. .	. .	. .	26 24.02	76.43	" 2 43.110	43 33.53	24.25	27 40.45	45 7 27.78
16	9	. .	58.0	. .	29.0	44.2	0.0	. .	. .	. .	29 29.02	76.49	" 5 50.410	18 28.02	25.03	30 45.51	44 42 23.05
17	8	. .	7.3	22.2	38.3	53.5	8.8	. .	. .	. .	11 2 38.11	76.95	" 5 43.910	22 15.81	31.96	11 3 55.06	44 46 17.77
18	8	. .	42.3	57.5	13.6	28.8	44.5	. .	. .	. .	8 13.45	77.02	" 2 49.188	39 59.94	33.04	9 30.47	45 4 2.98
19	8.9	. .	. .	. .	34.0	48.2	4.3	19.8	. .	. .	9 33.68	77.03	" 6 37.290	17 17.63	33.27	10 50.71	44 41 20.90
20	8.9	. .	38.5	54.0	9.5	25.0	. .	. .	. .	. .	12 9.56	77.09	" 4 40.050	30 24.28	33.75	13 26.65	44 54 28.03 M.
21	9	. .	14.5	30.5	. .	. .	7.0	. .	. .	. .	12 45.94	77.09	" 3 34.070	39 56.83	33.85	14 3.03	45 4 0.68
22	8.9	. .	47.0	2.3	18.0	33.0	58.8	. .	. .	. .	17 17.93	77.16	" 3 35.090	39 23.35	34.65	18 35.09	45 3 28.00 B.
23	9.10	. .	28.0	43.0	59.0	14.2	29.6	. .	. .	. .	19 58.86	77.21	" 3 46.085	32 55.67	35.11	21 16.07	44 57 0.78 M.
24	9.10	. .	. .	47.0	2.0	18.0	32.5	. .	. .	. .	23 2.24	77.26	" 1 38.825	52 1.84	35.62	24 19.50	45 16 7.46
25	9	. .	4.8	20.0	35.5	. .	6.8	. .	. .	. .	29 35.69	77.36	" 4 38.825	31 7.16	36.71	30 53.05	44 55 13.87
26	9	29.5	45.0	. .	16.0	. .	. .	. .	. .	. .	31 16.01	77.38	" 3 44.170	34 2.01	36.95	32 33.39	44 58 8.96
27	9.10	. .	. .	. .	. .	. .	40.0	56.0	. .	. .	31 9.50	77.38	VI. 2 44.150	42 56.73	36.93	32 26.88	45 7 3.66
28	9.10	. .	. .	. .	. .	. .	. .	7.2	. .	. .	33 21.24	77.43	VII. 5 39.325	24 56.45	37.27	34 38.67	44 49 3.72
29	7	. .	31.0	46.5	2.0	17.1	33.0	. .	. .	. .	37 2.01	77.49	IV. 4 45.185	27 24.05	37.83	38 19.50	44 51 31.88
30	8.9	. .	11.5	27.0	42.6	58.2	14.0	. .	. .	. .	11 40 42.79	77.54	" 1 42.310	49 59.58	38.36	11 42 0.33	45 14 7.94

CORRECTIONS.

	Cor. to Clock.	Hourly Cor.	m.	n.	c.	Zenith Point.	Coinc.
	s.	s.	s.	s.	s.	° ′ ″	r.
April 13, at 10h...	+67.851	+ 0.032	+0.521	−0.342	+0.246	359° 59′ 58″.79	40.070

INSTRUMENT READINGS.

	Circle. A.	B.	C.	D.	Mean.	Bar.	Thermom. At.	Ex.
h.						I.		
Zone III.—April 13, 9.6	276° 21′ 3″.5	5″.6	7″.3	6″.0	5″.60	29.996	51°.3	41°.8
10.5	0.5	3.8	5.1	2.0	2.85	30.032	49.0	40.0
11.0	0.7	3.6	5.0	2.0	2.82	30.046	48.3	38.7
12.1	0.5	3.5	5.0	2.0	2.75	30.056	46.5	36.8

Zone III. April 13. H. *D.* = −44° 23′ 30″.0. n′. = −4″.49. n″. = −26″.00. (Continued.)

Number.	Magnitude.	SECONDS OF TRANSITS. I.	II.	III.	IV.	V.	VI.	VII.	10.	11.	T.	a.	MICROMETER.	D.	d.	Mean Right Ascension, 1850.0.	Mean South Declination, 1850.0.
											h. m. s.	s.	r.	′ ″	″	h. m. s.	° ′ ″
31	9	. .	31.2	47.0	3.0	18.0	34.0	. .	. .	. .	11 41 2.77	+77.54	IV. 1 47.898	−46 42.77	−38.42	11 42 20.31	45 10 51.19
32	7.8	. .	45.5	1.2	16.8	32.0	47.4	. .	. .	. .	50 16.68	77.71	" 3 41.280	35 43.59	39.71	51 34.39	44 59 53.30
33	9	. .	0.0	15.5	30.5	46.2	1.8	. .	. .	. .	58 30.89	77.86	" 5 46.682	20 38.39	40.74	59 48.75	44 44 49.13 M.
34	8.9	. .	27.5	42.8	58.2	13.6	29.0	. .	. .	. .	12 1 58.31	77.90	" 6 47.802	11 8.62	41.12	12 3 16.21	44 35 19.74 M.

Zone IV. April 13. H. *D.* = −43° 38′ 20″.0. n′. = −8″.26. n″. = −22″.00

Number.	Magnitude.	I.	II.	III.	IV.	V.	VI.	VII.	10.	11.	T.	a.	MICROMETER.	D.	d.	Mean Right Ascension, 1850.0.	Mean South Declination, 1850.0.
1	7	. .	. .	. .	. .	4.2	20.0	35.0	. .	. .	14 9 49.05	80.35	V. 1 40.195	51 6.22	7.49	14 11 9.40	44 29 33.71 B.
2	9	. .	. .	. .	12.0	27.0	42.5	57.3	. .	. .	11 11.88	80.35	IV. 5 48.313	19 39.22	7.39	12 32.23	43 58 6.61 M.
3	9	. .	. .	36.4	52.0	7.0	. .	. .	. .	. .	13 51.88	80.43	" 2 38.292	46 16.31	7.14	15 12.31	44 24 43.45
4	7	. .	41.0	56.2	11.5	27.0	42.2	. .	. .	. .	15 11.64	80.46	" 1 35.200	54 1.49	7.04	16 32.10	44 32 28.53 B.
5	9	. .	. .	43.2	59.0	14.0	. .	. .	. .	. .	17 58.81	80.51	" 1 39.973	51 13.96	6.80	19 19.32	44 29 40.76
6	8.9	. .	17.4	32.3	48.0	3.0	18.4	. .	. .	. .	20 47.83	80.54	" 4 41.000	29 46.98	6.55	22 8.37	44 8 13.53 M.
7	8.9	. .	21.8	36.8	52.0	7.0	22.4	. .	. .	. .	33 52.01	80.80	" 5 42.315	23 9.16	5.23	35 12.81	44 1 34.39
8	8	. .	18.0	33.5	48.5	4.0	19.0	. .	. .	. .	34 48.62	80.83	" 3 41.702	35 23.59	5.13	36 9.45	44 13 48.72 M.
9	8	. .	31.3	46.3	2.0	17.0	32.5	. .	. .	. .	41 1.85	80.94	" 2 49.332	39 49.39	4.43	42 22.79	44 18 13.82
10	9	. .	2.5	18.0	33.3	48.5	. .	. .	. .	. .	44 33.24	80.99	" 4 46.570	26 31.67	4.01	45 54.23	44 4 55.68
11	7.8	. .	38.5	54.0	9.0	24.0	40.0	. .	. .	. .	45 9.11	81.00	" 4 45.610	27 5.34	3.93	46 30.11	44 5 29.27
12	9	. .	. .	. .	. .	. .	36.7	. .	. .	. .	45 6.01	81.02	VI. 2 49.410	39 46.46	3.94	46 27.03	44 18 10.40
13	9	. .	. .	. .	. .	. .	50.0	. .	. .	. .	47 19.26	81.08	" 1 39.580	45 36.31	3.66	48 40.34	44 23 59.97
14	8.9	. .	. .	. .	33.6	52.0	7.2	22.2	. .	. .	54 36.50	81.20	IV. 2 37.750	46 35.00	2.73	55 57.70	44 24 57.73
15	9	. .	50.2	. .	. .	35.2	51.0	6.0	. .	. .	57 20.40	81.26	" 6 40.546	15 21.36	2.35	58 41.66	43 53 43.71
16	9	. .	7.2	22.2	38.0	53.0	8.0	. .	. .	. .	15 0 37.73	81.32	" 1 45.290	48 7.70	1.93	15 1 59.05	44 26 29.63
†17	8.9	. .	57.0	12.0	27.5	43.0	58.2	. .	. .	. .	1 27.58	81.33	" 2 40.270	45 6.97	1.81	2 48.91	44 23 28.78

Zone V. April 15. M. *D.* = −43° 53′ 00″.0. n′. = −9″.44. n″. = −23″.00.

Number.	Magnitude.	I.	II.	III.	IV.	V.	VI.	VII.	10.	11.	T.	a.	MICROMETER.	D.	d.	Mean Right Ascension, 1850.0.	Mean South Declination, 1850.0.
1	10	. .	57.0	12.8	27.8	43.0	58.5	. .	. .	. .	9 15 27.85	16.18	IV. 3 35.16	39 14.36	13.81	9 15 44.03	44 32 28.17
2	6.7	37.7	53.0	8.0	23.5	38.5	54.0	9.0	. .	. .	40 23.44	16.41	" 7 38.63	10 33.32	20.55	40 39.85	44 3 53.87 B.
3	6.7	. .	36.2	52.0	7.1	22.1	38.0	. .	. .	. .	48 7.12	16.44	" 2 46.73	41 20.19	22.50	48 23.56	44 34 42.69 B.
*4	8	. .	40.0	55.0	10.5	26.0	41.0	56.5	. .	. .	54 10.53	16.52	" 5 46.07	20 58.32	24.11	54 27.05	44 14 22.43
5	6.7	. .	. .	. .	29.5	44.5	0.0	15.0	. .	. .	10 5 29.47	16.65	" 7 46.14	6 11.23	26.79	10 5 46.12	43 59 38.02
6	6.7	. .	45.5	1.0	16.2	31.3	46.5	. .	. .	. .	25 16.11	16.84	" 5 40.00	24 30.86	31.30	25 32.95	44 18 2.16
7	9.10	25.1	41.0	56.0	11.1	26.1	41.5	57.0	. .	. .	53 11.16	17.19	" 6 45.90	12 14.63	37.03	53 28.35	44 5 51.66
8	8	. .	6.5	22.3	38.0	53.3	8.5	24.0	. .	. .	11 3 37.77	17.32	" 1 37.62	52 38.07	38.95	11 3 55.09	44 46 17.02
9	8	. .	8.8	23.6	39.0	54.0	9.5	. .	. .	. .	23 39.00	17.62	" 6 41.56	14 46.91	42.31	23 56.62	44 8 29.22
10	10	. .	. .	. .	27.0	. .	. .	. .	. .	. .	36 26.96	17.81	" 1 40.31	51 4.60	44.24	36 44.77	44 44 48.84
11	4	. .	51.4	6.5	21.5	36.8	52.2	. .	. .	. .	43 21.70	17.92	" 5 46.62	20 42.03	45.18	43 39.62	44 14 27.21
12	10	. .	43.0	58.0	14.0	. .	. .	0.0	. .	. .	11 52 13.74	18.06	" 7 43.46	7.44.18	46.32	11 52 31.80	44 1 30.50

CORRECTIONS.

	COR. TO CLOCK.	HOURLY COR.	*m.*	*n.*	*c.*	ZENITH POINT.	COINC.
	s.	s.	s.	s.	s.	° ′ ″	r.
April 13, at 10*h*...	+67.851	+ 0.032	+0.521	−0.342	+0.246	359 59 59.08	40.070
April 15, at 12*h*...	+ 8.214	+ 0.004	+0.521	−0.342	+0.246	0 0 0.94	40.075

† Zone IV, 17.—Moon within half an hour of the meridian.

INSTRUMENT READINGS.

	CIRCLE. A.	B.	C.	D.	Mean.	BAR.	THERMOM. At.	Ex.
h.	° ′ ″	″	″	″	″	I.	°	°
Zone IV.—April 13, 14.0	277 6 2.3	4.0	7.8	6.2	5.07	30.082	45.5	35.8
15.0	4.0	5.8	9.5	7.2	6.62	30.084	44.5	34.0
Zone V.—April 15, 9.2	276 50 54.0	54.5	58.2	52.4	54.77	30.235	56.0	50.0
11.0	. . . .	. .	. .	. .	. .	30.282	52.0	43.0
12.0	. . . .	. .	. .	. .	. .	. .	51.0	40.5
14.0	. . . .	. .	. .	. .	. .	30.320	47.5	38.5
15.5	. . . .	. .	. .	. .	. .	30.350	46.0	38.5

Number.	Magnitude.	SECONDS OF TRANSITS. I.	II.	III.	IV.	V.	VI.	VII.	10.	11.	T.	a.	MICROMETER.	D.	d.	Mean Right Ascension, 1850.0.	Mean South Declination, 1850.0.
Zone V. April 15. M. $D. = -43° 53' 00''.0$. n. = −9''.44. n. = −23''.09. (Continued.)																	
											h. m. s.	s.	r.			h. m. s.	
13	7.8	44.5	0.0	15.5	31.0	. .	2.0	17.0	. .	. .	11 59 30.97	+18.18	IV. 1 40.6	—50' 54''.08	—47''.22	11 59 49.15	44° 44' 41''.30 M.
14	6	11.5	27.0	42.5	58.0	13.5	29.0	44.5	. .	. .	12 2 58.05	18.24	" 2 46.5	41 30.10	47.61	12 3 16.29	35 17.71 M.
15	7.8	32.0	48.0	3.5	19.0	. .	50.0	. .	. .	. .	24 18.86	18.60	" 2 42.57	43 50.83	49.65	24 37.46	37 40.48
16	6	8.2	23.8	38.3	54.0	9.2	24.5	40.0	. .	. .	13 4 54.03	19.33	" 4 42.16	29 7.42	51.98	13 5 13.36	22 59.40 M.
17	8.9	. .	3.0	18.5	34.0	49.0	4.5	20.5	. .	. .	14 33.92	19.52	III. 1 36.25	53 26.43	52.22	14 53.44	47 18.65
18	9	7.8	23.2	38.7	54.0	9.1	24.5	40.0	. .	. .	18 53.93	19.60	IV. 5 41.86	23 26.63	52.30	19 13.53	17 18.93
19	6.7	. .	. .	. .	. .	. .	. .	. .	12.0	26.5	21 2.33	19.64	10. 1 39.30	51 38.20	52.33	21 21.97	45 30.53
*20	6.7	27.0	41.8	57.0	12.5	27.5	43.0	58.5	. .	. .	32 12.52	19.83	IV. 1 42.53	49 46.32	52.33	32 32.35	43 38.65 M.
21	6.7	. .	. .	11.0	26.2	41.2	57.0	. .	. .	. .	34 26.19	19.89	VI. 2 37.51	46 44.59	52.32	34 46.09	40 36.91 M.
22	3.4	20.5	35.5	50.6	6.3	21.4	37.0	51.8	. .	. .	49 6.20	20.15	VI. 7 39.20	10 13.59	52.12	49 26.35	4 5.71
23	6.7	2.5	18.0	33.0	49.0	3.3	19.0	34.0	. .	. .	14 5 48.44	20.46	" 5 41.49	23 38.93	51.51	14 6 8.90	17 30.44
24	4.5	. .	18.5	34.0	49.0	4.5	19.5	35.0	. .	. .	10 49.09	20.56	" 3 41.34	35 37.81	51.29	11 9.65	29 29.10 B.
25	3.4	. .	41.0	. .	11.5	. .	42.0	. .	. .	. .	16 11.46	20.66	VII. 3 36.31	38 27.88	51.00	16 32.12	32 18.88 B.
26	3.4	. .	. .	58.0	. .	28.0	. .	. .	. .	. .	16 13.14	20.67	11. 2 35.22	48 3.62	51.00	16 33.81	41 54.62
27	4.5	. .	38.0	53.5	9.6	24.0	40.0	. .	. .	. .	20 9.06	20.75	IV. 2 40.55	44 58.88	50.77	20 29.81	38 49.65
28	7	. .	. .	. .	. .	2.5	18.0	33.3	. .	. .	21 47.46	20.74	V. 6 42.20	14 24.20	50.66	22 8.20	8 14.86 M.
29	7	2.3	18.0	33.2	49.0	3.5	19.0	. .	. .	. .	35 48.52	21.01	VI. 5 47.92	19 53.17	49.61	36 9.53	13 42.78 M.
30	9	. .	31.1	46.2	1.1	17.0	32.5	. .	. .	. .	42 1.59	21.13	IV. 5 40.36	24 17.34	49.08	42 22.72	18 6.42
31	8	. .	18.0	33.5	. .	. .	. .	. .	. .	. .	45 48.63	21.19	III. 7 37.52	11 12.00	48.74	46 9.82	5 0.74
32	6	. .	. .	. .	. .	23.8	39.2	54.5	. .	. .	46 8.64	21.19	V. 6 36.58	17 41.18	48.71	46 29.83	11 29.89
33	3	38.2	53.5	9.0	24.5	40.0	55.4	10.5	. .	. .	58 24.51	21.46	IV. 2 35.20	48 6.28	47.46	58 45.97	41 53.74
34	7	. .	. .	51.5	7.0	22.1	38.0	53.0	. .	. .	15 1 6.95	21.50	" 2 34.34	48 36.54	47.17	15 1 28.45	42 23.71
35	7.8	16.0	31.5	47.0	2.2	17.5	32.8	48.1	. .	. .	11 2.19	21.66	" 4 41.17	29 42.10	46.36	11 23.85	23 28.46
36	3	. .	. .	. .	. .	. .	. .	. .	18.0	33 5	12 9.48	21.66	10. 6 41.17	14 59.02	45.69	12 31.14	8 44.71
37	8.9	53.7	9.0	24.5	40.0	55.0	11.2	. .	. .	. .	17 40.01	21.80	IV. 2 34.55	48 29.30	45.20	18 01.81	42 14.50
38	6	. .	4.0	19.3	34.5	50.0	5.3	20.5	. .	. .	21 34.61	21.86	" 3 35.13	39 15.45	44.68	21 56.47	33 0.13
39	3.4	26.3	42.1	57.5	13.0	28.1	43.5	59.0	. .	. .	25 12.83	21.92	" 4 34.0	33 53.34	44.30	25 34.75	27 37.64
40	8.9	. .	. .	10.8	25.7	41.5	56.3	12.0	. .	. .	15 29 25.93	21.99	" 3 37.64	37 47.13	43.61	15 29 47.92	44 31 30.74
Zone VI. April 16. H. $D. -40° 21' 0''.0$. n. = −9''.61. n. = −12''.00.																	
1	10	. .	47.0	1.5	16.0	30.6	45.1	. .	. .	. .	11 4 16.05	17.52	IV. 4 41.023	29 36.44	10.27	11 4 33.57	40 50 46.71
2	10	. .	37.2	. .	. .	. .	. .	. .	. .	. .	8 6.00	17.58	II. 5 47.080	20 16.38	10.86	8 23.58	40 41 27.24
3	8.9	. .	. .	. .	48.3	2.8	. .	. .	. .	. .	9 48.39	17.57	IV. 6 44.370	13 5.28	11.12	10 5.96	40 34 16.40
4	9	. .	. .	. .	. .	. .	. .	. .	7.8	22.5	10 2.50	17.58	10. 2 39.060	45 30.82	11.15	10 20.08	41 6 41.97
5	10	. .	. .	. .	. .	. .	. .	. .	7.5	22.0	18 2.64	17.71	10. 6 44.181	13 10.48	12.33	18 20.35	40 34 22.81
6	8	. .	39.4	54.0	8.4	23.3	37.5	52.2	. .	. .	23 8.55	17.73	IV. 1 40.650	50 30.93	13.03	23 26.28	41 11 43.96
7	10	. .	. .	22.5	38.0	. .	. .	. .	. .	. .	29 37.52	17.85	10. 5 49.538	18 50.01	13.89	29 55.37	40 40 3.90
8	9	. .	13.8	28.0	42.0	56.5	11.2	. .	. .	. .	35 42.31	17.93	V. 5 45.249	21 20.22	14.62	36 0.24	40 42 34.84
9	9	. .	. .	. .	42.5	57.0	11.4	. .	. .	. .	44 42.62	18.07	VII. 7 50.360	3 43.55	15.65	45 0.69	40 24 59.20
10	8.9	. .	. .	. .	. .	21.2	36.0	51.0	. .	. .	11 45 7.04	18.05	VI. 3 41.088	35 32.70	15.70	11 45 25.09	40 56 48.40

CORRECTIONS.

	COR. TO CLOCK.	HOURLY COR.	m.	n.	c.	ZENITH POINT.	COINC.
	s.	s.	s.	s.	s.		r.
April 16, at 12h. . . .	+ 8.190	+ 0.006	+0.521	—0.342	+0.246	359° 59' 59''.96	40.062

INSTRUMENT READINGS.

	CIRCLE. A.	B.	C.	D.	Mean.	BAR.	THERMOM. At.	Ex.
h.						I.		
Zone VI.—April 16, 11.0	280° 21' 5''.3	6''.8	11''.2	8''.4	7''.92	30.338	51°.0	46°.4
12.3	5.3	. .	. .	. .	. .	30.320	50.1	45.0
14.4	0.1	0.4	5.5	2.5	2.12	30.308	48.8	43.1
15.2	5.1	5.1	10.1	7.2	6.87	30.300	48.0	42.1

Number.	Magnitude.	SECONDS OF TRANSITS. I.	II.	III.	IV.	V.	VI.	VII.	10.	11.	T.	a.	MICROMETER.	D.	d.	Mean Right Ascension, 1850.0.	Mean South Declination, 1850.0.
Zone VI. April 16. H. $D.-40^{\circ}\ 21'\ 0''.0$. n. = $-9''.61$. n'' = $-12''.00$. (Continued.)																	
											h. m. s.	s.	r.	′ ″	″	h. m. s.	° ′ ″
11	9	. .	. .	. .	. .	52.2	7.0	. .	. .	. .	11 46 37.80	+18.06	VI. 2 39.045	—45 32.73	—15.87	11 46 55.86	41 6 48.60
12	8.9	. .	. .	. .	31.0	45.4	59.8	14.4	. .	. .	47 30.84	18.07	V. 2 43.473	42 58.79	15.97	47 48.91	41 4 14.76
13	8.9	3.3	18.0	32.8	47.0	1.5	16.0	31.0	. .	. .	53 47.14	18.16	IV. 3 36.165	38 24.45	16.60	54 5.30	40 59 41.05 M.
14	10	. .	. .	. .	. .	19.8	34.2	48.0	. .	. .	56 5.00	18.20	V. 4 38.248	31 12.91	16.82	56 23.20	40 52 29.73
15	10	. .	38.4	52.5	7.0	. .	36.5	. .	. .	. .	12 5 7.22	18.33	IV. 3 38.862	36 55.15	17.64	12 5 25.55	40 58 12.79
16	7.8	43.0	57.5	12.1	26.5	41.2	55.8	10.2	. .	. .	7 26.67	18.37	IV. 2 43.110	43 11.36	17.85	7 45.04	41 4 29.21 M.
17	8	3.3	17.5	32.0	46.5	0.8	15.5	30.0	. .	. .	11 46.56	18.43	IV. 7 39.051	10 16.91	18.19	12 4.99	40 31 35.10
18	9.10	28.0	42.2	56.8	11.0	. .	40.0	. .	. .	. .	15 11.27	18.49	III. 3 34.310	39 28.61	18.46	15 29.76	41 0 47.07 M.
19	7.8	. .	. .	15.8	30.5	45.0	59.6	13.8	. .	. .	16 30.56	18.50	V. 7 36.765	11 36.46	18.56	16 49.06	40 32 55.02
20	8.9	54.8	9.2	24.0	38.8	52.5	7.2	22.0	. .	. .	21 38.39	18.58	IV. 4 35.398	32 52.08	18.90	21 56.97	40 54 10.98 B.
21	8	35.5	50.0	4.8	18.8	33.5	47.8	2.5	. .	. .	14 3 19.02	20.20	IV. 3 42.511	34 43.58	18.70	14 3 39.22	40 56 2.28 M.
22	7.8	. .	38.3	53.2	7.8	22.5	37.0	. .	. .	. .	5 7.80	20.24	V. 2 37.390	46 30.30	18.57	5 28.04	41 7 48.87
23	10	. .	34.0	48.4	. .	. .	31.5	. .	. .	. .	7 2.76	20.25	IV. 7 38.460	10 37.52	18.44	7 23.01	40 31 55.96
24	10	. .	. .	. .	26.0	. .	55.0	9.5	. .	. .	14 26.11	20.37	VI. 7 36.414	11 48.59	17.91	14 46.48	40 33 6.50
25	7.8	58.5	13.8	28.2	42.2	57.0	11.8	26.2	. .	. .	25 42.56	20.57	IV. 4 40.312	30 1.24	16.96	26 3.13	40 51 18.20 B.
26	9	16.4	31.8	46.0	0.2	14.0	30.0	44.0	. .	. .	38 0.39	20.78	" 3 35.871	38 34.27	15.74	38 21.17	40 59 50.01
27	10	. .	. .	54.5	. .	. .	. .	52.5	. .	. .	40 9.00	20.83	" 1 38.500	51 45.71	15.53	40 29.83	41 13 1.24
28	9	12.5	27.0	41.7	56.5	. .	. .	. .	. .	. .	44 56.17	20.87	I. 5 41.590	23 26.71	14.98	45 17.04	40 44 41.69
29	9.10	. .	. .	. .	. .	. .	37.0	52.0	. .	. .	45 8.46	20.87	VII. 7 41.100	9 5.41	14.96	45 29.33	40 30 20.37
30	10	1.0	. .	. .	. .	58.0	. .	. .	. .	. .	51 44.23	21.02	IV. 1 37.620	52 16.08	14.18	52 5.25	41 13 30.26
31	10	. .	. .	27.8	. .	. .	11.8	. .	. .	. .	51 42.57	21.02	" 1 38.082	52 0.12	14.18	52 3.59	41 13 14.30
32	9	. .	. .	. .	. .	. .	. .	. .	21.3	36.0	52 16.02	21.02	VI. 2 41.190	44 17.91	14.11	52 37.04	41 5 32.02
33	9	. .	. .	. .	. .	. .	. .	. .	20.8	35.2	53 15.74	21.00	" 5 48.682	19 20.57	13.98	53 36.74	40 40 34.55
34	7.8	. .	. .	. .	14.2	28.8	42.2	. .	. .	. .	55 14.04	21.02	IV. 7 43.858	7 30.19	13.73	55 35.06	40 28 43.92 B.
35	10	. .	. .	19.8	. .	. .	. .	. .	. .	. .	58 34.51	21.13	III. 1 41.772	49 51.61	13.30	58 55.64	41 11 4.91
36	10	. .	. .	. .	52.5	6.5	. .	36.0	. .	. .	59 52.49	21.10	IV. 6 41.195	14 55.50	13.14	15 0 13.59	40 36 8.64
37	10	44.3	59.0	. .	28.4	. .	. .	. .	. .	. .	15 3 28.13	21.18	" 3 43.095	34 23.18	12.66	3 49.31	40 55 35.84
38	7.8	. .	. .	37.0	51.5	5.8	20.8	35.2	. .	. .	5 51.57	21.23	IV. 3 42.680	34 37.48	12.34	6 12.80	40 55 49.82 B.
39	10	22.2	37.0	. .	. .	. .	. .	. .	. .	. .	8 5.91	21.25	II. 4 40.643	49 29.95	12.03	8 27.16	41 11 41.98
40	8	. .	. .	. .	57.0	11.2	26.2	40.2	. .	. .	7 57.07	21.22	IV. 7 40.945	9 11.03	12.06	8 18.29	40 30 23.09 M.
†41	6.7	5.0	. .	34.0	. .	2.4	17.0	. .	. .	. .	15 19 48.32	21.41	" 6 35.072	18 28.27	10.35	15 20 9.73	40 39 38.62
Zone VII. April 17. M. $D.=-39^{\circ}\ 20'\ 10''.0$. $n'.=-3''.75$. $n''.=-12''.00$.																	
1	7.8	34.5	48.5	3.3	17.5	31.5	. .	0.0	. .	. .	9 20 17.36	17.07	IV. 4 38.45	31 5.91	3.86	9 20 34.43	39 51 19.77 B.
2	4	47.8	2.6	16.6	31.5	45.5	59.8	14.0	. .	. .	24 31.14	17.10	" 4 42.97	28 28.92	4.89	24 48.24	39 48 43.81 B.
3	7	. .	. .	. .	. .	20.0	34.5	48.5	. .	. .	26 5.73	17.09	VI. 3 35.02	39 2.87	5.30	26 22.82	39 59 18.17 B.
4	6	54.5	9.4	23.5	38.0	52.1	6.5	21.0	. .	. .	49 37.91	17.22	IV. 2 37.27	46 33.04	10.86	49 55.13	40 6 53.90
5	6.7	. .	. .	. .	6.0	. .	35.0	49.0	. .	. .	10 7 6.28	17.38	10. 6 39.40	15 56.57	14.75	10 7 23.66	39 36 21.32 B.
‡6	6.7	. .	. .	. .	16.0	30.0	. .	. .	. .	. .	7 15.96	17.39	10. 6 43.30	13 38.12	14.79	7 33.55	39 34 2.91 B.

CORRECTIONS.

	COR. TO CLOCK.	HOURLY COR.	m.	n.	c.	ZENITH POINT.	COINC.
	s.	s.	s.	s.	s.	° ′ ″	r.
April 17, at 12*h*...	+8.564	+0.008	+0.521	—0.342	+0.246	0 0 1.89	40.078

† Zone VI, 41.—Cloudy.

‡ Instrument disturbed.

April 17, stars very steady.

INSTRUMENT READINGS.

	CIRCLE. A.	B.	C.	D.	Mean.	BAR.	THERMOM. At.	Ex.
						I.		
Zone VII.—April 17, 9.2*h*.	281° 21′ 5″.2	6′.8	10′.8	9″.2	8″.00	30.200	61°.0	64°.5

Number.	Magnitude.	SECONDS OF TRANSITS. I.	II.	III.	IV.	V.	VI.	VII.	10.	11.	T.	a.	MICROMETER.	D.	d.	Mean Right Ascension, 1850.0.	Mean South Declination, 1850.0.
Zone VIII. April 17. M. $D. = -28° 58' 50''.0.$ $n'. = -1''.10.$ $n''. = -2''.80.$																	
											h. m. s.	s.	r.			h. m. s.	
1	7.8	. .	23.8	36.4	. .	. .	. .	. .	. .	. .	11 11 48.94	+18.46	IV. 6 37.92	—16' 44''.78	— 1''.41	11 12 7.40	29° 15' 36''.19
2	7.8	. .	38.4	51.5	3.5	16.0	28.6	. .	. .	. .	26 3.62	18.55	10. 4 38.88	30 40.70	4.94	26 22.17	29 35.64
3	7.8	. .	. .	2.0	14.5	27.2	40.0	52.5	. .	. .	32 14.64	18.57	III. 1 33.08	54 35.60	5.72	32 33.21	53 31.32
4	5	. .	. .	15.0	27.7	40.1	53.0	5.6	. .	. .	39 27.71	18.65	I. 4 44.16	27 38.72	6.61	39 46.36	26 35.33
5	8	. .	47.0	59.5	12.4	24.7	37.4	. .	. .	. .	46 12.22	18.72	IV. 7 39.79	9 49.03	7.33	46 30.94	8 46.36 z.
*6	5	47.5	0.0	12.7	25.2	. .	50.5	3.0	. .	. .	51 25.27	18.76	I. 6 41.00	14 57.97	7.89	51 44.03	13 55.86 z.
7	7.8	. .	. .	. .	. .	. .	52.0	5.0	. .	. .	52 27.08	18.75	IV. 6 38.22	16 34.41	7.98	52 45.83	15 32.39
8	7.8	. .	. .	. .	. .	27.0	39.7	52.5	. .	. .	54 14.51	18.76	VI. 2 35.48	47 20.89	8.16	54 33.27	46 19.05 z.
9	8	2.2	15.0	27.5	40.3	52.5	5.5	18.0	. .	. .	12 12 40.20	18.92	11. 2 38.27	45 43.49	9.74	12 12 59.12	44 43.23 z.
*10	7	. .	. .	25.3	38.1	50.5	3.5	16.2	. .	. .	15 38.15	18.95	I. 4 37.60	31 25.42	9.94	15 57.10	30 25.36 z.
11	8	52.8	4.8	18.1	31.8	43.0	55.6	. .	. .	. .	19 30.67	19.00	11. 6 38.71	16 16.27	10.22	19 49.67	15 16.49
12	8	. .	16.5	29.5	42.0	54.5	7.0	. .	. .	. .	22 41.98	19.00	IV. 1 37.82	51 51.86	10.42	23 0.98	50 52.28 z.
13	6.7	. .	11.0	23.5	36.0	48.5	1.5	14.5	. .	. .	24 36.10	19.04	" 6 42.77	13 57.11	10.52	24 55.14	12 57.63 z.
14	3	8.5	21.5	34.1	46.5	59.0	11.6	24.5	. .	. .	12 30 46.57	19.09	" 3 38.63	36 46.80	10.88	12 31 5.66	29 35 47.68 z.
Zone IX. April 17. M. $D. = -28° 57' 20''.0.$ $n'. = -27''.19.$ $n''. = -3''.00.$																	
1	3.4	. .	41.3	53.4	6.6	19.0	31.5	44.3	. .	. .	15 30 6.43	20.95	V. 6 43.88	13 18.95	26.18	15 30 27.38	29 11 5.13
2	8	41.0	54.0	6.8	19.0	31.5	44.0	57.0	. .	. .	32 19.09	21.01	II. 2 45.15	41 46.98	25.92	32 40.10	39 32.90 z.
3	7	. .	45.5	58.4	11.0	23.4	36.0	. .	. .	. .	36 10.88	21.03	VII. 3 39.71	36 9.39	25.49	36 31.91	33 54.79 z.
4	8	. .	11.0	23.5	36.0	49.0	. .	. .	. .	. .	39 36.25	21.09	VI. 2 36.18	46 56.96	25.11	39 57.34	44 42.07
*5	5.6	59.0	11.5	24.1	36.5	49.4	2.3	14.5	. .	. .	42 36.78	21.10	IV. 4 43.00	28 19.34	24.74	42 57.88	26 4.08
6	8	. .	13.3	26.0	38.5	51.1	4.0	. .	. .	. .	47 38.60	21.16	VII. 3 40.84	35 30.27	24.15	47 59.76	33 14.42
7	7.8	21.5	34.4	47.0	59.5	. .	24.5	37.0	. .	. .	49 59.45	21.19	" 2 46.04	41 16.09	23.84	50 20.64	38 59.93
8	8	. .	. .	8.0	20.5	33.5	46.0	. .	. .	. .	53 20.72	21.24	" 1 36.26	52 45.80	23.42	53 41.96	50 29.22
9	8	. .	41.0	53.6	6.2	19.0	32.0	. .	. .	. .	16 4 6.38	21.35	" 1 38.12	51 41.51	21.99	16 4 27.73	49 23.50 z.
10	7.8	31.0	43.5	56.3	9.1	21.6	34.5	46.5	. .	. .	7 8.97	21.34	10. 5 40.01	24 13.87	21.55	7 30.31	21 55.42 z.
11	8	12.5	25.3	37.7	50.2	3.0	15.5	28.0	. .	. .	10 50.38	21.36	VII. 7 37.19	11 18.66	21.03	11 11.74	8 59.69 z.
12	4	16.0	28.5	41.0	53.5	6.3	19.0	31.5	. .	. .	14 53.72	21.41	10. 5 41.65	23 7.25	20.45	15 15.13	20 47.70 z.
*13	7.8	19.0	31.5	44.5	56.4	9.3	21.5	34.0	. .	. .	21 56.66	21.47	VII. 7 37.08	11 22.44	19.42	22 18.13	9 1.86
14	5.6	. .	2.0	14.5	27.2	39.9	52.7	5.0	. .	. .	29 27.26	21.55	" 3 33.54	39 42.79	18.29	29 48.81	37 21.08 z.
15	8	29.0	41.5	54.0	6.0	19.3	. .	. .	. .	. .	34 6.59	21.59	V. 5 46.60	20 27.63	17.54	34 28.18	18 5.17 z.
16	7	19.2	31.5	44.5	. .	9.5	. .	. .	. .	. .	50 57.00	21.75	I. 4 41.87	29 32.51	14.72	51 18.75	27 7.23
17	8	. .	. .	. .	. .	33.0	45.8	58.5	. .	. .	51 20.59	21.76	10. 4 40.22	29 54.62	14.65	51 42.35	27 29.27 z.
18	8	. .	47.3	0.0	12.5	25.2	38.0	. .	. .	. .	55 12.64	21.83	VII. 1 38.71	51 21.11	13.97	55 34.47	48 55.08 z.
19	7	58.5	. .	24.0	36.5	49.0	2.0	. .	. .	. .	58 36.59	21.86	VI. 1 41.88	49 31.67	13.35	58 58.45	46 51.67 z.
20	7.8	49.5	2.5	15.0	28.0	40.5	52.8	6.0	. .	. .	17 8 27.81	21.93	VII. 2 39.67	44 56.58	11.59	17 8 49.74	42 28.17 z.
21	7.8	. .	9.5	22.0	34.4	47.0	0.0	. .	. .	. .	10 34.61	21.90	VI. 6.41.21	14 51.02	11.22	10 56.51	12 22.24 z.
22	7	. .	33.5	46.0	58.5	. .	. .	. .	. .	. .	13 58.66	21.97	II. 2 43.14	42 56.45	10.58	14 20.63	40 27.03 z.
23	3.4	. .	0.0	12.2	25.0	37.5	. .	. .	. .	. .	17 25.06	22.01	I. 2 37.98	45 54.65	9.93	17 47.07	43 24.58 z.
24	5	. .	. .	. .	. .	. .	7.5	19.5	. .	. .	17 41.92	21.99	II. 2	. . .	9.89	18 3.91	. . . z.
25	6.7	. .	. .	. .	. .	20.0	32.5	. .	. .	. .	24 7.37	22.04	VII. 3 42.27	34 40.91	8.77	24 29.41	32 9.68
26	5.6	46.5	59.5	. .	25.0	37.3	50.1	2.7	. .	. .	17 29 24.77	22.07	IV. 4 42.10	28 50.45	7.58	17 29 46.84	29 26 18.03 z.

CORRECTIONS.

	COR. TO CLOCK.	HOURLY COR.	m.	n.	c.	ZENITH POINT.	COINC.
	s.	s.	s.	s.	s.		r.
April 17, at 12h...	+8.564	+0.008	+0.521	—0.342	+0.246	0° 0' 1''.89	40.078

April 17, stars very steady.

INSTRUMENT READINGS.

	h.	CIRCLE. A.	B.	C.	D.	Mean.	BAR.	THERMOM. At.	Ex.
							I.		
Zone VIII.—April 17,	11.1	291° 40' 41''.8	48'.0	54''.0	46''.0	47''.45	30.220	61°.5	63°.5
	12.7	39.0	45.6	52.2	45.0	45.45	. .	. .	. .
Zone IX.—April 17,	15.5	291 41 43.0	46.0	52.0	49.0	46.50			
		41.0	44.0	50.0	47.0		. .	. .	. .
	16.0	. . .	. .	. .	. .	. .	30.210	62.0	59.0
	16.7	. . .	. .	. .	. .	. .	30.210	62.0	57.5
	17.5	31.0	33.6	39.8	35.0	35.13	. .	. .	. .
	17.6	28.0	34.5	42.0	37.2		30.210	60.2	56.3

Zone X. April 18. H. $D. = -28^{\circ}\ 27'\ 10''.0.$ $n'. = -4''\ 62.$ $n''. = -3.00.$

Number.	Magnitude.	SECONDS OF TRANSITS. I.	II.	III.	IV.	V.	VI.	VII.	10.	11.	T.	a.	MICROMETER.	D.	d.	Mean Right Ascension, 1850.0.	Mean South Declination, 1850.0.
											h. m. s.	s.	r.	′ ″	″	h. m. s.	° ′ ″
1	9	30.0	42.2	54.8	8.0	20.2	. .	. .	. .	. .	10 30 7.68	+18.75	IV. 2 39.315	−45 8.63	− 9.16	10 30 26.43	29 12 27.79
2	10	. .	31.5	. .	56.5	. .	. .	. .	. .	. .	31 56.53	18.76	" 2 49.145	39 29.02	9.92	32 15.29	29 6 48.94 z.
3	9	. .	46.0	. .	11.0	. .	. .	48.4	. .	. .	33 10.93	18.78	IV. 4 38.938	30 39.68	10.52	33 29.71	28 58 0.20 z
4	8.9	. .	6.5	. .	31.0	43.0	. .	. .	. .	. .	34 31.02	18.78	VII.4 39.157	30 32.13	11.01	34 49.80	28 57 53.14
5	10	23.4	. .	48.4	. .	13.6	26.0	. .	. .	. .	36 1.06	18.80	IV. 6 30.488	21 1.94	11.66	36 19.86	28 48 23.60
6	8	5.0	. .	30.0	43.0	55.0	7.8	. .	. .	. .	37 42.72	18.80	" 5 36.162	26 28.37	12.38	38 1.52	28 53 50.75 z
7	8.9	35.6	48.0	0.8	13.0	. .	. .	50.8	. .	. .	42 13.44	18.82	" 2 40.068	44 42.61	14.22	42 32.26	29 12 6.83
8	9	45.0	57.7	10.0	22.8	35.0	47.8	. .	. .	. .	44 22.69	18.84	" 5 40.472	23 59.50	15.06	44 41.53	28 51 24.56 z.
9	9	. .	25.5	38.0	50.5	. .	. .	. .	. .	. .	45 50.60	18.83	" 2 40.220	44 37.37	15.66	46 9.43	29 12 3.03
10	9	. .	. .	. .	18.2	31.0	43.5	. .	. .	. .	46 18.36	18.85	" 3 33.950	39 28.57	15.85	46 37.21	29 6 54.42 z.
11	10	48.0	. .	. .	26.0	. .	51.0	. .	. .	. .	54 25.85	18.90	VI. 3 49.016	30 47.87	18.92	54 44.75	28 58 16.79
12	10	. .	. .	15.0	27.3	. .	52.7	. .	. .	. .	56 27.49	18.91	IV. 3 44.274	33 31.95	19.69	56 46.40	29 1 1.64 z.
13	9	12.5	25.0	38.0	. .	2.9	. .	. .	. .	. .	58 50.41	18.91	I. 2 34.540	47 54.43	20.57	59 9.32	29 15 25.00
14	8	50.5	2.8	15.0	. .	. .	. .	. .	. .	. .	11 0 28.02	18.92	II. 1 33.836	54 8.89	21.06	11 0 46.94	29 21 39.95 z.
15	7.8	. .	. .	. .	. .	55.2	8.0	21.0	. .	. .	10 59 43.29	18.92	V. 2 29.518	50 47.09	20.95	0 2.21	29 18 18.04
16	7.8	. .	. .	. .	. .	. .	. .	. .	3.0	16.0	11 0 6.87	18.93	10. 4 42.440	28 37.94	21.01	0 25.80	28 56 8.95
17	8	. .	. .	. .	. .	38.0	51.0	3.0	. .	. .	2 25.95	18.95	V. 4 37.748	31 20.74	21.37	2 44.90	28 58 52.11
18	8.9	. .	. .	. .	. .	. .	. .	34.4	. .	. .	2 56.86	18.95	II. 5 42.550	23 20.36	21.44	3 15.81	28 50 51.80
19	7.8	. .	. .	. .	44.5	57.0	9.4	22.0	. .	. .	4 44.43	18.96	VI. 4 39.153	30 32.06	21.71	5 3.39	28 58 3.77 z.
20	10	. .	. .	. .	13.5	. .	39.0	. .	. .	. .	6 13.65	18.96	" 1 45.495	47 26.54	21.94	6 32.61	29 14 58.48 z.
21	9	. .	. .	. .	45.0	58.0	. .	. .	. .	. .	7 45.29	18.98	IV. 5 41.560	23 21.86	22.17	8 4.27	28 50 54.03
22	8.9	. .	. .	. .	10.0	. .	35.0	. .	. .	. .	8 9.93	18.98	11. 5 37.695	25 33.53	22.33	8 28.91	28 53 5.86
23	9	. .	7.2	. .	. .	. .	. .	. .	. .	. .	13 32.32	19.02	II. 2 44.550	42 7.56	22.98	13 51.34	29 9 40.54 z.
24	9	. .	12.5	25.0	38.0	. .	. .	15.0	. .	. .	13 37.65	19.02	IV. 2 48.978	39 34.79	23.01	13 56.67	29 7 7.80 z.
25	8	. .	. .	. .	. .	. .	. .	. .	41.5	54.2	13 45.38	19.02	10. 5 49.415	18 49.04	23.01	14 4.40	28 46 22.05
26	9	41.8	. .	. .	19.5	. .	. .	56.5	. .	. .	19 19.30	19.06	II. 3 39.018	36 33.29	23.78	19 38.36	29 4 7.07
27	9	. .	19.3	. .	44.0	56.0	9.2	. .	. .	. .	21 43.99	19.08	IV. 6 43.815	13 21.43	24.06	22 3.07	28 40 55.49
28	10	. .	19.8	. .	44.2	56.5	9.0	. .	. .	. .	24 44.24	19.09	" 6 36.432	17 36.51	24.43	25 3.33	28 45 10.94
29	8	39.0	52.0	4.5	17.0	29.7	42.0	55.0	. .	. .	11 27 17.07	19.11	" 2 40.202	44 38.01	24.76	11 27 36.18	29 12 12.77

Zone XI. April 19. M. $D. = 39^{\circ}\ 52'\ 50''.0.$ $n'. = -10''.00.$ $n''. = -0''.22.$

Number.	Magnitude.	I.	II.	III.	IV.	V.	VI.	VII.	10.	11.	T.	a.	MICROMETER.	D.	d.	Mean Right Ascension, 1850.0.	Mean South Declination, 1850.0.
1	7	. .	8.2	22.2	36.5	50.8	5.5	. .	. .	. .	9 49 36.58	17.70	IV. 6 42.81	13 58.21	2.67	9 49 54.28	40 6 50.88
2	7	. .	47.3	1.5	16.0	31.0	45.4	. .	. .	. .	52 16.22	17.66	" 2 38.00	46 6.16	3.26	52 33.88	38 59.42
3	7.8	. .	13.5	27.2	41.7	56.0	11.0	. .	. .	. .	54 41.81	17.73	VII. 6 39.29	16 0.07	3.86	54 58.54	8 53.93
4	8	. .	59.0	. .	. .	42.5	56.0	11.0	. .	. .	57 27.65	17.74	" 5 43.77	22 9.51	4.53	57 45.39	15 4.04
5	7	29.5	44.0	58.0	12.5	26.8	41.4	55.5	. .	. .	10 5 12.52	17.82	I. 6 40.06	15 33.28	6.36	10 5 30.34	8 29.64
6	8.5	. .	17.8	32.0	46.5	1.5	16.0	. .	. .	. .	17 46.69	17.89	VII. 4 40.41	29 55.37	9.19	18 4.58	22 54.56
7	8	. .	. .	. .	. .	29.5	44.3	58.5	. .	. .	20 15.17	17.92	" 4 39.50	30 27.01	9.74	20 33.09	23 26.75
8	7.8	. .	. .	18.8	33.5	47.6	2.0	16.5	. .	. .	33.28	17.96	" 6 34.43	18 48.81	10	51.24	11 48.00
9	7	. .	. .	. .	45.0	59.0	13.4	28.0	. .	. .	10 24 44.80	17.99	IV. 7 40.34	9 31.32	10.73	10 25 2.79	40 2 32.05

CORRECTIONS.

	COR. TO CLOCK.	HOURLY COR.	m.	n.	c.	ZENITH POINT.	COINC.
	s.	s.	s.	s.	s.	° ′ ″	r.
April 18, at 12h...	+9.100	+0.009	+0.521	−0.342	+0.246	0 0 2.39	40.065

INSTRUMENT READINGS.

	CIRCLE. A.	B.	C.	D.	Mean.	BAR.	THERMOM. At.	Ex.
Zone X.—Apr.18, 10.3h..	292° 12′ 6″.0	11′.5	16″.8	13″.8	12″.02	I. 30.092	68°.5	67°.5
10.6..	0.7	. .	. .	. .	. .	. .	. .	. .
10.8..	56.0	. .	. .	. .	. .	. .	. .	. .
11.5..	11 55.5	60.9	65.5	63.4	1.32	30.082	69.0	67.5

Zone XI. April 19. M. $D. = 39° 52' 50''.0$. $n' = -10''.00$. $n'' = -0''.22$. (Continued.)

Number.	Magnitude.	SECONDS OF TRANSITS. I.	II.	III.	IV.	V.	VI.	VII.	10.	11.	T.	a.	MICROMETER.	D.	d.	Mean Right Ascension, 1850.0.	Mean South Declination, 1850.0.
											h. m. s.	s.	r.	' ''	''	h. m. s.	° ' ''
10	7	. .	. .	49.0	3.5	18.0	32.5	46.5	. .	. .	10 30 3.41	+17.99	10. 2 47.12	—40 48.13	—11.83	10 30 21.40	40 33 49.96
11	7	. .	. .	. .	. .	. .	. .	. .	20.5	35.5	31 16.08	18.03	11. 5 40.20	24 12.21	12.07	31 34.11	17 14.28
12	7.8	. .	. .	. .	42.5	. .	. .	. .	. .	. .	37 42.46	18.06	I. 1 42.33	49 28.86	13.41	38 0.52	42 32.27
13	7.8	. .	. .	. .	15.0	29.0	43.5	58.0	. .	. .	39 14.59	18.08	VII. 1 46.80	46 53.45	13.70	39 32.67	39 57.15
14	7.8	. .	26.0	40.0	54.5	. .	23.5	. .	. .	. .	48 54.59	18.20	II. 4 38.67	30 56.15	15.56	49 12.79	24 1.71
15	7.8	. .	57.4	12.0	. .	40.5	55.0	9.0	. .	. .	50 26.15	18.23	VII. 5 46.10	20 48.69	15.86	50 44.38	13 54.55
16	7	. .	. .	45.5	0.0	14.5	29.0	43.2	. .	. .	55 0.00	18.27	I. 5 38.28	25 20.28	16.69	55 18.27	18 26.97
17	8.9	. .	. .	. .	56.0	10.4	25.0	39.5	. .	. .	58 55.92	18.29	VII. 2 39.50	45 13.37	17.41	59 14.21	38 20.78
18	6.7	. .	. .	. .	43.8	58.1	12.3	26.5	. .	. .	11 8 43.58	18.43	11. 5 44.57	21 40.31	45.72	11 9 2.01	15 16.03
19	7	. .	. .	. .	. .	. .	. .	. .	53.0	8.5	10 48.58	18.43	11. 2 41.95	43 47.07	46.06	11 7.01	37 23.13
20	9	18.0	. .	46.5	0.8	15.2	30.0	44.5	. .	. .	18 1.01	18.53	VII. 3 41.74	35 7.44	47.39	18 19.54	28 44.83
21	9	7.5	21.8	. .	51.0	. .	19.6	. .	. .	. .	50.84	18	VI. 2 41.85	43 52.17	. . . .	. . . . . .	37 30
22	8	55.0	9.5	23.5	38.0	52.0	7.4	21.8	. .	. .	26 38.16	18.64	IV. 4 37.202	31 47.24	48.63	26 56.80	25 25.87
23	9	. .	. .	42.0	56.5	. .	. .	. .	. .	. .	28 56.51	18.66	VII. 2 50.422	38 54.27	49.01	29 15.17	32 33.28
24	9	. .	. .	. .	. .	. .	6.0	20.5	. .	. .	29 37.08	18.66	" 2 37.28	46 30.78	49.10	29 55.74	40 9.88
25	8.9	39.6	54.2	. .	. .	. .	. .	. .	. .	. .	33 22.72	18.73	" 7 40.212	9 35.22	49.64	33 41.47	3 14.86
26	8	. .	. .	. .	41.0	55.0	9.5	24.0	. .	. .	32 40.76	18.73	10 6 37.70	16 55.39	49.55	32 59.49	10 34.94
27	9	. .	. .	27.0	41.0	55.5	. .	24.6	. .	. .	34 41.13	18.72	VII. 1 43.90	48 34.22	49.84	34 59.85	42 14.06
28	9	. .	. .	39.8	54.5	8.8	23.4	. .	. .	. .	41 54.43	18.86	I. 7 42.46	8 17.22	50.87	42 13.29	1 58.09
29	8	. .	. .	. .	56.0	. .	25.0	39.2	. .	. .	42 56.00	18.85	IV. 4 38.22	31 11.88	51.00	43 14.85	24 52.88
30	9	26.0	. .	. .	. .	. .	. .	. .	. .	. .	9.59	18	I. 2 35.92	47 17.88	. . . .	. . . . . .	40 58
31	9	. .	. .	36.5	51.0	5.0	19.5	. .	. .	. .	47 50.71	18.92	I. 6 39.08	16 7.28	51.63	48 9.63	9 48.91
32	7	41.0	56.5	10.5	25.2	39.0	54.0	8.4	. .	. .	49 24.93	18.95	IV. 6 44.30	13 6.57	51.85	49 43.88	6 48.42
33	9	10.5	. .	38.7	. .	. .	. .	. .	. .	. .	59 53.68	19.06	III. 2 38.37	45 53.36	53.12	12 0 12.74	39 36.48
34	6	. .	22.0	36.2	50.8	5.1	19.5	34.7	. .	. .	12 0 50.78	19.09	VII. 4 40.17	30 3.65	53.22	1 9.87	23 46.87 B.
35	7	. .	27.0	41.0	55.5	10.0	24.0	38.5	. .	. .	1 55.45	19.12	V. 6 43.92	13 19.60	53.32	2 14.57	7 2.92
36	7	9.5	24.5	38.5	53.0	7.4	22.0	36.2	. .	. .	5 52.99	19.16	II. 5 39.93	24 23.17	53.76	6 12.15	18 6.93
37	8.9	45.0	0.0	14.0	28.5	43.0	57.4	12.0	. .	. .	8 28.53	19.20	II. 5 39.88	24 24.90	54.04	8 47.73	18 8.94
38	7	2.6	16.8	31.8	45.8	0.0	14.9	29.0	. .	. .	10 45.77	19.22	III. 3 36.99	37 52.93	54.27	11 4.99	31 37.20
39	7.8	9.2	24.0	38.2	52.5	. .	21.6	36.0	. .	. .	13 52.66	19.27	VII. 5 34.075	27 46.04	54.57	14 11.93	21 30.61
40	7	. .	. .	15.0	29.7	44.0	58.5	13.0	. .	. .	15 29.55	19.29	" 3 34.60	39 15.40	54.71	15 48.84	33 0.11
41	9	. .	. .	3.8	18.2	32.5	47.0	1.5	. .	. .	17 18.09	19.32	" 2 32.66	49 11.12	54.89	17 37.41	42 56.01
42	8	46.0	0.0	15.0	29.6	44.0	. .	. .	. .	. .	21 29.37	19.38	I. 2 47.12	40 48.91	55.26	21 48.75	34 34.17
*43	7.8	14.6	29.0	43.5	58.0	12.5	27.0	41.5	. .	. .	21 58.01	19.39	IV. 1 46.93	46 49.48	55.30	22 17.40	40 34.78 H.
44	6	23.0	37.6	52.0	6.6	21.0	35.3	49.6	. .	. .	25 6.43	19.43	II. 2 46.12	41 23.91	55.57	25 25.86	35 9.48 B.
45	5	39.5	53.6	8.3	23.1	37.1	51.5	6.0	. .	. .	27 22.71	19.46	I. 6 35.88	17 58.30	55.74	27 42.17	11 44.04 B.
46	7	17.7	32.6	47.5	1.5	15.5	30.5	44.7	. .	. .	35 1.27	19.58	II. 3 39.88	36 12.35	56.32	35 20.85	29 58.67
47	9.10	44.6	. .	. .	28.7	. .	57.3	11.5	. .	. .	41 28.32	19.67	VII. 4 36.35	32 16.38	56.75	41 47.99	26 3.13
48	8	. .	. .	8.0	22.2	36.8	51.2	6.0	. .	. .	46 22.40	19.75	I. 6 37.14	17 14.59	57.03	46 42.15	11 1.62
49	8	. .	. .	46.4	1.0	15.4	. .	. .	. .	. .	50 0.88	19.80	" 6 38.12	16 40.60	57.24	50 20.68	10 27.84
50	9	. .	. .	. .	25.8	40.0	54.7	. .	. .	. .	12 50 25.63	19.81	VII. 4 37.49	31 36.71	57.26	12 50 45.44	40 25 23.97

CORRECTIONS.

	COR. TO CLOCK.	HOURLY COR.	m.	n.	c.	ZENITH POINT.	COINC.
	s.	s.	s.	s.	s.	° ' ''	r.
April 19, at 12h. .	+8.987	+0.010	+0.521	—0.342	+0.246	0 0 1.08	40.080

At 17. The instrument disturbed and reading changed.

INSTRUMENT READINGS.

	CIRCLE. A.	B.	C.	D.	Mean.	BAR.	THERMOM. At.	Ex.
h.	° ' ''	''	''	''	''	I.	°	°
Zone XI.—April 19, 9.6	280 48 46.5	52.0	55.0	50.5	51.00	30.302	65.0	65.1
10.9	21.0	25.6	28.0	23.1	24.42	. .	. .	. .
11.5	. . . .	. .	. .	. .	. .	30.332	63.5	57 0
13.7	20.0	24.6	27.0	22.1	23.42	30.343	62.0	54.0
16.6	. . . .	. .	. .	. .	. .	30.362	60.0	49.5
16.5	. . . .	. .	. .	. .	. .	. .	. .	48.5
16.8	20.0	25.7	26.5	24.0	24 05	30.384	58.5	46.5

Number.	Magnitude.	SECONDS OF TRANSITS. I.	II.	III.	IV.	V.	VI.	VII.	10.	11.	T.	a.	MICROMETER.	D.	d.	Mean Right Ascension. 1850.0.	Mean South Declination. 1850.0.
Zone XI. April 19. M. D.= 39° 52′ 50″.0. n′.= —10″.00. n″.= —0″.22. (Continued.)																	
											h. m. s.	s.	r.	′ ″	′	h. m. s.	° ′ ″
51	8	. .	. .	. .	. .	. .	52.0	7.0	. .	. .	12 51 23.29	+19.82	VII. 2 31.51	—49 51.30	—57.30	12 51 43.11	40 43 38.60
52	7	. .	. .	48.7	2.5	. .	. .	. .	. .	. .	55 2.80	19.87	IV. 7 41.56	8 48.96	57.45	55 22.67	2 36.41
53	6	. .	. .	. .	2.5	16.6	31.0	45.7	. .	. .	56 2.24	19.89	VII. 4 41.09	29 31.44	57.49	56 22.13	23 18.93 B.
54	6	. .	. .	. .	. .	1.0	15.7	30.0	. .	. .	57 46.49	19.92	V. 1 35.84	53 14.72	57.56	58 6.41	47 2.28 B.
55	7	47.5	2.5	17.0	31.0	45.5	0.0	. .	. .	. .	13 0 31.09	19.96	I. 5 33.68	27 59.90	57.67	13 0 51.05	21 47.57
56	7.8	. .	. .	. .	25.0	39.5	. .	8.3	. .	. .	2 24.89	19.99	VI. 2 42.57	43 27.36	57.73	2 44.88	37 15.09
57	8	40.5	54.5	9.6	24.0	. .	. .	. .	. .	. .	5 23.81	20.04	I. 4 38.36	31 6.56	57.83	5 43.85	24 54.39
58	8	. .	. .	. .	43.6	. .	. .	. .	. .	. .	6 43.56	20.06	III. 5 35.33	27 3.18	57.87	7 3.62	20 51.05
59	7	. .	. .	. .	51.5	6.0	21.0	34.6	. .	. .	7 51.54	20.08	VI. 3 41.07	35 31.07	57.90	8 11.62	29 18.97
60	7	22.0	36.5	50.8	5.6	19.1	34.0	48.6	. .	. .	9 5.26	20.09	I. 4 39.86	30 14.34	57.95	9 25.35	24 2.29
61	9	57.5	. .	. .	. .	. .	. .	. .	. .	. .	17 41.06	20.23	I. 2 41.28	44 15.25	58.06	18 1.29	38 3.31
62	4	. .	. .	39.0	53.5	7.5	22.5	36.8	. .	. .	17 53.35	20.23	IV. 1 42.97	49 7.06	58.07	18 13.58	42 55.13 B.
63	7	. .	. .	9.1	23.5	38.0	52.4	6.7	. .	. .	22 23.41	20.30	" 1 33.17	54 47.92	58.24	22 43.71	48 36.16 M.
64	7	. .	. .	. .	34.0	48.0	3.0	17.2	. .	. .	24 33.80	20.34	" 3 35.19	38 55.57	58.28	24 54.14	32 43.85 M.
65	7.8	. .	. .	54.0	9.5	23.5	38.5	52.0	. .	. .	28 9.13	20.38	VII. 6 42.82	13 57.11	58.32	28 29.51	7 45.43
66	6	58.2	13.0	27.0	41.8	56.0	11.0	. .	. .	. .	33 41.72	20.50	IV. 2 40.58	44 36.74	58.30	34 3.22	38 25.04 M.
67	8	. .	. .	. .	. .	58.5	13.0	. .	. .	. .	34 43.92	20.51	VII. 2 46.05	41 26.08	58.29	35 4.43	35 14.37
68	8	. .	. .	. .	. .	22.2	. .	50.8	. .	. .	36 7.54	20.53	" 2 50.18	39 3.61	58.28	36 28.07	32 51.89
69	8	. .	. .	. .	57.5	11.5	26.5	40.5	. .	. .	49 57.40	20.72	" 6 40.46	15 19.42	57.95	50 18.12	9 7.37
70	8.9	21.0	35.7	50.0	4.5	18.3	33.1	. .	. .	. .	53 4.25	20.77	" 7 36.93	11 29.24	57.83	53 25.02	5 17.07
71	9	. .	. .	. .	. .	. .	. .	. .	4.8	19.3	53 59.81	20.83	V. 1 34.52	54 0.53	57.79	54 20.64	47 48.32
72	4	. .	. .	19.0	33.5	48.0	2.5	17.0	. .	. .	56 33.52	20.84	IV. 4 33.93	33 40.84	57.70	56 54.36	27 28.54 B.
73	8	. .	54.0	8.3	22.0	37.0	. .	. .	. .	. .	14 3 22.51	20.93	I. 6 43.16	13 45.39	57.42	14 3 43.44	7 32.81 M.
74	9	. .	. .	. .	. .	. .	24.4	39.0	. .	. .	3 55.60	20.95	VII. 3 42.70	34 34.10	57.40	4 16.55	28 21.50
75	7.8	. .	. .	. .	. .	21.0	36.0	50.5	. .	. .	5 6.93	20.98	" 5 35.69	26 50.08	57.34	5 27.91	20 37.42
76	8	. .	34.8	49.0	3.5	18.0	32.3	. .	. .	. .	8 3.45	21.01	IV. 6 39.44	15 55.34	57.20	8 24.46	9 42.54 M.
77	8	. .	. .	. .	55.0	9.5	24.0	38.4	. .	. .	9 55.07	21.02	VII. 5 44.41	21 47.45	57.11	10 16.09	15 34.56
78	9	. .	33.0	47.5	2.0	. .	. .	. .	. .	. .	13 2.02	21.14	IV. 1 43.35	48 53.99	56.93	13 23.16	42 40.92
79	9	. .	. .	. .	. .	. .	54.0	. .	. .	. .	14 25.06	21.13	VI. 2 49.68	39 21.15	56.86	14 46.19	33 3.01
80	6	. .	. .	. .	. .	. .	. .	47.0	. .	. .	15 4.04	21.11	VII. 6 48.93	10 25.25	56.81	15 25.15	4 12.06 M.
81	5.6	. .	44.0	58.3	12.4	27.0	. .	. .	. .	. .	21 12.53	21.21	I. 6 38.10	16 41.28	56.44	21 33.74	10 27.72
82	8.9	. .	. .	7.0	21.3	35.5	. .	. .	. .	. .	27 21.21	21.31	VII. 6 42.49	14 8.94	55.98	27 42.52	7 54.92
83	7	. .	59.3	13.5	27.8	42.0	56.8	. .	. .	. .	30 27.82	21.36	III. 6 36.29	17 44.56	55.73	30 49.18	11 30.29 M.
84	8	. .	. .	14.3	29.0	43.0	57.7	12.0	. .	. .	33 28.74	21.42	II. 4 41.78	29 7.94	55.47	33 50.16	22 53.41
85	9	31.0	. .	59.8	14.5	28.7	43.1	57.5	. .	. .	38 14.33	21.50	I. 4 41.67	29 11.68	55.04	38 35.83	22 56.72
86	8.9	17.8	32.8	47.0	1.3	15.5	29.5	44.3	. .	. .	42 1.15	21.54	" 6 37.10	17 15.99	54.68	42 22.69	11 0.67
87	7.8	12.5	27.0	41.5	. .	10.5	. .	. .	. .	. .	44 56.00	21.63	" 1 39.69	51 1.53	54.40	45 17.63	44 45.93
88	8	. .	. .	. .	. .	. .	. .	. .	. .	28.3	45 8.81	21.62	11. 3 39.245	36 32.60	54.38	45 30.43	30 16.98
89	8	. .	. .	. .	. .	30.0	44.8	. .	. .	. .	14 53 15.55	21.76	V. 2 36.535	46 57.16	53.54	14 53 37.31	40 40.70
90	. .	. .	. .	. .	. .	. .	. .	. .	. .	. .	. . . . . .	. . . .	VI. 5 43.50	22 17.29	. . . .	. . . . . .	16
91	. .	. .	. .	. .	. .	. .	. .	. .	18.6	33.0	14 55 13.70	21.77	10. 3 42.15	34 52.54	53.33	14 55 35.47	40 28 35.87 B.
92	. .	. .	. .	. .	. .	18.5	. .	. .	. .	. .	58 3.85	21.81	. . . . . .	. . . . .	53.02	58 25.66	. . . . . .
93	3.4	. .	. .	. .	. .	. .	. .	. .	11.8	. .	58 7.53	21.79	10. 7 45.94	6 15.83	53.02	58 29.32	39 59 58.85 M.
94	8	. .	. .	. .	. .	. .	. .	. .	. .	12.0	59 52.42	21.85	11. 2 44.42	42 21.45	52.82	15 0 14.27	40 36 4.27
95	8	. .	. .	. .	. .	. .	. .	25.0	. .	. .	15 1 41.96	21.84	11. 6 41.26	14 50.20	52.60	2 3.80	40 8 32.80
96	6	. .	28.0	42.5	56.8	11.0	. .	. .	. .	. .	7 56.74	21.97	I. 3 39.11	36 40.20	51.85	8 18.71	40 30 22.05 M.
97	4	. .	. .	. .	. .	59.3	14.0	28.6	. .	. .	8 45.20	21.95	VI. 6 41.72	14 35.76	51.75	9 7.15	40 8 17.51
98	2	. .	42.0	56.5	10.8	24.9	39.3	53.5	. .	. .	11 10.59	21.98	IV. 7 35.39	12 23.09	51.45	11 32.57	40 6 4.54 B.
99	6	. .	. .	. .	. .	. .	. .	. .	. .	42.0	11 22.94	21.99	11. 6 35.96	17 57.26	51.43	11 44.93	40 11 38.69 M.
100	7	. .	8.5	22.3	36.5	. .	. .	. .	. .	. .	17 36.75	22.08	III. 7 32.17	14 14.77	50.58	17 58.83	40 7 55.35
101	9	. .	. .	. .	. .	. .	. .	. .	18.0	32.5	18 13.46	22.10	10. 6 34.50	18 45.59	50.50	18 35.56	40 12 26.09
102	6	. .	38.0	52.4	6.5	21.0	35.0	. .	. .	. .	23 6.52	22.14	IV. 7 48.50	4 48.46	49.83	23 28.66	39 58 28.29
103	2	. .	. .	33.0	47.9	2.0	16.5	31.0	. .	. .	15 24 47.57	22.23	VI. 1 48.65	45 49.74	49.59	15 25 9.80	40 39 29.33 B.

Number.	Magnitude.	SECONDS OF TRANSITS I.	II.	III.	IV.	V.	VI.	VII.	10.	11.	T.	a.	MICROMETER.	D.	d.	Mean Right Ascension, 1850.0.	Mean South Declination, 1850.0.
Zone XI. April 19. M. $D.=30° 25' 50''.0.$ $n.'=-10''.00.$ $n.''=-0''.22.$ (Continued.)																	
											h. m. s.	s.	r.	′ ″	″	h. m. s.	° ′ ″
104	8	..	..	..	23.0	..	..	..	..	..	15 26 22.96	+22.25	IV. 2 49.02	—39 43.38	—49.38	15 26 45.21	40 33 22.76 M.
105	7	..	..	..	..	..	..	32.5	..	..	26 49.19	22.25	VII. 3 37.97	37 18.47	49.31	27 11.44	40 30 57.78 M.
106	9	..	6.5	21.5	..	..	..	..	..	..	36 35.82	22.42	I. 7 39.88	50 53.98	47.85	36 58.24	40 44 31.83
107	7.8	..	..	41.5	56.5	10.0	25.0	..	..	..	36 55.97	22.40	IV. 3 33.95	39 38.62	47.80	37 18.37	40 33 16.42
108	7.8	..	23.5	38.0	52.8	..	..	..	..	..	43 52.61	22.52	II. 2 36.70	46 51.09	46.71	44 15.13	40 40 27.80
109	7.8	..	..	..	..	..	23.8	38.0	..	..	43 54.70	22.52	VII. 1 41.83	49 46.15	46.71	44 17.22	40 43 22.86
110	9	..	..	..	..	..	..	..	42.0	56.5	45 37.39	22.53	10. 5 44.27	21 51.51	46.43	45 59.92	40 15 27.93
111	6	..	..	14.0	28.5	..	..	..	..	..	49 28.47	22.55	IV. 5 48.24	19 34.91	45.81	49 51.02	40 13 10.72
112	5	..	..	..	..	38.2	..	7.5	..	..	50 24.13	22.55	VII. 7 44.97	6 49.87	45.67	50 46.68	40 0 25.54
113	8	..	14.5	29.5	..	..	..	..	..	..	53 43.65	22.63	III. 4 37.22	31 46.54	45.10	54 6.28	40 25 21.64
114	8	..	..	..	..	33.0	..	2.0	..	..	54 18.58	22.64	V. 5 37.89	25 34.14	44.98	54 41.22	40 19 9.12
115	7	..	..	..	..	14.0	28.2	4.3	..	..	55 59.53	22.65	VI. 5 41.91	23 14.40	44.68	56 22.18	40 16 49.08
116	9	31.5	..	..	14.5	..	..	..	..	..	59 14.76	22.74	I. 1 48.40	45 58.09	44.12	59 37.50	40 39 32.21
117	5.6	..	13.5	28.0	42.5	57.0	11.3	26.0	..	..	16 0 42.45	22.76	IV. 1 42.41	49 26.67	43.85	16 1 5.21	40 43 0.52 B.
118	8	..	..	6.5	21.0	35.0	49.5	4.2	..	..	9 20.76	22.85	" 4 34.97	33 4.72	42.29	9 43.61	40 26 37.01
119	8	..	..	44.5	59.3	13.6	28.1	42.5	..	..	12 59.08	22.93	I. 1 42.38	49 27.20	41.62	13 22.01	40 42 58.82
120	7	..	..	42.5	57.5	12.0	26.0	..	..	..	18 57.21	23.01	" 1 36.56	52 50.04	40.48	19 20.22	40 46 20.52 M.
121	9	..	..	28.5	..	57.0	12.0	..	..	..	20 42.84	22.99	VI. 5 38.22	25 22.60	40.14	21 5.83	40 18 52.74
122	8	..	..	..	..	..	..	42.0	..	..	21 58.59	23.05	VII. 2 33.18	48 53.21	39.89	22 21.64	40 42 23.10
123	7.8	..	..	..	..	..	..	..	58.5	13.6	22 53.98	23.03	10. 4 34.64	33 14.86	39.71	23 17.01	40 26 44.57
124	7	..	..	..	..	2.0	17.0	31.0	..	..	25 47.98	23.02	VII. 7 46.93	5 41.90	39.12	26 11.00	39 59 11.02
125	8.9	..	40.0	54.3	9.1	23.5	38.0	52.3	..	..	32 8.94	23.13	2. 5 36.79	26 11.16	37.85	32 32.07	40 19 39.00
126	6	..	..	..	..	..	26.0	40.0	..	..	33 56.87	23.18	VI. 3 34.08	39 34.93	37.50	34 20.05	40 33 2.43 B.
127	8	..	..	50.6	5.2	..	..	..	..	..	37 5.18	23.24	IV. 1 44.79	48 3.83	36.78	37 28.42	40 41 30.61
128	8	..	29.5	..	..	12.5	..	41.0	..	..	16 38 57.99	23.19	II. 6 48.28	16 33.01	36.39	16 39 21.18	40 9 59.40
Zone XII. April 20. H. $D.=-43° 22' 30''.0.$ $n.'=-3''.15.$ $n.''=-20''.00$																	
1	7.8	36.4	51.8	6.5	22.2	37.2	52.8	8.0	..	..	9 40 22.18	17.66	III. 2 46.750	41 16.98	3.27	9 40 39.84	44 3 50.25 B.
2	10	..	..	..	..	..	..	31.3	..	..	43 46.00	17.73	VII. 7 38.835	10 24.93	4.19	44 3.73	43 32 59.12
3	9	17.0	32.4	47.2	3.0	18.2	33.3	49.0	..	..	47 2.90	17.73	IV. 4 40.083	30 17.14	5.07	47 20.63	43 52 52.21
4	9	23.2	38.4	53.5	9.0	24.5	40.0	55.0	..	..	53 9.15	17.75	" 1 39.070	51 41.58	6.66	53 26.90	44 14 18.24 M.
5	9	..	..	..	..	42.8	58.0	13.8	..	..	10 5 27.75	17.88	" 3 39.070	36 53.42	9.71	10 5 45.63	43 59 33.13
6	8.9	45.0	0.5	15.0	30.3	45.6	1.0	16.0	..	..	8 30.52	17.94	" 5 46.327	20 47.51	10.48	8 48.46	43 43 27.99
†7	10	..	26.4	41.0	..	..	..	..	..	..	14 56.48	18.00	11. 5 39.940	24 28.66	12.03	15 14.48	43 47 10.69
8	10	..	..	..	9.3	25.0	..	..	17.2	..	17 9.56	18.05	V. 7 45.810	6 21.72	12.53	17 27.61	43 29 4.25
9	9	15.0	30.2	45.1	1.0	15.3	31.0	46.0	..	..	21 0.56	18.08	IV. 6 46.230	12 2.32	13.47	21 18.64	43 34 45.79
10	9	29.0	44.2	59.0	..	..	..	..	..	..	24 14.38	18.11	I. 6 44.130	12 45.19	14.22	24 32.49	43 35 29.41
11	10	..	..	45.2	1.0	15.5	..	..	..	..	25 0.65	18.10	III. 5 37.320	26 2.36	14.39	25 18.75	43 48 46.75
12	8	..	..	..	..	5.0	20.3	35.8	..	..	25 49.98	18.11	V. 4 43.930	28 2.49	14.57	26 8.09	43 50 47.06
13	10	..	55.4	10.5	..	..	56.0	11.5	..	..	10 34 25.76	18.17	" 1 36.570	53 9.20	16.48	10 34 43.93	44 15 55.68

† Zone XII.—Clouds.

INSTRUMENT READING.

	CIRCLE. A.	B.	C.	D.	Mean.	BAR.	THERMOM. At.	Ex.
Zone XII.—April 20, 9.5 h.	277° 21′ 2″.4	6″.8	13″.0	7″.0	7″.30	30.338	66°.0	60°.0
10.5	0.9	..	..	..	5.80	30.332	64.4	58.5

Zone XIII. April 20. H. $D. = -40° 50' 50''.0.$ $n. = -30''.23.$ $n. = -15''.00.$

Number	Magnitude.	SECONDS OF TRANSITS. I.	II.	III.	IV.	V.	VI.	VII.	10.	11.	T.	a.	MICROMETER.	D.	d.	Mean Right Ascension, 1850.0.	Mean South Declination, 1850.0.
											h. m. s.	s.	r.	' ''	''	h. m. s.	° ' ''
1	8	. .	. .	. .	. .	. .	54.0	8.3	. .	. .	10 41 24.51	+18.44	VII. 2 43.012	— 43 18.00	—30.55	10 41 42.95	41 34 38.55
2	7	54.0	8.5	22.6	. .	. .	. .	. .	. .	. .	47 37.58	18.52	I. 5 43.335	22 29.06	31.86	47 56.10	41 13 50.92
3	10	. .	. .	. .	53.0	. .	21.5	. .	. .	. .	47 52.62	18.53	IV. 5 43.420	22 26.61	31.91	48 11.15	41 13 48.52
4	7.8	. .	. .	. .	. .	. .	. .	. .	0.8	15.5	47 55.03	18.53	II. 3 40.590	35 51.85	31.92	48 13.56	41 27 13.77
5	10	. .	. .	. .	. .	. .	. .	16.5	. .	. .	49 32.67	18.54	VI. 4 42.213	28 57.87	32.25	49 51.21	41 20 20.12
6	8	. .	. .	. .	. .	4.0	19.0	33.3	. .	. .	50 49.64	18.56	V. 5 42.652	22 53.04	32.50	51 8.20	41 14 15.54 M.
7	5	14.3	29.0	43.8	58.3	13.0	. .	42.0	. .	. .	52 58.33	18.58	IV. 3 43.848	34 0.12	32.92	53 16.91	41 25 23.04 B.
8	10	. .	31.0	45.3	0.5	15.0	30.0	44.4	. .	. .	55 0.40	18.59	" 1 41.278	50 13.10	33.32	55 18.99	41 41 36.42
9	10	. .	. .	. .	37.0	51.3	. .	21.0	. .	. .	58 37.08	18.66	" 6 41.993	14 30.26	34.04	58 55.74	41 5 54.30 M.
10	9	. .	18.5	. .	48.0	2.8	17.0	31.8	. .	. .	11 0 47.91	18.66	II. 2 42.710	43 28.68	34.44	11 1 6.57	41 34 53.12
11	7.8	7.0	21.8	36.2	51.0	5.2	20.0	34.8	. .	. .	9 50.89	18.79	I. 6 40.150	15 33.89	36.12	10 9.68	41 7 0.01
12	9.10	. .	16.0	32.0	. .	. .	. .	. .	. .	. .	22 45.91	18.92	II. 4 43.860	28 0.48	38.34	23 4.83	41 19 28.82
13	8	. .	. .	. .	22.5	36.5	51.0	6.0	. .	. .	23 22.21	18.96	IV. 6 41.900	14 33.47	38.43	23 41.17	41 6 1.90 M.
14	10	8.0	22.8	36.8	. .	6.0	. .	. .	. .	. .	28 51.66	19.03	II. 6 40.932	15 6.92	39.33	29 10.69	41 6 36.25
15	10	4.5	. .	34.0	. .	2.5	. .	32.0	. .	. .	34 48.36	19.09	III. 5 39.200	24 53.24	40.24	35 7.45	41 16 23.48
16	10	3.4	. .	32.8	. .	. .	16.0	31.0	. .	. .	37 47.21	19.13	" 5 41.775	23 23.57	40.68	38 6.35	41 14 54.25
17	8	52.0	7.0	23.0	. .	. .	. .	. .	. .	. .	45 36.54	19.23	" 5 45.580	21 11.48	41.79	45 55.77	41 12 43.27
18	9	. .	. .	. .	56.0	10.5	25.5	. .	. .	. .	46 56.03	19.24	IV. 2 44.960	42 10.66	41.98	47 15.27	41 33 42.64
19	9	. .	. .	. .	. .	. .	. .	52.0	. .	28.4	46 7.96	19.24	VII. 2 54.995	36 20.92	41.89	46 27.20	41 27 52.81
20	10	. .	. .	41.0	55.7	. .	. .	. .	. .	. .	50 55.67	19.32	VI. 6 38.128	16 44.67	42.52	51 14.99	41 8 17.19
21	8	. .	17.0	31.6	. .	0.0	15.0	. .	. .	. .	53 45.93	19.36	II. 7 42.950	8 3.57	42.87	54 5.29	40 59 36.44
22	5.6	51.0	5.5	20.2	35.0	49.2	4.0	18.2	. .	. .	55 34.79	19.36	IV. 2 41.582	44 8.46	43.11	55 54.15	41 35 41.57 B.
23	10	22.5	37.0	52.0	5.8	. .	. .	49.0	. .	. .	12 0 6.00	19.44	II. 7 45.078	6 49.66	43.70	12 0 25.44	40 58 23.36
24	10	. .	. .	51.2	6.0	. .	36.0	49.5	. .	. .	5 6.21	19.51	IV. 7 45.560	6 33.25	44.29	5 25.72	40 58 7.54
25	7.8	42.0	56.8	11.0	25.6	39.8	54.4	9.2	. .	. .	7 25.58	19.54	I. 6 45.013	12 45.06	44.58	7 45.12	41 4 19.64 M.
26	10	6.0	21.0	. .	49.4	. .	18.4	32.8	. .	. .	11 49.52	19.60	" 6 40.693	15 15.15	45.17	12 9.12	41 6 50.32
27	8	. .	. .	. .	. .	7.0	21.8	36.2	. .	. .	12 52.34	19.61	V. 1 37.910	52 10.17	45.28	13 11.95	41 43 45.45 M.
28	9.10	. .	41.0	55.0	10.0	. .	39.0	53.0	. .	. .	15 9.78	19.66	II. 7 40.728	9 20.72	44.80	15 29.44	41 0 55.52
29	7.8	. .	24.0	38.5	53.0	7.2	22.2	36.5	. .	. .	16 52.94	19.67	" 1 42.720	49 22.59	44.90	17 12.61	41 40 57.49 B.
30	10	7.3	21.3	36.0	51.0	5.5	20.0	34.5	. .	. .	21 50.84	19.75	I. 6 42.575	14 9.68	45.18	22 10.59	41 5 44.86
31	9	34.0	48.5	3.0	. .	. .	. .	. .	. .	. .	25 17.65	19.80	" 6 40.702	15 14.53	45.36	25 37.45	41 6 49.89
32	10	. .	. .	. .	. .	39.0	54.0	8.5	. .	. .	25 24.61	19.80	V. 3 42.270	34 55.11	45.36	25 44.41	41 26 30.47
33	9	. .	12.0	26.4	41.0	55.5	10.0	24.4	. .	. .	27 40.92	19.83	III. 3 37.800	37 30.52	45.49	28 0.75	41 29 6.01
34	8	37.0	52.0	6.3	21.2	36.0	51.0	5.0	. .	. .	30 21.27	19.87	I. 2 38.598	45 51.54	45.62	30 41.14	41 37 27.16
35	9	4.8	19.4	34.0	49.0	3.2	18.0	32.3	. .	. .	35 48.70	19.96	" 5 41.830	23 21.24	45.84	36 8.66	41 14 57.08
36	9.10	46.1	1.0	15.5	30.0	44.2	. .	13.5	. .	. .	39 29.96	20.01	" 5 40.738	23 57.47	46.00	39 49.97	41 15 33.47
37	10	10.5	25.2	39.4	54.0	8.5	23.1	37.4	. .	. .	41 54.05	20.05	" 6 43.400	13 40.94	46.08	42 14.10	41 5 17.02
38	7.8	42.2	57.0	11.8	26.0	41.0	55.3	10.0	. .	. .	46 26.21	20.12	IV. 3 38.673	37 0.14	46.25	46 46.33	41 28 36.39
39	9	. .	. .	55.0	10.0	24.2	39.0	53.8	. .	. .	48 9.91	20.15	III. 6 41.978	14 30.75	46.33	48 30.06	41 6 7.08
40	8.9	49.5	4.0	18.6	34.0	48.0	. .	. .	. .	. .	12 51 33.58	20.20	IV. 1 41.862	49 53.01	46.32	12 51 53.78	41 41 29.33

CORRECTIONS.

	COR. TO CLOCK.	HOURLY COR.	m.	n.	c.	ZENITH POINT.	COINC.
	s.	s.	s.	s.	s.	° ' ''	r.
April 20, at 12h...	+9.353	+0.008	+0.521	—0.342	+0.246	0 0 0.46	40.083
April 20, at 15h...	. . .	. . .	. .	. .	. .	0.95	. .

INSTRUMENT READINGS.

	h.	CIRCLE. A.	B.	C.	D.	Mean.	BAR.	THERMOM. At.	Ex.
		° ' ''	''	''	''	''	I.	°	°
Zone XIII.—April 20,	10.7	279 50 54.2	59.5	64.2	58.5	59.10	. .	. .	. .
	11.7	. . . .	. .	. .	. .	. .	30.304	62.0	55.1
	12.0	51.7	. .	. .	. .	56.60	. .	. .	. .
	12.7	. . . .	. .	. .	. .	. .	30.286	60.6	54.4
	13.0	. . . .	. .	. .	. .	. .	30.284	60.5	53.5
	14.3	. . . .	. .	. .	. .	. .	30.276	59.0	51.3
	14.7	52.0	57.5	63.4	57.8	57.68	. .	. .	. .
	15.6	. . . .	. .	. .	. .	. .	30.244	58.4	50.1
	16.5	. . . .	. .	. .	. .	. .	30.240	58.0	49.8
	17.5	53.5	59.2	64.9	59.1	59.17	30.228	57.7	48.5

Zone XIII. April 20. H. D. = −40° 50″ 50′.0. n′. = −30″.23. n″. = −15″.00. (Continued.)

Number.	Magnitude.	Seconds of Transits. I.	II.	III.	IV.	V.	VI.	VII.	10.	11.	T.	a.	Micrometer.	D.	d.	Mean Right Ascension, 1850.0.	Mean South Declination, 1850.0.
											h. m. s.	s.	r.	′ ″	″	h. m. s.	° ′ ″
41	10	..	..	..	..	37.0	52.0	..	..	..	12 56 22.82	+ 20.27	V. 7 45.567	− 6 32.66	−46.39	12 56 43.09	40 58 9.05
42	8.9	2.0	16.8	31.4	46.3	1.2	15.6	30.0	..	..	14 30 46.24	21.80	III. 2 43.830	42 50.21	42.20	14 31 8.04	41 34 22.41
43	9	24.5	39.0	53.8	8.5	23.3	37.5	..	..	..	36 8.47	21.88	IV. 2 50.060	39 13.21	41.61	36 30.35	41 30 44.82
44	8	..	31.0	45.0	59.2	14.0	28.5	..	..	..	37 59.56	21.90	II. 7 43.280	7 52.16	41.40	38 21.46	40 59 23.56
45	8.9	24.4	39.3	53.5	8.2	..	37.8	52.0	..	..	40 8.32	21.94	IV. 5 44.872	21 35.94	41.17	40 30.26	41 13 7.11
46	8.9	52.2	7.0	21.5	36.2	..	5.4	20.2	..	..	44 36.21	22.01	“ 3 43.484	34 13.01	40.64	44 58.22	41 25 43.65
47	8	24.0	38.6	53.1	8.0	22.2	37.3	52.2	..	..	47 7.96	22.05	“ 2 48.461	40 8.99	40.34	47 30.01	41 31 39.33
48	5.6	..	34.0	48.4	3.3	17.4	32.4	47.0	..	..	49 3.12	22.09	“ 3 36.198	38 26.44	40.10	49 25.21	41 29 56.54 B.
49	9	..	..	44.8	59.2	13.5	..	..	..	..	50 59.24	22.13	“ 1 41.971	49 48.94	39.86	51 21.37	41 41 18.80
50	10	..	..	..	..	43.5	58.0	3.0	..	..	51 29.05	22.14	V. 5 44.223	21 58.83	39.80	51 51.19	41 13 28.63
51	10	..	..	..	..	..	1.0	..	..	..	51 31.62	22.11	VI. .725	. . .	39.80	51 53.73	. . . .
52	9	..	..	..	..	..	..	..	20.4	35.0	52 15.07	22.20	10. 6 42.600	14 7.77	39.70	52 37.27	41 5 37.47
53	10	41.5	..	10.8	25.5	40.0	55.0	9.0	..	..	56 25.48	22.24	IV. 3 40.343	36 2.25	39.15	56 47.72	41 27 31.40
54	10	..	..	38.5	..	7.5	..	37.0	..	..	57 53.10	22.31	“ 2 39.995	45 3.54	38.94	58 15.41	41 36 32.48
55	7.8	..	..	36.0	50.8	5.0	..	..	..	..	15 5 50.68	22.37	“ 7 49.340	4 21.78	37.85	15 6 13.05	40 55 49.63 B.
56	8.9	..	..	46.8	1.7	16.0	..	45.0	..	..	7 1.42	22.57	“ 4 39.202	30 42.82	37.67	7 23.99	41 22 10.49
57	7.8	14.6	29.2	44.0	58.4	13.0	28.0	42.4	..	..	19 58.53	22.56	“ 4 36.310	32 23.49	35.63	20 21.09	41 23 49.12 M.
58	9.10	..	..	..	..	..	..	..	28.0	42.4	20 22.48	22.59	10. 6 38.178	16 41.66	35.59	20 45.07	41 8 7.25
59	10	..	..	..	..	..	..	50.0	12.5	28.0	22 7.12	22.62	VII. 6 37.198	17 16.51	35.29	22 29.74	41 8 41.80
60	8.9	..	35.0	49.5	5.0	18.6	33.0	48.0	..	..	25 4.28	22.66	IV. 7 42.442	8 21.27	34.82	25 26.94	40 59 46.09
61	8.9	..	..	31.5	45.2	59.3	..	..	..	..	27 45.42	22.68	III. 6 45.755	12 19.32	34.40	28 8.10	41 3 43.72
62	8	29.8	44.5	59.0	13.4	28.0	42.1	57.0	..	..	29 13.44	22.71	IV. 6 42.082	14 27.15	34.13	29 36.16	41 5 51.28
63	9	..	..	..	..	21.0	35.0	50.0	..	..	30 6.10	22.72	VII. 3 40.932	35 41.12	33.99	30 28.82	41 27 5.11
64	9	43.0	57.2	12.8	..	..	..	..	..	..	33 27.05	22.76	IV. 2 48.118	40 20.73	33.42	33 49.81	41 31 44.15
65	7.8	..	..	..	54.0	8.0	22.8	37.2	..	..	33 53.60	22.77	“ 4 42.380	28 52.32	33.32	34 16.37	41 20 15.64 M.
66	8.9	56.0	11.0	25.6	40.2	..	9.8	24.2	..	..	36 40.31	22.83	II. 1 37.810	52 14.15	32.87	37 3.14	41 43 37.02
67	9	59.4	14.5	28.5	43.5	58.0	13.0	27.0	..	..	38 43.44	22.85	IV. 4 43.722	28 5.45	32.51	39 6.29	41 19 27.96
68	9	1.6	16.0	30.8	45.0	59.2	..	..	..	..	47 45.15	22.97	II. 5 44.270	21 56.79	30.90	48 8.12	41 13 17.69
69	6	..	26.0	40.2	55.2	10.0	24.2	38.6	..	..	48 55.04	22.99	IV. 4 43.239	27 12.84	30.68	49 19.03	41 18 33.52 B.
70	8.9	48.4	3.8	18.2	33.0	47.2	2.4	..	..	..	56 32.90	23.13	I. 1 44.750	48 12.02	29.23	56 56.03	41 39 31.25
71	9.10	..	31.0	46.0	0.0	15.0	29.0	44.2	..	..	16 11 0.24	23.33	IV. 1 46.680	47 5.65	26.33	16 11 23.57	41 38 21.98 M.
72	7.8	9.3	24.2	39.0	53.7	8.0	23.0	37.4	..	..	20 53.56	23.45	“ 3 37.040	37 57.10	24.25	21 17.01	41 29 11.35
73	8.9	59.0	13.5	28.0	42.8	57.0	..	26.8	..	..	35 42.76	23.63	I. 4 42.854	28 35.19	21.00	36 6.39	41 19 46.19 M.
74	9	15.5	..	45.0	0.0	..	29.0	..	..	..	35 59.72	23.62	VII. 5 46.123	20 52.05	20.91	36 23.34	41 12 2.96
75	10	..	..	..	..	..	..	..	36.4	51.2	36 30.63	23.66	10. 2 47.492	40 41.49	20.80	36 54.29	41 31 52.29 M.
76	9	..	..	..	53.0	8.0	22.4	..	..	..	38 53.14	23.72	IV. 1 37.810	52 14.07	20.26	39 16.86	41 43 24.33
77	9	..	..	..	0.2	..	29.2	44.0	..	..	40 0.03	23.70	“ 2 44.102	42 40.51	20.02	40 23.73	41 33 50.53
78	8	..	10.0	25.0	39.0	54.0	..	..	..	..	41 39.38	23.73	VI. 2 41.020	44 27.35	19.65	42 3.11	41 35 37.00
79	9	..	24.0	38.2	..	..	22.0	37.0	..	..	41 52.99	23.73	“ 3 32.742	40 26.39	19.61	42 16.72	41 31 36.00 M.
80	7.8	..	..	..	7.2	22.0	36.8	..	..	..	43 07.37	23.74	IV. 3 30.180	41 58.36	19.29	43 31.11	41 33 7.65
81	9	..	..	..	..	..	..	..	..	38.5	43 17.98	23.73	11. 4 36.800	32 4.44	19.25	43 41.71	41 23 13.69
82	9	13.5	28.5	43.0	..	..	..	..	..	..	47 57.52	23.76	III. 5 48.360	19 34.73	18.17	48 21.28	41 10 42.90
83	9	24.8	40.0	54.0	9.0	23.5	38.2	42.8	..	..	57 8.94	23.89	IV. 3 45.088	33 17.05	15.99	57 32.83	41 24 23.04
84	9.10	24.5	39.0	53.5	..	23.0	37.4	52.0	..	..	17 0 8.29	23.94	“ 3 34.970	39 9.13	15.27	17 0 32.23	41 30 14.40
85	9	..	25.5	40.0	..	9.2	23.8	38.8	..	..	2 54.71	23.97	“ 3 35.287	38 58.22	14.59	3 18.68	41 30 2.81
86	8	..	48.0	2.2	17.0	31.3	46.0	0.3	..	..	11 16.90	24.00	“ 7 45.111	6 48.63	12.54	11 40.90	40 57 51.17
87	9	7.8	22.5	36.5	..	5.5	20.5	35.0	..	..	13 51.38	24.08	“ 4 39.939	30 17.11	11.88	14 15.46	41 21 18.99
88	10	53.0	..	23.0	37.2	51.8	6.0	21.0	..	..	16 37.21	24.08	“ 5 48.128	19 42.80	11.19	17 1.29	41 10 43.99
89	7.8	25.2	40.0	54.2	9.0	23.5	38.0	52.5	..	..	22 8.96	24.13	I. 6 45.556	12 26.03	9.79	22 33.09	41 3 25.82 M.
90	9	..	12.0	26.0	41.0	55.3	9.8	..	..	..	17 23 40.83	24.16	IV. 5 44.532	21 47.96	9.47	17 24 4.99	41 12 47.43

Number.	Magnitude.	SECONDS OF TRANSITS. I.	II.	III.	IV.	V.	VI.	VII.	10.	11.	T.	a.	MICROMETER.	D.	d.	Mean Right Ascension, 1850.0.	Mean South Declination, 1850.0.
											Zone XIV. May 3. M. D. = −42° 51′ 10″.0. n.′ = −41″.94. n.″ = −40″.00.						
											h. m. s.	s.	r.	′ ″	″	h. m. s.	° ′ ″
1	8	. .	. .	59.0	14.3	29.2	44.5	. .	. .	. .	16 2 14.21	+29.27	I. 1 44.6	−48 46.17	−41.54	16 2 43.48	43 40 37.71
2	6.7	. .	56.8	11.2	26.5	41.3	56.6	. .	. .	. .	11 26.41	29.39	2. 2 47.35	41 13.73	39.64	11 55.80	43 33 3.37 B.
3	9	. .	. .	0.8	16.0	31.5	46.3	. .	. .	. .	13 16.13	29.41	10. 4 39.94	30 40.80	39.25	13 45.54	43 22 30.05
4	9	. .	. .	28.5	43.0	59.0	. .	29.5	. .	. .	16 43.68	29.43	2. 1 43.29	49 31.13	38.52	17 13.11	43 41 19.65
5	8.9	. .	. .	. .	30.0	45.0	0.6	15.7	. .	. .	21 30.44	29.53	I. 4 36.75	32 33.27	37.49	21 59.97	43 24 20.76
6	5	. .	. .	42.0	57.0	12.0	27.5	42.1	. .	. .	22 56.98	29.53	IV. 1 39.74	51 36.44	36.86	23 26.51	43 43 23.30 B.
7	6	. .	. .	6.0	20.8	36.0	51.0	6.0	. .	. .	27 21.00	29.58	I. 6 44.12	13 36.55	36.21	27 50.58	43 5 22.76 B.
8	9	. .	. .	. .	21.0	. .	. .	. .	. .	. .	31 20.96	29.67	" 3 42.11	35 26.07	35.33	31 50.63	43 27 11.40
9	9	. .	. .	47.4	2.9	17.7	33.0	. .	. .	. .	32 2.73	29.67	VII. 4 41.44	30 23.45	35.17	32 32.40	43 22 8.62
10	9	. .	. .	. .	. .	50.7	5.8	20.9	. .	. .	36 35.49	29.76	2. 2 35.76	47 58.48	34.13	37 5.25	43 39 42.61
11	8.5	. .	. .	. .	. .	. .	48.8	4.0	. .	. .	38 18.46	29.79	III. 1 44.79	48 5.66	33.75	38 48.25	43 39 49.41
12	9	. .	33.0	48.3	3.5	18.0	33.3	. .	. .	. .	41 3.23	29.78	I. 5 39.29	25 13.16	33.14	41 33.01	43 16 56.30
13	8	. .	0.6	15.3	30.7	45.0	0.6	. .	. .	. .	43 30.44	29.82	2. 5 36.57	18 5.95	32.33	44 0.26	43 9 48.28
14	8	. .	. .	. .	25.5	40.5	55.6	10.5	. .	. .	44 25.57	29.81	VII. 7 36.26	12 16.27	32.30	44 55.38	43 3 58.57 B.
15	9	. .	. .	30.7	46.5	1.1	16.5	. .	. .	. .	48 46.28	29.85	" 7 44.45	6 55.92	31.30	49 16.13	42 58 37.22
16	8	. .	. .	2.0	16.7	32.0	47.0	2.0	. .	. .	53 16.98	29.92	2. 6 44.36	13 27.81	30.22	53 46.90	43 5 8.03
17	8.9	. .	20.0	35.0	50.0	5.0	20.0	. .	. .	. .	59 50.01	30.03	2. 5 36.66	26 44.28	28.87	17 0 20.04	43 18 23.15
18	4	. .	. .	. .	55.5	10.6	25.8	40.5	. .	. .	17 0 55.64	30.01	VII. 7 39.35	10 28.28	28.27	1 25.65	43 2 6.55 B.
19	9	. .	. .	. .	44.5	. .	14.7	30.0	. .	. .	6 44.51	30.10	I. 4 36.31	32 48.21	26.81	7 14.61	43 24 25.02
20	9	5.8	21.5	36.5	51.5	6.5	. .	. .	. .	. .	12 51.63	30.24	VI. 2 36.15	47 45.90	25.28	13 21.87	43 39 21.18
21	8	. .	45.0	59.8	14.6	29.7	45.0	. .	. .	. .	16 14.82	30.23	I. 4 36.78	32 30.53	24.43	16 45.05	43 24 4.96
22	8	. .	. .	54.0	9.0	. .	. .	. .	. .	. .	19 9.12	30.31	I. 2 38.98	46 5.99	23.85	19 39.43	43 37 39.82
23	8	. .	. .	. .	. .	31.6	46.9	1.8	. .	. .	19 16.78	30.23	VII. 6 42.68	14 26.93	23.81	19 47.01	43 6 0.74
24	7.8	. .	. .	30.5	45.0	0.5	. .	. .	. .	. .	27 45.42	30.31	2. 7 38.32	11 3.59	21.63	28 15.73	43 2 35.22
25	8.9	. .	. .	. .	. .	. .	33.4	48.5	. .	. .	28 3.42	30.32	VII. 7 35.60	12 39.24	21.57	28 33.74	43 4 10.81
26	8	. .	. .	48.0	3.4	18.2	33.3	48.7	. .	. .	31 3.22	30.42	I. 3 37.94	37 51.67	20.76	31 33.64	43 29 22.43
27	8.9	. .	. .	. .	6.3	21.3	. .	. .	. .	. .	34 6.28	30.46	" 3 33.09	40 41.18	20.97	34 36.74	43 32 12.15
28	8.9	. .	. .	22.3	37.5	52.5	8.0	. .	. .	. .	35 37.55	30.46	VI. 4 34.11	33 5.58	19.57	36 8.01	43 24 35.15
29	8.9	. .	. .	. .	. .	3.7	19.0	34.1	. .	. .	40 48.90	30.46	I. 6 36.69	17 55.87	18.20	41 19.36	43 9 24.07
30	8	. .	. .	. .	17.2	32.0	47.1	2.7	. .	. .	17.01	. . . .	10. 1 44.15	49 1.02	17.00	. . . . . .	43 40
31	8.9	. .	11.8	26.5	41.5	56.4	12.0	. .	. .	. .	51 41.66	30.62	I. 3 41.34	35 51.84	15.29	52 12.28	43 27 17.13
32	4.5	44.0	59.0	14.0	29.3	44.1	59.0	14.3	. .	. .	55 29.14	30.66	2. 3 44.30	34 9.07	14.26	55 59.80	43 25 33.33 B.
33	8.9	. .	. .	. .	. .	. .	50.0	5.0	. .	. .	56 19.68	30.67	VII. 4 36.65	32 36.34	14.03	56 50.35	43 24 0.37
34	8.9	. .	. .	13.3	28.5	43.0	58.4	. .	. .	. .	18 1 28.35	30.65	2. 6 41.89	14 54.00	12.64	18 1 59.00	43 6 16.64
35	7	. .	. .	14.5	28.5	44.4	59.3	. .	. .	. .	2 29.18	30.68	I. 5 43.60	22 42.47	12.36	2 59.86	43 14 4.83
36	8.7	. .	. .	16.0	31.5	46.0	1.5	16.5	. .	. .	4 31.29	30.69	I. 5 46.36	21 6.46	11.81	5 1.98	43 12 28.27
37	9	. .	. .	55.5	11.0	25.6	. .	. .	. .	. .	12 10.79	30.70	V. 7 44.67	7 23.44	9.78	12 41.49	42 58 43.22
38	5.6	. .	5.6	20.5	35.6	51.0	6.3	. .	. .	. .	20 35.84	30.91	I. 2 40.96	44 57.41	7.20	21 6.75	43 36 14.61
39	8.9	. .	. .	8.0	23.0	38.0	. .	. .	. .	. .	26 23.09	30.84	2. 6 45.01	13 4.97	5.77	26 53.93	43 4 20.74
40	6	. .	48.0	2.8	18.0	33.2	47.4	. .	. .	. .	28 17.89	30.91	I. 4 45.82	27 16.10	5.24	28 48.80	43 18 31.34
41	8	. .	59.5	14.4	29.5	45.2	. .	. .	. .	. .	36 29.81	31.05	" 1 41.20	50 44.73	2.94	37 0.86	43 41 57.67
42	8	. .	. .	. .	. .	. .	19.0	34.0	. .	. .	36 48.55	31.06	VII. 1 38.28	52 26.84	2.86	37 19.61	43 43 39.70
43	5.6	. .	. .	. .	17.0	32.0	47.1	2.2	. .	. .	18 38 16.85	31.06	" 2 41.91	44 24.19	2.44	18 38 47.91	43 35 36.73

CORRECTIONS.

	COR. TO CLOCK.	HOURLY COR.	m.	n.	c.	ZENITH POINT.	COINC.
	s.	s.	s.	s.	s.	° ′ ″	r.
May 3, at 13h.	+16.149	+ 0.034	+0.590	+0.458	+0.207	0 0 0.31	40.139

INSTRUMENT READINGS.

	CIRCLE. A.	B.	C.	D.	Mean.	BAR.	THERMOM. At.	Ex.
h.	° ′ ″	′	″	″	″	I.	°	°
Zone XIV.—May 3, 16.0	277 51 8.5	9.7	15.5	1.5	8.80	30.000	60.8	53.0
17.6	. . . . . .	. .	. .	. .	. . .	30.000	59.5	54.5
18.6	8.9	11.0	17.5	3.0	10.40	30.000	59.0	53.0

Number.	Magnitude.	Seconds of Transits. I.	II.	III.	IV.	V.	VI.	VII.	10.	11.	T.	a.	Micrometer.	D.	d.	Mean Right Ascension, 1850.0.	Mean South Declination, 1850.0.
Zone XV. May 4. H. $D. = -28° 26' 20''.0.$ $n'. = -40''.00.$ $n''. = -35''.63.$																	
											h. m. s.	s.	r.	′ ″	″	h. m. s.	° ′ ″
1	9	..	..	32.6	45.0	57.5	10.2	23.0	..	..	12 2 45.12	+26.48	IV. 1 37.078	−52 50.33	−40.17	12 3 11.60	29 19 50.50 z.
2	9	12.0	25.0	37.3	50.0	2.5	15.0	27.5	..	..	7 49.95	26.46	" 5 47.751	20 20.56	40.48	8 16.41	28 47 21.04 z.
3	9.10	..	16.2	..	41.5	..	6.2	19.0	..	..	9 41.30	26.51	" 5 47.054	20 44.66	40.60	10 7.81	28 47 45.26
4	9	..	..	..	..	45.4	58.4	10.8	..	..	10 33.12	26.53	V. 2 47.223	41 8.09	40.65	10 59.65	29 8 8.74
5	8.9	30.0	43.0	55.2	7.5	20.2	33.0	45.2	..	..	13 7.76	26.54	IV. 4 47.248	26 25.15	40.74	13 34.30	28 53 25.89
6	9.10	..	12.0	24.2	37.0	49.2	2.2	..	..	..	15 36.97	26.57	" 1 37.290	52 43.03	40.84	16 3.54	29 19 43.87
7	8	..	52.5	5.0	17.5	30.2	42.8	..	..	..	17 17.63	26.57	II. 2 41.128	44 3.96	40.92	17 44.20	29 11 4.88
8	9.10	..	..	..	..	46.6	59.0	11.5	..	..	17 33.94	26.58	VII. 5 42.991	23 7.48	40.93	18 0.52	28 50 8.41
9	8	..	45.0	57.2	10.0	23.0	35.0	47.5	..	..	19 10.04	26.59	IV. 1 45.127	48 12.22	40.99	19 36.63	29 15 13.21 z.
10	9.10	..	..	..	..	43.0	56.0	7.5	..	..	20 30.55	26.60	VI. 6 39.748	16 14.33	41.04	20 57.15	28 43 15.37
*11	8	..	40.0	..	..	..	29.4	42.0	..	..	21 4.57	26.60	" 6 40.710	15 41.34	41.06	21 31.17	28 42 42.40
12	7	50.8	3.3	16.0	28.2	41.0	53.4	6.0	..	..	24 28.50	26.63	IV. 2 38.871	45 56.70	41.17	24 55.13	29 12 57.87 z.
13	9.10	..	..	..	..	..	..	..	32.0	44.5	24 35.69	26.63	10. 5 40.900	24 16.58	41.17	25 2.32	28 51 17.75 z.
14	8.9	24.0	36.5	49.2	2.0	14.4	27.0	39.0	..	..	27 1.79	26.65	IV. 1 44.770	48 23.83	41.27	27 28.44	29 15 25.10
15	9.10	..	..	..	..	..	..	30.0	49.0	..	27 53.69	26.65	VI. 6 35.331	18 46.92	41.30	28 20.34	28 45 48.22
16	7.8	22.2	35.0	47.2	..	..	..	..	..	..	30 58.83	26.67	I. 6 40.740	15 39.92	41.37	31 25.50	28 42 41.29 z.
17	7.8	46.0	..	..	23.5	..	..	1.0	..	..	31 23.53	26.68	IV. 5 43.508	22 47.51	41.38	31 50.21	28 49 48.89 z.
18	8.9	..	..	..	..	4.8	19.5	32.0	..	..	31 53.75	26.68	VII. 5 47.810	20 18.21	41.39	32 20.43	28 47 19.60 z.
19	9	..	..	54.0	6.2	..	..	..	..	..	34 5.89	26.70	IV. 5 51.132	18 23.81	41.43	34 32.59	28 45 25.24
20	8.9	..	..	..	..	..	44.0	56.4	..	..	34 18.79	26.70	VII. 1 48.602	46 11.81	41.44	34 45.49	29 13 13.25
21	8.9	..	..	40.0	52.2	5.0	17.0	30.0	..	..	35 52.67	26.71	IV. 6 44.498	13 30.46	41.47	36 19.38	28 40 31.93
22	8	..	..	..	53.0	5.2	17.5	30.5	..	..	36 52.76	26.72	VI. 4 40.060	30 33.38	41.50	37 19.48	28 57 34.88 z.
23	9	..	29.5	..	..	..	..	32.0	..	..	38 54.45	26.74	IV. 6 34.605	19 12.17	41.54	39 21.19	28 46 13.71
24	7.8	..	48.0	0.5	..	..	38.0	..	9.5	22.5	39 13.15	26.74	10. 4 38.545	31 25.24	41.54	39 39.89	28 58 26.78 z.
25	9	27.5	..	52.5	..	..	30.5	..	..	..	44 5.25	26.77	III. 6 44.302	13 37.11	41.58	44 32.02	28 40 38.69
26	7.8	..	..	..	..	58.0	10.5	23.0	..	..	44 45.39	26.78	V. 2 40.680	44 54.24	41.59	45 12.17	29 11 55.83 z.
*27	8.9	..	..	..	..	53.5	6.0	18.4	..	..	45 41.07	26.79	IV. 7 43.364	8 18.87	41.59	46 7.86	29 35 20.46 z.
28	6.7	..	34.4	46.0	59.2	11.8	24.0	36.4	..	..	46 59.22	26.80	" 1 45.038	48 15.32	41.60	47 26.02	29 15 16.92 z.
29	9	..	..	..	..	..	28.5	41.0	..	..	48 3.34	26.81	" 2 41.620	44 21.82	41.60	48 30.15	29 11 23.42
30	7.8	..	57.5	10.1	23.0	..	47.5	..	..	..	50 22.68	26.83	" 2 41.930	44 11.06	41.61	50 49.51	29 11 12.67 z.
31	8.9	..	..	..	..	..	16.5	29.0	..	..	50 51.54	26.83	VII. 6 45.478	12 56.27	41.62	51 18.37	28 39 57.89 z.
32	7	9.5	22.0	..	..	59.5	..	24.2	..	..	54 46.98	26.86	IV. 5 40.906	24 17.13	41.62	55 13.84	28 51 18.75 z.
33	9	13.0	26.0	38.0	51.0	3.0	16.0	..	..	..	54 50.81	26.86	" 3 40.906	36 0.99	41.62	55 17.67	29 3 2.61 z.
34	9	..	..	..	37.0	49.2	2.0	14.2	..	..	56 36.76	26.88	V. 1 40.490	50 52.50	41.60	57 3.64	29 17 54.10
35	9	..	..	..	0.2	12.5	25.4	38.0	..	..	58 0.33	26.89	IV. 7 37.702	11 34.10	41.61	58 27.22	28 38 35.71
36	8.9	..	..	..	10.4	22.6	35.2	48.0	..	..	59 10.37	26.90	" 7 34.854	13 12.50	41.61	59 37.27	28 40 14.11 z.
37	9.10	..	..	..	..	..	27.5	40.0	..	..	13 0 2.34	26.91	VI. 2 36.283	47 26.00	41.61	13 0 29.25	29 14 27.61
38	9	..	9.2	21.0	34.0	..	..	..	..	..	4 34.01	26.94	III. 1 39.592	51 23.47	41.53	5 0.95	28 18 25.00
39	8.9	..	58.5	11.0	23.8	36.2	48.8	1.3	..	..	5 23.66	26.95	" 3 38.200	37 34.49	41.52	5 50.61	29 4 36.01 z.
40	8	..	41.5	54.0	6.5	19.0	32.0	44.2	..	..	13 7 6.63	26.96	IV. 6 41.178	15 25.15	41.50	13 7 33.59	28 42 26.65 z.

CORRECTIONS.

	Cor. to Clock.	Hourly Cor.	m.	n.	c.	Zenith Point.	Coinc.
	s.	s.	s.	s.	s.		r.
May 4, at 12.0h...	+16.495	+ 0.028	+0.590	+0.458	+0.207	359° 59′ 59″.41	40.114

INSTRUMENT READINGS.

	Circle. A.	B.	C.	D.	Mean.	Bar.	Thermom. At.	Ex.
h.						I.		
Zone XV.—May 4, 12.0	292° 11′ 54″.9	59″.5	73″.7	71″.6	64″.92	30.076	68°.0	62°.0
13.0	......	..	..	..	...	30.086	66.2	60.2
14.0	54.0	58.1	71.4	71.2	63.67	30.086	65.2	59.1
15.0	51.2	55.2	68.3	67.4	60.52	30.088	64.5	57.5
17.0	51.5	55.1	67.5	69.1	60.80	30.084	63.3	56.5

Zone XV. May 4. H. $D. = -28° 26' 20''.0$. $n.' = -40''.00$. $n.'' = -35''.63$. (Continued.)

Number.	Magnitude.	SECONDS OF TRANSITS. I.	II.	III.	IV.	V.	VI.	VII.	10.	11.	T.	a.	MICROMETER.	D.	d.	Mean Right Ascension, 1850.0.	Mean South Declination, 1850.0.
											h. m. s.	s.	r.	′ ″	″	h. m. s.	° ′ ″
41	8.9	. .	. .	. .	. .	15.0	27.2	. .	. .	. .	13 8 2.28	+26.97	V. 1 41.518	−50 16.96	−41.46	13 8 29.25	29 17 18.42
42	8	17.0	30.0	42.0	55.0	. .	21.0	. .	. .	. .	11 55.02	27.01	IV. 6 34.085	19 30.21	41.38	12 22.03	28 46 31.59
43	8	51.0	3.8	. .	29.0	. .	53.5	6.0	. .	. .	12 28.67	27.01	VI. 7 36.950	11 59.91	41.40	12 55.68	28 39 1.31 z.
44	9	34.0	. .	. .	12.0	. .	. .	49.4	. .	. .	19 11.87	27.07	IV. 4 34.640	33 49.85	41.21	19 38.94	29 0 42.06
45	9	. .	. .	48.5	. .	14.2	26.0	0.9	. .	. .	21 1.27	27.08	" 1 41.056	50 32.95	41.15	21 28.35	29 17 34.10
46	7	7.5	20.2	32.5	45.2	57.4	10.0	22.5	. .	. .	23 45.07	27.10	" 5 47.580	20 26.61	41.04	24 12.17	28 47 27.65 z.
*47	9	36.0	. .	1.0	14.0	26.4	. .	. .	. .	. .	25 13.83	27.12	" 4 48.470	25 43.01	40.99	25 40.95	28 52 44.00
48	7	. .	. .	53.8	6.2	. .	31.8	44.0	. .	. .	26 6.41	27.13	" 2 45.532	42 6.66	40.98	26 33.54	29 9 7.64
49	7.8	. .	. .	. .	. .	. .	15.2	27.5	. .	. .	26 50.17	27.14	VI. 7 41.272	9 30.70	40.93	27 17.31	28 36 31.63
50	. .	. .	18.0	30.2	43.0	55.0	. .	. .	. .	. .	28 42.90	27.15	II. 1 38.470	52 2.15	40.88	29 10.05	29 19 3.03 z.
51	7	. .	. .	17.5	30.2	43.0	55.5	. .	. .	. .	29 29.94	27.16	IV. 3 38.482	37 24.82	40.83	29 57.11	29 4 25.65 z.
52	6	. .	. .	. .	. .	. .	15.0	27.8	46.2	59.0	29 50.44	27.16	VI. 6 42.240	14 48.28	40.81	30 17.60	28 41 49.09
53	8.9	29.8	42.2	55.0	. .	. .	. .	. .	. .	. .	32 7.46	27.18	II. 4 39.140	31 5.23	40.70	32 34.64	28 58 5.93 z.
54	8.9	. .	. .	. .	20.5	33.0	46.0	. .	. .	. .	32 20.63	27.18	IV. 2 45.828	41 56.38	40.69	32 47.81	29 8 57.07 z.
55	9	. .	. .	. .	. .	. .	10.0	22.2	. .	. .	32 44.67	27.18	VI. 1 39.103	51 40.25	40.68	33 11.85	29 18 40.93
56	9	. .	. .	. .	. .	. .	46.0	59.0	18.0	. .	33 21.33	27.19	" 3 45.250	33 30.73	40.64	33 48.52	29 0 31.37
57	9	. .	. .	. .	. .	. .	. .	0.8	19.5	. .	33 23.23	27.19	IV. 4 40.114	30 31.80	40.64	33 50.42	28 57 32.44 z.
58	9	. .	. .	. .	. .	. .	. .	. .	12.0	24.2	34 15.85	27.18	VI. 6 45.620	12 51.53	40.58	34 43.03	28 39 52.11
59	9	. .	. .	39.2	51.8	. .	17.0	. .	. .	. .	36 51.82	27.21	IV. 5 40.303	24 38.02	40.27	37 19.03	28 51 38.29 z.
60	9	47.0	59.5	12.5	. .	. .	. .	. .	. .	. .	39 24.91	27.24	I. 1 42.712	49 35.37	40.29	39 52.15	29 16 35.66
*61	7	. .	30.5	42.5	55.0	7.0	20.0	32.7	. .	. .	39 55.03	27.25	IV. 4 44.238	28 9.29	40.26	40 22.28	28 55 9.55
*62	7.8	7.0	20.0	32.5	45.0	57.4	10.0	22.5	. .	. .	41 44.94	27.26	" 2 48.126	40 37.00	40.17	42 12.20	29 7 37.17 z.
63	9	. .	. .	. .	. .	. .	. .	51.0	10.0	22.2	42 13.38	27.26	VII. 1 38.032	52 17.11	40.12	42 40.64	29 19 17.23
64	8	. .	. .	. .	. .	. .	. .	17.2	. .	49.0	43 40.68	27.28	VI. 1 43.088	49 22.88	40.03	44 7.96	29 16 22.91
65	7.8	. .	. .	. .	52.8	5.0	18.0	30.8	. .	. .	44 52.69	27.28	IV. 1 43.565	49 6.30	39.95	45 19.97	29 16 6.25
*66	7.8	23.5	36.2	49.0	1.2	13.8	26.2	38.5	. .	. .	47 1.25	27.30	II. 2 45.092	42 21.64	39.80	47 28.55	29 9 21.44
67	9	. .	. .	58.0	. .	23.0	. .	. .	. .	. .	47 10.63	27.30	IV. 6 48.261	11 20.49	39.79	47 37.93	28 38 20.28
68	7	. .	. .	. .	8.0	20.8	33.5	46.1	. .	. .	49 8.32	27.32	" 3 45.318	33 28.60	39.66	49 35.64	29 0 28.26 z.
69	8.9	9.6	22.8	35.0	47.2	. .	12.5	25.0	. .	. .	51 47.44	27.33	" 6 40.775	15 39.17	39.47	52 14.77	28 42 38.64 z.
70	8.9	. .	. .	23.0	. .	47.0	. .	. .	. .	. .	52 35.13	27.33	" 6 44.712	13 23.05	39.41	53 2.46	28 40 22.46
71	9	. .	. .	. .	. .	56.2	. .	21.5	. .	. .	53 43.96	27.35	V. 6 44.750	13 21.70	39.33	54 11.31	28 40 21.03
72	9	. .	. .	. .	. .	. .	51.5	4.5	. .	. .	54 27.26	27.36	VI. 6 40.250	15 57.09	39.27	54 54.62	28 42 56.36
73	9	. .	. .	. .	. .	. .	52.0	5.0	. .	. .	54 27.26	27.36	" 6 41.040	15 29.79	39.27	54 54.62	28 42 29.06
74	8	. .	. .	. .	. .	. .	. .	. .	15.0	28.0	55 18.82	27.37	10. 2 43.070	43 30.99	39.21	55 46.19	29 10 30.20 z.
75	9	. .	. .	. .	18.0	30.2	42.8	55.2	. .	. .	57 18.11	27.40	IV. 7 39.485	10 32.55	39.06	57 45.51	28 37 31.61 z.
76	8.9	17.4	30.5	43.0	55.2	8.0	. .	. .	. .	. .	59 55.39	27.42	I. 5 43.020	23 3.78	38.87	14 0 22.81	28 50 2.65
77	9	. .	21.0	. .	. .	57.5	10.2	23.0	. .	. .	14 0 45.43	27.42	IV. 6 39.128	16 36.05	38.81	14 1 12.85	28 43 34.86
78	7	. .	. .	59.0	11.2	24.0	36.5	49.0	. .	. .	2 11.42	27.44	" 3 38.433	37 26.56	38.68	14 2 38.86	29 4 25.24 z.
*79	9	. .	. .	. .	. .	33.0	. .	58.1	. .	. .	15 0 20.52	27.96	V. 2 44.211	42 52.36	34.54	15 0 48.48	29 9 46.90
80	8.9	29.5	42.4	55.0	7.4	20.0	32.8	44.8	. .	. .	4 7.47	27.99	IV. 2 41.190	44 36.78	33.82	4 36.46	29 11 30.60
*81	8.9	46.6	59.2	11.3	24.1	36.3	49.0	. .	. .	. .	9 24.03	28.04	" 7 44.870	7 26.56	33.04	9 52.07	28 34 19.60
82	9.10	14.0	27.0	40.2	51.8	. .	17.0	. .	. .	. .	11 52.00	28.06	" 4 37.528	32 1.25	32.62	12 20.06	28 58 53.87
83	6.7	33.0	46.0	58.8	11.0	24.0	36.0	48.0	. .	. .	13 11.00	28.08	III. 5 46.538	21 2.67	32.42	13 39.08	28 47 55.09
84	9.10	. .	. .	. .	. .	. .	17.5	29.8	. .	. .	13 52.47	28.08	VI. 6 48.890	10 58.63	32.30	14 20.55	28 37 50.93
85	9	51.2	. .	16.5	. .	41.5	. .	6.7	. .	. .	16 29.07	28.10	IV. 4 46.344	26 56.65	31.87	16 57.17	28 53 48.52 z.
86	10	. .	. .	45.0	. .	. .	23.0	. .	. .	. .	17 57.75	28.12	" 3 45.945	33 7.03	31.62	18 25.87	28 59 58.65 z.
87	8.9	. .	. .	52.2	5.0	17.4	30.0	42.5	. .	. .	19 4.91	28.13	" 3 41.522	35 39.89	31.43	19 33.04	29 2 31.32 z.
88	8.9	33.8	46.2	58.4	11.5	. .	. .	. .	. .	. .	23 11.34	28.16	I. 3 39.280	36 56.98	30.72	23 39.50	29 3 47.70 z.
89	8.9	. .	. .	17.0	. .	42.0	54.8	7.0	. .	. .	23 29.56	28.17	IV. 2 45.795	41 57.67	30.67	23 57.73	29 8 48.34 z.
90	9	36.1	48.6	1.2	13.6	26.2	39.0	51.2	. .	. .	26 13.72	28.19	" 3 38.773	37 14.82	30.19	26 41.91	29 4 5.01 z.
91	9	. .	. .	. .	. .	22.0	35.0	47.3	. .	. .	27 9.85	28.19	V. 6 42.573	14 37.00	30.02	27 38.04	28 41 27.02 z.
92	8.9	. .	. .	. .	. .	. .	. .	24.0	. .	. .	27 46.47	28.20	VII. 5 45.295	21 45.24	29.93	28 14.67	28 48 35.17 z.
93	9	. .	. .	. .	. .	54.8	7.2	20.0	. .	. .	15 29 42.26	28.21	VI. 2 51.053	38 55.79	29.56	15 30 10.47	29 5 45.35

Number.	Magnitude.	SECONDS OF TRANSITS. I.	II.	III.	IV.	V.	VI.	VII.	10.	11.	T.	a.	MICROMETER.	D.	d.	Mean Right Ascension, 1850.0.	Mean South Declination, 1850.0.
Zone XV. May 4. H. $D. = -28° 26' 20''.0$. $n'. = -40''.00$. $n''. = -35''.63$. (Continued.)																	
											h. m. s.	s.	r.	′ ″	″	h. m. s.	° ′ ″
94	5	. .	. .	. .	. .	. .	24.0	. .	. .	. .	15 29 58.84	+28.21	11. 1 42.150	−49 54.12	−29.51	15 30 27.05	29 16 43.63
95	8.9	. .	. .	. .	. .	. .	39.2	52.0	. .	. .	30 14.19	28.21	VI. 1 44.890	48 20.38	29.48	31 42.40	29 15 9.86
96	8.9	. .	. .	. .	44.0	. .	8.8	21.5	. .	. .	31 43.81	28.22	11. 1 41.240	50 25.53	29.20	32 12.03	29 17 14.73
97	7.8	. .	. .	. .	. .	. .	18.5	31.2	. .	. .	31 53.49	28.22	VI. 5 45.252	21 46.91	29.16	32 21.71	28 48 36.07 z.
98	7.8	. .	. .	. .	. .	. .	. .	36.2	. .	. .	31 58.65	28.22	VII. 5 41.870	23 43.63	29.14	32 26.87	28 50 32.77
99	8	. .	. .	. .	41.0	53.5	6.0	. .	. .	. .	33 41.03	28.25	IV. 6 40.552	15 46.96	28.81	34 09.28	28 42 35.77
100	8	. .	. .	. .	. .	. .	. .	. .	50.8	3.8	34 54.61	28.26	10. 2 42.230	44 0.18	28.59	35 22.87	29 10 50.77
101	8.9	. .	33.0	. .	. .	10.0	22.0	. .	. .	. .	35 57.49	28.27	IV. 6 37.132	17 45.07	28.39	36 25.76	28 44 33.46
102	8.9	41.0	54.0	. .	. .	. .	44.0	57.0	. .	. .	36 19.01	28.28	" 6 41.110	15 27.66	28.33	36 47.29	28 42 15.99
103	9	35.2	47.8	0.8	12.8	. .	. .	. .	. .	. .	38 12.96	28.30	" 5 42.150	23 34.27	27.96	38 41.26	28 50 22.23
104	7.8	42.0	55.0	7.2	20.0	32.0	44.5	. .	. .	. .	39 19.75	28.31	" 3 44.210	34 7.00	27.75	39 48.06	29 0 54.75
105	9	. .	. .	. .	. .	. .	22.5	34.5	. .	. .	39 57.13	28.32	VI. 4 39.495	30 53.06	27.63	40 25.45	28 57 40.69
106	9	. .	. .	. .	41.0	53.0	6.0	. .	. .	. .	40 40.81	28.32	IV. 4 40.630	30 14.11	27.49	41 9.13	28 57 1.60
107	9	. .	. .	. .	11.0	23.0	. .	48.4	. .	. .	41 10.78	28.32	" 3 41.265	35 48.77	27.39	41 39.10	29 2 36.16
108	9	. .	. .	26.0	38.3	. .	. .	. .	. .	. .	42 38.46	28.33	I. 3 38.055	37 39.33	27.08	43 6.79	29 4 26.41
109	9	. .	. .	. .	. .	7.5	20.0	32.8	. .	. .	42 55.08	28.34	V. 4 38.548	31 26.03	27.03	43 23.42	28 58 13.06 z.
110	9	13.0	26.2	38.2	. .	. .	. .	. .	. .	. .	44 50.84	28.36	I. 6 41.402	15 17.18	26.64	45 19.20	28 42 3.82 z.
111	7.8	10.8	23.2	36.2	48.8	. .	. .	. .	. .	. .	45 48.50	28.36	IV. 6 47.022	10 54.38	26.46	46 16.86	28 37 40.84
112	5	32.0	44.5	. .	. .	. .	34.0	46.8	. .	. .	47 9.34	28.37	" 6 44.140	13 42.93	26.16	47 37.71	28 40 29.09
*113	9	. .	. .	12.8	24.0	37.4	. .	59.8	. .	. .	47 24.19	28.37	" 6 40.175	15 59.95	26.11	47 52.56	28 42 46.06
114	8	15.4	28.0	40.4	53.0	5.8	18.2	30.4	. .	. .	49 53.03	28.38	" 2 40.370	45 5.16	25.59	50 21.41	29 11 50.75
115	9	39.0	51.5	3.5	16.6	29.0	. .	. .	. .	. .	52 16.57	28.40	" 1 41.140	50 30.23	25.10	52 44.97	29 17 15.33
116	6.7	. .	. .	41.5	54.0	6.4	19.2	31.5	. .	. .	52 54.07	28.43	" 6 40.278	15 56.42	24.98	53 22.50	28 42 41.40 z.
117	8.9	11.5	24.0	36.4	49.0	1.5	14.2	26.4	. .	. .	57 49.00	28.46	" 3 39.242	36 58.68	23.97	58 17.46	29 3 42.65
118	9	49.0	. .	. .	26.5	39.0	52.0	4.2	. .	. .	59 26.66	28.48	" 4 45.890	27 12.39	23.54	59 55.14	28 53 55.93 z.
119	8	. .	. .	23.8	. .	. .	. .	14.0	. .	. .	16 0 36.43	28.49	" 4 47.642	26 11.79	23.37	16 1 4.92	28 52 55.16 z.
120	5.6	8.2	21.5	. .	45.0	. .	. .	22.5	. .	. .	2 45.59	28.50	VII. 3 44.222	34 6.29	22.93	3 14.09	29 0 49.22
*121	9	42.0	55.0	7.5	. .	. .	45.2	58.0	. .	. .	3 20.12	28.51	IV. 1 43.333	49 14.48	22.80	3 48.63	29 15 57.28
122	7.8	. .	. .	. .	. .	. .	16.5	29.2	. .	. .	3 51.64	28.52	VI. 6 44.950	13 14.81	22.69	4 20.16	28 39 57.50 z.
123	9	. .	35.3	47.4	0.3	13.0	. .	. .	. .	. .	6 0.26	28.55	IV. 7 38.770	10 57.35	22.23	6 28.71	28 37 39.58 z.
124	8.9	. .	. .	14.4	27.0	39.2	. .	4.0	. .	. .	6 26.82	28.55	VII. 5 39.825	24 54.28	22.04	6 55.37	28 51 36.32 z.
125	9	15.0	. .	. .	53.2	. .	18.0	31.0	. .	. .	9 53.04	28.56	II. 3 38.300	37 31.07	21.40	10 21.60	29 4 12.47
126	7	5.2	18.0	31.0	43.2	55.6	8.2	20.8	. .	. .	10 43.14	28.57	IV. 2 45.422	42 10.66	21.23	11 11.71	29 8 51.89 z.
127	6	8.0	20.0	33.0	46.5	. .	. .	. .	. .	. .	14 45.83	28.59	" 1 33.770	54 45.45	20.37	15 14.42	28 21 25.82
128	7.8	10.0	23.0	35.2	48.2	0.2	13.0	25.2	. .	. .	15 47.83	28.59	" 3 40.398	36 18.76	20.14	16 16.42	29 2 58.90 z.
129	9	49.0	. .	. .	. .	39.0	. .	. .	. .	. .	17 26.70	28.62	" 3 33.275	40 24.91	19.77	17 55.32	29 7 4.68 z.
130	9	54.8	. .	19.4	. .	44.4	. .	. .	. .	. .	17 32.54	28.62	" 4 32.630	*34 50.49	19.75	18 1.16	29 1 30.24 z.
131	7	1.0	. .	26.0	. .	51.0	. .	. .	. .	. .	17 38.63	28.63	10. 4 41.182	29 54.35	19.74	18 7.26	28 56 34.09 z.
132	7.8	12.0	24.4	37.0	49.4	2.2	14.6	27.2	. .	. .	20 49.56	28.64	IV. 2 45.270	42 15.91	19.07	21 18.20	29 8 54.98 z.
133	7	56.0	8.3	41.0	. .	46.0	. .	10.8	. .	. .	22 33.48	28.65	I. 6 39.800	16 12.59	18.68	23 2.13	28 42 51.27 z.
134	9	. .	55.0	. .	21.0	. .	46.0	. .	. .	. .	24 20.94	28.69	IV. 4 41.786	29 34.16	18.26	24 49.63	28 56 12.42
135	8	. .	. .	19.0	31.2	43.5	56.2	8.8	. .	. .	25 31.22	28.67	V. 2 38.470	46 10.84	18.00	25 59.89	29 12 48.84 z.
136	8.9	. .	. .	34.5	47.0	59.3	12.5	24.5	. .	. .	26 47.04	28.69	IV. 2 36.318	47 25.22	17.70	27 15.73	29 14 2.92
137	9	. .	14.5	. .	39.0	. .	4.0	. .	. .	. .	28 39.11	28.75	II. 7 39.520	10 31.24	17.29	29 7.86	28 37 8.53
138	8	37.5	. .	2.5	. .	. .	. .	. .	. .	. .	29 15.05	28.76	IV. 7 41.767	9 13.80	17.15	29 43.81	28 35 50.95 z.
139	7	. .	53.8	6.0	. .	31.0	43.5	56.0	. .	. .	30 18.60	28.76	" 7 37.640	11 36.40	16.91	30 47.36	28 38 13.31 z.
140	8	35.8	48.5	1.0	13.4	26.0	38.4	51.0	. .	. .	32 13.44	28.77	" 5 43.490	22 48.07	16.45	32 42.21	28 49 24.52 z.
141	8	22.0	34.8	47.2	. .	. .	. .	. .	. .	. .	33 59.92	28.75	" 1 39.630	51 22.46	16.02	34 28.67	29 17 58.48 z.
142	9	. .	. .	. .	. .	14.0	26.4	39.0	. .	. .	34 1.52	28.78	" 6 40.500	15 48.81	16.00	34 30.30	28 42 24.81
143	9	. .	10.6	. .	. .	49.0	. .	. .	. .	. .	35 36.07	28.79	" 5 46.142	21 16.38	15.65	36 4.86	28 47 52.03
144	8	. .	35.5	48.0	. .	. .	25.7	38.2	. .	. .	36 0.57	28.79	" 4 43.250	28 43.82	15.54	36 29.36	28 55 19.36 z.
145	8	. .	. .	. .	. .	. .	. .	. .	. .	9.5	36 0.52	28.79	11. 4 43.230	28 43.33	15.54	36 29.31	28 55 18.87 z.
146	8	. .	. .	49.5	2.0	14.5	27.4	. .	. .	. .	16 39 2.15	28.84	IV. 6 43.112	14 18.46	14.81	16 39 30.99	28 40 53.27

Number.	Magnitude.	SECONDS OF TRANSITS. I.	II.	III.	IV.	V.	VI.	VII.	10.	11.	T.	a.	MICROMETER.	D.	d.	Mean Right Ascension, 1850.0.	Mean South Declination, 1850.0.
Zone XV. May 4. H. $D. = -28° 26' 20''.0$. $n'. = -40''.00$. $n''. = -35''.63$. (Continued.)																	
											h. m. s.	s.	r.	′ ″	″	h. m. s.	° ′ ″
*147	7.8	. .	56.2	9.0	21.5	34.0	. .	0.0	. .	. .	16 40 21.66	+28.85	IV. 5 40.552	−24 29.64	−14.50	16 40 50.51	28 51 4.14
148	8	59.8	. .	25.0	37.2	49.7	2.2	15.2	. .	. .	41 37.39	28.82	" 2 45.493	42 8.23	14.20	42 6.21	29 8 42.43 z.
149	8.9	12.0	24.5	37.5	50.0	. .	. .	. .	. .	. .	43 49.88	28.84	" 2 48.378	40 28.52	13.67	44 18.72	29 7 2.19
*150	8.9	35.0	48.0	. .	13.5	. .	38.2	. .	. .	. .	44 13.10	28.84	" 2 46.730	41 25.43	13.55	44 41.94	29 7 58.98
151	9	. .	. .	. .	6.5	19.0	. .	. .	. .	. .	45 6.52	28.85	" 3 39.732	36 41.75	13.35	45 35.37	29 3 15.10
152	7.8	. .	. .	24.0	36.0	48.5	. .	13.5	. .	. .	45 36.15	28.86	VII. 3 42.618	35 1.66	13.23	46 5.01	29 1 34.89
153	8.9	52.7	5.5	17.5	30.0	43.0	. .	. .	. .	. .	48 30.37	28.86	I. 2 43.161	43 28.44	12.53	48 59.23	29 10 0.97
154	9	. .	. .	48.0	. .	12.0	24.8	37.6	. .	. .	48 59.98	28.87	V. 4 43.180	28 46.01	12.42	49 28.85	28 55 18.43
155	8	5.8	18.4	31.0	43.7	55.5	8.4	21.0	. .	. .	50 43.40	28.89	IV. 2 42.690	43 45.06	11.99	51 12.29	29 10 17.05
156	9	54.0	6.5	19.0	. .	. .	. .	. .	. .	. .	52 31.52	28.93	" 6 45.500	12 56.00	11.53	53 0.45	28 39 27.53
157	8.9	. .	14.0	. .	39.0	. .	. .	17.0	. .	. .	52 39.14	28.92	VII. 3 36.340	38 39.01	11.51	53 7.06	29 5 10.52
158	8	. .	35.8	48.2	. .	13.0	26.0	. .	. .	. .	56 0.78	28.94	IV. 7 35.070	13 5.21	10.67	56 29.72	28 39 35.88 z.
159	8	55.5	. .	. .	. .	45.0	57.5	9.0	. .	. .	56 32.32	28.94	" 6 32.450	20 26.91	10.08	57 1.26	28 46 56.99 z.
160	9	. .	. .	. .	22.0	34.5	. .	59.5	. .	. .	58 21.96	28.96	" 2 43.780	43 7.41	10.07	58 50.92	29 9 37.48
161	8	. .	. .	. .	23.5	36.0	. .	1.0	. .	. .	16 58 23.46	28.96	" 2 44.402	42 45.95	10.07	16 58 52.42	29 9 16.02
Zone XVI. May 19. H. $D. = -40° 51' 20''.0$. $n'. = -12''.29$. $n''. = -20''.00$.																	
1	7.8	13.0	28.2	42.2	57.2	11.2	26.2	41.0	. .	. .	13 1 57.00	40.16	IV. 4 43.260	28 26.70	11.96	13 2 37.16	41 19 58.66
2	9	37.5	. .	6.2	21.0	. .	50.0	4.2	. .	. .	4 20.88	40.20	" 3 46.012	32 49.82	11.90	5 1.08	41 24 21.72
3	9	. .	. .	. .	. .	. .	50.5	5.2	. .	. .	6 21.36	40.22	VII. 5 40.712	24 4.84	11.68	7 1.58	41 15 36.52
4	9.10	40.0	54.5	. .	23.5	38.2	53.0	8.0	. .	. .	11 23.78	40.28	II. 4 42.174	29 4.20	10.92	12 4.06	41 20 35.12
5	9	55.2	10.0	24.0	. .	53.0	. .	22.2	. .	. .	13 38.76	40.31	IV. 6 40.180	15 38.36	10.51	14 19.07	41 7 8.87
6	9	. .	. .	. .	8.5	22.2	36.0	52.0	. .	. .	16 7.89	40.35	" 6 42.340	14 23.32	9.98	16 48.24	41 5 53.30
7	8	. .	. .	53.0	. .	22.0	36.5	. .	. .	. .	17 7.57	40.35	" 6 45.403	12 36.86	9.77	17 47.92	41 4 6.63
8	8	. .	32.0	46.0	1.5	15.5	30.0	44.4	. .	. .	19 0.96	40.38	II. 5 47.430	20 11.97	9.31	19 41.34	41 11 41.28
9	9	. .	. .	. .	. .	. .	41.5	57.0	. .	. .	20 12.89	40.39	VI. 6 41.720	14 44.45	8.97	20 53.28	41 6 13.42
10	8.9	. .	. .	39.0	53.5	8.0	23.0	37.5	. .	. .	21 53.57	40.43	IV. 1 42.059	49 50.39	8.54	22 34.00	41 41 18.93
11	7	11.5	25.5	41.0	55.5	9.8	24.5	39.2	. .	. .	13 39 55.28	40.67	" 1 38.255	52 2.81	1.66	13 40 35.95	41 43 24.47 B.
Zone XVII. May 19. H. $D. = -28° 27' 00''.0$. $n'. = -20''.00$. $n''. = -11''.72$.																	
1	7.8	. .	. .	. .	. .	. .	. .	36.0	54.5	7.2	14 1 58.24	40.60	VII. 3 38.330	37 5.70	19.74	14 2 38.84	29 4 25.44 z.
2	8.9	. .	. .	. .	. .	. .	. .	12.2	. .	. .	3 34.52	40.61	VI. 1 40.430	50 30.35	19.60	4 15.13	29 17 49.95 z.
3	6.7	. .	. .	27.5	41.0	52.0	5.2	17.8	. .	. .	5 40.28	40.60	IV. 7 44.330	7 21.24	19.41	6 20.88	28 34 40.65 z.
4	9	. .	. .	. .	. .	. .	49.0	. .	. .	. .	6 23.85	40.63	" 3 46.264	32 31.91	19.35	7 4.48	28 59 51.26
5	8.9	39.0	52.0	4.0	16.4	28.8	41.2	54.0	. .	. .	8 16.56	40.62	I. 7 38.010	10 59.21	19.18	8 57.18	28 38 18.39
6	8.9	51.2	4.2	16.4	29.5	42.0	. .	6.5	. .	. .	14 13 29.18	40.68	" 4 36.620	32 8.12	18.69	14 14 9.86	28 59 26.81

CORRECTIONS.

	COR. TO CLOCK.	HOURLY COR.	$m.$	$n.$	$c.$	ZENITH POINT.	COINC.
	s.	s.	s.	s.	s.		r.
May 19, at 12h...	+29.708	+0.026	+0.505	+0.353	+0.207	0° 0′ 2″.57	40.137

INSTRUMENT READINGS.

	CIRCLE. A.	B.	C.	D.	Mean.	BAR.	THERMOM. At.	Ex.
Zone XVI.—May 19, 13.0 h.	279° 50′ 39″.9	52′.0	60″.4	64″.5	54″.20	I. 30.066	50°.5	53°.1
13.6	46.2	59.2	67.6	71.2	61.05	. . .	. .	. .
Zone XVII.—May 19, 14.0	292 11 57.5	70.7	81.0	83.2	73.10	30.066	59.5	50.5
	56.7	70.3	80.5	83.0	72.62	30.058	58.5	50.7

Number.	Magnitude.	SECONDS OF TRANSITS. I.	II.	III.	IV.	V.	VI.	VII.	10.	11.	T.	a.	MICROMETER.	D.	d.	Mean Right Ascension, 1850.0.	Mean South Declination, 1850.0.
Zone XVII. May 19. H. $D. = -28° 27' 00''.0$. $n'. = -20''.00$. $n''. = -11''.72$. (Continued.)																	
											h. m. s.	s.	r.	' ''	''	h. m. s.	° ' ''
7	9	33.2	46.0	58.2	11.0	23.2	36.0	. .	. .	. .	14 15 10.90	+40.69	I. 4 40.453	—28 46.65	—18.53	14 15 51.59	28 56 5.18 z.
8	6.7	6.0	18.2	31.0	43.2	55.5	8.2	21.0	. .	. .	18 43.30	40.71	" 5 45.023	21 30.58	18.19	19 24.01	28 48 48.77 z.
9	9	. .	37.0	49.0	2.0	14.0	. .	. .	. .	. .	20 1.81	40.73	II. 3 42.395	34 45.39	18.06	20 42.54	29 2 3.45 z.
10	8.9	. .	6.2	19.0	. .	43.3	56.2	9.0	. .	. .	20 31.24	40.73	VII. 4 39.740	30 20.35	18.01	21 11.97	28 57 38.36 z.
11	8	. .	. .	. .	. .	. .	. .	46.2	5.0	17.4	21 8.84	40.72	" 7 37.853	11 4.63	17.94	21 49.56	28 38 22.57 z.
12	9	. .	. .	21.5	34.0	46.2	59.0	11.5	. .	. .	23 33.98	40.73	IV. 6 36.400	17 46.30	17.71	24 14.71	28 45 4.01 z.
13	9	. .	. .	. .	. .	43.0	55.5	8.0	. .	. .	24 30.44	40.77	" 4 34.970	33 5.50	17.58	25 11.21	29 0 23.08 z.
14	9	43.0	55.5	. .	21.0	33.0	. .	. .	. .	. .	26 20.69	40.77	" 5 40.630	24 2.74	17.39	27 1.46	28 51 20.13
*15	8	20.2	33.0	45.2	58.0	10.5	25.0	35.2	. .	. .	27 58.16	40.79	I. 3 43.280	34 15.02	17.21	28 38.95	29 1 32.23 z.
16	7.8	17.0	. .	42.0	55.0	7.0	. .	. .	. .	. .	30 54.71	40.78	III. 7 36.600	11 48.20	16.90	31 35.49	28 39 5.10 z.
17	7	35.2	47.8	0.2	13.0	25.2	38.0	50.0	. .	. .	32 12.77	40.81	IV. 3 40.580	35 48.31	16.65	32 53.58	29 3 4.96 z.
18	9	. .	. .	. .	. .	35.0	. .	. .	. .	. .	32 22.65	40.82	" 6 40.702	15 17.62	16.64	33 3.47	28 42 34.26 z.
19	9	. .	. .	. .	38.0	50.8	3.2	. .	. .	. .	33 38.13	40.80	" 2 45.150	41 55.15	16.62	34 18.93	29 9 11.77 z.
20	9	. .	. .	. .	24.0	. .	49.0	2.0	. .	. .	35 24.17	40.82	VI. 6 42.190	14 26.04	16.40	36 4.99	28 41 42.44 z.
21	8	. .	16.0	28.2	41.0	53.2	. .	18.4	. .	. .	45 40.88	40.91	IV. 4 43.950	27 55.26	15.19	46 21.79	28 55 10.45 z.
22	9	. .	. .	. .	18.0	30.0	43.0	55.2	. .	. .	47 17.85	40.91	" 6 42.788	14 5.57	14.99	47 58.76	28 41 20.56
23	8	51.2	4.2	16.5	29.0	41.3	54.0	6.3	. .	. .	51 28.93	40.95	" 3 42.788	34 31.98	14.46	52 9.88	29 1 46.44 z.
*24	8	20.0	32.8	45.0	57.0	10.0	22.8	35.0	. .	. .	53 57.52	40.96	" 1 44.582	48 7.09	14.22	54 38.48	29 15 21.31 z.
25	7.8	55.5	8.3	21.2	33.0	45.2	58.2	10.8	. .	. .	57 33.17	41.00	" 4 43.000	28 28.08	13.64	58 14.17	28 55 41.72
26	7.8	. .	36.0	48.2	1.0	13.3	25.5	38.2	. .	. .	59 0.79	40.99	" 5 47.998	19 48.14	13.42	59 41.78	28 47 1.56 z.
*27	9	. .	. .	. .	. .	. .	33.0	45.0	. .	. .	15 0 7.58	40.99	VI. 1 43.110	48 57.72	13.37	15 0 48.57	29 16 10.99
Zone XVIII. May 19. H. $D. = -27° 27' 00''.0$. $n'. = -20''.27$. $n''. = -8''.00$.																	
1	8.9	20.5	33.0	46.0	58.0	. .	. .	. .	. .	. .	15 21 58.02	41.12	I. 5 37.060	26 2.01	19.58	15 22 39.14	27 53 21.59 z.
2	7.8	. .	. .	10.0	22.2	34.5	46.2	59.5	. .	. .	22 22.16	41.11	IV. 7 36.570	11 45.76	19.57	23 3.27	27 39 5.33 z.
3	9	25.0	37.0	49.0	. .	. .	. .	. .	. .	. .	25 1.78	41.12	I. 7 39.533	10 2.99	18.83	25 42.90	27 37 21.82
4	8	. .	. .	13.3	26.0	38.0	50.5	3.2	. .	. .	25 25.81	41.15	IV. 4 39.248	30 33.98	18.71	26 6.96	27 57 52.69 z.
5	9	. .	. .	. .	. .	. .	20.0	32.3	. .	. .	25 55.20	41.13	VI. 6 41.630	14 41.82	18.60	26 36.33	27 42 0.42
6	5	. .	. .	. .	. .	27.0	39.4	51.5	. .	. .	27 14.62	41.14	V. 7 38.350	10 44.22	18.27	27 55.76	27 38 2.49 z.
*7	7.8	. .	. .	16.0	28.2	40.3	53.0	5.0	. .	. .	28 28.16	41.15	IV. 6 40.792	15 10.92	17.95	29 9.31	27 42 28.87 z.
8	9	. .	. .	. .	44.0	56.0	8.5	. .	. .	. .	29 43.75	41.18	" 3 44.521	33 26.40	17.63	30 24.93	28 0 44.03 z.
9	9	46.3	. .	. .	. .	36.0	48.5	1.0	. .	. .	33 23.78	41.17	I. 6 45.128	12 40.82	16.70	34 4.95	27 39 57.52 z.
10	8.9	45.0	57.8	. .	. .	34.5	47.2	59.5	. .	. .	35 22.36	41.22	IV. 3 40.198	35 57.70	16.18	36 3.58	28 3 13.88
11	7	. .	. .	. .	24.2	36.2	49.0	. .	. .	. .	36 24.14	41.18	" 7 43.220	7 56.03	15.92	37 5.32	27 35 11.95 z.
12	7	52.5	5.6	18.0	30.5	43.0	55.4	. .	. .	. .	39 30.46	41.28	I. 1 37.828	51 56.18	15.11	40 11.74	28 19 11.29
13	9	41.8	. .	6.0	19.0	31.3	44.0	56.0	. .	. .	40 18.92	41.28	" 2 45.738	41 36.29	14.89	41 0.20	28 8 51.18
14	9	4.5	17.0	. .	42.0	54.0	6.5	. .	. .	. .	44 41.78	41.24	IV. 7 35.192	12 33.33	13.73	45 23.02	27 39 47.06 z.
15	7.8	. .	27.2	39.2	52.0	4.2	17.0	29.0	. .	. .	45 51.90	41.28	V. 5 34.249	27 39.44	13.42	46 33.18	27 54 52.86 z.
16	8.9	. .	. .	0.2	13.0	25.0	37.8	50.0	. .	. .	15 47 12.79	41.32	IV. 2 36.112	47 4.22	13.06	15 47 54.11	28 14 17.28 z.

INSTRUMENT READINGS.

Zone.	h.	CIRCLE. A.	B.	C.	D.	Mean.	BAR.	THERMOM. At.	Ex.
		° ' ''	'	''	''	''	I.	°	°
XVIII.—May 19....	15.0	293 11 43.2	58.8	66.0	71.4	59.85	. . .	. .	. .
	16.2	45.5	61.8	69.8	74.5	62.90	30.048	58.0	49.8

Zone XVIII. May 19. H. $D.=-27^{\circ}\ 27'\ 00''.0$. $n'.=-20''.27$. $n''.=-8''.00$. (Continued.)

Number.	Magnitude.	I.	II.	III.	IV.	V.	VI.	VII.	10.	11.	T.	a.	MICROMETER.	D.	d.	Mean Right Ascension, 1850.0.	Mean South Declination, 1850.0.
											h. m. s.	s.	r.	° ′ ″	″	h. m. s.	° ′ ″
17	9	. .	. .	28.5	. .	53.5	. .	18.0	. .	. .	15 48 41.17	+41.29	IV. 5 39.433	−24 40.40	−12.67	15 49 22.46	27 51 53.07 z.
18	9	39.0	51.5	. .	. .	29.0	. .	. .	. .	. .	51 16.44	41.32	I. 4 45.352	27 2.80	11.97	51 57.76	27 54 14.77 z.
19	9	. .	15.0	27.0	. .	52.0	4.3	17.0	. .	. .	55 39.64	41.38	II. 2 44.160	42 25.95	10.71	56 21.02	28 9 36.66
20	7	41.5	54.5	. .	19.2	. .	. .	. .	. .	. .	16 2 19.14	41.41	I. 3 43.280	34 10.91	8.91	16 3 0.55	28 1 19.82
21	6	41.0	54.0	. .	18.5	31.5	44.0	56.2	. .	. .	8 18.84	41.48	IV. 2 36.226	47 0.29	7.25	9 0.32	28 14 7.54 z.

Zone XIX. May 20. M. $D.=-41^{\circ}\ 21'\ 00''.0$. $n'.=-40''.00$. $n''.=-17''.47$.

Number.	Magnitude.	I.	II.	III.	IV.	V.	VI.	VII.	10.	11.	T.	a.	MICROMETER.	D.	d.	Mean Right Ascension, 1850.0.	Mean South Declination, 1850.0.
1	7.8	. .	. .	. .	. .	50.5	5.5	. .	. .	. .	13 3 35.90	40.39	V. 3 35.49	38 55.09	39.99	13 4 16.29	42 0 35.08
2	9	. .	. .	. .	. .	19.8	34.2	49.1	. .	. .	5 4.87	40.41	" 2 45.965	41 38.44	39.98	5 45.28	42 3 18.42
3	9.5	. .	. .	. .	. .	. .	9.0	24.0	. .	. .	12 39.47	40.51	II. 1 34.57	54 8.91	39.94	13 19.98	42 15 48.85
4	8.9	. .	. .	. .	. .	8.5	23.0	37.8	. .	. .	21 53.78	40.60	2. 6 33.95	19 11.52	39.82	22 34.38	41 40 51.34
5	8.9	. .	. .	53.2	8.3	. .	37.4	. .	. .	. .	25 8.12	40.65	2. 7 40.99	9 11.32	39.76	25 48.77	41 30 51.08
6	8.9	. .	. .	. .	. .	8.0	22.8	37.5	. .	. .	26 53.47	40.68	II. 6 37.38	17 12.61	39.72	27 34.15	41 38 52.33 M.
7	5	. .	26.0	40.5	55.0	9.8	24.8	. .	. .	. .	39 55.24	40.84	2. 5 44.58	21 48.45	39.29	40 36.08	41 43 27.74 B.
8	9	. .	35.0	49.6	4.5	19.0	33.5	. .	. .	. .	43 4.33	40.88	2. 5 43.23	22 35.00	39.14	43 45.21	41 44 14.14
9	8.9	. .	22.3	. .	51.2	. .	21.4	. .	. .	. .	14 8 51.57	41.21	2. 4 37.125	31 55.46	37.67	14 9 32.78	41 53 33.13
10	8.9	. .	. .	. .	46.5	1.0	16.5	31.0	. .	. .	10 46.73	41.23	I. 5 43.755	22 17.54	37.52	11 27.96	41 43 55.06
11	8.9	. .	43.0	57.6	12.6	. .	. .	. .	. .	. .	13 12.35	41.25	II. 6 45.87	12 17.40	37.36	13 53.60	41 33 54.76 M.
12	8	. .	39.0	53.2	8.2	22.5	37.8	. .	. .	. .	16 8.15	41.29	I. 6 38.44	16 34.97	37.11	16 49.44	41 38 12.08 B.
13	2.3	34.8	49.9	4.3	19.0	33.5	48.2	3.0	. .	. .	25 18.99	41.41	IV. 7 42.975	8 14.07	36.36	26 0.40	41 29 40.43 B.
14	8.9	6.3	21.2	35.7	50.5	5.7	. .	. .	. .	. .	31 50.71	41.51	2. 2 36.80	46 56.59	35.75	32 32.22	42 8 32.34 M.
15	9	. .	4.5	18.8	34.5	49.5	4.2	. .	. .	. .	40 34.35	41.64	I. 1 41.36	20 11.10	34.88	41 15.99	41 41 45.98
16	8.9	4.5	19.5	33.6	48.3	2.7	17.6	. .	. .	. .	46 48.39	41.67	I. 7 39.58	9 28.86	34.22	47 30.06	41 31 3.08
17	3.4	59.6	14.9	29.0	43.7	58.0	13.0	27.5	. .	. .	48 43.70	41.69	I. 7 42.60	8 16.36	34.02	49 25.39	41 29 50.38 B.
18	9	. .	. .	58.8	14.0	28.0	43.0	. .	. .	. .	15 4 13.63	41.89	I. 5 41.23	22 43.50	32.17	15 4 55.52	41 44 15.67
19	8.9	. .	. .	. .	0.1	15.0	30.0	. .	. .	. .	6 0.33	41.92	I. 4 45.71	26 56.99	31.93	6 42.25	41 48 28.92
20	9	. .	58.8	. .	28.2	. .	58.0	12.5	. .	. .	8 28.28	41.95	I. 4 38.07	31 23.46	31.61	9 10.23	41 52 55.07
21	5	. .	46.5	1.1	16.0	51.0	45.7	0.1	. .	. .	27 16.04	42.20	I. 2 44.07	42 43.26	29.00	27 58.24	42 4 12.26 B.
22	7	. .	51.5	6.5	. .	35.5	50.5	. .	. .	. .	36 21.03	42.27	I. 5 44.17	22 3.25	27.61	37 3.30	41 43 30.86
23	9	. .	34.4	49.5	3.0	. .	34.0	. .	. .	. .	39 3.85	42.35	VII. 1 42.36	49 36.60	27.19	39 46.20	42 11 3.79
24	8	. .	. .	. .	19.1	34.1	49.0	3.7	. .	. .	44 19.31	42.40	I. 2 35.25	47 50.71	26.35	45 1.71	42 9 17.06
25	8	. .	. .	. .	9.5	24.0	38.9	. .	. .	. .	51 9.34	42.49	VII. 1 33.92	54 30.99	25.22	51 52.23	42 15 56.21
26	8	. .	. .	58.5	13.6	28.0	43.4	58.0	. .	. .	56 13.66	42.48	2. 6 35.95	18 1.54	24.35	56 56.14	41 39 25.89
27	8	. .	. .	26.3	40.7	55.5	10.3	25.0	. .	. .	16 10 40.93	42.64	2. 6 37.87	16 55.27	21.78	16 11 23.57	41 38 17.05 M.
28	6	. .	5.5	. .	35.5	49.0	3.6	18.2	. .	. .	20 34.65	42.71	I. 7 43.46	7 46.73	18.94	21 17.36	41 29 5.67
*29	8.9	. .	. .	. .	11.8	26.1	40.8	55.4	. .	. .	36 11.62	42.87	" 7 37.74	11 5.99	16.94	36 54.49	41 32 22.93
30	8	. .	. .	19.5	34.6	48.5	4.0	19.0	. .	. .	16 38 34.46	42.88	2. 5 43.225	22 35.29	16.41	16 39 17.34	41 43 51.70

CORRECTIONS.

	COR. TO CLOCK.	HOURLY COR.	m.	n.	c.	ZENITH POINT.	COINC.
	s.	s.	s.	s.	s.		r.
May 20, at 16h...	+29.991	+0.018	+0.505	+0.353	+0.207	0° 0′ 3″.58	40.115

INSTRUMENT READINGS.

	CIRCLE. A.	B.	C.	D.	Mean.	BAR.	THERMOM. At.	Ex.
						I.		
Zone XIX.—May 20, 13.0 h.	279° 20′ 43″.1	56″.0	63″.0	68″.3	57″.60	29.920	67°.0	61°.5
14.2	42.4	. .	. .	. .	. .	. .	. .	.
15.6	. . . .	. .	. .	. .	. .	29.932	63.2	59.0
17.0	43.5	55.8	0.8	7.8	56.97	. .	. .	. .

Number.	Magnitude.	SECONDS OF TRANSITS.									T.	a.	MICROMETER.	D.	d.	Mean Right Ascension, 1850.0.	Mean South Declination, 1850.0.
		I.	II.	III.	IV.	V.	VI.	VII.	10.	11.							
Zone XIX. May 20. M. $D. = -41° 21' 00''.0$. $n'. = -40''.00$. $n''. = -17''.47$. (Continued.)																	
											h. m. s.	s.	r.	' ''	''	h. m. s.	° ' ''
31	8	. .	36.8	51.0	6.0	20.6	. .	. .	. .	. .	16 41 5.95	+42.92	IV. 6 42.315	−14 20.39	−15.89	16 41 48.87	41 35 36.28 M.
32	8	. .	. .	. .	34.0	. .	. .	. .	. .	. .	41 33.96	42.92	" 7 39.22	10 16.45	15.79	42 16.88	41 31 32.24 M.
*33	7.8	. .	. .	. .	33.0	48.8	. .	. .	. .	. .	42 33.63	42.93	" 7 36.52	11 49.65	15.59	43 16.56	41 33 5.24
34	5	. .	. .	. .	. .	. .	. .	. .	25.5	41.0	43 19.45	43.00	10. 2 40.81	44 35.35	15.46	44 2.45	42 5 50.81 B.
35	8.9	. .	19.5	34.0	48.5	3.6	18.1	. .	. .	. .	49 48.74	43.03	2. 4 42.5	28 50.01	14.11	50 31.77	41 50 4.12
36	9	. .	. .	34.4	. .	. .	18.3	33.0	. .	. .	16 59 49.12	43.07	I. 7 41.53	8 53.35	11.97	17 0 32.19	41 30 5.32
Zone XX. May 21. H. $D. = -40° 51' 00''.0$. $n'. = -8''.09$. $n''. = -30''.00$.																	
1	7.8	. .	34.7	48.7	3.5	18.0	33.0	47.2	. .	. .	13 34 3.56	41.01	IV. 4 45.202	27 29.17	7.55	13 34 44.57	41 18 36.72 B.
2	9	. .	3.5	18.0	32.5	47.0	. .	. .	. .	. .	38 32.69	41.07	" 3 43.822	34 15.92	7.34	39 13.67	41 25 23.26
3	5	. .	. .	. .	55.5	9.8	24.2	39.2	. .	. .	39 55.17	41.09	" 1 37.910	52 24.18	7.29	40 36.26	41 43 31.47 B.
4	8	. .	35.3	49.4	5.0	19.5	34.0	. .	. .	. .	43 4.75	41.12	" 1 36.553	53 11.66	7.10	43 45.87	41 44 18.76
5	7.8	15.4	30.0	44.4	59.0	13.5	28.8	43.0	. .	. .	45 59.16	41.15	" 5 40.730	24 15.01	6.94	46 40.31	41 15 21.95 M.
6	6.7	45.2	0.2	15.0	29.3	44.0	58.5	13.5	. .	. .	48 29.44	41.19	" 4 39.330	30 53.40	6.78	49 10.63	41 22 0.18 B.
7	9	10.0	24.8	39.2	54.0	8.3	23.0	37.2	. .	. .	50 53.79	41.22	" 6 36.942	17 40.90	6.65	51 35.01	41 8 47.55
8	8.9	39.0	53.5	7.5	23.5	. .	. .	. .	. .	. .	54 22.71	41.25	I. 6 43.170	14 3.82	6.42	55 3.96	41 5 10.24
9	9	. .	. .	. .	. .	. .	59.5	14.2	. .	. .	54 30.55	41.25	VI. 6 47.852	11 21.41	6.41	55 11.80	41 2 27.82
10	7.8	. .	17.4	32.3	47.0	1.2	16.2	30.5	. .	. .	14 4 46.75	41.40	IV. 6 38.243	16 55.79	5.72	14 5 28.15	41 8 1.51
11	9	. .	. .	32.2	47.0	. .	. .	31.0	. .	. .	10 46.99	41.45	" 1 36.975	52 57.10	5.26	11 28.44	41 44 2.36 M.
12	9	28.0	42.5	57.0	. .	26.5	41.2	56.0	. .	. .	13 11.93	41.49	I. 2 44.056	42 56.66	5.03	13 53.42	41 34 1.69 M.
13	8	24.2	39.0	54.0	8.2	23.0	37.3	52.2	. .	. .	16 8.27	41.52	IV. 2 36.815	47 8.60	4.66	16 49.79	41 38 13.26 M.
14	9	2.0	16.5	. .	46.0	. .	. .	. .	. .	. .	22 46.05	41.60	" 1 36.304	53 20.55	4.17	23 27.65	41 44 24.72 M.
15	8	13.1	27.8	42.5	57.2	11.5	. .	. .	. .	. .	23 57.12	41.62	III. 3 42.342	35 7.50	4.05	24 38.74	41 26 11.55 B.
16	5	34.4	49.3	4.0	19.0	33.2	47.8	2.5	. .	. .	25 18.60	41.64	IV. 3 36.150	38 42.86	3.91	26 0.24	41 29 46.77 B.
17	8.9	42.6	57.5	12.0	26.2	41.4	55.5	11.0	. .	. .	14 30 26.60	41.69	" 2 44.314	42 47.99	3.41	14 31 8.29	41 33 51.40
Zone XXI. May 21. H. $D. = 40° 20' 20''.00$. $n'. = -45''.70$. $n''. = -12''.00$.																	
1	9	41.0	55.5	10.0	. .	. .	54.0	8.2	. .	. .	14 58 24.72	42.04	II. 1 41.480	50 1.46	43.39	14 59 6.76	41 11 4.85
2	9	24.2	38.4	. .	. .	. .	. .	51.0	. .	. .	15 3 7.58	42.07	VII. 3 42.860	34 30.50	42.93	15 3 49.65	40 55 33.43
3	8	47.2	2.2	16.4	31.0	45.3	0.3	14.8	. .	. .	5 31.07	42.10	IV. 3 42.390	34 47.66	42.60	6 13.17	40 55 50.26 B.
*4	8.9	53.5	8.2	22.5	37.0	51.0	5.0	20.2	. .	. .	6 36.82	42.07	" 7 40.633	9 22.18	42.46	7 18.89	40 30 24.64
5	9	20.0	34.7	49.0	4.0	18.2	32.7	47.3	. .	. .	20 3.76	42.27	" 2 36.340	47 6.53	40.63	20 46.03	41 8 7.16
6	9	. .	18.2	33.0	47.5	2.0	. .	31.0	. .	. .	21 47.47	42.29	" 2 45.541	41 46.70	40.37	22 29.76	41 2 47.07
7	5	44.0	59.0	13.0	27.5	. .	. .	. .	. .	. .	24 27.59	42.38	III. 6 34.961	18 32.27	39.98	25 9.97	40 39 32.25 B.
8	9	. .	. .	. .	45.0	59.4	14.0	28.4	. .	. .	24 44.90	42.32	IV. 3 35.462	38 48.49	39.95	25 27.22	40 59 48.44
9	9	. .	. .	. .	3.0	17.0	31.5	. .	. .	. .	26 2.77	42.30	" 7 35.250	12 29.30	39.76	26 45.07	40 33 29.06
10	9	. .	. .	. .	. .	. .	58.5	13.0	. .	. .	15 26 29.71	42.30	VI. 7 39.400	10 4.95	39.69	15 27 12.01	40 31 4.64

INSTRUMENT READINGS.

	CIRCLE.					BAR.	THERMOM.	
	A.	B.	C.	D.	Mean.		At.	Ex.
Zone XX.—May 21, h. 13.5	279° 50' 60''.3	58''.1	66''.0	62''.8	61''.80	I. 30.104	65°.3	60°.7
14.5	60.7	58.6	66.9	63.5	62.42	30.140	64.8	60.9

Zone XXI. May 21. H. $D.=-40°\ 20'\ 20''.00$. $n.=-45''.70$. $n.=-12''.00$. (Continued.)

Number.	Magnitude.	SECONDS OF TRANSITS. I.	II.	III.	IV.	V.	VI.	VII.	10.	11.	T.	a.	MICROMETER.	D.	d.	Mean Right Ascension, 1850.0.	Mean South Declination, 1850.0.
											h. m. s.	s.	r.	′ ″	″	h. m. s.	° ′ ″
11	9	10.0	24.8	39.0	53.4	8.2	23.0	37.4	. .	. .	15 28 53.74	+42.38	IV. 2 40.540	—44 40.28	—39.33	15 29 36.12	41 5 39.61
12	9	32.3	47.2	1.5	16.2	. .	. .	. .	. .	. .	36 16.06	42.42	I. 5 41.280	23 37.67	38.17	36 58.48	40 44 35.84
13	7.8	. .	. .	22.0	36.0	50.0	5.0	19.4	. .	. .	36 36.10	42.41	IV. 6 45.630	12 21.57	38.12	37 18.51	40 33 29.69
14	9	. .	4.0	18.2	. .	47.0	. .	. .	. .	. .	43 32.75	42.49	II. 5 48.460	19 28.68	36.99	44 15.24	40 40 25.67
15	9	. .	6.2	. .	35.3	49.4	. .	. .	. .	. .	43 35.12	42.49	VII. 5 43.350	22 25.76	36.99	44 17.61	40 43 22.75
16	9	. .	57.0	11.2	26.0	40.3	55.7	9.5	. .	. .	47 26.04	42.59	IV. 1 37.440	52 22.16	36.33	48 8.63	41 13 18.49
17	7.8	. .	. .	. .	. .	37.0	51.2	5.8	. .	. .	16 0 22.42	42.67	V. 5 43.938	22 5.88	34.11	16 1 5.09	40 42 59.99 B.
18	8	56.0	10.8	25.0	39.2	. .	. .	. .	. .	. .	12 39.49	42.80	IV. 5 43.931	22 6.16	31.86	13 22.29	40 42 58.02
19	8.9	. .	. .	. .	. .	59.0	13.4	. .	. .	. .	12 44.47	42.81	V. 3 46.360	32 29.67	31.85	13 27.28	40 53 21.52
20	8.9	54.0	. .	23.0	37.3	52.0	6.3	21.0	. .	. .	18 37.49	42.86	IV. 5 38.090	25 29.14	30.71	19 20.35	40 46 19.85
21	9	55.5	10.4	24.4	39.2	. .	. .	22.2	. .	. .	21 39.05	42.89	" 5 44.910	21 32.14	30.13	22 21.94	40 42 22.27
22	9	. .	7.6	. .	36.8	. .	5.3	19.3	. .	. .	28 36.32	42.97	" 4 42.392	28 48.99	28.78	29 19.29	40 49 37.77
23	8	55.8	10.2	25.0	39.2	. .	. .	21.8	. .	. .	32 39.13	43.01	" 4 42.240	28 54.23	28.05	33 22.14	40 49 42.28 B.
24	8	4.0	18.2	33.0	47.2	. .	15.0	29.5	. .	. .	32 46.91	43.01	" 4 42.960	28 29.15	28.03	33 29.92	40 49 17.18 B.
25	7.8	. .	. .	. .	. .	. .	6.0	20.2	. .	. .	33 37.02	42.98	VI. 6 45.562	12 23.92	27.77	34 20.00	40 33 11.69 B.
26	9	47.0	2.0	16.5	31.0	45.2	. .	. .	. .	. .	39 31.01	43.12	IV. 1 40.380	50 39.92	26.58	40 14.13	41 11 26.50
27	6.7	. .	. .	9.4	24.0	38.3	53.0	7.2	. .	. .	40 23.88	43.08	" 3 38.136	37 15.45	26.39	41 6.96	40 58 1.84 B.
28	9	12.0	27.0	41.3	55.8	. .	. .	. .	. .	. .	42 55.82	43.10	" 4 42.482	28 45.89	25.87	43 38.92	40 49 31.76
29	8	5.0	19.5	34.0	48.2	2.8	17.5	32.0	. .	. .	43 48.45	43.09	" 3 45.142	33 6.67	25.79	44 31.54	40 53 52.46
*30	7.8	. .	59.0	13.0	27.2	42.0	56.0	10.5	. .	. .	45 27.41	43.10	" 6 42.982	13 53.91	25.34	46 10.51	40 34 39.25
31	8	21.5	35.8	50.2	5.0	19.5	. .	48.3	. .	. .	57 4.93	43.22	" 4 43.050	28 26.06	22.84	57 48.15	40 49 8.90
32	9	18.6	34.0	48.2	2.5	17.2	31.3	46.0	. .	. .	17 4 2.57	43.28	" 4 42.755	28 36.23	21.35	17 4 45.85	40 49 17.58
33	7.8	13.3	28.2	43.0	57.2	12.0	26.2	41.0	. .	. .	10 57.31	43.35	" 3 38.172	37 14.24	19.83	11 40.66	40 57 54.07
34	8.9	. .	17.2	31.8	46.2	0.3	15.0	29.2	. .	. .	14 46.07	43.33	" 6 38.733	16 21.20	18.98	15 29.40	40 37 0.18
35	9	. .	. .	. .	58.5	12.4	. .	41.0	. .	. .	16 57.79	43.43	" 1 41.720	49 53.11	18.49	17 41.22	41 10 31.60
36	9	. .	. .	46.8	1.3	. .	30.5	. .	. .	. .	18 1.40	43.35	" 6 38.610	16 25.44	18.23	18 44.75	40 37 3.67
37	9	. .	. .	26.2	40.2	55.0	. .	. .	. .	. .	19 40.55	43.36	" 7 36.825	11 34.49	17.94	20 23.91	40 32 12.43
38	8	. .	. .	. .	26.0	40.4	55.2	10.0	. .	. .	20 26.13	43.42	" 3 43.062	34 27.23	17.71	21 9.55	40 55 4.94
39	7	. .	. .	35.0	49.5	4.2	19.0	. .	. .	. .	21 49.71	43.43	" 3 43.783	33 59.10	17.40	22 33.14	40 54 36.50
40	8.9	. .	. .	44.8	59.3	13.5	28.4	43.0	. .	. .	22 59.29	43.44	" 3 43.425	34 11.71	17.12	23 42.73	40 54 48.83
41	8	. .	. .	48.5	. .	17.2	. .	. .	. .	. .	26 3.00	43.42	" 5 49.300	18 47.72	16.42	26 46.42	40 39 24.14
42	9	. .	53.0	7.0	22.0	36.0	. .	5.0	. .	. .	26 21.73	43.48	VII. 2 43.882	42 43.78	16.37	27 5.21	41 3 20.15
43	9	. .	. .	. .	. .	. .	. .	24.0	. .	. .	27 40.43	43.47	" 3 42.662	34 37.35	16.06	28 23.90	40 55 13.41
44	8	. .	33.0	47.2	2.0	16.2	31.0	45.0	. .	. .	30 1.82	43.48	IV. 4 35.860	32 35.86	15.50	30 45.30	40 53 11.36
45	8.9	40.0	55.0	9.2	24.0	38.2	53.0	. .	. .	. .	34 23.93	43.55	" 1 40.050	50 51.32	14.49	35 7.48	41 11 25.81
46	8	49.8	5.0	19.0	33.8	48.0	3.0	. .	. .	. .	35 33.80	43.57	" 1 37.412	52 23.14	14.24	36 17.37	41 12 57.38
47	8.9	. .	. .	. .	. .	. .	18.0	32.6	. .	. .	35 49.02	43.51	VI. 5 35.350	27 4.23	14.17	36 32.53	40 47 38.40
48	6.7	33.0	47.5	2.5	16.4	31.0	46.0	0.2	. .	. .	40 16.69	43.53	IV. 5 42.988	22 38.95	13.10	41 0.22	40 43 12.05
49	8.9	48.0	3.1	17.2	. .	46.5	1.0	15.5	. .	. .	42 31.96	43.60	" 2 35.553	47 33.96	12.60	43 15.56	41 8 6.56
50	9	1.0	. .	31.0	46.0	. .	. .	. .	. .	. .	45 45.40	43.57	" 5 37.440	25 51.86	11.83	46 28.97	40 46 23.79
51	9	. .	. .	. .	. .	12.5	27.2	42.0	. .	. .	45 58.31	43.56	V. 5 43.278	22 28.92	11.77	46 41.87	40 43 0.69
52	9	. .	. .	. .	. .	37.0	52.0	6.0	. .	. .	17 47 22.83	43.55	VI. 6 42.540	14 8.93	11.45	17 48 6.38	40 34 40.38

CORRECTIONS.

	COR. TO CLOCK.	HOURLY COR.	m.	n.	c.	ZENITH POINT.	COINC.
	s.	s.	s.	s.	s.	° ′ ″	r.
May 21, at 16h...	+30.231	+0.021	+0.505	+0.353	+0.207	0 0 2.12	40.119

INSTRUMENT READINGS.

	CIRCLE. A.	B.	C.	D.	Mean.	BAR.	THERMOM. At.	Ex.
h.	° ′ ″	″	″	″	″	I.	°	°
Zone XXI.—May 21, 14.9	280 20 61.0	59.5	65.6	64.0	62.52	30.148	65.0	60.3
16.0	. . .	. .	. .	. .	. .	30.152	64.8	59.8
17.0	. . .	. .	. .	. .	. .	30.150	64.4	58.5
17.9	60.5	59.0	66.5	64.1	62.52	30.154	64.0	57.3

Number.	Magnitude.	SECONDS OF TRANSITS. I.	II.	III.	IV.	V.	VI.	VII.	10.	11.	T.	a.	MICROMETER.	D.	d.	Mean Right Ascension, 1850.0.	Mean South Declination. 1850.0
Zone XXII. May 25. M. $D. = 27° 56' 50''.00.$ $n. = -40''.00.$ $n. = -7''.54.$																	
											h. m. s.	s.	r.	′ ″	″	h. m. s.	° ′ ″
1	8	..	..	41.5	54.3	6.5	..	..	..	..	15 12 54.17	+44.94	III. 1 39.101	−51 11.81	−37.89	15 13 39.11	28 48 39.70
2	8	..	..	..	7.6	20.1	32.6	45.0	..	..	18 7.62	44.95	I. 5 42.15	23 5.92	37.03	18 52.57	20 32.95
3	8	..	..	..	..	48.8	..	..	..	..	31 36.39	45.06	" 1 38.92	51 17.85	34.68	32 21.45	48 42.53 z.
4	8.9	..	..	..	..	..	..	..	37.5	..	31 41.49	45.05	10. 2 40.545	44 29.86	34.66	32 26.54	41 54.52 z.
5	9	..	1.9	14.0	26.5	..	..	..	..	..	38 26.58	45.07	VI. 5 44.40	21 48.37	33.31	39 11.65	19 11.68 z.
6	8	..	..	..	..	44.2	56.5	..	..	..	45 31.63	45.15	I. 2 35.60	47 21.08	32.08	46 16.78	44 43.16 z.
*7	5	..	..	..	..	5.4	17.5	30.0	..	..	46 52.65	45.16	II. 1 43.80	48 29.49	31.81	47 37.81	45 51.30
8	9	56.0	8.5	21.3	33.5	..	..	..	..	..	49 33.65	45.18	11. 2 40.18	44 42.29	31.33	50 18.83	42 3.62
9	7	..	..	..	37.5	50.0	2.5	..	..	..	52 37.51	45.19	2. 2 39.45	45 7.83	30.71	53 22.70	42 28.59
10	8	..	..	16.7	29.5	41.5	54.3	..	..	..	54 29.29	55.19	I. 4 34.20	33 27.66	30.33	55 14.48	30 47.99 z.
11	8.9	..	..	..	27.0	39.5	5.2	..	..	..	58 27.02	45.22	" 3 39.17	36 32.47	29.53	59 12.24	33 52.00 z.
12	8.9	..	..	..	..	26.0	38.6	..	..	..	16 2 13.60	45.24	" 3 34.55	39 12.05	28.77	16 2 58.48	36 30.82 z.
13	7.8	..	..	..	..	47.5	..	12.5	..	..	3 35.07	45.26	IV. 2 43.59	42 45.31	28.49	4 20.33	40 3.80 z.
14	8	..	..	30.5	..	..	8.0	21.0	..	..	6 43.19	45.28	11. 3 32.43	40 24.77	27.85	7 28.47	37 42.62
15	5.6	..	..	..	15.0	27.2	40.0	52.5	..	..	8 14.99	45.27	I. 5 37.79	25 36.44	27.52	9 0.26	22 53.96
16	8.9	..	..	..	..	29.1	41.8	54.1	..	..	22 16.69	45.39	" 2 38.41	45 44.02	24.51	23 2.08	42 58.53 z.
17	8	..	..	..	..	9.6	..	..	..	..	25 57.33	45.35	V. 7 47.62	5 23.68	23.69	26 42.68	2 37.37 z.
18	9	..	..	..	..	..	..	..	34.0	..	26 38.01	45.41	10. 2 38.711	45 33.34	23.55	27 23.42	42 46.89
19	8.9	..	..	..	..	..	..	36.0	..	..	28 58.50	45.43	VII. 2 35.39	47 28.37	23.03	29 43.93	44 41.40
20	6.7	..	..	..	..	..	..	39.5	..	..	30 2.02	45.43	" 3 31.29	41 4.69	22.34	30 47.45	38 17.03 z.
21	5.6	..	..	..	..	..	52.5	..	..	..	32 27.44	45.46	10. 1 37.01	52 23.73	22.23	33 12.90	49 35.96
22	5	..	..	..	..	..	17.8	..	..	..	34 52.90	45.42	II. 6 38.79	16 19.62	21.72	35 38.32	13 31.34 z.
23	8	..	..	..	..	..	..	..	21.0	..	35 24.98	45.45	IV. 3 39.64	36 16.46	21.62	36 10.43	33 28.08
24	8	..	..	..	..	..	..	11.0	..	..	36 33.53	45.47	VII. 2 47.28	40 37.69	21.37	37 19.00	37 49.06
25	7.8	..	..	..	..	..	..	23.0	..	..	37 45.51	45.48	" 2 41.85	43 45.21	21.18	38 30.99	40 56.39 z.
26	8	..	..	..	..	..	29.5	..	..	..	39 4.43	45.50	VI. 1 34.27	53 58.75	20.75	39 49.93	51 9.50 z.
27	8.9	..	..	..	..	10.5	23.0	..	..	..	40 58.02	45.50	VII. 2 34.78	47 49.41	20.32	41 43.52	44 59.73
28	8	..	..	..	4.0	16.5	..	..	..	..	43 4.09	45.46	IV. 6 42.35	14 16.73	19.84	43 49.55	11 26.57
29	8	..	..	..	..	..	..	24.0	..	..	43 46.51	45.52	VII. 2 40.15	44 43.91	19.68	44 32.03	41 53.59
30	9	..	..	..	..	..	50.0	..	..	..	45 25.18	45.47	VI. 7 43.58	7 43.06	19.24	46 10.65	4 52.30
31	8.9	..	..	..	..	..	..	..	..	49.3	45 40.43	45.53	11. 1 44.23	48 14.02	19.18	46 25.96	45 23.20
32	9	..	..	..	..	..	3.0	..	..	..	48 38.09	45.50	II. 6 38.44	16 31.73	18.53	49 23.59	13 40.26
33	8	..	..	..	..	..	..	29.5	..	..	48 52.14	45.51	VI. 5 43.44	22 21.48	18.47	49 37.65	19 29.95
34	7.8	..	..	..	..	..	..	..	..	26.5	50 17.83	45.53	IV. 4 45.44	26 59.67	18.14	51 3.36	24 7.81
35	6	..	..	3.0	15.5	28.0	..	..	..	..	54 15.57	45.54	I. 5 40.40	24 6.33	17.19	55 1.11	21 13.52 z.
36	7.8	..	..	..	44.0	56.2	..	..	..	..	55 43.90	45.58	" 2 43.98	42 31.65	16.84	56 29.48	39 38.49 z.
37	8.9	..	..	..	..	28.0	..	..	..	..	56 15.59	45.60	V. 1 41.48	49 49.82	16.71	57 1.19	46 56.53 z.
38	8	..	..	..	..	50.0	..	..	..	..	57 37.68	45.56	IV. 5 38.28	25 19.77	16.40	58 23.24	22 26.17
39	8.9	..	..	11.5	24.0	..	..	..	..	..	17 4 24.01	45.59	V. 6 38.35	16 34.88	14.70	17 5 9.60	13 39.58 z.
40	9	..	27.2	..	..	..	..	..	..	..	6 52.12	45.63	III. 4 34.40	33 21.00	14.16	7 37.75	30 25.16
41	8.9	..	..	..	..	40.0	52.1	..	..	..	17 7 27.32	45.65	IV. 2 32.92	48 53.98	13.99	17 8 12.97	28 45 57.97

CORRECTIONS.

	COR. TO CLOCK.	HOURLY COR.	m.	n.	c.	ZENITH POINT.	COINC.
	s.	s.	s.	s.	s.	° ′ ″	r.
May 25, at 16*h*...	+33.686	+ 0.044	+0.505	+0.353	+0.207	0 0 0.70	40.115

INSTRUMENT READINGS.

	CIRCLE. A.	B.	C.	D.	Mean.	BAR.	THERMOM. At.	Ex.
h.	° ′ ″	′	″	″	″	I.	°	°
Zone XXII.—May 25, 15.0	292 41 45.0	46.0	50.2	50.0	47.80	30.020	75.5	72.0
17.3	......	..	..	..	...	30.020	73.5	70.5

Number.	Magnitude.	SECONDS OF TRANSITS. I.	II.	III.	IV.	V.	VI.	VII.	10.	11.	T.	a.	MICROMETER.	D.	d.	Mean Right Ascension, 1850.0.	Mean South Declination, 1850.0.
Zone XXII. May 25. M. $D. = 27° 56' 50''.0$. $n' = -40''.00$. $n'' = -7''.54$. (Continued.)																	
											h. m. s.	s.	r.	' ''	''	h. m. s.	° ' ''
42	8	. .	44.8	56.5	9.5	. .	. .	. .	. .	. .	17 14 9.42	+45.66	I. 3 44.67	−33 22.50	−12.36	17 14 55.08	28 30 24.86 z.
43	8	. .	. .	. .	52.0	4.0	. .	. .	. .	. .	15 51.79	45.70	III. 1 40.89	50 10.18	11.94	16 37.49	47 12.12
44	7.8	. .	. .	. .	. .	. .	. .	32.0	. .	. .	15 54.59	45.67	IV. 4 45.735	26 49.38	11.93	16 40.26	23 51.31 z.
45	7	. .	. .	. .	. .	. .	. .	. .	58.5	. .	16 2.64	45.65	10. 6 38.52	16 28.49	11.88	16 48.29	13 30.37
46	7.8	. .	. .	. .	. .	. .	. .	. .	58.0	. .	17 1.99	45.70	10. 2 46.75	40 55.72	11.63	17 47.69	37 57.35 z.
*47	8	. .	. .	. .	. .	2.0	14.5	. .	. .	. .	17 21 49.53	45.74	I. 2 38.4	45 44.41	10.45	17 22 35.27	28 42 44.86
Zone XXIII. May 27. M. $D. = -27° 56' 40''.0$. $n' = -20''.00$. $n'' = -9''.62$.																	
1	9	58.4	. .	. .	. .	. .	. .	. .	. .	. .	13 11 36.09	45.71	III. 1 42.12	49 29.92	19.43	13 12 21.80	28 46 29.35
2	8.9	. .	. .	. .	9.8	22.0	34.7	. .	. .	. .	12 9.68	45.71	VI. 2 44.90	42 2.20	19.40	12 55.39	39 1.60 z.
3	8.9	. .	. .	. .	4.3	16.5	29.3	. .	. .	. .	18 4.28	45.73	" 6 32.60	19 55.40	19.13	18 50.01	16 54.53 z.
4	8.9	. .	. .	33.6	46.3	58.3	11.0	. .	. .	. .	20 46.14	45.75	I. 7 34.38	12 27.68	19.00	21 31.89	9 26.68
5	7	. .	1.5	14.0	. .	. .	. .	. .	. .	. .	23 26.60	45.78	I. 1 40.55	50 23.82	18.86	24 12.38	47 22.68 z.
6	8	. .	. .	. .	. .	. .	. .	4.2	. .	. .	23 26.76	45.77	VII. 3 43.18	34 16.04	18.86	24 12.53	31 14.90 z.
7	8.9	. .	. .	. .	. .	. .	. .	. .	. .	20.0	24 11.11	45.79	10. 1 39.96	50 44.02	18.80	24 56.90	47 42.82
8	8	. .	. .	. .	. .	. .	46.2	. .	. .	. .	26 21.20	45.79	VI. 5 37.10	26 2.50	18.67	27 6.99	23 1.17
9	8	. .	. .	. .	. .	. .	. .	. .	. .	40.0	26 31.19	45.80	11. 3 34.10	39 29.23	18.66	27 16.99	36 27.89
10	7	53.5	6.7	18.8	31.7	43.5	. .	. .	. .	. .	29 31.43	45.82	I. 1 40.28	50 33.20	18.50	30 17.25	47 31.70 z.
11	9	. .	. .	. .	. .	42.0	54.5	7.0	. .	. .	32 29.67	45.82	" 6 38.51	16 30.99	18.30	33 15.49	13 29.29
12	8.9	. .	. .	32.4	45.0	57.5	10.0	22.4	. .	. .	33 5.10	45.83	2. 6 41.88	14 34.38	18.25	33 50.93	11 32.63
13	8.9	. .	. .	. .	. .	. .	30.0	42.5	. .	. .	36 5.12	45.84	II. 6 34.74	18 41.48	18.05	36 50.96	15 39.53 z.
14	8	. .	1.0	13.5	26.0	. .	. .	. .	. .	. .	40 26.04	45.89	2. 2 40.07	44 48.63	17.75	41 11.93	41 46.38
15	8	. .	. .	. .	. .	5.0	18.0	30.0	. .	. .	41 52.68	45.90	IV. 1 45.81	47 22.47	17.65	42 38.58	44 20.12
16	8	. .	. .	. .	. .	. .	38.6	51.0	. .	. .	44 13.67	45.90	" 5 48.86	19 16.32	17.45	44 59.57	16 13.77
17	8	. .	. .	. .	. .	. .	58.0	10.1	. .	. .	46 32.98	45.91	III. 6 42.52	14 12.77	17.28	47 18.89	11 10.05
18	8	. .	26.5	39.0	. .	. .	. .	. .	. .	. .	47 51.57	45.94	2. 2 40.93	44 18.91	17.17	48 37.51	41 16.08 z.
19	8	. .	. .	. .	. .	. .	55.3	8.0	. .	. .	49 30.48	45.93	II. 5 43.25	22 29.59	17.03	50 16.41	19 26.62
20	8	. .	4.0	16.3	28.8	41.4	53.5	. .	. .	. .	51 28.84	46.96	2. 2 38.38	45 47.03	16.86	52 14.80	42 43.89 z.
21	8.9	. .	. .	55.0	7.5	. .	. .	. .	. .	. .	54 7.54	45.98	2. 2 37.91	46 3.22	16.61	54 53.52	42 59.83
22	7.8	. .	. .	52.2	5.0	17.5	. .	. .	. .	. .	55 4.90	45.97	II. 5 41.67	23 24.62	16.54	55 50.87	20 21.16
*23	8	. .	. .	. .	. .	41.3	54.1	6.2	. .	. .	55 28.95	45.98	VII. 4 44.62	27 29.66	16.51	56 14.93	24 26.17
24	8	. .	. .	. .	. .	12.0	24.3	36.5	. .	. .	56 59.30	45.99	" 2 47.38	40 1.85	16.37	57 45.29	36 58.22
25	8	. .	. .	. .	. .	. .	. .	57.7	. .	. .	58 20.34	45.99	" 5 44.91	21 32.44	16.23	59 6.33	18 28.67
26	8.9	. .	. .	. .	. .	. .	. .	14.0	. .	. .	59 36.48	46.02	" 1 38.80	51 24.31	16.13	14 0 22.50	48 20.44
27	8.9	. .	. .	. .	. .	. .	. .	. .	22.7	36.0	14 0 26.92	46.02	11. 2 36.87	46 38.89	16.04	1 12.94	43 34.93
28	8	. .	. .	. .	. .	. .	36.3	49.0	. .	. .	2 11.64	46.00	VII. 7 43.19	7 58.28	15.86	2 57.64	4 54 14 z.
29	8	. .	. .	. .	. .	. .	. .	. .	34.2	47.0	2 38.48	46.01	11. 6 42.87	13.59.90	15.81	3 24.49	10 55.71 z.
30	8.9	. .	40.0	52.0	4.5	. .	. .	. .	. .	. .	14 5 4.67	46.05	IV. 3 42.22	34 49.54	15.57	14 5 50.72	28 31 45.11

CORRECTIONS.

	COR. TO CLOCK.	HOURLY COR.	m.	n.	c.	ZENITH POINT.	COINC.
	s.	s.	s.	s.	s.		r.
May 27, at 16h....	+35.269	+0.038	+0.505	+0.353	+0.207	0° 0' 0''.70	40.110

INSTRUMENT READINGS.

		CIRCLE. A.	B.	C.	D.	Mean.	BAR.	THERMOM. At.	Ex.
Zone	h.						I.		
XXIII.—May 27....	13.2	292° 42' 21''.0	21'.0	27'.3	25''.3	23''.65	29.740	78°.0	75°.0
	14.8	....	...	...	...	....	29.720	76.5	73.5

Number.	Magnitude.	SECONDS OF TRANSITS. I.	II.	III.	IV.	V.	VI.	VII.	10.	11.	T.	a.	MICROMETER.	D.	d.	Mean Right Ascension, 1850.0.	Mean South Declination, 1850.0.
Zone XXIII. May 27. M. D. = −27° 56′ 40″.0. n′. = −20″.00. n″. = −9″.62. (Continued.)																	
											h. m. s.	s.	r.	′ ″	″	h. m. s.	° ′ ″
31	7	. .	. .	. .	. .	. .	. .	12.3	. .	. .	14 5 34.84	+46.05	VII. 3 37.26	−37 40.57	−15.52	14 6 20.89	28 34 36.49 z.
32	8	. .	. .	. .	25.0	37.0	. .	. .	. .	. .	8 24.77	46.06	I. 5 35.19	27 8.26	15.24	9 14.83	24 3.50
33	8.9	. .	. .	. .	. .	. .	. .	48.5	. .	. .	9 11.02	46.07	III. 3 30.73	41 26.43	15.16	9 57.09	38 21.59
34	8.9	. .	. .	. .	. .	. .	14.0	26.2	. .	. .	9 48.91	46.07	V. 5 39.40	24 43.13	15.09	10 34.98	21 38.22
35	7.8	. .	. .	. .	12.4	24.3	37.0	. .	. .	. .	12 12.19	46.07	I. 7 45.37	6 8.48	14.83	12 58.26	3 3.31
36	8.9	. .	. .	. .	41.4	54.0	6.9	. .	. .	. .	14 41.95	46.10	II. 5 40.20	24 15.41	14.55	15 28.05	21 9.96
37	7.8	. .	32.0	44.5	57.0	9.0	22.0	34.2	. .	. .	15 56.88	46.10	I. 6 39.90	15 42.99	14.43	16 42.98	12 37.42 z.
38	6.7	. .	13.0	25.5	37.9	50.1	. .	. .	. .	. .	18 37.95	46.16	2. 1 37.80	51 58.66	14.11	19 24.11	48 52.77 z.
39	8.7	. .	12.0	25.3	39.5	. .	. .	. .	. .	. .	19 38.08	46.13	IV. 4 41.20	29 28.20	13.98	20 24.21	26 22.18
40	8	. .	. .	51.1	3.9	16.0	28.2	41.0	. .	. .	21 3.59	46.15	" 3 45.89	32 42.73	13.81	21 49.74	29 36.54
41	8	. .	. .	0.2	12.9	25.0	. .	. .	. .	. .	27 12.77	46.18	I. 4 41.03	29 33.72	13.07	27 58.95	26 26.79
42	8	. .	. .	. .	. .	. .	51.5	4.8	. .	. .	28 27.14	46.17	VII. 7 45.01	6 55.38	12.91	29 13.31	3 48.29
43	8	. .	24.5	36.5	49.5	02.0	. .	. .	. .	. .	30 49.43	46.22	2. 2 44.60	42 12.11	12.61	31 35.65	39 04.72 z.
44	8	39.5	52.3	5.0	17.4	. .	. .	. .	. .	. .	32 17.38	46.23	I. 2 38.63	45 38.58	12.43	33 3.61	42 31.01 z.
45	8	. .	. .	. .	. .	. .	. .	1.5	. .	. .	32 24.24	46.20	10. 6 43.78	13 28.74	12.42	33 10.44	10 21.16 z.
46	9	. .	0.8	13.8	. .	. .	. .	. .	. .	. .	37 25.91	46.23	2. 7 37.64	11 9.77	11.77	38 12.14	8 01.54 z.
47	8.9	. .	. .	. .	47.5	. .	. .	. .	. .	. .	39 47.47	46.26	I. 5 36.99	26 6.05	11.43	40 33.73	22 57.48
48	7.8	. .	. .	7.3	. .	32.0	44.3	57.0	. .	. .	40 19.60	46.27	" 5 34.34	27 37.63	11.36	41 5.87	24 28.99
49	8.9	. .	. .	. .	. .	22.0	34.0	47.0	. .	. .	43 9.46	46.27	" 5 46.34	20 43.05	10.95	43 55.73	17 34.00
50	8.9	35.0	47.4	. .	12.5	. .	. .	. .	. .	. .	47 12.52	46.33	2. 2 40.52	44 33.14	10.39	47 58.85	41 23.53
51	7.8	. .	. .	. .	. .	. .	56.0	8.5	. .	. .	48 31.00	46.33	IV. 3 40.24	35 57.98	10.20	49 17.33	32 48.18
52	8.9	. .	. .	. .	. .	9.3	22.0	. .	. .	. .	52 56.98	46.35	VI. 4 44.27	27 41.93	9.56	53 43.33	24 32.49 z.
53	8.9	. .	. .	. .	. .	. .	. .	. .	37.8	50.7	53 41.88	46.34	10. 4 39.54	30 24.95	9.31	54 28.22	27 14.26 z.
54	8	. .	. .	. .	57.0	8.2	21.0	. .	. .	. .	55 56.35	46.35	IV. 7 38.50	10 40.59	8.98	56 42.70	7 29.57
55	8	. .	. .	9.0	21.5	. .	. .	. .	. .	. .	57 21.51	46.36	V. 6 36.84	17 29.00	8.74	58 7.87	14 17.74
56	8.9	. .	. .	. .	. .	. .	. .	32.5	. .	. .	57 55.15	46.37	VII. 6 29.91	21 28.10	8.71	58 41.52	18 16.81
57	7.8	. .	. .	. .	. .	. .	. .	. .	51.5	4.5	59 55.57	46.42	" 1 35.56	53 16.30	8.47	15 0 41.99	50 4.77
58	9	. .	59.5	11.5	24.5	. .	. .	. .	. .	. .	15 3 24.25	46.40	2. 6 41.43	14 49.95	7.93	4 10.65	11 37.88
59	8	. .	. .	20.7	33.5	45.4	58.3	10.5	. .	. .	4 33.22	46.43	I. 3 44.40	33 33.91	7.74	5 19.65	40 21.65
60	7.8	. .	41.0	. .	. .	. .	. .	. .	. .	. .	10 6.02	46.48	2. 2 42.65	43 19.49	6.84	10 52.50	40 6.33
61	8	. .	. .	. .	30.0	42.4	55.0	7.8	. .	. .	10 30.10	46.46	IV. 4 42.85	28 31.16	6.76	11 16.56	25 17.92
62	7	. .	28.0	40.1	52.7	5.1	. .	. .	. .	. .	12 52.80	46.51	2. 1 39.18	51 10.99	6.42	13 39.31	47 57.41 z.
63	8	. .	. .	. .	. .	. .	. .	. .	59.0	12.0	14 3.08	46.50	11. 3 31.25	41 7.72	6.17	14 49.58	37 53.89
64	7	. .	41.7	53.6	6.5	. .	. .	. .	. .	. .	19 6.39	46.51	2. 5 41.29	23 37.30	5.30	19 52.90	20 22.60 z.
65	8	. .	. .	. .	35.0	47.0	. .	12.3	. .	. .	15 19 34.86	46.52	IV. 5 43.19	22 32.20	5.23	15 20 21.38	28 19 17.43 z.
Zone XXIV. May 27. M. D. = −26° 55′ 20″.00. n′. = −62″.00. n″. = −3″.51.																	
*1	8.9	. .	. .	. .	6.0	18.3	31.0	. .	. .	. .	16 30 6.09	46.91	I. 2 38.95	45 17.76	59.62	16 30 52.98	27 41 37.38 z.
2	7	. .	6.5	19.0	31.1	43.5	55.7	8.2	. .	. .	31 31.17	46.90	II. 3 42.72	34 25.93	59.30	32 18.07	30 45.23 z.
*3	7.8	. .	48.0	0.1	12.4	24.9	. .	. .	. .	. .	34 12.53	46.89	I. 6 42.35	14 12.43	58.67	34 59.42	10 31.10
*4	8.9	. .	. .	. .	45.0	57.0	9.5	22.0	. .	. .	34 44.92	46.90	" 6 42.35	14 12.43	58.56	35 31.82	10 30.99
5	8	. .	32.3	45.0	. .	. .	. .	. .	. .	. .	40 57.31	46.98	2. 2 36.48	46 46.35	57.13	41 44.29	43 3.48 z.
6	8.9	. .	. .	3.5	. .	. .	. .	53.0	. .	. .	41 15.93	46.98	VII. 2 32.10	49 17.84	57.04	42 2.91	45 34.84 z.
7	8	. .	. .	. .	20.0	32.2	. .	. .	. .	. .	44 19.99	46.95	IV. 5 42.63	22 45.47	56.31	45 6.94	19 1.78 z.
8	8	. .	. .	8.5	20.5	. .	. .	. .	. .	. .	17 6 20.71	47.07	2. 4 45.33	26 58.88	50.99	17 7 7.78	23 9.87 z.
9	7.8	. .	52.0	4.0	16.8	. .	. .	. .	. .	. .	7 16.66	47.11	III. 2 48.93	39 36.82	50.77	8 3.77	35 47.59 z.
10	8	. .	. .	. .	. .	. .	. .	19.5	. .	. .	7 42.39	47.11	VII. 2 48.39	39 55.18	50.68	8 29.50	36 05.86 z.
11	8	. .	31.5	43.7	56.3	. .	. .	. .	. .	. .	9 56.24	47.12	I. 2 47.34	40 31.45	50.09	10 43.36	36 41.54
12	8	. .	. .	. .	. .	. .	. .	22.5	. .	. .	10 45.54	47.07	VII 6 41.15	14 53.84	49.90	11 32.61	11 03.74 z.
*13	7.8	. .	. .	. .	. .	. .	. .	. .	. .	3.5	10 55.70	47.08	11. 6 33.90	19 3.82	49.86	11 42.78	15 13.68
14	8.9	. .	. .	. .	. .	. .	. .	. .	30.5	43.0	12 34.95	47.12	" 3 41.24	35 16.38	49.44	13 22.07	31 25.82 z.
15	8	17.8	30.4	42.1	55.5	. .	19.5	31.7	. .	. .	17 15 54.91	47.13	2. 4 37.77	31 19.97	48.61	17 16 42.04	27 27 28.58 z.

Zone XXIV. May 27. M. $D. = -26^\circ 55' 20''.00.$ $n'. = -62''.00.$ $n''. = -3''.51.$ (Continued.)

Number.	Magnitude.	Seconds of Transits. I.	II.	III.	IV.	V.	VI.	VII.	10.	11.	T.	a.	Micrometer.	D.	d.	Mean Right Ascension, 1850.0.	Mean South Declination, 1850.0.
											h. m. s.	s.	r.	′ ″	″	h. m. s.	° ′ ″
16	8.9	. .	. .	11.2	24.0	36.2	48.5	. .	. .	. .	17 20 23.88	+47.11	III. 7 41.95	− 8 35.51	−47.47	−17 21 10.99	27 4 42.98 z.
17	8	. .	. .	. .	8.8	. .	. .	. .	. .	. .	18 10 8.77	47.38	I. 4 36.71	31 56.79	34.44	18 10 56.15	27 51.23 z.
18	7.8	. .	40.3	52.2	5.0	17.0	29.3	41.5	. .	. .	22 4.72	47.41	2. 5 41.45	23 25.74	31.23	22 52.13	19 16.97 z.
19	8	. .	. .	. .	25.0	37.5	. .	. .	. .	. .	23 25.11	47.44	IV. 2 48.88	39 38.58	30.89	24 12.55	35 29.47
20	8	. .	. .	. .	. .	. .	50.0	2.5	. .	. .	25 25.28	47.45	VI. 2 39.62	44 58.32	30.33	26 12.73	40 48.65
21	7.8	. .	. .	. .	. .	. .	. .	59.5	. .	. .	25 22.42	47.43	VII. 4 37.61	31 25.69	30.33	26 10.25	27 16.02
22	8	. .	. .	. .	. .	. .	. .	. .	. .	27.0	26.19.28	47.41	11. 7 34.61	12 48.20	30.08	27 7.09	8 38.28
23	8	. .	11.5	23.5	. .	. .	. .	. .	. .	. .	31 36.11	47.48	2. 3 34.85	38 57.34	28.65	32 23.59	34 45.99 z.
24	8	. .	. .	. .	. .	. .	0.5	13.2	. .	. .	31 36.06	47.43	VII. 7 35.28	12 25.58	28.63	32 23.49	8 14.21 z.
25	8	. .	. .	. .	. .	. .	. .	19.5	. .	. .	32.42.35	47.50	" 1 38.58	51 25.56	28.36	33 29.85	47 13.92 z.
26	7	15.0	27.5	40.0	. .	. .	. .	. .	. .	. .	35 52.36	47.50	1 2 42.61	43 14.32	27.53	36 39.86	39 1.85
27	8	. .	. .	. .	6.0	18.0	30.0	. .	. .	. .	36 5.65	47.48	VII. 3 43.78	33 49.08	27.44	36 53.13	29 36.52
28	8	. .	. .	. .	55.0	7.5	. .	. .	. .	. .	37 53.14	47.46	IV. 5 49.63	18 43.69	26.94	38 42.60	14 30.63
29	8	. .	. .	. .	. .	39.4	51.8	4.0	. .	. .	40 27.09	47.48	VII. 5 44.92	21 26.06	26.26	41 14.57	17 12.32
30	7.8	. .	. .	. .	. .	29.0	41.3	. .	. .	. .	41 16.67	47.48	I. 5 40.23	24 8.06	26.05	42 4.15	19 54.11 z.
31	8.9	. .	. .	10.0	22.5	34.5	. .	. .	. .	. .	43 22.40	47.52	2 2 45.96	41 18.91	25.48	44 9.92	37 4.39
32	8.9	. .	. .	. .	. .	. .	54.3	6.7	. .	. .	44 29.76	47.47	III. 7 42.21	8 26.52	25.16	45 17.23	4 11.68 z.
33	8.9	. .	. .	. .	16.0	29.0	. .	. .	. .	. .	46 16.35	47.53	II. 2 38.90	43 23.21	24.69	47 3.88	41 7.90
34	9	. .	. .	. .	. .	. .	. .	12.0	. .	. .	46 34.92	47.51	IV. 4 40.23	44 35.94	24.63	47 22.43	40 20.57
35	8	. .	. .	. .	. .	. .	. .	. .	14.0	27.0	47 18.69	47.53	VII. 2 43.11	42 57.56	24.40	48 6.22	38 41.96 z.
36	8.9	. .	. .	. .	. .	. .	35.0	47.0	. .	. .	49 10.08	47.51	" 4 45.90	26 39.38	23.90	49 57.59	22 23.28
37	8.9	. .	. .	. .	6.5	18.5	31.5	. .	. .	. .	51 6.46	47.56	VI. 1 41.59	49 41.83	23.37	51 54.02	45 25.20
38	8.9	. .	. .	. .	51.0	3.2	15.5	. .	. .	. .	52 50.87	47.54	" 3 36.21	38 10.85	22.90	53 38.41	33 53.75 z.
39	8	. .	29.0	41.0	53.2	6.0	. .	. .	. .	. .	54 53.56	47.57	VII. 1 43.48	48 36.36	22.35	55 41.13	44 18.71 z.
40	7.8	. .	. .	. .	10.5	23.0	35.3	. .	. .	. .	56 10.58	47.55	III. 3 42.16	34 45.38	22.00	56 58.13	30 27.38 z.
*41	7.8	. .	. .	. .	. .	13.3	25.5	38.3	. .	. .	58 1.15	47.51	II. 7 42.90	8 2.61	21.50	58 48.66	3 44.11 z.
42	7.8	. .	. .	24.1	36.5	. .	1.0	. .	. .	. .	59 36.50	47.54	VI. 5 38.48	25 8.85	21.06	19 0 24.04	20 50.91 z.
43	8	. .	. .	. .	. .	. .	25.0	37.0	. .	. .	19 1 0.13	47.55	III. 5 44.60	21 37.38	20.70	1 47.68	17 18.08 z.
44	8	. .	. .	. .	. .	. .	. .	2.0	. .	. .	1 24.97	47.55	VII. 5 41.85	23 12.08	20.60	2 12.52	18 52.68 z.
45	7.8	. .	25.0	38.0	50.4	. .	. .	. .	. .	. .	3 50.10	47.53	VI. 7 36.80	11 33.29	19.98	4 37.63	7 13.27
46	7.8	. .	. .	. .	. .	. .	. .	9.0	. .	. .	4 31.89	47.57	VII. 3 35.48	38 36.08	19.75	5 19.46	34 15.83 z.
47	8.9	56.1	8.7	21.1	. .	. .	. .	. .	. .	. .	7 33.44	47.59	1. 3 41.37	35 11.90	18.96	8 21.03	30 50.86 z.
48	9	. .	. .	. .	13.4	25.8	. .	50.5	. .	. .	10 13.54	47.56	2. 7 39.74	9 51.28	18.22	11 1.10	5 29.50 z.
49	8.9	43.0	56.0	8.3	. .	. .	. .	. .	. .	. .	13 20.62	47.61	2. 2 42.75	43 9.78	17.39	14 8.23	38 47.17 z.
50	8.9	. .	. .	. .	. .	. .	. .	. .	33.5	. .	13 58.05	47.61	IV. 2 38.94	45 21.95	17.22	14 45.66	40 59.17
51	8.9	. .	. .	. .	. .	. .	22.5	35.2	. .	. .	14 57.98	47.57	11. 5 44.64	21 35.20	16.95	15 45.35	17 12.15
52	7	10.7	23.0	. .	. .	. .	. .	. .	. .	. .	19 47.75	47.59	1. 5 44.60	21 36.58	15.67	20 35.34	17 12.25
53	8.9	. .	. .	. .	. .	56.7	. .	21.5	. .	. .	20 44.39	47.64	VII. 1 43.35	48 40.86	15.42	21 32.03	44 16.28
54	8.9	. .	. .	8.5	20.7	33.0	45.5	. .	. .	. .	24 20.77	47.62	2. 4 35.40	32 41.88	14.44	25 8.39	28 16.32 z.
55	8.9	. .	. .	. .	18.5	30.9	. .	. .	. .	. .	28 18.55	47.66	I. 2 37.95	45 55.81	13.38	29 6.21	41 29.19
56	8	. .	. .	. .	. .	. .	. .	29.2	. .	. .	19 28 52.06	47.66	VII. 2 36.50	46 45.94	13.25	18 29 39.72	27 42 19.19 z.

CORRECTIONS.

	Cor. to Clock.	Hourly Cor.	m.	n.	c.	Zenith Point.	Coinc.
	s.	s.	s.	s.	s.		r.
May 27, at 16h....	+35.269	+0.038	+0.505	+0.353	+0.247	0° 0′ 03″.79	40.110

INSTRUMENT READINGS.

	Circle. A.	B.	C.	D.	Mean.	Bar.	Thermom. At.	Ex.
Zone. h.						I.		°
XXIV.—May 27, 16.5..	293° 42′ 33″.5	32″.8	40″.1	41″.6	37″.00	29.720	76°.5	73.5
19.6..	. . . . . .	. .	. .	. .	. . .	29.700	72.8	69.5

Zone XXIV. May 27. M. $D. = -26°\ 55'\ 20''.00.$ $n' = -62''.00.$ $n'' = -3''.51.$ (Continued.)

Number.	Magnitude.	SECONDS OF TRANSITS. I.	II.	III.	IV.	V.	VI.	VII.	10.	11.	T.	a.	MICROMETER.	D.	d.	Mean Right Ascension. 1850.0.	Mean South Declination, 1850.0.
											h. m. s.	s.	r.	′ ″	″	h. m. s.	° ′ ″
57	8.9	. .	. .	. .	. .	. .	. .	. .	23.0	35.6	19 30 27.48	+47.65	V. 2 43.69	−42 37.82	−12.81	19 31 15.13	27 38 10.63 z.
58	8.9	14.0	26.5	38.8	. .	. .	. .	. .	. .	. .	34 51.09	47.66	1. 7 42.73	8 7.73	11.66	35 38.75	3 39.39
59	8	. .	. .	. .	. .	23.5	36.0	48.5	. .	. .	35 11.26	47.67	I. 1 41.90	49 30.93	11.57	35 58.93	45 2.50 z.
60	8	. .	. .	. .	16.5	29.0	41.0	. .	. .	. .	36 16.47	47.66	" 2 44.80	41 59.19	11.29	37 4.13	37 30.48 z.
61	8	. .	. .	. .	. .	. .	. .	59.3	. .	. .	37 22.34	47.63	VII. 6 39.80	15 40.42	11.00	38 9.97	11 11.42 z.
62	8	. .	. .	. .	. .	. .	. .	2.0	. .	. .	38 24.92	47.65	IV. 4 36.68	31 57.57	10.73	39 12.57	27 28.30
63	8	45.0	8.0	20.0	. .	. .	. .	. .	. .	. .	40 32.34	47.63	I. 7 40.20	9 35.61	10.15	41 19.97	5 5.76
64	8.9	. .	. .	. .	. .	. .	53.0	5.3	. .	. .	19 41 28.18	47.68	VII. 2 41.44	43 55.30	9.92	19 42 15.86	27 39 25.22

Zone XXV. June 3. M. $D. = -26°\ 56'\ 40''.00.$ $n' = -42''.00.$ $n'' = -4''.58.$

Number.	Magnitude.	I.	II.	III.	IV.	V.	VI.	VII.	10.	11.	T.	a.	MICROMETER.	D.	d.	Mean Right Ascension. 1850.0.	Mean South Declination, 1850.0.
1	7.8	. .	. .	8.5	20.5	33.1	. .	58.0	. .	. .	13 22 20.82	53.09	I. 5 42.32	22 56.94	41.89	13 23 13.91	27 20 18.83 z.
2	9	. .	6.3	18.5	31.0	. .	. .	. .	. .	. .	25 31.03	53.12	IV. 2 35.67	47 15.98	41.65	26 24.15	44 37.63 z.
3	8.9	. .	. .	. .	30.5	. .	55.5	. .	. .	. .	31 30.59	53.14	2. 4 37.61	31 26.56	41.31	32 23.73	28 47.87
4	8.9	. .	. .	. .	. .	. .	52.0	4.0	. .	. .	32 27.08	53.14	11. 4 44.12	27 41.44	41.24	33 20.22	25 2.68
5	8	. .	. .	. .	. .	29.0	41.0	54.0	. .	. .	36 16.78	53.14	I. 7 41.99	8 34.81	40.99	37 9.92	5 55.80 z.
6	7.8	. .	. .	. .	41.4	. .	6.5	. .	. .	. .	39 41.54	53.19	" 3 33.75	39 36.64	40.74	40 34.73	36 57.38 z.
7	7	. .	. .	. .	. .	. .	57.4	10.0	. .	. .	40 32.77	53.18	VII. 4 42.14	28 50.32	40.70	41 25.95	26 11.02 z.
8	8	. .	. .	. .	37.5	49.5	2.5	14.5	. .	. .	55 37.43	53.28	I. 1 40.35	50 25.58	39.45	56 30.71	47 45.03 z.
9	8	. .	. .	. .	26.0	38.2	. .	. .	. .	. .	58 25.98	53.27	" 4 43.94	27 48.14	39.19	59 19.25	25 7.33
10	9	. .	. .	. .	. .	. .	9.8	. .	. .	. .	58 45.05	53.28	10. 5 40.68	23 53.35	39.16	59 38.33	21 12.51
11	7	. .	. .	16.0	28.0	41.0	53.2	. .	. .	. .	14 1 28.40	53.30	2. 2 46.31	41 7.91	38.90	14 2 21.70	38 26.81 z.
12	7.8	. .	. .	. .	12.7	25.0	37.3	. .	. .	. .	5 12.77	53.28	I. 7 46.30	6 5.98	38.53	6 6.05	3 24.51 z.
13	8.9	. .	. .	. .	. .	2.0	. .	. .	. .	. .	5 49.83	53.30	" 6 46.635	11 45.40	38.48	6 43.13	9 3.88
14	8.9	. .	. .	31.5	44.4	. .	. .	. .	. .	. .	7 44.15	53.31	IV. 6 45.88	12 11.83	38.29	8 37.46	9 30.12
15	7	. .	11.0	23.4	35.5	47.5	0.5	. .	. .	. .	10 35.59	53.32	2. 5 44.43	21 43.87	37.99	11 28.91	19 1.86
16	7	. .	. .	. .	28.5	40.5	52.8	5.5	. .	. .	12 28.28	53.35	I. 3 33.33	39 51.17	37.79	13 21.63	37 8.96 z.
17	5	. .	. .	. .	. .	47.0	59.0	12.0	. .	. .	13 34.80	53.33	VII. 7 45.88	6 20.53	37.67	14 28.13	3 38.20
18	7	. .	. .	. .	38.0	50.0	3.0	. .	. .	. .	15 37.99	53.36	" 4 40.93	29 32.11	37.45	16 31.35	26 49.56
19	8	. .	. .	. .	53.4	. .	18.2	. .	. .	. .	17 53.41	53.36	VI. 5 38.80	24 58.74	37.18	18 46.77	22 15.92
20	7	. .	. .	. .	. .	. .	23.1	35.7	. .	. .	18 58.49	53.36	IV. 5 37.00	26 1.02	37.06	19 51.85	23 18.08
21	8	. .	. .	37.0	49.0	1.5	. .	. .	. .	. .	20 49.24	53.37	I. 5 42.21	23 0.73	36.86	21 42.61	20 17.59 z.
22	8.9	. .	5.8	18.0	. .	. .	. .	. .	. .	. .	22 30.42	53.37	" 5 39.30	24 41.25	36.65	23 23.79	21 57.90
23	8.9	. .	. .	. .	. .	. .	5.0	17.0	. .	. .	22 40.20	53.37	VII. 6 43.28	13 41.31	36.63	23 33.57	10 57.94
24	8.9	. .	. .	43.1	55.2	. .	. .	. .	. .	. .	25 55.35	53.40	I. 5 39.48	24 35.05	36.25	26 48.75	21 51.30 z.
25	8	. .	. .	. .	. .	3.5	16.0	. .	. .	. .	26 51.22	53.40	II. 3 35.50	38 36.46	36.12	27 44.62	35 52.58
26	7.8	. .	51.5	4.0	16.0	. .	. .	. .	. .	. .	32 16.19	53.44	2. 4 43.75	27 54.48	35.44	33 9.63	25 9.92 z.
27	7.8	. .	. .	. .	. .	57.7	10.0	22.3	. .	. .	33 45.38	55.44	VII. 6 37.30	17 7.86	35.25	34 38.82	14 23.11
*28	7.8	. .	. .	. .	. .	. .	25.5	37.8	. .	. .	34 0.88	53.43	" 7 38.34	10 40.93	35.21	34 54.31	7 56.14
29	5	. .	11.4	23.3	36.0	48.0	0.5	. .	. .	. .	14 40 35.85	53.47	2. 5 42.63	28 30.82	34.34	14 41 29.32	27 25 45.16

CORRECTIONS.

	COR. TO CLOCK.	HOURLY COR.	m.	n.	c.	ZENITH POINT.	COINC.
	s.	s.	s.	s.	s.	° ′ ″	r.
June 3, at 16h....	+42.761	+ 0.008	+0.198	+0.396	+0.247	0 0 1.27	40.110

INSTRUMENT READINGS.

	CIRCLE. A.	B.	C.	D.	Mean.	BAR.	THERMOM. At.	Ex.
Zone XXV.—June 3....13.3 h.	293° 42′ 0″.0	0″.0	6″.5	4″.7	2″.80	30.062 I.	75°.0	71°.5
17.3	. . . .	. .	. .	. .	. .	30.032	71.0	66.8

Number	Magnitude.	SECONDS OF TRANSITS. I.	II.	III.	IV.	V.	VI.	VII.	10.	11.	T.	a.	MICROMETER.	D.	d.	Mean Right Ascension, 1850.0.	Mean South Declination, 1850.0.
Zone XXV.	June 3.	M.	$D. = -26° 56' 40''.0.$	$n. = -42''.23.$	$n. = -4''.58.$												
											h. m. s.	s.	r.	' ''	''	h. m. s.	° ' ''
30	8	. .	. .	. .	. .	. .	34.0	46.0	. .	. .	14 41 9.03	+53.50	IV. 2 40.00	−44 46.41	−34.29	14 42 2.53	27 42 0.70 z.
31	8	. .	35.5	47.7	. .	. .	. .	. .	. .	. .	44 0.28	53.52	2. 1 40.83	50 8.74	33.86	44 53.80	47 22.60 z.
32	7	. .	. .	. .	34.5	46.5	59.5	. .	. .	. .	44 34.46	53.52	II. 2 36.40	46 50.68	33.79	45 27.98	44 4.47 z.
33	8	. .	. .	. .	12.5	24.5	. .	49.5	. .	. .	59 12.34	53.60	I. 1 41.28	49 53.43	31.55	15 0 5.94	47 4.98 z.
34	7.8	. .	. .	. .	23.0	35.5	. .	. .	. .	. .	15 5 23.14	53.59	" 5 46.68	20 26.30	30.66	6 16.73	17 36.96 z.
35	6	. .	. .	. .	. .	0.5	13.0	25.4	. .	. .	5 48.44	53.58	IV. 7 48.375	4 54.68	30.60	6 42.02	2 5.28 z.
36	7	. .	12.0	24.4	37.0	48.5	. .	. .	. .	. .	10 36.75	53.65	II. 2 35.91	47 7.58	29.80	11 30.40	44 17.38 z.
37	9	. .	. .	35.0	. .	. .	. .	. .	. .	. .	12 47.42	53.61	VI. 7 42.73	8 9.54	29.47	13 41.03	5 19.01
38	9	. .	. .	. .	. .	. .	. .	26.0	. .	. .	13 48.94	53.64	VII. 4 44.40	27 32.29	29.30	14 42.58	24 41.59
39	8	. .	. .	. .	45.0	. .	9.5	. .	. .	. .	16 44.83	53.67	" 3 39.44	36 20.10	28.69	17 38.50	33 28.79 z.
*40	8	. .	. .	. .	. .	5.5	18.0	30.0	. .	. .	16 53.14	53.66	" 4 40.17	29 58.38	28.76	17 46.80	27 7.14
41	8.9	. .	. .	. .	. .	. .	40.0	52.5	. .	. .	18 15.50	53.64	" 7 41.27	8 59.75	28.53	19 9.14	6 8.28
42	8.9	. .	. .	. .	. .	21.5	34.0	46.3	. .	. .	22 9.21	53.71	II. 2 45.10	41 50.13	27.85	23 2.92	38 57.98 z.
43	6	2.0	14.0	26.3	. .	51.0	. .	. .	. .	. .	24 38.87	53.71	I. 3 41.53	35 7.40	27.42	25 32.58	32 14.82 z.
44	9	. .	20.0	32.3	. .	. .	. .	. .	. .	. .	25 44.80	53.71	IV. 2 39.87	44 50.88	27.24	26 38.51	41 58.14 z.
45	4.5	. .	. .	49.5	2.0	14.4	27.0	. .	. .	. .	27 2.07	53.72	VI. 2 46.30	41 8.70	26.98	27 55.79	38 15.68 z.
46	7	. .	. .	. .	27.8	40.3	52.5	. .	. .	. .	28 27.83	53.73	VII. 2 38.78	45 28.18	26.72	29 21.56	42 34.90
47	8	. .	. .	. .	. .	. .	. .	14.0	. .	. .	29 37.07	53.70	" 7 36.29	11 51.76	26.54	30 30.77	8 58.30 z.
48	9	. .	. .	. .	. .	. .	. .	1.5	. .	. .	31 24.47	53.72	" 5 42.20	23 1.09	26.20	32 18.19	20 7.29
49	9	. .	. .	. .	. .	. .	28.3	. .	. .	. .	33 3.51	53.75	" 3 46.27	32 24.19	25.89	33 57.26	29 30.08 z.
50	7	. .	. .	. .	12.0	24.0	36.5	. .	. .	. .	36 11.82	53.77	I. 3 36.32	38 7.86	25.30	37 5.59	35 13.16 z.
51	8.9	. .	. .	. .	42.1	54.5	. .	. .	. .	. .	38 42.20	53.74	" 7 39.91	9 46.71	24.73	39 35.94	6 51.44 z.
52	8.9	. .	. .	. .	49.3	. .	14.0	. .	. .	. .	40 49.25	53.78	VI. 4 44.70	27 22.13	24.44	41 43.03	24 26.57
53	8	. .	. .	13.4	26.0	. .	. .	. .	. .	. .	43 25.90	53.77	2. 6 37.11	17 14.25	23.93	44 19.67	14 18.18
54	8	. .	. .	. .	. .	36.0	48.7	. .	. .	. .	44 23.96	53.76	II. 7 40.25	9 35.23	23.74	45 17.72	6 38.97 z.
55	8.9	. .	. .	. .	. .	. .	. .	35.5	. .	. .	44 58.42	53.80	VII. 4 39.74	30 13.21	23.63	45 52.22	27 16.84 z.
56	8	. .	. .	. .	. .	. .	. .	. .	39.5	52.0	45 43.96	53.81	11. 4 34.51	53 13.34	23.48	46 37.77	50 16.82
57	7	. .	. .	. .	. .	. .	. .	. .	6.0	18.5	47 10.69	53.79	" 6 41.20	14 52.70	23.21	48 4.48	11 55.91 z.
58	8.9	. .	. .	. .	2.7	15.0	27.0	. .	. .	. .	56 2.56	53.85	I. 4 44.21	27 38.85	21.44	56 56.41	24 40.29
*59	8	. .	. .	. .	. .	. .	. .	29.0	. .	. .	56 51.98	53.84	IV. 5 44.10	21 55.86	21.28	57 45.82	18 57.14
60	7	. .	. .	. .	. .	. .	25.7	38.0	. .	. .	58 0.97	53.85	VII. 5 43.26	22 24.49	21.03	58 54.82	19 25.52 z.
61	8	. .	. .	. .	. .	46.3	58.5	11.0	. .	. .	16 0 33.89	53.87	" 3 46.30	32 23.13	20.51	16 1 27.76	29 23.64
62	8	. .	. .	32.0	44.5	. .	. .	. .	. .	. .	1 44.45	53.85	I. 6 45.58	12 21.94	20.27	2 38.30	9 22.21 z.
63	5	. .	. .	. .	10.5	23.0	34.7	. .	. .	. .	2 10.39	53.88	VII. 3 47.78	31 32.00	20.18	3 4.27	28 32.18
64	8	. .	. .	. .	. .	. .	. .	. .	37.0	50.2	2 41.79	53.91	11. 1 45.50	47 27.15	20.08	3 35.70	44 27.23 z.
65	8	. .	. .	. .	. .	. .	31.5	43.5	. .	. .	8 6.54	53.93	VI. 2 43.11	42 58.86	18.94	9 0.47	39 57.80 z.
66	8	. .	. .	50.0	2.2	14.5	. .	. .	. .	. .	15 2.30	53.93	I. 5 44.20	21 52.01	17.44	15 56.23	18 49.45 z.
67	8	. .	. .	. .	20.0	32.0	44.7	. .	. .	. .	16 19.91	53.93	I. 5 41.36	23 30.13	17.17	17 13.84	20 27.30 z.
68	7	. .	39.2	51.5	4.0	16.3	28.7	. .	. .	. .	20 3.97	53.97	1. 3 36.57	37 58.71	16.35	20 37.94	34 55.06 z.
69	8	. .	. .	. .	0.5	12.5	25.0	. .	. .	. .	23 0.30	53.99	2. 1 49.30	45 16.15	15.69	23 54.29	42 11.84
*70	8	. .	. .	39.0	51.0	3.7	. .	. .	. .	. .	28 51.30	54.02	VI. 2 42.83	43 8.53	14.40	29 45.32	40 2.93
71	8.9	. .	. .	. .	. .	. .	23.5	. .	. .	. .	29 58.70	54.02	VI. 2 40.23	44 38.35	14.14	30 52.72	41 32.49 z.
72	7	. .	. .	. .	. .	36.2	48.8	1.0	. .	. .	32 23.96	54.02	VII. 3 43.90	33 46.01	13.60	33 17.98	30 39.61
*73	6.7	28.0	40.5	52.5	. .	. .	. .	. .	. .	. .	34 5.02	53.99	I. 6 43.10	13 47.07	13.21	34 59.01	10 40.28
74	8	. .	. .	. .	. .	50.0	2.2	14.7	. .	. .	35 37.71	53.99	IV. 6 42.98	13 52.05	12.86	36 31.70	10 44.91
75	8	. .	. .	. .	. .	. .	48.0	0.5	. .	. .	37 23.44	54.01	III. 6 40.62	15 13.51	12.45	38 17.45	12 5.96
76	9	. .	30.0	42.5	. .	7.0	. .	. .	. .	. .	54.78	54.03	VII. 5 45.40	21 10.58	. . . .	48.81	18
77	8	. .	. .	. .	. .	. .	56.0	8.4	. .	. .	40 31.24	54.07	V. 2 46.12	41 14.95	11.74	41 25.31	38 6.69 z.
78	8	. .	. .	. .	. .	. .	. .	. .	4.5	17.0	41 8.93	54.08	11. 1 43.36	48 41.06	11.62	42 3.01	45 32.68 z.
79	8	. .	. .	. .	13.0	. .	37.5	. .	. .	. .	44 12.87	54.05	VI. 5 43.74	22 8.12	10.89	45 6.92	18 59.01 z.
80	8	. .	. .	. .	. .	. .	. .	11.3	. .	. .	44 33.21	54.07	VII. 3 45.28	32 58.37	10.82	45 27.28	29 49.19
*81	8	. .	. .	26.5	39.0	51.0	. .	. .	. .	. .	47 38.90	54.07	I. 4 48.27	25 18.63	10.09	48 32.97	22 8.72 z.
82	8	. .	. .	. .	. .	16.5	29.0	. .	. .	. .	16 49 4.24	54.09	I. 2 50.76	38 34.40	9.75	16 49 58.33	27 35 24.15

Zone XXV. June 3. M. $D. = -26° 56' 40''.00$. $n' = -42''.23$. $n'' = -4''.58$. (Continued.)

Number.	Magnitude.	SECONDS OF TRANSITS I.	II.	III.	IV.	V.	VI.	VII.	10.	11.	T.	a.	MICROMETER.	D.	d.	Mean Right Ascension, 1850.0.	Mean South Declination, 1850.0.
											h. m. s.	s.	r.	° ' ''	''	h. m. s.	° ' ''
83	8	. .	. .	. .	52.0	4.5	. .	. .	. .	. .	16 50 52.09	+54.12	IV. 1 45.69	—47 21.37	— 9.31	16 51 46.21	27 44 10.68
84	7.8	. .	. .	. .	5.0	. .	. .	. .	. .	. .	51 4.97	54.05	" 7 49.32	4 22.12	9.28	51 59.02	1 11.40 z.
85	7	. .	. .	. .	. .	. .	. .	16.5	. .	. .	51 39.36	54.12	VII. 1 48.26	45 52.28	9.13	52 33.48	42 41.41
86	8	54.5	7.0	. .	. .	. .	. .	. .	. .	. .	53 31.61	54.09	I. 6 32.50	19 53.17	8.20	56 25.70	16 41.37
87	8	. .	. .	26.0	. .	. .	3.0	. .	. .	. .	55 38.39	54.08	VII. 7 34.16	13 5.34	8.18	56 32.47	9 53.52
88	8	. .	. .	. .	19.5	32.0	. .	. .	. .	. .	56 19.62	54.12	I. 4 32.20	34 33.64	8.01	57 13.74	31 21.65
89	8	. .	. .	. .	. .	. .	55.4	7.5	. .	. .	59 30.52	54.13	VII. 5 30.92	29 30.73	7.25	17 0 24.65	26 17.98
90	7.8	. .	. .	. .	. .	. .	16.5	28.5	. .	. .	59 51.55	54.14	" 3 37.15	37 39.16	7.17	0 45.69	34 26.33 z.
91	7	. .	. .	55.0	7.5	19.8	32.3	. .	. .	. .	17 1 7.50	54.14	I. 3 37.37	37 31.58	6.85	2 1.64	34 18.43
92	7	. .	. .	. .	. .	56.2	9.0	. .	. .	. .	3 44.07	54.15	" 3 33.06	40 0.53	6.23	4 38.22	36 46.76
93	8	. .	. .	50.7	3.4	15.5	. .	. .	. .	. .	5 3.26	54.18	V. 1 39.66	50 49.62	5.90	5 57.44	47 35.52 z.
94	8	. .	. .	. .	. .	. .	. .	50.5	. .	. .	6 13.44	54.14	III. 5 36.385	26 22.29	5.61	7 7.58	23 7.90
95	8	. .	. .	. .	. .	21.5	34.2	. .	. .	. .	7 9.32	54.18	VII. 3 34.57	39 8.25	5.38	8 3.50	35 53.63 z.
96	8	. .	. .	. .	. .	. .	. .	. .	30.8	43.5	7 35.35	54.18	11. 3 34.53	39 9.16	5.28	8 29.53	35 54.44 z.
97	8	. .	. .	. .	. .	. .	. .	26.0	. .	. .	9 48.89	54.19	VII. 3 33.27	33 53.21	4.74	10 43.08	30 37.95
98	7.8	. .	. .	. .	. .	50.0	2.3	. .	. .	. .	11 37.73	54.14	IV. 6 42.29	14 15.91	4.30	12 31.87	11 0.21
99	8	. .	23.0	35.2	47.5	. .	. .	. .	. .	. .	17 15 47.59	54.19	2. 4 38.97	30 39.60	3.26	17 16 41.78	27 27 22.86 z.

Zone XXVI. June 15. H. $D. = -40° 49' 50''.0$. $n. = -70''.00$. $n. = -14''.57$.

Number.	Magnitude.	I.	II.	III.	IV.	V.	VI.	VII.	10.	11.	T.	a.	MICROMETER.	D.	d.	Mean Right Ascension, 1850.0.	Mean South Declination, 1850.0.
1	7.8	. .	. .	. .	31.5	45.6	59.7	15.4	. .	. .	14 39 31.20	58.66	IV. 5 43.830	22 11.97	69.96	14 40 29.86	41 13 11.93
2	9	24.5	39.0	54.0	8.0	. .	. .	52.3	. .	. .	42 8.38	58.70	" 3 39.842	36 18.82	69.62	43 7.08	41 27 18.44
3	7.8	15.6	30.5	45.0	59.4	14.0	29.0	43.3	. .	. .	43 59.58	58.72	" 3 42.490	34 46.93	69.36	44 58.30	41 25 46.29
4	7	47.2	2.0	16.6	31.5	46.0	1.0	. .	. .	. .	46 31.43	58.76	II. 2 47.402	40 44.74	69.02	47 30.19	41 31 43.76
5	8.9	. .	. .	. .	44.0	58.2	. .	. .	. .	. .	46 43.80	58.76	IV. 1 43.375	48 58.86	68.99	47 42.56	41 39 57.85
6	5.6	42.2	57.2	11.6	26.0	41.0	55.4	10.3	. .	. .	48 26.28	58.77	" 3 35.190	39 0.69	68.76	49 25.05	41 29 59.45 B.
7	8.9	28.5	43.0	7.5	22.5	. .	. .	. .	. .	. .	50 22.35	58.78	II. 1 0.972	. . . . .	68.48	51 21.13	. . . . . .
8	9	. .	37.5	52.5	7.2	21.0	. .	. .	. .	. .	51 6.87	58.76	III. 5 43.230	22 32.92	68.38	52 5.63	41 13 31.30
9	9	. .	51.5	5.0	19.2	. .	. .	. .	. .	. .	51 19.20	58.77	VI. 5 43.730	22 15.29	68.36	52 17.97	41 13 13.65
10	8.9	5.0	19.5	34.0	49.0	3.3	18.2	32.2	. .	. .	55 48.78	58.83	IV. 3 39.522	36 27.85	67.72	56 47.61	41 27 27.57
11	8.9	. .	. .	. .	16.0	. .	. .	. .	. .	. .	57 15.96	58.85	" 2 38.925	45 39.52	67.51	58 14.81	41 36 37.03
12	8	. .	. .	52.4	7.2	22.0	36.3	51.0	. .	. .	58 7.22	58.83	V. 5 37.450	25 53.90	67.38	59 6.05	41 16 51.28
13	9	. .	20.3	34.5	49.0	4.2	18.2	33.4	. .	. .	15 0 49.30	58.88	IV. 2 38.150	46 6.55	66.99	15 1 48.18	41 37 3.54
14	7	. .	. .	42.0	57.0	11.4	26.0	40.6	. .	. .	3 56.76	58.92	" 1 34.022	54 23.75	66.52	4 55.68	41 45 20.27
15	7.8	40.2	55.2	10.0	25.0	39.2	54.0	8.5	. .	. .	6 24.63	58.91	" 4 38.250	31 15.50	66.14	7 23.54	41 22 11.64
16	9	44.6	59.3	14.0	28.4	43.0	58.0	12.3	. .	. .	16 28.54	59.00	" 4 44.280	27 45.86	64.56	17 27.54	41 18 40.42
17	9	. .	. .	. .	35.3	49.2	4.2	. .	. .	. .	16 34.90	59.03	" 1 36.080	53 12.09	64.55	17 33.93	41 44 6.64
18	9	12.5	27.0	42.0	57.0	. .	. .	. .	. .	. .	17 56.64	59.02	" 4 33.770	33 51.11	64.30	18 55.66	41 24 45.41
19	6.7	38.2	53.0	7.3	22.0	36.5	51.2	5.8	. .	. .	19 22.04	59.02	V. 4 35.320	32 56.92	64.09	20 21.06	41 23 51.01 M.
20	8	. .	. .	. .	. .	. .	. .	50.3	. .	. .	15 20 6.64	59.01	VII. 6 37.260	17 14.50	63.97	15 21 5.65	41 8 8.47

CORRECTIONS.

	COR. TO CLOCK.	HOURLY COR.	m.	n.	c.	ZENITH POINT.	COINC.
	s.	s.	s.	s.	s.	° ' ''	r.
June 15, at 16h...	+47.338	+0.020	+0.198	—0.396	+0.247	0 0 1.64	40.122

INSTRUMENT READINGS.

	CIRCLE. A.	B.	C.	D.	Mean.	BAR.	THERMOM. At.	Ex.
h.						I.		
Zone XXVI.—June 15, 14.7	279° 51' 6''.2	3''.0	13''.0	8''.9	7''.78	29.914	73°.0	70°.7
15.6	7.7	. .	. .	. .	6.28	29.906	72.2	69.6
18.0	7.0	4.0	15.2	10.0	9.05	29.888	70.3	67.5
18.5	. . . . .	. .	. .	. .	. . .	29.886	70.3	67.4
20.0	6.5	3.9	15.0	9.0	8.60	29.884	69.5	66.4

Number.	Magnitude.	SECONDS OF TRANSITS. I.	II.	III.	IV.	V.	VI.	VII.	10.	11.	T.	a.	MICROMETER.	D.	d.	Mean Right Ascension, 1850.0.	Mean South Declination, 1850.0.
Zone XXVI. June 15. H. $D. = -40° 49' 50''.0.$ $n.' = -70''.00.$ $n.'' = -14''.57.$ (Continued.)																	
											h. m. s.	s.	r.	' "	"	h. m. s.	° ' "
21	9			15.5	30.6	44.6	. .	. .	. .	. .	15 21 30.32	+59.02	IV. 7 36.250	—11 56.73	—63.74	15 22 29.34	41 2 50.47
22	9	. .	. .	. .	. .	. .	24.0	. .	. .	. .	21 54.89	59.03	VI. 5 46.152	20 51.27	63.68	22 53.92	41 11 44.95
23	9	. .	. .	. .	. .	. .	8.2	22.8	. .	. .	23 39.03	59.05	" 5 43.250	22 32.13	63.39	24 38.08	41 13 25.52
24	7	. .	. .	. .	. .	. .	57.0	11.5	. .	. .	23 27.98	59.03	" 7 41.554	8 52.09	63.40	24 27.01	40 59 45.49
25	7.8	24.8	39.4	54.0	8.5	23.5	. .	. .	. .	. .	27 8.60	59.06	IV. 7 44.882	6 56.67	62.80	28 7.66	40 57 49.47
26	8	53.2	8.0	22.2	37.0	51.2	. .	. .	. .	. .	28 36.92	59.07	" 6 41.530	14 46.19	62.55	29 35.99	41 5 38.74
27	7	. .	. .	15.0	29.4	44.0	58.8	13.5	. .	. .	29 29.54	59.12	" 3 39.890	36 17.15	62.39	30 28.66	41 27 9.54
28	9	. .	. .	. .	. .	48.0	2.2	17.2	. .	. .	30 33.20	59.14	V. 2 44.696	42 18.72	62.22	31 32.34	41 33 10.94
29	9	6.8	21.5	. .	50.6	5.0	20.5	. .	. .	. .	32 50.78	59.15	I. 3 31.920	40 54.05	61.91	33 49.93	41 31 45.96
30	6.7	. .	48.0	2.5	17.0	. .	. .	1.0	. .	. .	33 17.12	59.14	VI. 4 41.395	29 26.04	61.72	34 16.26	41 20 17.76 M.
31	7.8	19.8	34.8	49.0	4.0	18.3	33.0	48.0	. .	. .	36 3.91	59.19	IV. 1 36.800	52 47.37	61.24	37 3.10	41 43 38.61
32	8	23.0	38.1	52.6	7.0	21.6	36.6	50.8	. .	. .	38 7.14	59.17	" 4 42.690	28 40.96	60.88	39 6.31	41 19 31.84
33	9	29.2	44.0	58.5	13.0	28.0	42.5	57.2	. .	. .	44 13.24	59.23	VI. 3 37.170	37 51.71	59.86	45 12.47	41 28 41.57
34	9	28.5	43.0	57.2	12.0	. .	. .	56.0	. .	. .	46 12.13	59.24	IV. 4 39.460	30 33.49	59.39	47 11.37	41 21 22.88
35	9	. .	. .	. .	. .	23.0	38.0	54.0	. .	. .	47 9.20	59.24	V. 5 43.346	22 28.90	59.20	48 8.44	41 13 18.10
36	5.6	35.0	49.6	. .	19.0	33.2	47.8	2.4	. .	. .	48 18.75	59.26	IV. 4 44.270	27 46.21	58.99	49 18.01	41 18 35.20 B.
37	9	10.5	25.2	39.3	54.0	8.8	23.5	37.0	. .	. .	52 54.07	59.29	" 4 46.188	26 39.50	58.12	53 53.36	41 17 27.62
38	7.8	12.5	27.2	41.5	56.5	11.2	26.0	40.5	. .	. .	55 56.55	59.34	" 2 33.530	48 47.09	57.51	56 55.89	41 39 34.60
39	9	36.0	50.2	4.8	19.5	34.0	48.4	3.0	. .	. .	16 4 19.45	59.36	" 5 38.702	25 10.46	55.81	16 5 18.81	41 15 56.27
40	8	39.2	54.5	9.2	23.5	38.4	53.2	7.5	. .	. .	10 23.70	59.45	" 2 35.390	47 42.64	54.57	11 23.15	41 38 27.21 M.
41	8.9	52.0	7.0	21.5	36.2	50.5	5.2	19.8	. .	. .	18 36.06	59.46	" 5 37.660	25 46.08	52.84	19 35.52	41 16 28.92
42	6	33.4	48.2	2.2	17.2	32.0	46.4	1.3	. .	. .	20 17.24	59.48	" 3 36.055	38 30.57	52.49	21 16.72	41 29 13.06
43	9	13.0	27.5	. .	. .	. .	26.5	41.0	. .	. .	22 57.02	59.50	VI. 3 39.336	36 36.42	51.94	23 56.52	41 27 18.36
44	9	29.3	45.0	59.0	13.8	28.0	42.8	57.0	. .	. .	31 13.59	59.57	IV. 4 36.361	32 21.21	50.15	32 13.16	41 23 1.36
45	9	4.0	18.8	33.3	. .	2.2	17.0	31.5	. .	. .	32 47.85	59.58	" 3 41.240	35 30.33	49.79	33 47.43	41 26 10.12
46	8	22.5	37.5	52.0	6.5	. .	. .	. .	. .	. .	35 6.60	59.58	I. 4 41.980	29 5.45	49.29	36 6.18	41 19 44.74 M.
47	8	54.5	9.0	23.5	38.0	. .	. .	. .	. .	. .	35 38.13	59.57	IV. 5 45.172	21 25.42	49.17	36 37.70	41 12 4.59
48	8	. .	. .	. .	. .	1.0	16.0	30.2	. .	. .	35 46.54	59.58	V. 4 40.622	29 52.80	49.14	36 46.12	41 20 31.94
49	8.9	49.0	4.0	18.2	33.0	47.2	. .	. .	. .	. .	38 32.96	59.60	II. 4 36.540	32 14.61	48.54	39 32.56	41 22 53.15
50	9	30.5	45.4	59.0	14.0	. .	. .	. .	. .	. .	39 14.12	59.59	IV. 5 47.332	20 10.41	48.38	40 13.71	41 10 48.79
51	9	. .	. .	. .	. .	55.0	9.6	24.0	. .	. .	39 40.36	59.60	V. 4 44.632	27 33.41	48.29	40 39.96	41 18 11.70
52	9	. .	. .	. .	48.4	3.5	18.2	. .	. .	. .	40 48.75	59.63	IV. 3 40.062	36 11.25	48.04	41 48.38	41 26 49.29
53	9	. .	. .	. .	. .	32.0	46.2	1.0	. .	. .	41 17.13	59.64	VI. 3 31.860	40 56.27	47.93	42 16.77	41 31 34.20 M.
54	7.8	. .	. .	. .	31.0	45.5	0.2	15.0	. .	. .	42 30.96	59.64	IV. 3 29.210	42 28.65	47.65	43 30.60	41 33 6.30 M.
55	8	37.5	52.5	6.5	. .	36.0	. .	. .	. .	. .	47 21.42	59.67	I. 6 32.350	20 5.18	46.57	48 21.09	41 10 41.75
56	9	. .	21.5	. .	50.5	. .	. .	. .	. .	. .	47 50.48	59.63	IV. 6 33.388	19 29.37	46.46	48 50.11	41 10 5.83
57	9	49.0	3.5	18.3	33.2	47.2	2.4	. .	. .	. .	56 32.95	59.69	" 3 44.160	33 48.77	44.45	57 32.64	41 24 23.22
58	7.8	47.8	3.0	17.3	32.0	46.5	1.0	16.0	. .	. .	58 31.99	59.74	" 3 34.190	39 35.47	44.00	59 31.73	41 30 9.47
59	9	. .	. .	48.0	2.0	17.5	32.5	47.0	. .	. .	17 0 2.76	59.75	V. 2 41.382	44 14.21	43.65	17 1 2.41	41 34 47.86
60	8.9	34.7	49.2	4.0	18.2	33.0	48.0	2.6	. .	. .	2 18.58	59.76	IV. 3 34.442	39 26.79	43.12	3 18.34	41 29 59.91
61	9	. .	. .	. .	. .	12.0	26.4	41.0	. .	. .	2 57.30	59.74	VII. 5 35.952	26 45.62	42.98	3 57.04	41 17 18.60
62	9	16.5	31.5	46.0	1.0	15.2	30.4	44.2	. .	. .	8 0.75	59.80	IV. 1 38.478	51 49.24	41.77	9 0.55	41 42 21.01
63	9	. .	8.0	22.4	37.2	51.5	6.2	. .	. .	. .	9 37.08	59.77	" 4 34.550	33 23.93	41.34	10 36.85	41 23 55.27
64	8	. .	. .	32.0	46.8	1.0	16.0	30.5	. .	. .	10 46.64	59.80	" 2 40.262	44 53.15	41.12	11 46.44	41 35 24.27
65	8	41.3	56.2	10.8	25.2	40.0	54.5	. .	. .	. .	13 25.36	59.79	" 4 39.090	30 46.24	40.50	14 25.15	41 21 16.74
66	9	. .	. .	. .	. .	. .	30.4	45.0	. .	. .	14 1.24	59.78	VI. 5 45.530	21 12.65	40.35	15 1.02	41 11 43.00
67	8	17.5	32.2	46.4	0.5	15.2	30.0	. .	. .	. .	16 0.93	59.79	IV. 5 47.752	19 55.65	39.88	17 0.72	41 10 25.53
68	9	. .	. .	. .	. .	34.0	50.5	5.0	. .	. .	18 20.60	59.83	V. 3 40.700	35 48.92	39.32	19 20.43	41 26 18.24
69	9	. .	. .	40.5	55.2	10.0	. .	. .	. .	. .	20 55.31	59.81	IV. 5 46.670	20 33.24	38.72	21 55.12	41 11 1.96
70	6	. .	. .	. .	32.5	47.0	1.8	16.5	. .	. .	21 32.68	59.80	V. 6 44.725	12 55.14	38.58	22 32.48	41 3 23.72 M.
71	8	. .	36.0	50.3	5.0	19.2	34.2	48.5	. .	. .	23 4.92	59.83	IV. 5 43.726	22 15.56	38.20	24 4.75	41 12 43.76
72	8.9	10.0	24.4	39.2	53.6	8.0	22.8	37.5	. .	. .	27 53.68	59.83	" 6 46.360	11 58.54	37.04	28 53.51	41 2 25.58
73	8.9	48.5	3.2	18.0	32.8	47.0	2.0	17.0	. .	. .	17 29 32.64	59.90	" 2 38.644	45 49.23	36.67	17 30 32.54	41 36 15.90

Number.	Magnitude.	SECONDS OF TRANSITS.									T.	a.	MICROMETER.	D.	d.	Mean Right Ascension, 1850.0.	Mean South Declination, 1850.0.
		I.	II.	III.	IV.	V.	VI.	VII.	10.	11.							
Zone XXVI. June 15. H. $D. = -40° 49' 50''.0$. $n'. = -70''.00$. $n''. = -14''.57$. (Continued.)																	
											h. m. s.	s.	r.	′ ″	″	h. m. s.	° ′ ″
74	9	. .	9.0	23.4	38.0	52.4	. .	22.0	. .	. .	17 31 38.06	+59.87	IV. 5 40.540	—24 6.27	—36.18	17 32 37.93	41 14 32.35
75	8	. .	. .	. .	34.5	48.5	3.4	18.0	. .	. .	32 34.13	59.90	" 2 40.718	44 37.14	35.96	33 34.03	41 35 3.10
76	9	. .	48.0	3.0	17.0	31.5	46.0	. .	. .	. .	34 17.11	59.87	III. 5 46.005	20 56.42	35.53	35 16.98	41 11 21.93
77	8	33.0	47.5	2.0	17.0	31.2	46.0	. .	. .	. .	35 16.70	59.87	IV. 5 43.407	22 26.84	35.28	36 16.57	41 12 52.12
78	8	44.0	59.2	14.0	28.0	43.0	. .	. .	. .	. .	37 28.32	59.91	II. 3 44.364	33 41.60	34.75	38 28.23	41 24 6.35
79	9	25.0	40.3	55.0	8.2	. .	39.0	53.0	. .	. .	39 9.23	59.93	III. 2 45.180	42 2.04	34.36	40 9.16	41 32 26.40
80	9	. .	. .	. .	38.0	52.0	. .	. .	. .	. .	39 37.72	59.93	IV. 2 45.040	42 6.91	34.25	40 37.65	41 32 31.16
81	8	. .	. .	. .	. .	. .	. .	. .	53.5	8.4	39 47.72	59.94	VI. 2 39.626	45 14.94	34.20	40 47.66	41 35 39.14
82	8.9	31.5	46.0	0.6	15.0	29.8	44.5	58.5	. .	. .	42 15.16	59.91	IV. 5 36.490	26 27.33	33.64	43 15.07	41 16 50.97
83	6	24.0	39.0	53.8	8.0	22.8	. .	52.0	. .	. .	46 8.23	59.96	" 1 40.050	50 54.42	32.77	47 8.19	41 41 17.19 B.
84	8	18.2	33.1	47.7	2.5	17.0	31.2	46.2	. .	. .	48 2.33	59.96	" 2 37.550	46 27.27	32.21	49 2.29	41 36 49.48
85	9	. .	8.4	23.0	37.4	52.0	6.2	21.5	. .	. .	50 37.46	59.96	" 4 33.738	33 52.22	31.58	51 37.42	41 24 13.80
86	9	5.0	. .	. .	38.8	52.5	8.0	22.0	. .	. .	53 38.40	59.97	V. 3 43.550	34 9.78	31.10	53 38.37	41 24 30.88
87	9	38.0	52.5	7.0	21.5	36.5	51.2	5.2	. .	. .	55 21.76	59.99	" 2 34.436	48 15.83	30.43	56 21.75	41 38 36.26
88	6.7	43.3	58.2	12.7	27.3	42.0	56.3	11.0	. .	. .	59 27.30	59.99	IV. 4 36.272	32 24.29	29.41	18 0 27.29	41 22 43.70
89	6	51.4	6.0	20.0	35.0	49.4	. .	. .	. .	. .	18 1 35.04	59.99	" 4 37.711	31 34.08	28.91	2 35.03	41 21 52.99
90	8.9	20.0	. .	. .	4.0	18.2	33.0	47.5	. .	. .	2 3.82	59.99	" 5 34.220	27 46.17	28.80	3 3.81	41 18 4.97
91	9	3.0	17.4	32.0	46.5	1.0	. .	. .	. .	. .	32 46.58	60.04	" 6 38.996	16 14.26	21.52	33 46.62	41 6 25.78
92	9	. .	45.5	1.0	15.3	30.0	44.8	59.2	. .	. .	34 15.34	60.09	" 2 37.092	46 43.36	21.14	35 15.43	41 36 54.50
93	9	. .	. .	. .	25.5	40.0	55.0	9.3	. .	. .	34 25.52	60.07	" 4 32.835	34 23.65	21.11	35 25.59	41 24 34.76
94	9	. .	47.0	1.8	16.2	30.4	45.3	. .	. .	. .	37 16.17	60.09	" 3 34.302	39 31.62	20.44	38 16.26	41 29 42.06
95	7.8	41.8	56.4	11.0	25.5	39.8	54.6	9.0	. .	. .	39 25.48	60.06	" 5 41.615	23 28.92	19.91	40 25.54	41 13 38.83
96	8	. .	15.2	29.8	44.2	58.5	13.2	27.5	. .	. .	40 44.14	60.05	" 6 41.210	14 57.47	19.61	41 44.19	41 5 7.08
97	9	. .	. .	. .	. .	. .	51.0	6.0	. .	. .	42 21.91	60.08	VII. 3 44.302	33 43.60	19.23	43 21.99	41 23 52.83
98	9	. .	10.5	25.0	40.0	54.2	9.0	23.8	. .	. .	44 39.79	60.09	IV. 2 45.555	41 48.86	18.67	45 39.88	41 31 57.53
99	8.9	24.5	39.5	54.2	9.0	. .	. .	. .	. .	. .	47 8.71	60.07	III. 5 37.992	25 41.84	18.09	48 8.78	41 15 49.93
100	9	. .	. .	. .	23.0	37.2	51.8	6.4	. .	. .	47 22.64	60.10	IV. 3 33.030	40 15.78	18.03	48 22.74	41 30 23.81
101	9	. .	44.5	58.8	14.0	28.0	42.8	57.2	. .	. .	49 13.57	60.11	" 2 36.595	47 3.53	17.58	50 13.68	41 37 11.11
102	9	8.5	23.4	37.8	. .	7.2	22.0	36.4	. .	. .	50 52.61	60.09	V. 3 36.268	38 23.22	17.19	51 52.70	41 28 30.41
103	9	. .	. .	. .	3.0	17.5	32.0	46.8	. .	. .	53 2.88	60.09	" 3 34.618	39 20.40	16.68	54 3.97	41 29 27.08
104	8.9	58.2	12.8	27.4	42.0	56.7	11.2	26.2	. .	. .	57 42.12	60.10	IV. 3 34.362	39 29.57	15.57	58 42.22	41 29 35.14
105	6.7	. .	16.2	31.0	45.2	59.5	14.5	29.0	. .	. .	19 1 45.32	60.05	" 7 41.342	8 59.73	14.62	19 2 45.37	40 59 4.35
106	9	36.0	50.5	5.2	20.0	34.0	49.0	3.5	. .	. .	4 19.78	60.09	" 4 37.639	31 36.56	14.00	5 19.87	41 21 40.56
107	8.9	46.0	0.8	15.2	30.0	. .	. .	. .	. .	. .	7 30.06	60.11	" 2 41.450	44 11.93	13.25	8 30.17	41 34 15.18
108	9	9.0	23.5	. .	. .	7.5	22.0	37.0	. .	. .	7 52.93	60.12	V. 1 40.890	50 25.16	13.18	8 53.05	41 40 28.34
109	8	57.2	11.5	26.0	41.0	. .	10.0	24.5	. .	. .	16 40.81	60.07	IV. 6 36.368	17 45.77	11.11	17 40.88	41 7 46.88
110	8.9	15.5	30.0	44.2	59.0	13.3	28.0	43.0	. .	. .	17 59.03	60.08	" 5 39.722	24 34.74	10.80	18 59.11	41 14 35.54
111	8.9	43.0	58.0	12.5	27.2	42.0	56.5	11.0	. .	. .	23 27.21	60.10	II. 3 36.290	38 22.36	9.52	24 27.31	41 28 21.88
112	8	24.0	38.8	53.0	8.0	22.2	37.0	51.8	. .	. .	24 7.84	60.10	IV. 3 39.498	36 31.00	9.27	25 7.94	41 26 30.27
113	9	55.0	10.0	. .	38.8	53.4	8.0	22.4	. .	. .	27 38.86	60.10	II. 3 37.800	37 29.72	8.56	28 38.96	41 27 28.28
114	8	21.5	36.2	51.0	5.0	20.0	35.0	49.5	. .	. .	28 5.51	60.11	IV. 3 31.510	41 8.77	8.45	29 5.62	41 31 7.22
115	9	. .	. .	. .	. .	. .	10.0	24.2	. .	. .	28 40.41	60.13	VI. 2 32.693	49 16.13	8.31	29 40.54	41 39 14.44
116	8	27.2	42.0	56.4	11.0	25.4	40.2	54.8	. .	. .	37 11.03	60.08	IV. 4 40.178	30 8.43	6.35	38 11.11	41 20 4.78
117	9	46.0	1.0	15.0	29.2	44.0	58.8	13.0	. .	. .	40 29.60	60.07	" 5 41.225	23 42.63	5.61	41 29.67	41 13 38.24
118	9	22.0	36.2	51.2	. .	20.4	. .	49.6	. .	. .	46 5.82	60.08	" 3 44.430	33 39.46	4.43	47 5.90	41 23 33.89
119	8.9	. .	. .	19.2	34.0	48.5	3.0	. .	. .	. .	47 33.90	60.09	" 2 43.902	42 46.45	3.98	48 33.99	41 32 40.43
120	9	. .	. .	30.0	45.0	59.2	14.0	28.2	. .	. .	48 44.74	60.06	" 5 43.282	22 31.15	3.73	49 44.80	41 12 24.88
121	7.8	. .	43.2	58.0	12.4	27.0	41.5	56.2	. .	. .	50 12.42	60.06	" 5 42.148	23 10.55	3.38	51 12.48	41 13 3.93
122	9	41.0	56.0	10.3	25.0	. .	54.2	. .	. .	. .	56 25.03	60.06	" 3 40.150	36 8.21	1.97	57 25.09	41 26 0.18
123	7.8	. .	13.0	27.0	41.0	55.4	10.2	24.5	. .	. .	57 41.25	60.03	V. 6 36.980	17 24.36	1.68	58 41.28	41 7 16.04
124	8.9	. .	. .	51.5	6.0	20.5	35.0	49.4	. .	. .	19 59 5.86	60.08	IV. 2 40.102	44 58.68	1.35	20 0 5.94	41 34 50.03

Zone XXVII. June 17. H. $D. = 27^\circ\ 26'\ 20''.0.$ $n.' = -40''.84.$ $n.'' = -8''.00.$

Number.	Magnitude.	SECONDS OF TRANSITS. I.	II.	III.	IV.	V.	VI.	VII.	10.	11.	T.	a.	MICROMETER.	D.	d.	Mean Right Ascension, 1850.0.	Mean South Declination, 1850.0.
											h. m. s.	s.	r.	′ ″	″	h. m. s.	° ′ ″
1	9	44.0	56.5	8.6	21.2	33.5	46.2	58.4	. .	. .	15 55 21.25	+59.50	V. 2 43.680	—42 42.68	—37.27	15 26 20.75	28 9 39.95
2	*9	. .	. .	. .	. .	15.5	. .	40.0	. .	. .	56 2.98	59.48	IV. 4 40.154	30 2.69	37.10	57 2.46	27 56 59.79
3	9	. .	. .	27.3	40.2	53.0	5.0	. .	. .	. .	57 40.20	59.49	III. 4 39.010	30 42.16	36.73	58 39.69	27 57 38.89
4	9	. .	. .	. .	. .	. .	. .	25.2	. .	. .	58 48.05	59.47	VII. 6 37.140	17 16.75	36.47	59 47.52	27 44 13.22
5	7	23.2	36.0	48.2	1.0	13.0	. .	. .	. .	. .	16 2 0.77	59.51	IV. 3 42.943	34 22.88	35.73	16 3 0.28	28 1 18.61 z.
6	9	50.5	. .	. .	28.5	40.5	. .	. .	. .	. .	2 28.20	59.50	" 4 42.220	28 51.32	35.61	3 27.70	27 55 46.93 z.
7	8.9	. .	. .	. .	. .	48.2	1.0	13.5	. .	. .	2 36.11	59.50	" 5 36.620	26 17.52	35.58	3 35.61	27 53 13.10
8	8	. .	. .	. .	43.0	55.2	7.8	20.4	. .	. .	3 43.01	59.50	" 5 39.050	24 53.62	35.32	4 42.51	27 51 48.94 z
9	9	29.4	42.0	. .	6.7	19.0	. .	. .	. .	. .	6 6.71	59.50	" 5 47.400	20 5.19	34.75	7 6.21	27 46 59.94
10	9	. .	. .	. .	29.5	42.0	. .	. .	. .	. .	6 29.40	59.51	V. 5 35.830	26 44.80	34.66	7 28.91	27 53 39.46
11	8	24.0	36.2	48.8	. .	. .	. .	. .	. .	. .	8 1.13	59.50	III. 6 44.342	13 8.31	34.30	9 0.63	27 40 2.61 z
12	7	. .	. .	. .	. .	13.0	25.5	38.0	. .	. .	8 0.64	59.55	IV. 2 35.710	47 18.05	34.30	9 0.19	28 14 12.35 z.
13	9	. .	. .	. .	51.5	3.8	16.2	28.3	. .	. .	8 51.34	59.52	V. 4 44.078	27 47.10	34.10	9 50.86	27 54 41.20 z.
14	7.8	21.2	34.0	46.2	58.2	10.8	23.5	36.2	. .	. .	19 58.60	59.53	IV. 7 43.020	8 2.95	31.40	20 58.13	27 34 54.35 z.
15	9	. .	. .	. .	18.5	30.0	42.8	55.2	. .	. .	21 17.99	59.59	V. 3 37.330	37 36.76	31.10	22 17.58	28 4 27.86
16	8	. .	30.0	42.6	55.0	7.0	19.6	32.0	. .	. .	22 54.85	59.56	IV. 5 46.558	20 34.22	30.73	23 54.41	27 47 24.95 z
17	5	56.2	. .	21.0	33.2	46.0	58.0	10.5	. .	. .	24 33.40	59.58	" 4 45.218	27 7.75	30.35	25 32.98	27 53 58.10
18	9	5.2	17.8	. .	42.5	55.0	. .	19.2	. .	. .	24 42.47	59.59	" 3 40.488	35 47.71	30.31	25 42.06	28 2 38.02
19	9	12.0	25.0	37.2	49.5	2.0	. .	. .	. .	. .	27 49.61	59.59	II. 5 35.322	27 2.30	29.60	28 49.20	27 53 51.90
20	9	. .	21.0	33.4	46.0	58.2	10.8	23.0	. .	. .	28 45.90	59.57	IV. 7 32.989	13 49.43	29.38	29 45.47	27 40 38.81 z
21	9	. .	. .	. .	. .	5.2	18.0	30.5	. .	. .	29 53.18	59.58	V. 6 41.394	14 50.14	29.11	30 52.76	27 41 39.25 z
†22	9	. .	. .	. .	13.4	26.0	38.2	51.0	. .	. .	31 13.50	59.64	IV. 1 40.172	50 35.52	28.81	32 13.14	28 17 24.33 z
23	8.9	28.0	40.3	53.0	5.2	17.2	30.0	42.5	. .	. .	33 5.20	59.62	" 3 42.838	34 26.50	28.40	34 4.82	28 1 14.90 z
24	7	0.6	13.2	26.0	38.0	50.2	3.0	15.2	. .	. .	34 38.09	59.64	" 2 36.644	46 45.78	28.05	35 37.73	28 13 33.83 z
25	8.9	57.8	10.2	22.8	35.2	47.2	. .	12.5	. .	. .	36 35.15	59.64	" 3 33.992	39 32.07	27.61	37 34.79	28 6 19.68
26	9	49.0	1.2	13.5	. .	. .	. .	. .	. .	. .	40 26.03	59.60	I. 7 37.130	11 26.06	26.74	41 25.63	27 38 12.80 z
*27	8	. .	. .	32.0	. .	. .	. .	. .	. .	. .	40 44.50	59.61	IV. 6 37.972	16 48.34	26.66	41 44.11	27 43 35.00
28	8	. .	38.5	51.0	. .	. .	28.2	40.3	. .	. .	42 3.30	59.62	" 6 34.462	18 49.62	26.36	43 2.92	27 45 35.98
29	9	. .	. .	. .	51.0	. .	. .	26.0	. .	. .	42 49.85	59.64	" 4 35.716	32 35.96	26.17	43 49.49	27 59 22.13
30	9	34.0	47.0	59.0	. .	. .	36.0	. .	. .	. .	45 11.47	59.66	" 3 36.326	38 11.47	25.61	46 11.13	28 4 57.08
31	9	. .	48.5	0.8	. .	25.5	37.8	. .	. .	. .	45 13.18	59.66	V. 3 38.092	37 10.47	25.60	46 12.84	28 3 56.07
32	8.9	. .	. .	. .	. .	. .	. .	30.5	49.0	2.0	45 53.43	59.64	VII. 5 39.868	24 25.00	25.44	46 53.07	27 51 10.44 z
33	8.9	46.2	58.8	11.0	. .	. .	38.5	. .	. .	. .	48 23.64	59.69	II. 2 36.385	46 54.66	24.85	49 23.33	28 13 39.51
34	8	. .	29.0	. .	. .	. .	. .	31.0	. .	. .	48 53.76	59.66	IV. 2 40.534	44 29.94	24.73	49 53.42	28 11 14.67
35	9	. .	. .	. .	47.0	59.0	11.5	. .	. .	. .	49 46.78	59.65	" 5 36.875	26 8.73	24.52	50 46.43	27 52 53.25
36	9	. .	. .	. .	29.5	42.2	54.8	7.0	. .	. .	50 29.74	59.68	" 2 42.580	43 20.71	24.35	51 29.42	28 10 5.06
37	8	. .	. .	21.2	34.0	46.0	58.2	11.0	. .	. .	51 33.74	59.64	" 6 39.260	16 3.88	24.09	52 33.38	27 42 47.97
38	8	57.5	10.2	. .	35.0	47.2	59.7	12.0	. .	. .	52 34.89	59.68	" 3 41.003	35 29.90	23.84	53 34.57	28 2 13.74
39	9	. .	25.0	37.5	50.0	2.2	15.0	. .	. .	. .	54 49.96	59.69	" 3 42.890	34 24.70	23.30	55 49.65	28 1 8.00
40	9	. .	. .	. .	. .	42.0	54.6	6.6	. .	. .	55 29.56	59.69	V. 3 36.688	35 58.90	23.13	56 29.25	28 2 42.03
41	8.9	17.5	30.5	42.7	. .	7.2	. .	32.8	. .	. .	16 57 55.37	59.68	II. 4 45.022	27 14.41	22.55	16 58 55.05	27 53 56.96

CORRECTIONS.

	COR. TO CLOCK.	HOURLY COR.	m.	n.	c.	ZENITH POINT.	COINC.
	s.	s.	s.	s.	s.	° ′ ″	r.
June 17, at 16h...	+48.420	+0.025	+0.198	+0.396	+0.247	359 59 58.16	40.154

† Double.

INSTRUMENT READINGS.

	CIRCLE. A.	B.	C.	D.	Mean.	BAR.	THERMOM. At.	Ex.
Zone XXVII.—June 17, 15.8... h.	293° 12′ 0″.6	2″.3	11″.4	7″.5	5″.45	I. 30.080	73°.0	69°.0
17.0...	1.4	. .	. .	. .	6.25	30.076	72.2	68.0
18.2...	2.4	5.2	14.0	9.0	7.65	30.060	71.0	65.7

Zone XXVII. June 17. H. $D. = -27° 26' 20''.0$. $n' = -40''.84$. $n'' = -8''.00$. (Continued.)

Number.	Magnitude.	SECONDS OF TRANSITS. I.	II.	III.	IV.	V.	VI.	VII.	10.	11.	T.	a.	MICROMETER.	D.	d.	Mean Right Ascension. 1850.0.	Mean South Declination. 1850.0.
											h. m. s.	s.	r.	′ ″	′	h. m. s.	° ′ ″
42	9	. .	. .	12.5	25.0	. .	49.5	. .	. .	. .	16 58 24.86	+59.70	IV. 3 43.232	−34 12.92	−22.42	16 59 24.56	28 0 55.34
43	8.9	. .	. .	. .	. .	. .	. .	18.0	37.0	49.0	58 41.06	59.66	VII. 6 41.230	14 55.49	22.36	59 40.72	27 41 37.85
44	7	1.3	14.0	26.2	38.6	51.0	3.2	15.4	. .	. .	17 3 38.56	59.67	IV. 7 39.373	10 8.93	21.15	17 4 38.23	27 36 50.08 z.
45	8.9	21.0	33.2	45.2	58.0	10.2	23.0	35.0	. .	. .	4 57.98	59.69	" 5 46.260	20 44.56	20.81	5 57.67	27 47 25.37 z.
46	8.9	. .	39.2	51.8	4.0	17.0	. .	41.0	. .	. .	7 4.14	59.68	" 7 41.200	9 5.84	20.30	8 3.82	27 35 46.14 z.
47	8	53.0	5.5	18.5	30.0	. .	. .	7.0	. .	. .	7 30.26	59.69	" 6 40.660	15 15.48	20.20	8 29.95	27 41 55.68
48	9	9.3	22.0	. .	46.5	58.7	11.2	23.4	. .	. .	9 46.46	59.72	" 4 41.420	29 18.97	19.64	10 46.18	27 55 58.61
49	8.9	14.2	27.0	39.3	52.0	4.0	16.5	29.0	. .	. .	11 51.74	59.72	" 5 40.160	24 15.28	19.10	12 51.46	27 50 54.38
50	6.7	18.2	31.0	43.2	55.5	7.8	20.6	33.0	. .	. .	12 55.64	59.73	" 3 45.550	32 52.79	18.85	13 55.37	27 59 31.64 z.
51	9	. .	. .	. .	. .	23.0	35.5	48.0	. .	. .	14 10.64	59.76	" 2 36.352	46 55.91	18.53	15 10.40	28 13 34.44
52	7.8	11.0	23.8	36.0	48.5	0.5	13.2	25.5	. .	. .	15 48.42	59.77	" 1 41.290	49 56.91	18.12	16 48.19	28 16 35.03 z.
*53	9	36.5	49.0	1.5	. .	26.0	39.0	. .	. .	. .	17 13.91	59.75	" 3 39.099	36 35.67	17.77	18 13.66	28 3 13.44
54	9	47.0	59.3	. .	. .	. .	. .	1.3	. .	. .	18 24.19	59.75	VI. 3 41.133	35 25.31	17.42	19 23.94	28 2 2.73
55	9	. .	. .	15.5	28.0	. .	53.0	5.2	. .	. .	20 27.99	59.79	IV. 1 39.442	51 0.76	16.95	21 27.78	28 17 37.71
56	9	. .	. .	. .	. .	43.0	. .	8.0	. .	. .	21 30.72	59.76	" 3 44.800	33 18.72	16.68	22 30.48	27 59 55.40 z.
57	9	. .	. .	28.0	41.0	. .	. .	. .	. .	. .	21 40.74	59.76	VII. 3 45.030	33 10.44	16.64	22 40.50	27 59 47.08
58	8	6.0	. .	31.0	43.0	55.5	8.2	21.0	. .	. .	24 43.36	59.78	IV. 3 34.570	39 12.07	15.85	25 43.14	28 5 47.92
59	9	36.0	39.0	51.0	. .	. .	. .	. .	. .	. .	27 3.64	59.79	II. 2 44.428	42 16.82	15.25	28 3.43	28 8 52.07
60	9	. .	4.0	16.0	29.0	. .	. .	. .	. .	. .	27 28.77	59.78	IV. 3 38.842	36 44.53	15.13	28 28.55	28 3 19.66
61	7	. .	. .	. .	45.4	58.2	10.2	22.5	. .	. .	27 45.45	59.77	V. 4 39.461	30 26.61	15.06	28 45.22	27 57 1.67
62	8	. .	. .	. .	. .	. .	58.0	10.3	. .	. .	28 33.00	59.81	IV. 1 37.050	52 23.38	14.85	29 32.81	28 18 58.23 z.
63	8.9	39.2	52.2	4.5	16.7	29.0	. .	54.0	. .	. .	30 16.77	59.76	II. 5 44.503	21 45.11	14.42	31 16.53	27 48 19.53 z.
64	9	. .	. .	. .	34.0	46.0	58.5	10.5	. .	. .	30 33.61	59.79	IV. 3 35.650	38 34.78	14.33	31 33.40	28 5 9.11
65	9	. .	. .	52.5	5.0	17.3	29.6	. .	. .	. .	32 4.92	59.81	" 2 35.462	47 26.66	13.93	33 4.73	28 14 0.59 z.
66	7.8	. .	. .	39.0	52.0	4.0	16.2	29.0	. .	. .	32 51.66	59.77	" 5 44.390	21 49.17	13.72	33 51.43	27 48 22.89
67	9	. .	. .	57.0	9.5	22.0	. .	. .	. .	. .	34 9.57	59.80	" 3 33.516	39 48.48	13.37	35 9.37	28 6 21.85 z.
68	9	. .	. .	44.0	. .	8.5	21.0	. .	. .	. .	34 56.27	59.79	" 4 36.830	31 57.49	13.17	35 56.06	27 58 30.66 z.
69	9	. .	. .	51.2	. .	. .	29.3	41.5	. .	. .	36 4.11	59.79	I. 4 34.693	33 10.48	12.87	37 3.90	27 59 43.35
*70	6.7	. .	43.0	55.0	7.2	20.0	32.4	. .	. .	. .	37 7.54	59.77	IV. 5 47.350	20 6.92	12.59	38 7.31	27 46 39.51
71	8.9	. .	58.0	. .	23.0	35.0	47.4	. .	. .	. .	38 22.76	59.82	" 2 40.080	44 47.10	12.25	39 22.58	28 11 19.35
72	9	. .	. .	. .	33.0	45.4	58.0	10.2	. .	. .	39 33.02	59.81	" 3 36.535	38 4.21	11.94	40 32.83	28 4 36.15
73	9	. .	. .	31.0	43.4	55.6	8.3	21.0	. .	. .	40 43.50	59.78	" 5 47.110	20 15.19	11.63	41 43.28	27 46 46.82
74	9	16.2	28.8	41.2	53.2	5.8	18.6	31.0	. .	. .	42 53.58	59.81	" 3 42.840	34 26.43	11.05	43 53.39	28 0 57.48
75	9	8.6	21.4	33.6	46.0	58.2	10.8	. .	. .	. .	44 46.01	59.81	" 4 38.160	31 11.56	10.56	45 45.82	27 57 42.12
76	7	36.2	49.0	51.8	14.0	26.0	. .	. .	. .	. .	46 13.78	59.82	" 3 40.722	35 39.59	10.16	47 13.60	28 2 9.75
77	9	. .	. .	19.5	32.0	44.0	57.0	. .	. .	. .	46 31.95	59.83	" 3 36.628	38 1.00	10.09	47 31.78	28 4 31.09
78	9	. .	. .	28.0	41.0	53.0	5.5	. .	. .	. .	47 40.68	59.83	" 2 45.235	41 49.04	9.78	48 40.51	28 8 18.82
79	9	. .	. .	29.0	42.0	54.0	6.3	. .	. .	. .	47 41.65	59.84	" 2 47.390	40 34.61	9.77	48 41.49	28 7 4.38
80	9	. .	. .	39.0	51.0	3.4	. .	28.4	. .	. .	48 51.18	59.83	" 3 40.678	35 41.10	9.48	49 51.01	28 2 10.58
81	9	. .	. .	. .	41.5	54.0	. .	29.0	. .	. .	49 41.65	59.82	" 4 43.682	28 0.78	9.25	50 41.47	27 54 30.03
82	8.9	. .	. .	12.2	25.0	. .	. .	. .	. .	. .	51 24.83	59.81	" 5 37.888	25 33.75	8.79	52 24.64	27 52 2.54
83	9	. .	. .	48.0	0.5	. .	. .	. .	. .	. .	52 0.49	59.82	" 4 40.154	30 2.69	8.63	53 0.31	27 56 31.32
84	7.8	. .	3.0	15.2	28.0	40.0	52.4	5.0	. .	. .	52 27.74	59.81	" 5 42.825	22 43.19	8.51	53 27.55	27 49 11.70
85	9	. .	. .	. .	. .	16.0	29.0	41.4	. .	. .	53 4.00	59.82	" 4 43.710	27 59.82	8.35	54 3.82	27 54 28.17
86	8.9	17.0	29.4	42.0	54.2	6.4	19.0	31.2	. .	. .	54 54.20	59.82	II. 5 41.060	23 44.08	7.85	55 54.02	27 50 11.93 z.
87	9	18.5	31.0	43.5	. .	. .	. .	. .	. .	. .	56 55.91	59.84	I. 3 44.444	33 30.72	7.30	57 55.75	27 59 58.02
88	8	31.0	43.0	55.0	8.0	. .	. .	. .	. .	. .	58 7.90	59.83	IV. 4 46.810	26 12.73	6.98	59 7.73	27 52 39.71 z.
89	8	. .	. .	15.2	27.5	40.0	52.0	. .	. .	. .	58 27.50	59.82	" 5 44.900	21 31.53	6.89	59 27.32	27 47 58.42 z.
90	8	. .	. .	. .	50.0	. .	15.0	27.2	. .	. .	58 50.07	59.82	" 5 50.030	18 34.32	6.79	59 49.89	27 45 1.11 z.
91	8.9	. .	. .	51.5	4.0	16.5	29.0	. .	. .	. .	18 0 4.07	59.87	" 2 41.290	44 5.31	6.48	18 1 3.94	28 10 31.79 z.
92	8.9	. .	52.0	4.4	17.0	29.2	42.0	. .	. .	. .	1 16.94	59.85	II. 3 38.382	37 0.36	6.13	2 16.79	28 3 26.49 z.
93	8.9	. .	. .	56.3	9.0	21.4	34.0	. .	. .	. .	2 9.00	59.87	IV. 2 31.828	49 32.14	5.90	3 8.87	28 15 58.04 z.
94	8.9	31.8	44.3	57.0	9.0	21.5	34.0	. .	. .	. .	18 4 9.18	59.84	II. 3 42.510	34 37.71	5.36	18 5 9.02	28 1 3.07

Number.	Magnitude.	I.	II.	III.	IV.	V.	VI.	VII.	10.	11.	T.	a.	MICROMETER.	D.	d.	Mean Right Ascension, 1850.0.	Mean South Declination, 1850.0.
		SECONDS OF TRANSITS.															
		Zone XXVII. June 17. H. $D. = -27° 26' 20''.0$. $n.' = -40''.84$. $n.'' = -8''.00$. (Continued.)															
											h. m. s.	s.	r.	' ''	''	h. m. s.	° ' ''
95	9	34.0	46.4	59.0	11.4	. .	. .	. .	. .	. .	18 5 11.41	+59.86	II. 2 47.052	—40 46.16	— 5.09	18 6 11.27	28 7 11.25 z.
96	9	. .	. .	27.2	40.0	52.0	. .	. .	. .	. .	5 39.80	59.86	IV. 2 45.080	41 54.38	4.96	6 39.66	28 8 19.34 z.
97	7.8	. .	. .	19.0	31.3	43.5	. .	. .	. .	. .	6 31.34	59.81	" 5 48.410	19 30.30	4.73	7 31.15	27 45 55.03
98	9	. .	. .	. .	8.8	21.0	33.3	45.7	. .	. .	7 8.58	59.83	" 4 43.228	28 16.50	4.57	8 8.41	27 54 41.07 z.
99	8.9	50.5	3.3	15.5	27.5	40.2	53.0	5.0	. .	. .	10 27.91	59.86	" 2 40.935	44 17.55	3.67	11 27.77	28 10 41.22
100	9	15.2	28.0	40.2	. .	5.0	17.5	30.0	. .	. .	18 10 52.72	59.86	V. 1 43.190	48 51.23	3.56	18 11 52.58	28 15 14.79
		Zone XXVIII. June 18. M. $D. = -26° 25' 20''.0$. $n.' = -70''.90$. $n.'' = -6''.00$.															
1	8	. .	. .	46.5	58.5	. .	. .	. .	. .	. .	16 50 58.69	60.56	2. 3 42.11	34 49.09	68.21	16 51 59.25	27 1 17.30 z.
2	9	. .	. .	. .	. .	. .	. .	32.0	. .	. .	50 55.06	60.57	VII. 3 39.62	36 15.33	68.23	51 55.63	27 2 43.56
3	8	. .	. .	. .	45.0	57.0	. .	. .	. .	. .	53 44.91	60.55	IV. 5 37.79	25 35.19	67.56	54 45.46	26 52 2.75
4	8	. .	. .	. .	. .	53.5	6.0	. .	. .	. .	53 41.32	60.57	VI. 4 34.50	33 15.81	67.57	54 41.89	26 59 43.38 z.
5	8.9	. .	. .	. .	. .	. .	. .	. .	21.0	33.7	54 26.30	60.59	11. 1 40.57	50 18.73	67.39	55 26.89	27 16 46.12 z.
6	9	. .	. .	. .	. .	. .	. .	26.5	. .	. .	55 49.69	60.55	10. 6 36.64	17 31.99	67.08	56 50.24	26 43 59.07 z.
7	8.9	. .	52.7	4.8	. .	. .	. .	. .	. .	. .	58 17.11	60.54	2. 7 36.75	11 37.24	66.50	59 17.65	26 38 3.74 z.
8	7.8	. .	26.0	38.0	. .	. .	. .	. .	. .	. .	17 1 50.43	60.57	2. 5 39.44	24 37.71	65.66	17 2 51.00	26 51 3.37 z.
9	9	. .	. .	. .	15.5	28.0	. .	. .	. .	. .	2 15.66	60.57	III. 5 41.39	23 30.86	65.56	3 16.23	26 49 56.42 z.
10	7	16.0	29.0	41.0	53.0	5.0	. .	. .	. .	. .	3 53.13	60.57	2. 5 44.67	21 37.04	65.16	4 53.70	26 48 2.20 z.
11	8	. .	. .	19.0	32.0	. .	. .	. .	. .	. .	10 31.71	60.63	2. 2 40.19	44 40.64	63.56	11 32.34	27 11 4.20 z.
12	8	. .	. .	. .	. .	54.0	6.3	19.0	. .	. .	11 41.80	60.64	IV. 1 42.38	49 17.05	63.27	12 42.44	27 15 40.32
13	9.10	. .	4.2	16.0	28.7	. .	53.0	. .	. .	. .	18 28.52	60.59	2. 7 40.45	9 29.48	61.61	19 29.11	26 35 51.09 z.
14	9	. .	. .	58.1	10.5	22.3	. .	. .	. .	. .	20 10.36	60.64	I. 3 35.70	38 30.72	61.20	21 11.00	27 4 51.92 z.
15	8.9	. .	0.5	12.3	24.8	. .	49.0	1.4	. .	. .	24 24.66	60.61	2. 7 36.85	11 33.79	60.16	25 25.27	26 37 53.95 z.
16	8	. .	19.0	31.0	43.1	55.3	. .	20.2	. .	. .	28 43.28	60.64	2. 5 40.21	24 11.11	59.09	29 43.92	26 50 30.20 z.
17	8.9	. .	. .	. .	40.0	52.5	. .	. .	. .	. .	30 40.10	60.69	V. 1 37.20	52 15.94	58.62	31 40.79	27 18 34.56
18	8	. .	. .	. .	. .	. .	. .	19.5	. .	. .	31 42.66	60.63	IV. 6 33.23	19 30.29	58.36	32 43.29	26 45 48.65 z.
19	8	. .	56.8	8.8	21.5	. .	. .	. .	. .	. .	34 21.40	60.68	2. 2 42.78	43 11.16	57.70	35 22.08	27 9 28.86 z.
20	7.8	. .	13.5	26.0	38.5	. .	. .	. .	. .	. .	35 38.29	60.66	2. 4 43.59	28 1.47	57.37	36 38.95	26 54 18.84 z.
21	7	. .	. .	52.0	4.2	. .	29.0	41.0	. .	. .	38 4.25	60.67	I. 4 42.365	28 44.09	56.76	39 4.92	26 55 0.85 z.
22	8	. .	. .	. .	43.0	55.0	. .	. .	. .	. .	39 42.93	60.66	VII. 6 33.63	19 16.20	56.35	40 43.59	26 45 32.55 z.
23	7	. .	. .	. .	. .	. .	22.0	34.2	. .	. .	39 57.29	60.68	" 4 32.92	34 10.27	56.29	40 57.97	27 0 26.56
24	8.9	. .	. .	. .	. .	. .	. .	55.0	. .	. .	41 18.12	60.66	" 5 41.49	23 27.20	55.96	42 18.78	26 49 43.16 z.
25	8.9	. .	. .	. .	. .	. .	. .	. .	36.7	49.0	41 41.92	60.66	11. 5 39.37	24 39.85	55.85	42 42.58	26 50 55.70 z.
26	7	. .	. .	. .	. .	. .	. .	45.5	. .	. .	43 8.52	60.71	VII. 1 44.60	48 0.10	55.49	44 9.23	27 14 15.59 z.
27	8	. .	. .	. .	. .	. .	. .	44.8	. .	. .	44 8.07	60.64	" 7 41.14	9 5.91	55.24	45 8.71	26 35 21.15
28	8	. .	. .	. .	2.0	14.0	. .	. .	. .	. .	46 1.92	60.66	I. 6 35.55	18 9.90	54.77	47 2.58	26 44 24.67 z.
29	8	. .	. .	. .	. .	44.8	51.2	9.6	. .	. .	46 32.58	60.70	VII. 3 32.63	40 16.76	54.64	47 33.28	27 6 31.40 z.
30	8	. .	48.0	. .	12.0	. .	. .	. .	. .	. .	17 49 12.28	60.70	2. 3 38.50	36 53.79	53.96	17 50 12.98	27 3 7.75 z.

CORRECTIONS.

	COR. TO CLOCK.	HOURLY COR.	m.	n.	c.	ZENITH POINT.	COINC.
	s.	s.	s.	s.	s.		r.
June 18, at 16h...	+49.390	+0.020	+0.198	+0.396	−0.247	359° 59' 59''.56	40.105

INSTRUMENT READINGS.

		CIRCLE. A.	B.	C.	D.	Mean.	BAR.	THERMOM. At.	Ex.
Zone.	h.						I.		
XXVIII.—June 18,	16.8	294° 12' 14''.0	16'.0	22''.4	20''.4	18''.20	29.997	73°.4	70°.1
	17.4	. . . .	. . .	. . .	. . .	. . . .	29.980	73.0	70.0
	19.0	. . . .	. . .	. . .	. . .	. . . .	29.950	71.6	69.0
	21.1	12.0	12.8	14.4	21.0	16.80	29.930	71.0	67.4

Zone XXVIII. June 18. H. $D. = -26^{\circ}\ 25'\ 20''.0$. $n' = -70''.90$. $n'' = -6''.00$. (Continued.)

Number.	Magnitude.	Seconds of Transits. I.	II.	III.	IV.	V.	VI.	VII.	10.	11.	T.	a.	Micrometer.	D.	d.	Mean Right Ascension, 1850.0.	Mean South Declination, 1850.0.
											h. m. s.	s.	r.	′ ″	″	h. m. s.	° ′ ″
31	8.9	. .	35.5	. .	. .	12.0	25.0	. .	. .	. .	17 51 0.07	+60.70	2. 4 37.51	−31 31.50	−53.51	17 52 0.77	26 57 45.01
32	8	. .	. .	. .	. .	. .	. .	58.0	. .	. .	52 21.05	60.71	VII. 3 36.50	38 3.14	53.17	53 21.76	27 4 16.31
33	7	. .	. .	. .	. .	. .	. .	54.0	. .	. .	53 17.11	60.69	" 5 37.56	25 42.87	52.93	54 17.80	26 51 55.80
34	7	. .	. .	. .	. .	. .	. .	54.0	. .	. .	54 17.12	60.69	" 5 39.27	24 43.85	52.68	55 17.81	26 50 56.53
35	8.9	. .	. .	. .	. .	. .	. .	. .	36.0	48.5	54 41.20	60.72	11. 2 45.99	41 20.04	52.58	55 41.92	27 7 32.62
36	8	. .	. .	. .	. .	. .	. .	. .	. .	42.0	55 34.21	60.70	" 3 45.99	32 34.80	52.34	56 34.91	26 58 47.14
37	8	. .	. .	. .	. .	. .	. .	17.0	. .	. .	57 39.99	60.75	VII. 1 35.29	53 21.69	51.82	58 40.74	27 19 33.51
38	8.9	. .	. .	. .	. .	. .	. .	4.5	. .	. .	58 27.79	60.67	" 7 43.13	7 57.19	51.61	59 28.46	26 34 8.80
39	8	17.0	29.0	41.5	54.0	6.5	19.0	31.0	. .	. .	18 2 54.05	60.75	I. 1 43.48	48 38.84	50.48	18 3 54.80	27 14 49.32
40	6	. .	. .	. .	39.0	51.0	3.6	. .	. .	. .	8 38.90	60.74	" 3 34.35	39 17.40	49.00	9 39.64	27 5 26.40
41	9	. .	. .	. .	2.5	14.5	. .	39.5	. .	. .	12 2.45	60.73	2. 4 36.10	32 20.19	48.14	13 3.18	26 58 28.33
42	9	. .	. .	5.6	17.8	. .	42.8	. .	. .	. .	14 18.01	60.69	2. 7 43.50	7 44.15	47.55	15 18.70	26 33 51.70
43	7	45.0	57.1	9.5	. .	. .	. .	. .	. .	. .	16 21.79	60.71	1. 6 37.54	17 0.60	47.03	17 22.50	26 43 7.63
44	7	. .	. .	. .	. .	. .	. .	20.5	. .	. .	17 43.62	60.73	VII. 5 39.91	24 21.73	46.68	18 44.35	26 50 28.41 z.
45	7.8	. .	. .	. .	. .	. .	. .	. .	31.0	43.0	18 36.23	60.71	11. 6 42.52	14 8.60	46.44	19 36.94	26 40 15.04 z.
46	8	. .	28.5	40.5	. .	. .	. .	. .	. .	. .	21 52.85	60.70	2. 7 40.58	9 24.95	45.59	22 53.55	26 35 30.54
47	8	. .	. .	. .	. .	. .	16.0	28.0	. .	. .	21 51.16	60.78	VII. 1 35.575	53 11.80	45.59	22 51.94	27 19 17.39 z.
48	9.10	. .	. .	. .	. .	21.5	33.5	. .	. .	. .	23 9.07	60.75	" 4 35.87	32 28.38	45.26	24 9.82	26 58 33.64 z.
49	8.9	. .	. .	. .	. .	. .	. .	. .	31.8	44.5	23 37.18	60.74	11. 5 33.50	28 2.54	45.15	24 37.92	26 54 7.65
50	8.9	. .	. .	. .	. .	. .	8.5	20.8	. .	. .	25 43.81	60.79	III. 1 37.55	52 3.81	44.59	24 44.60	27 18 8.40
51	9	7.5	20.2	32.3	45.0	. .	. .	. .	. .	. .	30 44.72	60.75	1. 5 36.30	26 25.87	43.30	31 45.47	26 52 29.17 z.
52	9	. .	. .	. .	. .	. .	47.5	. .	. .	. .	32 22.82	60.78	VII. 3 28.70	42 32.48	42.88	33 23.60	27 8 35.36 z.
53	5	. .	. .	. .	16.5	28.8	41.0	53.3	. .	. .	35 16.43	60.78	IV. 2 44.51	42 11.92	42.12	36 17.21	27 8 14.04
54	8.9	. .	. .	20.0	32.0	. .	. .	. .	. .	. .	37 32.21	60.79	" 1 43.71	48 31.09	41.53	38 33.00	26 14 32.62
55	9	. .	. .	. .	48.3	. .	. .	. .	. .	. .	38 48.27	60.73	II. 7 43.38	7 48.71	41.20	39 49.00	26 33 49.91
56	8	. .	. .	. .	. .	26.0	38.4	. .	. .	. .	39 13.73	60.80	VII. 1 39.11	51 9.74	41.09	40 14.53	27 17 10.83 z.
57	8	. .	. .	. .	. .	41.0	53.0	. .	. .	. .	40 28.58	60.77	IV. 4 39.94	30 8.08	40.76	41 29.35	26 56 8.84
58	6.7	. .	. .	55.7	7.5	. .	. .	. .	. .	. .	42 7.77	60.76	I. 5 41.71	23 19.56	40.34	43 8.53	26 49 19.90
59	8	. .	. .	. .	38.0	50.0	2.0	. .	. .	. .	42 37.80	60.73	IV. 7 43.30	7 51.57	40.21	43 38.53	26 33 51.78
60	8	. .	. .	4.7	17.0	29.2	. .	. .	. .	. .	44 17.03	60.79	V. 3 36.14	38 15.75	39.78	45 17.82	27 4 15.53 z.
61	9	. .	. .	. .	. .	. .	11.5	24.0	. .	. .	45 46.95	60.78	VI. 3 37.66	37 23.16	39.39	46 47.73	27 3 22.55
62	9.10	. .	. .	44.0	56.2	. .	. .	. .	. .	. .	47 56.31	60.80	I. 2 35.80	47 12.52	38.83	48 57.11	27 13 11.35
63	9	. .	. .	. .	7.0	19.0	31.5	. .	. .	. .	49 6.93	60.75	IV. 6 39.78	15 44.08	38.52	50 7.68	26 41 42.60
64	8.9	. .	. .	. .	50.0	. .	. .	. .	. .	. .	51 49.97	60.74	I. 7 42.36	8 23.80	37.82	52 50.71	26 34 21.62
65	7.8	. .	. .	. .	. .	. .	13.0	25.0	. .	. .	57 48.19	60.80	VII. 3 36.89	37 49.63	36.26	58 48.99	27 3 45.89 z.
66	7.8	. .	. .	. .	. .	. .	55.2	7.5	. .	. .	19 0 30.62	60.77	" 5 46.42	20 36.92	35.57	19 1 31.39	26 46 32.49
67	8	. .	. .	. .	. .	. .	. .	. .	54.0	6.3	0 59.37	60.76	11. 6 41.28	14 51.47	35.44	2 0.13	26 40 46.91
68	9	. .	. .	27.0	39.0	. .	. .	. .	. .	. .	2 39.21	60.82	III. 1 43.36	48 43.17	35.02	3 40.03	27 14 38.19
69	7	. .	. .	25.0	37.5	49.5	. .	. .	. .	. .	3 37.40	60.81	V. 2 46.80	40 52.81	34.78	4 38.21	27 6 47.59
70	9	. .	. .	31.5	44.1	56.3	. .	. .	. .	. .	5 44.03	60.79	2. 4 46.47	26 23.05	34.24	6 44.82	26 52 17.29 z.
71	9.10	. .	26.0	37.6	50.5	. .	. .	. .	. .	. .	9 50.29	60.78	2. 6 37.40	17 5.78	33.21	10 51.07	26 42 58.99
72	9.10	. .	. .	32.5	. .	57.5	. .	20.0	. .	. .	13 45.09	60.80	IV. 3 43.35	34 6.88	32.24	14 45.89	26 59 59.12
73	9.10	. .	. .	. .	. .	. .	38.7	51.0	. .	. .	14 14.01	60.83	VII. 1 37.69	51 58.77	32.12	15 14.84	27 17 50.89 z.
74	7.8	. .	. .	14.3	26.7	39.0	51.5	. .	. .	. .	16 26.80	60.77	1. 7 38.27	10 45.04	31.57	17 27.56	26 36 36.61 z.
†75	6.7	. .	10.0	22.0	34.5	46.5	59.0	11.0	. .	. .	19 34.37	60.84	2. 1 38.65	51 25.34	30.79	20 35.21	27 17 16.13
76	8.9	. .	. .	. .	. .	. .	. .	16.5	. .	. .	25 39.74	60.77	IV. 7 36.85	11 34.30	29.27	26 40.51	26 37 23.57
77	8	. .	. .	58.0	10.3	22.5	35.0	. .	. .	. .	32 10.35	60.79	I. 5 44.76	21 34.21	27.65	33 11.14	26 47 21.86 z.
78	9	. .	. .	. .	. .	. .	11.0	. .	. .	. .	33 46.35	60.80	IV. 4 43.66	27 59.58	27.25	34 47.15	26 53 46.83
79	9	. .	. .	. .	. .	. .	37.5	50.0	. .	. .	34 13.01	60.79	VII. 5 42.96	22 36.40	27.14	35 13.80	26 48 23.54 z.
80	8	. .	. .	. .	. .	. .	. .	. .	33.0	45.6	34 38.25	60.83	11. 2 41.82	43 44.04	27.05	35 39.08	27 9 31.09 z.
81	7.8	. .	. .	. .	48.0	. .	. .	. .	. .	. .	36 47.97	60.80	IV. 4 48.55	25 10.69	26.50	37 48.77	26 50 57.19 z.
82	8.9	. .	. .	. .	. .	. .	. .	45.5	. .	. .	19 37 8.53	60.84	VII. 1 49.21	45 20.90	26.42	19 38 9.37	27 11 7.32 z.

† 75. A double star.

Number.	Magnitude.	Seconds of Transits. I.	II.	III.	IV.	V.	VI.	VII.	10.	11.	T.	a.	Micrometer.	D.	d.	Mean Right Ascension, 1850.0.	Mean South Declination, 1850.0.
Zone XXVIII. June 18. M. $D. = -26° 25' 20''.00$. $n.' = -70''.90$. $n.'' = -6''.00$. (Continued.)																	
											h. m. s.	s.	r.	′ ″	″	h. m. s.	° ′ ″
83	8	. .	. .	32.5	. .	57.0	. .	. .	. .	. .	19 39 44.88	+60.79	I. 5 50.70	—18 9.07	—25.77	19 40 45.67	26 43 54.84 z.
84	8	. .	. .	. .	. .	21.5	34.0	46.0	. .	. .	40 9.22	60.83	VII. 3 34.40	39 15.66	25.67	41 10.05	27 5 1.33 z.
85	8	. .	. .	. .	58.0	10.0	. .	. .	. .	. .	43 57.90	60.81	IV. 3 49.70	30 27.44	24.73	44 58.71	26 56 12.17
86	6	. .	. .	25.0	38.0	50.0	. .	. .	. .	. .	45 37.74	60.79	V. 6 39.68	15 47.48	24.32	46 38.53	26 41 31.80 z.
87	8	. .	. .	. .	. .	. .	. .	. .	. .	49.3	45 41.54	60.81	11. 4 39.00	30 39.74	24.31	46 42.35	26 56 24.05
88	9	. .	. .	. .	. .	. .	. .	42.5	. .	. .	47 5.75	60.78	VII. 7 37.66	11 6.07	23.97	48 6.53	26 36 50.04 z.
89	6	. .	. .	. .	47.5	. .	12.5	. .	. .	. .	48 47.78	60.78	V. 7 39.47	10 3.81	23.54	49 48.56	26 35 47.35
90	9	. .	. .	. .	. .	. .	. .	. .	45.0	. .	48 50.91	60.79	10. 6 39.44	15 55.34	23.53	49 51.70	26 41 38.87
91	8.9	. .	. .	. .	. .	. .	. .	22.8	. .	. .	50 46.03	60.78	V. 7 35.97	12 4.67	23.07	51 46.81	26 37 47.74
92	8.9	. .	. .	57.0	9.0	21.5	. .	. .	. .	. .	54 9.24	60.79	2. 6 34.28	18 53.52	22.23	55 10.03	26 44 35.75 z.
93	8	. .	. .	49.5	1.5	14.0	. .	. .	. .	. .	55 1.72	60.84	VI. 2 34.00	48 14.84	22.02	56 2.56	27 13 56.86 z.
94	8.9	. .	. .	. .	. .	. .	2.7	15.0	. .	. .	56 38.08	60.81	II. 5 37.29	25 52.38	21.62	57 38.89	26 51 34.00 z.
95	7.8	. .	33.2	45.2	57.5	9.0	. .	34.2	. .	. .	58 53.34	60.78	I. 6 43.68	13 29.14	21.09	59 54.12	26 39 10.23
96	9.10	. .	. .	37.5	. .	2.0	14.5	. .	. .	. .	20 2 49.91	60.78	VII. 6 45.56	12 24.22	20.13	20 3 50.69	26 38 4.39
97	9	. .	12.5	24.5	37.0	49.0	. .	. .	. .	. .	10 36.90	60.78	2. 7 37.25	11 19.98	18.30	11 37.68	26 36 58.28 z.
98	8	51.0	3.7	16.0	28.5	40.0	53.0	. .	. .	. .	13 28.26	60.84	I. 2 36.20	46 58.73	17.62	14 29.10	26 12 36.35 z.
99	8	. .	19.8	32.0	44.5	56.2	9.0	21.5	. .	. .	15 44.36	60.82	2. 3 38.90	36 39.93	17.09	16 45.18	26 2 17.02
100	9.10	. .	. .	. .	. .	38.0	. .	3.5	. .	. .	17 26.16	60.82	VII. 2 46.69	40 56.39	16.70	18 26.98	26 6 33.09
101	10.9	. .	53.5	5.3	17.6	30.1	. .	. .	. .	. .	19 17.83	60.82	II. 3 35.89	38 24.30	16.25	20 18.65	26 4 0.55 z.
102	7	14.0	26.4	38.7	51.0	3.5	. .	28.0	. .	. .	25 51.11	60.84	IV. 1 38.39	51 34.87	14.75	26 51.95	26 17 9.62 z.
103	7	. .	. .	22.7	35.5	47.5	59.8	12.0	. .	. .	31 35.21	60.83	" 2 40.55	44 28.70	13.45	32 36.04	26 10 2.15
104	7	. .	. .	. .	. .	. .	. .	2.5	. .	. .	31 25.80	60.76	VII. 7 46.53	5 59.78	13.49	32 26.56	26 31 33.27 z.
105	9	. .	18.0	30.5	42.8	54.8	7.0	. .	. .	. .	33 42.63	60.79	VI. 5 45.10	21 22.63	12.97	34 43.42	26 46 55.60 z.
106	9	. .	. .	10.0	22.5	. .	. .	. .	. .	. .	36 22.42	60.78	2. 6 36.62	17 32.69	12.38	37 23.20	26 43 5.07
107	7.8	45.0	57.0	9.7	22.0	34.0	46.5	59.0	. .	. .	37 21.90	60.80	I. 4 36.64	32 1.78	12.17	38 22.70	26 57 33.95 z.
108	9	. .	. .	12.0	24.6	36.8	. .	. .	. .	. .	39 24.53	60.79	VII. 4 43.87	27 52.09	11.70	40 25.32	26 53 23.79
*109	8	. .	. .	47.5	. .	12.0	24.5	36.6	. .	. .	43 59.82	60.79	2. 4 44.19	27 40.79	10.71	45 0.61	26 53 11.50
110	6.7	14.4	27.0	39.0	51.1	3.3	16.0	28.0	. .	. .	46 51.29	60.79	2. 5 36.50	26 19.25	10.10	47 52.08	26 51 49.35
111	9	14.0	26.8	39.0	51.2	3.5	. .	. .	. .	. .	48 51.20	60.76	IV. 7 40.62	9 24.09	9.66	49 51.96	26 34 53.75
112	9.8	. .	. .	25.0	37.5	49.5	. .	14.3	. .	. .	58 37.37	60.81	2. 1 46.40	46 57.70	7.60	59 38.18	27 12 25.30 z.
113	9	. .	42.0	. .	6.5	18.2	31.0	43.3	. .	. .	21 0 6.37	60.77	II. 5 46.58	20 31.49	7.28	21 1 7.14	26 45 58.77 z.
114	8	. .	. .	. .	56.8	9.0	21.7	34.0	. .	. .	2 56.83	60.82	I. 1 35.27	53 22.38	6.68	3 57.65	27 18 49.06 z.
115	8	. .	. .	. .	57.0	9.0	21.5	33.8	. .	. .	21 4 57.00	60.74	VII. 7 46.25	6 9.44	6.27	21 5 57.74	26 31 35.71 z.
†Zone XXIX. June 21. M. $D. = -39° 49' 10''.0$. $n.' = -30''.01$. $n.'' = -15''.00$.																	
1	7	28.8	43.0	51.5	. .	26.5	41.0	55.7	. .	. .	18 36 12.08	63.21	1. 2 41.61	44 4.66	26.14	18 37 15.29	41 33 40.80
2	8	. .	. .	52.3	7.0	21.0	35.7	. .	. .	. .	46 6.80	63.15	VII. 7 37.32	11 20.78	23.87	47 9.95	41 0 54.65
3	6	. .	22.0	36.5	51.0	5.5	20.0	34.2	. .	. .	56 50.94	63.23	II. 1 34.81	53 55.37	21.43	57 54.17	41 43 26.80
4	8.9	. .	. .	. .	. .	. .	43.0	57.5	. .	. .	58 14.39	63.15	10. 7 32.60	14 4.11	21.11	59 17.54	41 3 35.22

CORRECTIONS.

	Cor. to Clock.	Hourly Cor.	m.	n.	c.	Zenith Point.	Coinc.
	s.	s.	s.	s.	s.		r.
June 21, at 16h...	+50.731	+ 0.008	+0.198	+0.396	+0.247	0° 0′ 0″.93	40.105

INSTRUMENT READINGS.

Zone.	h.	Circle. A.	B.	C.	D.	Mean.	Bar.	Thermom. At.	Ex.
XXIX.—June 21,	18.6	280° 51′ 23″.0	22″.0	26″.5	26″.0	24″.38	I. 29.980	63°.8	56°.3
	20.2	22.0	20.0	28.0	27.2	24.27	29.976	54.5	55.0

† The sky cloudy and unfavorable.

Number.	Magnitude.	SECONDS OF TRANSITS. I.	II.	III.	IV.	V.	VI.	VII.	10.	11.	T.	a.	MICROMETER.	D.	d.	Mean Right Ascension, 1850.0.	Mean South Declination, 1850.0.
Zone XXIX. June 21. M. $D. = -39^{\circ} 49' 10''.0$. $n'. = -30''.01$. $n''. = -15''.00$. (Continued.)																	
											h. m. s.	s.	r.	′ ″	″	h. m. s.	° ′ ″
5	9.10	. .	. .	. .	. .	41.5	56.0	10.3	. .	. .	19 4 26.90	+63.21	I. 2 36.87	−46 50.10	−19.69	19 5 30.11	41 36 19.79
6	9	. .	. .	. .	. .	25.2	. .	54.8	. .	. .	9 11.28	63.17	" 5 37.28	26 0.21	18.61	10 14.45	41 15 28.82
7	9	36.5	51.0	5.8	. .	34.5	. .	. .	. .	. .	16 19.97	63.18	VII. 3 44.32	33 43.19	17.01	17 23.15	41 23 10.20
8	8	4.5	19.0	33.2	47.0	. .	16.6	31.0	. .	. .	23 47.53	63.16	IV. 4 37.58	31 38.95	15.34	24 50.69	41 21 4.29
9	7	52.8	7.5	21.4	35.9	50.0	4.7	19.0	. .	. .	40 35.87	63.12	" 5 38.40	25 21.63	11.64	41 38.99	41 14 43.27
10	8.9	. .	. .	30.5	44.8	59.0	13.4	28.1	. .	. .	56 44.71	63.08	I. 5 36.17	26 38.74	8.16	57 47.79	41 15 56.90
11	9	. .	31.6	. .	0.8	14.5	. .	. .	. .	. .	20 4 0.29	63.05	10. 5 46.51	20 39.12	6.62	20 5 3.34	41 9 55.74
12	8.9	. .	. .	28.5	42.3	57.0	10.5	25.5	. .	. .	6 42.24	63.10	11. 1 42.84	49 15.55	6.05	7 45.34	41 38 31.60
13	8.9	. .	. .	. .	. .	2.7	17.0	31.5	. .	. .	20 8 48.24	63.03	VII. 5 49.14	19 8.31	5.61	20 9 51.27	41 8 23.92
Zone XXX. June 22. H. $D. = -28^{\circ} 26' 30''.0$. $n'. = -15''.77$. $n''. = -6''.00$.																	
1	9	. .	. .	. .	. .	36.5	50.0	2.2	21.5	34.0	17 1 24.70	61.88	V. 1 40.120	50 35.52	15.28	17 2 26.58	29 17 20.80
2	9	39.2	51.8	4.2	16.5	29.3	41.8	54.5	. .	. .	5 16.80	61.86	IV. 3 43.010	34 18.61	14.44	6 18.66	29 1 3.05
3	8.9	34.0	46.5	59.0	11.2	24.0	36.2	49.0	. .	. .	7 11.45	61.84	V. 5 38.992	24 53.53	14.02	8 13.29	28 51 37.55
4	8.9	20.0	33.0	45.0	58.0	. .	. .	. .	. .	. .	8 57.90	61.88	III. 2 46.470	41 4.49	13.63	9 59.78	29 7 48.12 z.
5	7	17.0	30.0	. .	55.0	. .	. .	33.0	. .	. .	9 55.08	61.89	I. 2 38.790	45 29.49	13.43	10 56.97	29 12 12.92 z.
6	9	22.0	34.5	47.2	. .	. .	24.7	. .	. .	. .	9 59.74	61.90	VI. 2 31.812	49 30.84	13.41	11 1.64	29 16 14.25
7	9	24.8	37.4	50.0	2.0	14.8	27.0	39.8	. .	. .	13 2.30	61.88	IV. 3 34.678	39 6.45	12.74	14 4.18	29 5 49.19
8	8	57.5	10.5	23.0	35.8	48.0	0.2	12.8	. .	. .	14 35.43	61.85	" 5 46.682	20 27.85	12.40	15 37.28	28 47 10.25 z.
9	7.8	8.0	20.5	33.1	45.2	58.0	10.5	. .	. .	. .	16 45.50	61.84	" 6 47.515	10 36.50	11.92	17 47.34	28 37 18.42
10	7.8	17.2	30.0	43.0	55.0	7.5	. .	. .	. .	. .	17 55.13	61.87	" 4 42.130	28 52.42	11.66	18 57.00	28 55 34.08 z.
11	9	. .	. .	. .	. .	16.0	28.3	41.0	. .	. .	18 3.37	61.88	V. 3 45.240	33 1.55	11.63	19 5.25	28 59 43.18
12	9	. .	. .	. .	. .	53.0	6.0	18.2	. .	. .	18 40.72	61.87	VI. 5 40.711	23 54.06	11.49	19 42.59	28 50 35.55 z.
13	9	. .	57.2	9.5	22.0	34.4	47.2	. .	. .	. .	20 22.07	61.88	IV. 4 42.505	28 39.48	11.13	21 23.95	28 55 20.61
14	8	56.2	9.0	21.2	34.0	46.2	. .	. .	. .	. .	21 33.87	61.86	" 6 38.875	16 15.02	10.85	22 35.73	28 42 55.87 z.
15	9	53.0	5.5	18.2	31.0	. .	. .	. .	. .	. .	22 30.78	61.89	" 4 33.870	33 37.79	10.64	23 32.67	29 0 18.43 z.
16	8.9	43.0	. .	8.0	21.0	33.1	45.8	. .	. .	. .	23 20.75	61.90	" 3 33.149	39 59.32	10.45	24 22.65	29 6 39.77 z.
17	9	. .	. .	. .	6.2	18.8	31.2	43.8	. .	. .	24 6.18	61.91	V. 2 44.686	42 6.07	10.28	25 8.09	29 8 46.35 z.
18	9	28.2	41.0	53.2	6.0	18.0	30.8	43.2	. .	. .	26 5.80	61.89	IV. 4 45.652	26 50.70	9.84	27 7.69	28 53 30.54 z.
19	9	. .	. .	. .	30.0	. .	55.0	. .	. .	. .	27 29.90	61.90	" 3 43.220	34 11.37	9.52	28 31.80	29 0 50.89
20	6.7	13.5	26.0	38.5	51.0	3.5	16.0	28.6	. .	. .	17 29 51.05	61.88	" 5 41.590	23 23.78	8.99	17 30 52.93	28 50 2.77
Zone XXXI. June 24. H. $D. = -25^{\circ} 56' 50''.0$. $n'. = -15''.17$. $n''. = -6''.00$.																	
1	9	51.0	3.4	15.6	27.5	40.0	52.2	4.7	. .	. .	15 1 27.82	61.31	IV. 1 44.662	47 58.18	14.83	15 2 29.13	26 45 3.01
2	8.9	19.0	31.2	43.5	55.8	7.8	20.3	32.8	. .	. .	5 55.80	61.30	" 4 39.165	30 34.84	14.20	6 57.10	26 27 39.04
3	8	17.8	30.0	. .	54.5	6.7	19.0	31.3	. .	. .	15 7 54.53	61.31	" 4 41.250	29 22.85	13.91	15 8 55.84	26 26 26.76

CORRECTIONS.

	COR. TO CLOCK.	HOURLY COR.	m.	n.	c.	ZENITH POINT.	COINC.
	s.	s.	s.	s.	s.	° ′ ″	r.
June 22, at 16h...	+50.529	+ 0.004	+0.198	+0.396	+0.247	359 59 57.75	40.097

INSTRUMENT READINGS.

Zone. h.	CIRCLE. A.	B.	C.	D.	Mean.	BAR.	THERMOM. At.	Ex.
	° ′ ″	′	″	″	″	I.	°	°
XXX.—June 22, 17.0	292 12 8.6	10.2	17.4	16.6	13.05	30.120	63.8	56.4
	8.2	9.5	17.1	15.2	12.50	30.114	63.8	56.0

Number.	Magnitude.	SECONDS OF TRANSITS. I.	II.	III.	IV.	V.	VI.	VII.	10.	11.	T.	a.	MICROMETER.	D.	d.	Mean Right Ascension, 1850.0.	Mean South Declination, 1850.0.
		Zone XXXI. June 24. H. $D. = -25° 56' 50''.0$. $n' = -15''.17$. $n'' = -6''.00$. (Continued.)															
											h. m. s.	s.	r.	′ ″	″	h. m. s.	° ′ ″
4	8.9	3.2	15.5	28.0	40.0	52.3	. .	. .	. .	. .	15 9 40.06	+ 61.29	IV. 6 40.705	—15 12.10	—13.66	15 10 41.35	26 12 15.76
5	8.9	0.8	12.8	25.5	37.4	49.5	1.6	14.2	. .	. .	10 37.44	61.32	" 4 37.668	31 26.51	13.52	11 38.76	26 28 30.03
6	8	35.6	48.2	0.8	12.5	24.6	36.8	49.2	. .	. .	12 12.57	61.32	" 4 39.160	30 35.02	13.28	13 13.89	26 27 38.30
7	7.8	. .	34.5	46.5	59.0	11.0	23.2	45.6	. .	. .	12 58.86	61.31	" 6 36.360	17 42.21	13.16	14 0.17	26 14 45.37
8	8.9	. .	. .	. .	2.0	14.1	26.2	39.0	. .	. .	14 1.92	61.35	" 1 43.155	48 50.26	13.00	15 3.27	26 45 53.26
9	8.9	. .	. .	. .	10.6	22.6	35.0	47.2	. .	. .	15 10.55	61.31	" 6 39.262	16 1.98	12.82	16 11.86	26 13 4.80
10	9	31.3	44.0	56.0	8.0	23.0	32.6	45.0	. .	. .	18 8.18	61.36	" 1 39.762	50 47.43	12.37	19 9.54	26 47 49.80
11	9	. .	2.2	14.5	26.2	38.2	51.0	3.3	. .	. .	19 26.49	61.31	" 7 43.255	7 53.09	12.17	20 27.80	26 4 55.26
12	9	13.0	25.8	38.0	. .	. .	15.0	27.5	. .	. .	24 50.36	61.37	" 2 45.390	41 41.56	11.32	25 51.73	26 38 42.88
13	9	. .	15.6	27.5	39.2	. .	4.2	. .	. .	. .	27 39.68	61.34	" 7 39.536	10 1.47	10.87	28 41.02	26 7 2.34
14	9	58.5	. .	23.2	35.0	47.0	59.5	11.3	. .	. .	36 35.07	61.36	" 6 37.460	17 4.21	9.40	37 36.43	26 14 3.61
15	7.8	. .	35.0	47.2	59.2	11.1	23.7	36.5	. .	. .	41 59.37	61.37	V. 7 44.791	6 59.98	8.48	43 0.74	26 3 58.46
16	9	. .	. .	. .	. .	. .	. .	12.2	31.0	43.2	42 35.69	61.42	VII. 2 46.341	41 8.37	8.38	43 37.11	26 38 6.75
17	7.8	58.6	10.8	23.2	35.2	47.2	59.7	. .	. .	. .	15 45 35.28	61.39	IV. 5 45.890	20 55.43	7.86	15 46 36.67	26 17 53.29
		Zone XXXII. June 24. H. $D. = -28° 26' 10''.0$. $n' = -40''.00$. $n'' = -3''.16$.															
1	7	23.7	36.5	48.2	1.2	13.6	26.2	38.4	. .	. .	17 30 1.15	61.78	IV. 5 41.810	23 13 36	37.77	17 31 2.93	28 50 1.13
2	9	. .	34.9	46.0	58.2	. .	. .	36.0	. .	. .	31 58.55	61.77	" 6 44.185	13 8.76	37.36	33 0.32	28 39 56.12
3	8	27.0	39.8	52.2	5.0	17.2	30.0	42.5	. .	. .	36 4.88	61.84	" 1 36.210	52 47.77	36.52	37 6.72	29 19 34.29
4	9	2.2	15.0	27.3	39.2	52.4	5.0	17.5	. .	. .	37 39.84	61.78	" 6 40.380	15 20.23	36.19	38 41.62	28 42 6.42
5	8.9	. .	. .	. .	53.0	5.4	18.0	30.8	. .	. .	38 52.97	61.84	" 1 43.276	48 43.62	35.94	39 54.81	29 15 29.56
6	9	. .	. .	. .	6.6	19.0	31.5	. .	. .	. .	40 6.49	61.84	" 2 36.370	46 50.60	35.69	41 8.33	29 13 36.29
7	9	. .	. .	8.5	21.2	33.0	. .	. .	. .	. .	41 20.98	61.77	" 7 43.498	7 41.43	35.43	42 22.75	28 34 26.86
8	9	30.0	42.0	54.0	7.5	. .	33.0	. .	. .	. .	43 7.33	61.80	I. 5 44.098	21 53.98	35.06	44 9.13	28 48 39.04
9	9	31.5	. .	55.2	9.0	. .	34.2	. .	. .	. .	43 9.02	61.81	IV. 3 47.850	31 28.52	35.05	44 10.83	28 58 13.57
10	8.9	. .	. .	. .	. .	. .	. .	. .	12.2	25.0	16.23	61.78	" 6 46.050	12 4.34	. . . .	18.01	. . . . . .
11	9	41.2	54.0	. .	18.5	. .	. .	. .	. .	. .	46 18.70	61.78	II. 7 39.328	10 5.37	34.40	47 20.48	28 36 49.77
12	6.7	29.0	41.2	. .	6.2	18.6	31.2	43.8	. .	. .	48 6.27	61.80	IV. 6 36.752	17 25.54	34.02	49 8.07	28 44 9.56
13	9	. .	. .	. .	. .	. .	. .	2.0	20.5	33.2	48 24.33	61.81	VII. 5 37.031	25 58.14	33.96	49 26.14	28 52 42.10
14	9	59.2	12.0	24.8	37.5	49.6	2.2	15.0	. .	. .	50 37.25	61.86	IV. 1 36.131	52 50.49	33.50	51 39.11	29 19 33.99
15	9	37.0	49.7	1.8	14.2	27.0	39.2	52.0	. .	. .	53 14.45	61.80	" 6 37.290	17 6.98	32.95	54 16.25	28 43 49.93
16	8	. .	49.8	2.6	15.0	27.5	30.2	. .	. .	. .	55 15.07	61.86	" 1 41.105	49 58.62	32.53	56 16.93	29 16 41.15
17	9	. .	. .	1.5	14.0	. .	39.2	52.0	. .	. .	56 14.13	61.84	" 3 40.282	35 48.04	32.32	57 15.97	29 2 30.26
18	9	44.0	. .	. .	21.5	. .	. .	. .	17.5	30.2	56 21.40	61.84	VI. 3 36.211	38 10.56	32.30	57 23.24	29 4 52.86
19	9	. .	54.0	7.0	19.2	31.5	44.2	57.0	. .	. .	58 19.24	61.81	" 6 33.250	19 26.45	31.88	59 21.05	28 46 8.33
20	9	7.0	18.2	30.8	43.1	55.7	8.2	21.0	. .	. .	59 43.47	61.86	" 2 35.530	47 19.46	31.59	18 0 45.33	29 14 1.05
21	7.8	47.0	59.6	12.1	24.4	37.0	49.2	2.0	. .	. .	18 1 24.50	61.83	" 4 42.020	28 53.27	31.24	2 26.33	28 55 34.51
22	9	36.0	49.0	. .	13.5	. .	. .	. .	. .	. .	3 13.71	61.82	II. 5 38.922	24 53.05	30.85	18 4 15.53	28 51 33.90

CORRECTIONS.

	COR. TO CLOCK.	HOURLY COR.	m.	n.	c.	ZENITH POINT.	COINC.
	s.	s.	s.	s.	s.		r.
June 24, at 13h…	+50.453	+0.002	+0.198	+0.396	+0.247	0° 0′ 0″.12	40.093

INSTRUMENT READINGS.

	h.	CIRCLE. A.	B.	C.	D.	Mean.	BAR.	THERMOM. At.	Ex.
Zone XXXI.—June 24…	14.9	294° 41′ 57″.9	58″.7	64″.5	65″.5	61″.65	I. 30.138	70°.3	67°.9
	15.3	. . . . . .	. .	. .	. .	. . .	30.134	70.0	67.0
	15.8	56.9	58.1	65.0	64.6	61.15	30.128	69.5	65.6

Number.	Magnitude.	SECONDS OF TRANSITS. I.	II.	III.	IV.	V.	VI.	VII.	10.	11.	T.	a.	MICROMETER.	D.	d.	Mean Right Ascension, 1850.0.	Mean South Declination, 1850.0.
											Zone XXXII. June 24. H. $D. = -28° 26' 10''.0$. $n'. = -40''.00$. $n''. = -3''.16$. (Continued.)						
											h. m. s.	s.	r.	′ ″	″	h. m. s.	° ′ ″
23	9	. .	35.0	47.5	0.1	12.2	25.2	37.5	. .	. .	18 6 0.00	+61.83	II. 5 37.410	—25 45.31	—30.69	18 7 1.83	28 52 26.00
24	9	. .	. .	. .	. .	54.0	6.4	19.0	. .	. .	4 41.55	61.80	VI. 7 35.360	12 22.47	30.55	5 43.35	28 39 3.02
25	9	. .	. .	. .	. .	59.2	12.0	24.2	. .	. .	5 46.75	61.84	V. 4 37.116	31 42.78	30.32	6 48.59	28 58 23.10
26	7	. .	. .	. .	52.0	4.0	16.8	29.2	. .	. .	6 51.74	61.83	IV. 5 40.690	23 52.05	30.08	7 53.57	28 50 32.13
27	9	12.5	25.5	36.5	50.5	. .	15.2	. .	. .	. .	8 50.10	61.85	" 3 39.270	36 24.98	29.67	9 51.95	29 3 4.65
28	8.9	. .	26.2	38.5	51.3	3.3	16.6	29.0	. .	. .	9 51.24	61.86	" 3 31.817	40 42.45	29.46	10 53.10	29 7 21.91
29	9	. .	. .	. .	. .	. .	51.2	3.2	. .	. .	10 25.91	61.82	VI. 6 33.445	19 19.72	29.33	11 27.73	28 45 59.05
30	9	. .	12.8	25.2	37.4	50.2	23.0	15.2	. .	. .	13 37.72	61.86	IV. 2 43.250	42 52.89	28.65	14 39.58	29 9 31.54
31	9	. .	. .	. .	. .	8.2	. .	33.2	. .	. .	17 55.73	61.84	V. 5 38.250	25 16.35	27.73	18 57.57	28 51 54.08
32	8.9	21.3	33.4	46.1	58.6	. .	23.2	36.0	. .	. .	19 58.84	61.84	IV. 5 36.835	26 5.24	27.29	21 0.68	28 52 42.53
33	9	. .	. .	9.0	21.0	. .	. .	. .	. .	. .	21 21.28	61.81	" 7 39.750	9 50.87	27.01	22 23.09	28 36 27.88
34	8	. .	. .	. .	. .	53.0	5.0	17.5	. .	. .	23 40.06	61.88	" 1 39.695	50 47.31	26.51	24 41.94	29 17 23.82
35	8	55.0	7.8	20.0	32.2	44.4	57.3	10.0	. .	. .	26 32.45	61.82	" 7 37.992	10 51.62	25.90	27 34.27	28 37 27.52
36	9	. .	. .	. .	44.0	56.0	8.8	21.0	. .	. .	28 43.75	61.82	IV. 7 36.480	11 43.89	25.43	29 45.57	28 38 19.32 z.
37	9	8.8	21.2	34.0	46.2	59.0	11.3	24.0	. .	. .	30 46.39	61.85	" 4 38.528	30 53.97	25.00	31 48.24	28 58 28.97
38	9	12.0	25.0	37.2	49.2	2.0	14.4	27.0	. .	. .	32 49.59	61.81	" 7 41.650	8 45.23	24.56	33 51.40	28 35 19.79
39	9	. .	. .	43.5	. .	. .	20.0	. .	. .	. .	33 56.50	61.87	V. 3 36.210	38 10.65	24.32	34 58.37	29 4 44.97
40	9	. .	. .	. .	4.5	17.0	. .	. .	. .	. .	35 4.53	61.85	IV. 4 42.008	28 53.78	24.08	36 6.38	28 55 27.86
41	9	. .	. .	. .	. .	. .	31.0	43.2	. .	. .	46 5.70	61.87	VII. 2 48.078	40 6.70	21.72	47 7.57	29 6 38.42
42	9	. .	8.0	21.0	34.1	. .	. .	11.5	. .	. .	49 33.65	61.85	IV. 4 44.400	27 31.17	20.98	50 35.50	28 54 2.15 z.
43	9	25.2	37.5	50.2	2.7	. .	28.0	. .	. .	. .	52 2.75	61.85	" 5 39.740	24 24.89	20.46	53 4.60	28 50 55.35
44	8	38.1	51.0	3.5	16.2	28.6	41.2	53.6	. .	. .	55 16.09	61.89	" 1 38.320	51 34.81	19.77	56 17.98	29 18 4.58 z.
45	7	24.5	37.2	49.5	2.4	14.7	27.0	39.5	. .	. .	57 2.14	61.85	" 5 38.310	25 14.34	19.40	58 3.99	28 51 43.74 z.
46	9	43.5	56.0	8.4	21.0	33.0	46.0	58.5	. .	. .	19 6 20.94	61.85	" 4 41.770	29 2.00	17.44	19 7 22.79	28 55 29.44 z.
47	9	. .	33.5	46.0	58.6	10.5	23.0	. .	. .	. .	8 58.37	61.89	" 1 39.505	50 53.81	16.88	10 0.26	29 17 20.69
48	9	50.5	3.0	15.8	28.2	40.8	53.5	. .	. .	. .	12 28.32	61.89	" 1 33.778	54 11.64	16.16	13 30.21	29 20 37.80 z.
49	9	49.0	. .	14.0	26.5	39.0	51.0	. .	. .	. .	18 26.48	61.89	" 1 41.430	49 47.37	14.91	19 28.37	29 16 12.28 z.
*50	9	0.8	13.5	. .	. .	. .	4.0	. .	. .	. .	19 25 38.66	61.86	II. 3 43.020	34 15.31	13.43	19 26 40.52	29 0 38.74
											Zone XXXIII. July 1. H. $D. = -25° 56' 30''.0$. $n'. = -25''.00$. $n''. = -3''.70$.						
1	8.9	. .	11.2	23.2	35.2	47.3	. .	12.0	. .	. .	15 28 35.35	66.51	IV. 5 41.030	23 41.01	23.29	15 29 41.86	26 20 34.30 z.
2	9	. .	. .	. .	. .	27.5	40.0	52.0	. .	. .	29 15.32	66.53	V. 2 41.650	43 48.38	23.17	30 21.85	26 40 41.55
3	9	. .	32.2	. .	. .	9.0	21.0	33.1	. .	. .	32 56.60	66.51	IV. 5 46.530	20 31.02	22.48	34 3.11	26 17 23.50
4	8	53.1	5.5	17.6	30.0	. .	. .	. .	. .	. .	36 29.91	66.52	III. 6 36.130	17 47.82	21.82	37 36.43	26 14 39.64
5	7.8	. .	. .	56.5	9.3	21.5	33.5	. .	. .	. .	37 9.07	66.55	IV. 3 32.722	40 11.50	21.69	38 15.62	26 37 3.19 z.
6	9	. .	. .	. .	38.0	49.5	2.0	14.0	. .	. .	37 37.50	66.54	VI. 4 33.922	33 33.52	21.61	38 44.04	26 30 25.13
7	9	. .	. .	. .	. .	. .	57.5	9.0	28.0	40.5	38 32.76	66.56	" 2 36.600	46 42.72	21.43	39 39.32	26 43 34.15
8	9	14.5	26.8	39.0	51.0	3.2	15.7	. .	. .	. .	40 51.18	66.53	IV. 5 42.515	22 49.69	21.00	41 57.71	26 19 40.69
9	9	45.0	57.8	. .	. .	33.0	45.8	. .	. .	. .	42 21.59	66.56	" 2 44.892	41 56.44	20.70	43 28.15	26 38 47.14 z.
10	9	54.4	. .	. .	30.5	42.5	. .	. .	. .	. .	15 42 30.72	66.56	" 2 46.020	41 17.49	20.68	15 43 37.28	26 38 8.17 z.

INSTRUMENT READINGS.

Zone	h.	CIRCLE. A.	B.	C.	D.	Mean.	BAR.	THERMOM. At.	Ex.
XXXII.—June 24....	17.4	292° 12′ 2″.2	2″.4	10″.3	10″.0	6″.22	I. 30.104	68°.6	65°.5
	18.2	. . . . .	. .	. .	. .	. . .	30.100	68.0	65.0
	19.0	292 11 57.1	58.5	66.2	64.3	61 52	30.100	67.5	64.5
	19.5	. . . . .	. .	. .	. .	. . .	30.086	67.0	63.7

Zone XXXIII. July 1. H. $D.=-25° 56' 30''.0.$ $n'.=-25''.00.$ $n''.=-3''.70.$ (Continued.)

Number.	Magnitude.	SECONDS OF TRANSITS. I.	II.	III.	IV.	V.	VI.	VII.	10.	11.	T.	a.	MICROMETER.	D.	d.	Mean Right Ascension, 1850.0.	Mean South Declination, 1850.0.
											h. m. s.	s.	r.	′ ″	″	h. m. s.	° ′ ″
11	8.9	. .	56.0	8.0	20.4	32.8	45.0	. .	. .	. .	15 44 20.47	+66.57	IV. 2 45.132	—41 48.16	—20.32	15 45 27.04	26 38 38.48
12	7.8	53.1	6.0	17.5	30.0	. .	54.5	. .	. .	. .	45 30.02	66.54	III. 5 45.550	21 4.82	20.09	46 36.56	26 17 54.91 z.
13	9	. .	. .	. .	48.0	. .	12.2	24.7	. .	. .	45 47.89	66.54	IV. 5 42.708	34 12.71	20.04	46 54.43	26 31 2.75
14	9	. .	. .	. .	36.0	. .	0.2	12.0	. .	. .	46 35.64	66.54	" 5 40.782	23 49.56	19.88	47 42.18	26 20 39.44
15	8.9	23.2	35.4	47.5	. .	. .	. .	. .	. .	. .	48 59.82	66.54	" 6 46.040	12 5.65	19.41	50 6.36	26 8 55.06
16	8	. .	. .	1.3	13.5	26.0	38.2	50.5	. .	. .	49 13.67	66.58	" 3 36.280	38 8.69	19.36	50 20.25	26 34 58.05
17	9	13.4	26.0	38.2	50.5	2.8	14.8	. .	. .	. .	50 50.48	66.59	II. 2 32.530	49 3.30	19.06	51 57.07	26 45 52.36
18	9	20.5	. .	45.0	57.0	. .	21.5	34.0	. .	. .	51 57.20	66.55	I. 6 40.720	15 9.00	18.83	52 3.75	26 11 57.83
19	8	25.8	38.2	. .	2.5	14.6	27.0	39.0	. .	. .	53 2.50	66.55	IV. 5 46.592	20 28.88	18.61	54 9.05	26 17 17.49 z.
20	8.9	9.2	22.0	34.2	46.5	. .	. .	. .	. .	. .	54 46.39	66.58	" 3 41.540	35 7.01	18.26	55 53.97	26 31 55.27
21	9	. .	. .	. .	54.0	. .	18.0	30.0	. .	. .	54 53.53	66.59	" 3 33.702	39 37.71	18.23	56 0.12	26 36 25.94
22	8.9	. .	. .	. .	. .	. .	38.8	51.0	. .	. .	55 14.22	66.59	" 3 40.270	35 50.86	18.16	56 20.81	26 32 39.02 z.
23	9	. .	32.1	44.4	56.8	. .	21.2	33.3	. .	4.4	56 56.69	66.60	" 2 40.205	44 38.36	17.82	58 3.29	26 41 26.18 z.
24	7	23.2	35.3	48.0	. .	12.1	24.8	. .	. .	. .	16 0 0.07	66.60	" 3 43.972	33 43.00	17.20	16 1 6.67	26 30 30.20
25	7.8	39.5	52.0	. .	17.0	. .	. .	53.5	. .	. .	1 16.69	66.62	I. 1 43.590	48 32.64	16.94	2 23.31	26 45 19.58
26	9	. .	55.0	. .	19.2	. .	. .	56.0	. .	. .	1 19.31	66.61	IV. 2 40.820	44 17.08	16.92	2 25.92	26 41 4.00
27	7.8	24.2	37.0	49.2	1.5	14.0	26.2	38.2	. .	. .	5 1.53	66.63	" 1 36.605	52 34.20	16.14	6 8.16	26 49 20.34 z.
28	8	33.8	46.0	58.5	. .	. .	. .	. .	. .	. .	14 10.78	66.65	I. 1 39.180	51 4.94	14.19	15 17.43	26 47 49.13 z.
29	9	45.5	58.0	. .	22.5	. .	47.0	59.0	. .	. .	14 22.39	66.62	VII. 4 39.220	30 30.31	14.17	15 29.01	26 27 14.48 z.
30	9	. .	. .	20.5	33.0	45.0	. .	9.6	. .	. .	15 32.91	66.60	IV. 6 38.442	16 28.03	13.90	16 39.51	26 13 11.93 z.
31	9	30.0	42.5	. .	. .	19.0	. .	. .	. .	. .	18 6.82	66.59	" 7 36.960	11 28.25	13.35	19 13.41	26 8 11.60
32	1	29.2	42.0	54.2	6.4	18.2	30.8	43.0	. .	. .	19 6.30	66.60	" 7 41.290	8 58.75	13.13	20 12.90	26 5 41.88 B.
33	8	27.5	40.0	52.0	4.2	16.1	28.8	40.6	. .	. .	21 4.21	66.61	" 6 39.788	15 41.53	12.71	22 10.82	26 12 24.24
34	8.9	47.0	59.3	11.8	24.0	36.2	48.8	. .	. .	. .	24 24.05	66.67	" 1 39.640	50 49.37	11.97	25 30.72	26 47 31.34 z.
35	9	. .	. .	. .	56.0	8.5	25.0	32.8	. .	. .	24 56.17	66.62	V. 6 44.496	12 58.95	11.85	26 2.79	26 9 40.80 z.
36	9	37.8	50.0	2.2	14.5	26.4	38.6	51.2	. .	. .	28 14.43	66.66	IV. 2 40.731	44 20.14	11.12	29 21.09	26 41 1.26 z.
37	9	15.0	28.0	39.7	52.0	3.8	16.0	28.4	. .	. .	29 51.88	66.63	" 6 45.390	12 28.11	10.75	30 58.51	26 9 8.86 z.
38	9	. .	49.0	1.5	. .	26.0	. .	50.5	. .	. .	32 13.75	66.69	IV. 1 37.760	51 54.31	10.22	33 20.44	26 48 34.53
39	9	50.0	3.0	. .	27.2	39.0	52.0	4.0	. .	. .	32 27.20	66.69	" 1 37.640	51 58.45	10.18	33 33.89	26 48 38.63
40	7.8	52.8	. .	17.5	30.0	42.0	54.0	6.3	. .	. .	33 29.72	66.66	" 3 42.946	34 18.43	9.94	34 36.38	26 30 58.37 z.
41	8	50.2	2.5	15.0	27.0	39.0	51.4	3.8	. .	. .	35 27.01	66.65	" 5 38.140	25 20.82	9.50	36 33.66	26 22 0.32 z.
42	9	33.0	45.8	58.0	10.0	22.2	34.5	46.2	. .	. .	37 10.00	66.68	" 2 47.247	40 35.12	9.11	38 16.68	26 37 14.23 z.
43	8	11.2	23.8	36.0	48.2	10.5	. .	35.0	. .	. .	39 48.23	66.67	II. 4 36.880	31 51.34	8.51	40 54.90	26 28 29.85
44	9	52.5	5.2	17.0	29.2	. .	. .	. .	. .	. .	40 29.36	66.66	IV. 5 38.905	24 54.39	8.36	41 36.02	26 21 32.75
45	9	. .	3.5	15.8	28.0	40.0	. .	. .	. .	. .	41 28.00	66.69	II. 3 32.850	40 6.98	8.13	42 34.69	26 36 45.11
46	9	. .	. .	. .	49.5	2.0	14.2	26.5	. .	. .	41 49.66	66.69	IV. 2 43.140	42 56.98	8.05	42 56.35	26 39 35.03 z.
47	9	. .	. .	. .	. .	. .	. .	9.5	27.8	40.0	42 32.69	66.67	VII. 4 34.920	32 58.80	7.88	43 39.36	26 29 36.68 z.
48	9	. .	. .	16.0	28.2	40.2	53.0	. .	. .	. .	44 28.25	66.68	IV. 3 44.230	33 34.09	7.43	45 34.93	26 30 11.52
49	9	57.0	. .	21.2	33.5	46.0	57.8	10.2	. .	. .	46 33.58	66.70	" 2 37.970	45 55.52	6.96	47 40.28	26 42 32.48
50	9	. .	. .	. .	6.0	. .	. .	. .	. .	. .	16 48 5.62	66.65	" 7 38.622	10 30.84	6.60	16 49 12.27	26 7 7.44 z.

CORRECTIONS.

	COR. TO CLOCK.	HOURLY COR.	m.	n.	c.	ZENITH POINT.	COINC.
	s.	s.	s.	s.	s.	° ′ ″	r.
July 1, at 13h....	+55.312	+0.034	+0.213	+0.298	+0.330	0 0 0.65	40.101

INSTRUMENT READINGS.

		CIRCLE. A.	B.	C.	D.	Mean.	BAR.	THERMOM. At.	Ex.
	h.	° ′ ″	″	″	″	″	I.	°	°
Zone XXXIII.—July 1,	15.4	294 42 2.2	10.2	14.0	8.2	8.65	29.846	77.0	74.9
	16.5	. . . .	. .	. .	. .	. .	. .	. .	74.5
	16.8	2.5	10.4	14.9	9.3	9.27	29.846	76.0	73.4

Zone XXXIV. July 7. H. $D. = -41° 51' 10''.0.$ $n'. = -15''.00.$ $n''. = -19''.91.$

Number	Magnitude.	SECONDS OF TRANSITS. I.	II.	III.	IV.	V.	VI.	VII.	10.	11.	T.	a.	MICROMETER.	D.	d.	Mean Right Ascension, 1850.0.	Mean South Declination, 1850.0.
											h. m. s.	s.	r.			h. m. s.	
1	9	59.2	14.2	28.5	43.4	58.2	13.1	28.0	. .	. .	15 40 43.53	+72.16	IV. 6 38.250	—16' 44''.34	—11''.44	15 41 55.69	42° 8' 5''.78
2	8.9	5.2	20.0	35.0	49.3	4.0	19.0	. .	. .	. .	44 49.52	72.18	II. 6 35.962	18 3.78	10.72	46 1.70	42 9 24.50
3	9	8.5	23.8	37.8	53.0	7.2	22.2	37.0	. .	. .	44 52.83	72.18	V. 7 34.350	13 6.38	10.71	46 5.01	42 4 27.09
4	9	31.2	46.0	0.8	16.0	30.2	45.2	. .	. .	. .	46 15.67	72.19	IV. 6 33.970	19 13.23	10.46	47 27.86	42 10 33.69
5	8.9	54.8	9.2	24.5	39.2	. .	9.2	. .	. .	. .	50 39.25	72.22	III. 5 39.750	24 38.51	9.68	51 51.47	42 15 58.19 M.
6	9	. .	46.0	. .	15.5	30.0	44.5	59.8	. .	. .	51 15.34	72.21	IV. 6 43.910	13 27.20	9.57	52 27.55	42 4 46.77
7	7.8	2.2	17.1	32.0	46.4	2.0	16.0	31.3	. .	. .	16 3 46.77	72.32	" 3 34.310	39 37.65	7.22	16 4 59.09	42 30 54.87 B.
8	9	. .	. .	. .	. .	. .	59.5	14.6	36.2	. .	4 29.64	72.34	VI. 1 36.180	53 16.75	7.08	5 41.98	42 44 33.83
†9	7	55.2	10.0	24.8	39.4	54.6	9.5	24.5	. .	. .	16 7 39.75	72.31	IV. 5 36.070	26 46.81	6.48	16 8 52.06	42 18 3.29

Zone XXXV. July 7. H. $D. = -25° 55' 40''.0.$ $n'. = -20''.00.$ $n''. = -5''.65.$

Number	Magnitude.	I.	II.	III.	IV.	V.	VI.	VII.	10.	11.	T.	a.	MICROMETER.	D.	d.	Mean Right Ascension, 1850.0.	Mean South Declination, 1850.0.
1	9	. .	. .	. .	45.0	57.0	9.2	. .	. .	. .	19 59 44.84	71.21	IV. 5 43.200	22 28.00	19.83	20 0 56.05	26 18 27.83 Z.
2	9	3.0	15.2	27.2	39.2	52.0	4.0	16.1	. .	. .	20 2 39.57	71.24	" 2 44.688	42 5.42	19.19	3 50.81	26 38 4.61
3	8.9	48.8	2.1	14.2	26.2	38.2	51.0	3.3	. .	. .	10 26.30	71.22	" 3 37.287	37 35.84	17.47	11 37.52	26 33 33.31
4	7.8	47.6	. .	11.9	24.0	36.3	48.8	0.9	. .	. .	14 24.22	71.19	" 5 42.621	22 48.02	16.59	15 35.41	26 18 44.61 Z.
5	8	13.3	25.5	38.0	50.0	2.0	14.2	27.0	. .	. .	17 50.04	71.23	" 7 39.670	9 56.52	15.84	19 1.27	26 5 52.36 Z.
6	10	45.3	. .	. .	. .	34.2	. .	. .	. .	. .	23 22.13	71.17	" 5 40.380	24 5.41	14.64	24 33.30	26 20 0.05
7	9	5.8	18.2	30.8	42.5	. .	7.0	19.3	. .	. .	25 42.65	71.15	" 6 44.180	13 11.76	14.14	26 53.80	26 9 5.90
8	7	58.7	51.0	3.2	15.0	27.8	40.0	52.3	. .	. .	31 15.46	71.18	" 3 40.455	35 46.44	12.96	32 26.64	26 31 39.40 Z.
9	8.9	7.1	19.6	31.4	44.0	56.0	8.1	20.5	. .	. .	33 43.84	71.15	" 5 37.366	25 49.51	12.43	34 54.99	26 21 41.98
10	9	35.3	48.0	. .	12.2	. .	37.0	49.0	. .	. .	36 12.33	71.19	" 2 35.672	47 15.82	11.91	37 23.52	26 43 7.73
11	6.7	34.5	47.2	59.3	11.4	. .	36.0	48.4	. .	. .	39 11.51	71.14	" 5 40.486	24 1.76	11.28	40 22.65	26 19 53.04 Z.
12	8.9	30.0	42.2	54.3	7.0	18.8	31.1	43.2	. .	. .	41 6.69	71.12	" 6 45.400	12 29.65	10.89	42 17.81	26 8 20.54 Z.
13	8	43.1	56.0	8.0	19.2	41.3	. .	. .	. .	. .	44 19.77	71.11	" 6 45.390	12 29.99	10.23	45 30.88	26 8 20.22
14	9	38.0	. .	3.5	15.8	. .	. .	52.4	. .	. .	45 15.56	71.16	" 2 39.780	44 54.95	10.04	46 26.72	26 40 44.99 Z.
15	9	. .	16.2	28.6	40.0	. .	5.3	17.5	. .	. .	48 40.62	71.15	" 3 34.595	39 8.77	9.35	49 51.77	26 34 58.12
16	8.9	. .	29.4	41.4	54.0	5.8	18.0	30.2	. .	. .	56 53.71	71.09	" 6 43.155	13 47.16	7.72	58 4.80	26 9 34.88
17	8.9	19.2	32.0	44.0	56.2	8.2	20.0	33.0	. .	. .	20 59 56.14	71.14	" 1 40.998	50 4.41	7.12	21 1 7.28	26 45 51.53 Z.

Zone XXXVI. July 9. H. $D. = -42° 21' 10''.0.$ $n'. = -26''.85.$ $n''. = -16''.00.$

Number	Magnitude.	I.	II.	III.	IV.	V.	VI.	VII.	10.	11.	T.	a.	MICROMETER.	D.	d.	Mean Right Ascension, 1850.0.	Mean South Declination, 1850.0.
1	8	2.0	17.2	32.0	47.0	1.8	. .	32.0	. .	. .	16 3 47.01	72.03	IV. 7 40.560	9 25.01	25.86	16 4 59.04	42 31 0.87 B.
2	9	45.0	0.5	15.0	30.4	45.0	. .	14.7	. .	. .	4 30.13	72.05	" 5 42.371	23 3.20	25.71	5 42.18	42 44 38.91
3	9	47.5	3.0	17.2	32.5	47.0	2.2	. .	. .	. .	10 32.42	72.09	" 4 42.595	28 45.40	24.45	11 44.51	42 50 19.85
4	9	10.0	. .	. .	55.0	. .	. .	39.3	. .	. .	19 54.81	72.14	" 4 37.475	31 44.21	22.45	21 6.95	42 53 16.66
5	9	22.0	36.4	52.2	7.2	. .	. .	. .	. .	. .	24 6.95	72.15	" 4 36.555	32 15.94	21.53	25 19.10	42 53 47.47 M.
6	7.8	. .	. .	. .	. .	52.5	7.8	22.8	. .	. .	16 24 38.01	72.12	V. 7 37.452	11 13.55	21.41	16 25 50.13	42 32 44.96 B.

CORRECTIONS.

	COR. TO CLOCK.	HOURLY COR.	m.	n.	c.	ZENITH POINT.	COINC.
	s.	s.	s.	s.	s.		r.
July 7, at 12h.....	+59.985	—0.022	+0.213	+0.298	+0.330	0° 0' 1''.70	40.110

† Moon too bright for observation.

INSTRUMENT READINGS.

Zone	h.	CIRCLE. A.	B.	C.	D.	Mean.	BAR.	THERMOM. At.	Ex.
							I.		
XXXIV.—July 7,	15.6.	278° 51' 1''.8	0''.1	3''.3	57''.0	0''.55	29.956	79°.0	73°.7
	16.2.	. . . .	. .	. .	. .	. .	29.962	77.6	72.7
	19.8.	. . . .	. .	. .	. .	. .	29.960	74.0	68.8
XXXV.—July 7,	20.0.	294 41 58.9	59.0	60.3	55.7	58.48	. .	. .	. .
	21.0.	. . . .	. .	. .	. .	. .	29.962	72.3	68.3

Zone XXXVI. July 9. II. $D. = -42^\circ\ 21'\ 10''.0.$ $n' = -26''.85.$ $n'' = -16''.00.$ (Continued.)

Number.	Magnitude.	Seconds of Transits. I.	II.	III.	IV.	V.	VI.	VII.	10.	11.	T.	a.	Micrometer.	D.	d.	Mean Right Ascension, 1850.0.	Mean South Declination, 1850.0.
											h. m. s.	s.	r.	′ ″	″	h. m. s.	° ′ ″
7	8	52.7	8.0	22.8	38.0	53.0	8.0	23.2	. .	. .	16 26 38.15	+ 72.19	IV. 2 42.000	−43 56.21	−20.98	16 27 50.34	43 5 27.19 B.
8	9	21.3	36.0	51.0	6.0	21.0	36.0	51.0	. .	. .	38 6.08	72.20	" 4 42.792	28 38.61	18.43	39 18.28	42 50 7.04
9	8.9	57.2	12.3	26.5	42.0	57.0	12.0	. .	. .	. .	40 42.04	72.20	" 5 43.516	22 22.99	17.85	41 54.21	42 43 50.84
10	7.8	7.8	22.0	36.8	52.0	6.8	22.0	37.0	. .	. .	41 52.09	72.21	" 5 37.002	26 10.18	17.58	43 4.30	42 47 37.76 B.
11	8.9	57.5	13.0	27.8	43.0	57.8	13.0	27.8	. .	. .	43 42.90	72.24	" 2 44.390	42 33.01	17.17	44 55.14	43 4 0.18
12	9	17.5	32.0	46.8	2.0	. .	. .	47.2	. .	. .	48 2.14	72.25	" 3 37.510	37 42.75	16.20	49 14.39	42 59 8.95
13	9	49.3	4.4	19.5	34.2	49.2	4.6	19.3	. .	. .	52 34.42	72.27	" 2 42.333	43 44.73	15.16	53 46.69	43 5 9.89
14	9	6.2	21.0	35.8	50.0	6.0	20.4	35.2	. .	. .	55 50.70	72.22	" 6 46.313	11 58.84	14.41	57 2.92	42 33 23.25
15	5.6	27.7	42.5	58.0	12.5	27.2	42.8	58.0	. .	. .	17 0 12.70	72.29	" 2 47.430	40 47.02	13.41	17 1 24.99	43 2 10.43 B.
16	9	. .	. .	56.0	. .	25.5	. .	. .	. .	. .	6 10.89	72.26	III. 5 43.690	22 16.96	12.18	7 23.15	42 43 39.14
17	9	. .	. .	36.0	. .	5.5	21.0	35.5	. .	. .	6 50.90	72.27	IV. 5 44.100	22 2.86	12.04	8 3.17	42 43 24.90
18	9	. .	. .	. .	. .	. .	. .	. .	. .	44.0	6 21.66	72.27	VII. 4 44.781	27 29.00	12.15	7 33.93	42 48 51.15
19	8.9	49.0	4.2	19.0	34.4	49.2	4.2	19.0	. .	. .	18 34.20	72.33	IV. 2 40.680	44 42.12	9.61	19 46.53	43 6 1.73
20	9	12.0	27.0	42.0	57.0	11.4	. .	. .	. .	. .	22 56.89	72.31	" 4 45.530	27 3.07	8.69	24 9.20	42 48 21.76
21	5	35.5	50.8	5.2	20.5	35.2	50.0	. .	. .	. .	25 20.40	72.32	" 4 36.180	32 29.25	8.19	26 32.72	42 53 47.44 B.
22	8.9	26.0	. .	55.5	11.2	25.8	41.0	55.5	. .	. .	26 10.92	72.31	" 5 38.150	25 30.23	8.02	27 23.23	42 46 48.25
23	9	. .	. .	. .	. .	55.0	10.0	25.0	. .	. .	26 40.25	72.29	" 6 37.806	16 55.01	7.91	27 52.54	42 38 12.92
24	9	. .	. .	. .	. .	. .	. .	. .	10.2	25.8	27 3.06	72.34	VI. 3 31.290	41 19.41	7.83	28 15.40	43 2 37.24
25	9	. .	10.2	25.0	. .	55.0	. .	. .	. .	. .	30 40.13	72.33	IV. 3 40.301	36 5.35	7.07	31 52.46	42 57 22.42
26	8	. .	. .	. .	44.5	59.3	13.8	28.7	. .	. .	32 44.23	72.30	V. 6 35.879	18 2.15	6.63	33 56.53	42 39 18.78 B.
27	9	55.8	. .	25.5	. .	55.2	. .	. .	. .	. .	40 40.61	72.33	IV. 4 40.362	30 3.51	4.95	41 52.94	42 51 18.46
28	9	. .	. .	. .	57.0	12.2	. .	41.5	. .	. .	42 56.91	72.36	V. 2 38.568	45 55.73	4.46	44 9.27	43 7 10.19
29	8.9	41.8	57.0	12.2	27.0	41.4	57.0	. .	. .	. .	50 26.93	72.34	IV. 4 36.364	32 22.90	2.87	51 39.27	42 53 35.77
30	8.9	11.0	26.0	40.2	56.0	10.2	25.0	40.2	. .	. .	56 55.55	72.32	" 6 34.165	19 2.00	1.47	58 7.87	42 40 13.47
31	9	1.5	16.5	. .	. .	1.3	. .	. .	. .	. .	59 46.57	72.36	II. 2 39.818	45 12.11	0.85	18 0 58.93	43 6 22.96
32	9	. .	. .	. .	. .	. .	. .	30.0	. .	8.2	17 59 45.69	72.32	IV. 6 34.694	18 43.40	0.85	0 58.01	42 39 54.25

Zone XXXVII. July 9. II. $D. = -27^\circ\ 26'\ 10''.0.$ $n' = -25''.00.$ $n'' = -3''.24.$

Number.	Magnitude.	I.	II.	III.	IV.	V.	VI.	VII.	10.	11.	T.	a.	Micrometer.	D.	d.	Mean Right Ascension, 1850.0.	Mean South Declination, 1850.0.
1	9	23.0	35.0	48.0	. .	13.0	. .	. .	. .	. .	18 5 0.40	+70.95	II. 2 47.152	−40 37.95	−23.40	18 6 11.35	28 7 11.35 z.
2	9	. .	. .	16.5	29.0	41.7	. .	. .	. .	. .	5 29.14	70.95	IV. 2 45.170	41 46.52	23.26	6 40.09	28 8 19.78 z.
3	8	. .	. .	8.0	20.5	33.0	45.5	. .	. .	. .	6 20.60	70.91	" 6 34.290	18 50.81	23.03	7 31.51	27 45 23.84
4	9	. .	. .	. .	58.0	10.2	22.2	35.0	. .	. .	6 57.74	70.93	" 4 43.296	28 9.39	22.86	8 8.67	27 54 42.25
5	9	. .	. .	. .	. .	49.0	1.0	13.5	. .	. .	7 36.35	70.93	VII. 4 38.990	30 37.79	22.69	8 47.28	27 57 10.48 z.
6	9	. .	42.3	54.0	7.0	. .	31.8	. .	. .	. .	9 6.85	70.89	IV. 7 44.650	7 1.89	22.28	10 17.74	27 33 34.17 z.
7	8.9	. .	52.5	5.0	17.0	29.5	. .	54.2	. .	. .	10 17.19	70.95	" 2 41.002	44 10.48	21.96	11 28.14	28 10 42.44
8	8.9	. .	. .	. .	42.0	54.5	7.0	19.2	. .	. .	11 42.02	70.96	" 1 43.235	48 44.94	21.58	12 52.98	28 15 16.52 z.
9	8.9	. .	. .	38.0	50.5	. .	15.2	. .	. .	. .	12 50.48	70.89	" 7 43.398	7 45.17	21.27	14 1.37	27 34 16.44
10	9	9.2	21.5	. .	46.2	59.0	. .	. .	. .	. .	18 46.50	70.95	II. 1 44.056	48 16.46	19.67	19 57.45	28 14 46.13
11	8.9	38.6	51.3	3.8	16.0	28.0	40.5	. .	. .	. .	18 20 15.96	70.93	IV. 3 39.361	36 20.87	19.25	18 21 26.89	28 2 50.12 z.

CORRECTIONS.

	Cor. to clock.	Hourly cor.	m.	n.	c.	Zenith point.	Coinc.
	s.	s.	s.	s.	s.	° ′ ″	r.
July 9, at 12h....	+59.630	−0.004	+0.213	+0.298	+0.330	0 0 1.68	40.106

INSTRUMENT READINGS.

Zone	h.	Circle. A.	B.	C.	D.	Mean.	Bar.	Thermom. At.	Ex.
		° ′ ″	″	″	″	″	I.	°	°
XXXVI.—July 9,	16.0..	278 21 2.0	0.0	4.0	1.0	1.75	30.002	81.0	77.5
	17.0..	4.4	2.5	5.9	2.0	3.70	30.010	79.5	74.8
	18.0..	4.8	2.2	5.9	2.2	3.77	30.012	78.5	74.5
XXXVII.—July 9,	18.0..	293 12 3.6	4.0	4.9	4.2	4.17	30.012	78.5	74.6
	19.0..	3.8	4.2	6.5	5.0	4.92	30.020	74.1	77.8

Zone XXXVII. July 9. H. $D. = -27^\circ\ 26'\ 10''.0.$ $n' = -25''.00.$ $n'' = -3''.24.$ (Continued.)

Number.	Magnitude.	I.	II.	III.	IV.	V.	VI.	VII.	10.	11.	T.	a.	MICROMETER.	D.	d.	Mean Right Ascension, 1850.0.	Mean South Declination, 1850.0
12	9	14.5	26.6	39.0	51.5	3.0	16.5	28.9	. .	. .	h. m. s. 18 22 51.48	s. +70.94	r. IV. 2 37.680	′ ″ −46 5.23	″ −18.55	h. m. s. 18 24 2.42	° ′ ″ 28 12 33.78
13	9	. .	. .	53.5	6.0	18.0	31.0	43.0	. .	. .	24 5.89	70.94	" 2 40.030	44 44.08	18.21	25 16.83	28 11 12.29
14	9	38.0	51.0	3.0	. .	. .	. .	. .	. .	. .	26 15.58	70.92	I. 3 43.320	34 3.76	17.63	27 26.50	28 0 31.39
15	9	. .	. .	10.0	22.0	34.0	. .	. .	. .	. .	26 22.07	70.90	IV. 5 39.860	24 20.88	17.60	27 32.97	27 50 48.48 z.
16	9	. .	. .	. .	. .	. .	27.0	39.8	59.0	. .	27 2.61	70.93	VI. 3 33.253	39 52.75	17.41	28 13.54	28 6 20.16
17	8.9	. .	. .	. .	. .	48.0	0.3	13.0	. .	. .	28 35.56	70.95	V. 1 37.700	51 56.12	16.99	29 46.51	28 18 23.11 z.
18	9	10.0	23.0	. .	47.5	. .	12.5	24.8	. .	. .	30 47.57	70.92	II. 3 34.650	39 4.45	16.39	31 58.49	28 5 30.84
19	9	. .	. .	. .	46.2	. .	11.0	. .	. .	. .	30 46.12	70.91	IV. 3 43.530	33 56.81	16.40	31 57.03	28 0 23.21
20	9	. .	. .	. .	. .	. .	. .	50.0	8.5	21.0	31 12.97	70.87	VII. 7 42.532	8 14.70	16.28	32 23.84	27 34 40.98
21	9	. .	. .	. .	. .	. .	43.8	56.2	. .	. .	32 18.99	70.88	VI. 5 46.140	20 43.85	15.98	33 29.87	27 47 9.83 z.
22	9	. .	. .	45.2	. .	10.2	. .	. .	. .	. .	33 57.82	70.93	IV. 2 39.950	44 46.84	15.52	35 8.75	28 11 12.36
23	6.7	51.2	4.0	16.4	28.5	41.0	54.0	5.3	. .	. .	35 28.67	70.87	" 7 34.880	12 39.38	15.11	36 39.54	27 39 4.49
24	9	. .	38.4	50.2	3.3	15.2	27.8	40.0	. .	. .	37 2.95	70.89	" 4 43.820	27 51.27	14.69	38 13.84	27 54 15.96
25	9	4.0	. .	28.2	41.2	. .	. .	18.2	. .	. .	38 41.06	70.89	" 4 45.519	26 52.63	14.25	39 51.95	27 53 16.88
*26	8	55.2	7.2	20.0	32.2	44.6	57.4	9.5	. .	. .	42 32.33	70.89	" 4 40.855	29 33.45	13.20	43 43.22	27 55 56.65
27	9	. .	. .	38.2	51.0	. .	16.0	28.2	. .	. .	43 50.93	70.87	" 5 42.770	22 40.34	12.85	45 1.80	27 49 3.19
28	8.9	. .	57.1	9.4	22.0	34.5	46.5	59.2	. .	. .	44 21.93	70.92	" 1 36.568	52 35.24	12.71	45 32.85	28 18 57.95
29	8.9	18.0	31.0	43.0	55.5	. .	20.4	. .	. .	. .	46 55.50	70.85	" 6 45.556	12 21.69	12.01	48 6.35	27 38 43.70 z.
30	9	. .	0.5	12.5	25.0	37.3	. .	. .	. .	. .	48 25.03	70.86	III. 5 39.910	24 19.11	11.62	49 35.89	27 50 40.73
31	9	. .	. .	. .	53.0	. .	17.4	. .	. .	. .	48 52.73	70.88	IV. 4 40.705	29 38.87	11.49	50 3.61	27 56 0.36
32	8.9	. .	. .	. .	. .	. .	. .	1.5	. .	. .	49 24.17	70.91	VII. 1 43.376	48 39.73	11.34	50 35.08	28 15 1.07 z.
33	9	. .	. .	. .	. .	. .	. .	45.5	4.2	17.0	50 8.50	70.87	IV. 5 39.778	24 23.70	11.14	51 19.37	27 50 44.84
34	9	35.5	48.2	0.8	13.0	25.2	. .	. .	. .	. .	53 13.01	70.87	" 4 41.100	29 25.25	10.31	54 23.88	27 55 45.56
35	4.5	46.0	58.2	11.0	23.5	35.5	48.0	0.2	. .	. .	56 23.23	70.86	" 4 45.848	26 41.22	9.45	57 34.09	27 53 0.67
36	9	31.0	43.5	56.0	. .	. .	. .	46.0	. .	. .	18 58 8.48	70.87	" 4 40.002	30 3.17	8.98	18 59 19.35	27 56 22.15

Zone XXXVIII. July 10. M. $D. = -39^\circ\ 49'\ 20''.0.$ $n' = -30''.00.$ $n'' = -14''.95.$

Number.	Magnitude.	I.	II.	III.	IV.	V.	VI.	VII.	10.	11.	T.	a.	MICROMETER.	D.	d.	Mean Right Ascension, 1850.0.	Mean South Declination, 1850.0
1	8.9	. .	38.0	52.0	. .	. .	. .	. .	. .	. .	16 52 6.83	71.98	2. 1 38.805	51 35.52	28.43	16 53 18.81	40 41 23.95
2	8.9	. .	29.3	44.0	58.3	. .	. .	. .	. .	. .	56 58.39	71.98	2. 1 43.26	49 0.92	27.77	58 10.37	40 38 48.69
3	8.9	. .	. .	. .	. .	. .	35.3	49.4	. .	. .	58 6.52	71.91	II. 7 37.05	11 30.56	27.62	59 18.43	40 1 18.18
4	8.9	. .	. .	. .	57.6	. .	. .	. .	. .	. .	17 8 57.56	71.98	I. 3 42.89	34 32.62	25.75	17 10 9.54	40 24 18.37
5	8.9	. .	. .	. .	44.0	58.1	12.9	. .	. .	. .	12 43.93	71.93	II. 7 41.80	8 45.68	25.05	13 55.86	39 58 30.73
6	8	. .	48.5	2.7	. .	32.0	46.0	. .	. .	. .	14 17.27	72.01	2. 2 36.08	47 16.80	24.77	15 29.28	40 37 1.57
7	8.9	0.5	15.1	29.2	43.6	. .	. .	. .	. .	. .	16 43.70	71.96	2. 5 43.60	22 20.28	24.31	17 55.66	40 12 4.59
8	9	. .	. .	. .	. .	. .	9.5	. .	. .	. .	17 40.73	71.96	III. 6 33.40	19 30.12	24.14	18 52.69	40 9 14.26
9	8	. .	. .	. .	. .	25.5	. .	. .	. .	. .	19 10.79	72.01	" 3 29.25	42 26.58	23.86	20 22.80	40 32 10.44
10	6.7	56.8	11.0	25.2	40.1	54.7	. .	. .	. .	. .	17 22 40.00	72.00	2. 3 41.29	35 27.90	23.21	17 23 52.00	40 25 11.11

CORRECTIONS.

	COR. TO CLOCK.	HOURLY COR.	m.	n.	c.	ZENITH POINT.	COINC.
July 10, at 17h...	s. +59.557	s. 0.000	s. +0.213	s. +0.298	s. +0.330	0° 0′ 1″.22	r. 40.105

INSTRUMENT READINGS.

	CIRCLE. A.	B.	C.	D.	Mean.	BAR.	THERMOM. At.	Ex.
Zone XXXVIII.—July 10, h. 16.8	280° 51′ 25″.1	22″.3	21″.5	17″.6	21″.62	I. 30.084	85°.0	82°.3
17.4	23.5	20.7	19.9	16.0	20.02	. .	. .	. .
18.1	21.0	18.0	17.3	13.4	17.42	. .	. .	.

Number.	Magnitude.	SECONDS OF TRANSITS. I.	II.	III.	IV.	V.	VI.	VII.	10.	11.	T.	a.	MICROMETER.	D.	d.	Mean Right Ascension, 1850.0.	Mean South Declination, 1850.0.
		Zone XXXVIII. July 10. M. $D. = -39° 49' 20''.0$. $n'. = -30''.00$. $n''. = -14''.95$. (Continued.)															
											h. m. s.	s.	r.	' ''	''	h. m. s.	° ' ''
11	7	. .	. .	. .	. .	30.0	44.5	59.1	. .	. .	17 15.84	+71.95	10. 7 43.30	— 7 53.22	—23.11	17 27.79	39 57 36.00
12	7	. .	9.7	23.7	38.0	. .	. .	. .	. .	. .	25 38.17	71.98	I. 5 41.67	23 27.69	22.66	26 50.15	40 13 10.35
13	7	. .	. .	. .	. .	. .	21.2	36.2	. .	. .	25 52.47	72.03	VII. 1 36.20	53 6.48	22.62	27 4.50	40 42 49.10
14	7.8	. .	. .	. .	. .	. .	54.0	9.0	. .	. .	30 25.70	71.96	I. 7 38.76	10 31.02	21.78	31 37.66	40 0 12.80
15	8	. .	. .	. .	. .	. .	. .	38.0	. .	. .	29 55.00	71.96	VII. 7 35.48	12 25.01	21.86	31 6.96	40 2 6.87
16	7	. .	. .	. .	. .	. .	. .	. .	37.2	51.8	30 32.43	72.00	" 4 35.22	33 0.69	21.75	31 44.43	40 22 42.44
17	8.9	. .	. .	. .	. .	. .	5.0	19.7	. .	. .	32 36.51	71.97	III. 7 35.50	12 24.56	21.36	33 48.48	40 2 5.92
18	8.9	. .	. .	. .	58.0	12.5	. .	. .	. .	. .	35 57.87	72.02	2. 2 46.54	41 13.45	20.73	37 9.89	40 30 54.18
19	7	. .	. .	. .	. .	. .	36.5	51.0	. .	. .	36 7.67	72.00	II. 4 40.74	29 49.05	20.70	37 19.67	40 19 29.75
20	2.3	. .	. .	. .	. .	8.0	22.3	36.7	. .	. .	36 53.57	71.97	IV. 6 42.75	14 5.49	20.55	38 5.54	40 3 46.04
21	5.6	. .	. .	15.6	30.0	44.0	58.7	13.0	. .	. .	38 29.89	71.97	I. 6 45.49	12 30.29	20.25	39 41.86	40 2 10.54 B.
22	6	. .	. .	. .	. .	2.0	16.5	31.2	. .	. .	39 47.49	72.05	V. 1 35.34	53 36.61	20.01	40 59.54	40 43 16.62
23	8.9	. .	27.5	. .	56.6	. .	25.0	39.5	. .	. .	42 56.31	71.99	I. 5 41.97	23 17.34	19.41	44 8.30	40 12 56.75
24	8.9	. .	. .	. .	4.6	19.0	. .	. .	. .	. .	45 4.45	72.00	2. 3 48.00	31 34.84	19.00	46 16.45	40 21 13.84
25	5.6	. .	. .	. .	. .	27.5	41.0	56.0	. .	. .	45 12.59	72.00	I. 4 45.85	26 51.55	18.98	46 24.59	40 16 30.53
26	9	. .	. .	. .	. .	. .	47.0	. .	. .	. .	48 18.07	72.02	IV. 3 39.76	36 21.55	18.39	49 30.09	40 25 59.94
27	8	. .	. .	. .	. .	. .	56.8	11.4	. .	. .	50 28.03	72.01	" 4 41.135	29 35.57	17.97	51 40.04	40 19 13.54
28	7	. .	23.8	38.1	53.0	7.1	21.3	36.0	. .	. .	52 52.62	72.04	I. 1 44.17	48 28.97	17.51	54 4.66	40 38 6.48
29	8.9	. .	. .	. .	1.0	15.0	30.0	44.0	. .	. .	55 0.98	71.96	I. 7 45.78	6 26.73	17.10	56 12.94	39 56 3.83
*30	8.9	. .	35.0	49.0	4.0	18.6	. .	. .	. .	. .	59 3.82	72.02	2. 3 37.75	37 30.69	16.32	18 0 15.84	40 27 7.01
31	8.9	. .	. .	. .	. .	15.0	29.8	44.0	. .	. .	18 0 0.72	71.99	IV. 5 39.92	24 28.77	16.14	1 12.71	40 14 4.91
32	8	. .	3.5	17.4	32.0	45.7	. .	. .	. .	. .	2 31.73	71.97	2. 7 40.785	9 20.38	15.66	3 43.70	39 58 56.04
33	8	55.7	10.5	24.8	39.0	53.4	8.0	22.8	. .	. .	4 39.17	72.03	I. 2 46.50	41 14.76	15.24	5 51.20	40 30 50.00
34	8.9	. .	40.7	. .	9.5	23.8	38.0	. .	. .	. .	7 9.29	72.02	2 3 33.581	39 55.41	14.77	8 21.31	40 29 30.18
35	8	. .	30.5	44.8	59.0	13.6	27.8	44.8	. .	. .	8 58.99	72.00	I. 4 40.290	30 4.66	14.41	10 10.99	40 19 39.07
36	6	. .	51.3	5.5	20.0	33.5	49.0	3.0	. .	. .	20 19.84	71.95	I. 7 40.91	9 16.44	12.24	21 31.79	39 58 48.68
37	8	. .	9.0	23.3	37.5	51.5	6.5	20.6	. .	. .	18 27 37.50	71.96	2. 7 30.34	15 22.99	10.84	18 28 49.46	40 4 53.83
		Zone XXXIX. July 10. M. $D. = 26° 58' 10''.0$. $n'. — 20''.00$. $n''. — 8''.17$.															
1	6.7	. .	. .	. .	. .	. .	9.5	21.7	. .	. .	19 40 44.62	70.74	I. 1 37.27	52 15.49	19.62	19 41 55.36	27 50 45.11 B.
2	6.7	. .	. .	. .	. .	. .	. .	. .	. .	24.0	41 15.95	70.70	VII. 4 43.15	28 53.57	19.53	42 26.65	27 27 23.10 B.
3	7	. .	. .	. .	. .	. .	. .	38.5	. .	. .	43 1.49	70.68	IV. 5 45.99	20 54.12	19.18	44 12.17	27 19 23.30 Z.
4	7.8	. .	. .	. .	. .	. .	13.0	25.0	. .	. .	43 48.27	70.66	" 7 46.24	6 12.04	19.03	44 58.93	27 4 41.07
5	8	. .	. .	. .	. .	. .	. .	21.0	. .	. .	44 43.92	70.69	VII. 4 38.19	31 10.36	18.84	45 54.61	27 29 39.20 Z.
6	4.5	. .	9.0	21.1	33.4	. .	58.0	. .	. .	. .	46 33.46	70.70	I. 3 41.41	35 15.65	18.50	47 44.16	27 33 44.15 B.
7	8.9	. .	. .	. .	. .	. .	11.0	22.8	. .	. .	48 45.94	70.70	II. 2 48.02	40 12.83	18.07	49 56.64	27 38 40.90 Z.
8	9	53.0	5.7	18.0	. .	. .	. .	. .	. .	. .	50 30.38	70.69	IV. 3 38.93	36 41.62	17.73	51 41.07	27 35 9.35 Z.
9	9	. .	. .	. .	. .	. .	. .	. .	30.5	. .	50 35.24	70.65	II. 7 40.92	9 14.94	17.71	51 45.89	27 7 42.65
10	6.7	14.4	27.0	39.2	51.7	3.8	16.5	. .	. .	. .	19 54 51.64	70.64	I. 6 40.37	15 25.46	16.70	19 56 2.28	27 13 52.16 Z.

INSTRUMENT READINGS.

	CIRCLE. A.	B.	C.	D.	Mean.	BAR.	THERMOM. At.	Ex.
Zone XXXIX.—July 10, h. 19.7	293° 39' 43''.5	35''.2	36''.2	36''.0	35''.47	I. 30.075	81°.5	79°.2
	32.0	32.5	34.2	34.0	33.27	. . .	. .	. .

Number.	Magnitude.	I.	II.	III.	IV.	V.	VI.	VII.	10.	11.	T.	a.	MICROMETER.	D.	d.	Mean Right Ascension, 1850.0.	Mean South Declination, 1850.0.
Zone XXXIX. July 10. M. D. = 26° 58′ 10″.0. n′. —20″.00. n″. —8″.17. (Continued.)																	
											h. m. s.	s.	r.	′ ″	″	h. m. s.	° ′ ″
11	7	. .	. .	. .	. .	46.0	58.0	10.5	. .	. .	19 56 33.44	+70.68	VI. 2 47.74	—40 22.59	—16.37	19 57 44.12	27 38 48.96 z.
12	8.9	. .	. .	. .	. .	. .	30.0	. .	. .	. .	58 5.23	70.66	VII. 4 44.42	27 35.17	16.27	59 15.89	27 26 1.44
13	9	. .	. .	. .	. .	30.0	42.0	55.0	. .	. .	20 3 17.64	70.65	IV. 4 37.72	31 26.91	15.29	20 4 28.29	27 29 52.20 z.
14	5	. .	. .	. .	44.7	56.8	9.5	21.8	. .	. .	4 44.67	70.65	II. 4 40.12	30 3.93	15.02	5 55.32	27 28 28.95 z.
15	8	. .	. .	16.8	. .	41.3	54.0	6.2	. .	. .	8 29.16	70.64	I. 3 43.985	33 46.68	14.32	9 39.80	27 32 11.00 z.
16	8	. .	. .	14.8	27.0	39.2	52.0	4.3	. .	. .	10 27.11	70.66	" 1 41.45	49 51.10	13.96	11 37.77	27 48 15.06 z.
17	7.8	. .	53.5	5.3	18.0	30.3	42.5	55.0	. .	. .	13 17.95	70.60	2. 6 42.47	14 12.74	13.44	14 28.55	27 12 36.18 z.
18	8	. .	. .	. .	. .	. .	40.8	52.8	. .	. .	16 16.07	70.58	III. 7 42.92	8 6.66	12.88	17 26.65	27 6 29.54 z.
19	8	. .	. .	. .	. .	21.5	34.0	. .	. .	. .	17 9.26	70.61	IV. 4 43.09	28 21.43	12.74	18 19.87	27 26 44.17
20	8	. .	. .	. .	23.0	35.2	47.1	. .	. .	. .	19 22.73	70.64	I. 1 41.24	49 58.34	12.16	20 33.37	27 48 20.50 z.
21	8.9	. .	. .	. .	. .	56.0	. .	21.0	. .	. .	20 43.85	70.60	VII. 4 40.30	29 57.48	11.91	21 54.45	27 28 19.39 z.
22	9	1.0	13.5	26.0	. .	. .	. .	. .	. .	. .	38.35	70.62	IV. 2 44.82	42 3.46	11.75	48.97	27 40 25.21
23	8	. .	. .	. .	. .	43.0	55.5	8.0	. .	. .	24 30.77	70.62	" 2 38.00	45 59.03	11.43	25 41.39	27 44 20.46
24	8	. .	. .	. .	. .	. .	5.6	18.0	. .	. .	25 41.02	70.56	V. 6 44.44	13 5.20	11.23	26 51.58	27 11 26.43
25	7	. .	. .	. .	25.0	37.0	49.5	2.0	. .	. .	30 24.94	70.55	I. 7 36.45	11 49.85	10.40	31 35.49	27 10 10.25
26	8	. .	. .	. .	. .	28.0	40.5	. .	. .	. .	34 15.71	70.59	1. 2 36.97	46 33.78	9.74	35 26.30	27 44 53.52 z.
27	6	. .	. .	. .	. .	. .	26.5	. .	. .	. .	35 1.70	70.58	VI. 3 38.04	37 12.28	9.61	36 12.28	27 35 31.89
28	5.6	. .	. .	. .	. .	. .	. .	54.5	. .	. .	36 17.45	70.56	V. 5 36.71	26 14.60	9.40	37 28.01	27 24 34.00 z.
29	7.8	. .	. .	. .	. .	. .	. .	. .	25.0	37.5	36 29.43	70.59	11. 2 34.25	48 7.75	9.36	37 40.02	27 46 27.11 z.
30	8.9	. .	. .	. .	. .	. .	57.0	9.2	. .	. .	39 32.15	70.56	VII. 3 41.91	34 58.34	8.84	40 42.71	27 33 17.18
31	9	. .	. .	. .	. .	. .	. .	. .	. .	23.5	39 15.44	70.55	11. 4 39.32	30 30.85	8.89	40 25.99	27 28 49.74 z.
32	8	. .	. .	11.5	24.0	. .	. .	. .	. .	. .	41 23.98	70.58	I. 1 41.91	49 35.18	8.54	42 34.56	27 47 53.72 B.
33	4	. .	. .	. .	41.0	53.5	6.0	18.0	. .	. .	41 41.09	70.55	IV. 4 39.89	30 11.97	8.33	42 51.64	27 28 30.30 B.
34	8	. .	. .	. .	52.5	5.0	17.7	. .	. .	. .	42 52.70	70.57	" 2 39.25	45 15.87	8.13	44 3.27	27 43 34.00 z.
35	8	48.5	1.0	13.5	25.9	38.0	. .	. .	. .	. .	49 25.82	70.54	I. 3 38.04	37 12.04	7.23	50 36.36	27 35 29.27
36	8.9	. .	22.0	. .	46.5	58.5	. .	. .	. .	. .	50 46.48	70.54	10. 3 34.19	39 24.80	7.02	51 57.02	27 37 41.82 z.
37	5	. .	. .	. .	. .	. .	4.6	17.0	. .	. .	51 39.86	70.52	11. 4 41.20	29 25.90	6.88	52 50.38	27 27 42.78
38	8.9	. .	. .	. .	. .	36.5	49.0	1.5	. .	. .	54 24.35	70.50	III. 5 45.42	21 13.78	6.44	55 34.85	27 19 30.22
39	7	. .	. .	. .	. .	30.0	42.8	54.6	. .	. .	57 17.71	70.54	I. 1 32.44	55 2.28	5.98	58 28.25	27 53 18.26 z.
40	8	. .	. .	51.0	3.4	15.5	28.1	40.5	. .	. .	20 59 3.35	70.52	" 2 40.89	44 18.87	5.70	21 0 13.87	27 42 34.57 z.
Zone XL. July 11. H. D. = —43° 21′ 50″.0. n′. = —20″.29. n″. = —20″.00																	
1	9	. .	. .	. .	31.3	46.0	1.3	16.4	. .	. .	16 1 31.03	72.18	IV. 6 34.510	18 52.60	19.82	16 2 43.21	43 41 2.42
2	7.8	57.7	13.3	28.0	43.2	58.1	13.5	29.2	. .	. .	10 43.33	72.21	" 7 38.072	10 53.25	18.12	11 55.54	43 33 1.37 B.
3	9	49.2	5.0	19.8	34.0	50.0	5.3	21.0	. .	. .	18 34.93	72.27	" 5 39.636	24 41.42	16.63	19 47.20	43 46 48.05
*4	7	28.2	43.5	59.0	13.8	29.0	44.0	59.8	. .	. .	22 3.94	72.27	" 5 45.578	21 13.85	15.96	23 16.21	43 43 19.81
5	9	. .	. .	53.2	8.3	24.0	. .	. .	. .	. .	26 8.58	72.32	" 3 38.355	37 18.26	15.16	27 20.90	43 59 23.42
6	9	. .	. .	45.2	0.2	15.8	31.0	46.2	. .	. .	27 0.50	72.31	" 4 42.395	28 56.50	15.00	28 12.81	43 51 1.50
7	9	. .	59.5	14.5	30.0	45.0	0.2	15.2	. .	. .	16 27 29.79	72.35	" 1 34.580	54 17.89	14.90	16 28 42.14	44 16 22.79

CORRECTIONS.

	COR. TO CLOCK.	HOURLY COR.	m.	n.	c.	ZENITH POINT.	COINC. °
	s.	s.	s.	s.	s.		r.
July 11, at 17h...	+59.647	—0.005	+0.213	+0.298	+0.330	0° 0′ 0″.87	41.123

INSTRUMENT READING.

	CIRCLE. A.	CIRCLE. B.	CIRCLE. C.	CIRCLE. D.	CIRCLE. Mean.	BAR.	THERMOM. At.	THERMOM. Ex.
Zone XL.—July 11.......16.0 h.	277° 21′ 2″.3	1′.5	2″.0	0″.2	1″.50	30.030 I.	87°.5	85°.6
17.0	2.0	1.4	2.0	0 3	1.42	30.030	87.0	84.9

Number.	Magnitude.	SECONDS OF TRANSITS. I.	II.	III.	IV.	V.	VI.	VII.	10.	11.	T.	a.	MICROMETER.	D.	d.	Mean Right Ascension, 1850.0.	Mean South Declination, 1850.0.
Zone XL. July 11. H. $D. = -43^{\circ} 21' 50''.0$. $n'. = -20''.29$. $n''. = -20''.00$. (Continued.)																	
											h. m. s.	s.	r.	′ ″	″	h. m. s.	° ′ ″
8	9.10	7.5	23.0	. .	. .	8.0	23.3	. .	. .	. .	16 35 53.07	+72.32	IV. 6 36.654	—17 37.36	—13.24	16 37 5.39	43 39 40.60
9	9	. .	5.5	21.0	36.0	51.0	6.5	21.2	. .	. .	37 35.97	72.33	" 6 35.438	18 20.17	12.90	38 48.30	43 40 23.07
10	9	9.0	. .	. .	54.0	. .	. .	. .	. .	. .	51 54.90	72.40	" 4 34.703	33 24.97	9.99	53 7.30	43 55 24.96
11	8	2.2	17.5	33.0	47.4	3.0	. .	. .	. .	. .	52 47.91	72.39	" 4 37.872	31 34.29	9.81	54 0.30	43 53 34.10
12	9	. .	. .	. .	. .	14.0	29.0	43.5	. .	. .	53 58.30	72.43	V. 2 35.852	47 37.12	9.56	55 10.73	44 9 36.68
13	8.9	. .	48.0	3.2	18.5	34.0	49.2	4.5	. .	. .	55 18.63	72.44	IV. 1 38.366	52 5.37	9.29	56 31.07	44 14 4.66
14	9	27.0	. .	58.0	12.8	. .	. .	. .	. .	. .	17 3 13.10	72.46	" 1 39.248	51 34.46	7.63	17 4 25.56	44 13 32.09
15	9.10	. .	38.0	. .	. .	. .	39.2	. .	. .	. .	12 8.56	72.45	VI. 3 35.622	38 53.31	5.74	13 21.01	44 0 49.05
Zone XLI. July 11. H. $D. = -25^{\circ} 56' 20''.0$. $n'. = -12''.46$. $n''. = -5''.00$.																	
1	8	55.8	8.2	20.2	33.0	45.0	57.2	9.6	. .	. .	17 31 32.77	70.90	IV. 1 42.372	49 9.52	9.49	17 32 43.67	26 45 39.01 z.
2	8.9	49.6	2.5	14.0	26.6	39.0	51.3	. .	. .	. .	33 26.65	70.84	III. 6 36.970	17 20.15	9.04	34 37.49	26 22 49.19
3	9	40.7	. .	5.0	17.5	29.5	41.9	. .	. .	. .	35 17.45	70.87	IV. 3 42.781	34 25.41	8.60	36 28.32	26 30 54.01
4	9	. .	. .	. .	. .	. .	20.0	32.2	. .	. .	35 55.60	70.83	VI. 7 36.808	11 34.74	8.42	37 6.43	26 8 3.16
5	9	. .	. .	. .	3.0	. .	27.5	. .	. .	. .	37 2.98	70.84	IV. 5 46.380	20 37.60	8.19	38 13.82	26 17 5.79
6	8	56.0	8.2	21.0	33.0	. .	. .	. .	. .	. .	39 33.04	70.90	III. 2 32.516	49 5.05	7.59	40 43.94	26 45 32.64 z.
7	8.9	. .	. .	. .	. .	59.6	12.0	25.2	. .	. .	39 47.85	70.84	V. 5 47.624	19 54.56	7.54	40 58.69	26 16 22.10 z.
8	9	. .	. .	. .	8.2	21.0	32.5	. .	. .	. .	41 8.29	70.90	IV. 1 35.452	53 14.60	7.22	42 19.19	26 49 41.82 z.
9	9	44.0	56.5	. .	21.0	33.0	. .	. .	. .	. .	42 20.89	70.84	" 5 45.715	21 0.52	6.94	43 31.73	26 17 27.46
10	9	21.5	34.0	46.0	58.0	. .	. .	. .	. .	. .	43 58.29	70.86	II. 3 44.970	33 9.71	6.55	45 9.15	26 29 36.26
11	9	. .	. .	. .	6.2	19.0	31.0	. .	. .	. .	44 6.55	70.83	VI. 6 40.340	15 23.70	6.52	45 17.38	26 11 50.22
12	9	. .	. .	. .	. .	51.0	3.4	. .	. .	. .	44 38.91	70.84	V. 5 48.150	19 36.42	6.42	45 49.75	26 16 2.84 z.
13	8	. .	. .	39.2	52.0	4.2	16.5	28.5	. .	. .	45 51.83	70.89	IV. 1 44.650	47 57.54	6.11	47 2.72	26 44 23.65 z.
14	9	40.0	. .	. .	17.0	29.0	42.0	54.0	. .	. .	48 17.07	70.90	" 1 37.561	52 3.28	5.53	49 27.97	26 48 28.81 z.
15	9	. .	52.0	4.0	16.0	. .	40.2	53.0	. .	. .	50 16.14	70.82	" 6 42.670	14 3.35	5.07	51 26.96	26 10 28.42 z.
16	9	50.0	2.0	14.0	26.2	38.8	51.0	3.5	. .	. .	50 26.53	70.83	" 6 39.090	16 6.99	5.03	51 37.36	26 12 32.02 z.
17	8	16.1	28.3	40.0	53.0	5.1	17.5	29.8	. .	. .	52 52.86	70.84	" 5 43.228	22 26.42	4.45	54 3.70	26 18 50.87 z.
18	9	7.2	19.2	31.6	: .	57.0	. .	. .	. .	. .	17 55 44.21	70.89	" 1 38.670	51 24.92	3.78	17 56 55.10	26 47 48.70
Zone XLII. July 14. H. $D. = -41^{\circ} 50' 30''.0$. $n'. = -50''.57$. $n''. = -17''.00$.																	
1	7.8	3.0	18.2	33.0	48.0	2.8	17.4	. .	. .	. .	16 3 47.90	71.48	VI. 3 34.360	39 32.87	49.67	16 4 59.38	42 30 52.54 B.
2	8	. .	. .	. .	. .	44.0	59.2	14.4	36.0	. .	4 29.36	71.50	IV. 2 36.090	47 26.11	49.54	5 40.86	42 38 45.65
3	7	56.0	11.2	25.5	40.8	55.0	10.2	25.0	. .	. .	7 40.56	71.48	" 5 36.012	26 43.82	48.96	8 52.03	42 18 2.78 B.
4	7	54.2	9.2	24.0	39.0	54.0	9.2	24.0	. .	. .	24 39.14	71.56	" 2 46.495	41 20.05	45.74	25 50.70	42 32 35.79 B.
5	9.10	. .	17.2	. .	47.0	1.8	. .	32.0	. .	. .	35 47.07	71.60	" 2 40.680	44 42.36	43.56	36 58.67	42 35 55.92
6	8	58.0	12.8	27.2	43.0	57.0	13.0	27.2	. .	. .	40 42.67	71.63	" 1 37.350	52 33.26	42.59	41 54.30	42 43 45.85 M.
7	7.8	. .	. .	59.0	14.0	29.0	. .	. .	. .	. .	16 42 14.08	71.57	III. 6 40.826	15 11 59	42.28	16 43 25.65	42 6 23.87 B.

INSTRUMENT READINGS.

	CIRCLE. A.	B.	C.	D.	Mean.	BAR.	THERMOM. At.	Ex.
Zone XLI.—July 11......18.0 h.	294° 42′ 3″.5	3″.0	4″.8	3″.5	3″.70	I. 30.016	86°.0	83°.5

Zone XLII. July 14. II. $D. = -41° 50' 30''.00$. $n'. = -50''.57$. $n''. = -17''.00$. (Continued.)

Number.	Magnitude.	Seconds of Transits. I.	II.	III.	IV.	V.	VI.	VII.	10.	11.	T.	a.	Micrometer.	D.	d.	Mean Right Ascension, 1850.0.	Mean South Declination, 1850.0.
											h. m. s.	s.	r.	′ ″	″	h. m. s.	° ′ ″
8	8	. .	. .	. .	40.0	55.2	10.0	. .	. .	. .	16 42 40.28	+71.58	V. 5 43.848	−22 12.94	−42.20	16 43 51.86	42 13 25.14
9	6.7	. .	. .	36.0	51.0	. .	. .	34.2	. .	. .	42 50.59	71.57	VII. 6 41.570	14 45.37	42.16	44 2.16	42 5 57.53 B.
10	9	. .	. .	. .	. .	. .	. .	59.0	21.2	36.4	45 14.33	71.64	" 1 40.022	50 59.73	41.67	46 25.97	42 42 11.40
11	9.10	6.5	. .	36.2	. .	. .	. .	. .	. .	. .	55 51.29	71.65	" 2 46.176	41 30.77	39.51	57 2.94	42 32 40.28
12	8.9	42.7	58.0	12.1	27.2	42.0	57.0	11.3	. .	. .	17 4 27.22	71.62	IV. 6 34.980	18 35.18	37.79	17 5 38.84	42 9 42.97 B.
13	9	27.0	41.2	55.8	11.0	26.2	. .	56.0	. .	. .	6 11.26	71.68	I. 1 37.483	52 28.41	37.63	7 22.94	42 43 36.04
14	9	. .	. .	. .	51.2	6.0	21.0	36.0	. .	. .	6 51.18	71.68	IV. 1 37.890	52 14.27	37.50	8 2.86	42 43 21.77
15	9	10.5	25.2	. .	. .	10.0	. .	. .	. .	. .	8 55.14	71.66	" 3 35.630	38 48.51	36.92	10 6.80	42 29 55.43
16	8.9	. .	. .	52.0	7.0	21.8	36.2	51.8	. .	. .	10 7.01	71.61	" 7 38.878	10 25.75	36.69	11 18.62	42 1 32.44
17	9	18.0	33.0	. .	2.2	. .	. .	. .	. .	. .	16 2.45	71.64	" 5 38.883	25 5.87	35.52	17 14.09	42 16 11.39
18	9	. .	. .	. .	25.2	40.0	. .	. .	32.0	46.5	17 25.26	71.63	" 5 45.843	21 3.50	35.25	18 36.89	42 12 8.75
19	9	43.2	58.2	12.5	27.2	. .	. .	. .	. .	. .	20 27.45	71.62	II. 6 45.342	12 34.46	34.65	21 39.07	42 3 39.11
20	9	51.0	6.2	21.0	36.0	50.2	5.3	19.8	. .	. .	21 35.66	71.65	IV. 5 37.450	25 55.96	34.42	22 47.31	42 17 0.38
21	9	41.8	57.0	11.5	27.0	. .	. .	. .	. .	. .	24 26.78	71.69	" 2 36.233	47 17.51	33.85	25 38.47	42 38 21.36
22	8.9	12.0	26.2	41.2	56.8	. .	. .	. .	. .	. .	25 56.41	71.67	I. 3 40.360	36 3.71	33.54	27 8.08	42 27 7.25
23	8.9	. .	10.8	26.0	41.0	55.3	10.8	25.2	. .	. .	26 40.76	71.69	IV. 2 36.630	47 3.46	33.40	27 52.45	42 38 6.86
24	9	25.0	. .	54.0	. .	23.8	38.2	. .	. .	. .	31 9.07	71.62	" 7 44.750	7 1.36	32.50	32 20.69	41 58 3.86
25	7.8	0.5	15.2	30.2	. .	. .	15.0	29.8	. .	. .	32 45.20	71.69	" 2 34.568	48 15.27	32.17	33 56.89	42 39 17.44 B.
26	9	. .	19.5	. .	49.2	3.2	18.0	. .	. .	. .	37 48.76	71.68	" 2 45.532	41 53.25	31.15	39 0.44	42 32 54.40
27	8.9	. .	27.5	42.2	57.0	12.1	27.0	42.0	. .	. .	38 57.23	71.65	" 5 38.270	25 27.35	30.92	40 8.88	42 16 28.27
28	8	. .	28.5	43.2	. .	12.4	27.5	. .	. .	. .	40 57.93	71.61	" 7 47.242	5 34.78	30.52	42 9.54	41 56 35.30 B.
29	8	24.8	40.2	54.5	9.2	24.2	39.0	53.8	. .	. .	44 9.44	71.65	" 5 36.823	26 17.57	29.87	45 21.09	42 17 7.44
30	8	. .	. .	2.8	17.8	32.5	. .	. .	. .	. .	45 17.79	71.61	" 7 46.650	5 55.20	29.64	46 29.40	41 56 54.84
31	9	4.0	18.2	33.3	48.0	2.8	18.2	33.0	. .	. .	46 48.28	71.70	" 1 39.290	51 25.61	29.34	47 59.98	42 42 24.95
32	8.9	1.8	16.4	31.2	46.0	1.0	15.3	30.3	. .	. .	52 46.05	71.61	" 7 44.783	7 0.18	28.14	53 57.66	41 57 58.36
33	9	15.0	30.0	45.2	. .	15.0	29.8	. .	. .	. .	55 0.07	71.70	" 1 37.973	52 11.41	27.69	56 11.77	42 43 9.10
34	8.9	11.4	26.5	41.8	56.0	. .	. .	. .	. .	. .	56 56.40	71.69	II. 1 43.060	49 14.00	27.30	58 8.09	42 40 11.30
35	9	5.0	20.0	35.0	49.2	. .	. .	. .	. .	. .	57 49.64	71.66	I. 3 43.530	34 13.01	27.12	59 1.30	42 25 10.13
36	9	. .	. .	. .	. .	34.0	49.0	. .	26.0	41.0	58 19.24	71.66	IV. 3 43.482	34 15.30	27.02	59 30.90	42 25 12.32
37	9	. .	37.5	52.2	7.2	22.0	36.5	. .	. .	. .	18 1 7.09	71.65	" 4 44.180	27 51.50	26.45	18 2 18.74	42 18 47.95
38	8	0.8	16.0	30.2	45.0	. .	14.8	29.2	. .	. .	6 45.16	71.65	" 4 41.783	28 14.84	25.28	7 56.81	42 19 10.12
39	9	. .	. .	28.0	42.5	. .	. .	. .	. .	. .	11 42.73	71.65	" 3 36.900	38 4.36	24.26	12 54.38	42 28 58.62
40	9	. .	. .	. .	. .	. .	5.8	20.2	. .	. .	11 35.82	71.64	VI. 4 36.462	32 20.25	24.28	12 47.46	42 23 14.53
41	9	. .	. .	. .	. .	. .	. .	40.0	2.5	. .	11 55.60	71.65	VII. 3 36.519	38 17.23	24.21	13 7.25	42 29 11.44
42	9	. .	. .	. .	. .	13.0	27.8	43.0	. .	. .	12 58.28	71.63	V. 5 35.438	27 5.99	23.99	14 9.91	42 17 59.98
43	8	. .	. .	14.8	29.2	44.5	59.0	14.0	. .	. .	14 29.44	71.67	IV. 2 38.500	45 58.25	23.67	15 41.11	42 36 51.92
44	9	. .	54.2	8.2	23.5	38.2	53.8	. .	. .	. .	17 23.59	71.51	" 7 36.650	11 43.24	23.07	18 35.18	42 2 36.31
45	7	27.0	41.8	56.4	11.2	26.0	40.8	55.6	. .	. .	19 11.30	71.59	" 7 40.460	9 30.89	22.70	20 22.89	42 0 23.59 B.
46	6.7	51.0	6.1	21.0	35.5	50.5	5.0	20.5	. .	. .	21 35.67	71.64	" 3 44.032	33 55.99	22.20	22 47.31	42 24 48.19 B.
47	9	. .	. .	7.2	22.2	37.0	52.0	7.2	. .	. .	18 22 22.24	71.66	" 1 40.206	50 53.67	22.04	18 23 33.90	42 41 45.71

CORRECTIONS.

	Cor. to Clock.	Hourly Cor.	m.	n.	c.	Zenith Point.	Coinc.
	s.	s.	s.	s.	s.		r.
July 14, at 17h...	+58.886	−0.011	+0.213	+0.298	+0.330	359° 59′ 58″.10	40.118

INSTRUMENT READINGS.

		Circle. A.	B.	C.	D.	Mean.	Bar.	Thermom. At.	Ex.
Zone	h.						I.		
XLII.—July 14.....	16.0	278° 50′ 58″.4	59″.8	60″.9	59″.2	59″.58	30.024	76°.6	71°.0
	16.3	59.4	. .	. .	. .	60.17	30.036	75.0	69.1
	17.0	59.5	. .	. .	. .	59.90	30.044	75.0	69.0
	18.6	59.7	59.6	61.3	58.8	59.85	. . .	. .	66.7

Zone XLII. July 14. H. $D. = -41° 50' 30''.00$. $n' = -50''.57$. $n'' = -17''.00$. (Continued.)

Number.	Magnitude.	Seconds of Transits. I.	II.	III.	IV.	V.	VI.	VII.	10.	11.	T.	a.	Micrometer	D.	d.	Mean Right Ascension, 1850.0.	Mean South Declination, 1850.0.
											h. m. s.	s.	r.	′ ″	″	h. m. s.	° ′ ″
48	9.10	20.2	36.0	51.0	. .	. .	. .	49.4	. .	. .	18 25 5.30	+71.60	IV. 5 43.290	−22 32.55	−21.47	18 26 16.90	42 13 24.02
49	9	35.8	50.2	5.2	20.0	. .	. .	. .	. .	. .	28 19.98	71.58	" 6 44.873	12 50.77	20.80	29 31.56	42 3 41.57
50	8.9	36.2	51.1	6.0	20.5	35.4	50.3	5.3	. .	. .	29 20.72	71.60	" 4 45.752	26 56.61	20.59	30 32.32	42 17 47.20
51	9	. .	. .	. .	. .	35.5	50.2	5.8	. .	. .	30 21.04	71.57	V. 7 37.265	11 21.98	20.38	31 32.61	42 2 12.36
52	9	55.0	10.0	25.0	39.5	55.0	. .	. .	. .	. .	32 39.93	71.65	IV. 1 37.759	52 18.79	19.90	33 51.58	42 43 8.69
53	9	10.2	. .	40.0	55.5	. .	. .	. .	. .	. .	33 55.22	71.64	" 1 42.010	49 50.72	19.64	35 6.86	42 40 40.36
54	8.9	15.0	30.0	45.0	. .	. .	28.2	43.5	. .	. .	33 59.41	71.65	V. 1 38.400	51 56.65	19.62	35 11.06	42 42 46.27
55	8	. .	. .	. .	. .	. .	. .	. .	34.2	49.4	34 28.05	71.64	10. 6 44.400	13 6.75	19.53	35 39.69	42 3 56.28
56	9	32.8	48.0	2.2	17.0	. .	46.0	1.5	. .	. .	38 17.08	71.59	IV. 4 37.890	31 30.46	18.73	39 28.67	42 22 19.19
57	8.9	22.5	37.0	52.0	6.4	21.3	36.3	51.2	. .	. .	46 6.76	71.57	" 4 42.270	28 58.02	17.13	47 18.33	42 19 45.15
58	8	. .	51.0	6.0	21.0	35.6	. .	5.2	. .	. .	50 20.82	71.53	" 6 39.150	16 10.68	16.26	51 32.35	42 6 56.94
59	6	33.0	. .	3.0	17.5	32.0	46.8	2.0	. .	. .	51 17.49	71.55	" 5 35.050	27 19.40	16.06	52 29.04	42 18 5.46 B.
60	9	16.2	31.8	46.0	1.0	. .	. .	. .	. .	. .	57 1.20	71.57	III. 1 44.580	48 20.96	14.89	58 12.77	42 39 5.85
61	7.8	27.0	42.3	57.0	12.0	26.0	41.2	56.0	. .	. .	18 58 11.69	71.50	IV. 6 38.133	16 45.48	14.65	18 59 23.19	42 7 30.13

Zone XLIII. July 14. H. $D. = -28° 26' 00''.0$. $n' = -13''.18$. $n'' = -5''.00$.

Number.	Magnitude.	I.	II.	III.	IV.	V.	VI.	VII.	10.	11.	T.	a.	Micrometer	D.	d.	Mean Right Ascension, 1850.0.	Mean South Declination, 1850.0.
1	8.9	. .	. .	. .	. .	. .	10.2	23.0	. .	. .	20 28 45.23	69.92	VI. 4 39.072	30 36.97	10.95	20 29 55.15	28 56 47.92 z.
2	8	. .	10.8	23.2	36.0	48.2	1.0	. .	. .	. .	30 35.87	69.92	IV. 3 35.935	38 22.13	10.57	31 45.79	29 04 32.70
3	8.9	. .	4.0	16.8	29.2	. .	54.7	. .	. .	. .	31 29.35	69.95	" 1 38.710	51 23.46	10.38	32 39.30	29 17 33.84 z.
4	9	. .	21.0	33.0	46.0	58.2	11.0	. .	. .	. .	32 45.89	69.92	" 1 37.670	51 59.40	10.15	33 55.81	29 18 9.55 z.
5	8	43.0	55.7	8.0	21.0	. .	. .	. .	. .	. .	34 20.71	69.88	" 6 35.278	18 18.22	9.82	35 30.59	28 44 28.04 z.
6	9	47.0	. .	12.2	25.0	. .	. .	. .	. .	. .	35 24.89	69.92	" 2 42.290	43 28.06	9.58	36 34.81	29 9 37.64
7	9	. .	36.2	49.0	. .	13.3	26.8	39.0	. .	. .	36 1.36	69.89	V. 3 45.668	32 45.73	9.45	37 11.25	28 58 55.18
8	9	49.2	1.5	14.0	. .	. .	. .	. .	. .	. .	38 26.58	69.85	IV. 7 37.858	10 57.86	8.81	39 36.43	28 37 6.67
9	9	. .	49.7	2.0	14.2	26.8	39.7	. .	. .	. .	39 14.49	69.88	" 4 44.090	27 43.68	8.77	40 24.37	28 53 52.45 z.
*10	9	. .	. .	. .	. .	26.8	40.2	53.0	. .	. .	40 15.12	69.85	V. 7 43.685	7 36.47	8.58	41 24.97	28 34 45.05
11	8	. .	. .	. .	24.4	36.5	49.5	2.0	. .	. .	41 24.43	69.84	" 7 44.795	6 58.13	8.38	42 34.27	28 33 6.51 z.
12	9	31.2	44.0	56.2	9.0	21.0	33.8	46.0	. .	. .	43 8.79	69.84	IV. 7 41.320	8 58.28	8.01	44 18.63	28 35 6.29 z.
13	9	19.0	31.8	44.0	56.2	9.2	21.3	34.1	. .	. .	44 56.55	69.87	" 3 37.800	37 17.66	7.65	46 6.42	29 3 25.31
14	9	32.5	45.2	57.7	10.0	22.4	35.2	48.0	. .	. .	47 10.17	69.85	" 4 42.412	28 41.68	7.19	48 20.02	28 54 48.87 z.
15	9	58.8	11.5	24.0	36.5	49.0	2.0	14.8	. .	. .	49 36.69	69.84	II. 4 43.640	27 59.09	6.76	50 46.53	28 54 5.85
16	9	12.5	25.1	37.0	50.1	3.0	15.2	27.2	. .	. .	50 50.05	69.83	IV. 5 43.220	22 26.45	6.50	51 59.88	28 48 32.95
17	9	. .	. .	8.0	20.5	32.4	. .	. .	. .	. .	53 20.37	69.86	V. 1 38.840	51 18.93	6.03	54 30.23	29 17 24.96
18	8	13.3	26.0	38.2	51.0	3.2	. .	. .	. .	. .	58 50.96	69.82	IV. 3 35.956	38 21.39	4.93	21 0 0.78	29 4 26.32 z.
19	9	. .	. .	. .	12.6	25.2	37.7	50.1	. .	. .	59 12.68	69.78	" 6 38.311	16 33.41	4.87	0 22.46	28 42 38.28
20	8	. .	. .	10.0	22.2	35.0	47.2	. .	. .	. .	21 0 22.36	69.82	" 3 33.507	39 46.00	4.64	1 32.18	29 5 50.64 z.
21	9	. .	. .	. .	. .	. .	. .	17.0	35.8	48.6	0 39.45	69.82	VII. 2 34.317	48 3.22	4.59	21 1 49.27	29 14 7.81

CORRECTIONS.

	Cor. to Clock.	Hourly Cor.	m.	n.	c.	Zenith Point.	Coinc.
	s.	s.	s.	s.	s.		r.
July 14, at 17h....	+58.886	− 0.011	+0.213	+0.298	+0.330	359° 59′ 58″.10	40.118

INSTRUMENT READINGS.

	Circle. A.	B.	C.	D.	Mean.	Bar.	Thermom. At.	Ex.
Zone XLIII.—July 14... 20.5 h.	292° 11′ 56″.5	56″.6	57″.8	56″.5	56″.85	I. 30.074	71°.9	63°.8
21.0	55.3	55.9	57.3	57.0	56.37	30.080	71.0	63.7

Number.	Magnitude.	SECONDS OF TRANSITS. I.	II.	III.	IV.	V.	VI.	VII.	10.	11.	T.	a.	MICROMETER.	D.	d.	Mean Right Ascension. 1850.0.	Mean South Declination. 1850.0.
Zone XLIV. July 15. M. D.=—43° 51′ 50″.0. n′.=—25″.48. n″.=—22″.00.																	
											h. m. s.	s.	r.	′ ″	′	h. m. s.	° ′ ″
1	9.10	. .	18.2	. .	49.0	4.7	20.0	. .	. .	. .	18 1 49.15	+71.38	VII. 1 44.55	—48 32.76	—24.90	18 3 0.53	44 40 47.06
2	7	. .	14.9	29.9	45.0	0.2	16.0	31.0	. .	. .	3 45.19	71.33	II. 5 43.65	22 21.79	24.52	4 56.52	44 14 36.31 B.
3	10.9	36.0	51.8	7.0	22.0	37.5	52.8	8.0	. .	. .	8 22.22	71.31	2. 6 40.22	15 31.59	23.61	9 33.53	44 6 45.20
4	6.7	. .	. .	56.6	12.1	26.8	42.1	57.5	. .	. .	12 11.78	71.31	I. 6 35.26	18 25.87	22.65	13 23.09	44 10 38.52 B.
5	8	. .	33.0	48.3	3.8	19.0	34.0	49.8	. .	. .	34 3.65	71.29	" 4 40.04	30 19.97	18.51	35 14.94	44 22 28.48
6	10.9	. .	32.5	47.6	3.3	18.5	34.0	49.2	. .	. .	40 3.18	71.31	2. 1 42.21	49 54.65	17.33	41 14.49	44 42 1.98
7	7.8	. .	. .	57.9	13.4	. .	. .	. .	. .	. .	45 13.33	71.23	1. 6 43.07	13 51.09	16.32	46 24.56	44 5 57.41 B.
8	9.10	. .	. .	. .	. .	. .	. .	0.5	. .	. .	44 14.41	71.28	10. 3 38.92	37 0.05	16.51	45 25.69	44 29 6.56
9	7.6	. .	8.8	24.0	39.0	54.5	10.4	25.4	. .	. .	19 10 39.35	71.21	2. 1 38.85	51 52.30	11.39	19 11 50.56	44 43 53.69 B.
10	9	. .	. .	. .	. .	16.4	31.8	47.5	. .	. .	13 1.19	71.17	VII. 3 39.84	36 28.35	10.95	14 12.36	44 28 29.30
11	9	. .	. .	. .	30.0	44.7	. .	15.2	. .	. .	16 29 56	71.14	" 5 35.02	27 23.77	10.19	17 40.70	44 19 23.96
12	8	6.5	22.0	37.3	52.7	8.0	23.5	38.6	. .	. .	31 52.70	71.09	2. 3 39.18	36 51.08	7.42	33 3.79	44 28 48.50
13	8	34.5	50.0	5.0	20.3	35.6	51.0	6.5	. .	. .	44 20.45	71.01	VII. 4 37.14	32 1.62	5.15	45 31.46	44 23 56.77
14	8	. .	. .	37.0	52.5	7.0	22.2	. .	. .	. .	48 51.99	70.98	VII. 4 39.33	30 45.00	4.33	50 2.97	44 22 39.33
15	9	. .	. .	. .	. .	. .	59.1	14.5	. .	. .	54 28.20	70.99	10. 1 35.70	53 43.29	3.34	55 39.19	44 45 36.63
16	9	. .	. .	. .	. .	3.5	. .	34.0	. .	. .	57 48.14	70.92	I. 4 42.43	28 56.46	2.75	58 59.06	44 20 49.21
17	8	. .	. .	. .	. .	. .	58.0	13.3	. .	. .	58 27.29	70.92	" 4 44.61	27 39.66	2.63	59 38.21	44 19 32.29
18	8	. .	. .	. .	. .	. .	. .	25.0	47.8	. .	19 59 39.25	70.88	VII. 6 42.95	13 56.50	2.42	20 0 50.13	44 5 48.92
Zone XLV. July 16. H. D.=—42° 20′ 40″.0. n′.—17″.91. n″.—17″.00.																	
1	8	56.0	10.8	. .	40.6	55.8	. .	. .	. .	. .	20 28 40.84	70.53	IV. 3 43.170	34 27.17	16.13	20 29 51.37	42 55 23.30
2	7.8	26.0	42.0	. .	10.4	25.0	40.2	55.2	. .	. .	30 10.67	70.48	" 6 34.728	18 43.73	15.86	31.21.15	42 39 39.59
3	9	. .	23.0	37.8	. .	7.3	22.2	37.2	. .	. .	31 52.58	70.47	" 6 38.561	16 30.04	15.56	33 3.05	42 37 25.60
4	9	38.2	53.2	9.0	. .	38.8	53.8	9.0	. .	. .	39 23.73	70.46	" 2 46.154	41 33.68	14.22	40 34.19	43 2 27.90
5	9	5.0	. .	35.0	. .	5.0	20.2	. .	. .	. .	40 50.18	70.47	V. 2 37.400	46 39.27	13.97	42 0.65	43 7 33.24
6	9	. .	. .	. .	55.8	10.8	. .	. .	. .	. .	41 55.83	70.46	" 2 35.295	47 52.68	13.78	43 6.29	43 8 46.46
7	8.9	8.5	23.4	38.2	53.2	7.5	23.0	38.0	. .	. .	50 52.14	70.34	IV. 6 34.402	18 55.35	12.28	52 2.48	42 39 47.63
8	9	. .	. .	32.5	47.0	2.2	. .	32.2	. .	. .	56 47.30	70.31	" 4 40.878	29 47.23	11.30	57 57.61	42 50 38.53
9	8.9	. .	44.0	59.0	13.8	29.0	43.5	58.2	. .	. .	21 1 13.80	70.26	" 6 34.266	19 0.04	10.59	21 2 24.06	42 39 50.63
10	9	14.5	29.2	44.0	59.2	. .	. .	. .	. .	. .	6 59.13	70.22	" 6 33.455	19 28.38	9.69	8 9.35	42 40 18.07
11	8.9	13.2	27.5	43.0	57.8	12.3	27.5	42.0	. .	. .	13 57.65	70.16	" 6 37.063	17 22.45	8.62	15 7.81	42 38 11.07
12	8.9	19.0	34.1	49.0	4.0	. .	. .	. .	. .	. .	16 3.95	70.15	III. 5 43.632	22 20.54	8.30	17 14.10	42 43 8.84
13	6.7	. .	. .	. .	13.0	28.0	43.0	57.9	. .	. .	16 12.93	70.20	IV. 1 40.301	50 53.20	8.28	17 23.13	43 11 41.48 B.
14	9	. .	. .	46.5	. .	15.5	30.4	. .	. .	. .	25 0.93	70.07	V. 5 45.706	21 8.25	7.00	26 11.00	42 41 55.25
15	7.8	16.6	31.2	46.2	1.8	16.8	31.2	46.2	. .	. .	29 1.49	70.09	IV. 2 37.740	46 27.16	6.43	30 11.58	43 7 13.59
16	9	34.0	49.0	3.5	. .	. .	. .	. .	. .	. .	33 18.83	70.02	III. 4 39.510	30 34.77	5.84	34 28.85	42 51 20.61
17	8.9	. .	39.0	54.0	9.0	24.0	38.8	. .	. .	. .	34 8.97	70.01	IV. 4 43.770	28 6.33	5.72	35 18.98	42 48 52.05
18	9	. .	. .	. .	. .	. .	46.0	. .	22.5	37.3	34 15.32	70.02	10. 3 38.095	37 22.93	5.71	35 25.34	42 58 8.64
19	9	5.8	21.0	35.0	50.0	4.4	19.5	35.0	. .	. .	21 40 50.14	69.92	IV. 6 41.808	14 36.94	4.82	21 42 0.06	42 35 21.76

CORRECTIONS.

	COR. TO CLOCK.	HOURLY COR.	m.	n.	c.	ZENITH POINT.	COINC.
	s.	s.	s.	s.	s.	° ′ ″	r.
July 15, at 17h...	+58.483	+0.010	+0.213	+0.298	+0.330	0 0 0.16	40.118
July 16, at 17h...	+58.354	+0.006	+0.213	+0.298	+0.330	2.30	40.119

INSTRUMENT READINGS.

		CIRCLE. A.	B.	C.	D.	Mean.	BAR.	THERMOM. At.	Ex.
Zone	h.	° ′ ″	′	″	″	″	I.	°	°
XLIV.—July 15....	17.8	276 51 21.1	20.0	21.0	18.5	20.15	. . .	. .	. .
	18.6	. . . . .	. .	. .	. .	. . .	30.228	66.0	58.0
	19.6	. . . . .	.	. .	. .	. . .	30.230	65.0	57.2
XLV.—July 16......	20.4	278 21 2.5	2.6	4.7	2.7	3.12	30.296	63.3	56.8
	22.0	2.5	2.1	4.7	2.0	3.82	30.288	63.0	55.7

Number.	Magnitude.	SECONDS OF TRANSITS I.	II.	III.	IV.	V.	VI.	VII.	10.	11.	T.	a.	MICROMETER.	D.	d.	Mean Right Ascension, 1850.0.	Mean South Declination, 1850.0.
Zone XLV. July 16. H. $D.=-42°\ 20'\ 40''.0.$ $n'.-17''.91.$ $n''.-17''.00.$ (Continued.)																	
											h. m. s.	s.	r.	′ ″	″	h. m. s.	° ′ ″
20	8.9	48.0	3.0	17.4	32.8	47.2	3.0	17.8	. .	. .	21 42 32.79	+69.94	IV. 4 35.548	—32 52.93	—4.60	21 43 42.73	42 53 37.53
21	7.8	. .	35.0	. .	4.5	19.2	34.5	49.2	. .	. .	48 4.59	69.85	V. 7 47.748	5 15.75	3.90	49 14.44	42 25 59.65
22	8.9	. .	35.0	49.2	5.0	. .	35.1	50.0	. .	. .	50 4.88	69.90	IV. 1 42.950	49 20.57	3.65	51 14.78	43 10 4.22
23	8.9	18.6	34.0	49.0	4.0	18.3	34.0	49.0	. .	. .	52 3.87	69.85	" 4 44.795	27 30.58	3.41	53 13.72	42 48 13.99
24	8	. .	16.0	31.0	45.8	1.0	16.2	31.1	. .	. .	21 56 46.04	69.85	" 1 36.400	53 9.43	2.85	21 57 55.89	43 13 52.28
Zone XLVI. July 24. H. $D.=-28°\ 25'\ 40''.0.$ $n'.=-20''.00.$ $n''.=-5''.29.$																	
1	8	3.8	16.3	28.8	41.5	53.8	. .	19.0	. .	. .	20 59 41.44	19.40	IV. 3 35.784	38 27.50	20.02	21 0 0.84	29 4 27.52 z.
2	9	. .	. .	. .	3.0	15.5	28.0	40.5	. .	. .	21 0 3.03	19.37	" 6 38.210	16 37.38	19.96	0 22.40	28 42 37.34
3	8.9	. .	. .	0.2	13.0	25.8	38.0	. .	. .	. .	1 13.01	19.39	" 3 33.410	39 49.56	19.76	1 32.40	29 5 49.32 z.
4	9	. .	. .	. .	. .	42.8	. .	7.5	. .	. .	1 30.09	19.40	V. 2 34.226	48 6.71	19.71	1 49.49	29 14 6.42
5	9	. .	. .	. .	5.0	17.1	. .	. .	. .	. .	4 4.82	19.38	IV. 3 36.000	38 20.05	19.27	4 24.20	29 4 19.32
6	9	. .	. .	34.5	. .	59.2	. .	24.8	. .	. .	4 46.71	19.36	V. 4 38.390	31 0.90	19.15	5 6.07	28 57 0.05 z.
7	8.9	4.2	17.0	29.2	. .	. .	. .	. .	. .	. .	6 42.04	19.38	11. 1 39.372	51 0.49	18.82	7 1.42	29 16 59.31
8	8.9	. .	. .	55.8	8.2	21.3	. .	. .	. .	. .	7 8.50	19.35	IV. 4 44.464	27 31.10	18.74	7 27.85	28 53 29.84 z.
9	9	. .	. .	. .	. .	26.5	38.4	51.0	. .	. .	7 13.56	19.37	V. 2 45.142	41 49.59	18.72	7 32.93	29 7 48.31 z.
10	8.9	15.0	27.5	40.0	52.2	5.0	17.3	30.1	. .	. .	13 52.48	19.30	IV. 6 35.384	18 15.02	17.61	14 11.78	28 44 12.63
11	9	39.2	52.0	4.2	17.0	29.2	. .	54.5	. .	. .	15 16.90	19.30	" 6 34.118	18 58.73	17.38	15 36.20	28 44 56.11
12	9	. .	. .	20.3	. .	. .	58.0	10.2	. .	. .	15 32.89	19.29	VI. 7 34.734	12 46.26	17.34	15 52.18	28 38 43.60
13	8.9	. .	12.8	25.0	37.5	49.8	2.5	15.0	. .	. .	17 37.54	19.28	IV. 7 37.750	11 2.18	16.99	17 56.82	28 36 59.17
14	9	. .	17.3	29.3	42.0	54.0	. .	19.3	. .	. .	19 41.90	19.27	" 7 38.481	10 36.97	16.65	20 1.17	28 36 33.62
15	9	29.5	42.0	54.5	7.0	. .	. .	. .	. .	. .	22 7.08	19.28	" 4 39.310	30 29.15	16.27	22 26.36	28 56 25.42
16	9	11.5	. .	37.0	. .	2.2	15.0	27.2	. .	. .	22 49.62	19.28	V. 3 43.902	33 47.03	16.16	23 8.90	28 59 43.19
17	9	. .	. .	. .	. .	59.2	. .	24.2	. .	. .	23 46.80	19.25	" 6 41.630	14 39.16	16.00	24 6.05	28 40 35.16
18	8	16.0	28.2	41.0	53.1	6.0	18.5	31.0	. .	. .	27 53.46	19.28	IV. 1 39.732	50 48.11	15.36	28 12.74	29 16 43.47 z.
19	8	49.2	2.2	14.4	27.0	39.0	51.7	4.4	. .	. .	29 26.86	19.22	" 7 43.019	8 0.17	15.12	29 46.08	28 33 55.29 z.
20	9	36.8	49.5	1.3	14.2	26.8	39.2	. .	. .	. .	35 14.28	19.23	" 3 41.340	35 15.60	14.25	35 33.51	29 1 9.85 z.
21	7.8	49.0	1.3	14.0	26.4	39.0	51.2	4.0	. .	. .	36 26.33	19.20	" 5 42.460	22 53.11	14.07	36 45.64	28 48 47.18 z.
22	8.9	33.1	46.0	58.1	10.8	23.1	36.0	48.2	. .	. .	39 10.78	19.20	" 4 43.205	28 14.58	13.66	39 29.98	28 54 8.24 z.
23	9	. .	. .	. .	. .	4.8	17.1	29.4	. .	. .	39 52.02	19.21	V. 2 39.778	44 54.88	13.56	40 11.23	29 10 48.44
24	7.8	9.0	21.3	34.0	46.2	58.8	11.6	23.9	. .	. .	41 46.44	19.17	IV. 6 46.341	11 56.51	13.29	42 5.61	28 37 49.80
25	9	. .	. .	. .	. .	. .	48.8	1.1	. .	. .	42 23.58	19.18	VI. 4 37.680	31 25.31	13.21	42 42.76	28 57 18.52
26	9	. .	0.5	12.3	25.0	. .	. .	. .	. .	. .	47 25.07	19.14	IV. 6 44.820	12 49.02	12.51	47 44.21	28 38 41.53
27	8	23.0	35.2	47.2	0.5	13.0	. .	37.8	. .	. .	49 0.31	19.15	V. 4 40.311	29 54.53	12.29	49 19.46	28 55 46.82
28	6	15.4	28.2	41.0	53.2	. .	18.5	. .	. .	. .	51 53.35	19.12	IY. 2 40.574	44 27.40	11.90	52 12.47	29 10 19.30 z.
29	9	. .	. .	6.0	18.5	31.0	43.2	56.0	. .	. .	52 18.43	19.13	" 4 38.772	30 47.70	11.85	52 37.56	28 56 39.55
30	9	. .	. .	. .	. .	. .	16.0	28.2	. .	. .	52 50.83	19.12	VI. 6 34.882	18 32.23	11.78	53 9.95	28 44 24.01
31	9	. .	. .	. .	26.5	39.2	51.1	. .	. .	. .	21 54 26.37	19.15	IV. 1 36.370	52 44.33	11.56	21 54 45.52	29 18 35.89

CORRECTIONS.

	COR. TO CLOCK.	HOURLY COR.	m.	n.	c.	ZENITH POINT.	COINC.
	s.	s.	s.	s.	s.	° ′ ″	r.
July 24, at 17h...	+8.856	+0.003	+0.079	+0.300	+0.230	0 0 0.17	40.117

INSTRUMENT READINGS.

		CIRCLE. A.	B.	C.	D.	Mean.	BAR.	THERMOM. At.	Ex.
	h.	° ′ ″	″	″	″	″	I.	°	°
Zone XLVI.—July 24....	21.0	292 11 60.2	60.3	63.0	59.8	60.82	29.908	78.0	73.0
	22.0	59.4	60.6	62.9	59.4	60 57	29.916	76.7	73.0
	23.0	60.3	62.6	65.3	61.0	62.30	29.924	75.8	71.5

Zone XLVI. July 24. H. $D. = -28° 25' 40''.0$. $n' = -20''.00$. $n'' = -5''.29$. (Continued.)

Number.	Magnitude.	SECONDS OF TRANSITS. I.	II.	III.	IV.	V.	VI.	VII.	10.	11.	T.	a.	MICROMETER.	D.	d.	Mean Right Ascension, 1850.0.	Mean South Declination, 1850.0.
											h. m. s.	s.	r.	' ''	''	h. m. s.	° ' ''
32	7.8	6.3	19.2	31.8	44.2	56.6	. .	22.0	. .	. .	21 55 44.27	+19.13	IV. 2 41.712	—43 48.10	—11.39	21 56 3.40	29 9 39.49 z.
33	9	. .	. .	. .	17.0	. .	42.0	54.2	. .	. .	56 16.82	19.11	" 4 42.574	28 36.33	11.32	56 35.93	28 54 27.65 z.
34	9	. .	. .	. .	16.0	28.0	41.0	. .	. .	. .	57 15.85	19.10	V. 5 48.910	19 10.22	11.19	57 34.95	28 45 1.41 z.
35	8	11.0	. .	. .	48.2	. .	. .	. .	. .	. .	58 48.44	19.10	IV. 5 36.191	26 29.66	10.99	59 7.54	28 52 20.65
36	7.8	14.0	26.2	38.0	51.0	. .	16.0	29.0	. .	. .	58 51.14	19.10	" 4 35.738	32 32.51	10.98	59 10.24	28 58 23.49
37	8	29.7	42.1	54.6	7.1	19.4	32.2	44.8	. .	. .	22 1 7.17	19.10	" 3 40.345	35 49.97	10.65	22 1 26.27	29 1 40.62 z.
38	9	41.0	53.2	. .	18.2	31.0	43.5	56.0	. .	. .	4 18.42	19.08	" 3 40.356	35 49.59	10.15	4 37.50	29 1 39.74 z.
39	8.9	8.3	21.0	33.2	46.0	. .	11.0	. .	. .	. .	9 45.93	19.04	" 5 36.843	26 7.11	9.28	10 4.97	28 51 56.39 z.
40	8	4.0	16.2	. .	. .	. .	6.8	19.1	. .	. .	10 41.53	19.04	VI. 4 37.272	31 39.44	9.14	11 0.57	28 57 28.58
41	9	. .	. .	. .	54.0	6.2	18.2	31.1	. .	. .	11 53.57	19.04	IV. 4 34.762	33 6.23	8.96	12 12.61	28 58 55.19 z.
42	8.9	7.0	20.0	32.2	45.0	57.2	9.6	. .	. .	. .	14 44.78	19.00	" 6 44.996	12 42.95	8.55	15 3.78	28 38 31.50 z.
43	9	. .	. .	. .	4.0	16.5	28.2	. .	. .	. .	15 3.80	19.00	" 7 43.649	7 38.39	8.50	15 22.80	28 33 26.89
44	8	48.0	0.7	13.0	25.8	. .	. .	. .	. .	. .	17 25.67	19.00	" 5 46.592	20 30.31	8.16	17 44.67	28 46 18.47
45	9	. .	. .	. .	40.0	52.2	5.0	17.5	. .	. .	17 39.86	19.02	" 2 46.863	40 50.15	8.12	17 58.88	29 6 38.27
46	9	32.3	45.2	57.7	10.0	22.2	35.0	47.5	. .	. .	21 10.03	18.97	" 7 38.692	10 29.61	7.63	21 29.00	28 36 17.24
47	9	5.2	18.0	30.3	43.0	55.5	8.0	20.8	. .	. .	24 43.00	18.97	" 4 41.350	29 18.68	7.16	25 1.97	28 55 5.84
48	9	25.2	38.0	. .	. .	. .	. .	. .	. .	. .	27 3.12	18.98	" 1 42.220	49 22.19	6.85	27 22.10	29 15 9.04 z.
49	9	56.5	. .	22.0	34.4	. .	59.3	12.0	. .	. .	27 34.37	18.97	" 3 34.211	39 21.88	6.78	27 53.34	29 5 8.66
50	9	32.3	44.8	57.2	9.8	. .	. .	. .	. .	. .	30 9.89	18.95	" 3 37.912	37 14.00	6.44	30 28.84	29 3 0.44
51	8.9	25.5	. .	51.0	3.3	. .	29.0	. .	. .	. .	31 3.52	18.95	" 3 32.308	40 27.63	6.32	31 22.47	29 6 13.95 z.
*52	8.9	28.2	41.0	53.0	6.0	18.0	31.0	. .	. .	. .	31 5.86	18.95	V. 3 29.992	41 47.58	6.32	31 24.81	29 7 33.90 z.
53	9	36.5	49.2	1.3	14.0	26.0	. .	. .	. .	. .	34 13.94	18.91	" 6 42.250	14 17.79	5.90	34 32.85	28 40 3.69 z.
54	8.9	. .	. .	. .	. .	44.2	57.0	9.3	. .	. .	34 31.77	18.92	" 4 39.432	30 24.91	5.87	34 50.69	28 56 10.78 z.
55	8	. .	. .	12.3	25.2	37.8	50.2	. .	. .	. .	39 25.13	18.92	IV. 1 36.259	52 48.15	5.22	39 44.05	29 18 33.37 z.
56	9	7.5	. .	32.5	45.2	. .	10.5	. .	. .	. .	43 45.22	18.88	" 4 37.056	31 47.00	4.73	44 4.10	28 57 31.73
57	8	. .	28.2	40.3	53.5	5.8	18.3	31.0	. .	. .	44 53.28	18.89	" 2 36.270	46 56.14	4.60	45 12.17	29 12 40.74
58	9	45.0	57.8	10.2	23.0	35.0	. .	. .	. .	. .	46 22.74	18.85	" 6 44.341	13 5.59	4.44	46 41.59	28 38 50.03
59	8.9	52.5	5.1	17.0	30.0	42.2	55.0	7.5	. .	. .	47 29.93	18.85	" 5 41.301	23 33.15	4.31	47 48.78	28 49 17.46 z.
60	9	34.0	47.0	59.2	11.4	24.0	. .	. .	. .	. .	49 11.68	18.84	" 5 47.080	20 13.48	4.12	49 30.52	28 45 57.60 z.
61	8.9	. .	44.0	56.2	9.0	. .	. .	. .	. .	. .	50 8.94	18.84	" 4 37.850	31 19.56	4.02	50 27.78	28 57 3.58 z.
62	9	. .	. .	. .	. .	21.0	34.0	46.0	. .	. .	50 8.59	18.85	VI. 3 31.992	40 38.43	4.02	50 27.44	29 6 22.45 z.
63	9	. .	. .	30.8	43.1	55.2	8.0	20.2	. .	. .	51 43.00	18.83	IV. 6 36.180	17 47.51	3.85	52 1.83	28 43 31.36
64	9	. .	. .	41.3	54.0	6.2	19.0	31.4	. .	. .	52 53.89	18.82	" 5 42.280	22 59.32	3.74	53 12.71	28 48 43.06 z.
65	8.9	1.2	14.0	26.2	39.0	51.0	3.8	16.5	. .	. .	55 38.86	18.83	" 3 38.340	36 59.24	3.47	55 57.69	29 2 42.71 z.
66	7.8	41.4	54.0	6.2	19.0	31.2	44.0	56.5	. .	. .	23 1 18.93	18.79	" 4 43.092	28 18.47	2.90	23 1 37.72	28 54 1 37

Zone XLVII. July 29. H. $D. = -40° 50' 10''.0$. $n' = -13''.00$. $n'' = -12''.85$.

Number.	Magnitude.	I.	II.	III.	IV.	V.	VI.	VII.	10.	11.	T.	a.	MICROMETER.	D.	d.	Mean Right Ascension, 1850.0.	Mean South Declination, 1850.0.
1	8	22.5	37.0	51.2	6.2	20.2	35.1	49.4	. .	. .	18 0 5.98	21.84	IV. 4 36.220	32 24.35	12.97	18 0 27.82	41 22 47.32
2	7.8	30.0	44.2	. .	13.5	28.0	. .	57.2	. .	. .	2 13.54	21.84	" 4 37.592	31 36.45	12.35	2 35.38	41 21 58.80
3	8.9	59.0	. .	. .	42.8	. .	11.2	26.0	. .	. .	18 2 42.40	21.83	" 5 34.088	27 48.99	12.21	18 3 4.23	41 18 11.20

CORRECTIONS.

	COR. TO CLOCK.	HOURLY COR.	m.	n.	c.	ZENITH POINT.	COINC.
	s.	s.	s.	s.	s.		r.
July 29, at 17h....	+ 9.228	+0.009	0.117	0.200	0.330	359° 59' 59''.86	40.120

INSTRUMENT READINGS.

	CIRCLE. A.	B.	C.	D.	Mean.	BAR.	THERMOM. At.	Ex.
Zone XLVII.—July 29... h. 17.9	279° 51' 2''.5	2''.9	4''.6	0''.2	2''.55	I. 29.960	76°.0	70°.9
18.5	5.5	5.8	8.7	3.8	5.95	29.960	75.2	70.7

Number.	Magnitude.	SECONDS OF TRANSITS. I.	II.	III.	IV.	V.	VI.	VII.	10.	11.	T.	a.	MICROMETER.	D.	d.	Mean Right Ascension, 1850.0.	Mean South Declination, 1850.0.
Zone XLVII. July 29. M. $D. = -40° 50' 10''.0.$ $n' = -13''.00.$ $n'' = -12''.85.$ (Continued.)																	
											h. m. s.	s.	r.	' "	"	h. m. s.	° ' "
4	9	24.2	39.2	54.0	8.2	23.0	37.8	52.2	. .	. .	18 5 8.43	+21.87	IV. 1 42.433	—49 29.91	—11.49	18 5 30.30	41 39 51.40
5	8.9	20.0	34.2	49.3	4.0	18.4	33.2	48.0	. .	. .	13 3.93	21.85	" 1 41.567	49 59.76	9.16	13 25.78	41 40 18.92
6	9	52.5	7.5	22.2	. .	51.0	. .	. .	. .	. .	19 36.61	21.78	" 5 42.150	23 8.74	7.25	19 58.39	41 13 25.99
7	9	. .	5.0	19.0	34.0	48.0	2.8	17.2	. .	. .	20 33.73	21.77	" 5 48.550	19 26.11	6.97	20 55.50	41 9 43.08
8	9	24.5	39.2	53.5	8.2	22.8	37.2	52.1	. .	. .	23 8.24	21.78	" 4 42.055	29 1.43	6.21	23 30.02	41 19 17.64
9	9	. .	. .	30.3	45.2	. .	. .	. .	. .	. .	26 45.15	21.82	" 1 35.200	53 41.31	5.15	27 6.97	41 43 56.46
10	9	. .	. .	. .	. .	44.5	59.4	14.0	. .	. .	28 30.02	21.79	VI. 2 42.252	43 42.01	4.64	28 51.81	41 33 56.65
11	9	. .	47.0	1.2	16.0	31.0	45.5	. .	. .	. .	18 30 16.18	21.79	IV. 2 41.562	44 6.04	4.12	18 30 37.97	41 34 20.16
Zone XLVIII. July 29. H. $D. = -28° 26' 00''.0.$ $n' = -33''.67.$ $n'' = -7''.00.$																	
1	9	. .	. .	25.0	37.2	49.8	. .	. .	. .	. .	18 34 37.40	20.57	IV. 3 36.075	38 19.20	30.03	18 34 57.97	29 4 49.23
2	9	. .	25.0	37.2	. .	2.2	. .	. .	. .	. .	35 49.88	20.55	" 4 41.900	29 1.35	29.73	36 10.43	28 55 31.08
3	9	. .	26.0	38.2	. .	3.2	. .	27.2	. .	. .	35 50.87	20.55	" 4 42.370	28 45.14	29.73	36 11.42	28 55 14.87
4	9	. .	. .	. .	. .	. .	30.0	42.0	1.0	. .	36 4.65	20.56	VI. 3 33.072	40 2.81	29.67	36 25.21	29 6 32.48
5	9	57.5	10.2	22.5	35.0	. .	0.2	. .	. .	. .	39 35.18	20.56	IV. 2 34.555	47 57.09	28.80	39 55.74	29 14 25.89
6	8	. .	. .	20.5	32.7	45.3	58.0	. .	. .	. .	40 32.91	20.52	" 6 32.403	19 59.68	28.57	40 53.43	28 46 28.25
7	9	. .	. .	. .	. .	26.4	39.2	. .	. .	. .	41 14.02	20.53	V. 4 40.410	29 52.82	28.40	41 34.55	28 56 21.22
8	9	17.5	30.5	42.8	55.2	7.8	20.3	32.8	. .	. .	42 55.30	20.52	IV. 4 44.128	27 44.38	27.99	43 15.22	28 54 12.37
9	9	. .	29.0	41.0	53.2	6.2	18.8	. .	. .	. .	43 53.65	20.52	" 4 42.950	28 25.07	27.75	44 14.17	28 54 52.82
10	9	8.5	21.0	. .	. .	59.0	11.2	24.0	. .	. .	44 46.26	20.52	V. 4 46.148	26 34.57	27.54	45 6.78	28 53 2.11
11	9	. .	. .	. .	. .	44.2	57.2	10.0	. .	. .	45 32.17	20.50	" 6 36.903	17 24.14	27.35	45 52.67	28 43 51.49
12	9	. .	. .	34.7	47.0	59.5	2.2	. .	. .	. .	46 47.11	20.53	IV. 3 37.630	37 25.46	27.04	47 7.64	29 3 52.50
13	9	47.3	0.2	12.2	25.0	38.0	. .	. .	. .	. .	48 25.13	20.51	" 4 39.616	30 20.24	26.65	48 45.64	28 56 46.89 z.
14	9	. .	55.0	7.2	19.4	32.5	44.8	. .	. .	. .	50 19.79	20.49	" 5 45.912	20 55.49	26.18	50 40.28	28 47 21.67
15	8.9	. .	. .	3.0	15.7	28.2	. .	. .	. .	. .	50 15.70	20.50	" 4 44.273	27 39.39	26.20	50 36.20	28 54 5.59 z.
16	8.9	. .	2.7	15.2	. .	40.2	. .	. .	. .	. .	51 27.77	20.50	" 4 43.002	28 23.28	25.90	51 48.27	28 54 49.18
17	9	. .	. .	. .	33.0	. .	57.3	9.5	. .	. .	51 32.33	20.51	" 3 41.658	35 6.27	25.89	51 52.84	29 1 32.16 z.
18	9	. .	. .	. .	. .	38.5	51.2	4.0	. .	. .	52 26.22	20.49	V. 5 39.155	24 48.93	25.67	52 46.71	28 51 14.60
19	8.9	. .	. .	. .	45.0	57.2	9.2	22.0	. .	. .	52 44.58	20.49	IV. 5 39.562	24 34.86	25.60	53 5.07	28 51 0.46
20	9	43.5	56.2	9.0	. .	. .	. .	. .	. .	. .	19 48 21.38	20.29	III. 4 34.660	33 11.42	12.51	19 48 41.67	28 59 23.93
21	9	. .	. .	. .	. .	30.0	42.5	55.0	. .	. .	48 17.53	20.26	V. 6 37.420	17 6.30	12.52	48 37.79	28 43 18.82
22	9	. .	. .	. .	11.0	23.4	36.0	48.2	. .	. .	49 10.84	20.29	IV. 3 38.435	36 57.69	12.31	49 31.13	29 3 10.00 z.
23	7.8	20.5	33.6	46.0	58.2	11.0	23.5	36.0	. .	. .	50 58.43	20.28	" 3 44.770	33 18.76	11.92	51 18.71	28 59 30.68 z.
24	9	. .	8.0	20.5	33.0	45.0	. .	. .	. .	. .	52 32.89	20.24	" 7 38.700	10 31.00	11.58	52 53.13	28 36 42.58
25	9	. .	. .	55.5	8.2	20.2	33.1	. .	. .	. .	53 8.03	20.25	" 5 45.460	21 11.13	11.44	53 28.28	28 47 22.57 z.
26	9	. .	. .	12.3	25.0	37.4	. .	. .	. .	. .	54 24.97	20.27	" 3 39.145	36 33.14	11.16	54 45.24	29 2 44.30
27	9	. .	. .	1.8	14.2	26.5	39.2	51.5	. .	. .	55 14.19	19.23	" 6 40.202	15 30.21	10.98	55 34.42	28 41 41.19
28	8	26.4	39.1	51.5	4.0	16.5	29.0	41.2	. .	. .	57 4.00	20.23	" 5 44.845	21 32.34	10.57	57 24.23	28 47 42.91 z.
29	8	6.0	18.4	31.0	43.0	. .	8.8	. .	. .	. .	19 59 43.47	20.23	" 5 36.912	26 6.44	9.98	20 0 3.70	28 52 16.42

CORRECTIONS.

	COR. TO CLOCK.	HOURLY COR.	m.	n.	c.	ZENITH POINT.	COINC.
	s.	s.	s.	s.	s.		r.
July 29, at 17*h*...	+ 9.228	+ 0.009	+0.117	+0.200	+0.330	359° 59' 59''.86	40.120

* The mean of the circle reading for 18.6*h* is corrected from the difference between the readings of A.

INSTRUMENT READINGS.

		CIRCLE. A.	B.	C.	D.	Mean.	BAR.	THERMOM. At.	Ex.
	h.	° ' "	"	"	"	"	I.	°	°
Zone XLVIII.—July 29,	18.6	292 12 0.9	. .	. .	. .	*1.78	29.960	75.2	70.7
	20.5	1.9	2.8	5.2	1.2	2.78	29.944	74.5	70.8

Number.	Magnitude.	SECONDS OF TRANSITS. I.	II.	III.	IV.	V.	VI.	VII.	10.	11.	T.	a.	MICROMETER.	D.	d.	Mean Right Ascension, 1850.0.	Mean South Declination, 1850.0.
Zone XLVIII. July 29. H. *D.* = —28° 26′ 00″.00. n′. = —33″.67. n″. = —7″.00. (Continued.)																	
											h. m. s.	s.	r.	′ ″	″	h. m. s.	° ′ ″
30	9	. .	. .	7.5	20.0	32.5	. .	. .	. .	. .	20 0 20.07	+20.21	IV. 6 37.412	—17 6.61	— 9.85	20 0 40.28	28 43 16.46
31	8	14.0	26.6	38.8	51.5	4.2	16.7	29.3	. .	. .	1 51.64	20.24	" 2 45.223	41 48.57	9.52	2 11.88	29 7 58.09 z.
32	9	. .	. .	. .	. .	. .	. .	18.5	37.2	50.5	2 41.07	20.24	VII. 2 44.706	42 6.08	9.34	3 1.31	29 8 15.42
33	9	15.0	27.7	39.8	52.2	5.0	17.2	30.0	. .	. .	5 52.44	20.21	IV. 4 40.570	29 47.27	8.65	6 12.65	28 55 55.92 z.
34	9	. .	. .	. .	. .	. .	42.0	54.5	13.3	. .	6 17.11	20.18	VI. 6 43.815	13 25.23	8.56	6 37.29	28 39 33.79
35	9	49.2	2.2	14.4	27.0	. .	52.2	. .	. .	. .	7 27.00	20.17	IV. 7 40.625	9 24.48	8.31	7 47.17	28 35 32.79
36	8.9	. .	12.4	25.0	37.2	50.0	3.0	. .	. .	. .	14 37.53	20.16	" 5 37.600	25 42.64	6.78	14 57.69	28 51 49.42
37	7	17.6	30.2	42.5	55.0	7.4	20.0	32.8	. .	. .	15 55.12	20.18	" 2 43.786	42 38.18	6.51	16 15.30	29 8 44.69 z.
38	9	. .	. .	. .	56.5	9.0	31.4	. .	. .	. .	16 56.44	20.16	" 4 37.292	31 40.57	6.29	17 16.60	28 57 46.86
39	8	. .	. .	. .	. .	9.8	22.5	35.0	. .	. .	17 57.32	20.18	V. 1 37.545	52 5.40	6.08	18 17.50	29 18 11.48 z.
40	9	. .	. .	. .	. .	. .	41.0	53.2	. .	. .	18 15.85	20.13	VI. 5 49.341	18 56.90	6.01	18 35.96	28 45 2.91
41	9	10.5	23.1	35.5	48.2	0.2	. .	. .	. .	. .	21 48.07	20.13	IV. 4 41.290	29 22.45	5.26	22 8.20	28 55 27.71
42	9	. .	27.2	39.8	53.0	5.0	17.7	30.0	. .	. .	22 52.53	20.14	" 3 32.778	40 13.09	5.04	23 12.67	29 6 18 13 z.
43	8	35.5	48.0	. .	13.0	25.5	38.2	50.5	. .	. .	23 13.07	20.14	" 3 33.375	39 52.51	4.97	23 33.21	29 5 57.48 z.
44	9	. .	0.5	12.7	25.3	38.0	50.6	. .	. .	. .	25 25.45	20.13	" 3 33.060	40 3.36	4.50	25 45.58	29 6 7.86 z.
45	9	14.8	27.8	40.2	53.0	. .	. .	. .	. .	. .	26 52.80	20.12	" 3 43.665	33 56.95	4.20	27 12.92	29 0 1.15
46	8	. .	22.0	34.8	47.1	59.8	12.8	. .	. .	. .	27 47.34	20.13	" 2 35.010	47 41.41	4.00	28 7.47	29 13 45.41 z.
47	8	57.3	10.2	22.5	35.0	47.5	. .	12.6	. .	. .	28 35.08	20.10	V. 4 38.836	30 47.17	3.84	28 55.18	28 56 51.01
48	7.8	47.8	0.4	13.0	25.5	38.0	50.2	3.2	. .	. .	20 31 25.48	20.10	IV. 3 35.702	38 32.06	3.26	20 31 45.58	29 4 35.32
Zone XLIX. August 11. H. *D.* = —40° 19′ 50″.0. n′. = —25″.83. n″. = —12″.00.																	
1	9	. .	. .	. .	34.0	47.5	. .	. .	. .	. .	17 48 33.57	23.32	IV. 5 43.720	22 13.54	23.85	17 48 56.89	40 42 27.39
2	9	. .	8.0	. .	. .	51.0	. .	20.2	. .	. .	50 36.75	23.34	" 4 41.923	29 5.17	23.39	51 0.09	40 49 18.56
3	8	58.0	12.5	26.8	41.4	56.0	10.2	24.5	. .	. .	53 41.38	23.30	" 6 36.000	17 56.39	22.69	54 4.68	40 38 9.08
4	8.9	. .	24.0	38.0	53.0	6.2	. .	. .	. .	. .	59 52.52	23.26	" 7 44.858	6 55.82	21.30	18 0 15.78	40 27 7.12
5	8	57.4	12.0	26.2	41.0	55.5	10.0	24.2	. .	. .	18 2 40.96	23.34	" 1 42.930	49 10.77	20.67	3 4.30	41 9 21.44
6	8.9	44.3	59.2	13.6	27.8	42.5	56.4	. .	. .	. .	5 27.89	23.24	" 7 38.426	10 39.32	20.03	5 51.13	40 30 49.35
7	9	. .	. .	. .	. .	. .	16.0	30.2	. .	. .	4 46.95	23.26	VI. 6 38.200	16 39.78	20.19	5 10.21	40 36 49.97
8	9	. .	29.3	44.0	58.0	13.0	27.0	. .	. .	. .	7 58.28	23.24	IV. 7 40.680	9 20.87	19.46	8 21.52	40 29 30.33
9	9	. .	53.5	7.6	22.3	36.2	51.0	. .	. .	. .	13 22.12	23.25	" 4 43.930	27 55.45	18.26	13 45.37	40 48 3.71
10	9	. .	3.2	17.5	32.0	. .	. .	. .	. .	. .	20 32.19	23.26	" 1 42.209	49 35.90	16.64	20 55.45	41 9 42.54
11	8	. .	51.2	5.5	20.0	34.0	49.0	. .	. .	. .	26 19.96	23.21	" 3 41.926	35 3.58	15.34	26 43.17	40 55 8.92
12	9	. .	22.8	37.0	51.4	6.0	20.5	. .	. .	. .	32 51.56	23.18	" 3 39.713	36 20.42	13.87	33 14.74	40 56 24.29
13	9	. .	. .	. .	24.0	38.2	52.5	7.0	. .	. .	33 23.59	23.20	" 2 37.410	46 29.06	13.75	33 46.79	41 6 32.81
14	6	. .	23.0	37.2	52.0	6.3	21.0	. .	. .	. .	36 51.91	23.11	" 6 43.560	13 33.71	12.97	37 15.02	40 33 36.68 B.
15	9	. .	. .	. .	42.5	57.0	12.0	26.2	. .	. .	37 42.64	23.17	V. 2 44.000	42 39.84	12.81	38 5.81	41 2 42.65
16	8	. .	34.0	48.3	2.3	17.2	32.0	. .	. .	. .	40 2.82	23.18	IV. 1 35.120	53 42.28	12.26	40 26.00	41 13 44.54
17	8	. .	52.5	7.0	21.5	36.0	51.0	. .	. .	. .	41 21.64	23.15	" 2 39.611	45 12.34	11.97	41 44.79	41 5 14.31
18	9	. .	19.0	33.2	47.5	2.0	16.2	. .	. .	. .	18 43 47.60	23.10	" 5 38.000	25 32.31	11.44	18 44 10.70	40 45 33.75

CORRECTIONS.

	COR. TO CLOCK.	HOURLY COR.	m.	n.	c.	ZENITH POINT.	COINC.
	s.	s.	s.	s.	s.	° ′ ″	r.
Aug. 11, at 18h...	+10.685	—0.003	+0.294	+0.300	+0.230	0 0 2.02	40.085

INSTRUMENT READINGS.

	h.	CIRCLE. A.	B.	C.	D.	Mean.	BAR.	THERMOM. At.	Ex.
		° ′ ″	′	″	″	″	I.	°	°
Zone XLIX.—August 11,	17.6	. . . .	. . .	. . .	. . .	. . . .	30.106	78.0	72.5
	17.8	280 20 59.5	61.8	64.0	60.8	61.52	. . . .	. . .	. . .
	18.5	. . . .	. . .	. . .	. . .	. . . .	30.108	76.5	70.6
	19.7	59.5	62.6	64.8	61.5	62.10	30.100	75.2	68.0
	19.9	. . . .	. . .	. . .	. . .	. . . .	30.114	75.0	69.2

Number	Magnitude	SECONDS OF TRANSITS. I.	II.	III.	IV.	V.	VI.	VII.	10.	11.	T.	a.	MICROMETER.	D.	d.	Mean Right Ascension, 1850.0.	Mean South Declination, 1850.0.
Zone XLIX. August 11. H. $D. = -40° 19' 50''.0.$ $n'. = -25''.83.$ $n''. = -12''.00.$ (Continued.)																	
											h. m. s.	s.	r.	′ ″	″	h. m. s.	° ′ ″
19	9	. .	6.2	20.7	35.2	49.2	4.0	. .	. .	. .	18 45 35.07	+23.09	V. 5 37.216	—25 59.53	—11.04	18 45 58.16	40 46 0.57
20	9	. .	20.8	35.0	49.8	4.0	18.8	. .	. .	. .	48 49.70	23.08	IV. 4 41.828	29 8.34	10.34	49 12.78	40 49 8.68
21	8.9	. .	41.2	55.8	10.2	24.4	39.0	. .	. .	. .	51 10.13	23.07	" 4 36.765	32 4.34	9.83	51 33.20	40 52 4.17
22	9	. .	31.5	45.5	. .	. .	. .	. .	. .	. .	53 0.13	23.02	" 7 35.340	13 35.93	9.43	53 23.15	40 33 35.36
23	5.6	. .	1.8	16.0	31.0	45.2	. .	. .	. .	. .	57 30.77	23.01	" 5 41.635	23 25.94	8.45	57 53.78	40 43 24.39
24	8.9	. .	54.0	8.2	23.0	37.0	52.1	. .	. .	. .	19 2 22.89	23.02	" 3 34.866	39 8.86	7.40	19 2 45.91	40 59 6.26
25	9	. .	. .	52.6	7.0	21.0	36.0	. .	. .	. .	4 6.98	22.96	" 6 38.638	16 24.68	7.03	4 29.94	40 36 21.71
26	5	. .	37.0	51.6	6.0	20.3	35.0	. .	. .	. .	19 13 6.00	22.93	" 3 44.425	33 36.90	5.10	19 13 28.93	40 53 32.00 B.
Zone L. August 11. H. $D. = -25° 55' 20''.0.$ $n'. = -22''.47.$ $n''. = -6''.00.$																	
1	8.9	. .	21.5	33.3	46.0	58.2	10.6	. .	. .	. .	21 0 45.96	21.12	IV. 1 40.720	50 14.32	22.28	21 1 7.08	26 45 56.60 Z.
2	8	. .	12.2	24.4	36.2	48.8	1.3	. .	. .	. .	5 36.60	21.07	" 3 40.055	36 0.56	21.29	5 57.67	26 31 41.85 Z.
3	9	. .	49.0	1.5	13.5	. .	38.0	. .	. .	. .	8 13.58	21.06	" 2 44.180	42 23.32	20.74	8 34.64	26 38 4.06 Z.
4	9	. .	. .	. .	9.5	22.0	34.5	46.7	. .	. .	9 9.81	21.04	" 4 39.888	30 9.86	20.55	9 30.85	26 25 50.41
5	9	. .	21.5	33.2	. .	57.0	. .	. .	. .	. .	13 45.47	21.02	" 3 43.243	34 10.48	19.64	14 6.49	26 29 50.12
6	8	. .	. .	58.0	10.3	22.4	34.4	47.0	. .	. .	15 10.24	20.98	" 6 38.623	16 24.02	19.36	15 31.22	26 12 3.38 Z.
7	8	. .	13.2	25.2	37.7	49.9	2.1	. .	. .	. .	19 37.63	20.97	" 5 44.058	21 58.72	18.48	19 58.60	26 17 37.20 Z.
8	7.8	. .	17.0	29.0	41.4	53.5	6.0	. .	. .	. .	21 41.39	20.96	" 5 36.550	26 18.00	18.08	22 2.35	26 21 56.08 Z.
9	8	. .	. .	37.5	49.8	1.8	14.0	. .	. .	. .	22 49.73	20.93	" 7 42.120	8 32.31	17.86	23 10.66	26 4 10.17 Z.
10	9	. .	. .	. .	31.0	42.5	55.0	7.2	. .	. .	27 30.55	20.94	" 3 43.025	34 17.99	16.97	27 51.49	26 29 54.96 Z.
11	8	. .	46.0	58.2	11.1	23.0	35.2	. .	. .	. .	29 10.71	20.90	" 6 47.311	11 24.01	16.66	29 31.61	26 7 0.67 Z.
12	9	. .	. .	55.2	7.2	19.8	. .	. .	. .	. .	30 7.47	20.91	" 4 43.581	28 2.30	16.48	30 28.38	26 23 38.78 Z.
13	8.9	. .	37.0	49.1	1.2	13.6	26.2	. .	. .	. .	32 1.44	20.91	" 3 40.430	35 47.62	16.13	32 22.35	26 31 23.75 Z.
14	8	. .	41.0	52.8	5.0	17.4	29.2	. .	. .	. .	33 5.10	20.91	" 3 38.715	36 46.81	15.94	33 26.01	26 32 22.75 Z.
15	9	. .	. .	39.0	50.5	2.8	15.0	. .	. .	. .	33 50.72	20.91	" 2 39.448	45 6.78	15.80	34 11.63	26 40 42.58 Z.
16	9	. .	37.1	. .	1.2	. .	25.6	. .	. .	. .	38 1.34	20.86	" 5 41.120	23 40.20	15.03	38 22.10	26 19 15.23
17	9	. .	48.0	. .	12.2	24.2	57.0	. .	. .	. .	39 12.29	20.87	" 3 35.516	38 37.34	14.82	39 33.16	26 34 12.16 Z.
18	9	. .	. .	36.0	49.0	1.2	. .	. .	. .	. .	40 48.80	20.84	" 5 39.343	24 41.57	14.53	41 9.64	26 20 16.10
19	9	. .	37.0	49.0	1.2	13.5	25.2	. .	. .	. .	45 1.19	20.83	" 3 44.750	33 18.39	13.80	45 22.02	26 28 52.19 Z.
20	8	. .	. .	23.3	36.0	48.0	. .	. .	. .	. .	47 35.83	20.82	" 6 37.501	17 2.75	13.36	47 56.65	26 12 36.11 Z.
21	9	38.0	51.0	2.5	14.5	. .	. .	. .	. .	. .	50 14.82	20.77	" 7 42.238	8 28.24	12.90	50 35.59	26 4 1.14
*22	9	. .	. .	. .	40.0	52.5	5.0	17.0	. .	. .	50 40.26	20.79	" 4 39.102	30 37.02	12.83	51 1.05	26 26 9.85
23	9	. .	. .	. .	. .	57.0	9.0	21.2	. .	. .	50 44.59	20.79	VI. 4 39.780	30 13.49	12.82	51 5.38	26 25 46.31 Z.
24	9	. .	. .	45.0	57.0	9.2	. .	. .	. .	. .	52 57.13	20.76	IV. 6 40.702	15 12.22	12.45	53 17.89	26 10 44.67 Z.
25	7.8	. .	13.5	26.0	38.0	50.1	2.5	. .	. .	. .	55 38.05	20.77	" 2 46.624	40 58.89	12.01	55 58.82	26 36 30.90
26	8	. .	32.0	44.0	56.0	8.5	20.8	. .	. .	. .	59 56.28	20.74	IV. 3 42.682	34 29.81	11.30	22 0 17.02	26 30 1.11 Z.
27	9	. .	. .	11.5	24.0	36.0	48.0	. .	. .	. .	22 2 23.83	20.71	" 7 38.110	10 50.79	10.92	2 44.54	26 6 21.71 Z.
28	8	44.2	57.0	9.0	21.2	. .	. .	. .	. .	. .	6 21.25	20.69	" 4 43.850	27 53.03	10.30	6 41.94	26 23 23.33
29	9	. .	. .	. .	24.0	. .	48.2	0.8	. .	. .	22 6 23.86	20.71	VI. 2 46.100	41 16.92	10.30	22 6 44.57	26 36 47.22

INSTRUMENT READINGS.

	CIRCLE. A.	B.	C.	D.	Mean.	BAR.	THERMOM. At.	Ex.
	° ′ ″	″	″	″	″	I.	°	°
Zone L.—August 11, 21.0 h.	294 42 1.5	5.6	6.5	5.0	4.65	30.100	73.8	71.7
23.0	4.1	8.1	10.3	8.1	7.65	30.118	73.8	68.7

Number.	Magnitude.	SECONDS OF TRANSITS. I.	II.	III.	IV.	V.	VI.	VII.	10.	11.	T.	a.	MICROMETER.	D.	d.	Mean Right Ascension, 1850.0.	Mean South Declination, 1850.0.
Zone L. August 11. H. $D. = -25° 55' 20''.0$. $n' = -22''.47$. $n'' = -6''.00$. (Continued.)																	
											h. m. s.	s.	r.	′ ″	″	h. m. s.	° ′ ″
30	7.8	. .	26.2	38.2	51.0	3.0	15.1	. .	. .	. .	22 7 50.73	+20.70	IV. 2 42.950	—43 5.81	—10.08	22 8 11.43	26 38 35.89 z.
31	8	. .	47.3	59.2	11.8	24.0	36.0	. .	. .	. .	13 11.66	20.63	" 6 46.900	11 38.20	9.28	13 32.29	26 7 7.48 z.
32	8	. .	2.0	14.2	26.5	38.8	51.0	. .	. .	. .	14 26.53	20.66	" 3 32.790	40 11.45	9.11	14 47.19	26 35 40.56 z.
33	9	. .	22.0	34.2	46.0	58.0	10.5	. .	. .	. .	16 46.15	20.61	" 7 37.531	11 10.75	8.77	17 6.76	26 6 39.52 z.
34	9	. .	41.3	53.5	6.0	18.0	30.2	. .	. .	. .	24 5.82	20.60	" 2 45.502	41 37.69	7.77	24 26.42	26 37 5.46 z.
35	9	. .	. .	. .	. .	. .	42.0	54.0	. .	. .	24 17.31	20.61	IV. 3 34.814	39 1.45	7.74	24 37.92	26 34 29.19
36	8	. .	9.7	21.6	34.2	46.2	59.0	. .	. .	. .	29 34.15	20.56	IV. 4 39.366	30 27.91	7.04	29 54.71	26 25 54.95 z.
37	8.9	. .	13.5	26.0	38.2	51.0	3.2	. .	. .	. .	30 38.40	20.54	" 5 47.230	20 9.18	6.90	30 58.94	26 15 36.08 z.
38	9	. .	. .	33.0	45.0	57.2	9.8	22.0	. .	. .	32 45.24	20.52	" 6 45.418	12 29.40	6.63	33 5.76	26 7 56.03 z.
39	9	. .	16.6	28.5	41.0	53.0	5.4	. .	. .	. .	34 40.91	20.53	" 4 37.587	31 29.30	6.39	35 1.44	26 26 55.69 z.
40	9	. .	46.0	. .	10.0	22.2	34.2	. .	. .	. .	38 10.04	20.49	" 6 39.850	15 41.66	5.95	38 30.53	26 11 7.61 z.
41	7.8	. .	57.0	9.0	21.1	33.4	46.0	. .	. .	. .	39 21.34	20.52	" 2 37.180	46 25.09	5.80	39 41.86	26 41 50.89 z.
42	9	. .	52.8	4.8	17.0	28.8	41.2	. .	. .	. .	44 16.93	20.46	" 5 42.191	23 3.22	5.21	44 37.39	26 18 28.43
43	9	. .	34.2	46.2	58.4	10.2	23.0	. .	. .	. .	45 58.41	20.44	" 7 36.360	11 51.25	5.01	46 18.85	26 7 16.26
44	9	. .	43.1	55.0	7.5	19.2	32.0	. .	. .	. .	49 7.39	20.43	" 6 33.322	19 27.12	4.63	49 27.82	26 14 51.75 z.
45	7	. .	31.0	43.1	55.2	7.3	19.5	. .	. .	. .	51 55.23	20.43	" 4 39.650	30 18.07	4.32	52 15.66	26 25 42.39
46	9	. .	. .	. .	. .	56.2	. .	. .	. .	. .	52 40.00	20.44	" 1 36.570	52 37.66	4.23	53 0.44	26 48 1.89
47	8.9	51.0	3.3	15.3	28.0	. .	. .	. .	. .	. .	55 27.85	20.41	" 3 35.949	38 22.35	3.92	55 48.26	26 33 46.27
48	8.9	. .	. .	55.0	7.2	19.2	31.8	43.8	. .	. .	56 7.15	20.40	" 3 43.320	34 7.81	3.84	56 27.55	26 29 31.65
49	9	. .	35.0	. .	59.4	11.2	23.5	. .	. .	. .	58 59.17	20.39	" 4 42.055	28 55.04	3.53	59 19.56	26 24 18.57
50	8	. .	4.2	16.3	28.2	41.0	53.2	. .	. .	. .	23 0 28.61	20.39	" 2 43.080	43 1.32	3.37	23 0 49.00	26 38 24.69
Zone LI. August 12. M. $D. -28° 56'' 3'.13$. $n' = -36''.59$. $n'' -4''.00$.																	
1	8.9	. .	. .	48.8	. .	14.0	. .	. .	. .	. .	18 8 1.51	21.93	2. 5 44.50	21 40.56	34.91	18 8 23.44	29 18 18.60
2	9.10	. .	. .	. .	. .	. .	41.2	54.0	. .	. .	9 16.02	21.96	II. 1 45.632	47 23.03	34.65	9 37.98	29 44 0.81 z.
3	8	. .	. .	. .	. .	. .	. .	23.5	. .	. .	9 45.65	21.95	VII. 2 41.65	43 48.72	34.54	10 7.60	29 40 26.39
4	8	. .	. .	. .	. .	. .	. .	. .	27.6	40.1	10 31.15	21.90	11. 7 38.22	10 43.40	34.38	10 53.05	29 7 20.91 z.
5	8	. .	. .	. .	28.6	. .	54.0	6.5	. .	. .	14 28.64	21.93	2. 3 32.97	40 2.78	33.56	14 50.57	29 36 39.47
6	8.9	. .	. .	. .	9.4	22.0	34.7	. .	. .	. .	17 9.44	21.90	IV. 3 45.39	32 54.40	33.01	17 31.34	29 29 30.54
7	7	39.6	52.5	5.0	. .	. .	. .	. .	. .	. .	19 17.59	21.88	2. 5 40.24	24 7.74	32.56	19 39.47	29 20 43.43
8	9	. .	. .	. .	. .	29.5	42.2	55.0	. .	. .	19 17.06	21.89	IV. 4 39.82	30 10.21	32.56	19 38.95	29 26 45.90
9	8.9	. .	. .	. .	. .	. .	. .	. .	32.2	45.0	19 35.63	21.89	11. 4 44.40	27 30.87	32.50	19 57.52	29 24 6.50
10	8	42.0	55.0	7.3	20.0	. .	. .	. .	. .	. .	22 19.97	21.87	I. 5 46.14	20 44.29	31.95	22 41.84	29 17 19.37 z.
11	7	. .	. .	51.0	3.5	16.0	. .	. .	. .	. .	26 3.56	21.90	" 1 37.27	52 11.78	31.19	26 25.46	29 48 46.10 z.
12	8.9	. .	57.5	. .	22.5	. .	. .	. .	. .	. .	27 22.59	21.87	II. 3 34.95	38 54.96	30.93	27 44.46	29 35 29.02 z.
13	8	. .	. .	52.0	5.0	. .	. .	. .	. .	. .	29 4.55	21.88	III. 2 31.5	49 39.69	30.58	29 26.43	29 46 13.40
14	10	. .	17.5	. .	42.5	. .	. .	. .	. .	. .	31 42.44	21.81	VII. 7 41.50	8 50.86	30.04	32 4.25	29 5 24.03
15	9	. .	2.5	15.0	27.5	. .	. .	. .	. .	. .	18 34 27.63	21.84	IV. 3 37.4	37 30.48	29.46	18 34 49.47	29 34 3.07 z.

INSTRUMENT READINGS.

	CIRCLE. A.	B.	C.	D.	Mean.	BAR.	THERMOM. At.	Ex.
Zone LI.—Aug. 12, 18.1 h.	291° 42′ 4″.3	8″.1	8″.3	9″.2	7″.48	30.124 i.	80°.0	77°.2
18.6	1.8	7.5	7.3	7.7	6.08	. . .	. .	. .

Zone LI. August 12. M. D. —28° 56′ 3″.13. n.′ = —36″.59. n.″ —4″.00. (Continued.)

Number.	Magnitude.	SECONDS OF TRANSITS. I.	II.	III.	IV.	V.	VI.	VII.	10.	11.	T.	a.	MICROMETER.	D.	d.	Mean Right Ascension, 1850.0.	Mean South Declination, 1850.0.
											h. m. s.	s.	r.	° ′ ″	″	h. m. s.	° ′ ″
16	9	. .	. .	20.0	32.0	. .	. .	. .	. .	. .	18 36 32.35	+21.84	I. 2 41.65	—43 48.72	—29.03	18 36 54.19	29 40 20.88 z.
17	6	. .	. .	. .	52.6	5.2	18.0	. .	. .	. .	36 52.65	21.85	IV. 1 40.40	50 23.94	28.95	37 14.50	29 46 56.02 z.
18	6	6.0	18.6	31.0	43.7	56.2	9.0	. .	. .	. .	42 43.76	21.80	2. 3 39.16	36 28.92	27.70	43 5.56	29 32 59.75
19	8.9	37.5	50.6	3.0	15.5	. .	. .	. .	. .	. .	44 15.53	21.76	VI. 6 33.83	19 7.15	27.37	44 37.29	29 15 37.65 z.
20	8.7	. .	. .	21.0	33.4	46.0	. .	. .	. .	. .	45 33.53	21.77	III. 5 34.89	27 13.25	27.08	45 55.30	29 23 43.46
21	8	. .	. .	. .	. .	. .	40.7	53.0	. .	. .	46 15.28	21.79	VII. 2 42.61	43 15.55	26.92	46 37.07	29 39 45.60 z.
22	9	. .	. .	15.0	27.8	40.0	52.5	. .	. .	. .	52 27.53	21.75	I. 3 39.30	36 24.51	25.54	52 49.28	29 32 53.18
23	9	. .	. .	. .	50.6	3.0	. .	. .	. .	. .	54 50.58	21.70	II. 7 42.76	8 7.51	25.00	55 12.28	29 4 35.64 z.
24	7.8	. .	31.5	43.8	56.5	9.0	. .	. .	. .	. .	55 56.50	21.71	IV. 5 44.84	21 29.50	24.75	56 18.21	29 17 57.38 z.
25	9	. .	. .	. .	16.0	. .	41.0	53.6	. .	. .	57 15.85	21.71	10. 4 46.11	26 32.18	24.45	57 37.56	29 22 59.76
26	9	. .	38.5	50.5	3.2	. .	. .	. .	. .	. .	19 1 3.25	21.67	2. 7 40.73	9 17.05	23.60	19 1 24.92	29 5 43.78 z.
27	6	. .	. .	. .	27.0	39.5	52.0	5.0	. .	. .	1 26.95	21.72	V. 1 44.56	48 0.10	23.52	1 48.67	29 44 26.75 z.
28	8.9	58.0	11.0	23.0	. .	. .	. .	. .	. .	. .	4 35.95	21.69	2. 3 41.87	34 55.26	22.82	4 57.64	29 31 21.21
29	7.8	. .	. .	37.3	49.7	2.5	15.4	27.4	. .	. .	4 49.88	21.68	VI. 3 45.9	32 36.62	22.77	5 11.56	29 29 2.52
30	9	. .	14.0	26.3	39.0	. .	4.0	. .	. .	. .	9 38.95	21.64	V. 5 46.7	20 25.19	21.71	10 0.59	29 16 50.03
31	7	. .	57.1	9.9	22.3	. .	. .	. .	. .	. .	12 22.45	21.67	2. 1 38.55	51 27.09	21.12	12 44.12	29 47 51.34
32	7	. .	53.5	6.2	18.3	. .	43.9	. .	. .	. .	13 18.60	21.63	I. 5 40.25	24 7.81	20.91	13 40.23	29 20 31.85
33	6.7	. .	50.5	3.0	15.6	28.2	40.9	. .	. .	. .	15 15.67	21.61	2. 3 34.41	39 13.06	20.49	15 37.28	29 35 36.68 z.
34	8	. .	. .	. .	. .	. .	28.0	41.4	. .	. .	18 3.10	21.64	VII. 1 38.83	51 17.84	19.88	18 24.74	29 47 40.85 z.
35	8	. .	. .	. .	. .	. .	. .	. .	3.6	16.3	19 7.10	21.59	11. 6 32.57	19 49.67	19.65	19 28.69	29 16 12.45 z.
36	7.8	. .	. .	. .	18.5	31.0	43.5	. .	. .	. .	21 18.39	21.62	VII. 1 37.22	52 13.51	19.18	21 40.01	29 48 35.82
37	8	. .	. .	. .	. .	. .	3.8	16.2	. .	. .	55 38.40	21.40	" 4 34.22	33 23.41	12.11	55 59.80	29 29 38.65
38	7.8	. .	. .	. .	. .	. .	39.5	51.8	. .	. .	57 14.04	21.41	" 1 34.2	53 57.79	11.79	57 35.45	29 50 12.71 z.
39	7.8	. .	. .	38.0	50.7	3.0	. .	. .	. .	. .	20 1 50.64	21.32	2. 7 36.58	11 40.44	10.90	20 2 11.96	29 7 54.47 z.
40	8	. .	14.0	26.8	39.4	52.0	. .	. .	. .	. .	10 39.40	21.31	2. 3 33.72	39 36.86	9.18	11 0.71	29 35 49.17 z.
41	6	. .	. .	. .	. .	. .	17.7	30.0	. .	. .	10 52.28	21.31	11. 2 42.5	43 18.59	9.14	11 13.59	29 39 30.86 z.
42	7	. .	43.5	56.0	8.6	21.0	. .	. .	. .	. .	15 8.62	21.28	2. 3 38.15	37 3.83	8.30	15 29.90	29 33 15.26
43	6	. .	. .	. .	54.0	6.7	19.6	31.5	. .	. .	15 54.13	21.24	VII. 6 45.56	12 21.70	8.15	16 15.37	29 8 32.98 z.
44	7	. .	. .	. .	. .	. .	24.0	37.0	. .	. .	16 58.95	21.27	" 3 37.94	37 11.48	7.94	17 20.22	29 33 22.55 z.
45	8	. .	. .	. .	. .	. .	. .	34.0	53.0	. .	17 56.36	21.24	10. 5 44.23	21 49.87	7.76	18 17.60	29 18 0.76 z.
46	7	. .	59.3	11.7	24.0	36.0	. .	. .	. .	. .	21 24.11	21.24	2. 2 47.47	40 27.28	7.10	21 45.35	29 36 37.51
47	7	. .	. .	59.2	12.0	24.5	37.0	. .	. .	. .	23 11.96	21.19	I. 7 40.12	9 38.57	6.77	23 33.15	29 5 48.47 z.
48	7.8	. .	. .	. .	16.4	29.0	41.7	54.5	. .	. .	24 16.46	21.24	IV. 1 38.2	51 39.95	6.57	24 37.70	29 47 49.65 z.
49	8.9	. .	21.8	. .	46.4	59.0	11.4	. .	. .	. .	28 46.50	21.16	I. 6 36.66	17 29.20	5.75	29 7.66	29 13 38.08
50	8.7	. .	. .	12.1	25.0	37.0	. .	. .	. .	. .	31 24.77	21.13	2. 7 42.34	8 21.48	5.29	31 45.90	29 4 29.90
51	7.8	. .	. .	5.8	. .	31.0	. .	. .	. .	. .	32 18.52	21.14	V. 5 45.19	21 17.38	5.14	32 39.66	29 17 25.65 z.
52	8.9	. .	. .	. .	35.0	. .	0.3	12.7	. .	. .	20 34 35.00	21.13	VII. 5 44.8	21 30.56	4.75	20 34 56.13	29 17 38.44

CORRECTIONS.

	COR. TO CLOCK.	HOURLY COR.	m.	n.	c.	ZENITH POINT.	COINC.
	s.	s.	s.	s.	s.		r.
August 12, at 20h.	+10.387	—0.009	+0.294	+0.300	+0.230	0° 0′ 2″.11	40.115

* Barometer, &c., from the Mural.

INSTRUMENT READINGS.

	CIRCLE. A.	B.	C.	D.	Mean.	BAR.	THERMOM. At.	Ex.
Zone LI.—August 12....20.6 h.	291° 42′ 1″.0	5″.5	5″.3	6″.0	4″.45	I. 30.098	76°.5	*72°.1

Number.	Magnitude.	SECONDS OF TRANSITS. I.	II.	III.	IV.	V.	VI.	VII.	10.	11.	T.	a.	MICROMETER.	D.	d.	Mean Right Ascension, 1850.0.	Mean South Declination, 1850.0.
Zone LII. August 13. H. $D. = -28° 26' 00''.0$. $n'. = -20''.88$. $n''. = -7''.00$.																	
											h. m. s.	s.	r.	′ ″	″	h. m. s.	° ′ ″
1	9	. .	. .	. .	16.8	29.2	. .	. .	. .	. .	18 51 16.80	+21.43	IV. 4 42.769	—28 31.32	—18.15	18 51 38.23	28 54 49.47 z.
2	9	. .	. .	12.5	25.0	38.0	. .	. .	. .	. .	52 25.24	21.42	" 5 38.920	24 57.09	17.87	52 46.66	28 51 14.96
3	9	. .	. .	. .	. .	8.3	20.8	. .	. .	. .	52 55.80	21.42	" 5 39.433	24 39.39	17.74	53 17.22	28 50 57.13
4	9	. .	. .	. .	51.0	3.1	16.0	. .	. .	. .	54 50.83	21.43	" 3 35.878	38 25.97	17.29	55 12.26	29 4 43.26 z.
5	7.8	. .	31.2	44.0	56.2	9.0	21.2	. .	. .	. .	55 56.36	21.45	" 1 37.995	51 49.89	17.03	56 17.81	29 18 6.92 z.
6	7	. .	18.0	30.0	42.5	54.5	7.2	. .	. .	. .	57 42.45	21.40	" 5 38.015	25 28.35	16.61	58 3.85	28 51 44.96 z.
7	9	. .	42.2	54.6	7.2	19.6	32.2	. .	. .	. .	59 7.17	21.40	" 4 36.990	31 50.99	16.27	59 28.57	28 58 7.26
8	9	25.7	38.2	50.3	3.5	. .	. .	. .	. .	. .	19 1 3.30	21.41	" 3 33.880	39 35.01	15.81	19 1 24.71	29 5 50.82 z.
9	9	. .	. .	. .	24.2	37.0	49.2	2.0	. .	. .	1 24.36	21.38	" 6 32.142	20 8.73	15.73	1 45.74	28 46 24.46 z.
10	8.9	. .	36.4	49.0	1.2	13.8	26.2	. .	. .	. .	7 1.33	21.36	" 4 41.440	29 17.29	14.40	7 22.69	28 55 31.69 z.
11	9	. .	. .	52.5	5.2	18.0	. .	. .	. .	. .	9 5.30	21.35	" 4 43.021	28 22.63	13.91	9 26.65	28 54 36.54
12	9	. .	. .	32.0	44.2	. .	. .	. .	. .	. .	9 44.39	21.34	" 5 42.272	23 1.32	13.76	10 5.73	28 49 15.08
13	9	. .	. .	. .	. .	6.0	. .	30.5	. .	. .	9 53.28	21.34	V. 5 36.836	26 9.04	13.72	10 14.62	28 52 22.76
14	9	. .	. .	5.2	18.0	. .	. .	. .	. .	. .	11 17.88	21.32	IV. 5 46.007	20 52.27	13.40	11 39.20	28 47 5.67
15	9	. .	. .	. .	. .	43.0	56.0	8.0	. .	. .	11 30.72	21.32	VII. 5 47.820	19 49.33	13.35	11 52.04	28 46 2.68 z.
16	9	. .	28.3	41.0	53.2	. .	. .	. .	. .	. .	13 53.37	21.33	IV. 4 38.662	30 53.20	12.81	14 14.70	28 57 6.01 z.
17	9	. .	36.1	48.8	1.0	13.6	. .	. .	. .	. .	14 1.18	21.33	" 4 37.723	31 25.65	12.77	14 22.51	28 57 38.42 z.
18	9	. .	. .	. .	47.0	59.4	12.0	24.6	. .	. .	14 46.97	21.32	" 4 44.156	27 43.43	12.59	15 8.29	28 53 56.02 z.
19	9	. .	. .	. .	. .	11.5	24.2	36.5	. .	. .	15 59.02	21.32	V. 4 36.822	31 56.75	12.31	16 20.34	28 58 9.06
20	9	. .	49.0	1.4	. .	26.0	39.0	. .	. .	. .	18 13.87	21.30	IV. 4 44.160	27 43.30	11.79	18 35.17	28 53 55.09 z.
21	8.9	. .	. .	. .	7.2	19.2	32.3	45.0	. .	. .	18 7.09	21.34	" 1 41.130	50 1.58	11.82	18 28.43	29 16 13.40
22	8.9	50.8	. .	16.0	28.2	40.5	53.0	. .	. .	. .	21 28.27	21.26	" 6 45.706	12 20.16	11.04	21 49.53	28 38 31.20
23	8.9	. .	5.8	18.0	30.0	43.0	55.4	. .	. .	. .	22 30.45	21.26	" 6 41.211	14 55.45	10.81	22 51.71	28 41 6.26
24	9	. .	32.5	45.0	57.0	9.5	22.0	. .	. .	. .	23 57.21	21.27	" 5 39.189	24 47.81	10.48	24 18.48	28 50 58.29
25	9	. .	. .	. .	. .	8.5	. .	33.8	. .	. .	24 56.13	21.28	V. 3 43.430	34 5.07	10.25	25 17.41	29 0 15.32
26	9	. .	. .	. .	0.0	12.1	. .	57.2	. .	. .	24 59.64	21.27	V. 3 44.395	33 31.74	10.24	25 20.91	28 59 41.98
*27	8.9	. .	. .	. .	19.0	31.5	44.0	56.2	. .	. .	26 18.87	21.27	IV. 3 43.670	33 56.77	9.94	26 40.14	29 0 6.71
28	8.9	. .	. .	29.0	41.8	54.0	. .	19.2	. .	. .	26 41.65	21.26	V. 3 43.915	33 48.29	9.85	27 2.91	28 59 58.14 z.
29	9	. .	. .	56.0	8.2	21.0	. .	. .	. .	. .	28 8.47	21.27	" 2 43.965	42 31.95	9.51	28 29.74	29 8 41.46 z.
30	9	. .	. .	39.0	51.2	3.5	. .	. .	. .	. .	28 51.30	21.25	" 4 36.168	32 19.35	9.35	29 12.55	28 58 28.70
31	8	. .	. .	. .	. .	25.5	38.0	50.4	. .	. .	29 12.93	21.25	" 4 39.656	30 18.83	9.21	29 34.18	28 56 28.04 z.
32	9	. .	42.5	55.0	7.2	19.8	32.5	. .	. .	. .	32 7.44	21.25	" 2 38.575	45 38.14	8.61	32 28.69	29 11 46.75
33	9	. .	2.5	15.0	27.5	40.0	52.5	. .	. .	. .	33 27.51	21.23	" 4 34.100	33 30.81	8.31	33 48.74	28 59 39.12 z.
34	9	. .	. .	. .	. .	12.8	25.0	38.0	. .	. .	36 0.22	21.21	" 4 40.263	29 57.89	7.73	36 21.43	28 56 5.62 z.
35	9	. .	. .	. .	16.5	29.0	42.0	. .	. .	. .	37 16.62	21.23	" 2 39.410	45 9.35	7.45	37 37.85	29 11 16.80
36	7.8	. .	. .	. .	. .	19.2	32.2	44.4	. .	. .	38 6.92	21.19	" 5 38.550	25 9.82	7.26	38 28.11	28 51 17.08
37	9	. .	. .	. .	. .	. .	4.0	16.0	. .	. .	38 38.61	21.21	VI. 3 37.390	37 33.64	7.17	38 59.82	29 3 40.81
38	7	. .	. .	. .	28.2	40.8	. .	6.0	. .	. .	39 28.30	21.21	IV. 2 43.118	43 1.26	6.95	39 49.51	29 9 8.21
39	9	58.0	11.0	23.3	. .	. .	. .	. .	. .	. .	41 35.86	21.17	" 5 40.438	24 4.68	6.48	41 57.03	28 50 11.16 z.
40	9	. .	35.2	47.5	0.2	. .	25.0	. .	. .	. .	42 0.09	21.18	" 4 40.380	29 53.89	6.39	42 21.27	28 56 0.28
41	9	. .	. .	. .	. .	31.0	43.2	56.0	. .	. .	42 18.37	21.17	VII. 5 36.330	26 26.28	6.32	42 39.54	28 52 32.60 z.
42	9	. .	59.0	. .	24.1	. .	49.2	. .	. .	. .	19 45 24.04	21.15	IV. 5 42.202	23 3.73	5.64	19 45 45.19	28 49 9.37

CORRECTIONS.

	COR. TO CLOCK.	HOURLY COR.	m.	n.	c.	ZENITH POINT.	COINC.
	s.	s.	s.	s.	s.	° ′ ″	r.
Aug. 13, at 20h. . .	+10.132	—0.012	+0.294	+0.300	+0.230	0 0 1.88	40.106

INSTRUMENT READINGS.

	CIRCLE. A.	B.	C.	D.	Mean.	BAR.	THERMOM. At.	Ex.
Zone h.	° ′ ″	″	″	″	″	I.	°	°
LII.—August 13. . 18.0	. . . . . .	. .	. .	. .	. . .	29.990	82.0	78.8
18.7	. . . . . .	. .	. .	. .	. . .	29.996	81.0	77.7
19.7	292 12 5.3	8.7	12.0	8.0	8.50	29.996	80.0	77.0

Zone LIII. August 13. H. $D. = -40^\circ\ 49'\ 30''.00.$ $n'. = -23''.00.$ $n''. = -15''.86.$

Number.	Magnitude.	I.	II.	III.	IV.	V.	VI.	VII.	10.	11.	T.	a.	MICROMETER.	D.	d.	Mean Right Ascension, 1850.0.	Mean South Declination, 1850.0.
											h. m. s.	s.	r.	′ ″	″	h. m. s.	° ′ ″
1	9	. .	50.5	4.2	19.0	34.8	49.0	. .	. .	. .	19 58 19.51	+22.06	IV. 6 36.857	—17 29.93	—19.17	19 58 41.57	41 7 19.10
2	8	. .	50.4	4.6	19.2	34.0	49.0	. .	. .	. .	20 5 19.45	22.03	" 4 37.460	31 44.20	17.78	20 5 41.48	41 21 31.98
3	9	. .	43.0	57.2	12.0	26.0	41.0	. .	. .	. .	9 11.86	21.96	" 6 38.042	16 48.79	17.01	9 33.82	41 6 35.80
4	8.9	. .	52.0	6.2	21.0	35.2	49.8	. .	. .	. .	11 20.85	21.96	" 5 41.181	23 45.46	16.60	11 42.81	41 13 32.06
5	9	. .	1.0	15.0	30.0	44.2	59.0	. .	. .	. .	14 29.81	21.92	" 5 42.456	23 1.21	15.99	14 51.73	41 12 47.20
6	7.8	. .	55.0	9.1	24.0	38.0	52.2	. .	. .	. .	15 23.67	21.92	" 4 46.190	26 40.72	15.82	15 45.59	41 16 26.54 B.
7	9	. .	59.2	13.2	28.0	42.5	57.2	. .	. .	. .	21 28.04	21.88	" 3 43.892	33 59.29	14.66	21 49.92	41 23 43.95
8	9	. .	57.0	11.0	25.5	40.0	55.0	. .	. .	. .	22 25.72	21.83	" 6 42.900	13 59.93	14.48	22 47.55	41 3 44.41
9	8	. .	. .	6.5	21.0	35.6	. .	. .	. .	. .	26 21.10	21.87	" 1 33.240	54 52.61	13.75	26 42.97	41 44 36.36
10	8.9	. .	58.0	12.0	27.0	41.5	56.0	. .	. .	. .	40 26.93	21.69	" 3 36.900	38 2.39	11.19	40 48.62	41 27 43.58
11	9	. .	43.2	58.0	12.2	27.0	41.4	. .	. .	. .	48 12.40	21.63	" 2 41.346	44 16.69	9.86	48 34.03	41 33 56.55
12	8	. .	45.0	59.1	14.0	28.0	43.0	. .	. .	. .	21 5 13.83	21.39	" 6 36.295	17 49.58	7.08	21 5 35.22	41 7 26.66
13	9	. .	1.3	16.0	30.6	45.0	. .	. .	. .	. .	9 30.64	21.41	" 1 39.528	51 13.64	6.42	9 52.05	41 40 50.06
14	6.7	. .	18.4	32.8	47.3	2.0	16.6	. .	. .	. .	10 47.44	21.37	" 3 39.043	36 47.91	6.22	11 8.81	41 26 24.13 B.
15	7.8	. .	59.0	13.8	29.0	43.0	58.0	. .	. .	. .	11 28.61	21.39	" 1 43.086	49 10.04	6.12	11 50.00	41 38 46.16
16	9	. .	8.4	23.0	37.0	51.2	6.2	. .	. .	. .	21 26 37.18	21.14	" 7 39.235	10 14.30	3.92	21 26 58.32	40 59 48.22

Zone LIV. August 13. H. $D. = -27^\circ\ 25'\ 30''.0.$ $n'. = -\ 6''.65.$ $n''. = -10''.00.$

Number.	Magnitude.	I.	II.	III.	IV.	V.	VI.	VII.	10.	11.	T.	a.	MICROMETER.	D.	d.	Mean Right Ascension, 1850.0.	Mean South Declination, 1850.0.
1	8	. .	12.0	24.1	36.4	49.0	1.2	. .	. .	. .	22 2 36.55	20.19	IV. 4 44.400	27 38.04	6.30	22 2 56.74	27 53 14.33 Z.
2	8	. .	22.3	35.0	47.0	59.3	12.0	. .	. .	. .	3 47.14	20.17	" 5 41.130	23 43.80	6.15	4 7.31	27 49 19.95 Z.
3	9	. .	. .	36.5	49.0	1.3	14.0	. .	. .	. .	4 49.02	20.18	" 2 37.561	46 16.08	6.02	5 9.20	28 11 52.10 Z.
4	8	. .	3.4	15.8	28.2	40.4	53.0	. .	. .	. .	8 28.19	20.16	" 2 44.242	42 25.33	5.56	8 48.35	28 8 0.89 Z.
5	9	. .	. .	24.0	36.6	49.0	. .	. .	. .	. .	9 36.60	20.15	" 3 38.550	36 56.58	5.41	9 56.75	28 2 31.99 Z.
6	8	. .	36.0	48.2	1.0	13.2	25.8	. .	. .	. .	11 0.87	20.14	" 2 43.601	42 47.43	5.25	11 21.01	28 8 22.68 Z.
7	9	. .	. .	. .	. .	59.5	. .	24.2	. .	. .	13 47.02	20.12	" 2 40.015	44 51.33	4.94	14 7.14	28 10 26.27 Z.
8	7.8	. .	37.5	49.6	1.5	14.1	27.0	. .	. .	. .	16 1.96	20.08	" 7 37.165	11 27.27	4.69	16 22.04	27 37 1.96 Z.
9	9	. .	2.5	. .	27.2	39.2	52.1	4.6	. .	. .	19 27.18	29.08	" 4 35.632	32 40.86	4.30	19 47.26	27 58 15.16 Z.
10	9	. .	16.0	28.0	40.5	53.0	5.2	. .	. .	. .	20 40.55	20.07	" 4 40.694	29 46.00	4.17	21 0.62	27 55 20.17 Z
11	7.8	. .	37.0	49.0	2.0	. .	. .	39.0	. .	. .	21 1.74	20.06	" 5 35.830	26 46.85	4.13	21 21.80	27 52 20.98 Z.
12	9	. .	. .	51.2	. .	16.0	. .	. .	. .	. .	25 3.70	20.05	" 2 34.650	47 56.64	3.71	25 23.75	28 13 30.35
13	9	. .	. .	. .	47.2	59.6	12.0	. .	. .	. .	25 47.18	20.04	" 2 40.050	44 50.13	3.63	26 7.22	28 10 23.76
14	9	. .	. .	. .	. .	36.2	49.0	1.5	. .	. .	26 24.04	20.04	VI. 1 42.775	49 12.46	3.57	26 44.08	28 14 46.03
15	9	. .	. .	. .	. .	32.5	45.0	57.2	. .	. .	27 20.17	29.01	V. 6 38.165	16 43.72	3.47	27 40.18	27 42 17.19
16	8	49.0	1.5	13.6	26.2	. .	. .	. .	. .	. .	29 26.32	20.02	IV. 2 34.950	47 46.30	3.25	29 46.34	28 13 19.55 Z.
17	8	. .	. .	. .	43.5	55.5	8.2	20.6	. .	. .	29 43.42	19.99	" 6 44.160	13 16.68	3.22	30 3.41	27 38 49.90
18	5.6	. .	. .	48.2	1.0	13.0	26.0	. .	. .	. .	22 32 0.89	19.98	V. 5 40.835	23 53.94	3.00	22 32 20.87	27 49 26.94

CORRECTIONS.

	COR. TO CLOCK.	HOURLY COR.	m.	n.	c.	ZENITH POINT.	COINC.
	s.	s.	s.	s.	s.	° ′ ″	r.
August 13, at 20h	+10.132	—0.012	+0.294	+0.300	0.230	0 0 2.50	40.106
22	. . . .	. . . .	. . .	. . .	. . .	3.12	. . .

INSTRUMENT READINGS.

	CIRCLE. A.	CIRCLE. B.	CIRCLE. C.	CIRCLE. D.	CIRCLE. Mean.	BAR.	THERMOM. At.	THERMOM. Ex.
Zone h.	° ′ ″	′	″	″	″	I.	°	°
LIII.—August 13...19.8	279 51 1.8	4.0	7.1	3.6	4.12	. . .	. .	. .
20.8	. . . .	. .	. .	. .	. . .	29.992	79.0	76.5
21.7	. . . .	. .	. .	. .	. . .	29.960	78.5	75.3
LIV.—August 13...22.0	293 12 1.0	6.1	8.2	6.0	5.32	. . .	. .	. .
22.6	1.0	6.3	8.0	5.9	5.30	29.974	78.0	74.6

Number.	Magnitude.	SECONDS OF TRANSITS. I.	II.	III.	IV.	V.	VI.	VII.	10.	11.	T.	a.	MICROMETER.	D.	d.	Mean Right Ascension, 1850.0.	Mean South Declination, 1850.0.
Zone LV. August 18. M. $D. = -27^\circ 55' 10''.0$. $n'. -42''.00$. $n''. -5''.14$.																	
											h. m. s.	s.	r.	′ ″	″	h. m. s.	° ′ ″
1	9	. .	. .	. .	. .	. .	. .	. .	22.8	35.5	18 29 26.85	+19.37	11. 5 43.6	−22 13.40	−39.96	18 29 46.22	28 18 3.36 z.
2	9	. .	. .	. .	. .	30.5	42.8	. .	. .	. .	31 17.98	19.37	VII. 4 44.59	27 26.20	39.56	31 37.35	28 23 15.76
3	9	. .	. .	. .	. .	. .	. .	. .	34.7	47.0	31 38.78	19.34	11. 7 40.13	9 38.68	39.49	31 58.12	28 5 28.17
4	9	. .	. .	. .	. .	. .	56.8	9.1	. .	. .	33 31.69	19.37	VII. 3 33.83	39 34.53	39.09	33 51.06	28 35 23.62
5	9	. .	. .	. .	. .	. .	. .	. .	18.3	31.0	35 22.33	19.34	11. 5 36.48	26 18.43	38.70	35 41.67	28 22 7.13
6	8	. .	25.5	37.5	50.3	2.9	. .	. .	. .	. .	37 50.32	19.34	I. 4 39.47	30 23.14	38.18	38 9.66	28 26 11.32
7	8.9	. .	9.0	21.2	34.0	. .	59.0	11.3	. .	. .	40 33.92	19.36	2. 1 39.84	50 43.54	37.60	40 53.28	28 46 31.14
8	8.9	. .	. .	0.2	12.6	25.0	. .	50.0	. .	. .	43 12.65	19.30	I. 5 41.45	23 27.50	37.05	43 31.95	28 19 14.55
9	10	55.7	. .	21.0	33.5	46.0	. .	. .	. .	. .	45 33.52	19.33	VI. 1 44.40	48 6.65	36.55	45 52.85	28 43 53.20
10	9	. .	. .	. .	. .	. .	. .	. .	9.2	21.9	46 13.28	19.28	11. 5 42.05	23 5.99	36.41	46 32.56	28 18 52.40
11	9	. .	55.7	8.4	21.0	33.3	46.0	. .	. .	. .	49 20.93	19.31	VI. 1 38.28	51 38.10	35.75	49 40.24	28 47 23.85
12	9	. .	. .	. .	. .	. .	40.0	52.6	. .	. .	50 15.16	19.25	10. 6 33.45	19 20.92	35.56	50 34.41	28 15 6.48 z.
13	9	. .	2.0	14.3	26.8	39.4	. .	. .	. .	. .	19 1 26.94	19.25	V. 1 39.93	50 41.13	33.22	19 1 46.19	28 46 24.35 z.
14	9	. .	. .	. .	. .	50.8	3.5	15.9	. .	. .	3 38.49	19.19	" 4 44.37	27 34.16	32.77	3 57.68	28 23 16.93
15	9	. .	. .	. .	. .	. .	. .	. .	. .	18.0	9 9.23	19.17	11. 3 43.302	34 6.56	31.63	9 28.40	28 29 48.19 z.
16	9	13.3	26.0	38.0	. .	. .	. .	. .	. .	. .	13 50.89	19.17	IV. 1 43.44	48 39.93	30.69	14 10.06	28 44 20.62
17	6.7	. .	. .	37.0	49.2	1.8	14.2	26.8	. .	. .	14 49.41	19.10	1. 6 43.83	13 22.74	30.49	15 8.51	28 9 3.23 z.
18	9	. .	5.4	17.9	30.5	42.8	. .	. .	. .	. .	21 30.46	19.11	" 2 43.27	42 53.83	29.15	21 49.57	28 38 32.98
19	8.9	. .	. .	10.0	22.5	34.8	. .	. .	. .	. .	22 22.50	19.10	IV. 3 40.43	35 46.88	28.98	22 41.60	28 31 25.86 z.
20	9	. .	. .	. .	. .	. .	. .	. .	28.8	41.6	22 32.78	19.11	11. 2 38.66	45 33.29	28.95	22 51.89	28 41 12.24
21	9	. .	. .	. .	. .	. .	. .	. .	47.5	. .	24 51.55	19.06	" 5 38.47	25 10.69	28.49	25 10.61	28 20 49.18
22	8	. .	. .	59.0	12.1	. .	36.5	. .	. .	. .	31 11.76	18.99	VII. 7 45.63	6 29.48	27.27	31 20.75	28 2 6.75
23	9.10	13.6	26.3	38.5	. .	. .	. .	. .	. .	. .	36 51.01	18.96	VI. 7 42.19	8 28.53	26.14	37 9.97	28 4 4.67
24	9	39.5	51.9	4.2	17.0	29.0	41.9	. .	. .	. .	38 16.84	18.96	VII. 7 39.29	10 8.47	25.87	38 35.80	28 5 44.34
25	9	. .	. .	. .	. .	. .	51.8	4.6	. .	. .	40 26.91	19.01	" 1 39.16	51 7.44	25.45	40 45.92	28 46 42.89
26	9	. .	. .	37.0	49.3	. .	. .	. .	. .	. .	41 49.41	18.96	VI. 5 36.51	26 18.39	25.18	42 8.37	28 21 53.57
27	9	. .	. .	. .	8.6	21.2	33.7	. .	. .	. .	43 8.69	18.97	VII. 3 40.49	35 44.47	24.94	43 27.66	28 31 19.41
28	8.9	. .	. .	20.0	32.1	45.0	. .	. .	. .	. .	52 32.44	18.89	2. 4 42.11	28 51.53	23.17	52 51.33	28 24 24.70 z.
29	9	. .	. .	. .	. .	. .	. .	11.0	. .	. .	52 33.52	18.91	11. 2 46.37	41 6.98	23.17	52 52.43	28 36 40.15
30	9	. .	. .	. .	. .	6.0	18.2	30.7	. .	. .	54 53.47	18.85	IV. 6 42.37	14 13.40	22.74	55 12.32	28 9 46.14 z.
31	8	. .	. .	. .	. .	57.5	9.8	22.5	. .	. .	56 45.08	18.84	10. 6 35.12	18 23.21	22.40	57 3.92	28 13 55.61
32	8.9	. .	. .	. .	. .	. .	30.0	42.8	. .	. .	57 5.09	18.90	I. 1 37.31	52 11.38	22.34	57 23.99	28 47 43.72 z.
33	9	. .	. .	20.8	33.0	45.5	. .	. .	. .	. .	59 33.17	18.84	2. 5 34.53	27 26.13	21.88	59 52.01	28 22 58.01
34	9	. .	. .	. .	. .	1.0	13.5	26.0	. .	. .	20 0 48.58	18.84	IV. 5 33.89	27 48.99	21.66	20 1 7.42	28 23 20.65
35	9	. .	. .	. .	. .	. .	. .	. .	30.4	. .	0 34.58	18.81	11. 7 35.37	12 23.14	21.70	0 53.39	28 7 54.84
36	9	. .	. .	. .	. .	21.5	34.0	. .	. .	. .	6 9.05	18.81	I. 3 39.50	36 18.60	20.71	6 27.86	28 31 49.31
37	9	. .	. .	. .	. .	. .	. .	. .	14.7	. .	6 18.70	18.82	11. 2 41.33	44 0.16	20.69	6 37.52	28 39 30.85
38	9	. .	. .	. .	. .	40.8	53.0	5.7	. .	. .	8 28.20	18.80	10. 3 33.10	39 59.38	20.30	8 47.00	28 35 29.68
*39	10	. .	. .	. .	. .	55.5	. .	. .	. .	. .	10 43.06	18.76	VII. 5 42.96	22 35.30	19.87	11 1.82	28 18 5.17
40	10	. .	. .	. .	. .	. .	. .	16.1	. .	. .	14 38.91	18.70	II. 7 44.65	7 3.51	19.21	14 57.61	28 2 32.72
41	10	. .	. .	. .	. .	. .	. .	. .	45.7	58.1	20 14 49.51	18.75	11. 3 45.13	33 3.39	19.18	20 15 8.26	28 28 32.57

CORRECTIONS.

	COR. TO CLOCK.	HOURLY COR.	m.	n.	c.	ZENITH POINT.	COINC.
	s.	s.	s.	s.	s.		r.
August 18, at 20*h*.	+7.943	−0.017	+0.294	+0.300	+0.230	0° 0′ 1″.75	40.110

INSTRUMENT READINGS.

	CIRCLE. A.	B.	C.	D.	Mean.	BAR.	THERMOM. At.	Ex.
h.						I.		
Zone LV.—Aug. 18, 18.5	292° 42′ 41″.0	44″.0	46″.7	43″.7	43″.85	30.118	74°.8	69°.5
19.3	. . . . .	. .	. .	. .	. . .	. . .	74.3	68.0
20.0	. . . . .	. .	. .	. .	. . .	30.130	. .	67.2
20.2	37.2	39.2	42.2	40.2	39.72	. . .	. .	. .
21.0	36.3	38.3	41.3	39.3	38.80	. . .	. .	. .

Number	Magnitude.	SECONDS OF TRANSITS. I.	II.	III.	IV.	V.	VI.	VII.	10.	11.	T.	a.	MICROMETER.	D.	d.	Mean Right Ascension, 1850.0.	Mean South Declination, 1850.0.
Zone LV. August 18. M. $D. = -27° 55' 10''.0.$ $n. -42''.00.$ $n. -5''.14.$ (Continued.)																	
											h. m. s.	s.	r.	' ''	''	h. m. s.	° ' ''
42	8.9	. .	. .	. .	27.0	. .	52.3	4.4	. .	. .	20 19 27.04	+18.74	11. 1 41.79	—49 35.78	—18.37	20 19 45.78	28 45 4.15
43	9	. .	. .	. .	. .	. .	24.0	36.4	. .	. .	21 59.05	18.67	VII. 6 33.25	19 28.21	17.93	22 17.72	28 14 56.14
44	8	. .	. .	20.2	33.0	45.2	. .	. .	. .	. .	30 32.87	18.61	2. 6 34.02	19 1.20	16.44	30 51.48	28 14 27.64
45	8	. .	. .	1.0	13.5	25.7	. .	. .	. .	. .	31 13.48	18.59	VI. 7 37.28	11 18.15	16.32	31 32.07	28 6 44.47
46	8	. .	. .	. .	. .	. .	35.0	47.3	. .	. .	32 9.90	18.63	VII. 3 40.20	35 54.47	16.15	32 28.53	28 31 20.62
47	8	. .	7.6	20.0	32.5	. .	. .	. .	. .	. .	34 32.51	18.61	2. 4 37.41	31 33.91	15.74	34 51.12	28 26 59.65
48	8	. .	. .	59.3	11.5	. .	36.6	. .	. .	. .	35 11.65	18.63	VI. 1 42.72	49 4.65	15.63	35 30.28	28 44 30.28
49	8	. .	31.7	44.0	56.5	. .	. .	. .	. .	. .	37 56.48	18.55	2. 6 43.74	13 25.40	15.15	38 15.03	28 8 50.55
50	8	. .	. .	19.7	32.0	44.4	57.0	. .	. .	. .	38 32.08	18.56	VI. 5 43.25	22 25.53	15.04	38 50.64	28 17 50.57
51	9.10	. .	. .	. .	. .	19.0	31.7	. .	. .	. .	41 6.65	18.58	II. 3 35.98	38 20.49	14.60	41 25.23	28 33 45.09
52	9.10	. .	. .	. .	. .	. .	. .	56.0	. .	. .	41 18.55	18.56	VII. 3 39.46	36 20.05	14.57	41 37.11	28 31 44.62
53	8	. .	. .	. .	. .	. .	. .	53.2	11.8	. .	41 15.76	18.57	11. 3 37.13	37 39.78	14.58	41 34.33	28 33 4.36
54	9	. .	. .	. .	. .	. .	24.6	37.0	. .	. .	43 59.54	18.55	VII. 3 33.57	39 43.49	14.12	44 18.09	28 35 7.61
55	8	. .	. .	. .	. .	. .	43.5	56.5	. .	. .	45 18.74	18.53	" 3 38.57	36 50.05	13.90	45 37.27	28 32 13.95
56	8.9	. .	. .	. .	. .	. .	13.0	26.0	. .	. .	45 48.25	18.53	11. 4 32.65	34 17.94	13.82	46 6.78	28 29 41.76
57	9	. .	. .	. .	23.0	. .	48.0	. .	. .	. .	48 22.99	18.49	VI. 5 41.80	23 15.60	13.38	48 41.48	28 18 38.98
58	9	. .	. .	. .	. .	. .	. .	43.0	. .	. .	52 5.63	18.46	2. 5 43.95	22 0.72	12.79	52 24.09	28 17 23.51
59	8	. .	. .	. .	. .	. .	42.0	54.3	. .	. .	52 16.94	18.47	I. 4 43.98	27 47.30	12.76	52 35.41	28 23 10.06
60	7	. .	30.0	42.2	. .	. .	. .	32.0	. .	. .	53 54.74	18.45	11. 5 41.20	23 35.37	12.51	54 13.19	28 18 57.88
61	9	27.0	40.0	. .	5.0	17.0	30.0	42.2	. .	. .	21 3 4.81	18.40	2 3 40.91	35 29.55	11.11	21 3 23.21	28 30 50.66
62	6	. .	. .	. .	5.0	17.1	29.6	41.1	. .	. .	4 4.55	18.37	VII. 6 35.23	18 19.81	10.96	4 22.92	28 13 40.77 z.
Zone LVI. August 29. M. $D. = 41° 19' 50''.0.$ $n. = 35''.39.$ $n. = 13''.00.$																	
1	9	. .	. .	. .	12.0	26.4	. .	56.0	. .	. .	18 31 11.81	20.74	10. 2 45.45	41 50.63	32.83	18 31 32.55	42 2 13.46
2	9	. .	10.7	25.5	. .	. .	. .	. .	. .	. .	33 40.04	20.65	IV. 6 48.24	10 50.81	32.29	34 0.69	41 31 13.10
3	9	. .	. .	. .	. .	. .	. .	25.5	. .	. .	33 41.39	20.68	10. 5 42.50	22 55.37	32.29	34 2.07	41 43 17.66
4	9.10	. .	. .	. .	. .	. .	24.5	39.0	. .	. .	34 54.94	20.68	10. 5 38.39	25 18.34	32.01	35 15.62	41 45 40.35
5	8.9	. .	. .	. .	. .	. .	. .	. .	25.0	40.0	35 18.71	20.71	11. 2 42.38	43 37.09	31.92	35 39.42	42 3 59.01
6	9.10	. .	26.0	41.0	55.5	10.0	24.5	. .	. .	. .	37 55.42	20.62	10. 7 40.59	9 22.11	31.34	38 16.04	41 29 43.45
7	9	42.0	57.0	12.0	. .	. .	. .	. .	. .	. .	40 26.41	20.63	III. 5 45.45	21 13.83	30.79	40 47.04	41 41 34.62
8	8	. .	. .	. .	14.8	29.3	44.5	59.0	. .	. .	41 14.78	20.65	VII. 3 46.63	32 20.71	30.61	41 35.43	41 52 41.32 B.
9	10	. .	19.5	33.6	49.0	3.5	18.0	32.6	. .	. .	47 48.68	20.59	2. 5 37.86	25 36.61	29.17	48 9.27	41 45 55.78
10	8.7	27.2	41.7	56.8	11.0	. .	41.0	55.5	. .	. .	51 11.36	20.61	2. 2 37.14	46 39.80	28.43	51 31.97	42 6 58.23
11	8	7.4	22.5	37.1	51.5	6.0	. .	35.6	. .	. .	55 51.62	20.54	1. 5 38.20	25 25.51	27.35	56 12.16	41 45 42.86
12	10	. .	52.2	7.2	. .	. .	. .	. .	. .	. .	58 21.93	20.56	III. 2 40.63	44 39.25	26.88	58 42.49	42 4 56.13
13	7	. .	. .	. .	2.4	17.0	32.0	46.8	. .	. .	59 2.38	20.55	V. 2 36.18	47 14.33	26.74	59 22.93	42 7 31.07
14	10	. .	. .	. .	35.0	49.5	4.5	. .	. .	. .	19 5 34.95	20.46	IV. 4 38.38	31 9.49	25.34	19 5 55.41	41 51 24.83
15	9.10	25.5	40.8	55.2	9.8	. .	. .	. .	. .	. .	8 9.81	20.40	2. 6 42.77	13 59.71	24.79	8 30.21	41 34 14.50
16	9	. .	38.0	52.3	. .	. .	. .	. .	. .	. .	24 7.06	20.26	III. 7 42.59	8 13.68	21.46	24 27.32	41 28 25.14
17	7.8	. .	. .	. .	. .	12.0	27.0	41.5	. .	. .	19 24 37.66	20.25	10. 7 45.84	6 19.64	21.28	19 25 17.91	41 26 30.92

CORRECTIONS.

	COR. TO CLOCK.	HOURLY COR.	m.	n.	c.	ZENITH POINT.	COINC.
	s.	s.	s.	s.	s.	° ' ''	r.
Aug. 29, at 21h...	+7.935	+0.010	+0.273	+0.347	+0.230	0 0 2.51	40.107

INSTRUMENT READING.

	h.	CIRCLE. A.	B.	C.	D.	Mean.	BAR.	THERMOM. At.	Ex.
Zone LVI.—Aug. 29.....	18.5	279° 21' 6''.8	9.1	9.0	9.0	8.48	I. 30.072	76.5	75.0
	19.0	. . . .	. .	. .	. .	. . .	. .	76.2	75.0
	19.3	. . . .	. .	. .	. .	. .	30.070	76.5	74.7
	19.7	. . . .	. .	. .	. .	. .	30.075	76.0	74.8
	19.9	. . . .	.	. .	. .	. .	. .	.	74.5
	20.9	6.8	7.2	9.2	6.5	7.42	. .	. .	74.0

Number.	Magnitude.	SECONDS OF TRANSITS. I.	II.	III.	IV.	V.	VI.	VII.	10.	11.	T.	a.	MICROMETER.	D.	d.	Mean Right Ascension, 1850.0.	Mean South Declination, 1850.0.
Zone LVI. August 29. M. $D.=41°\ 19'\ 50''.0$. $n'.=35''.39$. $n''.=13''.00$. (Continued.)																	
											h. m. s.	s.	r.	′ ″	″	h. m. s.	° ′ ″
18	8.9	. .	. .	39.5	54.0	9.0	. .	. .	. .	. .	19 26 54.25	+20.27	VI. 4 45.65	−26 55.82	−20.89	19 27 14.52	41 47 6.71
19	8	. .	. .	. .	. .	. .	54.2	9.2	. .	. .	27 24.71	20.32	VII. 1 45.32	47 49.96	20.78	27 45.03	42 8 0.74
20	9	. .	. .	. .	. .	. .	15.0	29.8	. .	. .	28 45.80	20.22	" 6 48.5	10•41.29	20.51	29 6.02	41 30 51.80
21	9	. .	. .	. .	. .	. .	23.5	38.0	. .	. .	29 53.77	20.29	" 1 45.16	47 55.48	20.27	30 14.06	42 8 5.75
22	9	. .	. .	. .	. .	32.8	48.0	2.6	. .	. .	32 18.39	20.23	" 4 43.56	28 8.42	19.79	32 38.62	41 48 18.21
23	8	59.7	14.5	29.0	44.0	58.0	13.5	28.2	. .	. .	34 43.86	20.22	IV. 3 37.82	37 27.92	19.29	35 4.08	41 57 37.21
24	9.10	. .	43.5	. .	13.0	. .	42.6	. .	. .	. .	37 12.97	20.18	VII. 5 34.50	27 33.99	18.79	37 33.15	41 47 42.78
25	8	. .	. .	42.0	56.5	11.3	26.3	41.0	. .	. .	39 56.65	20.21	III. 1 35.14	53 44.82	18.24	40 16.86	42 13 53.06 B.
*26	5	. .	. .	. .	. .	48.7	3.5	18.1	. .	. .	44 33.85	20.16	VI. 1 32.33	55 22.57	17.33	44 54.01	42 15 29.90
27	9	. .	. .	59.5	. .	29.0	. .	. .	. .	. .	48 14.39	20.04	V. 7 34.95	12 39.43	16.60	48 34.43	41 32 46.03
28	9.10	. .	. .	. .	29.5	. .	59.5	. .	. .	. .	49 29.69	20.08	VII. 3 34.46	39 24.52	16.36	49 49.77	41 59 30.88
29	9	. .	35.5	49.5	4.5	19.0	34.0	48.5	. .	. .	52 4.48	20.04	" 4 41.13	29 33.16	15.87	52 24.52	41 49 39.03
30	8	. .	. .	. .	. .	54.4	9.0	. .	. .	. .	56 39.53	20.04	VI. 1 34.85	53 54.65	15.01	56 59.57	42 13 59.66
31	8.9	. .	. .	. .	. .	. .	. .	. .	59.1	14.0	57 52.69	20.02	11. 1 38.41	51 49.58	14.79	58 12.71	42 11 54.37
32	9	. .	17.2	32.0	46.5	. .	15.7	30.3	. .	. .	20 0 46.45	19.92	VII. 6 41.39	14 48.50	14.25	20 1 6.37	41 34 52.75
33	8	59.0	14.4	. .	43.5	58.0	13.2	27.9	. .	. .	5 43.55	19.90	I. 3 40.63	35 49.51	13.34	6 3.45	41 55 52.85
34	8	12.0	27.0	41.5	56.5	11.0	26.0	40.6	. .	. .	13 56.42	19.84	VII. 1 43.69	48 46.51	11.86	14 16.26	42 8 48.37
35	9	40.0	55.0	9.3	24.0	39.0	. .	. .	. .	. .	16 24.13	19.74	V. 7 41.53	8 50.81	11.43	16 43.87	41 28 52.24
36	8	26.6	41.0	55.5	10.7	25.4	. .	. .	. .	. .	19 10.62	19.75	VI. 3 44.54	33 33.73	10.93	19 30.37	41 53 34.66
37	9	. .	. .	. .	. .	. .	49.2	4.3	. .	. .	21 19.88	19.72	VII. 4 40.51	29 54.85	10.56	21 39.60	41 49 55.41
38	7.8	. .	31.0	45.8	0.5	. .	. .	. .	. .	. .	23 0.56	19.68	VI. 2 46.42	41 17.79	10.28	23 20.24	42 1 18.07
39	8.9	. .	. .	. .	. .	. .	. .	53.5	. .	. .	23 9.66	19.66	VII. 7 45.78	6 22.33	10.25	23 29.32	41 26 22.58
40	7.8	39.3	54.0	8.3	23.1	37.3	52.8	7.4	. .	. .	27 23.19	19.64	I. 5 39.61	24 36.25	9.52	27 42.83	41 44 35.77
41	9.10	52.8	7.5	22.0	36.5	. .	. .	. .	. .	. .	29 36.66	19.59	VI. 7 40.15	9 38.50	9.15	29 56.25	41 29 37.65
42	9	. .	. .	42.2	57.0	11.4	26.5	40.8	. .	. .	34 57.88	19.57	2. 4 40.39	29 58.37	8.28	35 17.45	41 49 56.65
43	9.10	20.0	35.0	49.6	. .	19.4	. .	. .	. .	. .	36 4.55	19.58	VI. 2 40.65	44 38.39	8.10	36 24.13	42 4 36.49
44	8	. .	. .	14.4	29.0	43.5	58.2	13.0	. .	. .	41 29.05	19.45	VII. 7 43.34	7 47.32	7.23	41 48.50	41 27 44.55
45	8.9	. .	. .	. .	23.5	38.0	53.0	. .	. .	. .	43 23.52	19.44	" 5 50.80	18 7.08	6.94	43 42.96	46 38 4.02
46	9.10	. .	44.5	59.1	14.0	28.7	. .	. .	. .	. .	47 13.94	19.40	VI. 6 33.69	19 16.38	6.35	47 33.34	41 39 12.73
47	8.9	. .	. .	. .	. .	29.0	43.7	58.5	. .	. .	48 14.48	19.38	VII. 7 32.53	14 2.98	6.19	48 33.86	41 33 59.17
48	9	. .	. .	17.5	32.0	46.7	1.9	16.5	. .	. .	50 32.25	19.37	" 5 38.60	25 11.39	5.84	50 51.62	41 45 7.23
*49	7.6	35.5	50.1	5.0	19.5	. .	. .	. .	. .	. .	56 19.70	19.32	2. 3 34.25	39 31.15	5.00	56 39.02	41 59 26.15
*50	9.10	. .	. .	. .	. .	46.0	0.8	15.4	. .	. .	20 56 31.24	19.32	VI. 3 35.42	38 51.39	4.97	20 56 50.56	41 58 46.36
Zone LVII. September 9. H. $D.=-40°\ 51'\ 10''.0$. $n'.=-40''.00$. $n''.=-15''.06$.																	
1	7.8	. .	36.5	51.3	6.2	20.6	36.0	. .	. .	. .	18 59 6.13	16.60	IV. 6 38.020	16 47.23	35.66	18 59 22.73	42 7 32.89
2	9	. .	44.0	59.0	. .	28.0	43.1	. .	. .	. .	19 6 13.55	16.52	V. 6 45.530	12 25.86	34.10	19 6 30.07	42 3 9.96
3	9	. .	12.2	27.1	42.0	56.5	11.3	. .	. .	. .	8 41.83	16.54	IV. 4 41.850	29 10.57	33.56	8 58.37	42 19 54.13

CORRECTIONS.

	COR. TO CLOCK	HOURLY COR.	m.	n.	c.	ZENITH POINT.	COINC.
	s.	s.	s.	s.	s.		r.
Sept. 9, at 22h...	+ 4.777	−0.021	−0.356	−0.527	+0.022	0° 0′ 4″.50	40.092

INSTRUMENT READINGS.

	CIRCLE. A.	B.	C.	D.	Mean.	BAR.	THERMOM. At.	Ex.
Zone LVII.—Sept. 9.....18.8 h.	278° 50′ 59″.5	60′.8	69″.3	60″.3	62″.47	I. 30.224	75°.0	66°.6
19.6	. . . .	. .	. .	. .	. .	. . . .	. .	64.7

Number.	Magnitude.	SECONDS OF TRANSITS. I.	II.	III.	IV.	V.	VI.	VII.	10.	11.	T.	a.	MICROMETER.	D.	d.	Mean Right Ascension, 1850.0.	Mean South Declination, 1850.0.
Zone LVII.	September 9.	H.	$D.=-40° 51' 10''.0.$	$n.=-40''.00.$	$n.=-15''.06.$	(Continued.)											
											h. m. s.	s.	r.	' ''	''	h. m. s.	° ' ''
4	7.8	. .	51.2	6.0	21.0	35.5	50.5	. .	. .	. .	19 11 20.85	+16.51	IV. 4 46.113	—26 43.18	— 32.98	19 11 37.36	42 17 26.16
5	9	. .	9.0	23.0	37.5	. .	. .	. .	. .	. .	16 38.10	16.49	" 2 42.522	43 36.25	31.84	16 54.59	42 34 18.09
6	9	. .	. .	. .	. .	. .	. .	27.4	. .	. .	16 42.91	16.45	VII. 4 47.061	26 8.58	31.82	16 59.36	42 16 50.40
7	8	. .	. .	. .	1.0	15.7	30.3	. .	. .	23.0	18 0.90	16.46	IV. 3 43.459	34 14.18	31.54	18 17.36	42 24 55.72
8	8.9	. .	28.5	43.2	58.3	13.3	. .	. .	. .	. .	20 58.37	16.47	" 1 35.288	53 43.25	30.90	21 14.84	42 44 24.15
9	9	. .	0.8	15.2	31.0	45.2	0.6	. .	. .	. .	24 30.59	16.40	" 3 34.265	39 34.39	30.17	24 46.99	42 30 14.56
10	9	. .	. .	48.0	2.4	17.0	32.0	. .	. .	. .	26 2.45	16.40	" 2 40.388	44 50.95	29.84	26 18.85	42 35 30.79
11	8	. .	59.0	13.2	28.4	43.0	57.8	. .	. .	. .	27 28.29	16.32	V. 6 36.940	17 24.74	29.54	27 44.61	42 8 4.28
12	8.9	. .	28.0	42.4	57.5	12.0	26.8	. .	. .	. .	29 57.35	16.30	IV. 6 36.743	17 31.61	29.02	30 13.65	42 8 10.63
13	8	. .	18.5	32.0	47.5	2.0	16.5	. .	. .	. .	33 47.32	16.23	" 7 44.728	6 59.83	28.23	34 3.55	41 57 38.06
14	8	. .	10.5	24.2	39.5	54.0	9.6	. .	. .	. .	37 39.58	16.25	" 3 40.556	35 54.98	27.42	37 55.83	42 26 32.40
15	8.9	16.0	31.0	45.6	0.2	15.2	30.5	. .	. .	. .	40 0.53	26.20	" 5 42.068	23 13.00	26.94	40 16.73	42 13 49.94 B.
16	9	. .	. .	32.0	46.0	1.0	16.0	30.8	. .	. .	40 46.32	16.22	" 3 38.053	37 22.36	26.79	41 2.54	42 27 59.15
17	5	. .	8.0	22.2	37.2	52.0	6.8	. .	. .	. .	44 37.25	16.15	" 5 39.212	24 52.51	26.01	44 53.40	42 15 28.52
18	9	. .	4.0	18.7	33.8	48.0	2.5	. .	. .	. .	48 33.41	16.10	V. 5 42.172	23 9.33	25.22	48 49.51	42 13 44.55
19	9	42.5	57.5	12.2	27.0	. .	. .	. .	. .	. .	50 27.03	16.07	II. 5 47.200	20 14.05	24.84	50 43.10	42 10 48.89
20	9	. .	. .	. .	. .	42.0	57.0	12.0	. .	. .	50 27.24	16.12	V. 2 41.851	43 59.69	24.84	50 43.36	42 34 34.53
21	9	. .	21.1	36.0	50.8	5.5	. .	. .	. .	. .	55 50.89	16.07	IV. 1 37.698	52 19.08	23.79	56 6.96	42 42 52.87
22	9	. .	13.2	28.5	43.0	58.0	12.5	. .	. .	. .	56 43.05	16.00	" 5 41.755	23 23.78	23.62	56 59.05	42 13 57.40
23	9	. .	27.0	42.0	57.0	11.0	26.0	. .	. .	. .	56 56.61	16.00	" 5 45.360	21 18.42	23.58	57 12.61	42 11 52.00
24	9	. .	57.2	12.0	27.0	42.0	57.0	. .	. .	. .	59 27.06	15.98	" 5 26.818	32 4.08	23.09	59 43.04	42 22 37.17
25	9	3.0	18.0	32.2	47.0	11.5	16.8	. .	. .	. .	20 5 47.17	15.85	" 7 47.598	5 19.87	21.90	20 6 3.02	41 55 51.77
26	5.6	. .	29.5	44.5	59.0	14.2	29.0	. .	. .	. .	11 59.27	15.84	" 3 32.460	40 37.34	20.76	12 15.11	42 31 8.10 B.
27	8	. .	5.8	20.0	35.0	50.0	5.0	. .	. .	. .	13 35.17	15.79	" 5 37.553	25 50.06	20.46	13 50.96	42 16 20.52
28	9	. .	. .	. .	. .	. .	29.5	44.2	. .	. .	13 59.84	15.78	VI. 6 35.310	18 21.44	20.39	14 15.62	42 8 51.83
29	9	. .	44.2	59.6	14.8	28.8	43.5	. .	. .	. .	15 14.22	15.80	IV. 2 45.350	41 57.98	20.16	15 30.02	42 32 28.14
30	7.8	. .	34.5	50.0	4.5	19.0	34.0	. .	. .	. .	23 4.41	15.65	" 7 38.093	10 50.94	18.76	23 20.06	42 1 19.70
31	8.9	. .	3.3	18.0	33.0	47.5	2.2	. .	. .	. .	24 32.84	15.68	" 3 34.800	39 15.58	18.51	24 48.52	42 29 44.09
32	7	. .	35.5	50.0	5.2	19.8	34.8	. .	. .	. .	31 5.11	15.61	" 2 32.850	49 13.48	17.39	31 20.72	42 39 40.87
33	9	. .	42.0	56.3	11.2	26.0	41.0	. .	. .	. .	22 0 11.31	14.25	" 7 44.647	7 2.63	5.78	22 0 25.56	41 57 18.41
34	9	. .	44.0	58.0	12.2	27.2	42.5	. .	. .	. .	5 12.80	14.14	" 6 40.840	15 8.99	5.78	5 26.94	42 5 24.77 B.
35	6.7	. .	49.3	4.1	19.0	33.2	48.5	. .	. .	. .	6 18.84	14.14	" 6 40.676	15 14.64	5.78	6 32.98	42 5 30.42 B.
36	5.6	. .	. .	55.0	9.0	24.0	39.0	53.6	. .	. .	7 9.29	14.14	" 4 36.910	32 2.67	5.79	7 23.43	42 22 18.46 B.
37	6.7	. .	12.1	26.5	41.1	56.0	11.0	. .	. .	. .	11 41.38	14.06	II. 5 46.395	20 42.16	5.79	11 55.44	42 10 57.85
38	9	42.0	56.8	11.0	26.0	. .	. .	. .	. .	. .	15 26.20	13.99	III. 5 44.940	21 32.86	5.79	15 40.19	42 11 48.65
39	8	45.5	0.2	15.0	30.0	. .	. .	. .	. .	. .	15 29.92	13.99	V. 5 45.050	21 29.06	5.79	15 43.91	42 11 44.85
40	9	. .	. .	. .	. .	55.0	9.5	24.5	. .	. .	15 40.12	13.98	IV. 6 35.290	18 22.37	5.80	15 54.10	42 8 38.17
41	8	. .	. .	. .	49.5	4.2	19.0	33.5	. .	. .	17 49.44	13.95	" 6 43.970	13 20.04	5.81	18 3 29	42 3 35.85
42	9	. .	48.1	3.0	17.8	32.2	47.1	. .	. .	. .	22 17.64	13.90	" 5 44.513	21 47.64	5.91	22 31.54	42 12 3.55
43	9	. .	. .	. .	. .	12.5	27.0	42.3	. .	. .	24 57.54	13.85	VI. 3 33.749	39 51.94	6.05	25 11.39	42 40 7.99
44	9	. .	. .	13.0	27.5	42.0	. .	12.0	. .	. .	22 32 27.62	13.70	IV. 6 46.144	12 4.42	6.51	22 32 41.34	42 2 20.93

CORRECTIONS.

	COR. TO CLOCK.	HOURLY COR.	m.	n.	c.	ZENITH POINT.	COINC.
	s.	s.	s.	s.	s.	° ' ''	r.
Sept. 9, at 22h...	+ 4.777	—0.021	—0.356	—0.527	+0.022	0 0 4.59	40.092

INSTRUMENT READINGS.

	CIRCLE. A.	B.	C.	D.	Mean.	BAR.	THERMOM. At.	Ex.
	° ' ''	''	''	''	''	I.	°	°
Zone LVII.—Sept. 9......h. 20.1	. . . . .	. .	. .	. .	. . .	. .	. .	64.6
20.5	. . . . .	. .	. .	. .	. . .	30.238	71.5	64.7
21.9	. . . . .	. .	. .	. .	. . .	30.248	69.3	63.5
23.0	278 50 59.3	61.8	70.3	61.8	63.30	30.268	68.7	61.8

Number.	Magnitude.	Seconds of Transits. I.	II.	III.	IV.	V.	VI.	VII.	10.	11.	T.	a.	Micrometer.	D.	d.	Mean Right Ascension, 1850.0.	Mean South Declination, 1850.0.
Zone LVII. September 9. H. $D. = -40° 51' 10''.00$. $n'. = -40''.00$. $n''. = -15''.06$. (Continued.)																	
											h. m. s.	s.	r.	′ ″	″	h. m. s.	° ′ ″
45	9	35.2	50.2	5.0	20.0	34.5	49.5	5.0	. .	. .	22 34 19.95	+13.70	I. 4 40.412	−30 0.29	−6.58	22 34 33.65	42 20 16.87
46	6	48.0	3.2	17.6	33.0	47.2	2.5	17.0	. .	. .	34 32.68	13.70	IV. 5 45.091	21 27.71	6.59	34 46.38	42 11 44.30 B.
47	8	. .	44.5	59.0	14.1	28.8	43.7	. .	. .	. .	38 14.05	13.65	" 3 35.781	38 41.40	6.85	38 27.70	42 28 58.25
48	9	. .	54.2	8.5	24.0	38.2	53.2	. .	. .	. .	41 23.63	13.59	" 5 36.886	26 13.41	7.00	41 37.22	42 16 30.41
49	9	. .	59.8	14.2	29.3	44.0	59.0	. .	. .	. .	42 29.28	13.57	" 4 36.480	32 17.85	7.06	42 42.85	42 22 34.91
50	9	. .	12.5	27.2	42.3	57.1	12.1	. .	. .	. .	45 42.29	13.55	" 2 35.712	47 33.70	7.17	45 55.84	42 37 50.87
51	8	. .	11.2	26.0	41.0	55.2	10.1	. .	. .	. .	51 40.71	13.40	V. 7 44.726	6 59.83	7.39	51 54.11	41 57 17.22
*52	6.7	. .	48.8	3.1	18.0	32.8	47.8	. .	. .	. .	22 55 18.11	13.36	11. 4 45.452	27 3.77	7.55	22 55 31.47	42 17 21.32
Zone LVIII. September 13. M. $D. = -28° 54' 50''.0$. $n'. = -34''.00$. $n''. = -3''.26$.																	
1	7.8	. .	. .	. .	. .	. .	. .	. .	12.5	25.1	20 13 15.75	13.56	11. 3 36.585	37 56.75	30.73	20 15 29.31	29 33 17.48
2	7	. .	. .	. .	. .	. .	. .	. .	10.5	. .	16 14.12	13.51	" 7 33.535	13 24.60	30.52	16 27.63	29 8 45.12
3	7	. .	. .	. .	. .	. .	. .	. .	3.0	15.5	17 6.21	13.55	" 3 36.376	38 3.95	30.33	17 19.76	29 33 24.28
4	7	. .	. .	. .	. .	. .	. .	. .	. .	12.5	18 3.21	13.51	" 5 42.66	22 43.01	30.13	18 16.72	29 18 3.14 z.
5	7.8	. .	6.5	18.7	31.5	43.8	56.4	. .	. .	. .	21 31.41	13.51	2. 3 46.01	41 16.87	29.41	21 44.92	29 36 36.28
6	9	21.0	33.8	45.0	. .	. .	. .	. .	. .	. .	22 58.41	13.45	IV. 7 37.862	10 56 26	29.11	23 11.86	29 6 15.37 z.
7	7	. .	. .	. .	. .	. .	44.0	56.6	. .	. .	23 18.95	13.44	VII. 7 38.45	10 35.64	29.04	23 32.39	29 5 54.68 z.
8	7.8	. .	. .	. .	. .	. .	59.0	11.5	. .	. .	24 33.64	13.50	" 1 36.45	52 39.20	28.79	24 47.14	29 47 57.99
9	8	. .	. .	40.7	53.5	6.0	18.8	31.3	. .	. .	27 53.53	13.41	2. 6 35.09	18 22.38	28.11	28 6.94	29 13 40.49 z.
10	10	. .	. .	. .	47.0	59.6	. .	. .	. .	. .	30 47.05	13.40	I. 4 42.78	28 26.86	27.53	31 0.45	29 23 44.39 z.
11	8	. .	. .	. .	. .	. .	28.0	40.4	. .	. .	31 2.62	13.43	VII. 1 44.27	48 9.00	27.48	31 16.05	29 43 26.48 z.
12	8	. .	. .	. .	25.5	38.0	50.5	. .	. .	. .	32 25.45	13.37	VI. 5 43.62	22 10.83	27.21	32 38.82	29 17 28.04 z.
13	8.9	. .	. .	. .	42.0	54.5	7.0	19.8	. .	. .	33 41.97	13.36	VII. 5 42.48	22 50.03	26.96	33 55.33	29 18 6.99 z.
14	9	. .	47.5	. .	12.6	. .	. .	. .	. .	. .	41 12.64	13.31	VI. 3 34.95	38 54.18	25.51	41 25.95	29 34 9.69 z.
15	10	. .	. .	. .	. .	. .	. .	. .	10.0	23.2	41 13.56	13.30	11. 5 34.42	27 27.73	25.51	41 26.86	29 22 43.24
16	9	. .	. .	. .	. .	5.3	18.1	30.5	. .	. .	45 52.96	13.21	I. 7 42.89	8 2.22	24.66	46 6.17	29 3 16.88
17	9	. .	. .	. .	56.0	8.3	21.2	33.5	. .	. .	45 55.83	13.27	VII 2 43.60	42 40.49	24.65	46 9.10	29 37 55.14
18	10	. .	12.5	. .	38.0	. .	3.5	. .	. .	. .	50 37.96	13.21	" 3 37.60	37 22.38	23.80	50 51.17	29 32 36.18
19	6	. .	. .	29.3	42.0	54.0	. .	. .	. .	. .	53 41.83	13.19	VI. 2 36.792	46 35.95	23.27	53 55.02	29 41 49.22 z.
20	8	. .	32.0	45.0	57.0	10.0	. .	. .	. .	. .	54 57.38	13.19	VII. 1 43.30	48 42.52	23.04	55 10.57	29 43 55.56 z.
21	7	9.5	22.4	34.7	47.5	. .	12.5	24.8	. .	. .	59 47.35	13.07	1. 7 40.86	9 12.35	22.20	21 0 0.42	29 4 24.55 z.
22	8	. .	. .	6.4	19.0	31.4	44.0	56.4	. .	. .	21 1 18.94	13.06	VII. 7 38.41	10 37.02	21.94	1 32.00	29 5 48.96 z.
23	9	. .	. .	59.5	12.1	24.7	. .	50.0	. .	. .	4 12.18	13.06	I. 4 42.684	28 30.16	21.46	4 25.24	29 23 41.62 z.
24	9	. .	. .	6.5	19.2	31.5	44.4	. .	. .	. .	7 19.18	13.00	VI 6 45.185	12 34.27	20.94	7 32.18	29 7 45.21 z.
25	9	. .	. .	45.5	. .	10.8	. .	. .	. .	. .	8 58.26	13.00	V. 5 40.70	23 51.80	20.67	9 11.26	29 19 2.47 z.
26	7	. .	. .	. .	49.0	. .	14.2	26.7	. .	. .	9 48.94	13.00	VII. 4 43.26	28 10.31	20.53	10 1.94	29 23 20.84 z.
27	7	. .	. .	. .	41.0	53.4	6.2	19.0	. .	. .	12 40.95	13.00	" 1 36.27	52 45.40	20.08	12 53.95	29 47 55.48 z.
28	8.9	. .	12.1	. .	37.0	50.1	2.3	15.0	. .	. .	17 37.22	12.94	2. 2 41.7	43 45.75	19.30	17 50.16	29 38 55.95 z.
29	9	. .	. .	. .	. .	. .	. .	. .	16.0	28.8	21 19.38	12.89	11. 3 42.81	34 21.65	18.73	21 32.27	29 29 30.38
30	8	. .	12.0	25.0	37.5	. .	2.9	15.3	. .	. .	21 25 37.50	12.85	2. 3 36.73	37 52.06	18.09	21 25 50.35	29 33 0.15 z.

CORRECTIONS.

	Cor. to clock.	Hourly cor.	m.	n.	c.	Zenith point.	Coinc.
	s.	s.	s.	s.	s.		r.
Sept. 13, at 22*h*..	+3.439	−0.020	−0.356	+0.527	+0.022	0° 0′ 2″.61	40.110

INSTRUMENT READINGS.

	Circle. A.	B.	C.	D.	Mean.	Bar.	Thermom. At.	Ex.
Zone LVIII.—Sept. 13, *h.* 20.2	291° 42′ 50″.2	55″.0	57″.4	51″.0	53″.40	I. 30.040	78°.1	74°.1
20.6	46.7	.	. .	. .	49.90	. .	. .	. .
20.7	. . . .	. .	. .	. .	. .	. .	. .	73.5
21.5	. . . .	. .	. .	. .	. .	. .	. .	73.5
22.0	. . . .	. .	. .	. .	. .	. .	. .	72.7
22.6	45.6	. .	. .	. .	49.02	. .	. .	73.2
0.5	45.7	51.5	56.0	50.0	50.80	30.008	75.3	72.0

Zone LVIII. September 13. M. $D. = -28^\circ 54' 50''.0.$ $n'. = -34''.00.$ $n''. = -3''.26.$ (Continued.)

Number.	Magnitude.	SECONDS OF TRANSITS. I.	II.	III.	IV.	V.	VI.	VII.	10.	11.	T.	a.	MICROMETER.	D.	d.	Mean Right Ascension, 1850.0.	Mean South Declination, 1850.0
											h. m. s.	s.	r.	′ ″	″	h. m. s.	° ′ ″
31	8	. .	. .	46.5	59.6	12.0	25.0	37.2	. .	. .	21 27 59.52	+12.80	I. 5 44.77	−21 30.88	−17.74	21 28 12.32	29 16 38.62 z.
*32	8	. .	10.0	22.2	34.4	. .	. .	12.2	. .	. .	36 34.70	12.72	" 4 40.22	29 55.33	16.52	36 47.42	29 25 1.85
33	9	. .	. .	. .	58.0	11.0	23.2	35.7	. .	. .	39 58.16	12.66	" 6 39.81	15 39.69	16.04	40 10.82	29 10 45.73
34	10	. .	. .	33.7	. .	59.0	. .	. .	. .	. .	43 46.47	12.66	VI. 3 32.15	40 30.94	15.55	43 59.13	29 35 36.49 z.
35	8	. .	. .	. .	. .	58.5	10.9	23.7	. .	. .	44 45.87	12.62	VII. 5 35.76	26 42.14	15.42	44 58.49	29 21 47.56 z.
36	10	. .	. .	. .	. .	. .	. .	. .	38.0	50.3	45 41.12	12.63	11. 3.37.62	37 20.94	15.30	45 53.75	29 32 26.24 z.
37	8	. .	. .	42.0	54.6	7.0	20.0	32.1	. .	. .	47 54.56	12.61	VII. 3 39.18	36 27.82	15.01	48 7.17	29 31 32.83 z.
38	8	. .	13.8	26.6	38.3	. .	. .	. .	. .	. .	50 38.92	12.60	2. 1 39.08	51 7.92	14.66	50 51.52	29 46 12.58
39	7.8	. .	. .	. .	57.0	9.5	22.0	34.7	. .	. .	50 56.94	12.56	VII. 5 38.96	24 51.61	14.62	51 9.50	29 19 56.23
40	7	. .	. .	. .	. .	. .	. .	. .	55.8	8.3	52 59.27	12.52	11. 6 40.63	15 10.58	14.38	53 11.79	29 10 14.96
41	7.8	13.0	25.5	37.8	50.8	. .	. .	. .	. .	. .	53 50.64	12.51	1. 6 41.86	14 28.87	14.28	54 3.15	29 9 33.15
42	8	. .	0.5	13.0	25.8	38.1	. .	. .	. .	. .	57 25.68	12.49	2. 4 38.64	30 49.49	13.84	57 38.17	29 25 53.33 z.
43	8	. .	. .	. .	. .	. .	49.0	1.8	. .	. .	57 23.79	12.53	VII. 1 36.17	52 48.85	13.84	57 36.32	29 47 52.69
44	7	. .	48.8	1.0	13.1	. .	. .	. .	. .	. .	22 1 13.47	12.42	IV. 7 45.62	6 28.32	13.39	22 1 25.89	29 1 31.71 z.
45	9.10	. .	30.5	43.0	55.5	8.1	21.0	33.4	. .	. .	12 55.63	12.34	2. 3 39.14	36 28.82	12.10	13 7.97	29 31 30.92 z.
46	9	. .	. .	19.0	32.0	44.2	57.0	9.4	. .	. .	15 31.75	12.30	I. 4 38.79	30 44.70	11.86	15 44.05	29 25 46.56 z.
47	9.10	. .	. .	2.2	15.0	27.4	40.0	. .	. .	. .	17 14.88	12.29	VI. 3 44.01	33 41.20	11.69	17 27.17	29 28 42.89 z.
48	7	9.8	22.5	35.0	47.5	59.8	12.5	. .	. .	. .	20 47.44	12.24	I. 4 39.40	30 23.67	11.36	20 59.68	29 25 25.03
49	9	. .	. .	. .	. .	. .	. .	. .	42.5	55.0	20 45.73	12.25	11. 3 42.99	34 15.44	11.36	20 57.98	29 29 16.80
50	8.9	. .	57.6	10.4	23.5	35.5	48.0	0.6	. .	. .	24 22.99	12.23	VII. 1 40.88	50 6.09	11.03	24 35.22	29 45 7.12 z.
51	9	. .	. .	56.5	9.1	21.7	34.2	46.6	. .	. .	27 9 08	12.16	2. 5 47.56	19 54.10	10.78	27 21.24	29 14 54.88 z.
*52	7	33.3	46.0	58.5	11.1	24.0	. .	. .	. .	. .	30 11.25	12.15	" 3 39.80	36 6.01	10.51	30 23.40	29 31 6.52
53	7	. .	45.0	57.2	10.3	. .	. .	. .	. .	. .	31 10.03	12.10	IV. 7 37.47	11 9.84	10.43	31 22.13	29 6 10.27 z.
*54	7.8	. .	. .	. .	. .	. .	. .	. .	8.8	21.3	31 12.33	12.10	11. 7 35.90	12 2.94	10.43	31 24.43	29 7 3.37
55	9.10	0.6	13.5	26.0	38.5	. .	. .	. .	. .	. .	34 38.58	12.09	VI. 4 40.26	29 54.19	10.17	34 50.67	29 24 54.36
56	10	. .	. .	. .	33.1	45.5	58.1	10.8	. .	. .	35 32.95	12.11	VII. 1 44.88	47 47.90	10.10	35 45.06	29 42 48.00
57	8.9	. .	35.0	47.2	. .	12.1	25.0	37.4	. .	. .	44 59.62	11.96	" 6 36.23	17 43.40	9.46	45 11.58	29 12 42.86 z.
58	9	. .	37.1	49.2	. .	14.4	27.0	39.8	. .	. .	48 1.96	11.95	2. 4 41.36	29 15.57	9.27	48 13.91	29 24 14.84 z.
59	10	37.1	49.7	2.4	15.0	27.5	. .	. .	. .	. .	50 14.94	11.90	VII. 7 37.17	11 19.84	9.14	50 26.84	29 6 18.98 z.
60	7	17.4	30.1	42.8	. .	7.7	20.6	33.0	. .	. .	52 55.33	11.92	2. 2 40.50	44 27.26	8.97	53 7.25	29 39 26.23 z.
61	9	8.0	20.6	32.9	45.3	57.8	10.4	. .	. .	. .	53 45.37	11.84	VII. 7 43.54	7 39.75	8.81	53 57.21	29 2 38.56
62	7	23.6	36.1	48.3	1.2	13.4	26.7	39.1	. .	. .	23 0 1.25	11.84	2. 2 43.105	42 57.23	8.56	23 0 13.09	29 37 55.79
63	8	. .	22.7	35.2	47.9	0.5	. .	. .	. .	. .	1 47.95	11.83	VI. 1 40.21	50 29.51	8.48	1 59.78	29 45 27.99 z.
64	9	. .	. .	. .	. .	. .	. .	. .	8.3	21.0	3 11.80	11.78	11. 6 33.19	19 27.64	8.42	3 23.58	29 14 26.06
65	8.9	22.3	35.3	47.4	0.5	. .	. .	. .	. .	. .	5 0.26	11.76	V. 6 34.50	18 43.41	8.34	5 12.02	29 13 41.75 z.
66	8	. .	50.5	2.8	. .	27.7	40.3	53.0	. .	. .	6 15.33	11.75	" 5 44.99	21 23.61	8.29	6 27.08	29 16 21.90 z.
67	7.8	. .	. .	11.0	23.5	36.2	. .	. .	. .	. .	8 23.63	11.75	IV. 3 41.61	35 4.18	8.19	8.35.38	29 30 2 37 z.
68	7	. .	. .	. .	. .	. .	18.0	30.5	. .	. .	8 52.80	11.72	VII. 5 47.30	20 3.50	8.17	9 4.52	29 15 1 67 z.
69	9	. .	. .	. .	14.1	26.5	. .	. .	. .	. .	10 14.07	11.71	V. 5 42.79	22 39.59	8.11	10 25.78	29 17 37.70 z.
70	7	. .	. .	. .	. .	. .	13.4	26.0	. .	. .	10 48.26	11.70	VII. 6 36.59	17 30.91	8.09	10 59.96	29 12 29.00 z.
71	8.9	37.4	50.5	3.0	15.3	. .	. .	. .	. .	. .	15 15.51	11.68	2. 3 42.53	34 31.68	7.94	15 27.19	29 29 29.62
72	9	. .	. .	. .	. .	43.0	55.8	8.1	. .	. .	16 30.46	11.65	VII. 4 41.25	29 19.75	7.90	16 42.11	29 24 17.65
73	8	. .	. .	44.5	57.0	8.8	22.0	34.7	. .	. .	20 56.91	11.59	" 7 38.94	10 18.68	7.76	21 8.50	29 5 16.44 z.
74	10	. .	49.8	. .	14.7	. .	. .	52.5	. .	. .	27 14.78	11.55	2. 3 34.77	38 59.77	7.63	27 26.33	29 33 57.40 z.
75	10	. .	. .	. .	. .	. .	. .	. .	24.5	. .	27 27.94	11.56	11. 2 37.55	46 8.81	7.62	27 39.50	29 41 6.43 z.
76	10	7.2	. .	32.0	44.5	. .	. .	. .	. .	. .	30 44.72	11.49	V. 7 37.95	10 53.19	7.56	30 56.21	29 5 50.75 z.
77	8	42.3	55.1	7.3	20.3	32.5	45.4	57.7	. .	. .	32 20.12	11.48	VII. 6 37.95	16 43.95	7.55	32 31.60	19 11 41.50
78	9	. .	19.5	. .	44.5	57.0	10.0	22.3	. .	. .	42 44.61	11.37	2. 6 40.01	15 32.40	7.48	42 55.98	29 10 29.88
79	9	17.6	30.5	43.0	55.5	8.0	20.0	. .	. .	. .	44 55.42	11.35	VII. 6 41.47	14 42.38	7.48	45 6.77	29 9 39.86
80	7	. .	. .	. .	. .	. .	. .	. .	24.5	37.1	53 27.76	11.29	11. 3 35.40	38 37.67	7.53	53 39.05	29 33 35.20 z.
81	8	. .	. .	. .	44.3	57.0	9.5	. .	. .	. .	55 44.35	11.25	VI. 6 31.89	20 13.54	7.56	55 55.60	29 15 11.10 z.
82	7.8	. .	. .	. .	. .	. .	. .	. .	55.8	8.7	56 59.42	11.24	11. 6 34.37	18 46.89	7.57	57 10.66	29 13 44.46
83	7	. .	. .	. .	. .	34.7	47.0	. .	. .	. .	0 13 21.93	11.10	V. 1 34.55	53 45.17	7.96	0 13 33.03	29 48 43.13

Number.	Magnitude.	SECONDS OF TRANSITS. I.	II.	III.	IV.	V.	VI.	VII.	10.	11.	T.	a.	MICROMETER.	D.	d.	Mean Right Ascension, 1850.0.	Mean South Declination, 1850.0.
Zone LVIII. September 13. M. $D. = -28° 54' 50''.0$. $n'. = -34''.00$. $n''. = -3''.26$. (Continued.)																	
											h. m. s.	s.	r.	′ ″	″	h. m. s.	° ′ ″
84	9	17.8	30.7	43.0	. .	. .	. .	. .	. .	. .	0 15 55.79	+11.07	V. 3 42.34	—34 38.98	—8.06	0 16 6.86	29 29 37.04
85	9	. .	50.0	2.8	15.0	. .	. .	. .	. .	. .	18 15.13	11.05	III. 7 37.21	11 18.76	8.15	18 26.18	29 6 16.91 z˙.
86	9	. .	. .	. .	49.5	2.0	. .	. .	. .	. .	18 49.52	11.05	VII. 6 32.982	19 35.58	8.17	19 0.57	29 14 33.75 z.
87	7.8	. .	. .	. .	. .	53.6	6.5	18.9	. .	. .	19 41.30	11.04	" 7 40.40	9 28.27	8.21	19 52.34	29 4 26.48 z.
88	8	. .	. .	. .	. .	16.0	29.0	41.5	. .	. .	21 3.60	11.03	" 1 43.15	48 47.69	8.27	21 14.63	29 43 45.96 z.
89	9	17.5	. .	43.0	55.3	8.0	20.3	33.1	. .	. .	24 55.35	10.99	" 3 33.64	39 39.25	8.46	25 6.34	29 34 37.71 z.
90	8.9	. .	. .	40.0	52.5	5.1	17.8	30.0	. .	. .	26 52.49	10.97	" 2 37.37	46 15.78	8.55	27 3.46	29 41 14.33 z.
91	8.9	. .	31.7	44.5	57.0	9.2	22.2	. .	. .	. .	0 28 56.95	10.95	" 2 38.23	45 46.05	8.65	0 29 7.90	29 40 44.70 z.
Zone LIX. September 14. H. $D. = -40° 19' 20''.0$. $n'. = -26''.59$. $n''. = -11''.00$.																	
1	8	. .	1.6	16.0	30.3	. .	. .	. .	. .	. .	19 2 30.53	15.03	IV. 3 34.431	39 23.10	25.96	19 2 45.56	40 59 9.06
2	8.9	. .	46.2	. .	14.2	29.0	43.3	. .	. .	. .	4 14.54	14.96	" 6 38.333	16 34.58	25.53	4 29.50	40 36 20.11
3	5	. .	44.8	59.0	13.5	28.0	43.0	. .	. .	. .	13 13.67	14.91	" 3 44.092	33 47.38	23.31	13 28.58	40 53 30.69 B.
4	9	. .	57.2	11.5	26.2	41.0	55.2	. .	. .	. .	17 26.33	14.90	" 2 34.546	48 7.23	22.29	17 41.23	41 7 49.52
5	9	. .	41.2	. .	. .	24.2	39.1	. .	. .	. .	20 10.00	14.83	" 5 37.362	25 53.61	21.62	20 24.83	40 45 35.23
6	9	. .	9.5	23.5	38.0	52.0	7.0	. .	. .	. .	37 38.01	14.62	" 6 38.320	16 35.02	17.47	37 52.63	40 36 12.49
7	9	. .	46.0	. .	15.0	29.5	44.2	. .	. .	. .	41 15.05	14.64	" 2 39.398	45 18.87	16.63	41 29.69	41 4 55.50
8	9	. .	23.0	. .	. .	6.0	. .	. .	. .	. .	42 51.78	14.58	V. 5 38.138	25 26.53	16.26	43 6.36	40 45 2.79
9	8.9	. .	. .	. .	41.5	56.0	10.8	25.0	. .	. .	43 41.69	14.55	" 6 42.438	14 11.96	16.07	43 56.24	40 33 48.03
10	9	. .	. .	50.0	4.5	. .	33.5	48.0	. .	. .	45 4.47	14.58	IV. 3 35.620	38 41.56	15.76	45 19.05	40 58 17.32
11	8.9	. .	43.0	57.2	11.2	26.2	41.0	. .	. .	. .	48 11.74	14.54	" 3 38.876	36 48.51	15.04	48 26.28	40 56 23.55
12	9	. .	1.5	15.2	30.0	44.5	. .	. .	. .	. .	49 30.17	14.56	III. 1 36.418	52 56.03	14.74	49 44.73	41 12 30.77
13	8	. .	1.5	16.2	31.0	. .	59.0	. .	. .	. .	50 30.51	14.48	IV. 6 38.250	16 37.43	14.52	50 44.99	40 36 11.95
14	9	. .	18.2	32.1	46.5	1.1	15.5	. .	. .	. .	57 46.70	14.41	" 4 42.181	28 55.28	12.90	58 1.11	40 48 28.18
15	8	. .	. .	. .	27.0	41.1	56.0	11.0	. .	. .	58 26.94	14.44	" 2 35.160	47 46.06	12.75	58 41.38	41 7 18.81
16	9	. .	42.0	56.0	10.0	. .	. .	. .	. .	. .	20 5 10.39	14.29	" 7 40.512	9 25.83	11.28	20 5 24.68	40 28 57.11
17	9	. .	46.2	0.5	15.0	29.5	. .	. .	. .	. .	6 15.06	14.29	III. 5 47.190	20 12.17	11.05	6 29.35	40 39 43.22
18	9	. .	. .	. .	. .	32.5	46.5	1.2	. .	. .	6 17.70	14.32	VI. 3 41.410	35 20.38	11.04	6 32.02	40 54 51.42
19	8	. .	. .	. .	30.5	45.0	59.5	13.5	. .	. .	7 30.45	14.28	IV. 6 34.040	19 3.58	10.78	7 44.73	40 38 34.36
20	9	. .	. .	. .	19.5	34.1	48.3	2.8	. .	. .	9 19.34	14.30	" 2 36.333	47 5.36	10.38	9 33.64	41 6 35.74
21	7.8	. .	59.2	13.6	28.2	43.0	57.3	. .	. .	. .	11 28.32	14.29	" 1 34.400	54 5.95	9.93	11 42.61	41 13 35.88 M.
22	7.8	. .	8.2	23.0	37.8	52.0	6.6	. .	. .	. .	14 37.58	14.25	" 1 35.760	53 19.05	9.28	14 51.83	41 12 48.33
23	8.9	. .	1.3	15.8	30.0	44.2	59.5	. .	. .	. .	16 30.18	14.19	" 3 43.130	34 20.79	8.89	16 44.37	40 53 49.68
24	7	. .	4.2	18.0	33.3	48.0	2.1	. .	. .	. .	20 23 33.16	14.12	" 2 41.176	44 17.01	7.45	20 23 47.28	41 3 44.46

CORRECTIONS.

	COR. TO CLOCK.	HOURLY COR.	m.	n.	c.	ZENITH POINT.	COINC.
	s.	s.	s.	s.	s.		r.
Sept. 14, at 22h...	+3.248	—0.024	—0.356	+0.527	+0.022	0° 0′ 2″.37	40.106

INSTRUMENT READINGS.

	CIRCLE. A.	B.	C.	D.	Mean.	BAR.	THERMOM. At.	Ex.
Zone LIX.—Sept. 14...19.0 h.	280° 21′ 1″.9	4′.5	12′.6	4″.1	5″.72	I. 29.940	81°.8	78°.5
19.2	1.5	. . .	. . .	. . .	5.68	. . . .	. . .	. . .
20.0	. . . . . .	. . .	. . .	. . .	. . . .	29.926	80.5	77.5
20.3	1.0	3.3	11.8	2.6	6.23	. . . .	. . .	. . .

Number.	Magnitude.	SECONDS OF TRANSITS. I.	II.	III.	IV.	V.	VI.	VII.	10.	11.	T.	a.	MICROMETER.	D.	d.	Mean Right Ascension, 1850.0.	Mean South Declination, 1850.0.
Zone LX. September 14. H. $D. = -27° 31' 30''.0$. $n' = -25''.60$. $n'' = 3''.00$.																	
											h. m. s.	s.	r.	' ''	''	h. m. s.	° ' ''
*1	8	35.5	48.2	0.5	. .	. .	. .	. .	. .	. .	20 35 12.87	+13.06	I. 6 43.293	—13 39.37	—22.56	20 35 25.93	27 45 31.93
*2	9	. .	. .	20.5	32.0	45.0	. .	. .	. .	. .	35 32.57	13.08	IV. 4 46.190	26 29.21	22.49	35 45.65	27 58 21.70
3	5.6	. .	. .	. .	59.0	11.5	24.0	36.2	. .	. .	35 59.13	13.06	" 6 40.340	15 21.70	22.40	36 12.19	27 47 14.10 z.
4	9	. .	2.0	14.2	27.0	. .	. .	. .	. .	. .	37 26.76	13.05	" 6 41.498	14 41.72	22.12	37 39.81	27 46 33.84 z.
5	9	. .	. .	. .	. .	44.0	56.2	9.0	. .	. .	38 31.71	13.04	" 6 46.548	11 47.27	21.91	38 44.75	27 43 39.18
6	8	. .	. .	. .	. .	. .	27.0	39.5	. .	. .	39 2.13	13.07	" 2 43.460	42 45.29	21.81	39 15.20	28 14 37.10
7	7.8	. .	. .	. .	38.0	50.0	. .	. .	33.3	. .	39 37.75	13.08	VI. 2 37.701	46 4.06	21.70	39 50.83	28 17 55.76
8	8	15.0	27.0	39.5	52.2	. .	. .	. .	. .	. .	40 52.06	13.03	I. 5 41.680	23 17.46	21.46	41 5.09	27 55 8.92 z.
9	9	. .	. .	48.0	1.0	13.2	. .	. .	. .	. .	41 0.80	13.04	IV. 4 38.450	30 56.56	21.43	41 13.84	28 2 47.99
10	8.9	. .	48.0	. .	12.5	. .	. .	. .	. .	. .	42 12.52	12.99	" 7 38.511	10 33.84	21.21	42 25.51	27 42 25.05 z.
11	7	. .	. .	8.5	. .	34.0	46.0	. .	. .	. .	42 21.33	13.00	" 6 38.932	16 10.31	21.18	42 34.33	27 48 1.49 z.
12	9	. .	25.5	37.5	50.3	2.5	15.0	. .	. .	. .	43 50.38	12.98	" 6 46.452	11 50.62	20.91	44 3.36	27 43 41.53 z.
13	9	13.5	26.1	38.2	51.0	3.2	. .	. .	. .	. .	45 50.87	12.99	" 4 42.272	28 44.54	20.53	46 3.86	28 0 35.07 z.
14	9	. .	. .	17.0	30.0	. .	. .	. .	. .	. .	46 29.74	12.98	" 4 42.462	28 37.99	20.41	46 42.72	28 0 28.40 z.
15	9	. .	. .	4.0	17.5	30.0	. .	. .	. .	. .	47 17.24	12.95	" 6 41.270	14 49.58	20.26	47 30.19	27 46 39.84 z.
16	8	. .	. .	16.2	28.5	41.0	. .	. .	. .	. .	48 28.63	12.99	" 2 35.522	47 19.41	20.04	48 41.62	28 19 9.45
17	9	. .	27.5	. .	. .	4.2	16.5	28.8	. .	. .	49 51.86	12.93	" 6 36.142	17 46.69	19.78	50 4.79	27 49 36.38
18	7.8	. .	44.2	56.5	9.0	21.5	33.8	. .	. .	. .	51 9.01	12.92	" 5 41.493	23 24.31	19.54	51 21.93	27 55 13.85 z.
19	9	. .	45.5	58.0	. .	33.0	. .	. .	. .	. .	52 10.56	12.95	" 2 38.430	45 39.02	19.37	52 23.51	28 17 28.39 z.
20	7	. .	. .	10.0	22.0	. .	47.0	. .	. .	. .	52 22.20	12.95	" 1 38.485	51 28.67	19.33	52 35.15	28 23 18.00 z.
21	6.7	22.3	35.2	47.1	59.2	12 12	24.5	. .	. .	. .	53 59.69	12.93	" 2 35.550	47 18.45	19.04	54 12.62	28 19 7.49 z.
22	9	34.0	47.0	59.2	11.5	24.0	36.2	. .	. .	. .	55 11.57	12.90	" 3 40.780	35 32.54	18.83	55 24.47	28 7 21.37 z.
23	9	5.0	17.5	30.0	42.3	54.4	. .	. .	. .	. .	57 42.36	12.89	" 2 41.520	43 52.23	18.38	57 55.25	28 15 40.61 z.
24	7.8	. .	. .	3.0	15.2	27.5	39.8	52.2	. .	. .	58 15.16	12.85	" 5 44.810	21 29.70	18.28	58 28.01	27 53 17.98 z.
25	8	23.2	36.1	. .	1.0	13.2	. .	. .	. .	. .	21 0 0.78	12.82	" 6 48.230	10 49.20	17.97	21 0 13.60	27 42 37.17 z.
26	9	. .	. .	34.0	46.5	59.0	12.0	. .	. .	. .	0 46.70	12.86	" 2 43.545	42 42.30	17.84	0 59.56	28 14 30.14
27	9	. .	. .	52.0	. .	17.0	29.2	. .	. .	. .	2 4.51	12.81	" 6 43.410	13 35.67	17.62	2 17.32	27 45 23.29
28	9	. .	44.0	57.0	9.0	. .	. .	. .	. .	. .	2 9.06	12.82	" 4 45.980	26 36.46	17.60	2 21.88	27 58 24.06
29	6	32.2	45.0	57.2	10.0	22.2	34.5	. .	. .	. .	4 9.80	12.82	" 2 44.990	41 52.41	17.26	4 22.62	28 13 39.67 z.
30	9	. .	. .	52.1	4.5	16.8	. .	. .	. .	. .	5 4.54	12.79	" 4 44.762	27 18.51	17.11	5 17.33	27 59 5.62
31	9	5.5	17.8	30.2	42.8	. .	47.2	19.5	. .	. .	8 42.58	12.75	" 6 33.085	19 32.26	16.49	8 55.33	27 51 18.75 z.
32	7.8	11.2	. .	36.1	49.0	0.8	13.3	. .	. .	. .	10 48.63	12.73	III. 6 34.752	18 34.64	16.14	11 1.36	27 50 20.78
33	8	21.5	3.4	. .	58.2	11.0	. .	36.0	. .	. .	10 58.65	12.73	IV. 5 40.088	24 12.81	16.11	11 11.38	27 55 58.92
34	9	. .	. .	53.0	5.2	17.5	30.0	. .	. .	. .	12 5.25	12.75	" 2 40.890	44 14.07	15.93	12 18.00	28 16 0.00
*35	9	. .	. .	. .	53.0	5.5	18.0	30.3	. .	. .	12 53.13	12.70	" 6 41.860	14 29.18	15.80	13 5.83	27 46 14.98
36	9	. .	. .	59.3	12.0	24.1	. .	. .	. .	. .	14 11.87	12.69	" 5 41.860	23 11.60	15.59	14 24.56	27 54 57.19
37	9	. .	22.2	38.0	47.1	59.3	11.5	. .	. .	. .	15 47.04	12.66	" 7 39.180	10 10.77	15.34	15 59.70	27 41 56.21
38	9	. .	. .	. .	. .	30.0	42.3	55.0	. .	. .	16 17.57	12.70	V. 2 35.000	47 37.43	15.26	16 30.27	28 19 22.69
39	9	. .	. .	. .	17.0	29.2	41.8	54.2	. .	. .	17 16.98	12.65	" 6 37.570	16 57.27	15.10	17 29.63	27 48 42.39 z.
40	8	. .	. .	19.0	31.2	43.5	56.0	. .	. .	. .	18 31.24	12.69	IV. 1 39.848	50 41.84	14.90	18 43.93	28 22 26.74
41	9	. .	22.0	34.5	47.0	. .	. .	. .	. .	. .	19 46.99	12.68	" 1 38.342	51 23.60	14.69	19 59.67	28 23 8.29
42	9	. .	. .	. .	8.0	20.0	32.3	. .	. .	. .	21 20 07.72	12.64	" 5 39.880	24 19.64	14.64	21 20 20.36	27 56 4.28

CORRECTIONS.

	COR. TO CLOCK.	HOURLY COR.	m.	n.	c.	ZENITH POINT.	COINC.
	s.	s.	s.	s.	s.	° ' ''	r.
Sept. 14, at 22h..	+ 3.248	— 0.024	—0.356	+0.527	+0.022	0 0 2.71	40.106

† The recorded circle reading of this zone has been changed six minutes.

INSTRUMENT READINGS.

	CIRCLE. A.	B.	C.	D.	Mean.	BAR.	THERMOM. At.	Ex.
†Zone. h.	° ' ''	'	''	''	''	I.	°	°
LX.—Sept. 14.... 20.0	. . . .	. .	. .	. .	. .	29.926	80.5	77.5
20.4	293 6 3.3	7.6	14.0	6.1	7.75	. .	. .	. .
21.0	2.2	. .	. .	. .	6.65	. .	. .	. .
22.0	2.0	7.3	13.8	5.8	6.97	. .	. .	. .
22.6	2.2	. .	. .	. .	7.17	. .	. .	. .
23.5	. . . .	. .	. .	. .	. .	29.900	78.0	74.0
0.5	3.6	9.4	15.8	7.8	9.15	29.882	77.5	74.2

Zone LX. September 14. H. D. = −27° 31′ 30″.0. n′. = −25″.60. n″. = 3″.00. (Continued.)

Number.	Magnitude.	Seconds of Transits. I.	II.	III.	IV.	V.	VI.	VII.	10.	11.	T.	a.	Micrometer.	D.	d.	Mean Right Ascension, 1850.0.	Mean South Declination, 1850.0.
											h. m. s.	s.	r.	′ ″	″	h. m. s.	° ′ ″
43	9	. .	. .	. .	. .	45.2	58.0	9.9	. .	. .	21 20 32.98	+12.62	V. 6 39.461	−15 52.04	−14.58	21 20 45.60	27 47 36.62 z.
44	9	. .	38.0	50.0	2.5	14.6	27.1	. .	. .	. .	22 2.45	12.60	II. 6 39.330	15 56.49	14.35	22 15.05	27 47 40.84
45	9	34.0	46.5	59.0	11.2	23.4	36.2	48.2	. .	. .	24 11.24	12.60	" 4 43.233	28 11.23	14.02	24 23.84	27 59 55.25
*46	9	39.5	52.0	4.6	17.0	29.1	. .	. .	. .	. .	25 16.91	12.59	IV. 4 43.910	27 47.95	13.86	25 29.50	27 59 31.81
47	9	. .	. .	54.0	6.5	19.0	. .	43.5	. .	. .	26 6.47	12.60	" 2 39.740	44 53.74	13.73	26 19.07	28 16 37.47 z.
48	9	47.2	. .	12.5	25.0	37.0	49.2	2.1	. .	. .	28 24.74	12.58	" 2 37.689	46 4.58	13.38	28 37.32	28 17 47.96 z.
49	7	32.5	45.2	57.7	10.0	22.0	. .	. .	. .	. .	30 9.94	12.54	" 4 45.532	26 51.90	13.12	30 22.48	27 58 35.02 z.
50	9	. .	. .	. .	30.2	42.5	55.0	7.2	. .	. .	30 30.11	12.54	" 4 42.252	28 45.23	13.07	30 42.65	28 0 28.30 z.
51	7.8	31.5	44.0	56.5	. .	. .	. .	. .	. .	. .	33 9.01	12.54	III. 1 40.515	50 18.52	12.69	33 21.55	28 22 1.31 z.
52	9	. .	. .	. .	6.8	19.0	32.0	44.0	. .	. .	33 6.82	12.52	IV. 3 37.632	37 21.27	12.70	33 19.34	28 9 3.97
53	9	. .	. .	. .	49.2	1.5	14.0	26.0	. .	. .	33 49.04	12.51	VI. 3 35.622	38 30.58	12.60	34 1.55	28 10 13.18 z.
54	9	. .	. .	9.0	21.0	33.3	46.0	. .	. .	. .	35 21.14	12.52	IV. 1 40.868	50 6.33	12.38	35 33.66	28 21 48.71
55	9	. .	. .	. .	. .	. .	. .	30.5	. .	. .	35 53.21	12.49	VII. 3 36.220	38 9.71	12.31	36 5.70	28 9 52.02
56	9	. .	. .	40.8	53.2	5.8	. .	. .	. .	. .	37 53.34	12.44	IV. 6 40.068	15 31.08	12.02	38 5.78	27 47 13.10
57	9	. .	. .	12.2	25.0	. .	. .	. .	. .	. .	38 24.83	12.44	" 6 38.255	16 33.72	11.95	38 37.27	27 48 15.67
58	9	. .	. .	41.2	53.5	6.0	. .	. .	. .	. .	38 53.63	12.45	" 4 34.910	32 58.80	11.88	39 6.08	28 4 40.68
59	9	. .	. .	. .	. .	20.0	32.2	45.0	. .	. .	39 7.64	12.44	VI. 5 44.200	21 50.68	11.84	39 20.08	27 53 32.52 z.
*60	7	24.2	37.0	49.2	1.7	14.0	26.5	. .	. .	. .	41 1.69	12.44	IV. 3 42.020	34 49.72	11.59	41 14.13	28 6 31.31
61	8	. .	. .	31.0	43.0	56.0	8.4	. .	. .	. .	41 43.42	12.42	" 4 39.925	30 5.59	11.52	41 55.84	28 1 47.11 z.
62	8	. .	. .	27.0	40.0	52.1	. .	17.1	. .	. .	42 39.78	12.42	" 3 43.169	34 10.05	11.38	42 52.20	28 5 51.43 z.
63	9	. .	13.5	26.0	38.2	50.8	3.3	15.5	. .	. .	43 38.35	12.40	" 4 41.350	29 16.39	11.26	43 50.75	28 0 57.65 z.
64	9	58.5	11.2	23.4	36.0	48.2	1.0	. .	. .	. .	46 35.96	12.37	" 4 36.730	31 55.94	10.88	46 48.33	28 3 36.82 z.
65	9	. .	5.0	. .	. .	42.2	55.0	. .	. .	. .	47 29.92	12.36	" 4 43.290	28 9.38	10.77	47 42.28	27 59 50.15 z.
66	9	. .	59.5	12.2	24.5	37.0	. .	. .	. .	. .	47 24.51	12.34	" 6 46.372	11 53.38	10.78	47 36.85	27 43 34.16
67	7.8	8.5	21.0	34.0	46.0	. .	. .	. .	. .	. .	50 46.12	12.35	II. 1 42.661	49 4.27	10.35	50 58.47	28 20 44.62
68	8	35.0	48.0	. .	13.0	25.5	38.0	. .	. .	. .	51 12.91	12.33	IV. 3 37.620	37 21.67	10.29	51 25.24	28 9 1.96 z.
69	9	. .	. .	. .	. .	. .	. .	37.3	. .	. .	51 0.04	12.32	VII. 4 41.300	29 17.77	10.32	51 12.36	28 1 58.09
70	7.8	17.5	30.1	43.0	55.0	. .	. .	. .	. .	. .	53 55.08	12.30	IV. 3 44.278	33 31.76	9.94	54 7.38	28 5 11.70 z.
71	8	45.3	. .	10.5	23.5	35.0	47.5	. .	. .	. .	54 22.91	12.27	" 6 41.428	14 44.13	9.88	54 35.18	27 46 24.01 z.
72	9	36.5	49.0	1.4	13.8	25.8	38.6	51.0	. .	. .	22 0 13.76	12.22	" 5 40.437	24 0.77	9.12	22 0 25.98	27 55 39.89 z.
73	8	. .	. .	12.3	25.0	37.3	50.0	. .	. .	. .	1 24.96	12.24	" 1 36.483	52 37.82	8.97	1 37.20	28 24 16.79 z.
74	6.7	6.8	19.5	31.8	44.0	56.5	12.5	. .	. .	. .	2 44.24	12.19	" 5 44.680	21 34.19	8.79	2 56.43	27 53 12.98 z.
75	8	18.0	30.0	42.3	55.0	. .	. .	. .	. .	. .	3 54.94	12.18	" 6 36.205	17 44.52	8.64	4 7.12	27 49 23.16 z.
76	9	19.2	32.0	44.2	57.0	9.0	21.2	. .	. .	. .	3 56.70	12.20	" 3 32.648	40 13.40	8.64	4 8.90	28 11 52.04
77	9	11.8	24.2	36.2	49.0	. .	. .	. .	. .	. .	30 48.98	11.91	" 4 35.182	32 49.42	5.33	31 0.89	28 4 24.75
78	6.7	. .	. .	56.5	8.8	21.0	33.6	. .	. .	. .	31 8.83	11.89	" 6 35.975	17 52.45	5.29	31 20.72	27 49 27.74
79	9	. .	. .	. .	56.2	8.2	20.8	33.5	. .	. .	32 56.05	11.90	" 4 38.872	30 41.96	5.11	33 7.95	28 2 17.07 z.
80	9	. .	. .	36.0	48.0	0.8	13.2	25.2	. .	. .	33 48.29	11.89	" 3 35.985	38 18.16	5.02	34 0.18	28 9 53.18 z.
81	8.9	51.0	3.3	15.8	28.2	40.8	53.0	5.5	. .	. .	35 28.25	11.86	" 4 44.283	27 34.91	4.85	35 40.11	27 59 9.76 z.
82	9	. .	. .	23.5	35.2	48.0	. .	. .	. .	. .	36 35.63	11.86	III. 3 45.050	33 5.04	4.73	36 47.49	28 4 39.77 z.
83	8	. .	. .	2.0	14.2	26.8	39.0	. .	. .	. .	37 14.37	11.83	IV. 6 42.150	14 19.18	4.66	37 26.20	27 45 53.84 z.
84	9	. .	. .	. .	. .	46.5	59.0	. .	. .	. .	38 34.13	11.84	V. 3 34.226	39 18.91	4.53	38 45.97	28 10 53.44
85	8	. .	31.1	43.6	56.0	8.2	. .	. .	. .	. .	38 56.01	11.85	IV. 2 35.182	47 31.19	4.49	39 7.86	28 19 5.68
86	7.8	. .	35.0	47.2	1.0	13.2	26.0	38.2	. .	. .	40 0.41	11.84	II. 1 42.018	49 26.50	4.38	40 12.25	28 21 0.88 z.
87	9	50.5	3.0	15.2	28.0	40.0	. .	5.0	. .	. .	42 27.80	11.79	IV. 4 35.600	32 34.98	4.16	42 39.59	28 3 9.11
88	9	25.3	38.0	50.5	2.5	15.0	27.6	. .	. .	. .	44 2.75	11.79	" 3 34.161	39 21.18	4.01	44 14.54	28 10 55.19 z.
89	9	36.0	48.4	0.8	13.0	25.0	. .	. .	. .	. .	45 13.07	11.75	" 6 40.780	15 6.48	3.91	45 24.82	27 46 40.39
90	8	. .	50.8	3.0	15.2	27.2	40.0	52.2	. .	. .	46 15.23	11.73	" 6 44.916	12 43.64	3.81	46 26.96	27 44 17.45 z.
91	9	. .	3.3	16.0	28.0	40.5	. .	. .	. .	. .	48 28.25	11.76	" 1 36.311	52 43.75	3.61	48 40.01	28 24 17.36
92	9	. .	. .	30.0	43.0	55.0	. .	. .	. .	. .	51 42.73	11.70	" 4 40.440	29 47.83	3.33	51 54.43	28 1 21.16
93	8	16.0	28.0	. .	. .	. .	18.2	30.3	. .	. .	51 53.13	11.69	VI. 5 43.272	22 22.74	3.31	52 4.82	27 53 56.05
94	9	11.0	23.5	36.0	48.0	1.0	13.0	. .	. .	. .	53 48.34	11.68	IV. 3 36.863	37 47.84	3.16	54 0.02	28 9 21.00
95	9	58.2	11.0	23.1	36.0	. .	. .	. .	. .	. .	22 55 35.82	11.68	" 2 36.440	46 47.76	3.01	22 55 47.50	28 18 20.77

Zone LX. September 14. H. $D. = -27° 31' 30''.0$. $n' = -25''.60$. $n'' = 3''.00$ (Continued.)

Number.	Magnitude.	Seconds of Transits. I.	II.	III.	IV.	V.	VI.	VII.	10.	11.	T.	a.	Micrometer.	D.	d.	Mean Right Ascension, 1850.0.	Mean South Declination, 1850.0.
											h. m. s.	s.	r.	' ''	''	h. m. s.	° ' ''
96	7.8	53.5	6.2	18.2	31.0	43.0	56.0	7.8	. .	. .	22 56 30.56	+11.64	IV. 5 38.550	−25 5.91	−2.94	22 56 42.20	27 56 38.85 z.
97	9	3.5	16.0	28.2	40.5	. .	. .	. .	. .	. .	23 0 40.70	11.60	" 5 36.410	26 19.86	2.61	23 0 52.30	27 57 52.47
98	9	. .	. .	53.0	5.5	18.0	30.5	43.0	. .	. .	1 5.63	11.59	" 5 42.136	23 2.08	2.58	1 17.22	27 54 34.66
99	9	. .	. .	. .	57.6	9.5	22.2	34.6	. .	. .	1 57.34	11.60	V. 3 42.680	34 26.87	2.52	2 8.94	28 5 59.39
100	8.9	. .	. .	. .	56.0	8.0	21.0	33.0	. .	. .	2 55.97	11.56	IV. 6 46.120	12 2.07	2.45	3 7.53	27 43 34.52 z.
101	9	51.0	3.5	16.0	28.2	41.0	. .	. .	. .	. .	5 28.43	11.57	" 3 40.315	35 48.64	2.27	5 40.00	28 7 20.91
102	9	. .	. .	58.8	11.2	24.0	36.0	. .	. .	. .	6 11.35	11.54	" 5 47.172	20 8.15	2.22	6 22.89	27 51 40.37 z.
103	9	51.0	4.0	16.0	28.2	40.6	53.0	. .	. .	. .	7 28.38	11.54	" 4 43.280	28 9.72	2.13	7 39.92	27 59 41.85 z.
104	7.8	39.0	51.5	. .	16.4	28.1	41.0	53.1	. .	. .	8 16.14	11.52	" 5 43.285	22 22.39	2.08	8 27.66	27 53 54.47 z.
105	9	. .	. .	. .	. .	16.2	28.8	51.0	. .	. .	9 3.95	11.51	" 6 40.435	15 18.42	2.02	9 15.46	27 46 50.44
106	6.7	26.5	39.0	51.2	3.5	16.0	28.3	40.5	. .	. .	13 3.61	11.47	" 6 37.602	16 56.23	1.78	13 15.08	27 48 28.01 z.
107	8	13.2	25.5	38.0	50.5	3.0	15.0	21.4	. .	. .	15 50.41	11.46	" 3 42.268	34 41.17	1.62	16 1.87	28 6 12.79 z.
108	7.8	. .	7.5	19.8	32.0	. .	57.0	9.5	. .	. .	16 32.19	11.46	" 3 34.980	38 52.87	1.58	16 43.65	28 10 24.45
109	7.8	24.0	. .	49.0	1.3	13.3	26.0	38.6	. .	. .	18 1.28	11.45	" 2 42.261	43 26.68	1.49	18 12.73	28 14 58.17
110	8.	44.8	58.2	10.6	23.0	35.0	47.6	0.0	. .	. .	19 22.78	11.42	" 3 42.290	34 40.41	1.41	19 34.20	28 6 11.82
111	9	29.5	42.3	54.1	7.0	19.3	. .	. .	. .	. .	21 6.90	11.40	" 5 40.969	23 42.39	1.32	21 18.30	27 55 13.71 z.
112	9	3.3	15.5	28.2	40.8	. .	. .	. .	. .	. .	22 40.64	11.39	" 3 40.480	35 42.94	1.25	22 52.03	28 7 14.19 z.
113	9	. .	. .	52.8	5.1	17.5	. .	. .	. .	. .	23 5.20	11.38	" 3 32.133	40 31.23	1.23	23 16.58	28 12 2.46 z.
114	9	. .	. .	41.0	53.6	5.7	. .	30.6	. .	. .	23 53.44	11.37	" 5 36.130	26 29.52	1.19	24 4.81	27 58 0.71
115	9	1.2	13.5	26.0	38.2	51.0	. .	. .	. .	. .	26 38.50	11.36	" 2 42.610	43 14.60	1.07	26 49.86	28 14 45.67
116	7	56.0	8.5	21.0	33.5	. .	. .	. .	. .	. .	27 33.49	11.35	" 2 35.519	47 19.51	1.02	27 44.84	28 18 50.53 z.
117	9	. .	. .	. .	38.0	51.0	3.3	. .	. .	. .	27 38.35	11.34	" 3 41.595	35 4.48	1.02	27 49.69	28 6 35.40 z.
118	7	. .	. .	. .	. .	. .	29.5	41.8	. .	. .	28 4.74	11.32	VII. 7 38.045	10 49.61	1.00	28 16.06	27 42 20.61
119	9	. .	. .	. .	53.2	6.0	18.0	30.5	. .	. .	29 53.40	11.32	IV. 4 34.050	33 28.52	0.92	30 4.72	28 4 59.44
120	9	. .	. .	6.0	18.5	30.8	43.1	55.5	. .	. .	31 18.39	11.30	" 5 33.910	27 46.19	0.86	31 29.69	27 59 17.05 z.
121	7.8	. .	. .	. .	16.5	28.8	41.5	53.5	. .	. .	32 16.55	11.28	" 7 36.520	11 42.61	0.83	32 27.83	27 43 13.44 z.
122	9	. .	. .	. .	13.0	25.4	38.0	50.0	. .	. .	33 12.98	11.29	" 2 44.160	42 21.08	0.79	33 24.27	28 13 51.87
123	9	28.2	40.8	53.0	5.5	18.0	30.5	. .	. .	. .	36 5.58	11.26	" 4 39.693	30 13.59	0.69	36 17.84	28 1 44.28
124	9	. .	12.5	25.4	37.8	. .	. .	. .	. .	. .	36 37.72	11.26	" 1 42.541	49 8.51	0.67	36 48.98	28 20 39.18
125	8	. .	. .	. .	49.0	1.5	14.0	26.5	. .	. .	36 49.25	11.23	" 7 43.810	7 30.85	0.66	37 0.48	27 39 1.51
126	9	. .	. .	. .	25.0	37.0	49.4	2.0	. .	. .	37 24.82	11.23	" 6 45.470	12 24.53	0.63	37 36.05	27 43 55.16
127	9	. .	. .	. .	. .	. .	21.0	33.0	52.0	4.5	38 56.02	11.23	" 3 36.850	37 48.28	0.58	39 7.25	28 9 18.86
128	9	. .	. .	. .	47.0	59.2	1.1	. .	. .	. .	40 46.66	11.23	" 1 38.406	51 31.39	0.52	40 57.89	28 23 1.91
129	9	33.5	46.0	58.2	10.8	23.1	35.5	. .	. .	. .	42 10.76	11.20	" 5 36.365	26 21.41	0.49	42 21.96	27 57 51.90
130	9	46.0	58.2	10.2	23.4	35.4	47.0	0.2	. .	. .	44 22.95	11.18	" 5 43.500	22 14.92	0.44	44 34.13	27 53 45.36
131	8	47.8	59.8	12.0	24.8	37.0	49.2	1.4	. .	. .	46 24.60	11.16	" 5 45.365	21 10.56	0.39	46 35.76	27 52 40.95 z.
132	9	. .	. .	23.0	35.5	48.0	0.2	. .	. .	. .	47 35.50	11.15	" 3 39.760	36 7.77	0.36	47 46.65	28 7 38.13
133	8	36.5	49.2	1.8	14.2	26.3	39.0	51.0	. .	. .	49 14.04	11.12	" 7 41.655	8 45.28	0.32	49 25.16	27 40 15.00
134	9	. .	13.0	25.2	37.5	. .	. .	. .	. .	. .	31 37.67	11.11	" 3 41.040	35 23.57	0.28	51 48.78	28 6 53.85
135	9	. .	54.0	5.5	18.0	30.5	43.0	. .	. .	. .	52 18.21	11.10	" 7 37.445	11 10.71	0.27	52 29.31	27 42 40.98
136	9	. .	1.5	13.8	26.0	. .	. .	. .	. .	. .	53 26.27	11.12	" 1 38.969	51 11.91	0.25	53 37.39	28 22 42.16
137	8	. .	58.0	10.0	22.5	34.5	47.0	. .	. .	. .	54 22.41	11.09	" 5 36.651	26 11.50	0.24	54 33.50	27 57 41.74
138	9	15.0	27.2	39.9	52.0	. .	. .	29.5	. .	. .	56 52.21	11.06	" 3 43.110	34 12.08	0.20	57 3.27	28 5 42.28
139	8.9	. .	10.0	22.5	. .	47.0	. .	. .	. .	. .	57 34.85	11.06	" 3 42.025	34 49.56	0.20	57 45.91	28 6 19.76
140	8.9	49.0	1.2	13.8	26.2	39.0	. .	. .	. .	. .	59 26.35	11.05	" 2 44.009	42 26.29	0.17	59 37.40	28 13 56.46
141	9	. .	. .	. .	1.5	13.5	26.2	38.5	. .	. .	59 1.27	11.05	" 2 37.670	46 5.24	0.17	59 12.32	28 17 35.41
142	9	3.5	16.0	28.0	40.2	52.5	5.1	17.2	. .	. .	0 0 40.39	11.03	" 6 38.480	16 25.95	0.16	0 0 51.42	27 47 56.11
143	9	55.6	8.0	20.5	33.0	45.0	. .	. .	. .	. .	3 32.86	11.00	" 6 33.330	19 23.81	0.14	3 43.86	27 50 53.95 z.
144	7.8	. .	. .	0.8	13.0	25.5	. .	. .	. .	. .	4 13.18	11.00	" 7 36.180	11 54.39	0.14	4 24.18	27 43 24.53 z.
145	7.8	. .	. .	. .	47.5	0.2	12.5	24.5	. .	. .	4 47.65	10.99	" 7 39.320	10 5.94	0.14	4 58.64	27 41 36.08 z.
146	7.8	55.8	8.2	21.0	33.5	. .	. .	. .	. .	. .	6 33.38	10.98	II. 1 40.870	50 6.15	0.13	6 44.36	28 21 36.28
147	8	. .	. .	. .	39.0	51.0	3.6	16.0	. .	. .	6 38.78	10.98	IV. 4 42.450	28 38.40	0.13	6 49.76	28 0 8.53
148	9	. .	. .	. .	. .	28.0	40.3	52.8	. .	. .	0 7 15.51	10.97	V. 1 43.168	48 46.86	0.12	0 7 26.48	28 20 16.98 z.

Number.	Magnitude.	SECONDS OF TRANSITS. I.	II.	III.	IV.	V.	VI.	VII.	10.	11.	T.	a.	MICROMETER.	D.	d.	Mean Right Ascension, 1850.0.	Mean South Declination, 1850.0.
											Zone LX. September 14. H. $D. = -27° 31' 30''.0$. $n.' = -25''.60$. $n.'' = 3''.00$. (Continued.)						
											h. m. s.	s.	r.	° ' ''	''	h. m. s.	° ' ''
149	9	. .	. .	22.5	36.0	47.0	. .	12.2	. .	. .	0 8 35.17	+10.96	IV. 4 44.990	—27 10.65	— 0.12	0 8 46.13	27 58 40.77
150	9	43.0	55.8	. .	20.5	33.0	45.1	37.5	. .	. .	9 20.45	10.95	" 6 44.300	13 4.93	0.11	9 31.40	27 44 35.04
151	9	47.5	. .	12.2	25.0	. .	. .	. .	. .	. .	14 24.90	10.91	III. 2 43.850	42 31.73	0.23	14 35.81	28 14 1.96
152	8	. .	. .	. .	37.2	49.2	2.0	14.5	. .	. .	14 37.16	10.91	IV. 5 48.520	19 21.54	0.23	14 48.07	27 50 51.77 z.
153	9	39.0	51.0	4.0	. .	. .	. .	. .	. .	. .	16 16.30	10.89	III. 2 42.550	43 16.63	0.27	16 27.19	28 14 46.90
*154	7.8	. .	. .	23.0	35.8	48.0	. .	. .	. .	. .	16 35.68	10.89	IV. 5 46.042	20 47.17	0.28	16 46.57	27 52 17.45
155	7.8	. .	. .	. .	. .	59.3	12.0	24.5	. .	. .	16 47.24	10.89	VI. 6 43.750	13 23.79	0.29	16 58.13	27 44 54.08 z.
156	9	43.7	56.2	8.2	21.3	. .	. .	. .	. .	. .	21 21.07	10.85	IV. 2 43.942	42 28.60	0.45	21 31.92	28 13 59.05
157	7.8	. .	. .	. .	27.0	39.2	51.3	4.0	. .	. .	21 26.81	10.85	" 5 49.452	18 49.41	0.46	21 37.66	27 50 19.87 z.
158	9	. .	. .	. .	. .	29.0	41.3	53.6	. .	. .	22 16.47	10.84	" 3 45.250	32 58.17	0.51	22 27.31	28 4 28.68 z.
159	8	23.2	35.5	48.0	0.5	. .	. .	. .	. .	. .	28 0.38	10.79	" 7 40.285	9 32.61	0.88	28 11.17	27 41 3.49 z.
160	8	26.8	39.2	51.3	4.0	. .	. .	. .	. .	. .	29 4.01	10.78	" 3 42.338	34 38.76	0.95	29 14.79	28 6 9.71 z.
161	8	. .	. .	. .	6.5	19.0	31.0	43.5	. .	. .	0 29 6.38	10.78	V. 2 42.476	43 19.23	0.95	0 29 17.16	28 17 50.18
											Zone LXI. September 15. M. $D. = -28° 59' 20''.0$. $n.' = -21''.97$. $n.'' = -4''.00$.						
1	8	. .	. .	. .	. .	. .	48.5	1.0	. .	. .	19 15 23.20	13.16	VII. 3 40.20	35 53.00	18.30	19 15 36.36	29 35 31.68 z.
2	9	48.8	1.5	14.0	. .	. .	. .	. .	. .	. .	17 26.73	13.14	III. 3 39.27	36 25.78	17.81	17 39.87	29 36 3.59 z.
3	9	. .	. .	. .	10.5	23.0	. .	. .	. .	. .	18 10.47	13.16	V. 1 44.53	48 1.05	17.64	18 23.63	29 47 38.69 z.
4	9	. .	. .	. .	. .	. .	. .	19.2	. .	. .	18 41.35	13.14	VII. 2 45.58	41 32.88	17.52	18 54.49	29 41 10.40 z.
5	9	. .	. .	. .	. .	. .	. .	. .	11.5	24.0	19 14.95	13.09	II. 6 38.18	16 36.15	17.39	19 28.04	29 16 13.54 z.
6	9.10	. .	. .	. .	10.5	23.0	. .	. .	. .	. .	21 10.49	13.12	VII. 3 30.14	41 40.94	16.94	21 23.61	29 41 17.88
7	8	. .	. .	. .	. .	. .	. .	. .	22.6	35.5	21 25.99	13.13	II. 2 33.59	48 26.50	16.88	21 39.12	29 48 3.38
8	9.10	26.2	39.1	. .	. .	. .	. .	. .	. .	. .	25 4.03	13.04	III. 7 39.44	10 2.45	16.01	25 17.07	29 9 38.46
9	9.10	. .	. .	. .	. .	. .	. .	45.2	. .	. .	25 7.61	13.03	VII. 7 41.47	8 52.05	16.01	25 20.64	29 8 28.06
10	8	. .	51.4	3.5	16.3	. .	. .	. .	. .	. .	28 16.25	13.00	III. 7 41.12	9 4.40	15.26	28 29.25	29 8 39.66
11	9	. .	. .	. .	. .	. .	28.4	40.9	. .	. .	29 3.28	13.00	VII. 6 45.98	12 7.30	15.07	29 16.28	29 11 42.37 z.
12	9	37.2	50.0	2.3	15.3	27.3	. .	52.5	. .	. .	32 15.00	12.98	2. 7 35.705	12 10.79	14.36	32 27.98	29 11 45.15
13	8.9	. .	. .	4.0	16.4	29.0	41.5	. .	. .	. .	38 16.48	12.96	2. 4 36.85	31 52.13	13.03	38 29.44	29 31 25.16 z.
14	9.10	. .	. .	. .	. .	17.6	30.3	. .	. .	. .	39 5.15	12.93	VI. 6 38.46	16 27.33	12.85	39 18.08	29 16 0.18 z.
15	2	. .	. .	. .	. .	. .	. .	. .	32.2	45.5	39 36.17	12.91	VII. 7 40.15	9 37.63	12.74	39 49.08	29 9 10.37 z.
16	9.10	. .	. .	14.8	27.5	40.0	. .	. .	. .	. .	45 27.50	12.92	2. 1 45.15	47 39.02	11.43	45 40.42	29 47 10.45
17	9	. .	. .	. .	56.5	. .	22.0	. .	. .	. .	46 56.60	12.88	VI. 4 40.91	29 32.46	11.11	47 9.48	29 29 3.57
18	9	. .	. .	. .	. .	. .	. .	. .	19.0	32.0	46 22.47	12.89	II. 3 41.31	35 14.43	11.24	46 35.36	29 34 45.67 z.
19	10	. .	. .	. .	. .	. .	33.0	45.2	. .	. .	48 7.57	12.87	VII. 4 41.60	29 8.38	10.85	48 20.44	29 28 39.23
20	9	. .	. .	. .	40.2	52.5	5.5	. .	. .	. .	49 40.20	12.83	VI. 6 39.66	15 45.82	10.50	49 53.03	29 15 16.32
21	8	. .	22.8	35.0	47.6	0.2	. .	. .	. .	. .	55 47.73	12.80	I. 4 39.80	30 9.97	9.18	56 0.53	29 29 39.15 z.
22	9.10	. .	. .	34.0	46.8	. .	. .	. .	. .	. .	56 46.74	12.80	II. 3 42.55	34 32.36	8.96	56 59.54	29 34 1.32 z.
23	8	. .	. .	. .	. .	34.5	47.2	. .	. .	. .	19 58 21.94	12.81	VII. 1 39.60	50 51.10	8.63	19 58 34.75	29 50 19.73

CORRECTIONS.

	COR. TO CLOCK.	HOURLY COR.	m.	n.	c.	ZENITH POINT.	COINC.
	s.	s.	s.	s.	s.	° ' ''	r.
Sept. 15, at 22h...	+2.484	—0.021	—0.356	+0.527	+0.022	0 0 3.52	40.110

† The circle reading recorded for this zone has been changed three minutes.

INSTRUMENT READINGS.

	CIRCLE. A.	B.	C.	D.	Mean.	BAR.	THERMOM. At.	Ex.
						I.	°	°
†Zone LXI.—Sept. 15......h. 19.3	291° 38' 46''.8	51''.1	50''.7	50''.2	51''.28	30.045	77.6	69.9
20.3	. . . . .	. .	. .	. .	. . .	30.051	75.8	65.5

Zone LXI. September 15. M. $D. = -28° 59' 20''.0$. $n' = -21''.97$. $n'' = -4''.00$. (Continued.)

Number.	Magnitude.	Seconds of Transits. I.	II.	III.	IV.	V.	VI.	VII.	10.	11.	T.	a.	Micrometer.	D.	d.	Mean Right Ascension, 1850.0.	Mean South Declination, 1850.0.
											h. m. s.	s.	r.	' ''	''	h. m. s.	° ' ''
24	7.8	. .	33.5	45.8	58.5	. .	23.5	36.0	. .	. .	20 1 58.44	+12.71	2. 7 42.27	— 8 24.03	— 7.85	20 2 11.15	29 7 51.88 z.
25	9	. .	. .	. .	6.7	19.5	32.0	44.6	. .	. .	8 6.76	12.72	I. 1 38.115	51 42.46	6.56	8 19.48	29 51 9.02 z.
26	10	. .	57.0	10.0	. .	. .	. .	. .	. .	. .	10 22.51	12.68	2. 1 39.56	50 51.45	6.09	10 35.19	29 50 17.54
27	8	. .	22.0	34.5	47.0	. .	. .	. .	. .	. .	10 47.12	12.67	III. 3 39.54	36 16.41	6.00	10 59.79	29 35 42.41
28	7.8	. .	. .	. .	. .	. .	25.3	38.0	. .	. .	11 0.08	12.67	VII. 3 32.36	40 24.26	5.96	11 12.75	29 39 50.22 z.
29	10	. .	4.5	17.0	29.7	. .	. .	. .	. .	. .	13 29.70	12.64	IV. 3 36.33	38 7.39	5.45	13 42.34	29 37 32.84 z.
30	7.8	. .	51.2	3.8	16.2	. .	. .	. .	. .	. .	15 16.35	12.62	2. 4 33.35	33 53.08	5.10	15 28.97	29 33 18.18
31	6.7	. .	. .	49.0	2.2	14.8	. .	. .	. .	. .	16 2.07	12.57	VI. 7 40.74	9 17.43	4.95	16 14.64	29 8 42.38 z.
32	8	. .	. .	. .	7.0	19.8	32.4	45.0	. .	. .	20 17 7.14	12.60	VII. 3 43.51	33 58.98	4.72	20 17 19.74	29 33 23.70 z.

Zone LXII. September 15. M. $D. = -26° 58' 50''.0$. $n' = -20''.82$. $n'' = -7''.00$

Number.	Magnitude.	I.	II.	III.	IV.	V.	VI.	VII.	10.	11.	T.	a.	Micrometer.	D.	d.	Mean Right Ascension, 1850.0.	Mean South Declination, 1850.0.
1	5	. .	. .	. .	. .	. .	. .	. .	34.5	47.2	20 42 39.09	12.23	II. 4 41.26	29 22.56	20.36	20 42 51.32	27 28 32.92 z.
2	9	. .	. .	. .	. .	. .	. .	. .	46.5	59.1	43 50.98	12.24	" 2 40.40	44 34.03	20.16	44 3.22	27 43 44.19 z.
3	10	40.7	53.0	5.7	. .	. .	. .	. .	. .	. .	47 17.98	12.21	III. 1 45.54	47 28.87	19.58	47 30.19	27 46 38.45 z.
4	10	. .	. .	. .	. .	. .	7.5	19.7	. .	. .	47 42.62	12.21	VII. 1 40.62	50 18.55	19.53	47 54.83	27 49 28.08 z.
5	10	15.0	27.8	40.5	. .	. .	. .	. .	. .	. .	49 52.67	12.19	III. 1 40.35	50 28.19	19.15	50 4.86	27 49 37.34
6	9	. .	. .	. .	24.0	36.3	. .	. .	. .	. .	50 24.01	12.16	IV. 3 39.40	36 24.23	19.07	50 36.17	27 35 33.30 z.
7	9	. .	20.0	32.3	44.7	. .	. .	. .	. .	. .	51 44.73	12.15	V. 3 35.52	38 38.16	18.86	51 56.88	27 37 47.02 z.
8	6.7	. .	. .	25.6	38.0	50.5	2.8	. .	. .	. .	52 38.08	12.13	VII. 4 42.52	28 39.61	18.72	52 50.21	27 27 48.33 z.
9	9.10	. .	21.5	34.0	46.0	. .	. .	. .	. .	. .	54 46.23	12.12	V. 3 35.46	38 40.28	18.40	54 58.35	27 37 48.68 z.
*10	9	. .	. .	. .	. .	34.3	47.2	59.8	. .	. .	55 22.46	12.08	" 6 31.60	20 27.48	18.31	55 34.54	27 19 35.79
11	8.9	38.5	51.1	3.4	16.0	28.0	. .	. .	. .	. .	58 15.88	12.10	II. 1 33.77	54 15.38	17.86	58 27.98	27 53 23.24 z.
12	9	. .	. .	. .	25.5	. .	50.2	. .	. .	. .	59 25.52	12.03	VII. 7 33.72	13 23.01	17.68	59 37.55	27 12 30.69 z.
13	7.8	. .	. .	. .	. .	. .	. .	. .	57.0	9.9	21 0 1.63	12.07	II. 2 42.30	43 28.40	17.59	21 0 13.70	27 42 35.99 z.
14	9	. .	. .	. .	8.3	20.0	. .	. .	. .	. .	2 8.05	12.01	V. 7 46.30	6 8.87	17.29	2 20.06	27 5 16.16 z.
15	10	. .	. .	. .	. .	. .	. .	. .	5.3	18.5	2 9.58	12.06	II. 2 40.40	44 34.03	17.29	2 21.64	27 43 41.32
16	9	. .	. .	. .	. .	. .	10.0	22.0	. .	. .	3 45.15	12.01	VII. 6 32.79	19 46.13	17.07	3 57.16	27 18 53.20 z.
17	9.10	39.3	52.0	4.0	. .	. .	. .	. .	. .	. .	6 16.57	12.00	IV. 3 43.25	34 11.25	16.71	6 28.57	27 33 17.96 z.
18	8.9	. .	. .	25.4	. .	50.5	. .	. .	. .	. .	8 38.08	11.94	2. 7 44.27	7 18.32	16.38	8 50.02	27 6 24.70 z.
19	9	. .	. .	. .	. .	. .	. .	20.3	. .	. .	8 43.14	12.00	VII. 1 37.69	51 59.77	16.37	8 55.14	27 51 6.14 z.
20	8.9	. .	. .	. .	. .	. .	11.8	23.8	. .	. .	9 46.98	11.94	10. 6 40.45	15 21.22	16.22	9 58.92	27 14 27.44 z.
21	7	. .	. .	. .	. .	. .	14.2	26.5	. .	. .	10 49.37	11.98	VII. 1 39.70	50 50.02	16.08	11 1.35	27 49 56.10
22	9	. .	. .	. .	. .	. .	2.2	14.6	. .	. .	11 37.55	11.92	" 6 34.76	18 38.08	15.98	11 49.47	27 17 44.06 z.
23	9	. .	. .	. .	. .	. .	. .	. .	48.5	1.0	12 53.19	11.91	II. 6 39.78	15 44.09	15.82	13 5.10	27 14 49.91
24	9.10	. .	. .	. .	. .	. .	. .	. .	49.5	2.4	13 54.13	11.94	" 2 36.96	46 32.83	15.68	14 6.07	27 45 38.51
25	10	. .	. .	. .	18.0	. .	42.6	. .	. .	. .	17 17.88	11.91	VII. 1 41.93	49 33.31	15.24	17 29.79	27 48 38.55 z.
26	8.9	45.0	57.5	9.2	22.2	34.0	. .	. .	. .	. .	19 21.95	11.83	V. 6 46.17	12 4.33	14.97	19 33.78	27 11 9.30 z.
27	9.10	. .	. .	. .	34.7	47.0	59.4	. .	. .	. .	20 34.67	11.88	VI. 1 43.83	48 27.89	14.82	21 20 46.55	27 47 32.71 z.

CORRECTIONS.

	Cor. to Clock.	Hourly Cor.	m.	n.	c.	Zenith Point.	Coinc.
	s.	s.	s.	s.	s.	° ' ''	r.
Sept. 15, at 22h.	+2.484	—0.021	—0.356	+0.527	+0.022	0 0 3.25	40.110

† The circle reading of this zone has been changed three minutes from the recorded reading.

INSTRUMENT READINGS.

	h.	Circle. A.	B.	C.	D.	Mean.	Bar.	Thermom. At.	Ex.
		° ' ''	''	''	''	''	I.	°	°
†Zone LXII.—Sept. 15.	20.7	293 38 40.5	45.2	50.8	42.7	45.30	30.052	75.0	64.5
	21 4	40.0	. .	. .	. .	45.25	30.096	72.0	. .
	22.1	38.0	. .	. .	. .	43.25	. .	. .	. .
	23.1	. . . .	. .	. .	. .	. .	30.104	69.5	57.5
	23.3	38.0	. .	. .	. .	43.25	. .	. .	. .
	23.5	. . . .	. .	. .	. .	. .	30.106	68.3	57.5
	0.0	. . . .	. .	. .	. .	. .	30.110	67.7	56.5
	1.5	. . . .	. .	. .	. .	. .	30.108	65.8	55.5
	1.7	36.3	39.6	46.0	40.8	40.67	. .	. .	. .

Zone LXII. September 15. M. D. = —26° 58′ 50″.0. n′. = —20″.82. n″. = —7″.00. (Continued.)

Number.	Magnitude.	SECONDS OF TRANSITS. I.	II.	III.	IV.	V.	VI.	VII.	10.	11.	T.	a.	MICROMETER.	D.	d.	Mean Right Ascension, 1850.0.	Mean South Declination, 1850.0.
											h. m. s.	s.	r.	′ ″	″	h. m. s.	° ′ ″
28	9.10	. .	. .	51.0	3.2	15.5	28.0	40.3	. .	. .	21 22 3.25	+11.86	VII. 1 43.63	—48 34.58	—14.63	21 22 15.11	27 47 39.21 z.
29	9	29.6	42.2	. .	7.0	19.1	31.5	. .	. .	. .	24 6.87	11.83	" 3 34.62	39 8.97	14.37	24 18.70	27 38 13.34 z.
30	9	. .	. .	55.5	. .	20.4	. .	. .	. .	. .	35 8.08	11.69	V. 7 34.46	12 57.77	13.06	35 19.77	27 12 0.83 z.
31	8	. .	. .	57.0	9.5	21.5	. .	. .	. .	. .	36 9.41	11.68	VI. 7 36.94	11 32.04	12.95	36 21.09	27 10 34.99 z.
32	8.9	. .	. .	. .	. .	. .	16.3	28.5	. .	. .	36 51.62	11.67	VII. 7 37.19	11 23.21	12.87	37 3.29	27 10 26.08 z.
33	9	. .	. .	. .	. .	. .	. .	. .	50.0	2.3	38 54.56	11.65	11. 6 36.33	17 43.28	12.64	39 6.21	27 16 45.92
34	9	. .	. .	. .	. .	. .	54.1	6.7	. .	. .	40 29.42	11.68	VII. 1 39.13	51 10.04	12.47	40 41.10	27 50 12.51
35	9.10	10.0	22.8	34.9	47.1	59.4	. .	. .	. .	. .	43 47.31	11.65	VI. 1 42.41	49 16.97	12.13	43 58.96	27 48 19.10 z.
36	10	. .	. .	38.3	50.6	3.0	. .	. .	. .	. .	46 50.70	11.58	IV. 5 45.37	21 14.39	11.82	47 2.28	27 20 16.21
37	9.10	35.7	48.1	0.5	13.0	. .	. .	. .	. .	. .	48 12.97	11.59	2. 2 40.41	44 33.93	11.68	48 24.56	27 43 35.61 z.
38	7.8	. .	. .	. .	. .	. .	40.5	52.7	. .	. .	48 15.87	11.55	VII. 7 45.72	6 28.60	11.68	48 27.42	27 5 30.28
39	9	30.6	43.2	55.5	8.0	20.4	. .	44.6	. .	. .	52 7.88	11.52	1. 6 40.38	15 23.39	11.31	52 19.40	27 14 24.70 z.
40	8.9	. .	59.2	11.2	23.8	35.9	48.0	. .	. .	. .	54 23.67	11.53	VI. 1 35.54	53 14.22	11.10	54 35.20	27 52 15.32
41	7	15.3	28.0	40.0	52.3	4.9	. .	29.8	. .	. .	55 52.56	11.50	V. 3 44.62	33 23.85	10.96	56 4.06	27 32 24.81
42	9.10	40.9	53.1	5.4	18.0	. .	42.5	54.9	. .	. .	22 0 17.87	11.44	2. 5 38.50	25 10.99	10.57	22 0 29.31	27 24 11.56
43	10	53.8	. .	18.5	31.0	. .	. .	. .	. .	. .	3 30.94	11.39	VI. 7 38.38	10 42.33	10.23	3 42.33	27 9 42.56
44	8.9	. .	. .	. .	. .	. .	20.5	32.8	. .	. .	3 55.67	11.43	VII. 1 40.55	50 20.96	10.18	4 7.10	27 49 21.14 z.
45	8.9	. .	. .	. .	. .	. .	. .	. .	20.0	32.3	4 24.60	11.38	11. 6 40.97	15 3.00	10.14	4 35.98	27 14 3.14 z.
46	9.10	31.4	44.5	56.3	8.4	. .	33.0	45.3	. .	. .	8 8.56	11.34	2. 6 43.545	13 34.29	9.71	8 19.90	27 12 34.00
47	8	. .	6.2	18.5	30.4	42.8	. .	. .	. .	. .	15 30.65	11.26	I. 7 41.76	8 45.35	8.87	15 41.91	27 7 44.22 z.
48	7.8	. .	. .	. .	10.5	23.0	35.4	47.5	. .	. .	16 10.56	11.29	VII. 3 36.58	38 1.28	8.79	16 21.85	27 37 0.07 z.
49	9.10	. .	. .	. .	. .	43.1	55.1	7.6	. .	. .	18 30.52	11.28	" 1 34.12	54 3.05	8.53	18 41.80	27 53 1.58
50	7.8	. .	. .	. .	5.3	17.3	30.0	42.0	. .	. .	19 5.21	11.23	" 7 36.51	11 46.66	8.46	19 16.44	27 10 45.12 z.
*51	10	. .	47.0	59.0	. .	. .	. .	. .	. .	. .	21 11.50	11.22	III. 6 31.762	20 21.91	8.24	21 22.72	27 19 20.15 z.
*52	6.7	. .	. .	. .	. .	. .	. .	. .	6.0	. .	21 10.61	11.25	10. 1 35.20	53 25.42	8.24	21 21.86	27 52 23.66 z.
53	9.10	. .	. .	. .	. .	. .	28.8	41.1	. .	. .	23 3.99	11.22	11. 2 43.01	43 3.86	8.06	23 15.21	27 42 1.92
54	10	. .	. .	. .	. .	. .	. .	. .	6.0	18.8	24 10.85	11.18	" 6 41.00	15 1.97	7.95	24 22.03	27 13 59.92
55	9.10	. .	4.5	16.6	29.0	. .	53.7	6.0	. .	. .	27 29.02	11.18	" 2 42.58	43 19.62	7.64	27 40.20	27 42 17.26
56	9	. .	27.2	39.5	52.0	4.3	16.8	29.0	. .	. .	29 51.97	11.15	2. 3 33.30	39 54.23	7.41	30 3.12	27 38 51.64
57	4	. .	45.0	57.4	9.5	22.1	34.0	47.0	. .	. .	32 9.68	11.14	I. 1 40.28	50 30.33	7.22	32 20.82	27 49 27.55
58	9.10	. .	50.7	3.0	15.4	27.9	. .	. .	. .	. .	35 15.49	11.10	" 2 47.44	40 31.51	6.96	35 26.59	27 39 28.47
59	9	. .	. .	. .	. .	14.7	27.0	. .	. .	. .	37 2.47	11.04	VII. 7 47.16	5 38.89	6.81	37 13.51	27 4 35.70
60	8	. .	. .	. .	. .	. .	. .	. .	10.7	23.0	37 15.03	11.09	11. 1 46.50	46 54.87	6.79	37 26.12	27 45 51.66 z.
61	9	50.8	3.3	15.7	28.0	. .	52.5	. .	. .	. .	40 27.95	11.02	VI. 5 46.70	20 28.31	6.53	40 38.97	27 19 24.84
62	9.10	. .	. .	. .	. .	. .	55.3	7.5	. .	. .	42 30.55	11.00	VII. 5 49.96	18 35.54	6.38	42 41.55	27 17 31.92
63	9	. .	. .	. .	. .	. .	. .	12.5	. .	. .	42 35.54	11.00	" 6 40.68	15 13.62	6.37	42 46.54	27 14 9.99 z.
64	10	36.5	49.4	. .	. .	. .	. .	. .	. .	. .	45 14.02	11.01	III. 1 45.24	47 39.28	6.18	45 25.03	27 46 35.46
65	3	. .	. .	4.0	15.9	28.5	41.0	. .	. .	. .	46 16.20	10.99	IV. 2 39.20	45 16.40	6.11	46 27.19	27 44 12.51 z.
66	8	. .	. .	. .	29.0	41.0	53.6	5.9	. .	. .	48 28.86	10.95	VII. 4 43.67	27 59.91	5.95	48 39.81	27 26 55.86
67	9.10	. .	. .	. .	. .	20.0	. .	45.0	. .	. .	49 7.83	10.95	" 3 38.54	36 53.58	5.90	49 18.78	27 35 49.48
68	9.10	11.5	23.7	36.0	48.0	. .	. .	. .	. .	. .	51 48.37	10.92	V. 4 41.76	29 6.16	5.73	51 59.29	27 28 1.89
69	9.10	. .	. .	. .	. .	. .	. .	. .	46.7	59.0	51 51.04	10.93	11. 3 37.20	37 39.28	5.73	52 1.97	27 36 35.01
70	8	41.9	54.0	6.5	19.0	31.1	44.0	56.0	. .	. .	55 18.97	10.89	2. 3 36.19	38 14.40	5.51	55 29.86	27 37 9.91 z.
71	8.9	. .	32.0	44.4	56.9	9.2	21.5	33.6	. .	. .	23 2 56.78	10.82	III. 2 40.26	44 39.76	5.12	23 3 7.60	27 43 34.88 z.
72	9	. .	36.0	48.0	. .	. .	. .	. .	. .	. .	5 0.47	10.78	" 6 42.98	13 54.49	5.02	5 11.25	27 12 49.51 z.
73	8.9	. .	. .	. .	. .	29.5	41.5	54.0	. .	. .	5 17.01	10.79	VI. 5 43.34	22 24.19	5.01	5 27.80	27 21 19.20 z.
74	9.10	. .	. .	. .	59.0	. .	23.8	. .	. .	. .	6 59.00	10.77	" 4 42.21	28 50.57	4.94	7 9.77	27 27 45.51
75	9.10	. .	. .	. .	. .	. .	34.0	46.2	. .	. .	8 9.32	10.76	VII. 7 36.15	11 59.13	4.90	8 20.08	27 10 54.03
76	9.10	. .	. .	. .	. .	. .	0.3	13.1	. .	. .	9 35.73	10.75	" 2 34.56	47 56.31	4.84	9 46.48	27 46 51.15
77	9	. .	. .	. .	. .	. .	. .	56.0	. .	. .	11 18.95	10.73	" 5 36.89	26 6.95	4.79	11 29.68	27 25 1.74
78	5	. .	. .	52.3	4.6	17.1	29.0	41.7	. .	. .	13 4.59	10.72	" 2 31.76	49 33.03	4.75	13 15.31	27 48 27.78 z.
79	9.10	. .	. .	. .	. .	35.5	47.8	. .	. .	. .	14 23.20	10.69	" 6 33.67	19 15.71	4.73	14 33.89	27 18 10.44 z.
80	9.10	. .	. .	. .	. .	. .	36.5	48.7	. .	. .	23 15 11.80	10.68	" 7 32.76	13 56.18	4.71	23 15 22.48	27 12 50.89 z.

Number.	Magnitude.	SECONDS OF TRANSITS. I.	II.	III.	IV.	V.	VI.	VII.	10.	11.	T.	a.	MICROMETER.	D.	d.	Mean Right Ascension, 1850.0.	Mean South Declination, 1850.0.
											Zone LXII. September 15. M. $D. = -26° 58' 50''.00.$ $n. = -20''.82.$ $n. = -7''.00.$ (Continued.)						
											h. m. s.	s.	r.	′ ″	″	h. m. s.	° ′ ″
81	10	..	38.0	50.0	2.0	..	27.0	39.5	..	..	23 18 2.35	+10.66	VII. 5 47.00	−20 17.77	— 4.64	23 18 13.01	27 19 12.41 z.
82	9	..	..	..	36.5	49.0	..	..	..	..	19 36.62	10.65	V. 4 37.99	31 16.38	4.61	19 47.27	27 30 10.99 z.
83	9	..	..	..	..	..	..	..	43.1	55.5	20 7.70	10.64	11. 6 36.30	17 44.31	4.60	20 18.34	27 6 38.91
84	9.10	..	..	..	48.0	..	12.7	..	..	..	26 47.94	10.59	VI. 2 38.12	45 53.59	4.52	26 58.53	27 44 48.11
85	7	..	..	..	6.0	17.8	30.5	42.5	..	..	28 5.65	10.57	VII. 2 42.44	43 24.20	4.50	28 16.22	27 42 18.70
86	8.9	42.2	54.3	7.0	19.3	..	..	..	..	..	32 19.34	10.53	IV. 2 40.94	44 16.28	4.47	32 29.87	27 43 10.75
*87	7	52.4	5.0	17.3	30.0	..	..	..	..	..	36 29.66	10.47	III. 7 47.90	5 13.60	4.45	36 40.13	27 4 8.05
88	9	..	..	..	..	..	..	9.8	..	..	36 32.81	10.48	VII. 5 48.55	19 24.20	4.45	36 43.29	27 18 18.65 z.
89	8.9	..	..	..	..	..	27.4	40.0	..	..	38 2.74	10.47	" 2 48.18	40 5.92	4.44	38 13.21	27 39 0.36 z.
90	8.9	..	..	..	..	..	..	..	..	34.0	38 25.82	10.47	11. 1 49.98	44 54.65	4.44	38 36.29	27 43 49.09 z.
91	7	..	..	12.6	24.7	37.0	..	..	..	..	46 24.83	10.41	V. 1 34.60	53 46.77	4.48	46 35.24	27 52 41.25 z.
92	9	..	..	..	39.6	..	4.4	16.8	..	..	47 39.64	10.38	VII. 5 34.78	27 19.82	4.49	47 50.02	27 26 14.31
93	6	..	..	..	13.0	25.0	38.0	..	..	..	49 12.99	10.36	VI. 4 42.68	28 34.30	4.50	49 23.35	27 27 28.80 z.
94	9	..	..	..	..	..	..	..	..	23.0	49 14.84	10.36	11. 2 46.07	41 18.17	4.50	49 25.20	27 40 12.67 z.
95	7	..	..	23.5	36.0	48.0	0.8	13.0	..	..	52 35.95	10.33	VII. 5 43.05	22 34.20	4.56	52 46.28	27 21 28.76
96	5	44.8	57.5	9.6	22.0	34.0	..	..	..	..	54 22.00	10.32	V. 4 36.92	31 53.35	4.60	54 32.32	27 30 47.95
97	5	..	..	21.3	33.3	45.0	..	..	..	..	55 33.28	10.31	" 6 39.23	16 4.01	4.62	55 43.59	27 14 58.63 z.
98	3	..	19.0	31.3	44.0	..	..	..	..	..	0 3 43.88	10.23	III. 1 37.76	51 57.64	4.82	0 3 54.03	27 50 52.46
99	6	..	..	..	14.0	26.5	38.8	..	..	..	4 14.07	10.23	VI. 2 40.60	44 27.91	4.84	4 24.30	27 43 22.75 z.
100	7	..	..	..	..	..	..	25.4	..	..	4 48.28	10.22	VII. 2 43.73	42 39.60	4.85	4 58.50	27 41 34.45 z.
101	9	..	..	..	..	..	..	..	23.6	36.0	5 28.31	10.22	11. 7 38.49	10 37.70	4.87	5 38.53	27 9 32.57 z.
102	9	..	..	..	..	..	..	..	..	5.1	6 57.50	10.21	" 7 42.64	8 14.34	4.92	7 7.71	27 7 9.26
103	6	..	..	..	44.5	..	9.3	..	..	..	12 44.58	10.16	VI. 7 41.46	8 55.97	5.14	12 54.74	27 7 51.11
104	7	..	..	..	..	..	..	58.8	..	..	13 21.94	10.15	VII. 7 45.26	6 44.51	5.16	13 32.09	27 5 39.67 z.
105	7	..	..	..	..	..	2.8	15.2	..	..	14 38.02	10.14	" 1 37.71	51 59.08	5.22	14 48.16	27 50 54.30 z.
106	3	..	12.0	24.1	36.3	..	..	..	..	..	16 36.59	10.12	III. 1 36.26	52 49.47	5.31	16 46.71	27 51 44.78 z.
107	7	..	..	..	..	..	12.7	25.0	..	..	16 47.88	10.12	VII. 2 38.00	45 57.52	5.32	16 58.00	27 47 52.84 z.
108	3	..	3.1	15.5	27.6	40.2	52.6	..	..	..	21 27.82	10.08	III. 1 38.60	51 28.60	5.55	21 37.90	27 50 24.15 z.
109	7	..	..	..	..	37.0	..	2.0	..	..	28 24.83	10.03	VII. 3 41.26	35 19.68	5.91	28 34.86	27 34 15.59
110	7	..	..	..	..	..	..	38.0	..	..	28 0.88	10.03	" 2 44.72	42 5.40	5.89	28 10.91	27 41 1.29 z.
111	9	..	..	..	..	..	..	..	..	44.0	28 35.88	10.02	11. 3 39.61	36 16.00	5.93	28 45.90	27 35 11.93 z.
112	2	44.3	56.3	8.4	21.0	..	45.5	58.0	..	..	32 20.99	9.99	2. 4 37.67	31 26.76	6.16	32 30.98	27 30 22.92
113	2	..	25.0	37.0	50.0	..	14.6	27.0	..	..	36 49.77	9.96	" 5 44.56	21 41.63	6.47	36 59.73	27 20 38.10 z.
114	2	..	44.4	57.0	9.4	22.0	34.5	..	..	..	40 9.50	9.93	II. 1 43.21	48 49.33	6.70	40 19.43	27 47 46.03 z.
115	7	..	..	..	..	12.0	24.3	37.0	..	..	40 59.85	9.92	VII. 6 45.51	12 26.81	6.77	41 9.77	27 11 23.58 z.
116	2	..	24.0	36.0	48.2	..	12.8	25.4	..	..	44 48.35	9.89	2. 6 43.30	13 42.80	7.07	44 58.24	27 12 39.87 z.
117	7	..	..	..	..	..	2.3	14.6	..	..	48 37.69	9.86	VII. 7 38.52	10 37.24	7.37	48 47.55	27 9 34.61
118	8	..	..	..	11.0	23.5	36.0	..	..	..	58 11.13	9.79	2. 2 37.60	46 10.94	8.23	58 20.92	27 45 9.17
119	9	..	..	..	..	..	57.3	9.7	..	..	59 32.55	9.78	" 4 35.14	32 54.17	8.36	59 42.33	27 31 52.53
120	9	..	0.5	12.4	24.8	37.3	49.7	2.0	..	..	1 0 24.96	9.78	VII. 1 43.96	48 23.19	8.44	1 0 34.74	27 47 21.63
*121	9	13.9	26.3	38.4	49.9	2.0	14.0	26.6	..	..	4 50.21	9.75	10. 7 43.23	7 54.23	8.87	4 59.96	27 6 53.10
122	9.10	..	..	..	..	..	..	57.7	..	..	6 20.74	9.73	11. 6 40.50	15 19.26	9.01	6 30.47	27 14 18.27
123	10	..	..	6.1	18.4	31.0	..	..	..	..	10 18.56	9.69	2. 1 42.36	49 18.10	9.41	10 28.25	27 48 17.51
124	9	..	..	11.3	23.5	35.6	48.0	0.5	..	..	11 23.49	9.69	6 34.04	19 3.27	9.53	11 33.18	27 18 2.80 z.
125	10	..	..	14.1	26.0	38.5	..	..	..	..	14 26.27	9.67	V. 4 43.11	28 19.54	9.87	14 35.94	27 27 19.41 z.
126	9	..	..	..	..	..	..	..	..	0.5	14 52.41	9.67	11. 3 46.27	32 26.02	9.92	15 2.08	27 31 25.94
*127	9	38.5	31.1	3.0	15.4	28.0	40.0	52.4	..	..	18 15.52	9.64	2. 6 41.44	14 47.04	10.30	18 25.16	27 13 47.34
128	7	..	..	..	48.0	..	13.0	..	..	..	20 48.08	9.62	VII. 1 33.39	54 28.33	10.60	20 57.70	27 53 28.93 z.
129	8.9	..	24.3	36.5	49.0	1.2	13.4	25.8	..	..	22 48.88	9.61	" 2 38.26	45 48.55	10.84	22 58.49	27 44 49.39
130	9.10	30.0	43.0	54.8	7.0	19.7	32.0	44.0	..	..	25 7.25	9.60	" 6 31.80	20 20.31	11.13	25 16.85	27 19 21.44 z.
131	10	4.0	16.4	28.5	41.0	..	5.2	17.0	..	..	34 40.75	9.55	" 7 39.91	9 49.25	12.38	34 50.30	27 8 51.63
132	7.8	29.5	4.2	34.0	..	..	..	..	..	..	38 6.49	9.53	III. 7 43.51	7 45.18	12.86	38 16.02	27 6 48.04 z.
133	9.10	..	..	..	..	38.0	51.0	3.0	..	..	38 26.10	9.53	VII. 7 39.68	9 57.18	12.90	38 35.63	27 9 0.08 z.
134	9	56.5	8.8	21.2	33.5	..	58.5	10.4	..	..	40 33.56	9.50	" 4 39.81	30 13.24	13.20	40 43.06	27 29 16.44 z.
135	9	..	..	..	11.5	24.0	36.5	..	..	..	1 42 11.62	9.48	VI. 1 41.38	49 52.54	13.46	1 42 21.10	27 48 56.00

Number.	Magnitude.	Seconds of Transits. I.	II.	III.	IV.	V.	VI.	VII.	10.	11.	T.	a.	Micrometer.	D.	d.	Mean Right Ascension, 1850.0.	Mean South Declination, 1850.0.
											h. m. s.	s.	r.	′ ″	″	h. m. s.	° ′ ″
Zone LXIII. September 16. H. $D. = -27° 26' 00''.0$. $n'. = -33''.00$. $n''. = -3''.18$.																	
1	5	. .	. .	9.3	22.0	34.2	46.6	59.0	. .	. .	18 57 21.85	+12.32	IV. 5 35.953	−26 35.79	−28.21	18 57 34.17	27 53 4.00 z.
2	9	. .	26.1	38.5	51.0	3.0	15.8	. .	. .	. .	19 0 50.89	12.30	" 4 40.218	29 55.65	27.26	19 1 3.19	27 56 22.91
3	8	. .	. .	. .	. .	30.0	42.5	54.8	. .	. .	1 17.55	12.34	VI. 1 35.823	53 0.78	27.14	1 29.89	28 19 27.92
4	9	. .	. .	14.5	27.2	40.0	52.2	. .	. .	. .	2 27.30	12.32	IV. 2 35.250	47 29.08	26.83	2 39.62	28 13 55.91
5	8.9	19.5	31.8	44.3	56.5	. .	. .	. .	. .	. .	4 56.64	12.25	II. 6 37.115	17 13.11	26.16	5 8.89	27 43 39.27
6	8.9	. .	. .	. .	6.5	19.0	31.5	43.8	. .	. .	5 6.70	12.23	VI. 7 43.190	7 52.27	26.12	5 18.93	27 34 18.39 z.
7	9	. .	. .	. .	. .	. .	. .	. .	13.0	25.8	5 17.45	12.25	VII. 5 46.812	20 20.39	26.07	5 29.70	27 46 46.46 z.
8	9	. .	32.0	44.0	56.5	9.0	21.5	. .	. .	. .	8 56.64	12.25	V. 3 36.368	38 5.12	25.08	9 8.89	28 4 30.20 z.
9	8.9	. .	37.3	49.5	2.2	14.4	27.0	. .	. .	. .	11 2.12	12.26	IV. 1 41.180	49 55.80	24.52	11 14.38	28 16 20.32
10	9	19.0	31.0	43.5	. .	. .	. .	. .	. .	. .	13 55.99	12.18	I. 6 35.244	18 17.74	23.75	14 8.17	27 44 41.49
11	9	. .	. .	. .	58.0	10.0	22.0	34.5	. .	. .	13 57.49	12.21	IV. 3 38.083	37 5.91	23.75	14 9.70	28 3 29.66 z.
12	6.7	. .	. .	. .	56.5	8.8	21.6	33.0	. .	. .	14 56.33	12.22	" 2 43.550	42 42.34	23.49	15 8.55	28 9 5.83
13	8.9	42.5	55.0	7.2	20.2	. .	45.0	57.0	. .	. .	20 19.73	12.12	II. 6 35.790	17 58.86	22.04	20 31.85	27 44 20.90 z.
14	8	. .	. .	19.0	31.2	43.5	56.0	. .	. .	. .	20 31.29	12.11	IV. 7 34.600	12 49.04	22.00	20 43.40	27 39 11.04 z.
15	9	. .	. .	. .	38.0	50.2	2.2	15.0	. .	. .	21 37.72	12.15	" 3 42.935	34 18.31	21.70	21 49.87	28 0 40.01 z.
16	9	. .	. .	29.0	41.4	54.0	. .	. .	. .	. .	22 41.53	12.14	" 3 37.715	37 18.60	21.42	22 53.67	28 3 40.02 z.
17	9.8	. .	. .	. .	. .	19.2	31.5	44.2	. .	. .	23 6.75	12.17	" 1 37.987	51 46.08	21.31	23 18.92	28 18 7.39 z.
18	9	. .	. .	. .	. .	. .	. .	. .	7.8	20.5	23 12.07	12.13	VI. 4 36.030	32 20.31	21.29	23 24.20	27 58 41.60
19	9	. .	. .	27.0	39.1	52.0	. .	. .	. .	. .	25 39.44	12.08	IV. 5 47.543	19 55.44	20.64	25 51.52	27 46 16.08
20	9	. .	. .	. .	. .	14.2	27.0	39.5	. .	. .	26 2.08	12.10	" 4 38.578	30 52.27	20.54	26 14.18	27 57 12.81 z.
21	8.9	. .	. .	14.8	27.3	39.8	52.2	. .	. .	. .	27 27.36	12.08	" 5 41.656	23 18.80	20.16	27 39.44	27 49 38.96 z.
22	9	. .	. .	. .	. .	. .	8.6	21.0	. .	. .	27 43.70	12.09	VI. 3 44.220	33 33.84	20.10	27 55.79	27 59 53.94 z.
23	9	. .	. .	. .	53.6	6.2	18.5	. .	. .	. .	28 53.68	12.10	IV. 2 46.643	40 55.50	19.78	29 5.78	28 7 15.28 z.
*24	9	. .	. .	. .	. .	39.5	52.0	4.6	. .	. .	29 27.31	12.04	" 6 40.198	15 26.73	19.63	29 39.35	27 41 46.36
25	9	. .	. .	. .	30.0	42.2	54.5	. .	. .	. .	30 29.83	12.06	" 5 36.912	26 2.67	19.36	30 41.89	27 52 22.03 z.
26	9	. .	. .	. .	3.0	15.0	27.5	. .	. .	. .	31 2.83	12.03	" 7 36.190	11 54.15	19.22	31 14.86	27 38 13.37 z.
27	8	. .	. .	. .	. .	. .	43.5	56.0	. .	. .	31 18.65	12.07	VII. 3 40.292	35 49.31	19.15	31 30.72	28 2 8.46 z.
28	7.8	15.5	28.2	40.5	53.0	5.2	18.0	. .	. .	. .	34 52.98	12.03	IV. 3 44.645	33 19.22	18.21	35 5.01	27 59 37.43 z.
29	9	. .	22.0	34.5	47.0	59.1	12.0	. .	. .	. .	35 46.93	12.00	" 6 34.260	18 51.84	17.98	35 58.93	27 45 9.82 z.
30	8	. .	27.0	39.3	52.0	4.2	17.0	. .	. .	. .	36 51.92	11.98	" 7 37.180	11 19.96	17.69	37 3.90	27 37 37.65 z.
31	8.9	46.2	59.0	11.2	24.0	36.0	48.6	. .	. .	. .	37 23.76	12.03	III. 3 35.941	39 28.94	17.55	37 35.79	28 5 46.49
32	8.9	27.0	39.0	51.5	. .	. .	. .	. .	. .	. .	41 3.96	11.94	II. 6 46.082	12 3.39	16.61	41 15.90	27 38 20.00 z.
33	8.9	. .	. .	7.2	19.5	32.1	. .	. .	. .	. .	41 19.67	11.95	V. 6 37.190	17 10.58	16.54	41 31.62	27 43 27.12 z.
34	7.8	. .	. .	. .	43.5	. .	8.0	20.5	. .	. .	41 43.29	11.96	" 5 39.516	24 32.65	16.44	41 55.25	27 50 49.09 z.
35	9	57.0	10.0	22.0	34.2	. .	. .	. .	. .	. .	46 34.44	11.92	III. 5 36.602	26 13.31	15.22	46 46.36	27 52 28.53
36	9	. .	. .	53.0	5.5	17.5	30.5	. .	. .	. .	47 5.48	11.90	IV. 6 35.520	18 8.27	15.10	47 17.38	27 44 23.37
*37	9	32.0	44.5	56.5	9.5	. .	. .	. .	. .	. .	47 9.31	11.93	I. 3 42.358	34 37.95	15.08	47 21.24	28 0 53.03
38	5.6	55.0	. .	19.5	32.0	44.1	56.5	9.0	. .	. .	47 31.98	11.87	IV. 7 43.816	7 30.73	14.99	47 43.85	27 33 45.72 z.
39	8.9	. .	20.0	32.1	44.0	56.8	9.6	. .	. .	. .	49 44.51	11.86	" 6 45.280	12 31.20	14.43	49 56.37	27 38 45.63 z.
40	9	. .	23.0	35.0	47.5	0.0	12.2	. .	. .	. .	50 47.56	11.90	" 3 39.615	36 12.96	14.18	50 59.46	28 2 27.14
41	9	. .	. .	17.0	29.0	40.2	. .	. .	. .	. .	19 51 28.80	11.84	" 7 41.250	8 59.38	14.01	19 51 40.64	27 35 13.39 z.

CORRECTIONS.

	Cor. to Clock	Hourly Cor.	m.	n.	c.	Zenith Point.	Coinc.
	s.	s.	s.	s.	s.		r.
Sept. 16, at 22h..	+ 1.622	−0.027	−0.356	+0.527	+0.022	0° 0′ 2″.79	40.094

INSTRUMENT READINGS.

	Circle. A.	B.	C.	D.	Mean.	Bar.	Thermom. At.	Ex.
Zone LXIII.—Sept. 16 ... 19.0 h.	293° 11′ 53″.5	58″.1	64″.6	58″.0	58″.55	30.138 I.	69°.8	61°.1
20.0	54.4	59.3	67.6	59.6	60.22	30.150	66.0	59.8

Zone LXIII. September 16. H. $D. = -27° 26' 00''.0$. $n'. = -33''.00$. $n''. = -3''.18$. (Continued.)

Number.	Magnitude.	SECONDS OF TRANSITS. I.	II.	III.	IV.	V.	VI.	VII.	10.	11.	T.	a.	MICROMETER.	D.	d.	Mean Right Ascension. 1850.0.	Mean South Declination. 1850.0.
42	5.6	36.1	48.5	1.2	13.5	26.0	38.4	50.5	. .	. .	h. m. s. 19 53 13.51	s. +11.89	r. IV. 2 46.300	−41′ 7″.39	−13″.58	h. m. s. 19 53 25.40	28° 7′ 20″.97 z.
43	9	. .	35.8	48.0	0.4	12.5	25.5	. .	. .	. .	55 0.47	11.88	III. 2 42.038	43 34.55	13.15	55 12.35	28 9 47.70 z.
44	8	. .	27.2	39.5	52.2	4.5	16.8	. .	. .	. .	55 52.08	11.87	IV. 1 45.030	47 42.80	12.93	56 3.95	28 13 55.73 z.
45	8.9	55.2	7.5	20.0	32.5	44.5	37.0	9.1	. .	. .	57 32.30	11.79	" 6 44.964	12 42.10	12.53	57 44.09	27 38 54.63
46	9	32.0	44.1	56.5	9.0	. .	34.0	. .	. .	. .	20 0 9.11	11.82	" 2 43.890	42 30.60	11.88	20 0 20.93	28 8 42.48
47	9	. .	. .	29.0	42.0	53.4	6.2	18.5	. .	. .	0 41.41	11.82	" 2 45.240	41 44.00	11.75	0 53.23	28 7 55.75
48	9	. .	. .	59.0	. .	23.5	36.1	. .	. .	. .	2 11.34	11.76	" 6 32.511	19 52.19	11.40	2 23.10	27 46 3.59 z.
49	9	34.8	47.2	. .	12.1	24.4	37.2	49.6	. .	. .	7 12.17	11.75	" 3 37.590	37 22.91	10.19	7 23.92	28 3 33.10 z.
50	9	51.2	3.8	15.5	28.5	. .	. .	. .	. .	. .	10 28.38	11.69	" 5 43.180	22 26.17	9.41	10 40.07	27 48 35.58
51	9	. .	1.5	14.0	26.5	38.8	31.2	. .	. .	. .	11 26.41	11.68	10. 5 43.730	22 6.46	9.18	11 38.09	27 48 15.64 z.
52	9	. .	39.5	. .	4.0	. .	28.8	41.1	. .	. .	13 4.01	11.71	IV. 2 38.105	45 50.45	8.80	13 15.72	28 11 59.25 z.
53	9	. .	. .	33.6	46.2	58.5	. .	. .	. .	. .	14 46.17	11.68	" 3 38.520	36 50.78	8.40	14 57.85	28 2 59.18
54	8.9	24.0	36.4	48.5	1.0	13.5	. .	. .	. .	. .	18 1.15	11.63	" 4 40.432	29 48.28	7.63	18 12.78	27 55 55.91
55	8.9	30.4	43.0	55.2	7.3	19.3	32.1	. .	. .	. .	19 7.45	11.60	" 5 47.380	20 1.12	7.37	19 19.05	27 46 8.49
56	8.9	44.6	57.2	9.5	22.0	34.0	46.4	59.0	. .	. .	20 21.85	11.60	" 5 43.388	22 19.00	7.09	20 33.45	27 48 26.09 z.
57	8	29.2	42.0	54.0	6.8	19.0	31.5	. .	. .	. .	22 6.71	11.63	" 1 43.189	48 46.41	6.68	22 18.34	28 14 53.09 z.
58	9	59.6	12.5	. .	37.0	. .	. .	. .	. .	. .	24 36.99	11.54	II. 6 42.015	14 23.86	6.12	24 48.53	27 40 29.98
59	9	. .	. .	. .	43.0	55.5	8.0	. .	. .	. .	24 43.17	11.53	IV. 7 38.956	10 18.59	6.09	24 54.70	27 36 24.68
60	8	. .	. .	. .	29.6	42.0	54.5	6.6	. .	. .	25 29.61	11.54	V. 5 50.382	18 17.40	5.92	25 41.15	27 44 23.32 z.
61	9	10.0	. .	. .	47.5	0.2	12.4	25.4	. .	. .	28 47.67	11.57	IV. 1 35.370	53 16.51	5.17	28 59.24	28 19 21.68 z.
62	7.8	2.6	15.0	27.5	40.0	52.5	. .	. .	. .	. .	30 40.05	11.54	" 1 43.888	48 22.25	4.74	30 51.59	28 14 26.99 z.
63	8	. .	56.0	8.2	20.5	33.0	45.8	58.0	. .	. .	31 20.72	11.52	" 3 31.812	40 42.50	4.60	31 32.24	28 6 47.10 z.
64	9	. .	. .	. .	. .	. .	4.3	16.5	. .	. .	32 39.41	11.47	VII. 6 34.610	18 39.39	4.30	32 50.88	27 44 43.69 z.
65	9	37.5	49.8	2.2	. .	. .	. .	. .	. .	. .	35 14.66	11.44	II. 6 34.208	18 53.52	3.73	35 26.10	27 44 57.25 z.
66	9	. .	. .	. .	16.0	28.2	. .	. .	. .	. .	35 15.97	11.44	IV. 6 40.900	15 2.47	3.73	35 27.41	27 41 6.20
67	9	. .	. .	. .	. .	. .	48.5	1.2	. .	. .	35 23.76	11.47	" 4 36.032	32 20.24	3.70	35 35.23	27 58 23.94 z.
68	7.8	. .	. .	. .	. .	. .	25.6	37.5	. .	. .	20 36 0.54	11.44	" 5 45.462	21 7.37	3.57	20 36 11.98	27 47 10.94 z.

Zone LXIV. September 16. H. $D. = 40° 49' 40''.0$. $n'. = -4''.84$. $n''. = -12''.00$.

Number.	Magnitude.	I.	II.	III.	IV.	V.	VI.	VII.	10.	11.	T.	a.	MICROMETER.	D.	d.	Mean Right Ascension. 1850.0.	Mean South Declination. 1850.0.
1	8	. .	6.2	20.7	35.2	49.8	4.3	. .	. .	. .	21 50 35.25	11.23	IV. 5 37.965	25 33.27	4.12	21 50 46.48	41 15 17.39
2	9	. .	18.5	33.0	. .	2.0	16.4	. .	. .	. .	56 47.50	11.10	" 7 42.244	8 25.55	3.76	56 58.60	40 58 9.31
3	9	. .	2.2	16.2	31.0	45.2	. .	. .	. .	. .	22 1 30.93	11.03	" 7 40.330	9 32.09	3.50	22 1 41.96	40 59 15.59
4	7.8	. .	21.0	35.2	50.1	4.2	19.0	. .	. .	. .	1 49.92	11.02	" 7 37.452	11 12.16	3.48	2 0.94	41 0 55.64
5	7	. .	. .	2.0	16.5	31.2	. .	. .	. .	. .	5 16.65	10.96	" 7 45.352	6 37.56	3.32	5 27.61	40 56 20.88
6	8.9	. .	56.0	10.5	25.0	39.1	53.8	. .	. .	. .	7 24.90	10.94	" 7 38.274	10 43.53	3.22	7 35.84	41 0 26.75
7	7.8	. .	44.2	59.2	13.4	28.0	42.5	. .	. .	. .	22 10 13.48	10.89	V. 7 35.423	12 22.60	3.08	22 10 24.37	41 2 5.68

CORRECTIONS.

	COR. TO CLOCK.	HOURLY COR.	m.	n.	c.	ZENITH POINT.	COINC.
Sept. 16, at 22h..	s. +1.622	s. −0.027	s. −0.356	s. +0.527	s. +0.022	0° 0′ 2″.56	r. 40.094

INSTRUMENT READINGS.

	CIRCLE. A.	B.	C.	D.	Mean.	BAR.	THERMOM. At.	Ex.
Zone LXIV.—Sept. 16..21.7 h.	279° 50′ 59″.0	60″.3	67″.6	60″.1	61″.75	I. 30.142	64°.5	58°.0
22.1	. . . .	. .	. .	. .	. .	. .	. .	56.4
22.4	. . . .	. .	. .	. .	. .	. .	. .	54.4
22.7	55.7	58.0	66.9	57.4	59.52	30.126	62.0	55.0
23.0	. . . .	. .	. .	. .	. .	30.118	61.5	56.4
23.2	. . . .	. .	. .	. .	. .	30.112	60.2	55.5
23.7	. . . .	. .	. .	. .	. .	. .	. .	52.5
0.0	. . . .	. .	. .	. .	. .	. .	. .	53.5
0.5	58.5	61.2	69.8	60.8	62.57	30.100	58.4	52.3

Zone LXIV. September 16. H. $D.=40^{\circ}\ 49'\ 40''.0.$ $n'.=-4''.84.$ $n''.=-12''.00.$ (Continued.)

Number.	Magnitude.	SECONDS OF TRANSITS.									T.	a.	MICROMETER.	D.	d.	Mean Right Ascension, 1850.0.	Mean South Declination, 1850.0.
		I.	II.	III.	IV.	V.	VI.	VII.	10.	11.							
											h. m. s.	s.	r.	′ ″	″	h. m. s.	° ′ ″
8	8.9	. .	44.0	58.2	13.0	27.2	41.8	. .	. .	. .	22 18 12.85	+10.77	IV. 5 42.439	−22 57.84	− 2.79	22 18 23.62	41 12 40.63
9	9	. .	48.1	2.4	17.0	31.5	46.3	. .	. .	. .	20 17.08	10.72	" 6 45.470	12 26.66	2.71	20 27.80	41 2 9.37
10	9	. .	24.0	38.8	54.0	8.0	23.0	. .	. .	. .	25 53.57	10.64	" 5 48.325	19 33.15	2.57	26 4.21	41 9 15.72
11	9	. .	35.0	48.8	3.8	. .	. .	. .	. .	. .	27 3.73	10.62	" 6 40.126	15 32.33	2.54	27 14.35	41 5 14.87
12	7	. .	. .	. .	32.0	46.2	1.0	15.2	. .	. .	27 31.79	10.61	" 6 37.680	16 57.23	2.53	27 42.40	41 6 39.76
13	7	. .	. .	47.2	2.0	. .	30.5	45.2	. .	. .	28 1.41	10.62	VI. 4 36.722	32 5.68	2.52	28 12.03	41 21 48.20
14	7.8	. .	9.8	24.0	39.0	53.2	8.0	. .	. .	. .	34 38.81	10.48	IV. 7 48.150	5 0.27	2.40	34 49.29	40 54 42.67
15	7.8	. .	29.5	43.5	58.0	13.0	27.6	. .	. .	. .	35 58.36	10.50	" 2 42.584	43 29.78	2.37	36 8.86	41 33 12.15
16	8	. .	46.8	1.2	15.8	30.1	45.2	. .	. .	. .	46 15.88	10.34	" 1 34.906	53 51.05	1.64	46 26.22	41 43 32.69
17	9	. .	3.0	17.0	31.5	. .	1.0	. .	. .	. .	54 31.74	10.17	" 7 37.270	11 18.43	0.73	54 41.91	41 0 59.16
18	7	. .	25.0	39.8	55.0	9.2	24.0	. .	. .	. .	54 54.65	10.18	" 1 45.380	47 46.77	0.68	55 4.83	41 37 27.45
19	9	. .	. .	. .	22.2	36.2	50.0	5.0	. .	. .	55 21.36	10.18	" 1 45.322	47 48.77	0.63	55 31.54	41 37 29.40
20	9	. .	34.0	48.2	2.5	17.2	32.1	. .	. .	. .	58 2.81	10.11	" 6 38.338	16 34.55	0.32	58 12.92	41 6 14.87
21	9	. .	. .	3.5	17.6	32.2	46.4	. .	. .	. .	23 0 17.71	10.08	" 6 41.390	14 48.47	0.10	23 0 27.79	41 4 28.57
22	7	. .	8.4	22.5	37.0	51.8	6.5	. .	. .	. .	1 37.26	10.06	" 3 42.920	34 29.29	0.12	1 47.32	41 24 9.41 B.
23	9	. .	37.6	52.0	. .	21.2	36.0	. .	. .	. .	6 6.72	9.99	" 5 37.980	25 32.75	0.18	6 16.71	41 15 12.93
24	9	. .	21.0	35.5	49.9	4.2	19.2	. .	. .	. .	7 49.79	9.97	" 3 34.681	39 15.77	0.21	7 59.76	41 28 55.98
25	6	. .	13.1	27.2	41.8	56.5	11.2	. .	. .	. .	9 42.01	9.94	" 1 43.785	48 42.09	0.24	9 51.95	41 38 22.33 B.
26	9	. .	21.2	35.2	50.2	5.0	19.5	. .	. .	. .	13 50.23	9.86	" 4 39.300	30 36.43	0.29	14 0.09	41 20 16.72
27	9	. .	54.1	8.0	23.2	37.1	52.2	. .	. .	. .	16 22.93	9.82	VI. 5 40.010	24 21.92	0.32	16 32.75	41 14 2.24
28	8.9	. .	48.3	3.0	17.1	31.7	46.2	. .	. .	. .	19 17.27	9.77	IV. 6 41.600	14 40.95	0.36	19 27.04	41 4 21.31
29	9	. .	. .	14.0	28.2	. .	57.2	. .	. .	. .	21 28.32	9.73	III. 7 35.050	12 35.46	0.35	21 38.05	41 2 15.81
30	9	. .	. .	36.2	51.0	. .	20.2	. .	. .	. .	21 50.97	9.73	IV. 6 35.400	18 16.70	0.34	22 0.70	41 7 57.04
31	8.9	. .	28.2	42.5	57.3	11.5	27.0	. .	. .	. .	24 57.35	9.69	" 1 40.150	50 48.67	0.29	25 7.04	41 40 28.96
32	9	. .	47.3	2.2	16.5	30.4	45.1	. .	. .	. .	28 16.32	9.62	" 7 39.600	9 57.27	0.23	28 25.94	40 59 37.50
33	9	. .	41.0	. .	9.5	24.0	39.5	. .	. .	. .	34 9.85	9.53	" 6 33.343	19 28.20	0.14	34 19.38	41 9 8.34
34	7	. .	36.0	50.6	5.0	19.4	34.2	. .	. .	. .	36 5.06	9.50	" 2 46.075	41 28.49	0.12	36 14.56	41 31 8.61
35	6.7	. .	26.8	41.2	55.5	10.1	24.6	. .	. .	. .	37 55.66	9.46	" 7 37.312	11 16.98	0.09	38 5.12	41 0 57.07 B.
36	9	. .	0.5	14.6	. .	43.5	58.3	. .	. .	. .	41 29.25	9.42	" 5 42.270	23 3.66	0.07	41 38.67	41 12 43.73
37	9	37.5	52.1	6.6	21.5	. .	. .	. .	. .	. .	43 21.38	9.39	" 4 41.160	29 31.71	0.07	43 30.77	41 19 11.78
38	9	. .	. .	. .	43.2	57.8	12.5	27.1	. .	. .	43 43.13	9.39	" 1 41.526	50 0.59	0.07	43 52.52	41 39 40.66 B.
39	9	. .	. .	4.5	18.8	33.5	49.0	. .	. .	. .	45 19.18	9.36	" 3 41.604	35 14.96	0.08	45 28.54	41 24 55.04
40	6	. .	7.0	21.2	35.5	50.4	5.2	. .	. .	. .	46 35.89	9.34	" 6 34.806	18 37.18	0.09	46 45.23	41 8 17.27 B.
41	8.9	36.0	50.8	4.8	19.5	. .	. .	. .	. .	. .	52 19.60	9.24	" 7 36.120	11 58.37	0.13	52 28.84	41 1 38.50 M.
42	7	. .	. .	. .	. .	54.0	9.0	23.0	. .	. .	52 39.40	9.24	VI. 2 45.285	41 55.79	0.13	52 48.64	41 31 35.92
43	7.8	. .	. .	. .	49.0	3.5	18.0	33.0	. .	. .	53 49.13	9.22	IV. 7 40.478	9 26.98	0.14	53 58.35	40 59 7.12 B.
44	9	. .	42.2	56.2	11.5	. .	. .	. .	. .	. .	59 11.21	9.14	" 5 38.344	25 20.20	0.20	59 20.35	41 15 0.40
*45	9	. .	. .	. .	35.2	49.2	4.3	18.5	. .	. .	59 34.90	9.13	" 4 41.570	29 17.28	0.20	59 44.03	41 18 57.48
46	8.9	. .	32.0	46.3	1.4	16.0	30.3	. .	. .	. .	0 2 1.26	9.08	" 1 35.013	53 47.36	0.26	0 2 10.34	41 43 27.62
47	8	. .	. .	18.0	33.0	47.2	2.1	16.3	. .	. .	3 32.78	9.07	V. 5 42.708	22 48.21	0.29	3 41.85	41 12 28.50 B.
48	9	. .	50.5	5.0	19.0	. .	. .	. .	. .	. .	5 19.40	9.05	IV. 5 41.780	23 20.57	0.34	5 28.45	41 13 0.91
49	9	. .	. .	. .	46.2	0	15.4	. .	. .	. .	5 45.98	9.04	" 5 44.032	22 2.34	0.35	5 55.02	41 11 42.69
50	9	. .	. .	. .	43.2	58.0	12.2	26.5	. .	. .	6 43.10	9.02	" 5 37.656	25 43.93	0.37	6 52.12	41 15 24.30
51	8	. .	. .	. .	48.2	2.6	17.3	32.0	. .	. .	7 48.14	9.01	" 4 44.602	27 31.86	0.40	7 57.15	41 17 12.26 B.
52	8	. .	28.0	. .	. .	11.2	. .	. .	. .	. .	10 56.83	8.97	" 7 44.750	6 58.32	0.49	11 5.80	40 56 38.81
53	7.8	. .	. .	27.0	41.8	56.2	. .	. .	. .	. .	11 41.75	8.96	" 7 44.738	6 58.73	0.52	11 50.71	40 56 39.25
54	7.8	. .	23.4	37.5	52.4	6.4	22.0	. .	. .	. .	21 52.37	8.78	" 2 48.464	40 5.51	0.94	22 1.15	41 29 46.45 B.
55	9	. .	27.0	41.3	56.2	. .	. .	. .	. .	. .	22 56.11	8.77	V. 4 43.980	27 53.53	0.99	23 4.88	41 17 34.52
56	8.9	. .	. .	. .	56.2	11.0	26.0	. .	. .	. .	25 56.43	8.72	IV. 2 42.361	43 37.77	1.14	26 5.15	41 33 18.91
57	9	. .	3.5	17.0	32.0	46.8	1.0	. .	. .	. .	27 32.07	8.72	" 7 38.610	10 31.69	1.22	27 40.79	41 0 12.91
58	9	46.0	0.4	15.2	30.0	44.1	59.0	13.5	. .	. .	30 29.78	8.66	" 4 41.602	29 16.18	1.37	30 38.44	41 18 57.55
59	9	32.0	46.2	0.8	15.2	30.0	44.8	59.6	. .	. .	0 31 15.56	8.65	" 4 43.270	28 18.37	1.42	0 31 24.21	41 17 59.79

Zone LXV. September 16. H. $D. = -27° 25' 20''.0$. $n.' = -15''.56$. $n.'' = -5''.00$.

Number.	Magnitude.	Seconds of Transits. I.	II.	III.	IV.	V.	VI.	VII.	10.	11.	T.	a.	Micrometer.	D.	d.	Mean Right Ascension, 1850.0.	Mean South Declination, 1850.0.
											h. m. s.	s.	r.	′ ″	″	h. m. s.	° ′ ″
1	8	13.9	26.5	39.1	51.4	4.0	16.1	. .	. .	. .	1 30 51.41	+ 8.64	IV. 4 39.080	—30 36.79	—14.25	1 31 0.05	27 59 11.04 z.
2	9	. .	. .	35.0	48.0	59.8	12.2	24.6	. .	. .	31 47.53	8.63	" 4 36.012	32 22.76	14.13	31 56.16	28 0 56.89 z.
3	9	. .	21.2	33.3	46.0	8.5	. .	. .	. .	. .	33 45.96	8.63	" 6 38.656	16 21.68	13.87	33 54.59	27 44 55.55
4	9	. .	. .	. .	. .	10.5	23.0	36.0	. .	. .	33 58.43	8.62	" 6 35.490	18 11.09	13.84	34 7.05	27 46 44.93
5	9	0.6	13.0	25.3	37.5	49.2	. .	. .	. .	. .	36 37.55	8.61	" 6 37.440	17 3.73	13.50	36 46.16	27 45 37.23
6	8.9	52.0	4.5	16.8	29.5	. .	. .	. .	. .	. .	38 29.44	8.57	II. 2 36.170	46 59.12	13.25	38 38.01	28 15 32.37
7	7	. .	. .	44.0	56.5	8.4	20.3	. .	. .	. .	38 56.12	8.	IV. 3 588	. . . . .	13.19	39 4.	. . . . . .
8	9	. .	. .	. .	. .	. .	. .	28.0	. .	. .	40 50.77	8.57	" 5 37.672	25 38.20	12.93	40 59.34	27 54 11.13
9	9	. .	. .	0.5	13.0	25.2	. .	. .	. .	. .	42 12.97	8.56	" 5 46.933	20 18.28	12.75	42 21.53	27 48 51.03
10	9	. .	. .	. .	46.5	. .	. .	24.0	. .	. .	42 46.62	8.56	" 5 40.500	24 0.55	12.67	42 55.18	27 55 33.22
11	9	. .	. .	. .	. .	. .	. .	25.8	. .	. .	42 48.66	8.56	" 6 38.126	16 40.02	12.66	42 57.22	27 45 12.68
12	9	20.8	33.6	46.0	58.5	10.5	. .	. .	. .	. .	44 58.33	8.54	" 5 42.710	22 44.15	12.36	45 6.87	27 51 16.51 z.
13	9	. .	16.8	29.0	41.6	54.0	. .	. .	. .	. .	45 41.59	8.54	" 4 39.115	30 35.58	12.26	45 50.13	27 59 7.84
14	8	1.5	13.6	26.0	38.5	51.0	. .	. .	. .	. .	49 38.58	8.52	" 1 42.255	49 18.13	11.71	49 47.10	28 17 49.84 z.
15	9	16.4	29.2	41.0	53.8	. .	. .	. .	. .	. .	50 53.71	8.51	" 6 34.662	18 39.64	11.52	51 2.22	27 47 11.16 z.
16	9	. .	. .	. .	. .	10.8	23.0	35.6	. .	. .	50 58.43	8.51	" 7 36.811	11 34.37	11.51	51 6.94	27 40 5.88 z.
17	9	. .	. .	. .	2.5	14.6	27.5	. .	. .	. .	52 2.46	8.50	" 4 39.602	30 18.73	11.35	52 10.96	27 58 50.08
18	9	. .	. .	. .	. .	47.5	0.0	12.5	. .	. .	52 35.14	8.49	" 2 37.170	46 24.68	11.26	52 43.63	28 14 55.94
19	9	. .	. .	. .	. .	2.0	14.1	. .	. .	. .	52 49.43	8.49	VII. 2 42.256	43 28.67	11.23	52 57.92	28 11 59.90
20	9	. .	. .	. .	8.5	20.8	33.6	46.0	. .	. .	54 8.56	8.48	IV. 1 38.545	51 28.81	11.02	54 17.04	28 19 59.83 z.
21	7.8	36.2	49.0	1.2	13.8	. .	. .	. .	. .	. .	2 1 13.77	8.44	" 2 43.542	42 44.51	9.92	2 1 22.21	28 11 14.43
22	9	. .	38.2	50.5	3.0	. .	. .	. .	. .	. .	2 3.02	8.44	" 3 35.250	38 45.63	9.79	2 11.46	28 7 15.42 z.
23	9	. .	. .	. .	. .	31.6	43.5	56.2	. .	. .	2 18.90	8.43	" 1 43.010	48 54.52	9.75	2 27.33	28 17 24.27
24	8.9	27.8	40.5	52.6	5.6	17.5	30.2	. .	. .	. .	4 5.27	8.43	" 4 45.150	27 7.10	9.46	4 13.70	27 55 36.56 z.
25	8.9	. .	53.0	5.5	17.8	30.0	42.3	. .	. .	. .	5 17.76	8.41	" 2 40.421	44 32.38	9.27	5 26.17	28 13 1.65 z.
26	9	. .	56.2	8.8	21.2	33.2	. .	. .	. .	. .	8 21.11	8.40	" 2 48.110	40 6.74	8.78	8 29.51	28 8 35.52
27	8	54.5	7.0	19.5	31.5	43.6	56.4	8.8	. .	. .	13 31.64	8.38	" 4 41.610	29 9.36	7.92	13 40.02	27 57 37.28 z.
28	7.8	56.0	8.4	20.5	32.6	45.4	58.0	10.6	. .	. .	15 33.25	8.38	" 7 36.090	11 59.30	7.57	15 41.63	27 40 26.87
29	8	16.4	28.8	41.5	53.8	6.0	18.5	30.8	. .	. .	17 53.72	8.36	" 5 46.221	20 42.90	7.17	18 2.08	27 49 10.07
30	9	. .	. .	. .	. .	. .	52.5	4.0	. .	. .	19 27.14	8.35	VII. 3 35.702	38 29.68	6.90	19 35.49	28 6 56.58
31	9	. .	. .	. .	42.5	54.9	7.5	19.5	. .	. .	20 42.44	8.33	VI. 1 42.110	49 25.51	6.69	20 50.77	28 17 52.20 z.
32	8.9	42.5	55.0	7.2	20.0	. .	. .	. .	. .	. .	22 19.86	8.33	III. 3 39.980	36 2.19	6.40	22 28.19	28 4 28.59
33	9	. .	. .	. .	27.5	39.8	52.6	4.6	. .	. .	22 27.52	8.33	V. 4 45.201	27 5.31	6.38	22 35.85	27 55 31.69
34	8	10.5	22.8	35.0	47.6	0.0	. .	. .	. .	. .	24 47.69	8.31	IV. 2 45.411	41 39.99	5.96	24 56.00	28 10 5.95 z.
35	7.8	6.0	18.3	31.0	43.5	55.2	8.0	. .	. .	. .	25 43.23	8.33	" 7 37.136	11 23.16	5.80	25 51.56	27 39 48.96 z.
36	9	. .	. .	. .	. .	32.0	44.0	56.2	. .	. .	26 19.27	8.31	VI. 4 45.540	26 53.49	5.69	26 27.58	27 55 19.18
37	9	37.7	50.6	2.6	15.2	27.0	39.5	52.0	. .	. .	2 29 14.97	8.30	IV. 5 45.798	20 57.48	5.16	2 29 23.27	27 49 22.64

CORRECTIONS.

	Cor. to Clock.	Hourly Cor.	m.	n.	c.	Zenith Point.	Coinc.
	s.	s.	s.	s.	s.	° ′ ″	r.
Sept. 16, at 22h...	+1.622	— 0.027	—0.356	+0.527	+0.022	0 0 2.56	40.094

† The reading of the circle has been changed three minutes from that recorded.

INSTRUMENT READINGS.

	h.	Circle. A.	B.	C.	D.	Mean.	Bar.	Thermom. At.	Ex.
		° ′ ″	″	″	″	″	I.	°	°
†Zone LXV.—Sept. 16....	1.5	293 9 5.0	. .	. .	. .	10.72	30.100	58.4	52.3
	1.7	6.5	11.8	19.1	9.5	12.72	. .	. .	50.5
	2.5	7.0	12.6	20.0	11.3	12.72	30.074	57.0	50.7

Number	Magnitude.	SECONDS OF TRANSITS. I.	II.	III.	IV.	V.	VI.	VII.	10.	11.	T.	a.	MICROMETER.	D.	d.	Mean Right Ascension, 1850.0.	Mean South Declination, 1850.0.
Zone LXVI. September 19. M. $D. = 25° 25' 10''.0$. $n'. = -42''.84$. $n''. = -3''.00$.																	
											h. m. s.	s.	r.	′ ″	″	h. m. s.	
1	9	..	..	..	42.2	54.0	6.5	18.5	..	..	19 26 41.99	+10.37	VII. 2 34.87	−47 41.41	−41.22	19 26 52.36	26°13′32″63
2	9.10	..	..	..	..	..	..	..	23.8	36.0	29 28.90	10.34	11. 2 37.81	45 59.26	40.55	29 39.24	26 11 49.81
3	9.10	..	29.0	41.1	53.6	..	..	..	..	..	35 53.38	10.23	2. 6 35.65	18 3.01	39.03	36 3.61	25 43 52.04 z.
4	9.10	..	..	..	18.8	..	43.5	..	..	..	36 19.00	10.21	VII. 7 46.48	5 58.40	38.93	36 29.21	25 31 47.33 z.
5	9	..	57.0	9.2	21.3	..	..	..	..	..	38 21.37	10.25	IV. 3 44.27	33 31.98	38.45	38 31.62	25 59 29.43 z.
6	9.10	..	..	..	..	..	12.6	24.8	..	..	38 48.13	10.27	VII. 1 41.21	49 53.97	38.34	38 58.40	26 15 42.31 z.
7	9	46.2	58.8	10.6	23.0	35.0	47.1	59.5	..	..	42 22.91	10.18	" 6 41.11	14 54.82	37.50	42 33.09	25 40 42.32
8	8.9	14.5	27.1	39.5	51.6	3.7	15.8	28.0	..	..	43 51.48	10.18	2. 5 39.30	24 39.37	37.16	45 1.66	25 50 26.53 z.
9	9	..	49.0	1.0	13.2	..	37.0	49.4	..	..	48 13.06	10.12	" 7 42.30	8 22.39	36.15	48 23.18	25 34 8.54 z.
10	9.10	..	14.0	25.7	38.0	..	..	..	..	..	50 38.17	10.17	IV. 1 40.86	50 6.35	35.59	50 48.34	26 15 51.94 z.
11	9.10	..	..	..	..	20.0	32.0	44.0	..	..	51 7.57	10.17	VII. 1 36.90	52 22.82	35.47	51 17.74	26 18 8.29 z.
12	9.10	..	..	..	..	..	..	..	..	27.6	51 20.29	10.16	11. 2 31.82	49 26.12	35.43	51 30.43	26 15 11.55
13	10	..	..	..	..	..	..	27.0	..	..	52 50.38	10.13	VII. 3 38.48	36 51.63	35.08	53 0.51	26 2 36.71
14	9.10	..	57.0	9.4	21.1	33.2	46.0	..	..	..	57 21.36	10.08	2. 3 43.00	34 15.13	34.10	57 31.44	25 59 59.23
15	10	15.0	27.5	40.0	52.0	4.5	..	..	..	..	59 52.05	10.05	VI. 4 38.74	30 46.40	33.48	20 0 2.10	25 56 29.88
16	9.10	..	..	..	..	58.0	10.0	22.0	..	..	20 0 45.57	10.08	VII. 1 36.16	52 48.40	33.28	0 55.65	26 18 31.68
17	8	..	..	..	..	..	..	..	..	0.5	0 53.58	10.02	11. 6 36.80	17 23.06	33.26	1 3.60	25 43 6.32
18	10	..	..	25.5	37.6	..	2.3	..	..	..	4 37.74	10.04	I. 2 38.15	45 48.15	32.43	4 47.78	26 11 30.58
19	9.10	23.8	36.0	47.8	0.6	..	..	..	..	..	7 0.30	9.96	IV. 7 33.15	13 39.07	31.90	7 10.26	25 39 20.97 z.
20	10	5.7	..	29.8	..	..	..	..	..	..	9 42.21	9.95	" 5 44.74	21 32.15	31.30	9 52.16	25 47 13.45
21	8	..	12.0	24.0	36.0	..	..	..	..	..	10 36.14	9.93	" 6 40.10	15 30.02	31.11	10 46.07	25 41 11.13 z.
*22	8.9	..	..	..	16.1	28.0	40.4	52.1	..	..	11 15.94	9.92	VII. 6 41.90	14 27.53	30.97	11 25.86	25 40 8.50
23	9.10	..	32.7	44.7	56.5	9.0	..	..	..	..	14 56.83	9.89	V. 6 37.49	17 0.14	30.17	15 6.72	25 42 40.31
24	10	..	..	54.7	6.5	19.0	31.0	..	..	..	17 6.76	9.88	VII. 6 40.35	15 21.09	29.71	17 16.64	25 41 0.80
25	8	..	27.0	39.0	51.0	5.4	15.6	27.8	..	..	18 51.22	9.90	" 3 32.67	40 12.21	29.33	19 1.12	26 5 51.54 z.
26	9.10	..	..	25.0	37.0	39.5	..	..	..	..	21 37.24	9.86	VI. 4 39.15	30 32.26	28.75	21 47.10	25 56 11.01
27	10	..	..	..	..	..	..	..	38.0	51.0	20 43.51	9.90	11. 1 39.42	50 55.19	28.94	20 53.41	26 16 34.13
28	9.10	..	..	..	..	..	..	56.0	..	..	22 19.62	9.81	VII. 7 46.45	5 59.44	28.60	22 29.43	25 31 38.04 z.
29	10	29.1	..	53.8	..	18.0	..	..	..	..	25 5.91	9.78	V. 7 44.36	7 11.89	28.02	25 15.69	25 32 49.91
30	9	..	..	..	..	..	27.5	39.5	..	..	26 2.95	9.82	VII. 3 43.65	33 53.05	27.82	26 12.77	25 59 30.87 z.
31	8.9	..	..	..	44.0	56.0	8.1	..	..	..	27 43.84	9.82	VI. 2 42.25	43 26.80	27.47	27 53.66	26 9 4.27 z.
32	7.8	..	..	..	46.0	58.0	10.2	22.2	..	..	28 45.90	9.76	VII. 6 46.25	11 57.33	27.26	28 55.66	25 37 34.59 z.
33	9	..	..	..	..	..	7.3	19.2	..	..	29 42.81	9.76	" 6 36.71	17 26.77	27.06	29 52.57	25 43 3.83 z.
34	8	..	21.0	33.0	45.0	..	9.3	21.8	..	..	31 45.15	9.73	" 7 41.35	8 55.57	26.65	31 54.88	25 34 32.22 z.
35	9	20.3	32.4	..	..	..	..	..	..	..	36 56.74	9.69	IV. 6 44.21	13 8.08	25.61	37 6.43	25 38 43.69 z.
36	5	..	..	..	..	..	27.0	29.0	..	..	37 2.52	9.70	VII. 5 42.57	22 46.83	25.59	37 12.22	25 48 22.42 z.
37	6	36.5	..	0.8	13.0	25.3	37.3	39.5	..	..	40 12.99	9.72	" 1 33.53	54 19.25	24.97	40 22.71	26 19 54.22 z.
38	8	..	..	..	..	41.4	53.5	..	..	..	41 29.32	9.63	" 7 45.93	6 17.37	24.73	41 38.95	25 31 52.10 z.
39	8	..	..	..	..	..	..	..	2.8	15.3	42 8.06	9.68	11. 2 43.50	42 42.82	24.60	42 17.74	26 8 17.42 z.
40	8.9	45.0	57.0	9.2	21.4	33.5	45.8	58.0	..	..	45 21.46	9.65	2. 2 43.44	42 45.13	23.98	45 31.11	26 8 19.11
41	10	..	44.0	..	8.3	20.3	..	..	..	..	20 48 8.26	9.58	VI. 6 32.2	20 2.77	23.45	20 48 17.84	25 45 36.22

CORRECTIONS.

	COR. TO CLOCK.	HOURLY COR.	m.	n.	c.	ZENITH POINT.	COINC.
	s.	s.	s.	s.	s.		r.
Sept. 19, at 18h...	+0.030	−0.019	−0.415	+0.429	+0.022	0° 0′ 2″.05	40.120

INSTRUMENT READINGS.

		CIRCLE. A.	B.	C.	D.	Mean.	BAR.	THERMOM. At.	Ex.
Zone	h.						I.		
LXVI.—Sept. 19.	19.5	295° 12′ 12″.0	15″.0	23″.0	19″.0	17″.25	30.208	71°.8	63°.7
	20.0	....	..	..	..	..	30.220	69.8	61.0
	21.0	....	..	..	..	..	30.216	69.0	60.6
	22.8	....	..	..	..	..	30.222	66.5	58.7
	0.0	....	.	..	..	..	..	65.0	57.0
	0.3	....	.	..	..	..	30.212	63.8	57.5
	1.8	....	..	..	..	..	..	63.2	55.2
	2.0	12.5	16.0	24.0	20.0	18.12	..	..	..

Number.	Magnitude.	SECONDS OF TRANSITS									T.	a.	MICROMETER.	D.	d.	Mean Right Ascension, 1850.0.	Mean South Declination, 1850.0.
		I.	II.	III.	IV.	V.	VI.	VII.	10.	11.							
Zone LXVI. September 19. M. $D.=25^{\circ}\ 25'\ 10''.0$. $n'.=-42''.84$. $n''.=-3''.00$. (Continued.)																	
											h. m. s.	s.	r.	′ ″	″	h. m. s.	° ′ ″
42	9	. .	. .	. .	. .	15.7	27.7	39.7	. .	. .	20 50 3.33	+ 9.59	VII. 4 37.87	—31 16.23	—23.08	20 50 12.92	25 56 49.31 z.
43	8	42.4	55.2	7.0	19.1	31.2	43.3	55.5	. .	. .	53 19.13	9.53	2. 6 42.42	14 9.23	22.47	53 28.66	25 39 41.70
44	9	. .	. .	43.0	55.0	. .	. .	. .	. .	. .	57 55.14	9.53	III. 2 41.23	44 2.08	21.61	58 4.67	26 9 33.69
45	5	. .	. .	. .	. .	. .	35.4	47.5	. .	. .	58 11.08	9.48	VII. 7 38.45	10 35.73	21.56	58 20.56	25 36 7.29 z.
46	10	23.5	35.6	. .	0.3	12.2	25.9	. .	. .	. .	21 1 0.25	9.50	VI. 2 40.07	44 42.07	21.04	21 1 9.75	26 10 13.11
47	10	. .	19.0	31.0	43.0	. .	. .	. .	. .	. .	4 43.16	9.43	IV. 5 44.08	21 54.96	20.38	4 52.59	25 47 25.34
48	9	. .	. .	. .	. .	35.1	47.5	59.7	. .	. .	5 23.06	9.43	VII. 4 41.84	28 59.14	20.27	5 32.49	25 54 29.41 z.
49	9.10	. .	58.5	10.5	23.0	. .	. .	. .	. .	. .	9 22.95	9.43	IV. 1 32.97	54 38.87	19.56	9 32.38	26 20 8.43 z.
50	9.10	. .	. .	. .	. .	. .	. .	. .	35.0	47.3	9 40.45	9.37	11. 7 33.21	13 36.07	19.51	9 49.82	25 39 5.58
51	10	54.8	6.9	19.0	31.2	. .	. .	. .	. .	. .	13 31.26	9.34	2. 5 43.27	22 22.25	18.87	13 40.60	25 47 51.12 z.
52	8	. .	. .	. .	3.0	15.0	27.5	. .	. .	. .	15 3.01	9.33	" 5 38.84	24 55.24	18.61	15 12.34	25 50 23.85 z.
53	8.9	. .	. .	. .	. .	. .	46.5	58.5	. .	. .	15 21.93	9.36	VII. 2 36.90	46 31.31	18.55	15 31.29	26 11 59.86 z.
54	8.9	. .	. .	. .	. .	8.5	20.7	32.8	. .	. .	16 56.31	9.32	" 5 34.55	27 23.76	18.29	17 5.63	25 52 52.05
55	9	40.5	52.5	5.0	16.6	. .	. .	. .	. .	. .	19 16.97	9.30	IV. 4 39.10	31 5.09	17.90	19 26.27	25 56 32.99
56	9.10	. .	. .	. .	. .	. .	56.2	8.2	. .	. .	20 31.76	9.27	VII. 6 33.55	19 15.89	17.70	20 41.03	25 44 43.59
57	8	. .	12.2	24.2	36.0	. .	. .	. .	. .	. .	21 36.31	9.27	IV. 5 38.19	25 18.40	17.53	21 45.58	25 50 45.93 z.
58	8	. .	25.2	37.8	50.0	. .	. .	. .	. .	. .	22 49.86	9.26	" 4 36.64	31 59.02	17.33	22 59.12	25 57 26.35 z.
59	8	. .	. .	. .	. .	. .	26.0	37.6	. .	. .	23 1.25	9.27	VII. 3 35.29	38 41.78	17.30	23 10.52	26 4 9.08 z.
60	8	. .	. .	. .	. .	. .	. .	. .	11.5	23.5	23 16.59	9.26	11. 5 34.18	27 35.95	17.27	23 25.85	25 53 3.22 z.
61	9.10	. .	. .	29.6	41.7	53.8	. .	. .	. .	. .	25 41.77	9.20	V. 7 37.12	11 21.92	16.87	25 50.97	25 36 48.79
62	9	. .	. .	. .	. .	40.3	52.7	5.0	. .	. .	27 28.29	9.22	VII. 4 33.93	33 32.30	16.59	27 37.51	25 58 58.89
63	10	. .	. .	. .	51.7	. .	16.0	. .	. .	. .	28 51.67	9.18	VI. 6 39.88	15 37.52	16.37	29 0.85	25 41 3.89 z.
64	8	. .	. .	. .	. .	. .	. .	59.2	17.5	30.0	29 22.69	9.21	11. 2 45.55	41 31.97	16.29	20 31.90	26 6 58.26 z.
65	8.9	. .	. .	. .	8.0	20.1	32.2	44.7	. .	. .	31 7.97	9.18	VII. 4 43.09	28 15.97	16.02	31 17.15	25 53 41.99 z.
66	8	24.0	36.2	48.1	0.5	12.8	25.0	37.0	. .	. .	33 0.54	9.15	" 5 45.04	21 21.50	15.74	33 9.69	25 46 47.24 z.
67	8.9	11.5	23.5	35.5	48.0	. .	12.0	24.3	. .	. .	35 47.84	9.10	2. 7 39.37	10 3.58	15.33	35 56.94	25 35 28.91 z.
68	8.9	39.0	51.2	3.0	15.3	. .	39.0	52.0	. .	. .	38 15.29	9.09	VII. 5 47.20	20 6.91	14.96	38 24.38	25 45 31.87
69	9	. .	45.6	57.6	. .	22.0	. .	. .	. .	. .	41 9.91	9.07	VI. 5 38.25	25 16.23	14.54	41 18.98	25 50 40.77 z.
70	10	. .	. .	. .	. .	. .	38.8	50.2	. .	. .	42 13.95	9.08	VII. 3 41.03	35 23.55	14.39	42 23.03	26 0 47.94 z.
71	9	. .	. .	. .	41.0	53.0	5.6	17.2	. .	. .	44 40.89	9.05	" 3 35.07	38 49.36	14.05	44 49.94	26 4 13.41
72	8.9	11.0	23.0	35.3	47.6	59.3	12.0	24.0	. .	. .	47 47.51	9.04	" 2 35.73	47 11.71	13.62	47 56.55	26 12 35.33 z.
73	10	25.2	37.8	50.0	. .	. .	. .	. .	. .	. .	50 2.23	9.02	IV. 1 38.24	51 36.87	13.31	50 11.25	26 17 0.18
74	9	. .	. .	. .	. .	38.5	51.0	3.0	. .	. .	50 26.44	8.99	VII. 3 35.44	38 36.60	13.26	50 35.43	26 3 59.86
75	8.9	. .	9.8	21.8	33.8	. .	. .	. .	. .	. .	52 33.95	8.94	2. 6 35.38	18 12.37	12.98	52 42.89	25 43 35.35 z.
76	8.9	. .	. .	. .	2.1	14.2	26.5	38.7	. .	. .	53 2.19	8.93	VII. 7 40.16	9 36.65	12.92	53 11.12	25 34 59.57 z.
77	9	36.5	49.0	1.0	. .	. .	. .	. .	. .	. .	55 13.15	8.90	IV. 7 41.72	8 43.08	12.51	55 22.05	25 34 5.59 z.
78	9	. .	. .	. .	. .	. .	36.7	49.0	. .	. .	55 12.53	8.91	VII. 7 44.73	6 58.81	12.64	55 21.44	25 32 21.45 z.
79	9.10	. .	. .	. .	. .	. .	31.7	43.9	. .	. .	56 7.31	8.92	" 5 38.61	25 3.58	12.52	56 16.23	25 50 26.10 z.
80	10.11	24.5	36.2	48.3	1.2	. .	. .	. .	. .	. .	22 2 0.96	8.89	VI. 1 37.55	52 0.57	11.78	22 2 9.85	26 17 22.35 z.
81	8.9	. .	. .	. .	. .	47.7	. .	12.0	. .	. .	2 35.48	8.87	VII. 2 46.58	40 57.03	11.71	2 44.35	26 6 18.74 z.
82	7.8	. .	45.0	57.0	. .	21.0	33.6	45.8	. .	. .	5 9.18	8.84	2. 4 40.30	29 51.96	11.41	5 18.02	25 55 13.37 z.
83	10	. .	21.0	33.0	45.3	. .	. .	. .	. .	. .	6 45.25	8.81	VI. 6 34.80	18 32.96	11.22	6 54.06	25 43 54.18 z.
84	9.10	. .	. .	. .	. .	. .	25.7	37.8	. .	. .	7 1.20	8.82	VII. 4 32.90	34 7.86	11.19	7 10.02	25 59 29.05
85	10	. .	. .	. .	. .	. .	. .	. .	23.0	35.5	7 28.26	8.82	11. 2 44.98	41 51.68	11.13	7 37.08	26 7 12.81
86	9	. .	. .	. .	16.0	28.0	40.2	. .	. .	. .	12 15.90	8.76	2. 5 35.80	26 40.23	10.58	12 24.66	25 52 0.81 z.
87	10	. .	. .	. .	. .	. .	7.0	19.1	. .	. .	12 42.55	8.76	I. 5 34.12	27 38.65	10.53	12 51.31	25 52 59.18
88	8	. .	. .	. .	. .	35.7	48.0	. .	. .	. .	13 23.57	8.76	VII. 2 45.21	41 44.36	10.46	13 32.33	26 7 4.82 z.
89	5.6	. .	. .	. .	. .	12.0	24.0	36.3	. .	. .	14 59.89	8.71	" 7 46.98	5 41.12	10.28	15 8.60	25 31 1.40 z.
90	9.10	. .	34.0	46.0	58.0	10.0	22.5	. .	. .	. .	16 58.13	8.73	VI. 2 46.11	41 13.49	10.06	17 6.86	26 6 33.55 z.
91	10	. .	. .	39.0	51.0	3.2	15.0	27.3	. .	. .	30 50.91	8.60	VII. 1 40.45	50 20.24	8.69	30 59.51	26 15 38.93 z.
92	8.9	20.5	32.8	45.0	57.0	9.3	21.5	34.0	. .	. .	32 57.20	8.57	VII. 2 43.79	42 33.38	8.50	33 5.77	26 7 51.88 z.
93	8	33.0	45.2	57.3	9.8	21.7	. .	. .	. .	. .	37 9.66	8.51	IV. 3 39.82	36 5.63	8.13	37 18.17	26 1 23.76 z.
94	9	. .	. .	. .	21.8	34.0	46.2	58.2	. .	. .	22 38 21.73	8.49	VII. 2 38.23	45 45.40	8.02	22 38 30.22	26 11 3.42 z.

Number.	Magnitude.	SECONDS OF TRANSITS. I.	II.	III.	IV.	V.	VI.	VII.	10.	11.	T.	a.	MICROMETER.	D.	d.	Mean Right Ascension, 1850.0.	Mean South Declination, 1850.0.
Zone LXVI.	September 19.	M.	$D.=25^{\circ}\ 25'\ 10''.0.$	$n.=-42''.84.$	$n.=-3''.00.$	(Continued.)											
											h. m. s.	s.	r.	′ ″	″	h. m. s.	° ′ ″
95	9	4.0	16.6	28.8	41.0	53.0	5.0	17.0	. .	. .	22 40 40.80	+8.47	VII. 6 36.85	—17 21.95	— 7.82	22 40 49.27	25 42 39.77 z.
96	9	56.3	8.8	21.0	. .	. .	. .	. .	. .	. .	44 33.17	8.44	IV. 3 42.08	34 47.59	7.53	44 41.61	26 0 5.12 z.
97	9	. .	. .	. .	. .	. .	. .	5.9	. .	. .	44 29.22	8.46	VII. 1 35.41	53 14.31	7.53	44 37.68	26 18 31.84
98	8.9	. .	. .	. .	. .	. .	. .	. .	. .	55.7	44 48.52	8.44	11. 4 37.93	31 13.55	7.51	44 56.96	25 56 31.06
99	8	. .	. .	. .	. .	. .	. .	. .	55.0	7.3	47 0.46	8.40	11. 6 45.40	12 26.06	7.34	47 8.86	25 37 43.40
100	9	. .	. .	7.3	19.5	31.6	44.0	56.0	. .	. .	49 19.49	8.41	VII. 1 41.84	49 32.19	7.16	49 27.90	26 14 49.35 z.
101	5.6	13.0	25.3	37.5	. .	. .	. .	. .	. .	. .	51 49.72	8.37	2. 4 35.73	32 29.76	6.99	51 58.09	25 57 46.75 z.
102	10	. .	. .	. .	54.3	6.5	. .	. .	. .	. .	52 54.36	8.35	(†) 5 36.49	26 17.12	6.92	53 2.71	25 51 34.04
103	9	. .	. .	. .	. .	. .	52.0	4.0	. .	. .	53 27.53	8.35	VII. 5 43.74	22 6.38	6.89	53 35.88	25 47 23.27
104	10	. .	. .	. .	. .	. .	. .	. .	4.8	17.0	53 9.99	8.35	11. 4 44.64	27 21.79	6.90	53 18.34	25 52 38.69 z.
105	9.10	. .	. .	. .	. .	. .	. .	. .	52.5	5.0	54 57.82	8.34	" 4 42.44	28 37.81	6.79	55 6.16	25 53 54.60
106	10	. .	34.0	. .	58.0	10.2	22.4	34.7	. .	. .	23 3 58.11	8.26	I. 1 44.84	47 48.63	6.24	23 4 6.37	26 13 4.87
107	8.9	. .	. .	. .	. .	22.0	34.5	46.2	. .	. .	7 9.96	8.21	VII. 6 41.27	14 49.31	6.07	7 18.78	25 40 5.38 z.
108	9.10	. .	. .	25.1	37.3	49.7	. .	. .	. .	. .	9 37.43	8.21	2. 1 39.20	51 3.02	5.93	9 45.64	26 16 18.95
109	9	. .	. .	. .	15.5	27.7	40.5	52.0	. .	. .	10 15.66	8.19	VII. 5 40.50	23 58.33	5.90	10 23.85	25 49.14.23 z.
110	8.9	. .	. .	. .	58.0	10.0	22.4	. .	. .	. .	12 57.94	8.16	V. 3 34.50	39 9.30	5.79	13 6.10	26 4 25.09 z
111	8.9	. .	. .	. .	. .	. .	. .	. .	10.4	22.5	13 15.70	8.15	11. 6 38.52	16 23.63	5.78	13 23.85	25 41 39.41 z.
112	10	. .	. .	. .	13.0	25.2	. .	. .	. .	. .	16 13.05	8.13	IV. 3 37.29	37 33.02	5.67	16 21.18	26 2 48.69
113	8	. .	. .	9.5	21.5	33.5	45.8	58.0	. .	. .	20 21.47	8.11	I. 1 41.97	49 27.71	5.51	20 29.58	26 14 43.22 z.
114	10	. .	. .	. .	. .	. .	16.5	28.3	. .	. .	20 51.82	8.11	VII. 1 34.54	53 44.31	5.49	20 59.93	26 18 59.80 z.
115	8	. .	. .	46.0	58.0	10.2	22.5	. .	. .	. .	25 58.15	8.03	1. 6 39.11	16 3.90	5.34	26 6.18	25 41 19.24 z.
116	8.9	. .	16.0	28.0	40.0	32.3	4.5	. .	. .	. .	28 40.19	8.01	VII. 3 35.03	38 50.74	5.26	28 48.20	26 4 6.00 z.
117	8.9	. .	. .	. .	51.5	3.5	. .	. .	. .	. .	29 51.47	8.00	V. 6 37.35	17 14.97	5.22	29 59.47	25 42 30.19
118	9	. .	. .	. .	. .	. .	. .	45.0	3.3	16.0	30 8.57	8.00	11. 3 37.43	37 27.27	5.22	30 16.57	26 2 42.49 z.
119	9.10	. .	. .	33.2	. .	17.8	30.0	42.3	. .	. .	33 5.61	7.97	I. 4 35.33	32 43.97	5.16	33 13.58	25 57 59.13 z.
120	9	47.0	59.1	11.1	23.4	35.5	. .	. .	. .	. .	35 23.53	7.96	" 2 37.28	46 18.21	5.11	35 31.49	26 11 33.32 z.
121	8.9	. .	. .	. .	0.8	12.8	25.0	37.1	. .	. .	36 0.74	7.94	VII. 7 38.61	10 30.17	5.10	36 8.68	25 35 45.27 z.
122	7.8	18.5	30.8	42.8	55.0	7.1	19.2	31.6	. .	. .	41 55.05	7.90	2. 2 40.24	44 35.63	5.02	42 2.95	26 9 50.65 z.
123	7.8	11.0	23.0	35.1	47.5	59.3	11.6	24.0	. .	. .	44 47.41	7.87	" 5 40.50	23 57.94	5.02	44 55.28	25 49 12.96 z.
124	7.8	. .	14.0	26.0	38.0	50.0	2.3	14.2	. .	. .	48 38.03	7.82	VII. 7 41.14	9 2.81	5.01	48 45.85	25 34 17.82 z.
125	9.10	40.8	53.0	5.1	17.1	29.3	. .	. .	. .	. .	55 17.35	7.77	VI. 2 47.40	40 28.96	5.00	55 25.12	26 5 43.96 z.
126	9.10	. .	. .	. .	. .	. .	. .	. .	37.8	50.0	55 43.35	7.76	11. 7 47.90	5 8.72	5.00	55 51.11	25 30 23.72
127	9.10	. .	. .	. .	. .	. .	. .	. .	51.8	4.0	57 56.91	7.75	" 1 38.34	51 32.49	5.00	58 4.66	26 16 47.49
128	8	. .	. .	20.8	33.0	45.0	57.3	9.5	. .	. .	59 33.93	7.73	VII. 2 37.90	45 56.77	5.00	59 40.76	26 11 11.77 z.
129	8	. .	. .	3.5	16.0	28.0	40.0	. .	. .	. .	0 12 15.81	7.63	VI. 4 37.07	31 44.09	5.24	0 12 23.44	25 56 59.33
130	8.9	. .	. .	. .	. .	. .	27.5	39.4	. .	. .	13 2 87	7.62	VII. 1 36.33	52 42.53	5.26	13 10.49	26 17 57.79
131	8.9	. .	. .	. .	. .	. .	. .	29.0	. .	. .	13 52.40	7.61	" 4 41.40	29 14.36	5.29	14 0.01	25 54 29.65
132	8.9	. .	. .	. .	. .	. .	. .	. .	27.0	40.0	14 32.52	7.61	11. 3 37.27	37 32.79	5.31	14 40.13	26 2 48.10 z.
133	10	. .	. .	. .	. .	6.0	18.1	30.2	. .	. .	16 53.87	7.59	VII. 7 41.43	8 52.81	5.38	17 1.46	25 34 8.19 z.
134	9.10	. .	. .	. .	. .	. .	16.8	29.0	. .	. .	17 52.42	7.58	" 5 42.44	22 51.32	5.40	18 0.00	25 48 6.72 z.
135	9.10	. .	48.3	0.5	. .	. .	. .	. .	. .	. .	20 12.77	7.56	2. 2 45.53	41 32.91	5.46	20 20.33	26 6 48.37 z.
136	9.10	. .	. .	. .	. .	26.5	38.7	51.0	. .	. .	20 14.43	7.56	VII. 5 39.95	24 17.29	5.47	20 21.99	25 49 32.76
137	9.10	. .	. .	. .	. .	. .	. .	13.7	32.0	44.0	21 37.19	7.55	11. 6 32.16	20 3.32	5.52	21 44.74	25 45 18.84 z.
138	9.10	. .	. .	. .	51.5	3.8	16.4	28.4	. .	. .	23 51.74	7.53	VII. 5 30.58	29 40.88	5.61	23 59.27	25 54 56.49
139	7.8	. .	. .	. .	. .	. .	27.8	40.0	. .	. .	25 3.33	7.52	" 2 38.00	45 53.33	5.66	25 10.85	26 11 8.99 z.
140	8.9	13.0	25.2	. .	. .	. .	. .	. .	. .	. .	27 49.52	7.50	2. 6 38.86	16 12.15	5.77	27 57.02	25 41 27.92
141	8.9	. .	. .	46.0	58.0	10.0	. .	. .	. .	. .	27 58.06	7.50	III. 2 33.83	48 17.59	5.78	28 5.56	26 13 33.37 z.
142	8.9	. .	. .	. .	. .	. .	. .	. .	9.4	21.8	28 14.83	7.49	11. 6 37.41	17 2.01	5.79	28 22.32	25 42 17.80
143	6.7	. .	. .	. .	. .	. .	54.4	6.6	. .	. .	30 30.14	7.47	VII. 7 38.93	10 19.12	5.88	30 37.61	25 35 35.00
144	7.8	. .	. .	. .	14.2	26.3	38.2	. .	. .	. .	31 14.05	7.47	" 4 39.00	30 37.22	5.92	31 21.52	25 55 53.14
145	9	. .	. .	. .	17.5	29.3	. .	54.0	. .	. .	32 17.39	7.46	" 5 37.19	25 52.63	5.98	32 24.85	25 51 8.61
146	7.8	. .	37.5	49.5	2.0	. .	. .	. .	. .	. .	0 34 1.88	7.45	IV. 3 40.23	35 51.49	6.06	0 34 9.33	26 1 7.55 z.

† Computed as if on IV.

Number.	Magnitude.	SECONDS OF TRANSITS. I.	II.	III.	IV.	V.	VI.	VII.	10.	11.	T.	a.	MICROMETER.	D.	d.	Mean Right Ascension, 1850.0.	Mean South Declination, 1850.0.
	Zone LXVI. September 19. M. D. = 25° 25′ 10″.0. n′ = −42″.84. n″ = −3″.00. (Continued.)																
											h. m. s.	s.	r.	′ ″	″	h. m. s.	° ′ ″
147	9	. .	. .	. .	. .	. .	. .	46.0	4.0	16.2	0 35 9.50	+ 7.44	II. 7 39.87	— 9 46.03	— 6.12	0 35 16.94	25 35 2.15
148	9	. .	. .	15.0	27.0	. .	. .	. .	. .	. .	36 27.11	7.43	IV. 6 38.57	16 22.84	6.19	36 34.54	25 41 39.03
149	10	. .	. .	. .	. .	. .	12.5	24.7	. .	. .	36 48.25	7.42	VII. 7 41.16	9 2.12	6.21	36 55.67	25 34 18.33
150	9	. .	. .	. .	31.5	43.8	56.0	. .	. .	. .	38 31.56	7.41	(†) 1 46.54	46 50.18	6.29	38 38.97	26 12 6.47
151	9	. .	. .	. .	. .	2.5	. .	26.7	. .	. .	39 50.22	7.40	VII. 1 46.52	46 50.55	6.36	39 57.62	26 12 6.91 z.
152	9.10	. .	. .	. .	. .	. .	. .	. .	59.5	12.0	41 4.76	7.39	II. 1 45.17	47 36.58	6.44	41 12.15	26 12 53.02
153	10	. .	. .	. .	. .	. .	. .	. .	46.7	59.5	41 52.11	7.39	" 1 44.57	47 57.27	6.48	41 59.50	26 13 13.75
154	10	. .	. .	. .	22.0	34.0	46.0	58.0	. .	. .	44 21.70	7.37	VII. 3 41.19	35 18.03	6.65	44 29.07	26 0 34.68 z.
155	6.7	. .	. .	. .	. .	. .	7.8	19.4	. .	. .	45 43.25	7.36	" 7 38.81	10 23.27	6.74	45 50.61	25 35 40.01 z.
156	9.10	. .	. .	. .	. .	. .	55.3	7.5	. .	. .	47 30.90	7.34	" 5 36.82	26 5.38	6.85	47 38.24	25 51 22.23
157	7.8	46.0	58.1	10.4	22.5	34.5	46.5	. .	. .	. .	49 22.50	7.33	2. 2 39.00	45 18.42	6.97	49 29.83	26 10 35.39 z.
158	9.10	4.1	16.9	29.0	41.1	53.0	5.0	17.5	. .	. .	53 40.55	7.31	VII. 7 42.78	8 6.16	7.28	53 47.86	25 33 23.44
159	9.10	. .	. .	17.3	29.5	. .	. .	. .	. .	. .	58 29.55	7.25	I. 1 37.41	52 5.24	7.64	58 36.80	26 17 22.88 z.
160	9.10	. .	. .	. .	. .	28.5	41.0	53.0	. .	. .	59 16.46	7.25	VII. 4 38.29	31 1.75	7.70	59 23.71	25 56 19.45 z.
161	8	. .	. .	. .	. .	. .	. .	25.0	43.0	55.5	59 48.53	7.25	II. 6 42.34	14 11.74	7.73	59 55.78	25 39 29.47
162	7	. .	. .	. .	. .	46.0	58.0	10.2	. .	. .	1 21 33.86	7.11	VII. 7 40.78	9 15.22	9.63	1 21 40.97	25 34 34.85 z.
163	7	. .	. .	47.0	59.5	11.2	23.8	36.0	. .	. .	29 59.36	7.05	" 5 44.55	21 38.39	10.56	30 6.41	25 46 58.95 z.
164	7	. .	. .	. .	. .	. .	5.0	17.0	. .	. .	31 40.53	7.04	" 5 44.28	21 47.76	10.77	31 47.57	25 47 8.53 z.
165	6	53.4	5.5	17.8	30.0	42.0	54.0	6.4	. .	. .	38 29.89	7.00	" 5 42.41	22 52.35	11.63	38 36.89	25 48 13.98 z.
166	9	. .	. .	3.1	15.2	28.0	40.0	52.0	. .	. .	45 15.51	6.96	" 5 44.12	21 53.28	12.50	45 22.47	25 47 15.78 z.
167	8	. .	. .	. .	12.3	24.6	. .	. .	. .	. .	48 12.39	6.94	2. 2 46.55	40 57.69	12.89	48 19.33	26 6 20.58 z.
168	6.7	. .	. .	. .	. .	. .	. .	. .	55.1	7.0	49 0.36	6.95	II. 6 45.58	12 19.81	12.99	49 7.31	25 37 42.80
169	8	. .	. .	. .	. .	. .	. .	50.5	8.8	21.0	50 13.92	6.93	" 3 40.78	35 31.55	13.15	50 20.85	26 0 54.70
170	9	. .	. .	. .	. .	. .	. .	7.5	25.8	38.0	50 30.89	6.92	" 1 42.36	49 13.64	13.19	50 37.81	26 14 36.83
171	10	0.3	12.6	24.8	37.0	. .	. .	. .	. .	. .	53 37.02	6.91	IV. 3 37.78	37 16.08	13.63	53 43.93	26 2 39.71 z.
172	9.10	. .	. .	. .	1.9	14.0	26.0	38.4	. .	. .	55 1.76	6.90	VII. 2 40.01	44 43.93	13.83	55 8.66	26 10 7.76 z.
173	9.10	. .	. .	. .	. .	. .	. .	1.2	19.4	31.8	1 56 24.69	6.90	II. 5 37.67	25 35.40	14.02	1 56 31.59	25 50 59.42 z.
	Zone LXVII. September 21. H. D. = −43° 21′ 00″.0. n′ = −31″.66. n″ = −19″.00.																
1	8	. .	. .	. .	41.5	56.2	12.5	27.2	. .	. .	19 36 41.61	11.38	VII. 5 46.411	20 43.37	27.27	19 36 52.99	43 42 10.64
2	6.7	. .	18.3	3.3	48.2	3.4	18.4	. .	. .	. .	48 48.36	11.20	IV. 7 47.316	5 29.07	24.18	48 59.56	43 26 53.25
3	9.10	. .	26.0	. .	56.0	11.0	27.0	41.0	. .	. .	53 56.01	11.18	" 3 38.450	37 14.14	22.91	54 7.19	43 58 37.05
4	8.9	27.2	43.0	58.0	. .	. .	. .	. .	. .	. .	20 0 13.35	11.11	II. 3 31.831	41 5.07	21.37	20 0 24.46	44 2 26.44
5	8	. .	. .	13.5	29.2	44.0	. .	. .	. .	. .	0 28.97	11.09	IV. 4 34.613	33 27.15	21.30	0 40.06	43 54 48.45
6	7.8	. .	. .	. .	. .	54.0	9.5	24.2	. .	. .	0 38.73	11.11	VI. 2 40.910	44 39.39	21.27	0 49.84	44 6 0.66
7	9	38.0	53.0	. .	24.5	39.0	. .	10.0	. .	. .	4 24.01	11.06	IV. 2 38.076	46 18.84	20.36	4 35.07	44 7 39.20
8	9	. .	. .	15.0	. .	45.8	1.0	16.5	. .	. .	12 30.54	10.95	" 2 36.122	47 27.23	18.46	12 41.49	44 8 45.69
9	9.10	. .	. .	. .	. .	23.0	. .	54.0	. .	. .	14 8.30	10.87	VII. 6 39.586	15 53.08	18.08	14 19.17	43 37 11.16
10	9	. .	13.5	28.5	43.0	. .	. .	. .	. .	. .	20 22 43.54	10.77	IV. 4 43.175	28 28.11	16.21	20 22 54.31	43 49 44.32

CORRECTIONS.

	COR. TO CLOCK.	HOURLY COR.	m.	n.	c.	ZENITH POINT.	COINC.
	s.	s.	s.	s.	s.	° ′ ″	r.
Sept. 21, at 18h . .	—0.419	—0.020	—0.415	+0.429	+0.022	0 0 3.12	40.100

† Taken for IV.

INSTRUMENT READINGS.

		CIRCLE. A.	B.	C.	D.	Mean.	BAR.	THERMOM. At.	Ex.
	h.	° ′ ″	″	″	″	″	I.	°	°
Zone LXVII.—Sept. 21 . . .	19.7	277 21 1.7	5.7	13.0	3.2	5.40	30.108	73.8	69.0
	20.3	3.5	5.5	16.0	6 2	7.80	30.122	72.5	. .
	21.3	. . .	. .	. .	. .	. .	30.130	71.0	6.50

Number.	Magnitude.	SECONDS OF TRANSITS. I.	II.	III.	IV.	V.	VI.	VII.	10.	11.	T.	a.	MICROMETER.	D.	d.	Mean Right Ascension, 1850.0.	Mean South Declination, 1850.0.
Zone LXVII. September 21. H. $D. = -43° 21' 00''.0$. $n. = -31''.66$. $n. = -19''.00$. (Continued.)																	
											h. m. s.	s.	r.	° ′ ″	″	h. m. s.	° ′ ″
11	7.8	. .	. .	36.0	57.2	6.4	21.8	37.0	. .	. .	20 23 51.29	+10.76	IV. 3 40.831	—35 50.58	—15.99	20 24 2.05	43 57 6.57
12	9	. .	. .	4.0	18.2	34.0	48.5	3.5	. .	. .	25 18.44	10.74	" 3 43.541	34 15.70	15.70	25 29.18	43 55 31.40
13	8.9	. .	34.2	49.2	4.3	. .	. .	. .	. .	. .	27 4.34	10.67	III. 7 35.712	12 14.03	15.34	27 15.01	43 33 29.37
14	9	. .	. .	. .	. .	33.0	48.2	3.2	. .	. .	27 17.66	10.72	V. 3 34.310	39 38.79	15.29	27 28.38	44 0 54.08
15	8.9	16.0	31.0	45.5	1.0	16.0	31.0	46.1	. .	. .	30 1.00	10.63	IV. 6 42.710	14 4.57	14.75	30 11.63	43 35 19.32
16	7.8	35.7	51.4	6.2	21.5	36.3	51.8	6.5	. .	. .	38 21.39	10.50	" 6 46.282	12 0.07	13.35	38 31.89	43 33 13.42
17	7.8	. .	. .	43.3	59.2	14.2	29.2	45.0	. .	. .	21 19 58.94	9.88	" 1 44.833	48 18.31	6.85	21 20 8.82	44 9 25.16
18	6	45.0	1.2	16.0	31.5	46.0	1.5	16.8	. .	. .	24 31.18	9.75	" 6 42.803	14 1.37	6.24	24 40.93	43 35 7.61
19	9	39.5	. .	9.0	24.5	40.0	. .	11.0	. .	. .	28 24.88	9.73	" 2 40.240	45 3.24	5.72	28 34.61	44 6 8.96
20	7	. .	38.5	54.0	9.0	23.8	39.8	. .	. .	. .	30 9.03	9.68	" 4 45.270	27 14.94	5.48	30 18.71	43 48 20.42
21	7.8	30.5	46.3	2.0	16.2	31.0	47.2	2.5	. .	. .	33 16.59	9.66	" 1 43.100	49 19.10	5.11	33 26.25	44 10 24.21
22	9	. .	. .	. .	30.2	45.5	0.5	16.0	. .	. .	40 30.15	9.52	" 2 37.810	46 28.02	4.25	40 39.67	44 7 32.27
23	9	47.0	1.5	17.0	32.5	. .	. .	. .	. .	. .	41 32.28	9.46	" 6 32.890	19 47.67	4.13	41 41.74	43 40 51.80
24	9	. .	. .	. .	7.5	. .	38.2	53.0	. .	. .	21 43 7.70	9.43	" 7 36.752	11 37.79	3.96	21 43 17.13	43 32 41.75
Zone LXVIII. September 22. M. $D. = 24° 55' 20''.0$. $n. = -38''.00$. $n. = -4''.01$.																	
1	9.10	16.1	28.5	40.2	. .	. .	. .	. .	. .	. .	19 25 52.60	9.46	IV. 4 39.10	30 35.09	36.60	19 26 2.06	25 26 31.69 z.
2	5.6	. .	. .	33.0	45.5	57.3	. .	. .	. .	. .	26 45.34	9.42	VII. 7 45.12	6 46.61	36.40	26 54.76	25 2 43.01 z.
3	5	. .	. .	. .	. .	36.8	49.0	. .	. .	. .	27 24.78	9.43	" 6 38.17	16 37.48	36.25	27 34.21	25 12 33.73 z.
4	9	. .	. .	. .	. .	. .	. .	. .	. .	51.5	27 44.63	9.45	11. 4 43.30	28 9.23	36.17	27 54.08	25 24 5.40
5	9	. .	. .	42.5	54.5	. .	18.6	. .	. .	. .	30 54.52	9.40	I. 6 43.27	13 41.40	35.45	31 3.92	25 9 36.85
6	9	. .	55.8	7.7	20.0	. .	. .	. .	. .	. .	32 19.92	9.39	VII. 6 41.23	14 51.84	35.12	32 29.31	25 10 46.96 z.
7	7	. .	42.7	54.7	6.6	18.7	31.0	. .	. .	. .	33 6.75	9.38	II. 6 38.68	16 20.10	34.95	33 16.13	25 12 15.05 z.
8	8.9	. .	. .	. .	29.0	41.0	. .	. .	. .	. .	34 29.01	9.36	V. 7 42.89	8 3.90	34.63	34 38.37	25 3 58.53 z.
9	9.10	. .	. .	. .	. .	. .	. .	. .	28.8	41.3	34 34.40	9.38	11. 5 37.67	25 36.55	34.61	34 43.78	25 21 31.16
10	9.10	. .	. .	. .	. .	. .	. .	30.6	. .	. .	35 54.09	9.41	VII. 1 44.61	47 57.42	34.31	36 3.50	25 43 51.73 z.
11	9.10	. .	. .	. .	. .	. .	. .	. .	14.4	26.5	36 19.72	9.39	11. 3 40.35	35 47.51	34.21	36 29.11	25 31 41.72 z.
12	8.9	. .	. .	. .	. .	. .	. .	. .	4.4	16.9	37 10.10	9.35	" 6 35.20	18 19.55	34.02	37 19.45	25 14 13.57
13	8.9	47.1	59.5	11.4	23.7	. .	. .	. .	. .	. .	41 23.74	9.36	1. 2 39.85	44 49.88	33.07	41 33.10	25 40 42.95 z.
14	7.8	. .	36.0	48.0	1.1	13.0	. .	. .	. .	. .	42 0.61	9.31	V. 5 46.56	20 30.35	32.93	42 9.92	25 16 23.28
15	8.9	52.2	4.8	16.8	. .	. .	. .	. .	. .	. .	43 28.92	9.31	IV. 4 46.14	26 32.00	32.60	43 38.23	25 22 24.60
16	8.9	. .	. .	. .	. .	. .	59.8	12.0	. .	. .	43 35.47	9.33	VII. 2 49.79	39 7.13	32.57	43 44.80	25 34 59.70
17	10	49.5	1.5	13.6	. .	. .	. .	. .	. .	. .	47 25.97	9.31	III. 2 38.30	45 44.21	31.72	47 35.28	25 41 35.93
18	8.9	. .	. .	. .	51.0	3.0	. .	. .	. .	. .	47 50.98	9.28	V. 4 34.88	33 0.74	31.63	48 0.27	25 28 52.37 z.
19	8.9	. .	. .	. .	. .	. .	. .	. .	58.8	11.0	49 4.19	9.27	11. 4 38.12	31 8.08	31.35	49 13.46	25 26 59.43 z.
20	8	. .	. .	. .	. .	. .	. .	. .	8.0	20.5	48 13.52	9.28	" 3 35.76	38 25.98	31.32	48 22.80	25 34 17.30 z.
21	9.10	29.5	. .	53.8	. .	17.8	. .	. .	. .	. .	54 5.96	9.23	V. 4 41.52	29 11.46	30.24	54 15.19	25 25 1.70
22	9	25.1	37.5	49.8	2.1	14.0	. .	38.6	. .	. .	19 56 1.95	9.22	2. 4 35.25	32 47.47	29.81	19 56 11.17	25 28 37.28 z.

CORRECTIONS.

	COR. TO CLOCK.	HOURLY COR.	m.	n.	c.	ZENITH POINT.	COINC.
	s.	s.	s.	s.	s.	° ′ ″	r.
Sept. 22, at 18h..	—0.888	—0.014	—0.415	+0.429	+0.022	0 0 3.55	40.110

INSTRUMENT READINGS.

	CIRCLE. A.	B.	C.	D.	Mean.	BAR.	THERMOM. At.	Ex.
Zone LXVIII.—Sept. 22, h. 19.4	295° 42′ 5″.0	7′.4	18″.0	10″.0	10″.10	I. 30.210	70°.1	61°.7
20.5	. .	.	. .	. .	. .	30.220	68.0	59.0
21.7	. . .	. .	. .	. .	. .	30.210	66.2	57.2
22.2	. . .	. .	. .	. .	. .	30.216	65.3	56.3
0.4	1.0	4.7	14.0	7.5	6.80	30.202	63.0	50.7

Number.	Magnitude.	SECONDS OF TRANSITS. I.	II.	III.	IV.	V.	VI.	VII.	10.	11.	T.	a.	MICROMETER.	D.	d.	Mean Right Ascension, 1850.0.	Mean South Declination, 1850.0
Zone LXVIII. September 22. M. $D.=24°\ 55'\ 20''.0.$ $n.=-38''.00.$ $n'.=-4''.01.$ (Continued.)																	
											h. m. s.	s.	r.	′ ″	″	h. m. s.	° ′ ″
23	10	. .	32.0	. .	56.2	. .	. .	. .	. .	. .	19 57 56.13	+ 9.17	IV. 6 39.16	—16 3.65	—29.39	19 58 5.30	25 11 53.04
24	8.9	. .	. .	59.0	11.2	23.5	. .	. .	. .	. .	59 11.31	9.15	VI. 7 47.99	5 7.74	29.12	59 20.46	25 0 56.86 z.
25	9.10	. .	. .	. .	. .	. .	15.2	. .	. .	. .	59 51.00	9.15	11. 6 46.70	11 42.46	28.97	20 0 0.15	25 7 31.43
26	7.8	. .	. .	. .	. .	7.0	19.0	31.0	. .	. .	20 0 54.69	9.19	VII. 1 45.79	47 16.68	28.75	1 3.88	25 43 5.43
27	7.8	. .	. .	. .	. .	7.0	19.0	31.0	. .	. .	0 54.70	9.19	" 2 45.15	41 47.37	28.75	1 3.89	25 37 36.12
28	7.8	. .	. .	. .	38.0	49.8	2.0	. .	. .	. .	3 37.84	9.12	" 5 49.27	18 56.50	28.17	3 46.96	25 14 44.67 z.
29	8	. .	. .	. .	. .	. .	. .	. .	53.5	6.2	4 59.22	9.12	11. 5 42.50	22 49.81	27.88	5 8.34	25 18 37.69
30	8.9	24.9	37.0	48.7	. .	13.2	25.5	37.5	. .	. .	7 1.20	9.14	1. 2 42.13	43 31.62	27.46	7 10.34	25 39 19.08 z.
31	8.9	23.0	35.2	47.1	59.2	. .	23.6	. .	. .	. .	8 59.35	9.10	VII. 4 35.72	32 31.44	27.04	9 8.45	25 28 18.48
32	8.9	. .	. .	. .	. .	. .	7.5	19.2	. .	. .	9 42.89	9.12	" 1 38.53	51 27.43	26.88	9 52.01	25 47 14.31
33	7.8	. .	. .	. .	. .	49.5	1.5	. .	. .	. .	10 37.29	9.10	II. 2 38.87	45 24.45	26.69	10 46.39	25 41 11.14 z.
34	8.9	. .	. .	. .	. .	29.0	41.2	. .	. .	. .	11 16.89	9.10	VII. 2 39.98	44 45.89	26.56	11 25.99	25 40 32.45 z.
35	7.8	. .	. .	. .	. .	. .	. .	13.7	32.0	44.0	11 37.39	9.05	11. 6 32.00	20 10.04	26.49	11 46.24	25 15 56.53
36	8	. .	. .	. .	48.0	. .	13.2	. .	. .	. .	13 48.41	9.05	VII. 5 33.20	28 11.40	26.04	13 57.46	25 23 57.44
37	8	. .	. .	. .	. .	. .	. .	. .	49.8	2.2	13 55.30	9.05	11. 4 36.75	31 55.38	26.02	14 4.35	25 27 41.40
38	8.9	. .	. .	. .	. .	12.0	24.3	. .	. .	. .	17 0.00	9.01	2. 5 40.60	23 55.64	25.39	17 9.01	25 19 41.03
39	7.8	. .	. .	. .	. .	. .	32.0	44.5	. .	. .	17 7.84	9.02	I. 4 40.17	29 57.80	25.36	17 16.86	25 25 43.16
40	8.9	. .	. .	. .	. .	. .	. .	36.4	. .	. .	18 0.11	8.98	VII. 7 37.82	10 58.65	25.18	18 9.09	25 6 43.83 z.
41	9	. .	. .	. .	. .	. .	25.0	37.0	. .	. .	19 0.57	9.02	" 3 34.82	38 58.91	24.97	19 9.59	25 34 43.88
42	9	. .	. .	58.5	. .	23.0	. .	. .	. .	. .	22 10.86	8.98	2. 3 40.51	35 42.27	24.34	22 19.84	25 31 26.61
43	9	. .	56.5	. .	20.5	. .	45.0	. .	. .	. .	22 20.62	8.98	" 3 40.27	35 50.54	24.31	22 29.60	25 31 34.35 z.
44	7	. .	. .	. .	. .	26.0	38.0	. .	. .	. .	23 13.86	8.96	VII. 4 46.15	26 31.31	24.13	23 22.82	25 22 15.44 z.
45	7	. .	. .	. .	. .	59.1	11.2	23.7	. .	. .	23 47.06	8.96	11. 3 48.75	30 57.43	24.02	23 56.02	25 26 41.45 z.
46	7	. .	23.0	34.7	47.0	. .	. .	. .	. .	. .	28 47.09	8.93	IV. 2 45.50	41 35.65	23.03	28 56.02	25 37 18.68
47	9.10	. .	. .	. .	. .	. .	. .	40.5	. .	. .	29 3.97	8.94	VII. 1 37.18	52 14.03	22.98	29 12.91	25 47 57.01
48	9.8	. .	. .	. .	. .	. .	8.6	20.4	. .	. .	29 44.06	8.93	10. 1 45.70	47 19.62	22.84	29 52.99	25 43 2.46 z.
49	7.8	. .	. .	34.0	46.0	. .	. .	. .	. .	. .	31 46.11	8.90	V. 2 50.35	38 48.12	22.45	31 55.01	25 34 30.57 z.
50	8.9	. .	. .	. .	. .	. .	58.0	10.0	. .	. .	32 33.80	8.84	11. 7 46.21	6 8.53	22.30	32 42.64	25 1 50.83
51	8.9	. .	7.9	19.8	32.0	44.0	. .	. .	. .	. .	34 32.00	8.84	V. 6 36.14	17 47.88	21.92	34 40.84	25 13 29.80
52	10	. .	. .	. .	. .	. .	. .	55.0	13.0	25.0	35 18.46	8.84	VII. 5 44.53	21 40.14	21.77	35 27.30	25 17 21.91
53	8.9	. .	. .	. .	. .	10.5	22.0	. .	. .	. .	36 58.04	8.85	11. 2 43.60	42 40.39	21.45	37 6.89	25 38 21.84
54	5	. .	. .	. .	. .	. .	. .	. .	10.5	. .	37 16.08	8.87	" 1 36.43	52 39.45	21.40	37 24.95	25 48 20.85
55	9.10	12.0	24.5	. .	. .	. .	. .	. .	. .	. .	40 48.62	8.79	II. 5 35.92	26 37.72	20.72	40 57.41	25 22 18.44
56	7.8	. .	6.1	18.1	30.2	42.0	. .	6.5	. .	. .	41 30.18	8.80	10. 3 39.65	36 11.92	20.60	41 38.98	25 31 52.52
57	9.10	32.5	44.8	56.8	. .	. .	. .	. .	. .	. .	47 9.15	8.76	III. 1 41.80	49 34.77	19.56	47 17.91	25 45 14.33
58	9	. .	20.0	31.8	. .	. .	. .	. .	. .	. .	48 44.13	8.73	I. 4 36.98	31 47.94	19.26	48 52.86	25 27 27.20 z.
59	7.8	. .	. .	. .	. .	. .	7.0	19.0	. .	. .	48 42.79	8.69	VII. 7 43.10	7 36.35	19.27	48 51.48	25 3 35.62 z.
60	9	. .	. .	. .	. .	. .	50.0	3.8	. .	. .	49 27.14	8.69	11. 6 45.22	12 33.59	19.13	49 35.83	25 8 12.72
61	8.9	. .	9.9	21.5	. .	. .	. .	. .	. .	. .	53 33.93	8.68	I. 4 36.72	31 56.91	18.40	53 42.61	25 27 35.31
62	7.8	44.0	56.0	8.0	20.0	32.2	. .	56.8	. .	. .	54 20.29	8.69	IV. 2 41.315	44 0.14	18.26	54 28.98	25 39 38.40 z.
63	10	58.5	10.5	. .	35.0	. .	. .	. .	. .	. .	56 34.89	8.64	" 5 38.85	24 56.64	17.88	56 43.53	25 20 34.52
64	9	21.2	33.0	. .	. .	. .	. .	. .	. .	. .	20 57 57.40	8.61	III. 6 33.62	19 14.87	17.62	58 6.01	25 14 52.49 z.
65	4	. .	. .	. .	12.0	24.3	36.5	48.5	. .	. .	58 12.09	8.64	VII. 3 32.31	40 25.62	17.58	58 20.73	25 36 3.20 z.
66	8.9	38.9	51.0	3.0	. .	. .	. .	. .	. .	. .	21 0 15.29	8.61	IV. 5 34.40	27 30.32	17.22	21 0 23.90	25 23 7.54
67	8.9	. .	. .	59.5	12.0	. .	. .	. .	. .	. .	1 11.84	8.60	" 4 40.25	29 55.38	17.06	1 20.44	25 25 32.44 z.
68	7.8	. .	43.4	55.9	8.0	20.0	. .	44.5	. .	. .	2 7.97	8.59	10. 4 39.38	30 24.87	16.91	2 16.56	25 26 1.78 z.
69	7	. .	1.0	13.2	25.4	37.5	49.5	1.5	. .	. .	4 25.29	8.57	2. 4 37.01	31 46.69	16.52	4 33.86	25 27 23.21 z.
70	9	58.0	. .	23.0	. .	. .	. .	11.0	. .	. .	4 34.78	8.57	VII. 4 33.80	33 37.74	16.50	4 43.35	25 29 14.24 z.
71	9	. .	17.2	29.2	41.2	53.0	5.8	. .	. .	. .	9 41.31	8.53	" 2 42.34	43 24.41	15.64	9 49.84	25 39 0.05
72	8.9	. .	14.5	26.7	38.8	50.8	3.0	. .	. .	. .	12 38.77	8.48	I. 5 39.04	24 49.44	15.17	12 47.25	25 20 24.61
73	9	. .	. .	. .	32.0	44.0	. .	. .	. .	. .	13 31.94	8.51	IV. 1 37.60	51 59.85	15.04	13 40.45	25 47 34.89 z.
74	8.9	. .	. .	. .	. .	. .	. .	36.5	54.5	6.6	14 0.08	8.45	11. 6 38.98	16 9.03	14.96	14 8.53	25 11 43.99
75	7	. .	. .	. .	. .	. .	55.5	7.7	. .	. .	21 15 31.40	8.43	VII. 7 42.97	8 0.83	14.72	21 15 39.83	25 3 35.55 z.

Zone LXVIII. September 22. M. $D. = -24° 55' 20''.0$. $n' = -38''.00$. $n'' = -4''.01$. (Continued.)

Number.	Magnitude.	SECONDS OF TRANSITS. I.	II.	III.	IV.	V.	VI.	VII.	10.	11.	T.	a.	MICROMETER.	D.	d.	Mean Right Ascension, 1850.0.	Mean South Declination, 1850.0.
											h. m. s.	s.	r.	' ''	''	h. m. s.	° ' ''
76	8.9	. .	. .	. .	. .	45.0	57.5	9.5	. .	. .	21 16 33.04	+ 8.46	VII. 3 38.25	—37 0.51	—14.56	21 16 41.50	25 32 35.07
77	8.9	. .	. .	. .	. .	. .	. .	. .	47.7	. .	16 53.20	8.44	" 5 32.96	28 19.68	14.51	17 1.64	25 23 54.19
78	7	. .	. .	. .	. .	. .	26.8	. .	. .	. .	18 2.59	8.41	II. 7 35.98	12 1.71	14.33	18 11.00	25 7 36.04
79	8.9	. .	. .	. .	32.8	45.0	57.1	. .	. .	. .	19 32.81	8.44	VII. 1 42.68	49 4.08	14.09	19 41.25	25 44 38.17
80	9	. .	. .	. .	. .	55.5	7.9	. .	. .	. .	20 43.52	8.41	VI. 4 37.50	31 30.24	13.91	20 51.93	25 27 4.15
81	8	. .	. .	. .	. .	48.1	0.6	. .	. .	. .	21 36.29	8.37	VII. 7 40.86	9 13.69	13.78	21 44.66	25 4 47.47 z.
82	9.10	. .	. .	. .	48.1	0.8	. .	. .	. .	. .	22 48.46	8.36	VI. 7 39.25	10 9.54	13.61	22 56.82	25 5 43.15
83	6.7	. .	. .	33.5	46.0	57.7	10.0	22.2	. .	. .	23 45.79	8.36	VII. 6 33.35	19 23.92	13.47	23 54.15	25 14 57.39 z.
84	8.9	. .	18.3	30.7	42.7	55.5	. .	. .	. .	. .	25 42.93	8.37	" 2 46.18	41 11.81	13.18	25 51.30	25 36 44.99 z.
85	9.10	54.0	6.5	18.5	. .	. .	. .	. .	. .	. .	28 30.63	8.32	2. 5 41.775	23 15.09	12.76	28 38.95	25 18 47.85
86	7.8	. .	. .	. .	49.8	2.0	13.8	. .	. .	. .	28 49.80	8.30	VII. 7 36.61	11 40.44	12.71	28 58.10	25 7 13.15 z.
87	7.8	. .	49.2	1.6	13.2	25.5	. .	. .	. .	. .	30 13.44	8.29	VI. 7 36.64	11 39.64	12.51	30 21.73	25 7 12.15 z.
88	8.9	. .	. .	14.3	26.5	39.0	50.5	. .	. .	. .	31 26.54	8.30	VII. 5 36.60	26 13.97	12.33	31 34.84	25 21 46.30
89	7	. .	37.5	49.5	1.7	13.8	26.0	. .	. .	. .	33 1.75	8.31	IV. 1 38.96	51 12.88	12.11	33 10.06	25 46 44.99 z.
90	7.8	. .	. .	. .	. .	. .	. .	. .	. .	22.5	33 15.69	8.28	II. 5 39.97	24 17.14	12.07	33 23.97	25 19 49.21 z.
91	7	. .	24.5	36.5	49.0	0.8	13.2	. .	. .	. .	35 48.83	8.27	VI. 3 33.23	39 54.09	11.70	35 57.10	25 35 25.79 z.
92	7.8	. .	6.5	18.2	30.5	. .	. .	. .	. .	. .	37 30.56	8.24	IV. 3 42.32	34 40.31	11.46	37 38.80	25 30 11.77
93	7.8	. .	. .	. .	16.5	28.2	40.8	53.0	. .	. .	38 16.38	8.26	VII. 1 41.40	49 48.30	11.35	38 24.64	25 45 19.65 z.
94	8.9	. .	42.0	54.0	6.0	18.0	30.0	42.3	. .	. .	40 6.01	8.19	" 6 43.26	13 41.74	11.10	40 14.20	25 9 12.84 z.
95	9	. .	25.9	37.3	49.5	. .	. .	. .	. .	. .	46 49.78	8.17	2. 1 44.97	47 44.79	10.22	46 57.95	25 43 15.01 z.
96	8	. .	22.0	34.0	46.0	58.0	. .	. .	. .	. .	50 46.13	8.08	1. 6 39.33	15 53.51	9.72	50 54.21	25 11 23.23
97	9	. .	. .	. .	. .	. .	17.2	29.2	. .	. .	50 52.82	8.10	2. 5 37.49	25 43.08	9.71	51 0.92	25 21 12.79
98	9	. .	. .	. .	. .	. .	4.0	16.0	. .	. .	51 39.58	8.10	VII. 3 40.31	35 49.37	9.61	51 47.68	25 31 18.98
99	7.8	. .	. .	. .	. .	47.0	59.0	. .	. .	. .	53 34.78	8.10	" 1 44.44	48 3.33	9.38	53 42.88	25 43 32.71
100	7.8	. .	. .	. .	. .	. .	. .	. .	57.8	10.3	54 3.32	8.08	II. 2 49.26	39 24.97	9.32	54 11.40	25 34 54.29 z.
101	8	. .	. .	1.8	13.6	26.0	. .	. .	. .	. .	55 13.86	8.07	VII. 3 38.46	36 53.26	9.18	55 21.93	25 32 22.44 z.
102	7	. .	. .	51.2	3.2	15.0	. .	40.0	. .	. .	59 3.33	8.00	2. 7 36.57	11 41.60	8.72	59 11.33	25 7 10.32
103	8	. .	46.0	. .	. .	22.0	34.0	46.2	. .	. .	59 9.93	8.00	I. 6 34.30	18 51.12	8.71	59 17.93	25 14 19.83
104	7.8	44.5	57.0	9.2	21.0	33.0	45.3	57.1	. .	. .	22 2 21.04	7.99	1. 4 37.81	31 18.77	8.35	22 2 29.03	25 26 47.12 z.
105	8	53.0	5.1	17.0	29.5	41.2	53.8	5.8	. .	. .	5 29.37	7.95	2. 5 36.36	26 22.09	8.01	5 37.32	25 21 50.10 z.
106	8	. .	. .	36.0	48.2	0.2	12.5	. .	. .	. .	6 48.17	7.96	VI. 1 43.96	48 20.12	7.86	6 56.13	25 43 47.98 z.
107	9	. .	48.0	. .	12.0	. .	. .	. .	. .	. .	14 12.11	7.87	2. 4 37.96	31 13.88	7.09	14 19.98	25 26 40.97 z.
108	5	. .	36.8	49.0	0.9	13.2	25.0	37.4	. .	. .	15 1.00	7.87	III. 3 40.80	35 32.79	7.00	15 8.87	25 30 59.79 z.
109	9.10	. .	48.0	0.1	12.2	. .	. .	. .	. .	. .	17 12.25	7.84	VI. 3 44.12	33 38.04	6.78	17 20.09	25 29 4.82 z.
110	9	. .	. .	. .	. .	. .	. .	20.5	38.0	50.2	18 43.77	7.81	II. 6 38.34	16 31.14	6.63	18 51.58	25 11 57.77
111	8	. .	. .	. .	. .	28.0	40.2	52.3	. .	. .	24 15.91	7.76	VII. 4 44.26	27 36.57	6.13	24 23.67	25 23 2.70 z.
112	8	. .	. .	. .	. .	. .	10.3	22.2	. .	. .	25 46.02	7.72	" 7 38.55	10 33.44	5.99	25 53.74	25 5 59.43 z.
113	9.10	. .	. .	20.3	. .	44.5	56.5	. .	. .	. .	27 32.38	7.75	" 2 33.65	48 24.44	5.84	27 40.13	25 43 50.28
114	9	. .	. .	. .	35.5	47.5	59.6	12.0	. .	. .	29 35.38	7.74	" 1 38.50	51 28.41	5.65	29 43.12	25 46 54.06 z.
115	8.9	. .	. .	33.0	45.0	57.0	9.0	21.4	. .	. .	32 45.05	7.65	" 7 47.10	5 38.24	5.40	32 52.70	25 1 3.64 z.
116	8.9	. .	43.2	55.0	7.2	19.5	31.5	43.5	. .	. .	35 7.29	7.64	2. 6 42.11	14 21.25	5.22	35 14.93	25 9 46.47 z.
117	8	. .	17.5	29.6	41.8	34.0	6.0	18.2	. .	. .	40 41.80	7.61	II. 2 35.13	47 33.54	4.79	40 49.41	25 42 58.33
118	8.9	37.0	49.5	1.7	13.4	25.7	37.8	. .	. .	. .	44 13.62	7.56	2. 5 36.79	26 7.21	4.56	44 21.18	25 21 31.77 z.
119	7	25.0	37.2	49.3	1.4	13.5	25.6	38.0	. .	. .	46 1.48	7.57	II. 1 38.85	51 16.58	4.43	46 9.05	25 46 41.01 z.
120	9	. .	. .	37.5	50.0	2.0	14.3	26.5	. .	. .	49 49.92	7.53	VII. 1 36.54	52 36.09	4.18	49 57.45	25 48 0.27
121	9	. .	27.8	. .	52.0	. .	. .	. .	. .	. .	51 51.98	7.49	IV. 5 38.32	25 14.96	4.07	51 59.47	25 20 39.03
122	8.9	. .	. .	. .	40.0	51.7	4.0	16.0	. .	. .	52 39.70	7.48	VII. 4 35.91	32 24.89	4.02	52 47.18	25 27 48.91 z.
123	6	. .	40.0	51.7	3.9	15.5	28.0	. .	. .	. .	56 3.84	7.44	2. 6 42.75	12 59.13	3.84	56 11.28	25 8 22.97
124	9.10	. .	. .	. .	. .	. .	43.1	55.0	. .	. .	57 18.80	7.43	VII. 7 37.05	11 25.25	3.77	57 26.23	25 6 49.02 z.
125	8.9	36.5	48.5	1.1	13.0	25.0	37.0	49.4	. .	. .	23 2 12.97	7.37	" 7 42.40	8 20.55	3.53	23 2 20.34	25 3 44.08 z.
126	7	35.0	46.5	59.0	11.1	23.1	35.4	47.4	. .	. .	7 11.12	7.33	I. 7 40.23	9 35.46	3.31	7 18.45	25 4 58.77
127	8.9	. .	. .	. .	29.0	41.0	53.1	5.2	. .	. .	8 28.86	7.33	VII. 4 41.50	29 11.88	3.25	8 36.19	25 24 35.13
128	8.9	. .	. .	. .	51.5	3.3	. .	. .	. .	. .	23 9 51.38	7.31	VI. 4 38.35	31 9.88	3.20	23 9 58.69	25 26 24.08 z.

Number.	Magnitude.	SECONDS OF TRANSITS.									T.	a.	MICROMETER.	D.	d.	Mean Right Ascension. 1850.0.	Mean South Declination, 1850.0.
		I.	II.	III.	IV.	V.	VI.	VII.	10.	11.							
Zone LXVIII. September 22. M. $D. = 24° 55' 20''.0$. $n'. = -38''.00$. $n''. = -4''.01$. (Continued.)																	
											h. m. s.	s.	r.	′ ″	″	h. m. s.	° ′ ″
129	9	. .	. .	. .	. .	. .	. .	. .	49.5	2.0	23 10 55.03	+ 7.30	11. 4 33.46	−33 49.02	− 3.16	23 11 2.33	25 29 12.18
130	9	. .	. .	. .	. .	. .	. .	. .	55.2	7.2	12 0.77	7.28	11. 7 38.46	10 36.10	3.13	12 8.05	25 5 59.23
131	8.9	. .	53.0	. .	17.0	29.0	41.0	. .	. .	. .	13 16.98	7.28	VII. 2 37.43	46 13.96	3.09	13 24.26	25 41 37.05 z.
132	8.9	. .	. .	. .	. .	26.5	39.0	. .	. .	. .	14 14.68	7.28	VI. 7 41.52	8 51.18	3.05	14 21.96	25 4 14.23 z.
133	8	. .	. .	. .	. .	21.0	33.3	45.0	. .	. .	15 8.83	7.26	VII. 4 39.35	30 26.12	3.02	15 16.09	25 25 49.14
134	8.9	52.4	4.8	16.8	29.0	40.6	53.0	. .	. .	. .	19 28.86	7.22	I. 5 43.40	22 19.20	2.87	19 36.08	25 17 42.07 z.
135	9.10	. .	. .	. .	57.2	9.2	21.5	33.2	. .	. .	20 57.13	7.20	VII. 6 41.325	14 48.56	2.83	21 4.33	25 10 11.39
136	7	. .	. .	. .	. .	. .	2.0	14.4	. .	. .	22 38.00	7.18	" 7 46.57	5 56.56	2.80	22 45.18	25 1 19.36 z.
137	10	. .	. .	. .	. .	. .	. .	. .	59.6	. .	24 5.19	7.18	11. 5 52.01	17 21.40	2.77	24 12.37	25 12 44.17
138	7.8	22.5	34.5	47.0	59.3	11.3	23.4	35.5	. .	. .	25 59.11	7.16	VII. 2 38.11	45 50.45	2.74	26 6.27	25 41 13.19 z.
139	7	16.0	28.0	40.2	52.5	4.7	17.0	29.0	. .	. .	29 52.54	7.13	2. 2 36.27	46 53.78	2.66	29 59.67	25 42 16.44
140	7.8	. .	. .	57.5	. .	21.5	24.0	46.0	. .	. .	36 9.59	7.06	VII. 2 47.77	40 16.89	2.61	36 16.65	25 35 39.50
141	7.8	. .	. .	44.3	. .	8.8	20.8	. .	. .	. .	38 56.65	7.03	2. 6 45.00	12 41.45	2.58	39 3.68	25 8 4.03
142	8	. .	. .	. .	. .	. .	55.0	7.1	. .	. .	39 30.69	7.03	VII. 5 41.83	23 13.40	2.57	39 37.72	25 18 35.97 z.
143	6	12.0	24.2	36.4	48.0	0.6	13.0	25.0	. .	. .	44 48.52	7.00	II. 1 34.45	53 48.51	2.58	44 55.52	25 49 11.09 z.
144	6	. .	. .	. .	. .	. .	. .	. .	22.7	34.5	45 28.22	6.96	11. 7 42.44	8 18.68	2.58	45 35.18	25 3 41.26
145	9.10	. .	. .	. .	. .	35.5	47.8	. .	. .	. .	47 23.60	6.95	VI. 7 42.32	8 23.54	2.59	47 30.55	25 3 46.13
146	8.9	. .	. .	. .	. .	. .	27.4	39.4	. .	. .	48 3.08	6.95	VII. 6 36.61	17 31.33	2.59	48 10.03	25 12 53.92
147	6	. .	. .	. .	. .	. .	. .	. .	33.7	46.0	48 39.12	6.95	11. 3 34.99	38 52.57	2.60	48 46.07	25 34 15.17
148	7.8	. .	. .	. .	. .	53.0	5.0	17.2	. .	. .	50 40.96	6.91	VII. 7 48.57	4 47.47	2.61	50 47.87	25 0 10.08 z.
149	7.8	. .	. .	. .	. .	6.5	18.9	30.9	. .	. .	51 54.48	6.92	" 3 44.71	33 17.40	2.62	52 1.40	25 28 40.02
150	7.8	45.6	58.0	10.0	22.0	. .	. .	. .	. .	. .	55 22.15	6.89	I. 4 40.17	29 57.80	2.66	55 29.04	25 25 20.46 z.
151	9.10	. .	. .	. .	44.7	36.5	9.0	. .	. .	. .	55 44.59	6.88	VII. 3 31.67	40 47.68	2.66	55 51.47	25 36 10.34
152	8	. .	4.0	16.2	28.3	40.5	. .	. .	. .	. .	58 28.34	6.86	2. 5 39.40	24 37.12	2.71	58 35.20	25 19 59.83
153	8	. .	. .	. .	53.0	5.2	17.7	30.0	. .	. .	58 53.26	6.86	VII. 4 37.21	31 40.00	2.72	59 0.12	25 27 2.72 z.
154	9	. .	6.0	18.0	30.0	42.0	. .	. .	. .	. .	0 7 30.10	6.78	2. 5 41.13	23 37.37	2.94	0 7 36.88	25 19 0.31 z.
155	9	. .	. .	. .	50.8	3.0	15.0	27.0	. .	. .	7 50.81	6.78	VII. 6 40.46	15 18.43	2.95	7 57.59	25 10 41.38 z.
156	8.9	. .	3.4	15.1	27.3	39.5	. .	. .	. .	. .	11 27.39	6.75	" 7 40.02	9 42.70	3.07	11 34.14	25 5 5.77 z.
157	9	. .	. .	. .	39.4	51.2	3.5	15.5	. .	. .	12 39.18	6.74	" 3 38.83	36 40.45	3.11	12 45.92	25 32 3.56 z.
158	9.10	. .	. .	13.2	25.3	. .	. .	. .	. .	. .	14 25.37	6.72	IV. 1 39.87	50 41.46	3.18	14 32.09	25 46 4.64
159	7.8	. .	. .	. .	. .	. .	10.5	22.6	. .	. .	14 46.10	6.72	(†) 1 34.45	53 48.61	3.20	14 52.82	25 49 11.81 z.
160	9.10	. .	30.8	42.5	55.0	. .	. .	. .	. .	. .	16 54.94	6.70	IV. 3 35.35	38 40.98	3.28	17 1.64	25 34 4.26 z.
161	7.8	. .	. .	. .	. .	. .	. .	42.7	0.9	12.4	18 6.28	6.69	11. 7 36.66	11 38.22	3.32	18 12.97	25 7 1.54
162	8.9	39.0	51.0	3.2	15.2	27.2	. .	. .	. .	. .	20 15.36	6.67	2. 2 38.89	45 23.30	3.41	20 22.03	25 40 46.71 z.
163	7	. .	49.0	1.0	13.1	25.5	. .	. .	. .	. .	21 13.26	6.66	IV. 4 35.69	32 32.81	3.47	21 19.92	25 27 56.28 z.
164	8.9	. .	. .	. .	. .	. .	. .	14.8	32.7	45.2	21 38.24	6.66	11. 1 41.24	49 53.33	3.49	21 44.90	25 45 16.82 z.
165	7	8.5	20.5	32.6	45.0	. .	. .	. .	. .	. .	24 44.91	6.64	2. 3 45.05	33 5.47	3.67	24 51.55	25 28 29.14 z.
166	9.10	. .	56.0	7.9	20.1	. .	. .	. .	. .	. .	0 25 20.16	6.63	IV. 4 39.51	30 20.95	3.70	0 25 26.79	25 25 44.65 z.
Zone LXIX. September 23. H. $D. = 24° 25' 10''.0$. $n'. = -45''.46$. $n''. = -5''.00$.																	
1	9	. .	. .	. .	. .	. .	. .	14.2	. .	. .	19 29 37.90	8.80	IV. 4 36.861	31 53.37	43.01	19 29 46.70	24 57 46.38
2	9	. .	. .	. .	47.5	. .	11.5	. .	. .	. .	31 47.35	8.81	" 2 36.550	46 45.59	42.47	31 56.16	25 12 38.06
3	9	. .	. .	. .	. .	32.2	44.4	56.5	. .	. .	32 20.16	8.80	" 2 39.570	45 1.31	42.34	32 28.96	25 10 53.65 z.
4	7.8	. .	. .	. .	7.0	19.2	21.5	43.5	. .	. .	33 7.13	8.80	" 2 37.140	46 25.24	42.14	33 15.93	25 12 17.38 z.
5	7.8	. .	. .	. .	. .	. .	48.0	0.4	. .	. .	33 24.01	8.75	" 6 36.345	17 41.92	42.07	33 32.76	24 43 33.99
6	9	. .	. .	. .	29.5	41.6	54.0	6.0	. .	. .	34 29.62	8.77	" 3 36.233	38 11.46	41.80	34 38.39	25 4 3.26 z.
7	9	. .	. .	. .	. .	. .	. .	11.5	. .	. .	34 35.18	8.77	" 3 41.096	35 23.54	41.78	34 43.95	25 1 15.32
8	8.9	34.0	46.4	58.1	10.5	22.2	34.6	46.8	. .	. .	37 10.42	8.77	" 1 43.840	48 25.31	41.14	37 19.19	25 14 16.45
9	9	. .	. .	55.5	7.5	19.6	42.0	. .	. .	. .	38 7.65	8.71	" 5 46.765	20 24.35	40.90	38 16.36	24 46 15.25
10	8	24.5	36.5	48.5	1.0	. .	. .	. .	. .	. .	19 42 0.88	8.73	" 1 39.990	50 38.25	39.94	19 42 9.61	25 16 28.19

† Taken as IV.

Zone LXIX. September 23. H. $D. = -24° 25' 10''.0$. $n. = -45''.46$. $n. = -5''.00$. (Continued.)

Number.	Magnitude.	Seconds of Transits. I.	II.	III.	IV.	V.	VI.	VII.	10.	11.	T.	a.	Micrometer.	D.	d.	Mean Right Ascension, 1850.0.	Mean South Declination, 1850.0.
											h. m. s.	s.	r.	' "	"	h. m. s.	° ' "
11	8.9	. .	. .	. .	11.0	22.8	35.0	47.0	. .	. .	19 42 10.79	+ 8.72	IV. 2 41.032	—44 10.85	—39.90	19 42 19.51	25 10 0.75
12	9	. .	. .	. .	52.5	4.4	16.8	28.5	. .	. .	42 52.44	8.68	" 5 42.095	23 5.62	39.73	43 1.12	24 48 55.35 z.
13	9	. .	. .	. .	53.5	5.5	. .	. .	. .	. .	44 53.83	8.67	" 4 45.238	27 4.14	39.23	45 2.50	24 52 53.37
14	8	23.0	35.2	47.0	. .	. .	. .	. .	. .	. .	44 59.29	8.67	" 4 43.105	28 17.79	39.21	45 7.96	24 54 7.00
15	9	. .	. .	. .	. .	. .	. .	3.0	. .	. .	45 26.86	8.64	" 6 46.692	11 44.64	39.10	45 35.50	24 37 33.74
16	8.9	15.0	27.2	39.2	51.2	. .	. .	. .	. .	. .	47 51.27	8.63	" 6 35.920	17 56.57	38.52	47 59.90	24 43 45.09 z.
17	9	. .	. .	. .	8.8	20.8	33.0	45.0	. .	. .	48 8.73	8.67	" 2 37.340	46 18.35	38.45	48 17.40	25 12 6.80 z.
18	8.9	. .	. .	. .	. .	. .	12.5	24.2	. .	. .	48 48.11	8.63	" 5 40.416	24 3.61	38.28	48 56.74	24 49 51.89 z.
19	9	. .	. .	11.0	24.0	35.4	. .	. .	. .	. .	50 23.53	8.62	" 5 39.041	24 51.08	37.90	50 32.15	24 50 38.98
20	9	. .	15.2	27.2	39.1	51.0	3.2	. .	. .	. .	51 39.15	8.58	" 7 40.033	9 43.68	37.60	51 47.73	24 35 31.28 z.
21	9	16.8	29.0	41.0	53.3	. .	17.2	. .	. .	. .	54 53.14	8.58	" 5 36.910	26 4.64	36.83	55 1.72	24 51 51.47
22	9	20.5	33.0	45.0	57.0	. .	. .	33.0	. .	. .	57 57.02	8.59	" 2 37.392	46 16.55	36.11	58 5.61	25 12 2.66
23	9	35.0	47.2	. .	12.0	24.0	36.0	48.0	. .	. .	59 11.72	8.56	" 3 41.160	35 21.33	35.81	59 20.28	25 1 7.14 z.
24	8	45.2	57.2	9.2	21.5	. .	. .	. .	. .	. .	20 2 21.38	8.50	" 6 42.433	14 11.72	35.08	20 2 29.88	24 39 56.80 z.
25	9	. .	. .	41.5	53.2	5.3	17.5	29.5	. .	. .	2 53.37	8.50	" 6 36.818	16 16.59	34.95	3 1.87	24 42 1.54
26	8	. .	. .	. .	. .	50.5	3.0	14.5	. .	. .	3 38.45	8.54	" 1 42.511	49 11.18	34.77	3 46.99	25 14 55.95 z.
27	8	. .	. .	. .	. .	. .	. .	35.5	. .	. .	3 59.12	8.55	" 1 35.916	53 58.92	34.70	4 7.67	25 18 43.62 z.
28	9	53.0	5.2	17.2	29.5	41.0	53.2	5.2	. .	. .	6 29.22	8.46	" 6 46.310	11 57.85	34.12	6 37.68	24 37 41.97
29	8.9	24.0	36.0	48.0	. .	. .	. .	. .	. .	. .	9 0.21	8.45	" 5 40.364	24 5.41	33.53	9 8.66	24 49 48.94 z.
30	8.9	. .	. .	. .	0.5	12.5	25.0	37.0	. .	. .	9 0.67	8.44	" 6 35.835	17 59.49	33.53	9 9.11	24 43 43.02 z.
31	8.9	. .	8.5	20.2	32.5	44.5	56.6	. .	. .	. .	10 32.50	8.48	" 2 34.690	47 49.81	33.18	10 40.98	25 13 32.99
32	9	. .	10.0	22.0	34.0	. .	58.0	. .	. .	. .	11 34.05	8.47	" 1 41.335	49 51.81	32.95	11 42.52	25 15 34.76
33	8	. .	13.8	25.5	38.0	50.0	2.0	14.0	. .	. .	11 37.86	8.47	" 1 40.605	50 16.99	32.94	11 46.33	25 15 59.93
34	9	. .	. .	. .	. .	. .	. .	44.0	. .	. .	12 7.76	8.42	" 5 43.690	22 10.52	32.82	12 16.18	24 47 53.34 z.
35	9	28.0	40.2	52.1	4.2	16.2	28.2	. .	. .	. .	14 4.24	8.42	" 4 34.928	33 0.11	32.38	14 12.66	24 58 42.49
36	9	. .	. .	. .	49.0	1.0	13.3	25.2	. .	. .	14 49.08	8.38	" 6 45.003	12 42.97	32.20	14 57.46	24 38 25.17 z.
37	9	. .	. .	. .	. .	. .	56.0	. .	. .	. .	15 31.73	8.41	" 3 41.010	35 26.50	32.05	15 40.14	25 1 8.55
38	9	. .	. .	. .	40.5	. .	. .	17.0	. .	. .	15 40.57	8.41	" 3 40.541	35 42.68	32.01	15 48.98	25 1 24.69 z.
39	9	24.4	36.6	49.0	0.8	. .	. .	. .	. .	. .	18 0.92	8.40	" 2 46.370	41 6.55	31.48	18 9.32	25 6 48.03 z.
40	8	. .	. .	. .	12.0	24.0	36.2	48.2	. .	. .	18 11.99	8.37	" 5 39.262	24 43.45	31.44	18 20.36	24 50 24.89 z.
41	7	. .	. .	13.6	25.8	37.5	50.0	2.0	. .	. .	19 25.77	8.35	" 6 43.955	13 19.14	31.15	19 34.12	24 29 0.29
42	9	. .	. .	44.0	56.0	. .	. .	. .	. .	. .	22 57.05	8.30	" 7 42.854	8 6.28	30.39	23 5.35	24 33 46.67
43	8	. .	. .	. .	12.5	25.0	37.0	. .	. .	. .	23 12.83	8.30	" 7 42.188	8 29.28	30.33	23 21.13	24 34 9.61 z.
44	9	10.2	22.5	34.5	46.2	59.0	10.8	22.6	. .	. .	24 46.56	8.33	" 2 49.755	39 9.64	29.99	24 54.89	25 4 49.63
45	7.8	10.5	22.5	35.0	46.8	58.8	. .	. .	. .	. .	26 46.86	8.30	" 4 44.488	27 30.05	29.45	26 55.16	24 53 9.50 z.
46	9	. .	8.2	. .	32.5	44.2	37.0	. .	. .	. .	27 32.45	8.27	" 6 37.782	16 52.27	29.39	27 40.72	24 42 31.66
47	8.9	. .	14.5	27.0	38.6	51.0	. .	. .	. .	. .	28 38.85	8.28	" 4 43.090	28 18.31	29.14	28 47.13	24 53 57.45
48	7.8	. .	. .	51.0	3.5	15.0	27.2	39.5	. .	. .	29 3.21	8.26	" 6 33.710	19 12.85	29.06	29 11.47	24 44 51.91
49	9	. .	. .	. .	. .	12.0	24.2	36.0	. .	. .	30 0.03	8.24	" 7 39.065	10 17.10	28.85	30 8.27	24 35 55.95
50	7.8	. .	. .	8.2	20.2	32.1	44.2	36.3	. .	. .	20 31 20.17	8.23	" 7 35.640	12 15.39	28.57	20 31 28.40	24 37 53.96 z.

CORRECTIONS.

	Cor. to Clock.	Hourly Cor.	m.	n.	c.	Zenith Point.	Coinc.
	s.	s.	s.	s.	s.	° ' "	r.
Sept. 23, at 20h.	—1.535	—0.011	—0.415	+0.429	+0.022	0 0 3.73	40.105

INSTRUMENT READINGS.

	h.	Circle. A.	B.	C.	D.	Mean.	Bar.	Thermom. At.	Ex.
		° ' "	"	"	"	"	I.	°	°
Zone LXIX.—Sept. 23,	19.5	296 12 3.2	5.3	17.2	5.0	7.68	30.134	71.4	67.3
	19 9	. . . .	. .	. .	. .	. .	30.140	71.2	66.5
	20.0	. . . .	. .	. .	. .	. .	. .	. .	65.7
	21.0	. . . .	. .	. .	. .	. .	. .	. .	64.7
	21.7	. . . .	. .	. .	. .	. .	30.138	69.0	63.4
	22.1	. . . .	. .	. .	. .	. .	. .	. .	63.1
	22.5	. . . .	. .	. .	. .	. .	30.136	68.3	63.0
	23.5	. . . .	. .	. .	. .	. .	30.142	67.8	62.0
	0.0	5.0	7.3	18.1	6.5	9.22	30.140	67.5	61.9
	1.5	. . . .	. .	. .	. .	. .	. .	. .	61.2

Number.	Magnitude.	SECONDS OF TRANSITS. I.	II.	III.	IV.	V.	VI.	VII.	10.	11.	T.	a.	MICROMETER.	D.	d.	Mean Right Ascension, 1850.0.	Mean South Declination, 1850.0.
		Zone LXIX.	September 23.	H.	$D.=24°\ 25'\ 10''.0.$		$n.=-45''.46.$		$n.=-5''.00.$	(Continued.)							
											h. m. s.	s.	r.	′ ″	″	h. m. s.	° ′ ″
51	7	. .	. .	. .	. .	16.0	29.0	41.0	. .	. .	20 32 4.50	+ 8.25	VII. 4 39.570	—30 19.49	—28.41	20 32 12.75	24 55 57.90
52	8.9	56.2	8.2	20.3	32.5	44.1	56.6	8.4	. .	. .	34 32.38	8.26	IV. 1 44.660	47 56.98	27.89	34 40.64	25 13 34.87 z.
53	9	. .	23.8	35.5	48.0	59.5	11.5	. .	. .	. .	36 47.68	8.22	" 3 40.255	35 52.59	27.41	36 55.90	25 1 30.00
54	9	39.5	. .	3.4	16.0	28.0	39.5	32.1	. .	. .	38 15.76	8.20	" 3 40.910	35 29.95	27.10	38 23.96	25 1 7.05
55	8	. .	. .	6.0	18.0	29.5	. .	. .	. .	. .	40 17.91	8.15	" 7 38.072	10 51.39	26.67	40 26.06	24 36 28.06
56	7	. .	33.3	45.1	57.2	9.2	21.5	. .	. .	. .	43 57.27	8.13	" 5 46.020	20 50.08	25.92	44 5.40	24 46 26.00 z.
57	8.9	27.5	39.8	51.5	4.0	15.5	28.0	39.8	. .	. .	45 3.75	8.12	" 5 38.850	24 57.66	25.70	45 11.87	24 50 33.36 z.
58	8.9	. .	58.0	9.6	22.0	34.0	46.0	. .	. .	. .	46 21.93	8.11	" 5 43.176	22 28.30	25.43	46 30.04	24 48 3.73
59	9	. .	43.0	55.0	7.0	19.0	. .	. .	. .	. .	48 7.06	8.09	" 5 46.811	20 22.77	25.07	48 15.15	24 45 57.84 z.
60	9	. .	. .	30.5	43.0	55.0	. .	. .	. .	. .	48 42.90	8.10	" 3 36.342	38 7.71	24.95	48 51.00	25 3 42.66 z.
61	9	. .	. .	. .	. .	9.5	26.5	33.2	. .	. .	48 57.20	8.11	VI. 2 43.554	42 43.65	24.89	49 5.31	25 8 18.54 z.
62	9	57.5	10.0	22.0	33.5	46.0	58.2	10.2	. .	. .	53 33.96	8.07	IV. 2 36.130	47 0.11	23.98	53 42.03	25 12 34.09
63	7	17.5	29.6	41.4	53.5	5.5	18.0	29.5	. .	. .	54 53.60	8.03	" 4 41.717	29 5.70	23.72	55 1.63	24 54 39.42 z.
64	9	30.5	42.0	54.8	6.5	18.2	31.0	43.0	. .	. .	57 6.60	8.00	" 5 44.450	21 44.33	23.29	57 14.60	24 47 17.62 z.
65	9	. .	. .	. .	58.0	10.0	22.3	34.1	. .	. .	57 57.93	8.03	VI. 1 42.202	49 21.78	23.12	58 5.96	25 14 54.90 z.
66	6.7	3.0	15.2	27.0	39.5	51.5	3.5	15.5	. .	. .	59 39.34	7.98	IV. 5 42.650	22 46.44	22.78	59 47.32	24 48 19.22 z.
67	9	22.6	34.5	46.4	58.8	10.5	23.2	35.0	. .	. .	21 0 59.74	7.98	" 3 42.120	34 48.18	22.53	21 1 7.72	25 0 20.71
68	7	35.5	47.1	59.1	11.0	23.0	35.2	47.1	. .	. .	3 11.17	7.94	" 6 35.150	18 23.16	22.12	3 19.11	24 43 55.28 z.
69	9	. .	20.0	. .	44.2	56.0	8.2	20.3	. .	. .	8 44.09	7.88	V. 6 43.370	13 39.32	21.08	8 51.97	24 39 10.40 z.
70	9	41.6	54.0	6.0	18.0	30.0	42.0	. .	. .	. .	13 18.01	7.85	IV. 5 36.832	26 7.34	20.25	13 25.86	24 51 37.59
71	9	. .	. .	48.0	0.6	12.3	25.0	. .	. .	. .	14 0.41	7.87	" 2 37.348	46 18.06	20.13	14 8.28	25 11 48.19
72	6	55.0	7.4	19.5	32.0	44.0	56.1	8.2	. .	. .	15 31.76	7.85	" 3 36.252	38 10.81	19.86	15 39.61	25 3 40.67 z.
73	9	. .	. .	21.5	33.3	45.0	. .	. .	. .	. .	16 33.34	7.80	" 6 38.159	16 39.26	19.67	16 41.14	24 42 8.93
74	7	. .	. .	8.0	20.0	32.0	. .	. .	. .	. .	17 20.06	7.83	" 2 44.502	42 11.01	19.53	17 27.89	25 7 40.54 z.
75	9	. .	. .	. .	. .	. .	. .	56.8	. .	. .	17 20.48	7.82	" 3 40.470	35 45.17	19.53	17 28.30	25 1 14.70 z.
76	9	. .	. .	. .	. .	. .	55.5	. .	. .	38.2	17 31.27	7.83	" 2 44.822	41 59.98	19.50	17 39.10	25 7 29.48 z.
77	9	28.5	40.0	52.5	4.6	16.6	29.0	. .	. .	. .	20 4.59	7.76	" 7 45.295	6 42.02	19.05	20 12.35	24 32 11.07
78	9	0.4	13.0	25.0	37.0	48.8	1.2	13.0	. .	. .	21 36.95	7.79	" 3 34.161	39 23.00	18.78	21 44.74	25 4 51.78 z.
79	9	. .	. .	37.0	49.2	1.5	13.5	. .	. .	. .	22 49.29	7.77	" 3 32.440	40 22.44	18.57	22 57.06	25 5 51.01
80	7.8	. .	. .	34.0	. .	58.1	10.5	22.5	. .	. .	23 46.17	7.78	" 1 41.990	49 29.19	18.41	23 53.95	25 14 57.60 z.
81	9	. .	. .	. .	. .	. .	. .	28.0	. .	. .	23 51.75	7.74	" 5 42.290	22 58.89	18.39	23 59.49	24 48 27.28 z.
82	9	. .	. .	. .	18.0	30.2	43.0	55.0	. .	. .	25 18.39	7.76	" 2 40.710	44 21.61	18.14	25 26.15	25 9 49.75
83	7.8	13.5	26.0	37.8	50.0	2.1	14.5	26.0	. .	. .	28 50.03	7.72	" 2 45.180	41 47.63	17.52	28 57.75	25 7 15.15 z.
84	7.8	37.2	50.0	1.8	14.0	26.0	37.8	50.0	. .	. .	30 13.87	7.70	" 2 45.145	41 48.84	17.29	30 21.57	25 7 16.13 z.
85	9	23.0	35.5	47.2	59.1	11.2	. .	. .	. .	. .	31 59.31	7.65	" 7 40.336	9 33.22	17.01	32 6.96	24 35 0.23 z.
86	9	. .	. .	. .	27.0	39.0	51.2	3.0	. .	. .	32 26.89	7.68	" 3 31.371	40 59.34	16.94	32 34.57	25 6 26.28
87	7.8	2.6	15.0	26.6	39.0	51.0	3.4	15.0	. .	. .	34 38.97	7.64	V. 5 40.629	23 56.19	16.60	34 46.61	24 49 22.79 z.
88	9	. .	. .	. .	. .	. .	45.0	57.0	. .	. .	35 20.68	7.66	IV. 2 36.668	46 41.51	16.49	35 28.34	25 12 8.00
89	8.	54.4	6.8	18.5	30.8	. .	. .	. .	. .	. .	38 30.75	7.59	" 6 33.240	19 29.11	15.99	38 38.34	24 44 55.10
90	9	. .	42.5	54.2	6.5	19.0	30.6	43.0	. .	. .	40 6.61	7.61	" 2 41.460	43 56.09	15.75	40 14.22	25 9 21.84 z.
91	9	6.5	18.6	30.8	43.0	54.5	7.0	19.0	. .	. .	44 42.80	7.53	" 5 47.171	20 10.36	15.06	44 50.33	24 45 35.42 z.
92	8.9	30.0	42.2	54.0	6.0	18.0	30.5	. .	. .	. .	48 6.18	7.49	V. 6 36.568	17 34.14	14.55	48 13.67	24 42 58.69 z.
93	8.9	0.2	12.4	24.0	36.5	. .	. .	. .	. .	. .	50 36.37	7.46	IV. 7 38.133	10 49.28	14.19	50 43.83	24 36 13.47 z.
94	7.8	. .	. .	. .	42.0	54.0	6.0	18.0	. .	. .	50 41.98	7.46	V. 7 44.170	7 20.81	14.17	50 49.44	24 32 44.98 z.
95	9	. .	. .	. .	. .	. .	. .	. .	41.0	53.2	50 46.61	7.50	IV. 2 37.671	46 6.89	14.16	50 54.11	25 11 31.05
96	9	59.8	11.4	23.8	36.0	47.6	. .	12.0	. .	. .	56 35.84	7.42	" 4 39.054	30 37.67	13.35	56 43.26	24 56 1.02 z.
97	8	27.2	39.6	52.0	4.0	. .	. .	. .	. .	. .	59 3.92	7.42	" 2 44.072	42 25.89	13.00	59 11.34	25 7 48.89
98	8	. .	. .	. .	. .	22.6	34.8	46.8	. .	. .	59 10.52	7.42	" 1 42.411	49 14.67	12.99	59 17.94	25 14 37.66
99	9	. .	. .	. .	. .	. .	. .	. .	0.2	14.2	59 7.86	7.38	" 6 40.780	15 8.76	12.99	59 15.24	24 40 31.75 z.
100	9	. .	44.2	56.4	8.5	20.2	33.0	. .	. .	. .	22 2 8.47	7.36	" 5 47.095	20 12.97	12.59	22 2 15.83	24 45 35.56 z.
101	9	56.8	9.2	21.2	33.1	. .	57.6	. .	. .	. .	4 33.25	7.33	" 6 42.000	14 26.65	12.28	4 40.58	24 39 48.93
102	9	. .	. .	3.5	16.0	27.8	40.0	52.0	. .	. .	6 15.83	7.31	" 5 48.613	19 20.53	12.06	6 23.14	24 44 42.59 z.
103	9	. .	3.3	. .	27.2	. .	51.3	. .	. .	. .	22 8 27.27	7.33	" 1 40.360	50 25.49	11.77	22 8 34.60	25 15 47.26

Zone LXIX. September 23. H. $D. = -24° 25' 10''.0$. $n' = -45''.46$. $n'' = -5''.00$. (Continued.)

Number.	Magnitude.	SECONDS OF TRANSITS. I.	II.	III.	IV.	V.	VI.	VII.	10.	11.	T.	a.	MICROMETER.	D.	d.	Mean Right Ascension, 1850.0.	Mean South Declination, 1850.0.
											h. m. s.	s.	r.	' "	"	h. m. s.	° ' "
104	9	23.0	35.1	47.0	59.1	. .	. .	. .	. .	. .	22 10 59.13	+ 7.26	IV. 7 43.420	− 7 46.76	−11.45	22 11 6.39	24 33 8.21 z.
105	9	. .	. .	. .	. .	12.5	25.1	37.0	. .	. .	11 0.82	7.26	" 7 37.235	11 20.29	11.45	11 8.08	24 36 41.74
106	9	. .	. .	. .	. .	. .	. .	. .	17.0	29.2	11 21.71	7.27	" 5 38.898	24 56.00	11.41	11 28.98	24 50 17.41 z.
107	9	. .	20.5	32.1	44.2	56.1	8.5	. .	. .	. .	17 44.40	7.23	" 2 36.556	46 45.37	10.63	17 51.63	25 12 6.00 z.
108	9	. .	. .	. .	. .	. .	17.0	29.0	. .	. .	18 52.87	7.18	" 7 34.362	12 59.49	10.49	19 0.05	24 38 19.98
109	7.8	. .	. .	19.5	31.5	43.5	56.0	7.5	. .	. .	20 31.53	7.18	" 4 42.950	28 23.14	10.30	20 38.71	24 53 43.44 z.
110	8.9	. .	. .	. .	28.5	40.0	52.2	4.2	. .	. .	21 28.21	7.15	" 6 46.593	11 48.06	10.20	21 35.36	24 37 8.26 z.
111	8.9	. .	. .	12.2	24.0	36.2	48.6	. .	. .	. .	22 24.23	7.16	" 4 38.850	30 44.71	10.10	22 31.39	24 56 4.81 z.
112	8.9	9.8	22.2	34.4	46.5	58.4	10.5	23.0	. .	. .	25 46.44	7.14	" 2 47.090	40 41.69	9.75	25 53.58	25 6 1.44 z.
113	5.6	37.0	49.2	1.2	13.5	25.2	. .	. .	. .	. .	26 13.34	7.12	" 5 46.550	20 31.77	9.70	26 20.46	24 45 51.47
114	9	. .	. .	. .	46.0	58.0	10.0	22.0	. .	. .	27 45.91	7.10	" 5 45.532	21 6.92	9.53	27 53.01	24 46 26.45 z.
115	9	9.5	21.2	33.6	45.4	57.5	9.5	12.2	. .	. .	32 45.56	7.07	" 3 40.300	35 51.04	9.02	32 52.63	25 1 10.06 z.
116	9	52.5	4.1	16.2	28.2	. .	. .	. .	. .	. .	33 28.50	7.07	" 1 41.526	49 45.18	8.94	33 35.57	25 15 4.12
117	9	. .	43.8	55.8	7.6	19.6	32.0	. .	. .	. .	35 7.80	7.05	" 2 40.320	44 35.45	8.78	35 14.85	25 9 54.23 z.
118	9	. .	. .	54.2	6.2	18.2	30.5	. .	. .	. .	36 6.32	7.00	" 7 43.570	7 41.54	8.68	36 13.32	24 33 0.22 z.
119	9	56.0	8.0	19.8	32.1	44.0	56.2	8.1	. .	. .	39 32.05	7.00	" 4 41.290	29 20.48	8.34	39 39.05	24 54 38.82 z.
120	6.7	25.0	37.0	49.1	1.2	13.4	25.0	37.5	. .	. .	43 1.22	6.94	" 7 42.610	8 14.70	8.03	43 8.16	24 33 32.73 z.
121	9	31.5	44.0	55.5	8.0	. .	. .	. .	. .	. .	45 7.87	6.93	" 6 35.591	18 7.91	7.85	45 14.80	24 43 25.76 z.
122	9	. .	. .	. .	. .	32.0	44.0	56.2	. .	. .	45 19.89	6.94	" 4 35.760	32 31.39	7.83	45 26.83	24 57 49.22 z.
123	9	19.0	31.0	43.2	55.0	7.2	19.5	. .	. .	. .	46 55.22	6.92	" 5 46.340	20 39.06	7.70	47 2.14	24 45 56.76 z.
124	9	. .	35.5	47.4	39.2	11.5	24.0	. .	. .	. .	47 59.53	6.91	" 4 37.274	31 39.13	7.60	48 6.44	24 56 56.73 z.
125	9	. .	. .	. .	. .	. .	. .	. .	55.0	7.2	48 0.92	6.90	" 6 43.420	13 37.64	7.60	48 7.82	24 38 55.24 z.
126	9	. .	. .	. .	. .	. .	29.0	40.8	. .	. .	49 4.77	6.89	" 6 44.418	13 3.18	7.51	49 11.66	25 38 20.69 z.
127	9	46.2	58.5	10.5	22.8	34.5	47.0	. .	. .	. .	51 22.66	6.88	" 4 42.403	28 42.04	7.33	51 29.54	24 53 59.37 z.
128	9	. .	33.6	45.5	37.2	9.4	. .	. .	. .	. .	55 57.47	6.81	" 7 39.030	10 18.31	6.98	56 4.28	24 35 35.29 z.
129	9	. .	. .	37.5	49.6	2.0	. .	. .	. .	. .	56 49.77	6.82	" 6 43.330	13 40.74	6.92	56 56.59	24 38 57.66 z.
130	8	. .	. .	. .	. .	14.8	28.2	40.0	. .	. .	57 3.46	6.83	" 2 40.950	44 13.68	6.90	57 10.29	25 9 30.58
131	9	. .	. .	. .	. .	. .	. .	53.5	. .	. .	57 17.16	6.83	" 2 45.451	41 38.29	6.88	57 23.99	25 6 55.17
132	5	. .	. .	. .	30.2	41.5	54.0	6.0	. .	. .	58 29.91	6.79	" 7 43.298	7 50.96	6.79	58 36.70	24 33 7.75 z.
133	9	23.3	35.5	47.1	59.2	. .	. .	35.5	. .	. .	23 0 59.38	6.77	" 5 46.970	20 17.29	6.62	23 1 6.15	24 45 33.91
134	9	. .	. .	. .	. .	. .	. .	49.5	. .	. .	2 13.17	6.77	" 3 35.595	38 33.46	6.54	2 19.94	25 3 50.00 z
135	9	45.0	57.2	9.2	21.0	. .	. .	. .	. .	. .	4 21.20	6.75	" 6 44.040	13 16.21	6.41	4 27.95	24 38 32.62
136	9	. .	. .	43.0	55.0	7.0	19.1	31.2	. .	. .	4 54.98	6.74	" 4 40.261	29 55.99	6.37	5 1.72	24 55 12.36 z.
137	9	2.5	15.4	27.0	39.0	51.0	3.6	. .	. .	. .	6 39.15	6.73	" 6 43.430	13 37.29	6.27	6 45.88	24 38 53.56 z.
138	9	23.1	35.1	47.0	59.6	11.5	23.5	35.5	. .	. .	8 59.35	6.71	" 5 43.310	22 23.67	6.12	9 5.06	24 47 39.79 z.
139	9	. .	. .	. .	1.5	13.6	25.8	37.4	. .	. .	11 1.42	6.68	" 2 46.911	40 47.85	6.01	11 8.10	25 6 3.86 z.
140	9	3.0	15.0	27.1	39.5	51.0	. .	. .	. .	. .	13 39.25	6.66	" 4 47.381	25 50.15	5.86	13 45.91	24 51 6.01
141	9	. .	. .	3.0	15.1	27.2	39.6	51.8	. .	. .	14 15.26	6.65	" 3 34.755	39 2.47	5.83	14 21.91	25 4 18.30 z.
142	9	. .	5.0	16.9	29.0	41.2	53.5	. .	. .	. .	18 28.17	6.61	" 1 36.593	52 35.54	5.60	18 34.78	25 17 51.14
143	9	. .	33.5	45.5	37.5	. .	. .	. .	. .	. .	20 57.65	6.59	" 2 39.520	45 3.08	5.48	21 4.24	25 10 18.56
144	8	. .	. .	12.0	24.0	36.0	48.1	0.4	. .	. .	21 24.04	6.58	V. 5 35.978	26 36.80	5.46	21 30.62	24 51 52.26 z.
145	8	. .	. .	26.2	38.1	50.4	2.4	. .	. .	. .	22 38.25	6.57	IV. 3 39.700	36 11.72	5.42	22 44.82	25 1 27.14 z.
146	9	. .	. .	. .	. .	18.5	30.5	42.2	. .	. .	30 6.32	6.50	" 6 38.660	16 21.95	5.13	30 12.82	24 41 37.08
147	9	. .	. .	. .	11.0	24.0	36.2	48.2	. .	. .	31 11.85	6.49	" 4 42.103	28 52.39	5.10	31 18.34	24 54 7.49
148	7	33.5	46.0	57.8	10.0	22.0	. .	. .	. .	. .	35 10.02	6.45	" 3 43.182	34 11.53	4.97	35 16.47	24 59 26.50
149	9	. .	. .	. .	31.0	43.0	37.0	9.5	. .	. .	35 32.05	6.45	" 6 36.812	17 25.76	4.96	35 38.50	24 42 40.72
150	9	2.0	. .	26.2	38.4	. .	. .	. .	. .	. .	38 38.36	6.42	" 6 38.216	16 37.30	4.86	38 44.78	24 41 52.16
151	9	. .	. .	. .	57.0	9.0	21.0	33.2	. .	. .	38 56.89	6.42	" 2 44.232	42 20.36	4.85	39 3.31	25 7 35.21 z.
152	9	28.5	40.2	52.5	4.5	16.3	29.0	41.0	. .	. .	42 4.60	6.39	" 3 42.280	34 42.67	4.79	42 10.99	24 59 57.46 z.
153	9	20.5	32.6	45.0	57.0	. .	21.1	33.0	. .	. .	43 56.89	6.38	" 4 40.431	29 50.13	4.76	44 3.27	24 55 4.89 z.
154	5	52.0	4.6	16.4	28.4	40.6	53.0	4.5	. .	. .	45 28.53	6.36	" 3 45.350	32 56.66	4.73	45 34.89	24 58 11.39
155	8	12.1	24.0	36.5	48.2	. .	. .	. .	. .	. .	47 48.38	6.34	" 3 45.448	32 53.28	4.70	47 54.72	24 58 7.98
156	8	. .	. .	. .	3.6	16.0	28.0	39.8	. .	. .	23 48 3.68	6.34	" 2 34.938	47 41.25	4.69	23 48 10.02	25 12 55.94

Zone LXIX. September 23. H. $D.=-24^\circ\ 25'\ 10''.0.$ $n'.=-45''.46.$ $n''.=-5''.00.$ (Continued.)

Number.	Magnitude.	I.	II.	III.	IV.	V.	VI.	VII.	10.	11.	T.	a.	MICROMETER.	D.	d.	Mean Right Ascension, 1850.0.	Mean South Declination, 1850.0.
											h. m. s.	s.	r.			h. m. s.	
157	9	. .	. .	. .	2.5	15.0	. .	39.2	. .	. .	23 49 2.76	+ 6.33	IV. 1 40.392	−50 24″.38	− 4″.68	23 49 9.09	25° 15′ 39″.06 z.
158	9	5.0	17.2	29.0	41.6	53.4	. .	17.2	. .	. .	50 41.31	6.32	" 3 41.690	35 3.01	4.66	50 47.63	25 0 17.67 z.
159	7	43.0	55.8	7.3	19.2	31.8	43.8	55.5	. .	. .	55 19.51	6.28	" 3 44.274	33 33.83	4.63	55 25.79	24 58 48.46 z.
160	9	. .	19.2	31.3	43.2	55.1	. .	. .	. .	. .	59 43.24	6.24	" 6 42.351	14 14.54	4.60	59 49.48	24 39 29.14 z.
161	1.8	5.5	17.6	29.5	41.1	53.2	6.0	17.5	. .	. .	0 0 41.51	6.24	" 4 39.270	30 30.23	4.60	0 0 47.75	24 55 44.83
162	9	. .	45.5	57.4	9.4	21.2	33.5	. .	. .	. .	0 35 0.41	5.97	" 7 39.210	10 12.10	4.55	35 15.38	24 35 26.65
163	9	. .	. .	45.2	57.2	. .	. .	. .	. .	. .	0 35 57.26	5.97	" 6 46.043	12 7.07	4.55	0 36 3.23	24 37 21.62

Zone LXX. September 24. M. $D.=-24^\circ\ 27'\ 47''.11.$ $n'.=-25''.16.$ $n''.=-4''.00.$

Number.	Magnitude.	I.	II.	III.	IV.	V.	VI.	VII.	10.	11.	T.	a.	MICROMETER.	D.	d.	Mean Right Ascension, 1850.0.	Mean South Declination, 1850.0.
1	9	. .	. .	. .	20.5	. .	44.5	. .	. .	. .	20 43 20.40	8.05	VI. 6 41.43	14 45.20	24.52	20 43 28.45	24 42 56.83 z.
2	8	. .	. .	. .	. .	. .	. .	33.2	51.7	3.7	43 57.27	8.05	II. 6 35.26	18 17.51	24.41	44 5.32	24 46 29.03 z.
3	7.8	. .	. .	. .	. .	. .	. .	. .	58.1	9.8	45 3.60	8.04	II. 5 43.37	22 19.74	24.23	45 11.64	24 50 31.08 z.
4	8	. .	. .	. .	. .	. .	. .	. .	16.5	28.0	46 21.96	8.03	II. 5 47.69	19 50.56	24.00	46 29.99	24 48 1.67
5	8	. .	. .	. .	7.0	18.5	. .	. .	. .	. .	48 6.77	8.01	V. 5 51.35	17 45.05	23.70	48 14.78	24 45 55.86 z.
6	8	. .	. .	. .	. .	. .	9.2	20.5	. .	. .	48 44.55	8.03	VII. 3 39.85	36 5.32	23.60	48 52.58	25 4 16.03
7	8	. .	. .	. .	. .	. .	. .	. .	51.5	4.3	49 57.42	8.02	II. 3 32.77	40 9.16	23.39	50 5.44	25 8 19.66
8	9	. .	. .	. .	34.0	. .	. .	. .	. .	. .	53 33.97	8.00	" 2 40.60	44 24.79	22.75	53 41.97	25 12 34.65
9	7.8	. .	29.9	. .	54.0	6.0	. .	30.0	. .	. .	54 53.94	7.95	VII. 5 36.24	26 26.54	22.56	55 1.89	24 54 36.21 z.
10	8	. .	34.0	. .	58.2	10.0	. .	. .	. .	. .	57 58.15	7.95	2. 2 36.45	46 47.49	22.04	58 6.10	25 14 56.64 z.
11	7	3.0	15.5	27.6	39.5	51.7	. .	. .	. .	. .	59 39.58	7.90	IV. 5 47.21	20 8.01	21.75	59 47.48	24 48 16.87 z.
12	7.8	. .	35.0	47.0	59.0	11.0	. .	35.3	. .	. .	21 0 59.07	7.90	II. 3 46.58	32 13.03	21.54	21 1 6.97	25 0 21.68
13	7.8	35.1	47.2	59.1	11.3	. .	. .	47.5	. .	. .	3 11.29	7.86	I. 6 39.61	15 47.90	21.17	3 19.15	24 43 56.18 z.
14	9	. .	. .	32.0	. .	56.0	. .	20.5	. .	. .	8 44.20	7.80	VII. 7 37.75	11 1.24	20.25	8 52.00	24 39 8.60 z.
15	9	. .	. .	. .	. .	. .	25.0	37.0	. .	. .	14 0.69	7.79	" 2 41.93	43 38.59	19.39	14 8.48	25 11 45.09
16	6.7	. .	. .	. .	32.1	44.1	56.1	. .	. .	. .	15 32.01	7.76	IV. 3 40.78	35 33.44	19.14	15 39.77	25 3 39.69 z.
17	8	. .	. .	. .	33.5	45.3	37.0	. .	. .	. .	16 33.25	7.72	VII. 6 42.66	14 2.60	18.97	16 40.97	24 42 8.68
18	7	. .	. .	. .	. .	32.3	44.3	56.1	. .	. .	17 20.03	7.75	" 2 49.14	39 29.66	18.84	17 27.78	25 7 35.61 z.
19	8	. .	13.0	24.9	37.0	49.0	. .	13.1	. .	. .	21 37.01	7.70	" 3 38.67	36 46.05	18.15	21 44.71	25 4 51.31 z.
20	6	10.1	22.3	34.1	46.4	. .	. .	. .	. .	. .	23 46.47	7.69	2. 2 36.28	46 53.35	17.82	23 54.16	25 14 58.28 z.
21	8	. .	. .	. .	. .	. .	16.4	28.5	. .	. .	23 52.24	7.66	VII. 6 31.49	20 28.30	17.80	23 59.90	24 48 33.21 z.
22	8	. .	. .	. .	. .	2.5	14.5	26.5	. .	. .	28 50.31	7.63	I. 3 34.32	39 16.28	17.04	28 57.94	25 7 20.43 z.
23	8	. .	50.1	2.0	14.0	26.4	38.3	50.3	. .	. .	30 14.15	7.62	IV. 3 34.43	39 12.72	16.83	30 21.77	25 7 16.66 z.
24	9.10	. .	. .	15.2	27.3	. .	51.3	3.2	. .	. .	32 27.14	7.59	VII. 3 36.12	38 14.12	16.50	32 34.73	25 6 17.73
25	8	. .	. .	. .	. .	. .	41.0	52.6	. .	. .	33 16.47	7.60	" 1 37.73	51 55.04	16.39	33 24.07	25 19 58.54 z.
26	6.7	. .	. .	. .	. .	51.1	3.5	15.5	. .	. .	34 39.23	7.55	" 5 45.26	21 15.09	16.18	34 46.78	24 49 18.38 z.
27	8	. .	6.8	18.5	. .	42.5	55.0	. .	. .	. .	39 30.72	7.50	2. 6 37.81	16 49.71	15.47	39 38.22	24 44 52.29 z.
28	8.9	. .	. .	. .	. .	. .	31.2	43.0	. .	. .	40 6.79	7.52	VII. 2 46.82	40 49.75	15.39	40 14.31	25 8 52.25
29	8	. .	. .	. .	. .	. .	30.3	42.2	. .	. .	48 6.09	7.41	" 6 41.20	14 53.03	14.32	48 13.50	24 42 54.46 z.
30	8.9	. .	22.4	34.5	46.3	. .	. .	. .	. .	. .	21 50 46.53	7.41	2. 2 42.25	43 27.21	13.97	21 50 53.94	25 11 28.29

CORRECTIONS.

	COR. TO CLOCK.	HOURLY COR.	*m.*	*n.*	*c.*	ZENITH POINT.	COINC.
	s.	s.	s.	s.	s.		r.
Sept. 24, at 20*h*..	−1.620	−0.015	−0.415	+0.429	+0.022	0° 3′ 4″.75	40.112

INSTRUMENT READINGS.

	CIRCLE.					BAR.	THERMOM.	
	A.	B.	C.	D.	Mean.		At.	Ex.
Zone LXX.—Sept. 24..20.7 *h.*	296° 12′ 30″.0	30″.7	41″.7	33″.6	34″.00	30.100 I.	. ° .	69°.5
21.5	. . . .	. .	. .	. .	. .	30.108	72.5	68.0
22.0	. . . .	. .	. .	. .	. .	30.114	73.2	68.3
22.3	28.5	29.2	44.2	32.1	33.50	. .	. .	. .
22.5	. . . .	. .	. .	. .	. .	30.110	72.0	67.0
23.0	. . . .	. .	. .	. .	. .	30.110	71.7	67.0

Zone LXX. September 24. M. *D.* = −24° 27′ 47″.11. n′. = −25″.16. n″. = −4″.00. (Continued.)

Number	Magnitude	SECONDS OF TRANSITS.									T.	a.	MICROMETER.	D.	d.	Mean Right Ascension, 1850.0.	Mean South Declination, 1850.0.
		I.	II.	III.	IV.	V.	VI.	VII.	10.	11.	h. m. s.	s.	r.	′ ″	″	h. m. s.	° ′ ″
31	8.9	. .	. .	. .	. .	5.5	17.5	29.5	. .	. .	21 50 53.27	+ 7.43	VII. 1 35.37	−53′ 16″.54	−13″.95	21 51 0.70	25° 21′ 17″.60
32	8	. .	. .	. .	. .	. .	28.4	40.0	. .	. .	59 3.90	7.32	" 3 34.40	39 13.52	12.93	59 11.22	25 7 15.56
33	8	. .	. .	. .	. .	. .	. .	. .	. .	17.5	59 10.77	7.33	11. 2 36.77	46 36.14	12.92	59 18.10	25 14 36.17
34	7	. .	52.0	3.6	16.3	28.0	40.0	52.1	. .	. .	22 6 15.98	7.23	I. 6 37.96	16 44.88	12.11	22 6 23.21	24 44 44.10 z.
35	9.10	. .	. .	. .	. .	. .	. .	. .	2.5	15.2	7 8.37	7.25	11. 1 38.18	51 38.90	12.01	7 15.62	25 19 38.02
36	7.8	. .	35.0	46.5	59.0	11.0	. .	. .	. .	. .	10 58.91	7.16	V. 7 48.12	5 3.42	11.58	11 6.07	24 33 2.11
37	9	. .	. .	. .	. .	. .	. .	59.1	17.1	29.3	11 22.85	7.19	11. 5 43.00	22 32.51	11.54	11 30.04	24 50 31.16 z.
38	9.10	. .	. .	. .	. .	. .	47.0	59.0	. .	. .	19 22.90	7.09	" 7 39.01	10 17.11	10.72	19 29.99	24 38 14.94
39	7.8	. .	. .	. .	. .	. .	. .	8.0	26.2	38.3	20 31.81	7.10	" 5 37.43	25 44.84	10.60	20 38.91	24 53 42.55 z.
40	7	. .	. .	. .	. .	. .	. .	. .	22.4	34.6	21 28.35	7.07	11. 7 40.97	9 9.44	10.51	21 35.42	24 37 7.06 z.
41	7.8	. .	. .	. .	. .	. .	. .	. .	19.0	31.1	22 24.62	7.08	" 4 43.43	28 4.73	10.42	22 31.70	24 56 2.26 z.
42	8	. .	22.5	. .	47.0	59.0	11.0	23.1	. .	. .	25 46.84	7.04	VII. 3 36.42	38 3.77	10.09	25 53.88	25 6 0.97 z.
43	5	. .	. .	. .	14.0	26.0	38.0	50.0	. .	. .	27 13.92	7.03	" 6 35.97	17 53.60	9.95	27 20.95	24 45 50.66 z.
44	9	9.8	. .	. .	. .	. .	10.2	22.5	. .	. .	27 46.15	7.02	10. 6 34.71	18 36.74	9.90	27 53.17	24 46 33.75 z
45	8	22.0	. .	45.5	. .	10.2	. .	24.2	. .	. .	32 58.06	6.97	2 4 34.56	33 11.22	9.41	33 5.03	25 1 7.74
46	8	. .	. .	56.0	8.1	20.1	32.1	44.2	. .	. .	35 8.01	6.96	I. 2 44.89	41 56.39	9.22	35 14.97	25 9 52.72 z.
47	8.9	. .	. .	. .	. .	18.1	30.7	42.0	. .	. .	36 6.27	6.92	VII. 7 48.19	5 0.80	9.13	36 13.19	24 32 57.04 z.
48	6.7	. .	. .	. .	1.8	. .	26.0	37.5	. .	. .	43 1.71	6.85	" 7 47.24	5 33.59	8.53	43 8.56	24 33 29.23 z.
49	7	. .	44.0	56.0	8.2	20.0	. .	. .	. .	. .	45 8.10	6.84	V. 6 40.27	15 25.34	8.35	45 14.94	24 43 20.80 z.
50	8	. .	. .	. .	. .	. .	. .	. .	15.0	27.0	45 20.55	6.85	11 4 40.37	29 50.37	8.33	45 27.40	24 57 45.81 z.
51	8	. .	. .	. .	. .	7.2	19.4	31.8	. .	. .	46 55.37	6.82	VII. 6 35.66	18 4.29	8.20	47 2.19	24 45 59.60 z.
52	8	. .	. .	. .	. .	. .	24.3	36.0	. .	. .	47 59.88	6.82	" 4 41.89	28 58.49	8.11	48 6.70	24 56 53.71 z.
53	8	. .	. .	. .	. .	. .	29.0	41.1	. .	. .	49 4.94	6.79	" 7 38.88	10 22.23	8.02	49 11.73	24 38 17.36 z.
54	9.10	. .	. .	. .	. .	35.0	. .	59.0	. .	. .	51 22.94	6.78	" 5 36.98	26 0.98	7.83	51 29.72	24 53 55.92 z.
55	9.10	20.8	33.0	45.3	. .	. .	. .	. .	. .	. .	55 57.15	6.72	III. 7 43.63	7 38.41	7.47	56 3.87	24 35 32.99 z.
56	8	. .	. .	. .	50.0	2.0	. .	. .	. .	. .	55 50.03	6.72	VI. 7 37.79	10 59.96	7.48	55 56.75	24 38 54.55
57	6	. .	. .	. .	. .	. .	. .	40.9	59.0	11.0	56 4.53	6.74	11. 2 45.51	41 34.35	7.46	56 11.27	25 9 28.92
58	4.5	. .	. .	. .	. .	. .	54.0	6.0	. .	. .	58 29.93	6.69	" 7 47.98	5 7.42	7.27	58 36.62	24 33 1.80 z.
59	9.10	. .	. .	47.3	0.0	. .	. .	. .	. .	. .	23 1 59.71	6.68	10. 6 36.30	17 41.88	7.03	23 2 6.39	24 45 36.02
60	8.9	. .	. .	. .	. .	. .	. .	50.1	8.3	20.5	2 13.88	6.68	11. 3 40.25	35 50.91	7.02	2 20.56	25 3 45.04 z.
61	8	. .	. .	9.5	21.5	33.5	. .	. .	. .	. .	4 21.57	6.66	IV. 7 39.38	10 5.23	6.89	4 28.33	24 37 59.23 z.
62	8	. .	. .	. .	. .	7.3	19.5	32.0	. .	. .	4 55.45	6.65	VII. 5 34.81	27 15.90	6.85	5 2.10	24 55 9.86 z.
63	9	. .	. .	27.0	39.4	51.5	3.5	. .	. .	. .	6 39.38	6.63	VI. 7 37.91	10 55.82	6.75	6 46.01	24 38 49.68 z.
64	8.9	. .	. .	47.5	59.5	11.8	24.0	36.0	. .	. .	8 59.72	6.61	VII. 6 32.66	19 47.87	6.61	9 6.33	24 47 41.59 z.
65	8.9	. .	. .	49.6	1.8	14.0	26.0	38.0	. .	. .	11 1.80	6.59	" 3 36.30	38 7.91	6.50	11 8.39	25 6 1.52 z.
66	8	39.5	51.5	3.5	15.5	27.5	. .	52.0	. .	. .	14 15.66	6.56	I. 3 39.35	36 21.97	6.35	14 22.22	25 4 15.43 z.
67	8	. .	5.7	17.3	29.9	. .	. .	. .	. .	. .	19 29.80	6.51	2. 1 41.23	49 53.85	6.09	19 36.31	25 17 47.05 z.
68	7	. .	. .	52.1	4.4	16.5	. .	. .	. .	. .	21 4.40	6.49	VI. 5 41.55	23 23.28	6.03	21 10.89	24 51 16.42
69	6	. .	14.5	26.3	38.5	50.8	3.0	14.8	. .	. .	22 38.62	6.48	VII. 3 44.34	33 30.31	5.97	22 45.10	25 1 23.39 z.
70	9	. .	7.0	18.8	31.0	43.0	. .	. .	. .	. .	25 31.08	6.45	V. 1 37.49	52 3.53	5.87	25 37.53	25 19 56.51 z.
71	5.6	34.1	46.3	58.1	10.3	22.4	34.4	46.5	. .	. .	34 10.33	6.37	VII. 4 37.40	31 33.54	5.61	34 16.70	24 59 26.26
72	9	. .	. .	. .	. .	48.0	59.8	12.0	. .	. .	35 35.72	6.36	I. 1 33.46	54 22.50	5.58	35 42.08	25 22 15.19
73	9	. .	15.0	27.0	. .	. .	. .	. .	. .	. .	38 39.26	6.33	2. 6 42.85	13 55.70	5.50	38 45.59	24 41 48.31
74	8	. .	. .	. .	57.2	9.2	21.8	33.7	. .	. .	38 57.31	6.32	VII. 3 33.55	39 42.83	5.49	39 3.63	25 7 35.43 z.
75	8.9	. .	. .	. .	. .	. .	. .	. .	26.0	38.2	39 31.62	6.32	(†) 2 29.33	50 53.96	5.48	39 37.94	25 18 46.55 z.
76	8	. .	. .	. .	5.0	16.7	29.2	41.0	. .	. .	42 4.84	6.30	VII. 4 36.54	32 3.20	5.45	42 11.14	24 59 55.76 z.
77	9	. .	. .	44.8	37.2	9.3	21.5	. .	. .	. .	43 56.19	6.28	VI. 5 35.50	26 52.22	5.43	43 2.47	24 54 44.76
78	5	. .	4.9	16.9	29.0	41.0	53.0	5.0	. .	. .	45 28.93	6.27	VII. 3 40.25	35 51.53	5.42	45 35.20	25 3 44.06 z.
79	8.9	. .	24.4	36.2	48.0	. .	. .	. .	. .	. .	47 48.31	6.25	2. 3 40.40	35 46.01	5.39	47 54.56	25 3 38.51
80	8	. .	. .	. .	. .	15.7	27.7	40.0	. .	. .	23 48 3.59	6.25	IV. 2 39.55	45 1.00	5.39	23 48 9.84	25 12 53.50

† Taken as IV.

Zone LXX. September 24. M. $D. = -24° 27' 47''.11.$ $n'. = -25''.16.$ $n''. = -4''.00.$ (Continued.)

Number.	Magnitude.	SECONDS OF TRANSITS. I.	II.	III.	IV.	V.	VI.	VII.	10.	11.	T.	a.	MICROMETER.	D.	d.	Mean Right Ascension, 1850.0.	Mean South Declination, 1850.0
											h. m. s.	s.	r.	' ''	''	h. m. s.	° ' ''
81	8	5.2	17.8	29.5	41.5	53.6	3.9	17.8	. .	. .	23 50 41.64	+ 6.22	VII. 4 36.05	—32 20.15	—5.37	23 50 47.86	25 0 12.63 z.
82	7	43.2	55.7	7.6	19.8	31.4	44.0	56.0	. .	. .	55 19.70	6.18	2. 4 38.49	30 55.57	5.35	55 25.88	24 58 48.03 z.
83	8	. .	19.1	30.9	43.3	. .	. .	. .	. .	. .	59 43.13	6.14	IV. 7 36.81	11 33.94	5.34	59 49.27	24 39 26.39 z.
84	6.7	. .	. .	30.0	42.0	. .	6.0	18.0	. .	. .	0 0 41.90	6.13	VII. 4 43.95	27 47.37	5.35	0 0 48.03	24 55 39.83 z.
85	7	. .	. .	. .	. .	45.5	57.5	9.7	. .	. .	5 33.56	6.09	" 7 46.28	6 6.74	5.40	5 39.65	24 33 59.25 z.
86	8	. .	. .	18.8	30.8	. .	. .	. .	. .	. .	7 30.90	6.07	IV. 1 39.01	51 11.08	5.42	7 36.97	25 19 3.61 z.
87	8	. .	. .	. .	. .	. .	. .	27.9	. .	58.1	7 51.48	6.07	II. 2 43.32	42 50.00	5.42	7 57.55	25 10 42.53 z.
88	8	. .	. .	7.5	19.7	31.5	. .	. .	. .	. .	11 19.62	6.04	2. 1 43.39	48 39.28	5.46	11 25.66	25 16 31.85 z.
89	8	. .	. .	. .	. .	. .	52.3	4.4	. .	. .	11 28.05	6.03	VII. 3 37.79	37 16.45	5.46	11 34.08	25 5 9.02 z.
90	5.6	4.0	16.1	28.0	40.0	52.0	. .	16.3	. .	. .	14 40.13	6.00	" 7 35.23	12 28.27	5.50	14 46.13	24 40 20.88
91	7.8	31.0	43.0	55.0	7.0	19.0	31.0	43.3	. .	. .	17 7.08	5.99	I. 3 34.43	39 12.49	5.54	17 13.07	25 7 5.14 z.
92	9.10	43.5	55.3	7.4	. .	. .	. .	. .	. .	. .	21 19.56	5.95	IV. 6 40.31	15 24.00	5.72	21 25.51	24 43 16.83 z.
93	4.5	. .	. .	34.4	46.5	58.0	10.4	22.5	. .	. .	22 46.36	5.94	VII. 7 41.20	9 2.14	5.77	22 52.30	24 36 55.02 z.
94	9	34.8	46.6	58.5	. .	. .	. .	. .	. .	. .	0 25 10.94	5.92	III. 2 47.61	40 22.68	5.86	0 25 16.86	25 8 15.65 z.

Zone LXXI. October 7. M. $D. = -26° 25' 10''.0.$ $n'. = -25''.00.$ $n''. = -4''.13.$

Number.	Magnitude.	I.	II.	III.	IV.	V.	VI.	VII.	10.	11.	T.	a.	MICROMETER.	D.	d.	Mean Right Ascension, 1850.0.	Mean South Declination, 1850.0
1	8	. .	. .	17.5	29.7	42.2	. .	6.8	. .	. .	20 55 29.86	5.39	VII. 1 34.10	54 0.81	22.20	20 55 35.25	27 19 33.01 z.
2	9.10	55.5	7.6	. .	. .	. .	. .	. .	. .	. .	59 32.44	5.33	III. 3 32.28	40 27.20	21.50	59 37.77	27 5 58.70 z.
3	8.7	. .	. .	. .	. .	. .	. .	10.1	27.9	40.7	59 33.21	5.34	II. 2 36.22	46 55.52	21.50	59 38.55	27 12 27.02 z.
4	8.9	. .	. .	. .	. .	. .	. .	. .	57.2	9.3	21 1 2.39	5.29	" 5 47.10	20 10.94	21.26	21 1 7.68	26 45 42.20
5	8	. .	. .	. .	. .	. .	. .	. .	. .	23.3	2 15.45	5.30	" 2 48.62	39 47.28	21.05	2 20.75	27 5 18.33 z.
6	8	. .	. .	. .	. .	. .	16.5	29.2	. .	. .	3 52.00	5.30	VII. 1 35.20	53 22.88	20.79	3 57.30	27 18 53.67 z.
7	8	. .	. .	40.2	52.5	4.3	16.7	29.3	. .	. .	5 52.41	5.22	" 7 46.36	6 3.81	20.46	5 57.63	26 31 34.27 z.
8	9.10	. .	5.0	17.4	29.4	. .	. .	. .	. .	. .	8 29.50	5.20	2. 6 45.40	12 27.58	20.03	8 34.70	26 37 57.61 z.
9	8	. .	. .	. .	45.2	57.4	10.1	. .	. .	. .	8 45.26	5.23	VI. 2 46.70	40 54.26	19.98	8 50.49	27 6 24.24 z.
10	8	. .	. .	. .	54.3	6.6	19.0	. .	. .	. .	9 54.32	5.23	" 1 43.25	48 44.95	19.80	9 59.55	27 14 14.75 z.
11	5.6	. .	. .	. .	0.1	12.3	24.5	36.8	. .	. .	10 59.97	5.20	VII. 4 35.83	32 27.89	19.62	11 5.17	26 57 57.51 z.
12	8.9	. .	. .	. .	. .	. .	. .	37.5	. .	. .	12 0.50	5.21	" 1 42.32	49 16.97	19.47	12 5.71	27 14 46.44 z.
13	8	. .	. .	. .	. .	. .	. .	. .	12.0	24.5	12 17.22	5.19	II. 3 39.17	36 28.40	19.42	12 22.41	27 1 57.82 z.
14	9.10	. .	57.7	9.6	21.8	. .	. .	58.5	. .	. .	16 21.89	5.13	2. 5 33.57	27 58.46	18.79	16 27.02	26 53 27.25
15	7	. .	5.1	17.3	29.5	41.6	54.0	6.5	. .	. .	19 29.54	5.12	" 2 38.41	45 40.16	18.30	19 34.66	27 11 8.46 z.
16	9.10	. .	. .	. .	7.5	19.5	. .	. .	. .	. .	26 7.40	5.03	I. 5 30.61	29 41.03	17.33	26 12.43	26 55 8.36
17	5	47.1	59.5	11.8	24.0	35.7	48.7	0.5	. .	. .	27 23.93	5.00	VII. 5 39.31	24 40.60	17.14	27 28.93	26 50 7.74 z.
18	8	. .	. .	5.5	17.8	29.0	. .	. .	. .	. .	32 17.51	4.93	" 7 46.77	5 49.62	16.44	32 22.44	26 31 16.06 z.
*19	6	. .	. .	8.7	21.2	. .	. .	. .	. .	. .	33 21.11	4.92	V. 7 44.10	7 22.05	16.30	33 26.03	26 32 48.35
20	9.8	. .	. .	. .	6.6	19.1	. .	. .	. .	. .	34 6.77	4.92	VI. 6 40.75	15 8.57	16.20	34 11.69	26 40 34.77 z.
21	9.10	. .	. .	. .	. .	. .	. .	15.2	. .	. .	34 38.40	4.91	VII. 6 38.92	16 11.68	16.12	34 43.31	26 41 37.80 z.
22	9	. .	. .	. .	. .	. .	. .	. .	10.0	22.5	35 15.70	4.94	II. 2 36.88	46 32.70	16.04	35 20.64	27 11 58.74 z.
23	7	. .	. .	. .	. .	. .	. .	. .	12.0	24.8	21 36 17.35	4.93	" 2 39.36	45 7.07	15.89	21 36 22.28	27 10 32.96 z.

CORRECTIONS.

	COR. TO CLOCK.	HOURLY COR.	m.	n.	c.	ZENITH POINT.	COINC.
	s.	s.	s.	s.	s.	° ' ''	r.
Oct. 7, at 21h	—4.757	+0.013	—0.261	+0.273	+0.022	0 0 4.93	40.110

INSTRUMENT READINGS.

		CIRCLE. A.	B.	C.	D.	Mean.	BAR.	THERMOM. At.	Ex.
Zone	h.	° ' ''	''	''	''	''	I.	°	°
LXXI.—Oct. 7......	20.9	294 12 15.5	20.4	27.0	20.3	20.89	30.268	67.8	64.8
	21.3	13.5	18.4	25 0	18.3	18.80	. .	. .	64.3
	22.0	. . .	. .	. .	. .	. .	30.302	67.1	26.6
	22.5	. . .	. .	. .	. .	. .	. .	66.8	62.3
	23.6	11.3	17.5	21.2	16.1	16.52	30.318	66.0	61.0

Zone LXXI. October 7. M. $D. = -26° 25' 10''.0$. $n'. = -25''.00$. $n''. = -4''.13$. (Continued.)

Number.	Magnitude.	SECONDS OF TRANSITS. I.	II.	III.	IV.	V.	VI.	VII.	10.	11.	T.	a.	MICROMETER.	D.	d.	Mean Right Ascension, 1850.0.	Mean South Declination, 1850.0.
											h. m. s.	s.	r.	′ ″	″	h. m. s.	° ′ ″
24	8	..	..	..	..	..	..	..	..	7.0	21 36 59.12	+ 4.93	11. 2 39.64	—44 57.37	—15.80	21 37 4.05	27 10 23.17 z.
25	9	..	..	..	54.0	6.3	..	..	..	..	38 54.08	4.86	V. 7 38.73	10 27.48	15.53	38 58.94	26 35 53.01 z.
26	7	..	..	..	..	..	53.2	5.0	..	..	39 28.50	4.85	VII. 7 41.89	8 38.15	15.45	39 33.35	26 34 3.60 z.
*27	9.10	..	..	..	..	..	..	..	4.0	16.3	40 9.28	4.86	11. 5 46.92	20 17.15	15.36	40 14.14	26 45 42.51
28	9.10	..	..	..	..	..	..	4.1	22.0	..	47 27.50	4.85	10. 4 43.60	27 59.19	15.20	41 32.35	26 53 24.39 z.
29	9	..	31.0	42.8	55.5	..	..	..	..	..	43 55.36	4.81	V. 6 36.11	17 48.94	14.89	44 0.17	26 43 13.83
30	9	..	..	..	..	..	..	16.8	..	..	44 39.80	4.84	VII. 1 39.62	50 50.19	14.79	44 44.64	27 16 14.98 z.
31	7	..	..	11.4	23.4	36.0	..	0.3	..	..	48 23.57	4.80	2. 2 38.34	45 42.58	14.32	48 28.37	27 11 6.90 z.
32	7.8	..	..	3.1	15.4	27.7	40.3	..	..	..	52 15.50	4.75	" 1 42.91	48 56.23	13.86	52 20.25	27 14 20.09 z.
33	6	17.7	30.0	42.0	54.1	6.3	18.5	31.0	..	..	55 54.27	4.67	" 7 37.78	10 59.74	13.44	55 58.94	26 36 23.18
34	5.6	..	..	12.8	25.4	37.5	..	..	..	..	22 4 25.30	4.60	1. 3 35.62	38 30.98	12.50	22 4 29.90	27 3 53.48 z.
35	8	..	..	..	..	..	56.8	8.8	..	..	4 31.97	4.61	I. 2 33.25	48 38.72	12.49	4 36.58	27 14 1.21 z.
36	9.8	3.1	15.7	27.9	40.2	..	5.0	..	..	..	6 40.22	4.55	VI. 6 37.16	17 12.57	12.26	6 44.77	26 42 34.83
37	5	..	..	54.7	7.0	19.0	31.5	43.5	..	..	8 6.93	4.53	VII. 7 34.60	12 49.89	12.11	8 11.46	26 38 12.00
38	8.9	5.7	18.3	30.5	42.5	55.0	7.0	..	..	..	14 42.67	4.45	VI. 7 39.16	10 12.54	11.45	14 47.12	26 35 33.99 z.
39	8.9	..	..	..	38.0	50.3	2.4	14.6	..	..	15 37.85	4.47	VII. 2 44.17	42 21.55	11.37	15 42.32	27 7 42.92 z.
40	7.8	36.0	48.3	0.1	12.3	25.0	37.1	49.5	..	..	19 12.68	4.44	I. 2 38.75	45 28.73	11.02	19 17.12	27 10 49.75 z.
41	9	..	54.8	..	19.3	..	43.8	..	..	..	21 19.31	4.42	VII. 1 34.24	53 55.99	10.83	21 23.73	27 19 16.82 z.
*42	5	..	..	..	29.0	40.5	53.2	5.5	..	..	22 28.65	4.38	" 5 39.80	24 23.65	10.74	22 33.03	26 49 44.39
43	9.10	..	..	32.3	44.2	56.8	..	21.6	..	..	31 44.54	4.28	2. 4 37.20	31 40.25	9.99	31 48.82	26 57 0.24
44	10	39.0	..	3.7	16.0	..	..	52.5	..	..	34 15.93	4.25	VII. 3 38.75	36 43.51	9.81	34 20.18	27 2 3.32
45	8	..	12.5	24.3	36.8	49.1	1.5	13.7	..	..	38 36.85	4.20	" 3 33.15	39 56.93	9.50	38 41.05	27 5 16.43 z.
46	9	..	..	23.2	35.7	48.0	..	..	..	..	40 35.69	4.20	V. 1 33.21	54 31.82	9.36	40 39.89	27 19 51.18
47	9	5.8	18.1	30.3	42.4	55.0	7.0	19.5	..	..	42 42.64	4.17	VII. 2 32.94	48 49.41	9.24	42 46.81	27 14 8.65 z.
48	9.10	50.8	3.1	..	..	..	..	..	..	..	48 27.79	4.09	2. 3 36.85	37 48.79	8.88	48 31.88	27 3 7.67 z.
*49	8	..	52.8	5.5	19.3	..	..	..	..	..	48 18.17	4.09	V. 4 31.70	34 50.72	8.90	48 22.26	27 0 9.62
50	8	..	..	..	..	..	57.3	10.0	28.0	40.7	49 33.12	4.07	11. 5 32.74	28 26.85	8.82	49 37.19	26 53 45.67 z.
51	7	..	..	..	5.8	18.0	..	..	..	..	52 5.80	4.04	V. 4 37.28	31 38.04	8.69	52 9.84	26 56 56.73 z.
52	9	..	..	..	..	..	..	..	8.0	20.5	52 13.25	4.04	11. 4 38.73	30 47.11	8.68	52 17.29	26 56 5.79 z.
53	8	..	19.5	31.9	44.0	..	..	..	..	..	55 44.02	3.98	IV. 7 42.34	8 22.88	8.52	55 48.00	26 33 41.40
54	9	..	..	..	27.0	39.0	..	..	..	..	56 26.89	3.99	V. 3 43.21	34 9.71	8.48	56 30.88	26 59 28.19 z.
55	6	8.4	20.9	33.1	44.7	57.0	9.6	22.0	..	..	23 0 45.13	3.92	VI. 6 44.45	13 0.83	8.28	23 0 49.05	26 38 19.11 z.
56	8.9	..	43.5	55.6	8.1	20.0	32.5	45.0	..	..	5 8.00	3.91	2. 1 45.35	47 31.98	8.12	5 11.91	27 12 50.10 z.
57	9.10	39.7	52.2	4.0	17.0	..	..	53.6	..	..	8 16.76	3.87	VII. 2 38.50	45 37.41	8.00	8 20.63	27 10 55.41
58	8	10.3	23.0	35.0	47.3	59.2	..	24.0	..	..	10 47.26	3.83	" 5 45.82	20 55.74	7.92	10 51.09	26 46 13.66
59	9.10	..	..	..	..	..	..	3.8	22.0	35.0	11 27.22	3.84	11. 1 39.33	50 59.61	7.91	11 31.06	27 16 17.52 z.
*60	9.10	..	6.3	18.3	..	..	..	..	..	..	14 30.90	3.80	IV. 1 36.80	52 27.84	7.83	14 34.70	27 17 45.67
61	9	..	..	..	19.3	31.7	44.0	56.3	..	..	15 19.33	3.79	VII. 2 35.21	47 31.01	7.81	15 23.12	27 12 48.82 z.
62	8	..	30.7	42.5	55.2	7.4	19.8	32.0	..	..	19 55.14	3.73	" 1 38.74	51 20.59	7.69	19 58.87	27 16 38.28 z.
63	6	20.9	33.2	45.4	58.0	10.0	..	34.2	..	..	23 57.75	3.67	2. 7 41.34	8 56.82	7.64	24 1.42	26 34 14.46 z.
64	9.10	..	..	..	..	..	..	..	51.5	4.5	24 57.20	3.66	11. 6 42.64	14 2.58	7.63	25 0.86	26 39 20.21
65	8.9	..	..	..	..	..	..	32.0	50.0	3.0	25 55.62	3.65	" 7 38.17	10 46.02	7.62	25 59.27	26 36 3.64
66	9.10	36.9	49.5	1.4	..	26.0	38.8	..	..	..	29 13.77	3.62	2. 6 38.66	16 20.30	7.57	29 17.39	26 41 37.87 z.
67	6.7	53.5	6.0	18.3	30.5	43.0	55.0	7.5	..	..	31 30.58	3.59	1. 3 39.44	36 19.09	7.56	31 34.17	27 1 36.65
68	5.6	..	12.3	24.6	37.0	49.3	..	..	..	..	36 37.00	3.54	I. 3 34.13	39 23.09	7.55	36 40.54	27 4 40.64 z.
69	9	..	..	..	..	..	5.4	17.5	..	..	23 36 40.60	3.55	VII. 1 35.69	53 5.93	7.55	23 36 44.15	27 18 23.48 z.

Zone LXXII. October 8. M. $D. = -27° 55' 10''.0$. $n'. = -18''.60$. $n''. = 3''.00$.

Number.	Magnitude.	I.	II.	III.	IV.	V.	VI.	VII.	10.	11.	T.	a.	MICROMETER.	D.	d.	Mean Right Ascension, 1850.0.	Mean South Declination, 1850.0.
1	9	35.0	47.6	..	12.4	24.5	36.7	49.2	..	..	21 12 12.17	5.61	2. 5 36.28	26 23.72	16.67	21 12 17.78	28 21 50.39
2	9	28.7	41.4	53.5	6.3	18.7	31.5	..	..	..	14 6.33	5.61	VI. 1 43.16	48 47.18	16.38	14 11.94	28 44 13.56
3	9	..	..	..	30.8	42.8	55.6	..	..	..	21 15 30.59	5.59	VII. 2 41.82	43 41.75	16.17	21 15 36.18	28 39 7.92

Zone LXXII. October 8. M. $D. = -27° 55' 10''.0.$ $n'. = -18''.60.$ $n''. = 3''.00.$ (Continued.)

Number	Magnitude.	SECONDS OF TRANSITS. I.	II.	III.	IV.	V.	VI.	VII.	10.	11.	T.	a.	MICROMETER.	D.	d.	Mean Right Ascension, 1850.0.	Mean South Declination, 1850.0.
											h. m. s.	s.	r.	′ ″	″	h. m. s.	° ′ ″
4	8.9	. .	. .	. .	. .	. .	. .	2.1	20.8	33.5	21 16 24.81	+ 5.55	11. 5 40.62	—23 53.49	—16.04	21 16 30.36	28 19 19.53
5	7.8	. .	. .	26.0	38.3	50.5	3.5	15.5	. .	. .	18 38.32	5.53	VII. 4 45.36	26 57.62	15.71	18 43.85	28 22 23.33
6	9	. .	. .	. .	. .	. .	19.0	31.5	. .	. .	19 54.04	5.52	" 4 43.91	27 47.69	15.51	19 59.56	28 23 13.20
7	9.10	. .	36.5	48.8	1.0	. .	. .	. .	. .	. .	24 1.33	5.49	2. 2 39.23	45 10.91	14.94	24 6.82	28 40 35.85
8	7	. .	. .	23.8	36.0	. .	. .	. .	. .	. .	24 36.18	5.47	IV. 3 37.36	37 30.76	14.86	24 41.65	28 32 55.62
9	8	. .	. .	. .	. .	28.7	41.4	53.7	. .	. .	25 16.31	5.47	VII. 3 36.11	38 13.68	14.76	25 21.78	28 33 38.44
10	9.10	. .	. .	19.7	32.0	. .	. .	. .	. .	. .	28 32.11	5.41	2. 5 43.32	22 20.53	14.30	28 37.52	28 17 44.83 z.
11	6.7	3.6	16.0	28.5	41.0	. .	5.5	18.2	. .	. .	29 40.91	5.42	I. 3 35.54	38 33.40	14.15	29 46.33	28 33 57.55
12	7	37.0	51.2	3.9	. .	. .	. .	. .	. .	. .	33 16.36	5.36	2. 5 35.98	26 34.07	13.66	33 21.72	28 21 57.73 z.
13	8	. .	. .	. .	23.8	35.8	48.6	0.9	. .	. .	33 23.69	5.33	VII. 7 43.17	7 52.54	13.64	33 29.02	28 3 16.18
14	6	. .	. .	28.0	40.2	32.8	5.5	18.0	. .	. .	36 40.42	5.35	2. 1 35.60	53 7.87	13.20	36 45.77	28 48 31.07 z.
15	7	17.0	30.0	42.5	55.0	. .	. .	. .	. .	. .	38 54.87	5.30	" 4 38.19	31 4.95	12.90	39 0.17	28 26 27.85
16	8	. .	. .	. .	. .	13.0	25.5	37.8	. .	. .	39 0.66	5.27	VII. 7 40.65	9 19.55	12.88	39 5.93	28 4 42.43
17	7	. .	43.7	56.3	9.0	. .	. .	. .	. .	. .	41 8.73	5.25	IV. 7 38.45	10 35.83	12.60	41 13.98	28 5 58.43
18	6.7	. .	. .	48.0	. .	13.0	. .	. .	. .	. .	42 0.62	5.28	V. 2 44.30	42 16.33	12.48	42 5.90	28 37 38.81
19	8.9	. .	. .	. .	. .	. .	. .	. .	. .	58.4	47 50.18	5.23	11. 7 45.66	6 25.94	12.50	41 55.41	28 1 48.44 z.
20	7.8	. .	. .	. .	. .	. .	. .	. .	. .	55.5	42 47.20	5.22	" 6 48.83	10 27.43	12.38	42 52.42	28 5 49.81 z.
21	9	. .	18.5	30.8	43.2	. .	8.0	. .	. .	. .	46 43.21	5.17	VII. 7 42.47	8 16.74	11.86	46 48.38	28 3 38.60 z.
22	6.7	15.7	28.0	40.5	32.7	5.0	17.8	30.0	. .	. .	50 52.84	5.15	2. 5 38.14	25 19.47	11.31	50 57.99	28 20 40.78 B.
23	8	. .	. .	. .	. .	. .	44.9	57.5	. .	. .	51 20.12	5.13	VII. 7 32.15	13 38.64	11.25	51 25.25	28 8 59.89 z.
24	8.9	. .	. .	. .	. .	1.0	13.8	26.0	. .	. .	52 48.63	5.14	" 2 46.38	41 4.27	11.06	52 53.77	28 36 25.33 z.
25	9	. .	. .	. .	. .	. .	. .	. .	. .	14.0	53 5.13	5.15	11. 1 42.68	49 3.01	11.03	53 10.28	28 44 24.04
26	6.7	. .	. .	. .	. .	. .	. .	. .	58.0	10.3	54 2.11	5.09	" 7 39.68	9 52.43	10.91	54 7.20	28 5 13.34 z.
27	9	. .	. .	. .	. .	. .	. .	. .	. .	14.2	55 5.31	5.13	" 1 39.73	50 44.91	10.77	55 10.44	28 46 5.68 z.
28	9	. .	5.0	17.2	30.0	. .	. .	. .	. .	. .	57 29.96	5.10	IV. 1 41.41	49 47.78	10.46	57 35.06	28 45 8.24 z.
29	9	. .	. .	. .	30.5	42.5	. .	. .	. .	. .	58 30.28	5.08	VI. 1 38.80	51 17.78	10.33	58 35.36	28 46 38.11 z.
30	8	. .	. .	. .	. .	. .	27.5	40.0	. .	. .	59 2.45	5.07	VII. 1 37.79	51 52.57	10.26	59 7.52	28 47 12.83
31	9	54.5	7.5	20.0	32.5	44.5	57.0	. .	. .	. .	22 1 32.27	5.02	" 4 42.30	28 43.32	9.96	22 1 37.29	28 24 3.28 z.
32	9.10	. .	39.2	51.5	. .	. .	. .	. .	. .	. .	5 4.00	4.97	2. 6 38.35	16 29.73	9.56	5 8.97	28 11 49.29
33	4.5	. .	18.4	30.5	42.9	55.2	7.3	20.4	. .	. .	5 43.02	4.98	IV. 3 41.43	35 10.17	9.48	5 48.00	28 30 29.65 z.
34	6	6.0	18.7	30.9	43.5	. .	8.2	20.6	. .	. .	8 43.41	4.92	2. 6 45.05	12 38.28	9.14	8 48.33	28 7 57.42 z.
35	9	. .	. .	39.0	51.3	3.6	. .	. .	. .	. .	9 51.37	4.90	V. 7 44.41	7 9.93	9.00	9 56.27	28 2 28.93 z.
36	8	. .	51.2	. .	16.0	28.4	. .	33.2	. .	. .	11 15.99	4.89	IV. 6 44.42	13 0.65	8.86	11 20.88	28 8 19.51 z.
37	9	. .	. .	. .	2.2	14.4	. .	. .	. .	. .	14 2.13	4.86	VI. 6 40.74	15 7.59	8.58	14 6.99	28 10 26.17 z.
*38	8.9	. .	. .	. .	. .	. .	47.2	39.8	. .	. .	14 22.33	4.86	VII. 5 42.90	22 35.37	8.55	14 27.19	28 17 53.92
39	8	. .	. .	. .	. .	. .	. .	. .	55.4	7.6	15 59.08	4.86	11. 2 42.52	43 16.94	8.38	16 3.94	28 38 35.32
40	7	. .	15.0	27.1	40.0	. .	. .	. .	. .	. .	17 39.93	4.85	IV. 1 39.19	51 4.47	8.21	17 44.78	28 46 22.68
41	9	. .	. .	. .	. .	. .	. .	16.6	35.4	48.0	17 39.54	4.80	11. 7 38.15	10 45.32	8.21	17 44.34	28 6 3.53 z.
42	9	. .	. .	. .	. .	. .	. .	. .	. .	29.0	18 20.09	4.84	" 1 36.89	52 23.05	8.14	18 24.93	28 47 41.19
43	9	47.0	. .	. .	24.7	36.8	49.3	. .	. .	. .	22 21 24.50	4.79	VII. 3 31.30	40 59.86	7.84	22 21 29.29	28 36 17.70

CORRECTIONS.

	COR. TO CLOCK	HOURLY COR.	m.	n.	c.	ZENITH POINT.	COINC.
	s.	s.	s.	s.	s.	° ′ ″	r.
Oct. 8, at 21h....	−4.427	+0.010	−0.261	+0.273	+0.022	0 0 5.13	40.104

INSTRUMENT READINGS.

		CIRCLE. A.	B.	C.	D.	Mean.	BAR.	THERMOM. At.	Ex.
Zone	h.	° ′ ″	′	″	″	″	I.	°	°
LXXII.—Oct. 8	21.2	292 42 30.2	32.6	40.2	35.2	34.55	30.366	69.1	64.5
	21.7	29.2	31.6	39.2	34.2	33.55	. .	68.0	62.7
	22.5	. . . .	. .	. .	. .	. .	30.366	67.2	61.6
	23.0	. . . .	. .	. .	. .	. .	. .	67.0	61.7
	23.7	. . . .	. .	. .	. .	. .	30.364	66.8	60.3
	0.1	29.0	31 7	36.3	30.0	31.75	. .	. .	. .

Zone LXXII. October 8. M. $D. = -27° 55' 10''.0.$ $n'. = -18''.60.$ $n''. = 3''.00.$ (Continued.)

Number.	Magnitude.	SECONDS OF TRANSITS. I.	II.	III.	IV.	V.	VI.	VII.	10.	11.	T.	a.	MICROMETER.	D.	d.	Mean Right Ascension, 1850.0.	Mean South Declination, 1850.0.
											h. m. s.	s.	r.	' ''	''	h. m. s.	° ' ''
44	9.10	29.2	42.0	54.0	6.9	19.1	31.2	. .	. .	. .	22 24 6.67	+ 4.74	2. 4 37.85	—31 16.67	— 7.60	22 24 11.41	28 26 34.27 z.
45	9	. .	. .	29.2	. .	. .	. .	. .	. .	. .	25 41.77	4.72	V. 4 39.96	30 4.35	7.46	25 46.49	28 25 21.81 z.
46	9	. .	. .	. .	. .	. .	19.5	32.0	. .	. .	25 54.56	4.72	VII. 5 40.90	23 44.46	7.44	25 59.28	28 19 1.90
47	8.9	. .	. .	. .	. .	. .	. .	. .	57.6	10.7	27 2.03	4.70	11. 6 41.78	14 30.95	7.34	27 6.73	28 9 48.29
48	9	. .	. .	. .	. .	. .	. .	. .	4.0	17.0	27 8.10	4.71	" 3 40.17	35 52.82	7.33	27 12.81	28 31 10.15
49	7.8	. .	16.5	29.0	. .	. .	. .	. .	. .	. .	29 41.41	4.66	IV. 6 35.69	18 2.17	7.10	29 46.07	28 13 19.27 z.
50	9	. .	. .	. .	. .	26.3	39.0	. .	. .	. .	30 13.99	4.65	VII. 7 43.23	7 50.47	7.05	30 18.64	28 3 7.52 z.
51	9	. .	. .	. .	. .	. .	. .	. .	29.5	42.0	30 33.46	4.66	11. 4 48.90	24 54.69	7.02	30 38.12	28 20 11.71
52	9	. .	. .	. .	. .	. .	. .	. .	41.8	54.8	31 46.27	4.63	" 7 40.93	9 9.27	6.92	31 50.90	28 4 26.19
53	7	. .	. .	. .	. .	. .	. .	40.6	. .	. .	33 3.41	4.61	VII. 7 44.64	7 1.73	6.81	33 8.02	28 2 18.54 z.
54	7	. .	. .	. .	. .	. .	20.4	33.0	. .	. .	33 55.61	4.61	" 6 41.61	14 37.42	6.74	34 0.22	28 9 54.16 z.
55	7.8	. .	. .	. .	. .	. .	. .	. .	24.5	37.0	34 28.33	4.63	11. 2 39.89	44 47.81	6.69	34 32.96	28 40 4.50 z.
56	9	. .	. .	30.5	42.7	55.2	. .	. .	. .	. .	36 42.87	4.57	V. 7 40.53	9 23.89	6.50	36 47.44	28 4 40.39 z.
57	7	. .	. .	51.0	3.5	. .	. .	. .	. .	. .	39 3.50	4.55	2. 6 40.86	15 3.00	6.30	39 8.05	28 10 19.30 z.
58	9.10	. .	. .	. .	17.0	29.0	. .	. .	. .	. .	39 16.84	4.55	V. 6 42.66	14 1.36	6.28	39 21.39	28 9 17.64 z.
59	6	. .	. .	. .	. .	20.6	33.1	45.5	. .	. .	40 8.16	4.55	VII. 5 37.46	25 43.32	6.21	40 12.71	28 20 59.53 z.
60	9	32.5	45.2	57.3	9.5	22.0	34.9	47.0	. .	. .	44 9.81	4.49	" 6 39.90	15 36.51	5.93	44 14.30	28 10 52.44 z.
61	9	. .	12.6	24.6	37.0	49.5	. .	. .	. .	. .	46 37.23	4.48	(†) 2 42.02	43 35.10	5.77	46 41.71	28 38 50.87
62	8	. .	19.6	32.0	44.5	. .	. .	. .	. .	. .	47 44.61	4.47	V. 1 34.00	54 3.72	5.69	47 49.08	28 49 19.41 z.
63	7	48.5	1.0	13.4	26.0	38.5	51.0	3.5	. .	. .	49 26.05	4.45	I. 2 29.48	50 48.09	5.57	49 30.50	28 46 3.66 z.
64	9	. .	32.6	44.5	57.5	9.8	. .	. .	. .	. .	51 57.41	4.41	2. 2 33.79	48 18.79	5.42	52 1.82	28 43 34.21
65	7.8	. .	. .	56.0	8.5	20.9	33.0	46.0	. .	. .	53 8.40	4.41	VII. 1 34.96	53 30.34	5.35	53 12.81	28 48 45.69 z.
66	8	. .	. .	52.5	. .	16.5	29.2	42.1	. .	. .	23 2 4.61	4.27	" 7 38.17	10 45.24	4.85	23 2 8.88	28 6 0.09
67	9.10	. .	. .	. .	. .	. .	0.6	12.4	. .	. .	5 35.44	4.23	" 7 35.71	12 10.19	4.69	5 39.67	28 7 24.88
68	8.9	. .	. .	. .	. .	48.0	. .	12.6	. .	. .	7 35.57	4.20	" 7 49.19	4 24.60	4.60	7 39.77	27 59 39.20 z.
69	9	. .	24.1	36.3	48.9	11.0	13.7	26.0	. .	. .	12 48.77	4.15	2. 3 42.36	34 37.46	4.39	12 52.92	28 29 51.85 z.
70	7	20.8	33.3	45.5	37.6	. .	. .	. .	. .	. .	15 57.97	4.10	" 7 37.35	11 13.23	4.28	16 2.07	28 6 27.51 z.
71	6.7	. .	14.7	27.0	39.5	52.0	4.5	. .	. .	. .	16 39.55	4.09	VI. 6 40.62	15 11.72	4.25	16 43.64	28 10 25.97 z.
72	6	31.2	43.4	56.1	8.5	21.0	33.5	46.0	. .	. .	18 8.57	4.07	VII. 6 48.00	10 56.71	4.20	18 12.64	28 6 10.91
73	7	. .	. .	. .	. .	42.5	55.0	7.2	. .	. .	19 30.11	4.06	" 6 48.00	10 56.71	4.16	19 34.17	28 6 10.87
74	9	. .	. .	. .	15.5	27.4	40.3	53.0	. .	. .	21 15.34	4.05	" 4 39.94	30 4.83	4.11	21 19.39	28 25 18.94 z.
75	8.9	. .	. .	. .	48.0	0.3	13.0	25.0	. .	. .	22 47.96	4.02	" 7 35.90	12 3.64	4.08	22 51.98	28 7 17.72 z.
76	8.9	14.9	27.4	40.0	. .	. .	. .	. .	. .	. .	26 52.49	3.98	2. 3 37.65	37 20.18	3.98	26 56.47	28 32 34.16
77	6	3.2	16.0	28.4	40.6	53.0	5.5	18.0	. .	. .	27 40.70	3.97	VII. 5 41.23	23 33.08	3.96	27 44.67	28 18 47.04 z.
78	7.8	. .	. .	8.6	21.1	. .	46.2	58.5	. .	. .	34 21.12	3.89	" 3 45.35	32 54.51	3.88	34 25.01	28 28 8.39 z.
79	9	. .	. .	0.5	13.0	25.0	. .	. .	. .	. .	36 12.91	3.86	" 7 45.58	6 29.32	3.87	36 16.77	28 1 43.19
80	9	. .	20.5	32.5	45.3	57.5	10.1	. .	. .	. .	37 45.19	3.85	" 4 47.21	25 53.70	3.86	37 49.04	28 21 7.56
81	8.9	50.0	2.5	15.0	. .	. .	. .	. .	. .	. .	40 27.62	3.83	IV. 1 43.76	48 26.56	3.84	40 31.45	28 43 40.44 z.
82	6	51.2	4.0	16.3	29.0	41.0	53.6	6.0	. .	. .	41 28.78	3.82	VII. 2 37.93	45 56.14	3.84	41 32.60	28 41 9.98 z.
83	9	. .	. .	. .	14.7	27.4	. .	. .	. .	. .	50 14.82	3.72	V. 1 32.59	54 52.40	3.87	50 18.54	28 50 6.27 z.
84	7.8	. .	. .	. .	. .	15.3	28.3	40.7	. .	. .	51 3.13	3.70	VII. 3 30.77	41 18.14	3.88	51 6.83	28 36 32.02 z.
85	7.8	21.0	33.5	. .	58.2	10.5	23.5	35.2	. .	. .	52 58.28	3.69	" 2 32.30	49 10.65	3.91	53 1.97	28 44 24.56 z.
86	9.10	52.3	4.6	17.2	29.4	41.9	. .	. .	. .	. .	57 29.55	3.61	V. 7 37.55	11 6.82	3.98	57 33.16	28 6 20.80
87	8.9	. .	. .	21.1	33.5	45.8	58.7	11.0	. .	. .	59 33.61	3.60	VII. 6 34.43	18 45.49	4.00	59 37.21	28 13 59.49
88	4	. .	. .	25.6	38.1	50.8	3.0	15.8	. .	. .	0 1 38.18	3.58	" 1 33.80	54 10.41	4.05	0 1 41.76	28 49 24.46 z.
89	4.5	16.0	28.6	41.0	53.0	. .	. .	. .	. .	. .	3 53.46	3.55	IV. 2 43.25	42 52.63	4.12	3 57.01	28 38 6.75
90	9	. .	. .	. .	. .	44.1	56.5	. .	. .	. .	4 31.59	3.54	VI. 2 44.85	41 57.19	4.13	4 35.13	28 37 11.32
91	8.9	. .	. .	. .	. .	41.6	54.0	6.8	. .	. .	5 29.17	3.53	VII. 2 42.10	43 32.10	4.16	5 32.70	28 38 46.26
92	7	. .	. .	. .	40.7	53.0	6.0	. .	. .	. .	0 6 40.79	3.52	VI. 4 46.52	26 17.59	4.19	0 6 44.31	28 21 31.78

† Declination reduced as if observed at IV.

Number.	Magnitude.	SECONDS OF TRANSITS. I.	II.	III.	IV.	V.	VI.	VII.	10.	11.	T.	a.	MICROMETER.	D.	d.	Mean Right Ascension. 1850.0.	Mean South Declination. 1850.0.
Zone LXXIII. October 9. M. $D. = -39° 48' 50''.0$. $n.' = -17''.74$. $n.'' = -11''.00$.																	
											h. m. s.	s.	r.	′ ″	″	h. m. s.	° ′ ″
1	9.10	. .	. .	. .	47.8	1.8	16.5	30.8	. .	. .	20 25 47.56	+ 7.51	VII. 5 43.11	−22 33.53	−16.64	20 25 55.07	40 11 40.17
2	9.10	. .	. .	. .	. .	. .	. .	52.8	. .	. .	27 9.50	7.51	" 3 37.90	37 21.70	16.38	27 17.01	40 26 28.08
3	7	11.8	26.8	40.7	55.0	9.5	. .	. .	. .	. .	32 55.09	7.40	2. 6 38.71	16 20.41	15.28	33 2.49	40 5 25.69
4	9	. .	. .	. .	. .	. .	2.5	17.5	. .	. .	33 33.82	7.44	VII. 2 37.30	46 30.76	15.16	33 41.26	40 35 35.92
5	8.9	38.9	53.0	7.3	22.0	. .	50.7	5.1	. .	. .	37 21.95	7.38	2. 2 42.50	43 29.51	14.44	37 29.33	40 32 33.95
6	8.9	. .	26.0	40.0	54.2	9.0	23.0	38.0	. .	. .	40 54.50	7.28	I. 7 43.15	7 54.33	13.77	41 1.78	39 56 58.10
7	5.6	3.3	18.0	32.5	46.7	0.7	. .	. .	. .	. .	43 46.65	7.27	2. 4 35.00	33 3.37	13.27	43 53.92	40 22 6.64 B.
8	8	. .	16.0	30.2	44.4	58.5	13.3	27.7	. .	. .	44 44.26	7.27	VII. 3 37.43	37 38.14	13.09	44 51.53	40 26 41.23
9	9	. .	31.1	45.5	. .	14.2	29.0	43.6	. .	. .	21 0 59.97	7.04	" 2 38.52	45 48.18	10.26	21 1 7.01	40 34 48.44
10	5.6	. .	51.0	4.9	19.4	33.8	48.1	2.5	. .	. .	3 19.40	6.96	10. 6 44.61	12 55.58	9.89	3 26.36	40 1 55.47 B.
Zone LXXIV. October 11. M. $D. = -39° 48' 20''.0$. $n.' = -7''.00$. $n.'' = -10''.86$.																	
1	5	16.8	31.3	45.6	0.0	14.3	. .	. .	. .	. .	22 28 0.06	4.64	2. 1 42.30	49 27.51	6.24	22 28 4.70	40 37 53.75
2	5.6	. .	42.2	56.7	11.2	24.7	39.7	53.8	. .	. .	30 10.86	4.55	VII. 7 44.04	7 22.92	6.04	30 15.41	39 55 48.96
3	9	. .	22.3	37.5	. .	6.7	. .	. .	. .	. .	35 51.76	4.49	" 2 43.77	42 46.01	5.57	35 56.25	40 31 11.58
4	8.9	52.0	6.5	20.5	35.0	49.0	3.1	17.7	. .	. .	38 34.81	4.42	" 4 47.02	26 6.49	5.34	38 39.23	40 14 31.83
5	7	. .	. .	. .	. .	28.5	43.3	57.3	. .	. .	40 13.97	4.42	" 1 39.29	51 15.44	5.19	40 18.39	40 39 40.63
6	4	. .	. .	. .	25.0	39.0	53.3	7.5	. .	. .	42 24.64	4.33	IV. 7 42.24	8 26.03	5.04	42 28.97	39 56 51.07 B.
7	9	. .	. .	. .	. .	3.7	18.0	. .	. .	. .	43 49.16	4.32	VI. 6 37.49	17 3.58	4.93	43 53.48	40 5 28.51
8	7	. .	. .	. .	. .	8.0	22.8	37.1	. .	. .	44 53.75	4.30	VII. 5 39.86	24 26.06	4.85	44 58.05	40 12 50.91
9	9.10	. .	. .	13.2	. .	. .	. .	. .	. .	. .	53 27.78	4.16	11. 2 39.84	45 1.66	4.28	53 31.94	40 33 25.94
10	8	45.6	59.7	14.5	28.7	43.0	57.8	11.8	. .	. .	57 28.70	4.07	VII. 5 38.80	25 2.87	4.05	57 32.77	40 13 26.92
11	9	. .	. .	. .	. .	. .	13.0	27.7	. .	. .	23 7 42.44	3.87	" 6 38.12	16 41.31	3.54	23 7 46.31	40 5 4.85
12	9	. .	. .	. .	. .	. .	37.3	51.8	. .	. .	9 8.34	3.88	" 1 36.71	52 44.68	3.47	9 12.22	40 41 8.15
13	6	. .	. .	. .	8.4	22.7	36.6	51.0	. .	. .	11 8.12	3.81	" 7 39.27	10 8.57	3.39	11 11.93	39 58 31.96
14	9	31.5	46.1	. .	14.7	28.8	43.5	. .	. .	. .	21 14.60	3.64	" 5 37.60	25 44.49	3.06	21 18.24	40 14 7.55
15	9	28.5	43.7	57.5	12.1	26.4	40.8	55.1	. .	. .	30 12.00	3.48	" 3 36.05	38 26.00	2.85	30 15.48	40 26 48.85
16	8.9	. .	. .	. .	21.9	36.0	50.4	4.5	. .	. .	34 21.61	3.39	" 6 41.70	14 36.90	2.81	34 25.00	40 2 59.71
17	9	. .	. .	24.8	. .	53.0	8.0	. .	. .	. .	40 39.03	3.27	VI. 7 44.15	7 19.45	2.76	40 42.30	39 55 42.21
18	9	. .	. .	. .	. .	32.3	46.7	. .	. .	. .	48 17.94	3.13	VII. 7 49.51	4 13.15	2.73	48 21.07	39 52 35.88
19	9	. .	23.6	. .	. .	6.5	. .	34.8	. .	. .	53 51.93	3.05	" 5 44.44	21 47.15	2.76	53 54.98	40 10 9.91
20	9	. .	49.5	3.4	17.7	. .	46.2	0.4	. .	. .	58 17.70	2.96	" 7 39.71	9 53.17	2.82	58 20.66	39 58 15.99
21	7	. .	. .	4.0	18.3	32.5	47.0	1.8	. .	. .	0 1 18.21	2.91	" 2 38.42	45 52.08	2.88	0 1 21.12	40 34 14.96
22	6.7	40.2	55.1	. .	23.2	37.3	51.8	6.5	. .	. .	13 23.25	2.70	I. 6 39.63	15 48.77	3.30	13 25.95	40 4 12.07 B.
23	6.7	. .	48.3	2.6	16.8	30.9	45.8	. .	. .	. .	15 16.84	2.67	" 6 37.31	17 9.48	3.39	15 19.51	40 5 32.87
24	6	10.9	25.7	40.0	54.0	. .	. .	. .	. .	. .	17 54.21	2.62	IV. 6 37.91	16 51.86	3.52	17 56.83	40 5 15.38
25	6	. .	. .	. .	47.0	1.9	. .	. .	. .	. .	18 47.08	2.61	V. 3 33.17	40 6.58	3.56	18 49.69	40 28 30.14
26	2.3	. .	. .	. .	. .	14.2	28.8	. .	. .	. .	20 59.61	2.58	" 1 30.65	56 16.01	3.66	21 2.19	40 44 39.67 B.
27	6	. .	. .	. .	. .	19.0	34.0	48.0	. .	. .	23 4.72	2.54	VII. 4 38.50	31 2.53	3.78	0 23 7.26	40 19 26.31 M.

CORRECTIONS.

	COR. TO CLOCK.	HOURLY COR.	m.	n.	c.	ZENITH POINT.	COINC.
	s.	s.	s.	s.	s.	° ′ ″	r.
Oct. 9, at 21h	−4.288	− 0.004	−0.261	+0.273	+0.022	0 0 4.51	40.105
Oct. 11, at 21h...	−4.896	− 0.008	−0.261	+0.273	+0.022	0 0 5.82	40.105

INSTRUMENT READINGS.

	CIRCLE. A.	B.	C.	D.	Mean.	BAR.	THERMOM. At.	Ex.
Zone h.	° ′ ″	″	″	″	″	I.	°	°
LXXIII.—Oct. 9..20.4	280 51 18.2	19.5	27.2	22.0	21.72	30.202	71.4	67.4
20.7	16.0	17.3	25.2	20.0	19.57	30.196	70.5	65.2
LXXIV.—Oct. 11, 22.5	280 51 45.8	46.2	54.5	48.5	48.75	30.436	60.4	54.7
23.0	. . . .	. .	. .	. .	. .	. .	57.0	48.2
23.5	. . . .	. .	. .	. .	. .	. .	56.8	50.1

Zone LXXIV. October 11. M. $D. = -39^{\circ}\ 48'\ 20''.0.$ $n'. = -7''.00.$ $n''. = -10''.86.$ (Continued.)

Number.	Magnitude.	I.	II.	III.	IV.	V.	VI.	VII.	10.	11.	T.	a.	MICROMETER.	D.	d.	Mean Right Ascension, 1850.0.	Mean South Declination, 1850.0.
											h. m. s.	s.	r.	′ ″	″	h. m. s.	° ′ ″
28	9	. .	. .	8.0	. .	37.0	. .	. .	. .	. .	0 25 22.44	+ 2.50	V. 5 46.34	—20 41.62	— 3.91	0 25 24.94	40 9 5.53
29	9	. .	. .	. .	. .	45.0	59.3	14.3	. .	. .	27 30.75	2.46	VII. 6 39.50	15 53.25	4.02	27 33.21	40 4 17.27
30	7	. .	. .	. .	. .	27.4	42.0	56.4	. .	. .	0 28 12.91	2.45	" 2 39.17	45 25.96	4.06	0 28 15.36	40 33 50.02

Zone LXXV. October 16. M. $D. = -41^{\circ}\ 19'\ 30''.0.$ $n'. = -20''.56.$ $n''. = -16''.00.$

Number.	Magnitude.	I.	II.	III.	IV.	V.	VI.	VII.	10.	11.	T.	a.	MICROMETER.	D.	d.	Mean Right Ascension, 1850.0.	Mean South Declination, 1850.0.
1	2.3	. .	. .	48.5	. .	17.8	32.8	47.0	. .	. .	21 11 3.48	4.88	IV. 7 45.42	6 38.20	18.56	21 11 8.36	41 26 26.76 B.
2	4	0.8	15.7	30.0	44.7	59.5	14.1	28.8	. .	. .	14 44.83	4.83	" 6 34.13	19 4.29	17.92	14 49.66	41 38 52.21 B.
3	3.4	45.6	0.9	15.0	30.0	44.7	59.5	14.0	. .	. .	22 29.99	4.71	2. 4 39.69	30 25.45	16.60	22 34.70	41 50 12.05 B.
4	6	14.6	30.1	44.4	. .	13.7	29.0	43.0	. .	. .	30 59.18	4.66	" 4 37.18	31 52.95	15.23	31 3.84	41 51 38.18
5	6	. .	28.7	43.5	57.7	12.6	27.5	42.3	. .	. .	42 58.09	4.35	" 2 36.44	47 7.34	13.40	43 2.44	42 6 50.74
6	7	. .	. .	. .	21.5	36.1	51.0	5.8	. .	. .	22 0 21.66	4.02	VII. 3 37.48	37 42.46	11.06	22 0 25.68	41 57 23.52
7	4	39.0	54.0	8.5	. .	. .	. .	. .	. .	. .	5 23.26	3.93	IV. 2 38.73	45 48.62	10.45	5 27.19	42 5 29.07
8	2	. .	59.8	14.5	29.5	44.0	59.1	13.8	. .	. .	6 29.49	3.91	" 2 38.48	45 57.57	10.32	6 33.40	42 5 37.89
9	4	. .	. .	21.9	36.5	51.0	. .	. .	. .	. .	14 36.54	3.75	" 1 37.77	52 16.39	9.39	14 40.29	42 11 55.78
10	6.7	. .	. .	. .	. .	. .	. .	. .	56.6	12.0	16 51.06	3.71	" 1 43.31	49 3.66	9.15	16 54.77	42 8 42.81
11	2	. .	14.0	28.8	43.5	. .	13.0	27.5	. .	. .	34 43.52	3.36	" 1 38.00	52 8.45	7.44	34 46.88	42 11 45.89
12	6	. .	. .	. .	. .	. .	34.8	49.5	. .	. .	36 5.80	3.30	VII. 6 43.49	13 38.23	7.32	36 9.10	41 33 15.55
13	7	. .	. .	. .	11.3	26.0	40.6	55.5	. .	. .	44 11.45	3.15	" 4 43.16	28 25.52	6.68	44 14.60	41 48 2.20
14	7	. .	. .	. .	. .	37.5	52.0	6.7	. .	. .	46 22.93	3.10	" 5 40.95	23 52.63	6.53	46 26.03	41 43 29.16
15	5	. .	. .	. .	. .	. .	. .	0.7	23.0	38.0	47 17.20	3.09	" 3 43.34	34 18.45	6.46	47 20.29	41 53 54.91
16	5	7.0	22.5	37.0	51.7	6.1	20.9	35.5	. .	. .	51 51.57	3.01	IV. 3 37.64	37 37.16	6.15	51 54.58	41 57 13.31
17	5	27.7	42.6	57.3	11.7	26.5	41.0	56.0	. .	. .	55 11.86	2.92	" 6 36.14	17 54.37	5.94	55 14.78	41 37 30.31
18	4	. .	6.0	20.7	35.5	50.0	4.6	19.5	. .	. .	23 6 35.42	2.71	" 3 41.30	35 29.99	5.33	23 6 38.13	41 55 5.32 B.
19	5	. .	0.2	15.0	29.7	44.4	59.3	14.0	. .	. .	8 29.80	2.67	VII. 2 46.43	41 20.22	5.23	8 32.47	42 0 55.45
20	3	. .	. .	. .	3.7	18.7	32.8	. .	. .	. .	10 3.82	2.64	V. 5 49.85	18 43.43	5.17	10 6.46	41 38 18.60 B.
21	6.7	. .	. .	. .	24.0	38.6	53.3	8.0	. .	. .	12 23.87	2.59	VII. 3 42.73	34 39.48	5.08	12 26.46	41 54 14.56
22	6	. .	. .	. .	. .	. .	. .	. .	18.1	32.7	36 12.26	2.11	11. 7 36.82	11 35.65	4.55	36 14.37	41 31 10.20
23	5	6.7	21.3	35.8	50.5	5.2	19.8	. .	. .	. .	43 50.58	1.97	IV. 5 47.66	19 59.64	4.50	43 52.55	41 39 34.14 B.
24	7	. .	. .	34.0	46.5	1.5	16.0	30.5	. .	. .	23 52 46.70	1.79	VII. 7 36.19	11 58.60	4.54	23 52 48.49	41 31 33.14

Zone LXXVI. October 17. M. $D. = -42^{\circ}\ 46'\ 47''.78.$ $n'. = -20''.12.$ $n''. = -19''.00.$

Number.	Magnitude.	I.	II.	III.	IV.	V.	VI.	VII.	10.	11.	T.	a.	MICROMETER.	D.	d.	Mean Right Ascension, 1850.0.	Mean South Declination, 1850.0.
1	7	. .	. .	. .	40.3	. .	10.5	. .	. .	. .	21 4 40.23	4.96	VI. 4 39.25	30 45.05	19.22	21 4 45.19	43 17 52.05
2	4	32.3	47.5	2.3	17.5	32.0	47.0	2.3	. .	. .	17 17.30	4.73	IV. 5 39.92	24 30.96	16.91	17 22.03	43 11 35.65 B.
3	6	50.1	5.0	20.5	35.5	. .	6.3	21.1	. .	. .	24 35.67	4.62	" 1 45.21	48 3.80	15.63	24 40.29	43 35 7.21
4	6	20.8	36.5	51.0	5.9	20.5	36.3	51.0	. .	. .	21 30 6.04	4.48	" 6 32.24	20 11.33	14.67	21 30 10.52	43 7 13.78

CORRECTIONS.

	COR. TO CLOCK.	HOURLY COR.	m.	n.	c.	ZENITH POINT.	COINC.
	s.	s.	s.	s.	s.	° ′ ″	r.
Oct. 16, at 22h. . .	—5.709	—0.010	—0.530	+0.507	+0.022	0 0 4.57	40.111
† Oct. 17.........	. . .	. . .	. . .	. . .	. . .	. . . . .	. .

† No determination of clock error, &c., for this date.
‡ The circle reading increased 3′ from that recorded.

INSTRUMENT READINGS.

Zone	h.	CIRCLE. A.	CIRCLE. B.	CIRCLE. C.	CIRCLE. D.	CIRCLE. Mean.	BAR.	THERMOM. At.	THERMOM. Ex.
		° ′ ″	″	″	″	″	I.	°	°
LXXV.—Oct. 16,	21.2	279 21 6.0	11.0	21.0	10.0	12.80	30.132	63.1	61.1
	21.7	. . . .	. .	. .	. .	. .	30.140	63.5	63.0
	22.4	. . . .	. .	. .	. .	. .	. .	64.3	63.5
	23.0	. . . .	. .	. .	. .	. .	30.154	64.5	62.5
	23.6	. . . .	. .	. .	. .	. .	30.144	64.5	61.2
‡ LXXVI. Oct. 17,	21.0	277 54 35.0	40.0	49.0	39.0	40.73	29.916	66.0	65.5
	21.6	. . . .	. .	. .	. .	. .	29.912	66.2	65.0
	22.2	. . . .	. .	. .	. .	. .	29.904	66.3	65.0
	22.7	. . . .	. .	. .	. .	. .	29.912	66.5	65.2
	23.2	34.2	39.0	48.3	38.3	39.95	29.918	66.8	64.8

Number.	Magnitude.	SECONDS OF TRANSITS. I.	II.	III.	IV.	V.	VI.	VII.	10.	11.	T.	a.	MICROMETER.	D.	d.	Mean Right Ascension, 1850.0.	Mean South Declination, 1850.0.
Zone LXXVI. October 17. M. $D. = -42° 46' 47''.78$. $n'. = -20''.12$. $n''. = -19''.00$. (Continued.)																	
											h. m. s.	s.	r.			h. m. s.	
5	7.8	. .	. .	. .	. .	. .	4.3	19.0	. .	. .	21 40 33.80	+ 4.29	VII. 3 40.69	—35' 54''.47	—13''.00	21 40 38.09	43° 22' 55''.25
6	7.8	. .	. .	. .	. .	52.0	7.1	22.3	. .	. .	42 36.78	4.28	" 1 35.55	53 40.88	12.69	42 41.06	43 40 41.35
7	8	. .	. .	. .	. .	. .	. .	. .	20.3	. .	43 12.45	4.26	II. 2 38.81	45 50.26	12.60	43 16.71	43 32 50.64
8	7	. .	. .	45.1	0.1	15.5	. .	45.3	. .	. .	50 0.19	4.12	IV. 2 41.11	44 31.55	11.59	50 4.31	43 31 30.92
9	6	. .	. .	. .	. .	. .	40.0	54.6	. .	. .	51 9.58	4.08	VII. 5 42.32	23 6.83	11.43	51 13.66	43 10 6.04
10	7	0.4	15.3	30.4	45.5	0.5	15.5	30.7	. .	. .	22 6 45.52	3.78	IV. 3 34.49	39 31.43	9.39	22 6 49.30	43 26 28.60
11	6	31.0	46.0	1.1	16.0	31.0	46.0	1.0	. .	. .	21 16.05	3.46	" 6 38.46	16 34.39	7.70	21 19.51	43 3 29.87
12	7.8	. .	. .	. .	. .	. .	34.3	. .	. .	. .	23 3.94	3.46	VII. 2 42.39	43 46.40	7.52	23 7.40	43 30 41.70
13	7.8	16.0	31.4	46.5	1.5	16.5	31.5	46.8	. .	. .	38 1.49	3.13	" 4 36.41	32 23.96	6.07	38 4.62	43 19 17.81
14	8	. .	19.5	. .	49.5	. .	19.5	35.0	. .	. .	43 49.50	3.02	" 2 34.85	48 9.51	5.59	43 52.52	43 35 2.88
15	7	31.0	46.3	1.1	16.0	31.0	46.4	1.0	. .	. .	47 16.15	2.94	IV. 4 33.16	34 17.89	5.32	47 19.09	43 21 10.99
16	4	47.7	3.3	18.0	33.0	48.3	. .	. .	. .	. .	23 1 33.34	2.66	" 1 35.71	53 35.48	4.37	23 1 36.00	43 40 27.63 B.
17	6	. .	. .	. .	. .	. .	20.7	36.0	. .	. .	1 50.42	2.64	VII. 2 36.35	47 17.35	4.36	1 53.06	43 34 9.49
18	6	56.6	11.5	. .	42.0	. .	. .	. .	. .	. .	26 42.04	2.12	IV. 2 42.10	43 56.96	3.34	26 44.16	43 30 48.08 B.
19	3.4	11.0	26.5	. .	. .	. .	26.7	42.2	. .	. .	23 26 56.63	2.11	II. 2 49.12	39 50.33	3.34	23 26 58.74	43 26 41.45 B.
Zone LXXVII. October 19. M. $D. = -43° 47' 40''.0$. $n. = -27''.00$. $n''. = -21''.87$.																	
1	3	10.7	26.3	41.3	56.5	11.5	. .	. .	. .	. .	20 23 56.56	5.41	IV. 7 41.25	9 0.47	26.21	20 24 1.97	43 37 6.68
2	6	. .	. .	. .	24.0	38.8	54.0	. .	. .	. .	26 23.76	5.47	VII. 7 43.68	7 34.53	26.90	26 29.23	43 55 41.43
3	6.7	. .	. .	. .	. .	37.7	53.0	8.4	. .	. .	27 22.59	5.36	" 6 44.93	12 46.66	25.54	27 27.95	44 0 52.20
4	6.7	. .	. .	56.3	11.8	26.9	42.2	37.4	. .	. .	35 11.61	5.25	" 4 41.82	29 17.43	24.06	35 16.86	44 17 21.49
5	2.3	26.0	41.4	56.8	. .	. .	. .	. .	. .	. .	38 12.31	5.22	III. 2 42.38	43 53.34	23.50	38 17.53	44 31 56.84 B.
6	7	. .	. .	. .	. .	45.2	0.5	15.7	. .	. .	38 29.71	5.21	VII. 2 42.30	43 55.61	23.44	38 34.92	44 31 59.05 B.
7	7	. .	. .	. .	. .	11.0	26.1	. .	. .	. .	41 55.44	5.16	" 1 37.71	52 33.20	22.81	42 0.60	44 40 36.01
8	7.8	0.1	16.0	31.0	46.1	1.4	17.0	32.0	. .	. .	46 46.26	5.05	" 5 37.26	26 5.30	21.95	46 51.31	44 14 7.25
9	4	. .	. .	. .	. .	. .	. .	. .	46.8	2.8	47 37.85	5.04	" 1 39.30	51 37.75	21.60	47 42.89	44 39 39.35 M.
10	7	. .	. .	13.0	28.7	43.4	38.5	14.1	. .	. .	50 28.39	4.95	" 7 43.34	7 46.78	21.28	50 33.34	43 55 48.06
11	5	44.6	0.1	15.2	30.5	45.5	0.8	16.0	. .	. .	55 30.42	4.87	IV. 6 34.62	18 48.12	20.42	55 35.29	44 6 48.54
12	4.5	25.5	40.9	55.8	10.9	26.0	41.0	56.5	. .	. .	21 0 10.99	4.78	" 7 37.27	11 19.84	19.63	21 0 15.77	43 59 19.47 B.
13	4.5	45.0	0.5	15.6	30.9	45.7	1.2	17.0	. .	. .	8 30.92	4.68	" 1 39.99	51 13.91	18.31	8 35.60	44 39 12.22
14	7	9.5	. .	40.1	55.5	10.3	25.7	41.0	. .	. .	11 55.35	4.56	VII. 6 42.70	14 4.64	17.78	11 59.91	44 2 2.42
15	7	14.5	30.2	45.3	. .	. .	31.3	47.0	. .	. .	16 0.78	4.52	IV. 3 38.53	37 15.33	17.16	16 5.30	44 25 12.49
16	4.5	. .	33.8	48.8	4.0	19.2	34.7	50.0	. .	. .	20 4.11	4.42	" 5 44.15	22 4.38	16.55	20 8.53	44 10 0.93
17	6.7	. .	. .	. .	. .	. .	1.0	16.0	. .	. .	28 30.27	4.28	VII. 6 35.35	18 22.40	15.31	28 34.55	44 6 17.71
18	3	36.3	51.0	6.6	22.0	37.0	52.2	7.7	. .	. .	33 21.87	4.16	IV. 5 43.15	22 39.41	14.61	33 26.03	44 10 34.02 B.
19	7	. .	5.0	20.0	35.2	. .	. .	. .	. .	. .	40 35.34	4.01	" 5 48.24	19 41.15	13.59	40 39.35	44 7 34.74
20	7	39.2	54.8	10.0	25.0	40.5	56.0	10.8	. .	. .	50 25.22	3.81	VII. 4 54.45	21 55.24	12.49	50 29.03	44 9 47.73
21	7	59.0	14.4	. .	45.0	. .	15.0	. .	. .	. .	53 44.77	3.73	" 6 50.86	9 18.99	12.18	53 48.50	43 57 11.17
22	4	54.8	10.2	25.8	40.8	. .	12.0	27.5	. .	. .	21 56 41.16	3.72	IV. 1 35.71	53 43.92	11.91	21 56 44.88	44 41 35.83

CORRECTIONS.

	COR. TO CLOCK.	HOURLY COR.	m.	n.	c.	ZENITH POINT.	COINC.
Oct. 19, at 22h . .	s. —6.303	s. —0.018	s. —0.530	s. +0.507	s. +0.022	359° 57' 8''.09	r. 40.123

INSTRUMENT READINGS.

	h.	CIRCLE. A.	B.	C.	D.	Mean.	BAR.	THERMOM. At.	Ex.
Zone LXXVII.—Oct. 19,	20.1	276° 51' 59''.6	4''.8	16''.7	5''.7	6''.70	I. 30.226	51°.3	41°.5
	21.0	58.4	. .	. .	. .	. .	. .	50.9	41.8
	21.6	58.0	. .	. .	. .	. .	30.228	50.2	40.2
	22.0	. . . .	. .	. .	. .	. .	. .	49.7	39.2
	22.5	52 0.4	. .	. .	. .	. .	30.244	48.7	38.4
	22.9	52 0.0	. .	. .	. .	. .	. .	48.3	38.0
	23.5	. . . .	. .	. .	. .	. .	30.242	47.8	36.6
	0.0	. . . .	. .	. .	. .	. .	30.235	47.1	35.1
	0.5	. . . .	. .	. .	. .	. .	30.231	46.0	35.0
	0.7	51 8.0	4.2	15.3	4.5	. .	. .	. .	. .
	1.0	. . . .	. .	. .	. .	. .	. .	45.0	35.3

13 □

Number.	Magnitude.	SECONDS OF TRANSITS. I.	II.	III.	IV.	V.	VI.	VII.	10.	11.	T.	a.	MICROMETER.	D.	d.	Mean Right Ascension, 1850.0.	Mean South Declination, 1850.0.
		Zone LXXVII. October 19. M. $D. = -43° 47' 40''.0$. $n'. = -27''.00$. $n''. = -21''.87$. (Continued.)															
											h. m. s.	s.	r.	′ ″	″	h. m. s.	° ′ ″
23	4	22.2	38.1	53.1	9.0	24.2	39.6	53.2	. .	. .	22 2 8.86	+ 3.60	IV. 1 37.01	−52 58.49	−11.40	22 2 12.46	44 40 49.89
24	6	. .	. .	. .	. .	. .	. .	. .	29.0	45.0	7 20.15	3.48	11. 3 31.88	41 6.66	10.92	7 23.63	44 28 57.58
25	6	27.4	43.1	. .	13.4	. .	. .	59.8	. .	. .	11 13.40	3.00	IV. 35.22	. . .	. .	11 16	44
26	6.7	12.5	28.0	43.0	58.0	13.5	. .	. .	. .	. .	13 58.36	3.32	" 5 44.50	21 52.31	10.32	14 1.68	44 9 42.63
27	7.8	. .	. .	. .	. .	. .	. .	. .	26.0	41 0	14 17.02	3.31	11. 5 44.45	21 52.21	10.29	14 20.33	44 9 42.50
28	2	27.1	43.2	58.2	13.3	. .	. .	. .	. .	. .	20 13.49	3.20	IV. 4 44.30	27 51.35	9.77	20 16.69	44 15 41.12 B.
29	2	. .	. .	. .	42.9	58.0	13.5	28.8	. .	. .	20 42.75	3.20	" 2 43.51	43 13.87	9.73	20 45.95	44 31 3.60
30	6	. .	27.1	42.4	57.8	13.0	28.6	. .	. .	. .	22 57.80	3.14	VII. 4 38.53	31 12.57	9.57	23 0.94	44 19 2.14
31	5.6	. .	. .	. .	. .	. .	. .	. .	20.0	36.0	23 11.73	3.12	10. 6 42.41	14 14.84	9.55	23 14.85	44 2 4.39 B.
32	5	56.5	12.1	27.1	42.5	57.5	12.4	28.0	. .	. .	27 42.34	3.03	IV. 4 45.65	27 4.69	9.23	27 45.37	44 14 53.92
33	7.8	. .	. .	. .	15.5	31.0	. .	. .	. .	. .	29 15.60	3.01	10. 2 43.28	43 20.55	9.11	29 18.61	44 31 9.66
34	7	. .	. .	. .	. .	41.8	57.3	13.0	. .	. .	29 26.62	3.01	11. 2 42.81	43 36.52	9.10	29 29.63	44 31 25.62
35	6	. .	. .	. .	43.7	. .	13.5	28.5	. .	. .	39 42.99	2.77	VII. 4 46.76	26 24.29	8.49	39 45.76	44 14 12.78
36	8	. .	. .	56.5	. .	. .	42.0	57.0	. .	. .	46 11.61	2.61	" 7 41.45	8 53.02	8.16	46 14.22	43 56 41.18
37	7	. .	. .	. .	54.8	10.0	25.0	. .	. .	. .	54 54.76	2.42	" 7 48.12	4 59.31	7.81	54 57.18	43 52 47.12
38	6	. .	41.0	56.1	. .	26.4	41.5	57.0	. .	. .	57 11.31	2.37	IV. 7 47.36	5 26.60	7.73	57 13.68	43 53 14.33
39	1.2	. .	. .	. .	. .	. .	52.0	7.9	30.5	46.4	58 21.64	2.37	VII. 3 47.51	31 59.42	7.70	58 24.01	44 19 47.12 B.
40	7.8	. .	. .	48.3	. .	19.3	34.5	49.7	. .	. .	23 7 3.79	2.18	" 3 38.30	37 22.72	7.48	23 7 5.97	44 25 10.20
41	7	. .	34.5	49.4	5.0	19.7	35.0	50.3	. .	. .	12 4.72	2.06	IV. 7 38.90	10 22.57	7.39	12 6.78	43 58 9.96
42	5	. .	. .	. .	55.8	11.5	26.5	41.4	. .	. .	13 55.96	2.02	VII. 7 34.37	13 0.89	7.38	13 57.98	44 0 48.27
43	3	. .	. .	. .	28.5	43.5	59.0	14.2	. .	. .	15 28.64	1.99	IV. 7 40.91	9 12.20	7.36	15 30.63	43 56 59.56 B.
44	7.8	. .	. .	. .	. .	. .	30.0	45.5	. .	. .	16 59.15	1.98	VII. 1 36.39	53 13.01	7.35	17 1.13	44 41 0.36
45	7.8	. .	. .	. .	52.8	7.9	23.7	39.0	. .	. .	23 52.80	1.81	" 3 38.27	37 23.75	7.34	23 54.61	44 25 11.09
46	8	. .	. .	48.0	. .	. .	. .	. .	. .	. .	49 3.45	1.26	10. 5 43.55	22 24.38	7.76	49 4.71	44 10 12.14
47	6	48.1	3.8	18.5	34.0	. .	. .	. .	. .	. .	0 4 34.01	0.93	IV. 6 46.40	11 56.00	8.46	0 4 34.94	43 59 44.46
48	6	. .	. .	. .	. .	49.5	4.8	19.8	. .	. .	5 34.33	0.91	VII. 7 46.10	6 10.02	8.52	5 35.24	43 53 58.54
49	6	. .	22.5	38.0	53.5	. .	. .	. .	. .	. .	8 53.47	0.84	IV. 1 43.65	49 5.31	8.70	8 54.31	44 36 54.01
50	7	. .	. .	. .	. .	. .	11.2	26.2	. .	. .	9 40.11	0.82	VII. 1 36.18	53 27.15	8.74	9 40.93	44 41 15.89
51	4	. .	. .	. .	. .	. .	. .	57.8	20.7	35.5	11 11.83	0.79	11. 7 28.33	16 31.47	8.84	11 12.62	44 4 20.31 B.
52	1.2	. .	. .	. .	. .	. .	. .	. .	56.8	12.3	19 47.70	0.61	" 2 43.84	43 0.40	9.44	19 48.31	44 30 49.84
53	5	14.0	29.5	44.5	. .	15.0	30.6	46.3	. .	. .	24 0.04	0.52	IV. 3 41.79	35 20.61	9.77	24 0.56	44 23 10.38
54	7	54.8	10.6	25.7	40.8	56.0	11.5	27.0	. .	. .	31 40.97	0.36	VII. 6 33.42	19 30.05	10.40	31 41.33	44 7 20.45
55	4.5	. .	. .	. .	. .	16.0	31.3	46.5	. .	. .	43 0.67	0.13	" 5 39.19	24 57.62	11.49	43 0.80	44 12 49.11
56	5	. .	. .	. .	50.8	6.4	21.5	36.8	. .	. .	0 44 50.80	0.10	IV. 2 42.55	43 46.97	11.68	0 44 50.90	44 31 38.65
		Zone LXXVIII. October 21. M. $D. = -39° 48' 50''.0$. $n'. = -11''.52$. $n''. = -10''.00$.															
1	6	46.5	0.7	15.9	29.8	44.0	58.0	. .	. .	. .	21 25 29.98	2.69	VII. 5 43.40	22 22.34	10.89	21 25 32.67	40 11 23.23
2	6	. .	. .	. .	. .	25.5	. .	54.5	. .	. .	27 10.97	2.67	" 2 46.52	41 9.59	10.70	27 13.64	40 30 10.29
3	4.5	56.8	11.5	25.5	40.0	54.0	. .	. .	. .	. .	21 29 39.92	2.61	V. 5 42.10	23 7.92	10.43	21 29 42.53	40 12 8.35

CORRECTIONS.

	COR. TO CLOCK.	HOURLY COR.	m.	n.	c.	ZENITH POINT.	COINC.
	s.	s.	s.	s.	s.		r.
Oct. 21, at 22*h*...	−7.708	−0.024	−0.530	+0.507	+0.022	0° 0′ 6″.23	40.123

INSTRUMENT READINGS.

	h.	CIRCLE. A.	B.	C.	D.	Mean.	BAR.	THERMOM. At.	Ex.
Zone LXXVIII.—Oct. 21,	21.2	280° 51′ 27″.0	32″.0	41″.8	35″.0	33″.95	I. . .	° . .	° . .
	21.5	. .	. .	. .	. .	. .	30.246	51.8	41.8
	22.1	24.5	. .	. .	. .	31.45	30.240	50.2	39.0
	22.4	24.5	30.0	40.0	32.5	31.75	. .	49.5	39.5

Number.	Magnitude.	SECONDS OF TRANSITS. I.	II.	III.	IV.	V.	VI.	VII.	10.	11.	T.	a.	MICROMETER.	D.	d.	Mean Right Ascension, 1850.0.	Mean South Declination, 1850.0.
Zone LXXVIII. October 21. M. $D. = -39^{\circ}\ 48'\ 50''.0$. $n' = -11''.52$. $n'' = -10''.00$. (Continued.)																	
											h. m. s.	s.	r.	′ ″	″	h. m. s.	° ′ ″
4	6	. .	. .	. .	. .	. .	34.0	48.2	. .	. .	21 37 5.33	+ 2.46	VII. 7 42.49	— 8 15.88	— 9.67	21 37 7.79	39 57 15.55
5	5	. .	. .	. .	. .	. .	. .	14.8	. .	. .	38 31.63	2.45	" 5 41.97	23 11.92	9.53	38 34.08	40 12 11.45
6	7	. .	. .	. .	. .	. .	30.2	. .	6.5	21.2	45 1.50	2.36	11. 1 41.58	49 53.94	8.91	45 3.86	40 38 52.85
7	6	. .	. .	. .	. .	. .	. .	47.7	. .	. .	48 4.73	2.26	10. 7 37.60	11 4.76	8.63	48 6.99	40 0 3.39
8	6	. .	. .	. .	. .	0.5	14.0	28.6	. .	. .	49 45.48	2.25	VII. 5 38.47	25 13.60	8.47	49 47.73	40 14 12.07
9	5	55.5	10.0	24.2	38.7	53.5	. .	22.0	. .	. .	53 38.79	2.18	IV. 3 44.15	33 44.35	8.16	53 40.97	40 22 42.51
10	6.7	. .	. .	37.7	. .	7.0	21.0	36.0	. .	. .	55 52.33	2.14	VII. 3 38.89	36 46.45	7.97	55 54.47	40 25 44.42
11	2	. .	. .	. .	. .	15.0	29.5	43.5	. .	. .	57 0.43	2.11	" 5 35.40	27 0.22	7.88	57 2.54	40 15 58.10 B.
12	6	58.7	13.0	27.3	41.5	56.0	10.3	24.5	. .	. .	59 41.59	2.05	" 5 42.68	22 47.18	7.66	59 43.64	40 11 44.84
13	5	30.1	44.3	59.0	13.2	27.5	41.8	. .	. .	. .	22 1 13.16	2.03	" 4 44.20	27 43.60	7.56	22 1 15.19	40 16 41.16
14	6	34.5	49.0	3.3	17.7	32.0	46.5	. .	. .	. .	5 17.72	1.97	" 2 47.96	40 19.67	7.28	5 19.69	40 29 16.95
15	6	. .	. .	. .	44.0	58.0	. .	. .	. .	. .	9 43.65	1.87	V. 4 41.78	29 8.05	6.97	9 45.52	40 18 5.02
16	5	. .	. .	. .	. .	. .	. .	37.5	38.4	. .	8 53.86	1.91	10. 1 38.66	51 35.67	7.02	8 55.77	40 40 32.69
17	5	. .	48.4	2.6	17.0	31.6	46.0	. .	. .	. .	13 17.08	1.79	VI. 2 39.81	45 3.39	6.75	13 18.87	40 34 0.14
18	6	. .	. .	. .	. .	44.5	58.7	12.5	. .	. .	16 29.85	1.72	VII. 7 39.52	9 58.76	6.56	16 31.57	39 58 55.32
19	2	. .	. .	33.8	48.3	2.5	16.5	. .	. .	. .	22 19 48.09	1.65	VI. 7 49.14	4 25.25	6.36	22 19 49.74	39 53 21.61 B.
Zone LXXIX. October 28. M. $D. = -42^{\circ}\ 50'\ 40''.0$. $n' = -0''.76$. $n'' = -21''.00$.																	
1	5	8.5	23.7	39.0	54.0	8.7	24.0	39.0	. .	. .	0 37 53.89	2.83	VII. 3 35.44	39 0.73	1.87	0 37 51.06	43 29 42.60 B.
2	7	16.8	. .	47.1	1.8	17.1	32.5	47.3	. .	. .	42 2.11	2.91	" 4 36.86	32 10.14	2.18	41 59.20	43 22 52.32
3	7	12.2	27.7	. .	57.6	. .	27.8	43.0	. .	. .	44 57.69	2.98	IV. 2 39.23	45 40.27	2.41	44 54.71	43 36 22.68
4	8.7	35.5	52.0	5.7	21.0	36.0	. .	6.0	. .	. .	1 0 21.12	3.28	VII. 4 37.25	31 56.69	3.76	1 0 17.84	43 22 40.45
5	8	. .	45.4	. .	. .	. .	. .	. .	. .	. .	3 15.62	3.34	III. 3 40.57	36 1.96	4.06	3 12.28	43 26 46.02
6	5	. .	. .	. .	. .	. .	46.8	. .	24.0	38.7	2 16.29	3.31	11. 5 45.28	21 23.42	3.95	2 12.98	43 12 7.37
7	9	. .	. .	. .	. .	. .	. .	. .	1.1	16.1	3 53.31	3.34	VII. 5 45.65	21 11.47	4.13	3 49.97	43 11 55.60
8	7	. .	. .	. .	7.5	22.8	. .	. .	. .	. .	7 7.67	3.41	IV. 5 42.87	22 49.31	4.46	7 4.26	43 13 33.77
9	4	. .	8.5	23.5	38.4	. .	. .	. .	. .	. .	9 38.52	3.46	10. 5 41.93	23 20.96	4.73	9 35.06	43 14 5.69
10	5	. .	. .	. .	21.7	36.0	51.2	6.7	. .	. .	10 21.27	3.48	VII. 4 42.82	28 41.77	4.80	10 17.79	43 19 26.57
11	5	25.0	40.2	55.0	10.6	. .	40.7	53.8	. .	. .	32 10.47	3.91	IV. 1 40.77	50 41.97	7.50	32 6.56	43 41 29.47 B.
12	5	27.3	. .	. .	12.0	. .	. .	. .	. .	. .	40 12.29	4.03	VII. 6 37.35	17 12.83	8.63	40 8.26	43 8 1.46
13	7	. .	. .	. .	. .	18.2	33.2	48.5	. .	. .	41 3.11	4.05	VI. 4 36.182	32 34.31	8.75	40 59.06	43 23 23.06
14	8	. .	1.5	16.2	. .	. .	. .	. .	. .	. .	43 31.52	4.10	IV. 4 41.16	29 40.53	9.12	43 27.42	43 20 29.65
15	6.7	. .	. .	. .	15.7	30.3	45.6	0.5	. .	. .	44 15.42	4.12	VII. 5 40.30	24 18.79	9.23	44 11.30	43 15 8.02
16	3.4	27.2	42.0	57.0	12.3	27.1	42.4	57.1	. .	. .	48 12.19	4.19	IV. 5 42.24	23 11.50	9.81	48 8.00	43 14 1.31 B.
17	6	. .	21.8	36.1	51.2	6.5	21.5	37.0	. .	. .	52 51.31	4.28	VI. 1 41.94	50 0.89	10.55	52 47.03	43 40 51.44
18	8	28.0	43.0	58.0	13.0	28.0	. .	58.5	. .	. .	59 13.02	4.38	VII. 3 42.11	35 7.41	11.60	59 8.64	43 25 59.01
19	7.8	0.5	15.5	30.7	. .	1.0	. .	31.0	. .	. .	2 10 45.93	4.60	IV. 1 37.60	52 32.73	13.62	2 10 41.33	43 43 26.35
20	7.8	. .	. .	. .	. .	43.0	58.1	13.4	. .	. .	22 28.17	4.72	VII. 6 41.45	14 50.06	15.82	22 23.45	43 5 45.88

CORRECTIONS.

	COR. TO CLOCK.	HOURLY COR.	m.	n.	c.	ZENITH POINT.	COINC.
	s.	s.	s.	s.	s.	° ′ ″	r.
Oct. 28, at 22h...	—10.649	—0.012	—0.168	+0.103	+0.351	0 0 4.27	40.122

INSTRUMENT READINGS.

	h.	CIRCLE. A.	B.	C.	D.	Mean.	BAR.	THERMOM. At.	Ex.
Zone LXXIX.—Oct. 28....	0.6	277° 51′ 6″.2	11″.7	21″.5	10″.5	12″.48	I. 30.074	48°.5	41°.1
	1.3	. .	. .	. .	. .	. .	. .	48.0	40.0
	1.5	5.5	. .	. .	. .	11.98	. .	. .	. .
	1.9	. .	. .	. .	. .	. .	30.074	47.1	39.0
	2.3	. .	. .	. .	. .	. .	. .	46.9	38.3
	2.7	6.2	. .	. .	. .	12.48	30.088	46.0	37.4
	3.5	. .	. .	. .	. .	. .	30.086	45.3	38.4
	4.1	. .	. .	. .	. .	. .	30.090	44.8	37.0
	4.5	6.3	13.3	23.0	9.5	13.62	. .	44.8	36.5

Zone LXXIX. October 28. M. $D. = -42° 50' 40''.0.$ $n. = -0''.76.$ $n. = -21''.00.$ (Continued.)

Number.	Magnitude.	SECONDS OF TRANSITS I.	II.	III.	IV.	V.	VI.	VII.	10.	11.	T.	a.	MICROMETER.	D.	d.	Mean Right Ascension, 1850.0.	Mean South Declination, 1850.0.
											h. m. s.	s.	r.	' ''	''	h. m. s.	° ' ''
21	3	24.0	39.4	54.4	9.4	24.4	39.7	. .	. .	. .	2 34 9.52	+ 4.94	IV. 2 46.67	—41 9.90	—18.15	2 34 4.58	43 32 8.05 B.
22	7.8	. .	1.6	16.6	31.7	46.5	1.5	16.5	. .	. .	36 31.55	4.93	VII. 5 48.75	19 23.17	18.64	36 26.62	43 10 21.81
23	4	14.0	29.6	44.3	59.5	14.1	29.8	44.7	. .	. .	39 59.47	5.01	IV. 3 38.62	37 9.72	19.36	39 54.46	43 28 9.08 B.
24	7.8	. .	. .	. .	. .	. .	. .	58.7	21.6	36.7	41 13.19	5.05	II. 2 36.58	47 11.12	19.61	41 8.14	43 38 10.73
25	8	8.3	23.7	38.4	. .	. .	. .	. .	. .	. .	45 53.80	5.10	IV. 3 40.34	36 9.95	20.60	45 48.70	43 27 10.55
26	7	5.0	20.0	35.5	50.5	5.4	20.0	35.4	. .	. .	48 50.29	5.11	VII. 5 48.07	19 47.10	21.22	48 45.18	43 10 48.32
27	8	. .	. .	53.0	. .	23.4	38.0	53.2	. .	. .	3 9 8.12	5.37	" 5 42.80	22 51.17	24.88	3 9 2.75	43 13 56.05
28	8	39.0	54.6	. .	. .	. .	. .	. .	. .	. .	13 24.46	5.41	II. 5 47.16	20 19.25	25.91	13 19.05	43 11 25.16
29	2	. .	. .	45.7	0.7	16.0	. .	. .	. .	. .	14 0.87	5.48	IV. 1 45.84	47 44.73	26.06	13 55.39	43 38 50.79 B.
30	7.8	. .	. .	. .	. .	. .	. .	0.8	23.1	38.2	14 15.62	5.41	II. 6 39.45	15 59.38	26.12	14 10.21	43 7 5.50 M.
31	7.8	. .	42.0	56.9	12.0	. .	42.0	56.8	. .	. .	21 11.88	5.52	VII. 4 39.38	30 42.29	28.83	21 6.36	43 21 51.12
32	7	31.7	47.0	1.9	16.8	. .	. .	. .	. .	. .	24 16.86	5.50	IV. 7 43.26	7 52.14	29.59	24 11.36	42 59 1.73
33	3	. .	. .	. .	46.7	1.8	17.0	31.8	. .	. .	24 46.78	5.53	VII. 6 36.30	17 49.98	29.71	24 41.25	43 8 59.69
34	8	. .	. .	. .	21.0	36.0	. .	. .	. .	. .	32 21.06	5.59	" 7 45.39	6 37.20	31.63	32 15.47	42 57 48.83
35	7	. .	. .	58.5	. .	28.5	43.5	58.2	. .	. .	34 3.39	5.64	" 5 41.65	23 31.30	32.07	33 57.75	43 14 43.37
36	5.6	. .	. .	. .	. .	. .	. .	4.3	. .	42.6	36 18.99	5.71	10. 1 37.97	52 18.71	32.66	36 13.28	43 43 31.37
37	7.8	. .	. .	. .	13.8	29.3	. .	. .	. .	. .	39 14.00	5.75	VII. 1 39.46	51 27.54	33.42	39 8.25	43 42 40.96
38	6.7	4.5	19.5	34.2	49.5	4.2	19.3	34.3	. .	. .	49.39	. .	IV. 6 32.87	19 50.20	. .	. . . .	43
39	7	. .	. .	. .	53.0	8.0	23.5	38.5	. .	. .	48 53.03	5.82	VII. 2 39.73	45 21.99	35.98	48 47.21	43 36 37.97
40	7	36.0	51.1	6.3	21.7	36.5	51.5	6.6	. .	. .	51 21.43	5.84	" 2 45.82	41 49.13	36.63	51 15.59	43 33 5.76
41	5	. .	4.7	19.7	34.7	. .	. .	. .	. .	. .	4 2 34.79	5.90	IV. 4 44.38	27 48.07	39.70	4 2 28.89	43 19 7.77 M.
42	7.8	. .	. .	6.3	21.0	35.8	51.0	6.0	. .	. .	3 20.77	5.89	VII. 5 40.96	23 55.56	39.91	3 14.88	43 15 15.47
43	7.8	. .	. .	. .	27.7	42.4	57.2	12.4	. .	. .	5 27.46	5.87	" 7 40.31	9 34.71	40.50	5 21.59	43 0 55.21
44	7.8	. .	50.6	5.0	20.0	35.0	50.0	5.0	. .	. .	11 20.12	5.90	" 7 41.79	8 42.74	42.14	11 14.22	43 0 4.88
45	6	15.0	30.5	45.1	0.5	15.0	30.2	45.5	. .	. .	17 0.29	5.96	" 6 36.92	17 28.13	43.76	16 54.33	43 8 51.89
46	7.8	. .	. .	. .	5.7	20.6	36.0	51.0	. .	. .	19 5.68	6.01	" 4 41.14	29 40.66	44.35	18 59.67	43 21 5.01
47	8	. .	. .	. .	. .	55.0	10.0	25.0	. .	. .	20 39.71	6.06	" 2 37.30	46 47.22	44.80	20 33.65	43 38 12.02
48	7.8	. .	48.5	. .	18.0	32.8	48.0	3.0	. .	. .	23 18.02	5.99	" 6 43.42	13 41.21	45.56	23 12.03	43 5 6.77
49	6	0.8	16.0	31.0	46.1	. .	. .	. .	. .	. .	25 46.25	6.06	IV. 2 47.21	41 1.28	46.27	25 40.19	43 32 27.55
50	6	. .	. .	. .	. .	. .	21.0	35.8	57.7	14.1	25 50.31	6.10	II. 1 37.50	52 35.17	46.28	25 44.21	43 44 1.45
51	8	51.5	7.0	21.7	36.5	51.8	7.0	22.0	. .	. .	46 36.83	6.12	VII. 5 35.47	27 7.71	52.39	46 30.71	43 18 40.10
52	7.8	. .	. .	. .	. .	. .	29.6	44.7	. .	. .	47 59.38	6.13	" 5 35.20	27 17.02	52.81	47 53.25	43 18 49.83
53	7.8	. .	. .	. .	4.0	18.4	34.0	. .	. .	. .	52 3.64	6.19	VI. 2 34.08	48 40.00	54.02	51 57.45	43 40 14.02
54	7.8	. .	. .	. .	. .	. .	35.0	50.0	. .	. .	53 4.78	6.14	VII. 5 40.40	24 15.34	54.32	52 58.64	43 15 49.02
55	7.8	. .	. .	. .	. .	. .	59.0	14.0	. .	. .	4 54 28.58	6.19	" 2 39.54	45 28.54	54.74	4 54 22.39	43 37 3.28

Zone LXXX. November 21. M. $D. = 42° 50' 50''.0.$ $n. = -4''.00.$ $n. = -19''.53.$

Number.	Magnitude.	I.	II.	III.	IV.	V.	VI.	VII.	10.	11.	T.	a.	MICROMETER.	D.	d.	Mean Right Ascension, 1850.0.	Mean South Declination, 1850.0.
1	7	. .	29.5	44.8	0.0	15.0	30.0	45.0	. .	. .	23 33 59.89	— 1.96	VII. 6 46.06	12 8.28	3.16	23 33 57.93	43 3 1.44
2	8	. .	. .	44.0	58.8	13.5	29.0	. .	. .	. .	37 58.85	2.04	VI. 6 33.34	19 32.77	3.04	37 56.81	43 10 25.81
3	9	27.0	41.8	. .	. .	. .	. .	. .	. .	. .	23 42 12.00	2.15	II. 6 39.60	15 53.91	2.75	23 42 9.85	43 6 46.66

CORRECTIONS.

	COR. TO CLOCK.	HOURLY COR.	m.	n.	c.	ZENITH POINT.	COINC.
	s.	s.	s.	s.	s	° ' ''	r.
Nov. 21, at 7h....	—11.589	—0.032	—0.168	+0.103	+0.351	0 0 25.17	40.120

INSTRUMENT READING.

		CIRCLE. A.	B.	C.	D.	Mean.	BAR.	THERMOM. At.	Ex.
	h.	° ' ''	''	''	''	''	I.	°	°
Zone LXXX.—Nov. 21..	23.5	277 51 6.0	13.0	23.2	13.0	18.40	30.196	49.7	42.6
	0.0	. . . .	. .	. .	. .	. .	29.955	49.0	38.0
	0.5	7.2	13.2	25.0	13.7	19.70	. .	. .	. .

Number.	Magnitude.	SECONDS OF TRANSITS. I.	II.	III.	IV.	V.	VI.	VII.	10.	11.	T.	a.	MICROMETER.	D.	d.	Mean Right Ascension, 1850.0.	Mean South Declination, 1850.0.
Zone LXXX. November 21. M. $D. = 42^\circ 50' 50''.0$. $n' = -4''.00$. $n'' = -19''.53$. (Continued.)																	
											h. m. s.	s.	r.	′ ″	″	h. m. s.	° ′ ″
4	8	. .	. .	. .	. .	. .	34.7	49.8	. .	. .	23 42 4.64	— 2.14	VII. 6 37.42	—17 10.05	—2.76	23 42 2.50	43 8 2.81
5	7	. .	. .	. .	. .	. .	. .	. .	5.8	21.0	44 57.82	2.19	II. 2 49.24	39 47.12	2.64	44 55.63	43 30 39.76
6	8	11.5	27.0	41.7	56.5	11.3	26.0	. .	. .	. .	48 56.55	2.32	VII. 7 38.17	10 49.06	2.47	48 54.23	43 1 41.53
7	7	. .	57.0	11.7	27.0	. .	. .	. .	. .	. .	51 26.89	2.37	IV. 6 43.77	13 28.64	2.40	51 24.53	43 4 21.04
8	8.9	. .	. .	. .	. .	. .	. .	. .	59.5	14.7	52 52.06	2.40	II. 6 38.96	16 15.51	2.37	52 49.66	43 7 7.88
9	7	5.7	21.0	36.1	51.0	6.4	. .	36.5	. .	. .	57 51.27	2.49	IV. 1 37.48	52 35.58	2.26	57 48.78	43 43 27.84
10	7	40.5	55.8	10.4	25.7	40.4	55.5	10.4	. .	. .	0 4 25.56	2.66	" 7 40.53	9 26.99	2.16	0 4 22.90	43 0 19.15 B.
11	8.9	1.6	17.0	31.3	46.4	1.5	16.3	. .	. .	. .	7 46.56	2.74	VII. 7 41.24	9 1.95	2.12	7 43.82	42 59 54.07
12	8.9	. .	. .	. .	. .	. .	. .	19.5	42.0	57.2	8 34.04	2.76	II. 3 34.45	39 32.70	2.11	8 31.28	43 30 24.81
13	2	9.2	24.5	39.3	54.4	9.0	24.0	39.0	. .	. .	18 54.24	3.01	IV. 6 38.76	16 23.55	2.14	18 51.23	43 7 15.69 B.
14	7	20.0	35.0	50.1	5.5	20.1	35.4	50.3	. .	. .	0 27 5.23	3.20	" 5 39.54	24 44.31	2.30	0 27 2.03	43 15 36.61 B.

Zone.	No.	
I.	8	One minute of right ascension less makes this star identique with Zone III, 20, and with 1924, Madrass.
	11	This star may be the same with Zone III, 23, and 1954, Madrass. A revolution of the micrometer being misread.
II.	7	One revolution of the micrometer? 2833, Madrass.
V.	4	One minute in right ascension? Zone XII, 4. 1502, Madrass.
	20	2453, Madrass?
VIII.	6	One revolution of micrometer? Argelander, 11808, 11809.
	10	Argelander, 12131?
IX.	5	One revolution of the micrometer? Argelander, 14950.
	13	One minute in right ascension? Argelander, 15686, 15687, 15688.
XI.	43	One minute in right ascension? 2191, Madrass.
XV.	3	One revolution of the micrometer? Argelander, 12056.
	4	One revolution of the micrometer? Argelander, 12070, 12071.
	11	Misreading of wire of the micrometer? Argelander, 12197, 12198.
	47	One revolution of the micrometer? Argelander, 12949.
	61	One revolution of the micrometer? Argelander, 13155.
	66	One revolution of the micrometer? Argelander, 13246.
	79	Misreading of wire of micrometer? Argelander, 14302.
	81	Misreading of wire of micrometer? Argelander, 14440.
	121	One revolution of the micrometer? Argelander, 15373.
	147	One minute in right ascension? Argelander, 15975.
	150	Many small stars here.
XVII.	15	A double star.
	27	One revolution of the micrometer? Argelander, 14302.
XIX.	29	One revolution of the micrometer? 2988, Madrass.
	33	A cluster of stars, of which the brightest has been taken.
XXI.	4	A minute in right ascension. 2785, Madrass.
	30	This star may be 5681, B. A. C. A misreading of + 20s. in right ascension.
XXII.	. .	This zone has but one reading of the circle.
	7	One revolution of the micrometer? Argelander, 15040.
	47	Misreading of micrometer? Argelander, 16891, 16892.
XXIII.	24	One revolution of the micrometer? Argelander, 13374.
XXIV.	1	A double star.
	3	One revolution of the micrometer? Argelander, 15885, 15886, 15887.
	4	15895, 15896, 15897, Argelander?
	13	One revolution of the micrometer? Argelander, 16630, 16631.
	41	A double star.
XXV.	28	One revolution of the micrometer? Argelander, 13871.
	40	One revolution of the micrometer? Argelander, 14548.
	59	One revolution of the micrometer? Argelander, 15217.
	70	One revolution of the micrometer? Argelander, 15792.

Zone.	No	
XXV.	73	One revolution of the micrometer? Argelander, 15885, 15886, 15887.
	81	A double star.
XXVII.	27	One revolution of the micrometer? Argelander, 16011.
	53	One revolution of the micrometer? Argelander, 16795.
	70	One revolution of the micrometer? Argelander, 17201.
XXVIII.	109	One revolution of the micrometer? Argelander, 20929, 20930, 20931.
XXXII.	50	Two revolutions of the micrometer? Argelander, 19737, 19738.
XXXVII.	26	Two revolutions of the micrometer? Argelander, 18774.
XXXVIII.	30	A double star. The following star observed.
XL.	4	This star may be B. A. C., 5521; an error of 10 seconds in the right ascension.
XLIII.	10	A revolution of the micrometer? Argelander, 20886.
XLVI.	52	A double star.
L.	22	A revolution of the micrometer? Argelander, 21780, 21781.
LII.	27	A revolution of the micrometer? Argelander, 19737, 19738.
LV.	39	The recorded transit readings disagree?
LVI.	26	6812, B. A. C.
	49 } 50 }	The declination given for 50 is probably that of 49. The star being 7314, B. A. C.
LVII.	52	8027, B. A. C.
LVIII.	32	A revolution of the micrometer? Argelander, 21615.
	52	A revolution of the micrometer? Argelander, 22295.
	54	A revolution of the micrometer? Argelander, 22316, 22317.
LX.	1	A revolution of the micrometer? Argelander, 20784, 20785.
	2	Ten seconds in right ascension? Argelander, 20792.
	35	One revolution of the micrometer? Argelander, 21322.
	47	One revolution of the micrometer? Argelander, 21470.
	60	One revolution of the micrometer? Argelander, 21669.
	154	One revolution of the micrometer? Argelander, 161.
LXII.	10	Ten seconds in right ascension? Argelander, 21075.
	51 } 52 }	The right ascensions of these stars are probably transposed. Argelander, 22181, 22182.
	87	One revolution of the micrometer? Argelander, 23022, 23023.
	121	One revolution of the micrometer? Argelander, 683, 684.
	127	One revolution of the micrometer? Argelander, 831.
LXIII.	24	One revolution of the micrometer? Argelander, 19809.
	37	20078, Argelander?
LXIV.	45	One revolution of the micrometer? 8376, B. A. C.
LXVI.	22	One revolution of the micrometer? Argelander, 20406.
LXXI.	19	One revolution of the micrometer? Argelander, 21573.
	27	One revolution of the micrometer? Argelander, 21656.
	42	One revolution of the micrometer? Argelander, 22192.
	60	One revolution of the micrometer? Argelander, 22791.
LXXII.	38	One revolution of the micrometer? Argelander, 22104.

ERRATA.

Zone XI.	No. 43, for H, read M.
XV.	3, for 3, read *3.
XV.	4, for 4, read *4.
XV.	27, for *27, read 27.
XV.	62, for *62, read 62.
XV.	113, for *113, read 113.
XVII.	24, for *24, read 24.
XVIII.	7, for *7, read 7.
XXIII.	23, for *23, read 23.
XXIII.	24, for 24, read *24.
XXIX.	In the column "Mean South Declination," throughout the zone, for 41°, read 40°.

Made in United States
Orlando, FL
21 October 2026

89529436R00068